STREET ATLAS
Cambridgeshire

First published in 2001

George Philip Ltd, a division of
Octopus Publishing Group Ltd
2–4 Heron Quays, London E14 4JP

First colour edition 2001
First impression 2001

ISBN 0-540-08096-9 (hardback)
ISBN 0-540-08097-7 (spiral)

© George Philip Ltd 2001

Ordnance Survey®

This product includes mapping data licensed
from Ordnance Survey® with the permission of
the Controller of Her Majesty's Stationery Office.
© Crown copyright 2001. All rights reserved.
Licence number 100011710

Printed and bound in Spain
by Cayfosa-Quebecor

Contents

III   **Key to map symbols**

IV   **Key to map pages**

VI   **Route planning**

VIII   **Administrative and Postcode boundaries**

1   **Street maps** at 3½ inches to 1 mile

208   **Street maps** at 1¾ inches to 1 mile

239   **Street maps** at 3½ inches to 1 mile

246   **Street map of Cambridge city centre**
at 7 inches to 1 mile

247   **Town maps** of King's Lynn and Saffron Walden

248   **Index** of towns and villages

250   **Index** of streets, hospitals, industrial estates, railway
stations, schools, shopping centres, universities
and places of interest

Digital Data

The exceptionally high-quality mapping found in this atlas is available as digital data in TIFF
format, which is easily convertible to other bit mapped (raster) image formats.

The index is also available in digital form as a standard database table. It contains all the details
found in the printed index together with the National Grid reference for the map square in which
each entry is named and feature codes for places of interest in eight categories such as education
and health.

For further information and to discuss your requirements, please contact Philip's on
020 7531 8440 or george.philip@philips-maps.co.uk

Motorway with junction number			Railway station
Primary route – dual/single carriageway			Private railway station
A road – dual/single carriageway			Bus, coach station
B road – dual/single carriageway			Ambulance station
Minor road – dual/single carriageway			Coastguard station
Other minor road – dual/single carriageway			Fire station
Road under construction			Police station
Pedestrianised area			Accident and Emergency entrance to hospital
Postcode boundaries			Hospital
County and unitary authority boundaries			Place of worship
Railway			Information Centre (open all year)
Railway under construction			Parking
Tramway, miniature railway			Park and Ride
Rural track, private road or narrow road in urban area			Post Office
Gate or obstruction to traffic (restrictions may not apply at all times or to all vehicles)			Camping site
Path, bridleway, byway open to all traffic, road used as a public path			Caravan site

The representation in this atlas of a road, track or is no evidence of the existence of a of a right of way

Adjoining page indicators
(The colour of the arrow indicates the scale of the adjoining page - see scales below)

Adjoining page indicator showing the pages adjoining the top and bottom halves of the current page

The map areas within the pink/blue bands are shown at a larger scale on the page, indicated by the red/blue blocks and arrows

Golf course

Picnic site

Important buildings, schools, colleges, universities and hospitals

Prim Sch

River Medway — Water name

River, stream

Lock, weir

Water

Tidal water

Woods

Houses

Church — Non-Roman antiquity

ROMAN FORT — Roman antiquity

Allot Gdns	Allotments	Meml	Memorial
Acad	Academy	Mon	Monument
Cemy	Cemetery	Mus	Museum
C Ctr	Civic Centre	Obsy	Observatory
CH	Club House	Pal	Royal Palace
Coll	College	PH	Public House
Crem	Crematorium	Recn Gd	Recreation Ground
Ent	Enterprise	Resr	Reservoir
Ex H	Exhibition Hall	Ret Pk	Retail Park
Ind Est	Industrial Estate	Sch	School
Inst	Institute	Sh Ctr	Shopping Centre
Ct	Law Court	TH	Town Hall/House
L Ctr	Leisure Centre	Trad Est	Trading Estate
LC	Level Crossing	Univ	University
Liby	Library	Wks	Works
Mkt	Market	YH	Youth Hostel

■ The small numbers around the edges of the maps identify the 1 kilometre National Grid lines ■ The dark grey border on the inside edge of some pages indicates that the mapping does not continue onto the adjacent page

The scale of the maps is 5.52 cm to 1 km
3½ inches to 1 mile 1: 18103

0	¼	½	¾	1 mile
0	250m 500m	750m	1 kilometre	

The scale of the maps on pages numbered in green is 2.76 cm to 1 km 1¾ inches to 1 mile 1: 36206

0	¼	½	¾	1 mile
0	250m 500m 750m	1 kilometre		

The scale of the maps on pages numbered in red is 11.04 cm to 1 km 7 inches to 1 mile 1: 9051.4

0	220 yards	440 yards	660 yards	½ mile
0	125m	250m 375m	½ kilometre	

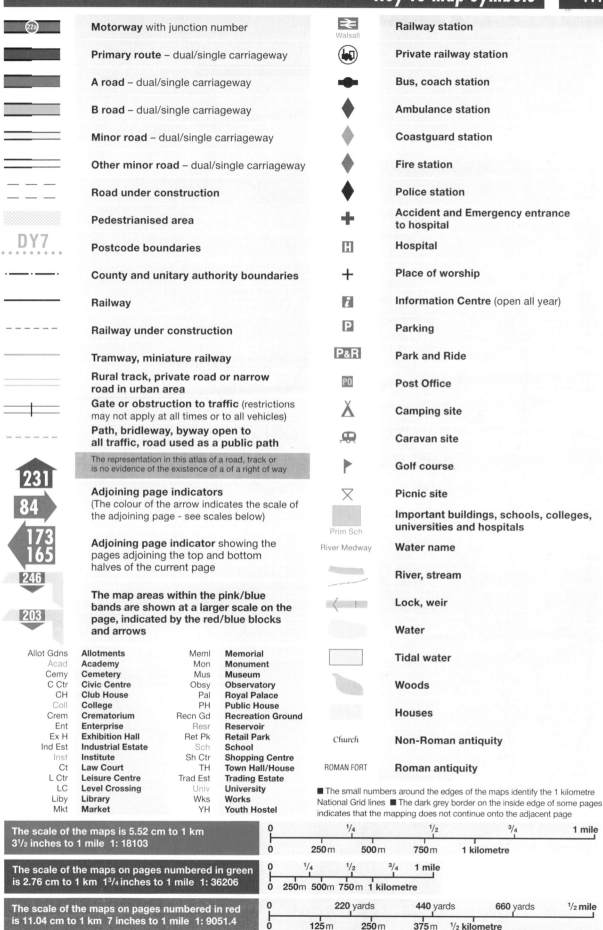

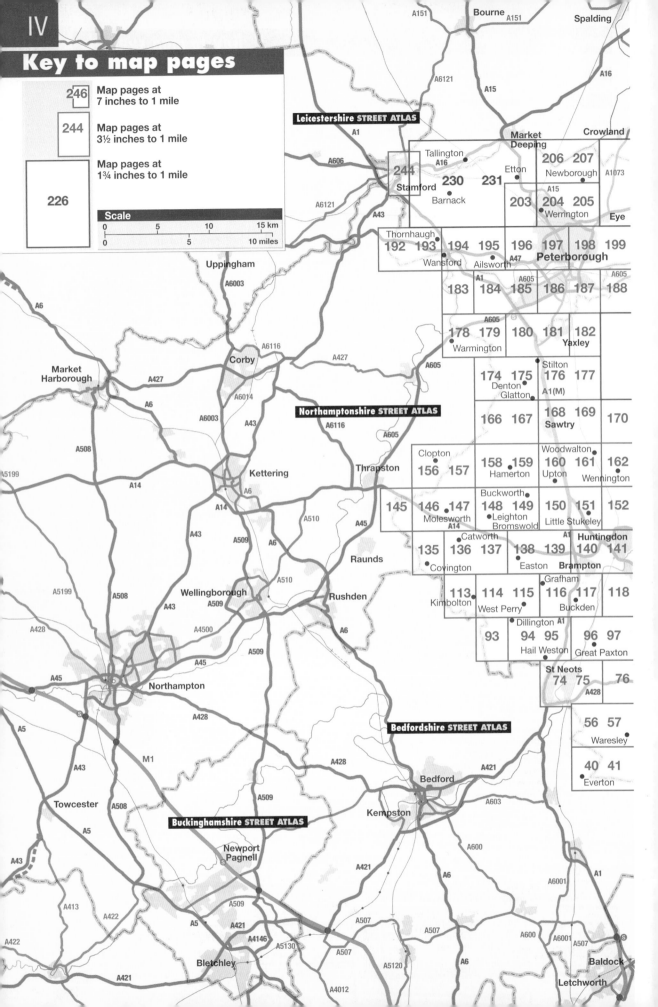

IV

Key to map pages

246	Map pages at 7 inches to 1 mile
244	Map pages at 3½ inches to 1 mile
226	Map pages at 1¾ inches to 1 mile

Scale

0   5   10   15 km
0   5   10 miles

Leicestershire STREET ATLAS

Northamptonshire STREET ATLAS

Bedfordshire STREET ATLAS

Buckinghamshire STREET ATLAS

Market Deeping Crowland

206 207
Newborough

230 231   203 204 205
Stamford   Etton   Werrington   Eye
Tallington   Barnack

192 193 194 195 196 197 198 199
Thornhaugh Wansford Ailsworth Peterborough
  Uppingham

183 184 185 186 187 188

178 179 180 181 182
Warmington   Yaxley

174 175 176 177
Denton Stilton
Glatton A1(M)

166 167 168 169 170
Sawtry

156 157 158 159 160 161 162
Clopton Hamerton Upton Woodwalton Wennington

145 146 147 148 149 150 151 152
Molesworth Buckworth Leighton Little Stukeley
  Bromswold

135 136 137 138 139 140 141
Covington Catworth Easton Huntingdon Brampton

113 114 115 116 117 118
Kimbolton West Perry Grafham Buckden

93 94 95 96 97
Hail Weston Dillington Great Paxton

74 75 76
St Neots

56 57
Waresley

40 41
Everton

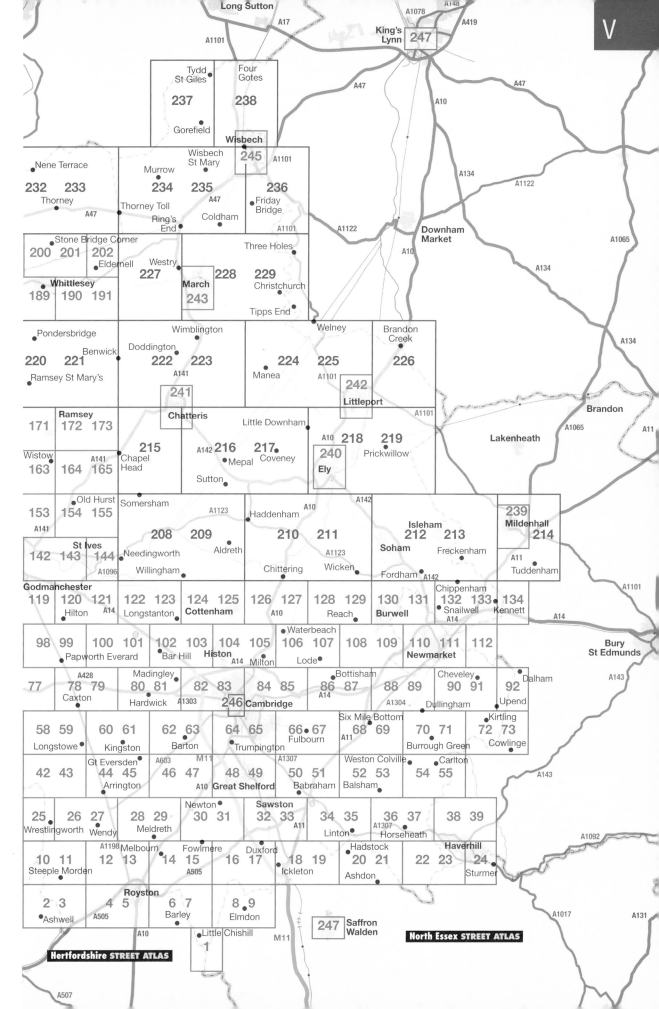

Long Sutton

A17

A1078

A419

A1101

King's Lynn **247**

A47

A47

A10

A134

A1122

A1065

Tydd St Giles **237**

Four Gotes **238**

Gorefield

Wisbech **245**

A1101

Downham Market

A1122

A10

A134

Nene Terrace

232 **233**

Thorney

Murrow **234**

Wisbech St Mary **235**

236 Friday Bridge

A47

Thorney Toll

Ring's End

Coldham

A1101

A134

Stone Bridge Corner

200 **201** **202**

Eldernell

Westry **227**

228

Three Holes **229** Christchurch

A1065

A1101

200 **201** **202**

Whittlesey

189 **190** **191**

March **243**

Tipps End

Welney

Brandon Creek

226

Brandon

A134

Pondersbridge

Benwick

220 **221**

Ramsey St Mary's

Doddington **222** **223**

A141

Wimblington **224**

Manea

225

A1101

Littleport **242**

A1101

Lakenheath

A1065

A11

Ramsey

171 **172** **173**

Wistow

163 **164** **165**

A141

Chapel Head

Chatteris **241**

215

A142 **216** Mepal

217 Coveney

Little Downham

A10 **218**

240 Ely

219 Prickwillow

Brandon

A1065

A11

Old Hurst

153 **154** **155**

A141

Somersham

A1123

Haddenham

Sutton

A10

A142

Isleham **212** **213**

Freckenham

239 Mildenhall **214**

A11 Tuddenham

A1101

St Ives

142 **143** **144**

A1096

208 **209**

Needingworth

Willingham

Aldreth

Chittering

210 **211**

A1123

Wicken

Soham **130** **131**

Fordham A142

A14

Godmanchester

119 **120** **121**

Hilton

A14

122 **123**

Longstanton

Cottenham **124** **125**

A10

126 **127**

Reach

128 **129**

Burwell **130** **131**

Chippenham

132 **133** **134**

Snailwell Kennett

A14

A1101

A14

Bury St Edmunds

Waterbeach

98 **99** **100** **101**

Papworth Everard

Bar Hill

Histon **102** **103** **104** **105**

A14 Milton

Lode **106** **107**

108 **109**

Newmarket **110** **111** **112**

A428

77 **78** **79**

Caxton

Madingley **80** **81**

Hardwick

A1303

82 **83**

246 Cambridge

84 **85**

Bottisham **86** **87**

A14

88 **89**

Cheveley **90** **91**

Dullingham

Dalham **92**

Upend

A143

Longstowe **58** **59**

Kingston **60** **61**

Barton **62** **63**

Trumpington

64 **65**

Fulbourn **66** **67**

A11

Six Mile Bottom **68** **69**

Burrough Green **70** **71**

Carlton

Kirtling **72** **73**

Cowlinge

A143

42 **43**

Gt Eversden **44** **45**

Arrington

A603

46 **47**

M11

Great Shelford **48** **49**

A1307

50 **51**

Babraham

Weston Colville **52** **53**

Carlton

54 **55**

Wrestlingworth **25** **26** **27**

Wendy

Meldreth **28** **29**

Newton **30** **31**

Sawston **32** **33**

A11

34 **35**

Linton

A1307 **36** **37**

Horseheath

38 **39**

Haverhill

A1092

Steeple Morden **10** **11**

A1198 Melbourn **12** **13**

Fowlmere **14** **15**

A505

Duxford **16** **17**

18 **19**

Ickleton

Hadstock **20** **21**

Ashdon

22 **23**

24

Sturmer

A1017

A131

Royston

2 **3**

Ashwell

A505

4 **5**

Barley **6** **7**

Elmdon **8** **9**

Little Chishill **1**

M11

247 Saffron Walden

A1017

A507

North Essex STREET ATLAS

Hertfordshire STREET ATLAS

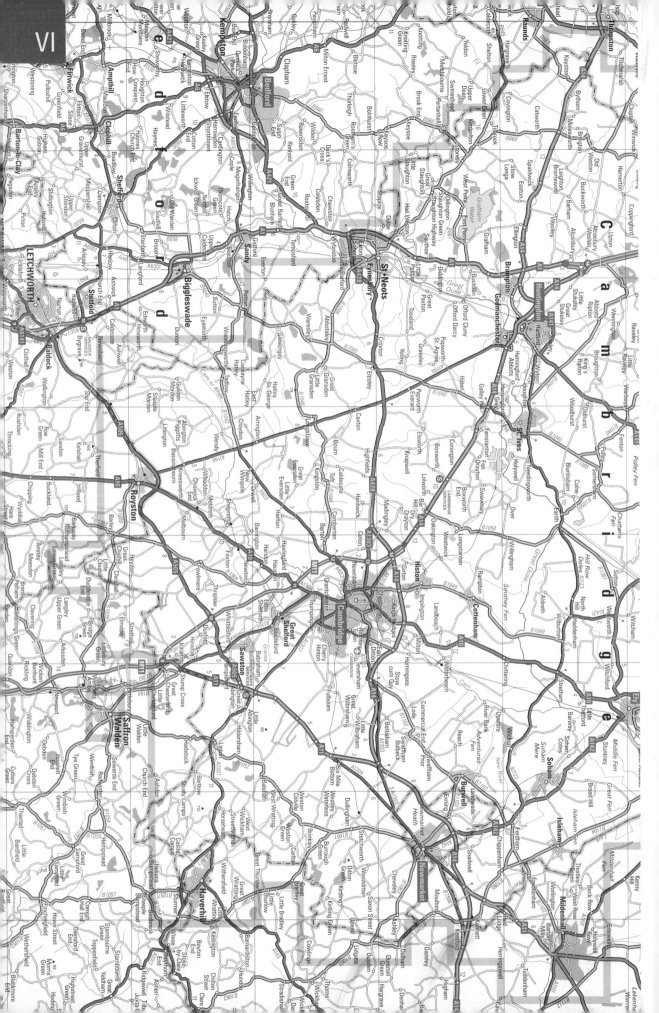

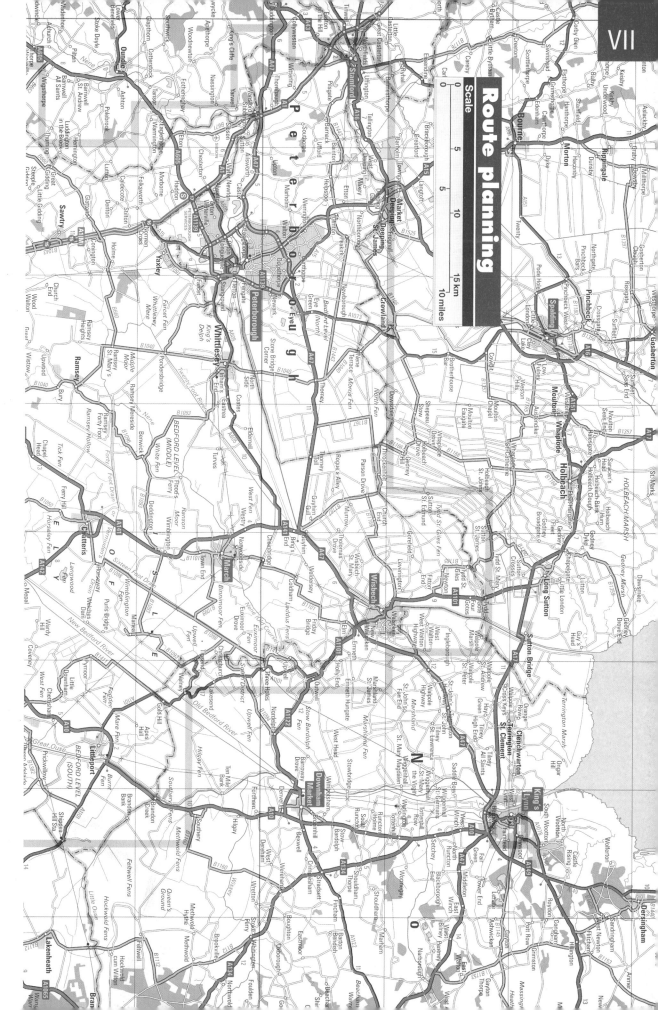

Route planning

Scale

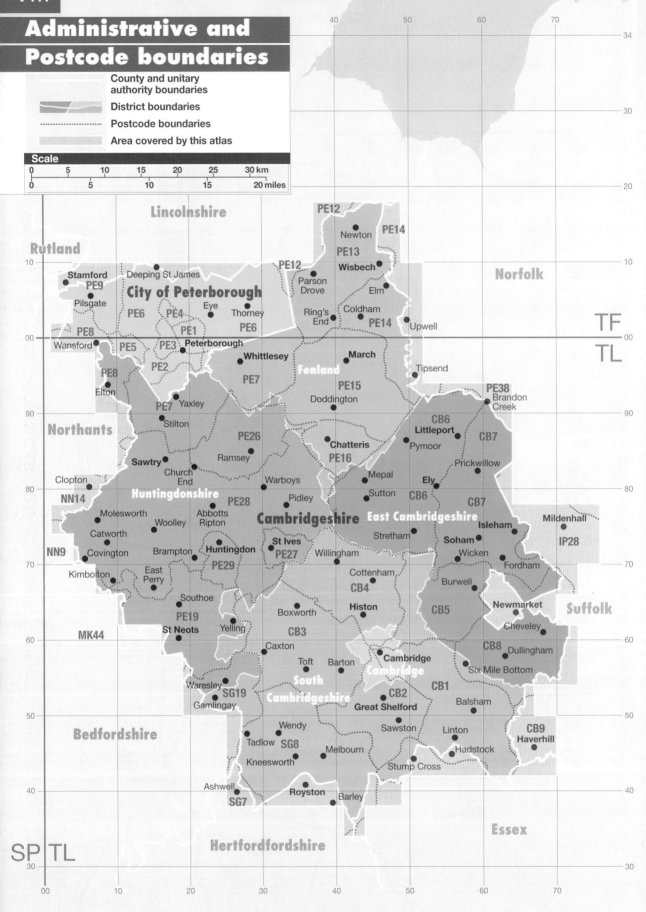

Administrative and Postcode boundaries

	County and unitary authority boundaries
	District boundaries
	Postcode boundaries
	Area covered by this atlas

Scale

0   5   10   15   20   25   30 km

0   5   10   15   20 miles

Lincolnshire

Rutland

Stamford
PE9

Deeping St James

Pilsgate

City of Peterborough

PE12

Newton

PE14

PE13

Wisbech

PE12

Parson Drove

Elm

Norfolk

TF
TL

Eye

Thorney

Ring's End

Coldham

PE6

PE4

PE6

PE14

Upwell

PE1

PE8

Wansford

PE5

PE3

Peterborough

Whittlesey

Fenland

March

Tipsend

PE2

PE7

PE15

PE38
Brandon Creek

PE8

Elton

PE7

Yaxley

Doddington

Stilton

CB6

Littleport

Pymoor

CB7

Northants

PE26

Chatteris

PE16

Prickwillow

Sawtry

Ramsey

Church End

Warboys

Mepal

Ely

CB7

Clopton

Huntingdonshire

PE28

Pidley

Sutton

CB6

CB7

NN14

Molesworth

Abbotts Ripton

Cambridgeshire

East Cambridgeshire

Isleham

Mildenhall

IP28

Catworth

Woolley

Stretham

Soham

NN9

Covington

Brampton

Huntingdon

Willingham

Wicken

Fordham

Kimbolton

East Perry

PE29

PE27

St Ives

Cottenham

Burwell

Southoe

CB4

Newmarket

Suffolk

Boxworth

Histon

CB5

Cheveley

PE19

St Neots

Yelling

CB3

MK44

Caxton

CB8

Dullingham

Toft

Barton

Cambridge

Six Mile Bottom

Cambridge

CB1

Waresley

SG19

South Cambridgeshire

CB2

Great Shelford

Balsham

Gamlingay

Wendy

Sawston

Linton

CB9
Haverhill

Bedfordshire

Tadlow

SG8

Melbourn

Hadstock

Kneesworth

Stump Cross

Ashwell

Royston

Barley

Essex

SG7

SP TL

Hertfordfordshire

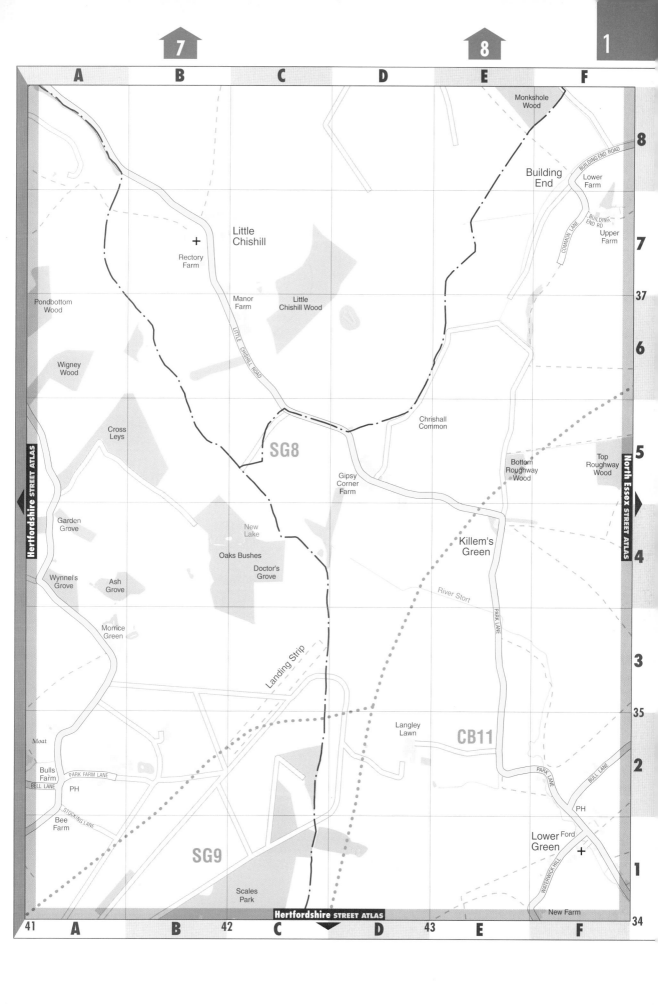

A   B   C   D   E   F

8

Monkshole
Wood

Building
End

Lower
Farm

BUILDING END ROAD

7

Little Chishill

Rectory
Farm

COMMON LANE

BUILDING
END RD

Upper
Farm

Pondbottom
Wood

Manor
Farm

Little
Chishill Wood

37

LITTLE CHISHILL ROAD

Wigney
Wood

6

Chrishall
Common

Cross
Leys

SG8

Bottom
Roughway
Wood

Top
Roughway
Wood

5

Gipsy
Corner
Farm

Garden
Grove

New
Lake

Killem's
Green

Wynnel's
Grove

Ash
Grove

Oaks Bushes

Doctor's
Grove

River Stort

PARK LANE

4

Morrice
Green

3

Landing Strip

Langley
Lawn

CB11

35

Moat

Bulls
Farm

PARK FARM LANE

PARK LANE

BULL LANE

BELL LANE

PH

PH

2

STOCKING LANE

Bee
Farm

Lower
Green

Ford

WATERWICK HILL

SG9

Scales
Park

New Farm

1

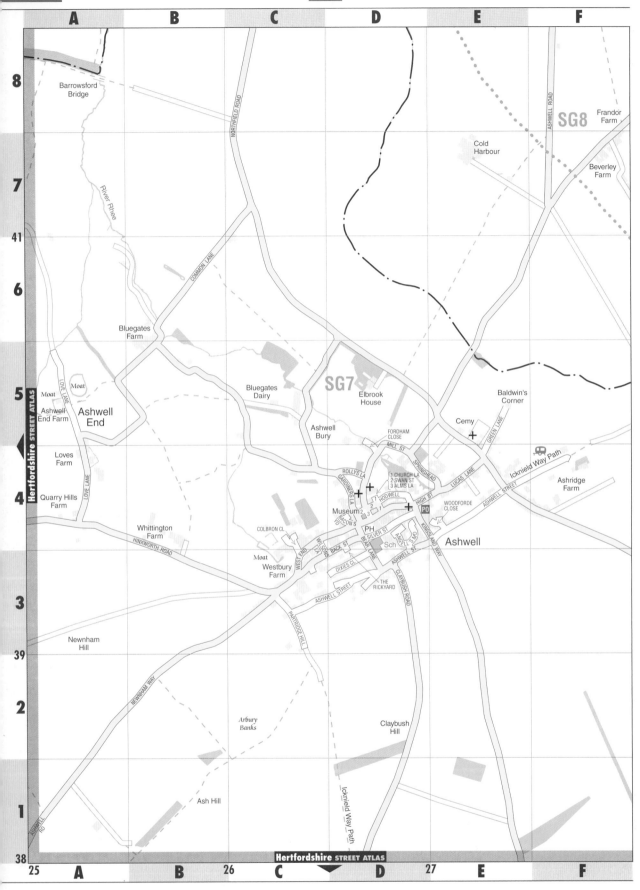

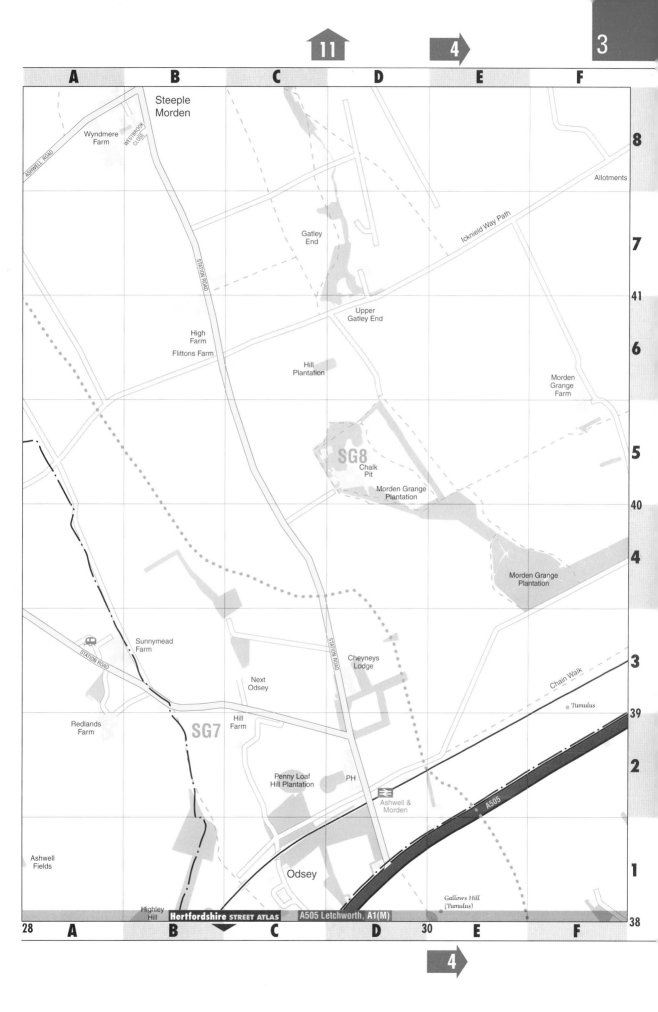

A B C D E F

8

Steeple
Morden

Wyndmere
Farm

ASHWELL ROAD

WESTBROOK CLOSE

Allotments

Gatley
End

Icknield Way Path

7

41

STATION ROAD

Upper
Gatley End

High
Farm

Flittons Farm

6

Hill
Plantation

Morden
Grange
Farm

SG8

Chalk
Pit

5

Morden Grange
Plantation

40

4

Morden Grange
Plantation

Sunnymead
Farm

STATION ROAD

STATION ROAD

Cheyneys
Lodge

Chain Walk

3

Next
Odsey

Redlands
Farm

SG7

Hill
Farm

• Tumulus

39

Penny Loaf
Hill Plantation

PH

2

Ashwell &
Morden

A505

Ashwell
Fields

Odsey

1

Gallows Hill
(Tumulus)

Highley
Hill

38

28 A B C D 30 E F 38

3
12

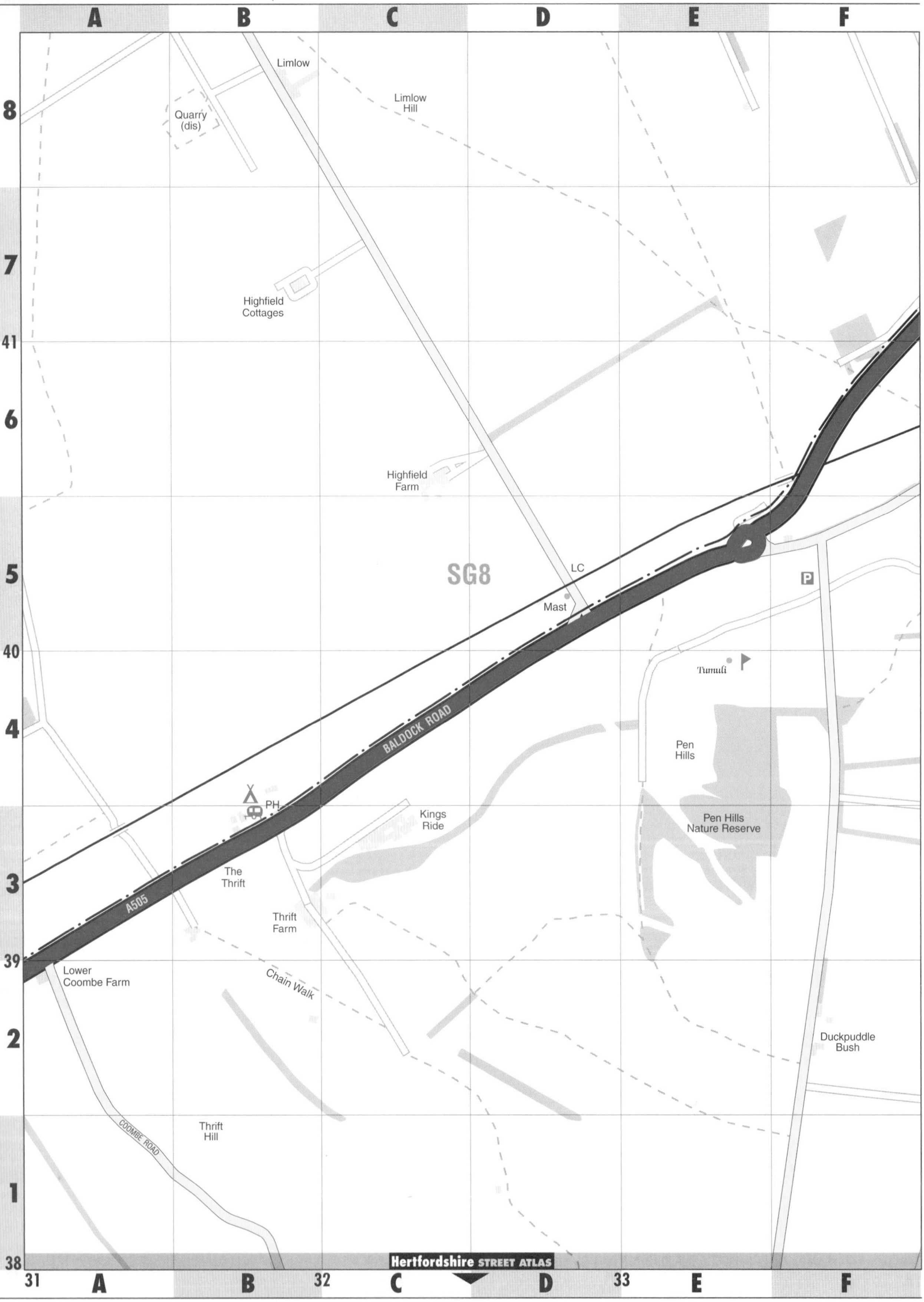
A
B
C
D
E
F
8
7
41
6
5
40
4
3
39
2
1
38
31
32
33
Limlow
Limlow Hill
Quarry (dis)
Highfield Cottages
Highfield Farm
SG8
LC
Mast
P
Tumuli
Pen Hills
Pen Hills Nature Reserve
BALDOCK ROAD
PH
Kings Ride
The Thrift
A505
Thrift Farm
Lower Coombe Farm
Chain Walk
Duckpuddle Bush
Thrift Hill
COOMBE ROAD

3

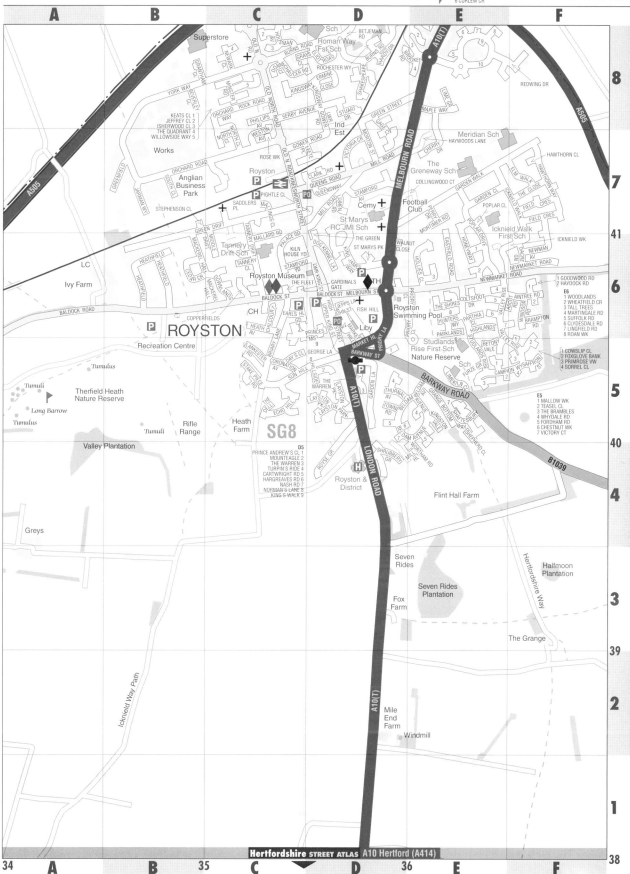

E8
1 KIPLING RD
2 ACKROYD RD
3 COOMBELANDS RD
4 BYRON RD
5 CORMAS CL
6 CURLEW CR

7 KESTREL WY
8 OWALL WK
9 SKYLARK PL
10 FIELDFARE WY

Superstore

Roman Way Fst Sch

BETJEMAN RD

REDWING DR

YORK WAY

KEATS CL 1
JEFFREY CL 2
ISHERWOOD CL 3
THE QUADRANT 4
WILLOWSIDE WAY 5

Works

Meridian Sch

HAYWOODS LANE

HAWTHORN CL

Orchard Road

Anglian Business Park

Royston

STEPHENSON CL

PIGHTLE CL

The Greneway Sch

COLLINGWOOD CT

Ind Est

Cemy

Football Club

Icknield Walk First Sch

ICKNIELD WK

LC

Ivy Farm

Tannery Drift Sch

Royston Museum

THE FLEET

St Marys RC JMI Sch

St Marys Pk

The Green

WALNUT CLOSE

NEWMAN AV

NEWMARKET ROAD

BALDOCK ROAD

CARDINALS GATE

BALDOCK ST

FISH HILL

Royston Swimming Pool

The Shires

1 GOODWOOD RD
2 HAYDOCK RD

E6
1 WOODLANDS
2 WHEATFIELD CR
3 TALL TREES
4 MARTINGALE RD
5 WHYDALE RD
6 CLYDESDALE RD
7 LINGFIELD RD
8 ROAN WK

COPPERFIELDS

ROYSTON

Liby

Studlands Rise First Sch Nature Reserve

1 COWSLIP CL
2 FOXGLOVE BANK
3 PRIMROSE VW
4 SORREL CL

Recreation Centre

Tumulus

BARKWAY ST

BARKWAY ROAD

E5
1 MALLOW WK
2 TEASEL CL
3 THE BRAMBLES
4 WHYDALE RD
5 FORDHAM RD
6 CHESTNUT WK
7 VICTORY CT

Tumuli

Long Barrow

Therfield Heath Nature Reserve

Tumulus

Rifle Range

Heath Farm

SG8

D5
PRINCE ANDREW'S CL 1
MOUNTEAGLE 2
THE WARREN 3
TURPIN'S RIDE 4
CARTWRIGHT RD 5
HARGREAVES RD 6
NASH RD 7
NORMAN'S LANE 8
KING'S WALK 9

Tumuli

Valley Plantation

Royston & District

Flint Hall Farm

B1039

Greys

Seven Rides

Halfmoon Plantation

Seven Rides Plantation

Hertfordshire Way

Fox Farm

Icknield Way Path

The Grange

A10(T)

Mile End Farm

Windmill

LONDON ROAD

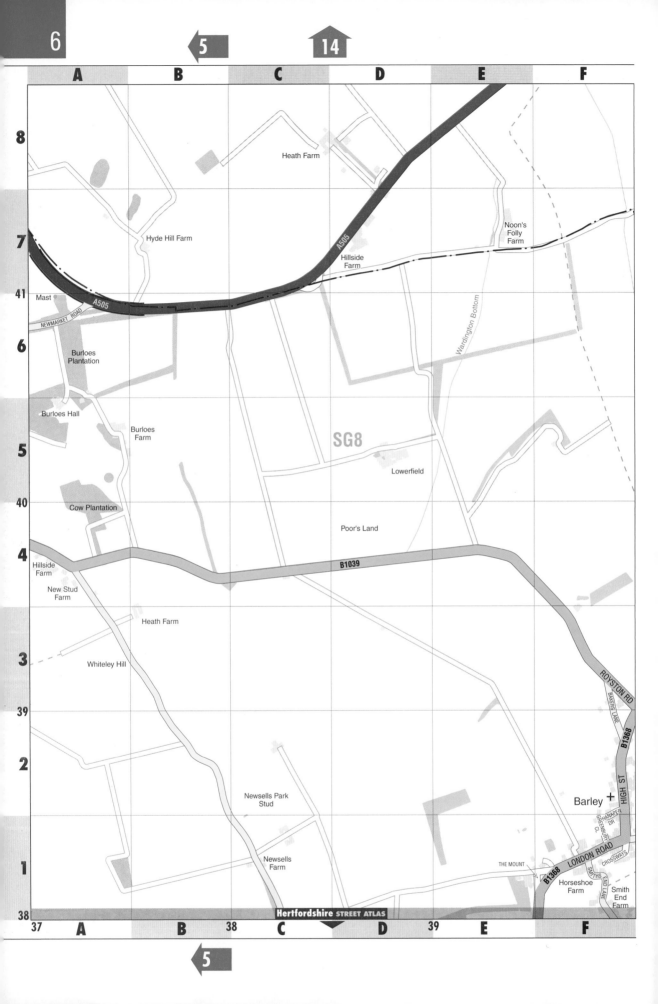

A B C D E F

8

Heath Farm

7

Hyde Hill Farm

Noon's
Folly
Farm

41

Mast

NEWMARKET ROAD

A505

Hillside
Farm

A505

Wardington Bottom

6

Burloes
Plantation

Burloes Hall

Burloes
Farm

5

SG8

Lowerfield

40

Cow Plantation

Poor's Land

4

Hillside
Farm

B1039

New Stud
Farm

Heath Farm

3

Whiteley Hill

ROYSTON RD

BAKERS LANE

39

B1368

2

Barley +

Newsells Park
Stud

GREENBURY
CL

HARPER
DR

HIGH ST

1

THE MOUNT

Newsells
Farm

LONDON ROAD

B1368

CROSSWAYS

SMITHS
END LANE

Horseshoe
Farm

Smith
End
Farm

38

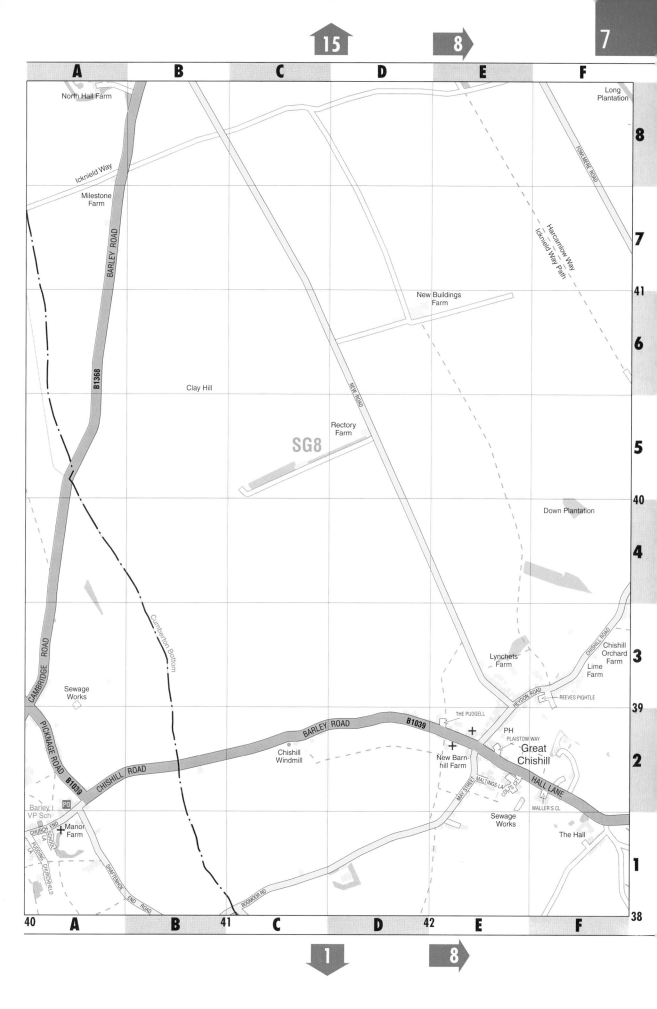

A B C D E F

North Hall Farm

Long Plantation

Icknield Way

8

Milestone Farm

FOWLMERE ROAD

BARLEY ROAD

Harcamlow Way
Icknield Way Path

7

B1368

New Buildings Farm

41

6

Clay Hill

SG8

Rectory Farm

5

40

Down Plantation

4

Cumberton Bottom

CAMBRIDGE ROAD

Lynchets Farm

CHISHILL ROAD

Chishill Orchard Farm

Lime Farm

3

Sewage Works

HEYDON ROAD

REEVES PIGHTLE

39

PICKNAGE ROAD

BARLEY ROAD

B1039

THE PUDGELL

PH

PLAISTOW WAY

Great Chishill

2

CHISHILL ROAD

B1039

Chishill Windmill

New Barn-hill Farm

MAY STREET

MALTINGS LA

COLTS CT

HALL LANE

Barley VP Sch

PO

WALLER'S CL

CHURCH END LA

SCHOOL LA

Manor Farm

Sewage Works

The Hall

PUDDING LA

CHURCHFIELD

SHAFTENHOE END ROAD

BOGMOOR RD

1

40 A 41 B C D 42 E F 38

A B C D E F

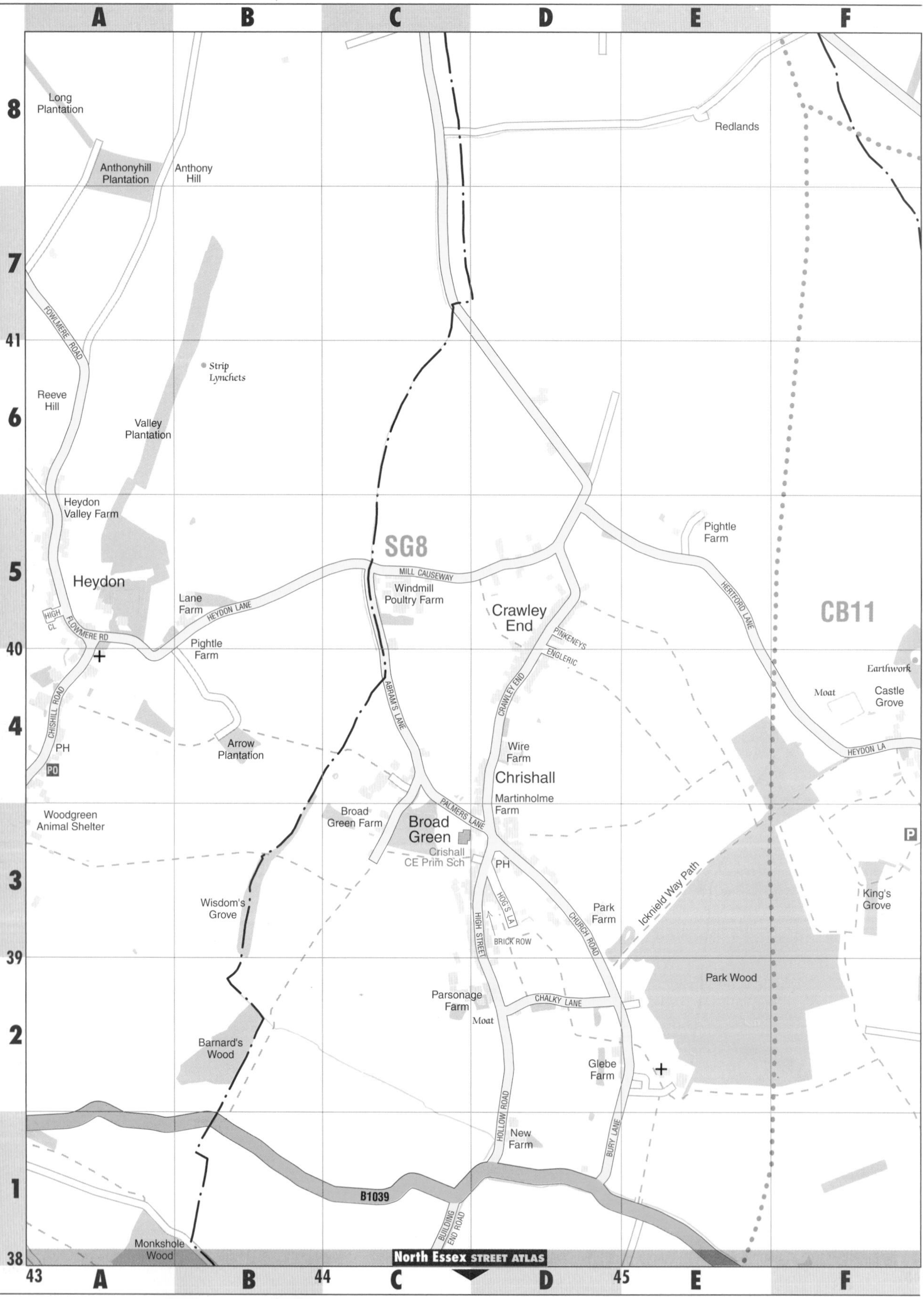

8
Long
Plantation

Anthonyhill
Plantation   Anthony Hill

Redlands

7

41

Strip
Lynchets

6
Reeve
Hill

Valley
Plantation

Heydon
Valley Farm

SG8

5

Pightle
Farm

MILL CAUSEWAY

Heydon

Lane
Farm

Windmill
Poultry Farm

Crawley
End

CB11

PINKENEYS

40

HIGH
CL

FLOWMERE RD

HEYDON LANE

Pightle
Farm

ENGLERIC

HERTFORD LANE

Earthwork

Moat   Castle
Grove

CHISHILL ROAD

+

ABRAM'S LANE

CRAWLEY END

4

Arrow
Plantation

Wire
Farm

HEYDON LA

PH

PO

Chrishall

Woodgreen
Animal Shelter

Broad
Green Farm

Broad
Green

Martinholme
Farm

P

King's
Grove

PALMERS LANE

Crishall
CE Prim Sch

Icknield Way Path

3

Wisdom's
Grove

PH

Park
Farm

HIGH STREET

NGG'S LA

BRICK ROW

CHURCH ROAD

39

Park Wood

2

Barnard's
Wood

Parsonage
Farm

Moat

CHALKY LANE

Glebe
Farm

+

HOLLOW ROAD

New
Farm

BURY LANE

1

B1039

BUILDING END ROAD

38

Monkshole
Wood

43 A B 44 C D 45 E F

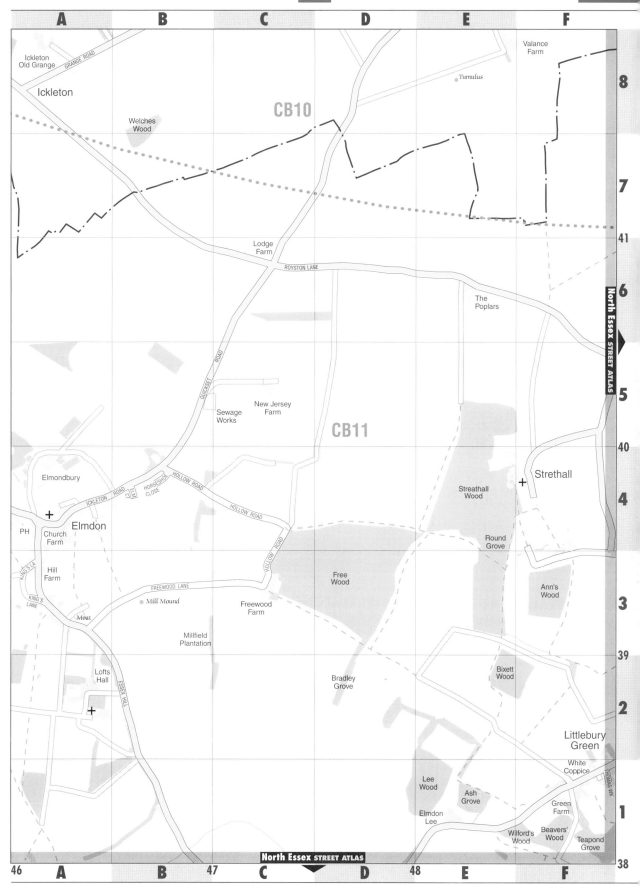

A B C D E F

8

CB10

7

41

6

Valance Farm

Ickleton Old Grange
GRANGE ROAD

Ickleton

Welches Wood

Tumulus

Lodge Farm

ROYSTON LANE

The Poplars

5

40

QUICKSET ROAD

Sewage Works

New Jersey Farm

CB11

Strethall

Streathall Wood

4

Elmondbury

HORSESHOE CLOSE

HOLLOW ROAD

ICKLETON ROAD

ELM CL

+

PH

Church Farm

Elmdon

HOLLOW ROAD

HOLLOW ROAD

Round Grove

Ann's Wood

39

KING'S LA

Hill Farm

KING'S LANE

FREEWOOD LANE

Mill Mound

Moat

Freewood Farm

Free Wood

Millfield Plantation

Bradley Grove

Bixett Wood

3

2

Lofts Hall

ESSEX HILL

+

Littlebury Green

White Coppice

THOMAS WK

Lee Wood

Ash Grove

Green Farm

1

Elmdon Lee

Wilford's Wood

Beavers' Wood

Teapond Grove

46 A B 47 C D 48 E F 38

North Essex STREET ATLAS

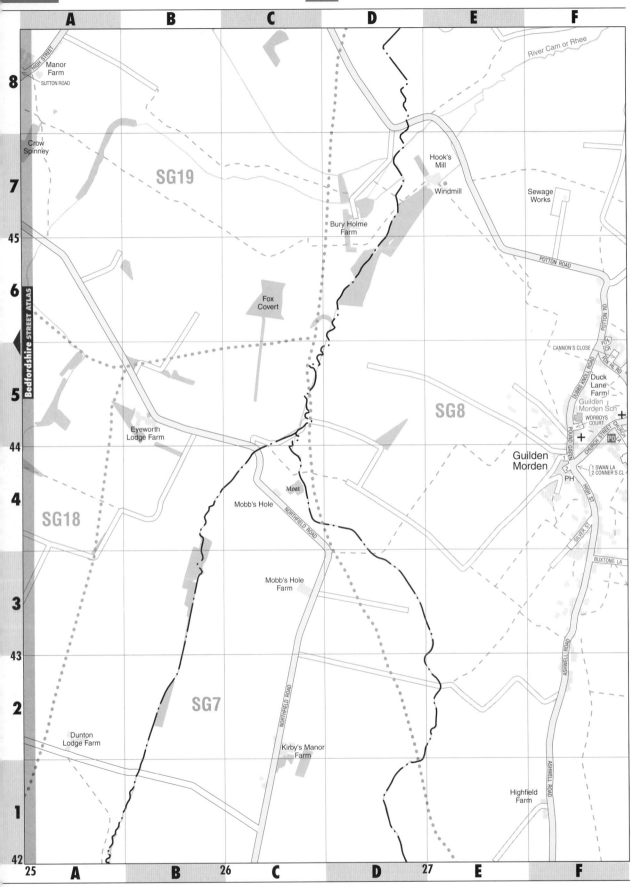

A   B   C   D   E   F

8

High Street
Manor
Farm
SUTTON ROAD

Crow
Spinney

SG19

River Cam or Rhee

Hook's
Mill

Windmill

Sewage
Works

7

45

Bury Holme
Farm

POTTON ROAD

6

Fox
Covert

Bedfordshire STREET ATLAS

POTTON RD

CANNON'S CLOSE

FOX
CR
FOX HL RD

Duck
Lane
Farm

Guilden
Morden Sch

WORBOYS
COURT

5

SG8

Eyeworth
Lodge Farm

DUBBS KNOLL ROAD

POUND GREEN

CHURCH STREET

CHURCH

PO

44

Guilden
Morden

1 SWAN LA
2 CONNER'S CL

PH

4

SG18

Mobb's Hole

NORTHFIELD ROAD

Moat

HIGH ST

SILVER ST

BUXTONS LA

3

Mobb's Hole
Farm

43

SG7

NORTHFIELD ROAD

ASHWELL ROAD

2

Dunton
Lodge Farm

Kirby's Manor
Farm

1

ASHWELL ROAD

Highfield
Farm

42

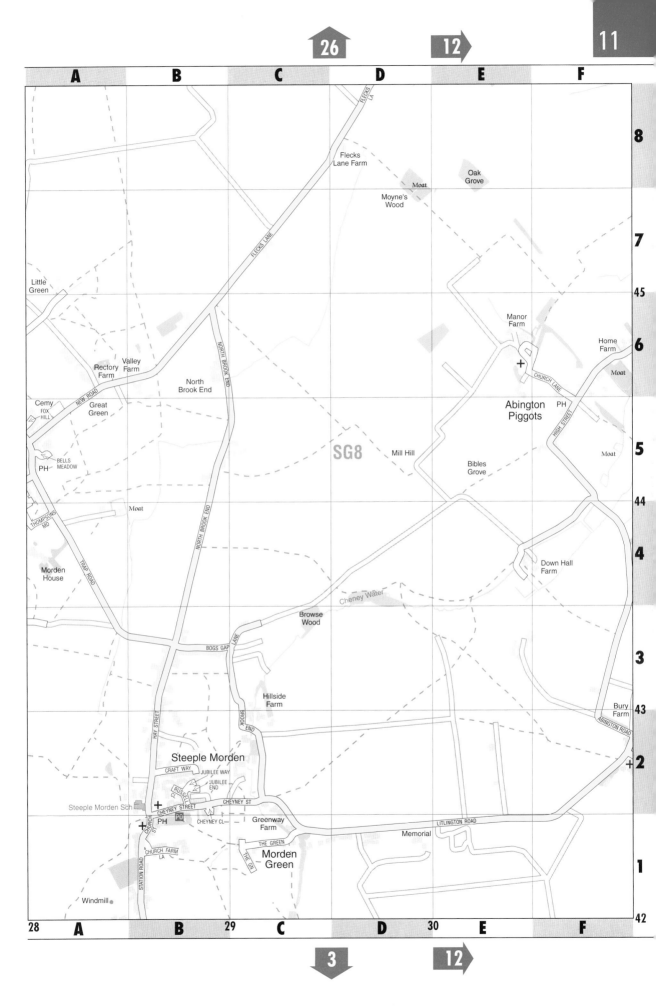

Flecks Lane Farm

Oak Grove

Moat

Moyne's Wood

Little Green

Manor Farm

Home Farm

Moat

Valley Farm

Rectory Farm

North Brook End

Abington Piggots

PH

Cemy
FOX HILL

Great Green

SG8

Mill Hill

Moat

PH
BELLS MEADOW

Bibles Grove

Moat

THOMPSONS MD

Moat

Down Hall Farm

MORDEN House

TRAP ROAD

Cheney Water

Browse Wood

BOGS GAP LANE

Bury Farm

ABINGTON ROAD

Hillside Farm

BROOK END

HAY STREET

Steeple Morden

CRAFT WAY   JUBILEE WAY

JUBILEE END

RUSSELL CL

CHEYNEY ST

Steeple Morden Sch

CHEYNEY STREET

PH   PO

CHEYNEY CL

Greenway Farm

Memorial

LITLINGTON ROAD

CHURCH ST

CHURCH FARM LA

THE GREEN

Morden Green

THE GN

STATION ROAD

Windmill

FLECKS LA

FLECKS LANE

NORTH BROOK END

NEW ROAD

CHURCH LANE

HIGH STREET

11
27

A B C D E F

8

Airfield (dis)

DANGER AREA

Mill River

Bassingboum Barracks

7

Boy Bridge

FEN ROAD

OXFORD CL

45

SAGGERS CL

GUISE LANE

Haygate Farm

6

Bleak Farm

NORTH END

Rectory Farm

Cemy

WALNUT TREE CL

PARK VW

THE FILLANCE

PH

5

SG8

MILL LANE

FORTUNE WY

CHURCH CL

ELBOURN WY

EL BOURN WY

KEFFORD CL

Manor Farm

THE LIMES

PLAYLES CL

HIGH ST

PH

44

POPLAR FARM CL

PO

LIMES CLOSE

PEPPER CL

EM TREE CL

WILLMOTT RD

CROFTS WY

DRIVE

KNUTSFORD ROAD

THE TANYAR

Ash Plantation

4

BROOK ROAD

Liby

Bassingbourn

Bassingbourn County Prim Sch

Bassingbourn Village Coll

Clear Farm

Sewage Works

Low Farm

SOUTH END

SPRING LANE

3

Moat

Brook Orchard Piggery

BASSINGBOURN ROAD

Bury Farm

43

Cemetery

Darwin Farm

CHAPEL CL

NEW CL

PH

MEETING LA

ABBOTTS CL

Icknield Way Path

2

Manor Farm

SILVER ST

MIDDLE ST

CHURCH ST

MALTING LA

Hill Farm

SOUTH ST

Litlington

ANVIL LA

COCKHALL LA

COCKHALL CL

CHERRY TREE CL

Sheen Farm

ROYSTON ROAD

1

42

11
4

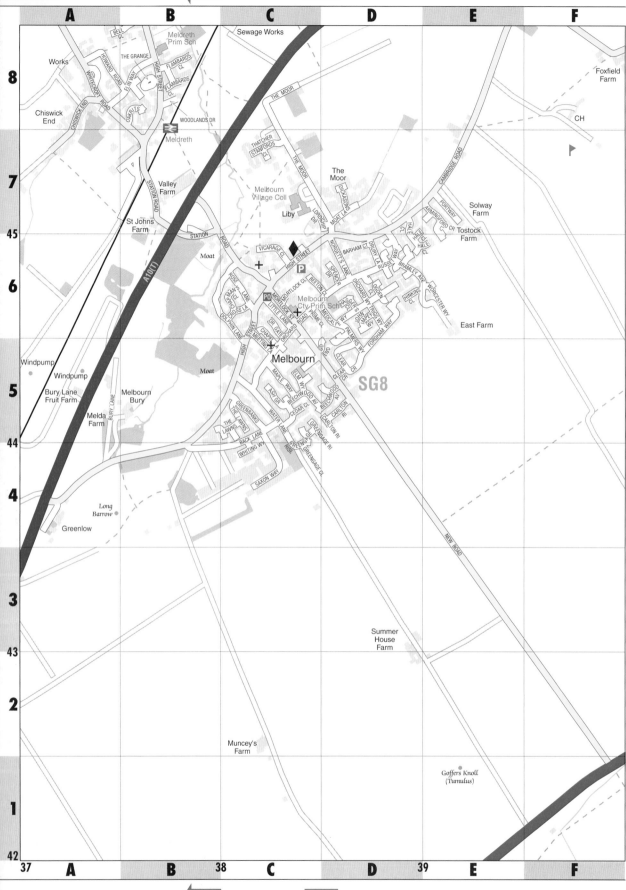

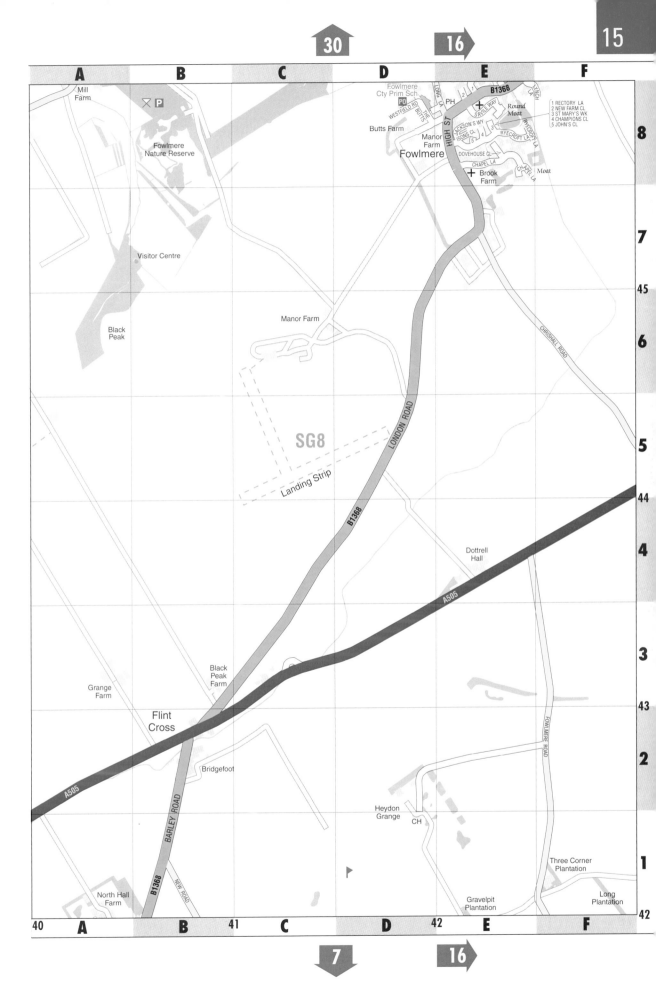

A   B   C   D   E   F

8

7

45

6

5

44

4

3

43

2

1

42

Newditch
Plantation

GRAVEL PIT HILL

Gravelpit Hill
Plantation

A505

Heath Farm

CHRISHALL
ROAD

Long
Plantation

American
Air Museum

Royal Anglian
Regiment Museum

CB2

Home
Plantation

Grange
Farm

Duxford
Grange House

Forty Acre
Plantation

Round
Plantation

SG8

Chrishall
Grange

Chrishall
Grange
Plantation

Laburnum
Plantation

CB10

43   A   B   44   C   D   45   E   F

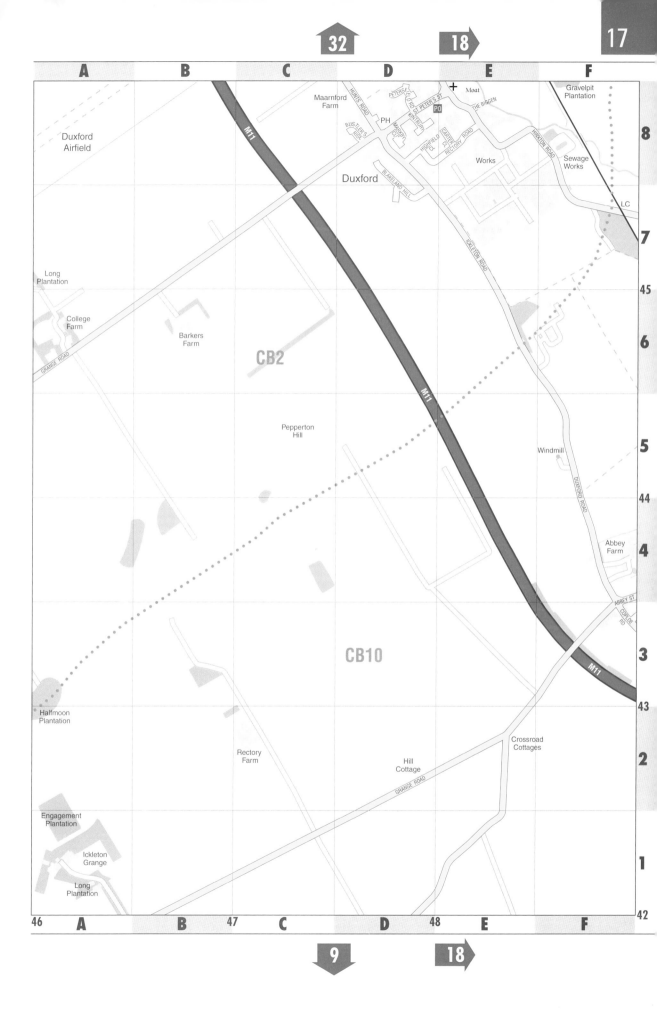

A B C D E F

Duxford
Airfield

Maarnford
Farm

Duxford

PETERSFIELD RD
ST PETER'S ST
PO
PH
KINTBURY
IMP END
HIGHFIELD CL
CARTER CL
RECTORY ROAD
THE BIGGEN
Moat
Works
HINXTON ROAD
Gravelpit
Plantation

BUSTLER'S RISE
HUNTS ROAD

BLAKELAND HILL

Sewage
Works

LC

Long
Plantation

College
Farm

Barkers
Farm

GRANGE ROAD

CB2

ICKLETON ROAD

M11

M11

Pepperton
Hill

Windmill

DUXFORD ROAD

44

Abbey
Farm

ABBEY ST
COLLEGE RD

M11

CB10

Halfmoon
Plantation

Rectory
Farm

Hill
Cottage

GRANGE ROAD

Crossroad
Cottages

Engagement
Plantation

Ickleton
Grange

Long
Plantation

46 A B 47 C D 48 E F 42

8
7
45
6
5
44
4
3
43
2
1

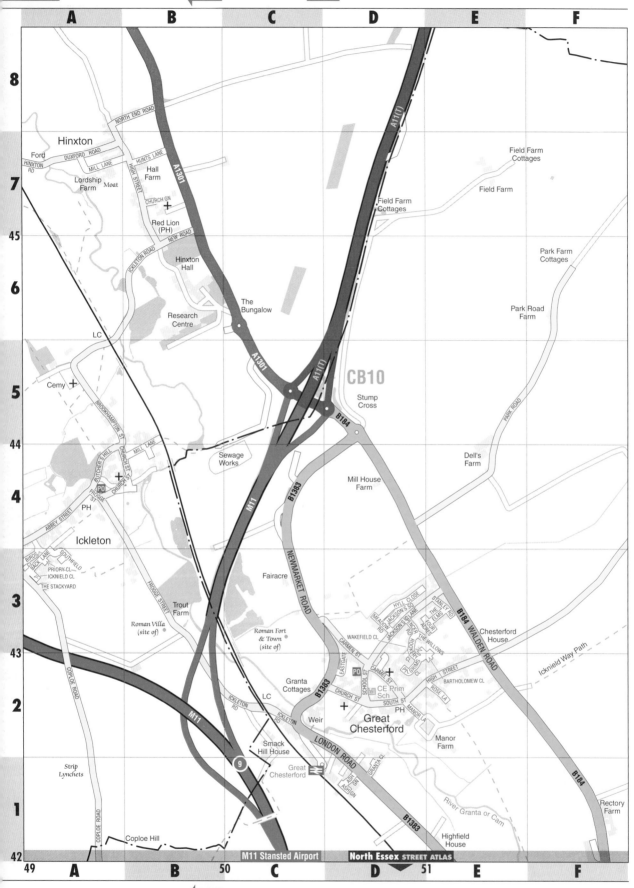

Hinxton

Ford

HINXTON RD

DUXFORD ROAD

MILL LANE

HUNTS LANE

NORTH END ROAD

Lordship Farm

Moat

HIGH STREET

Hall Farm

A1301

CHURCH GN

Red Lion (PH)

NEW ROAD

ICKLETON ROAD

Hinxton Hall

LC

Research Centre

The Bungalow

A1301

A11(T)

CB10

Field Farm Cottages

Field Farm Cottages

Field Farm

Park Farm Cottages

Park Road Farm

Stump Cross

B184

Cemy

BROOKHAMPTON ST

CHURCH ST

MILL LANE

BUTCHER'S HILL

Sewage Works

M11

B1383

Mill House Farm

Dell's Farm

PARK ROAD

PO

FORGE ST

CHURCH ST

PH

ABBEY STREET

Ickleton

BIRDS

BACK LANE

SOUTHFIELD

PRIORY-CL

ICKNIELD CL

THE STACKYARD

FROGGE STREET

Trout Farm

Roman Villa (site of)

Roman Fort & Town (site of)

Fairacre

NEWMARKET ROAD

HYLL CLOSE

STANLEY RD

MEADOW RD

JACKSON'S SQ

JACKSON'S LANE

GINGER CL

THE ELMS

THE WILLOWS

ROOKERY CL

ROOKERY CL

Chesterford House

B184 WALDEN ROAD

Icknield Way Path

WAKEFIELD CL

CARMEL ST

EASTGATE

SCHOOL ST

PO

CARMEL ST

CHURCH ST

CE Prim Sch

HIGH STREET

BARTHOLOMEW CL

ROSE LA

MANOR LA

Granta Cottages

B1383

SOUTH ST

PH

Great Chesterford

Strip Lynchets

COPLOE ROAD

M11

ICKLETON RD

LC

ICKLETON RD

Weir

LONDON ROAD

Smack Hill House

9

Great Chesterford

GRANTA CL

Manor Farm

B184

COPLOE ROAD

Coploe Hill

B1383

Highfield House

River Granta or Cam

Rectory Farm

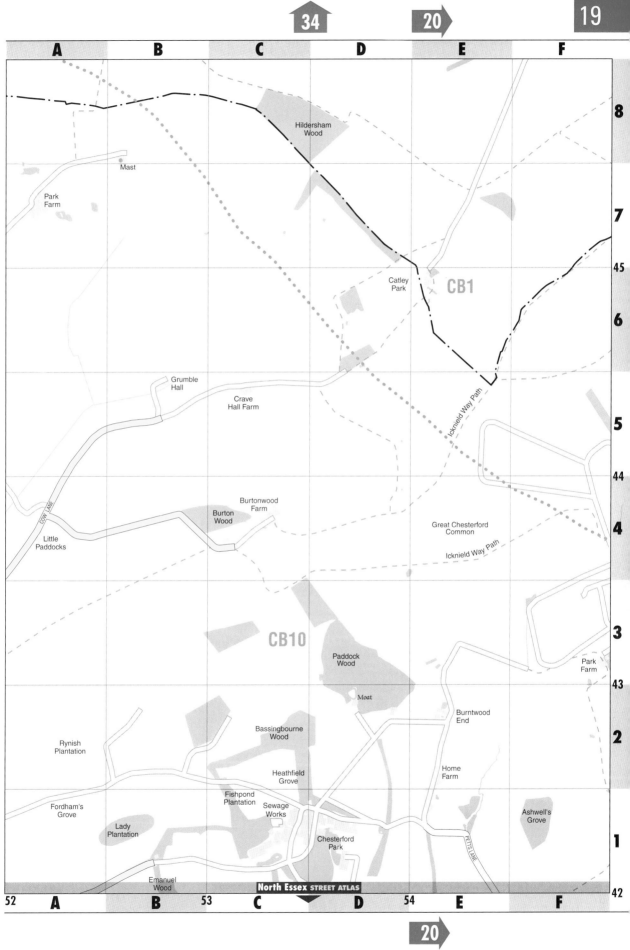

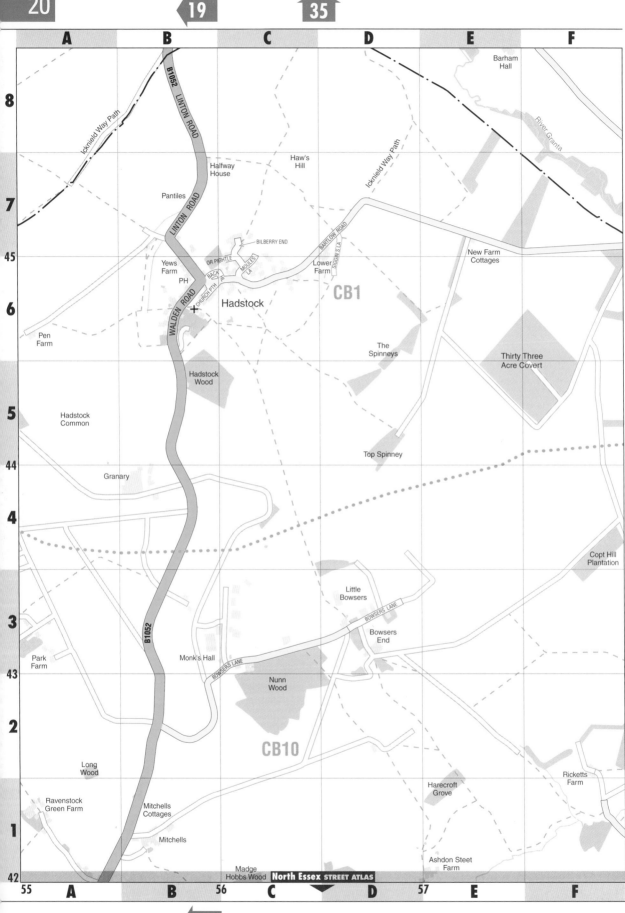

A B C D E F

8

7

45

6

5

44

4

3

43

2

1

42

55 A B 56 C D 57 E F

Barham Hall

River Granta

Icknield Way Path

B1052 LINTON ROAD

Halfway House

Pantiles

Haw's Hill

Icknield Way Path

BILBERRY END

OR PIGHTLE

MOULES LA

BARTLOW ROAD

SIGGIN'S LA

Yews Farm

PH

BACK

CHURCH PTH

WALDEN ROAD

Lower Farm

New Farm Cottages

CB1

Hadstock

Pen Farm

The Spinneys

Thirty Three Acre Covert

Hadstock Wood

Hadstock Common

Top Spinney

Granary

Copt Hill Plantation

Little Bowsers

BOWSERS LANE

B1052

Monk's Hall

BOWSERS LANE

Bowsers End

Park Farm

Nunn Wood

CB10

Long Wood

Harecroft Grove

Ricketts Farm

Ravenstock Green Farm

Mitchells Cottages

Mitchells

Madge Hobbs Wood

Ashdon Steet Farm

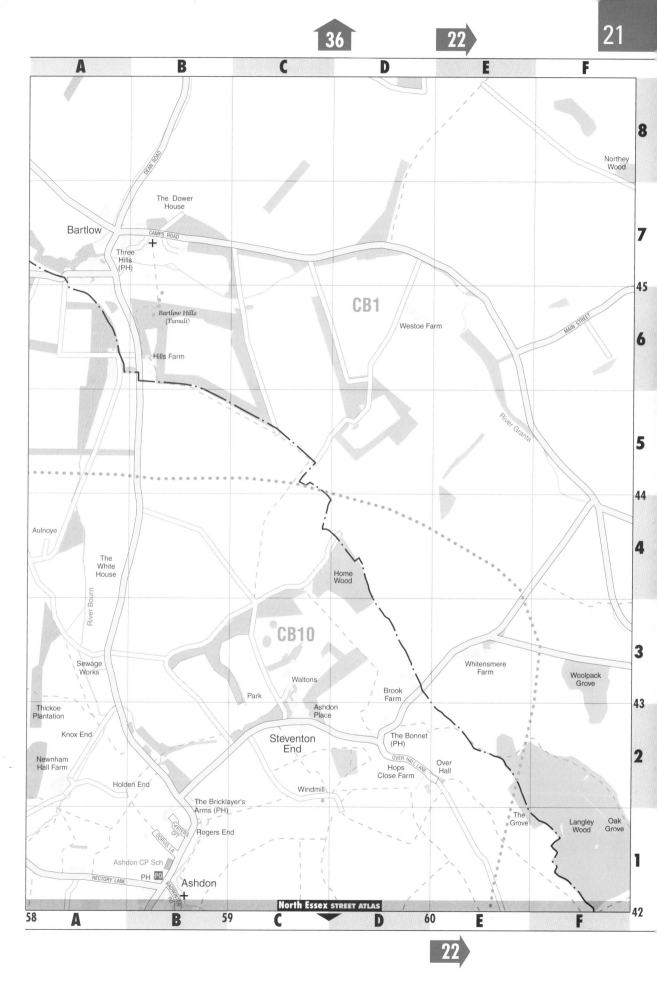

A B C D E F

8
7
45
6
5
44
4
3
43
2
1
42

Northey Wood

The Dower House

Bartlow

CAMPS ROAD

Three Hills (PH)

DEAN ROAD

CB1

Bartlow Hills (Tumuli)

Westoe Farm

MAIN STREET

Hills Farm

River Granta

Aulnoye

The White House

River Bourn

Home Wood

CB10

Whitensmere Farm

Woolpack Grove

Sewage Works

Waltons

Brook Farm

Thickoe Plantation

Park

Ashdon Place

Knox End

Steventon End

The Bonnet (PH)

Over Hall

Newnham Hall Farm

Holden End

Windmill

OVER HALL LANE

Hops Close Farm

The Grove

Langley Wood

Oak Grove

The Bricklayer's Arms (PH)

CARTERS CFT

OGRUS LA

Rogers End

Ashdon CP Sch

PH PO

RECTORY LANE

ROWITTER RD

Ashdon

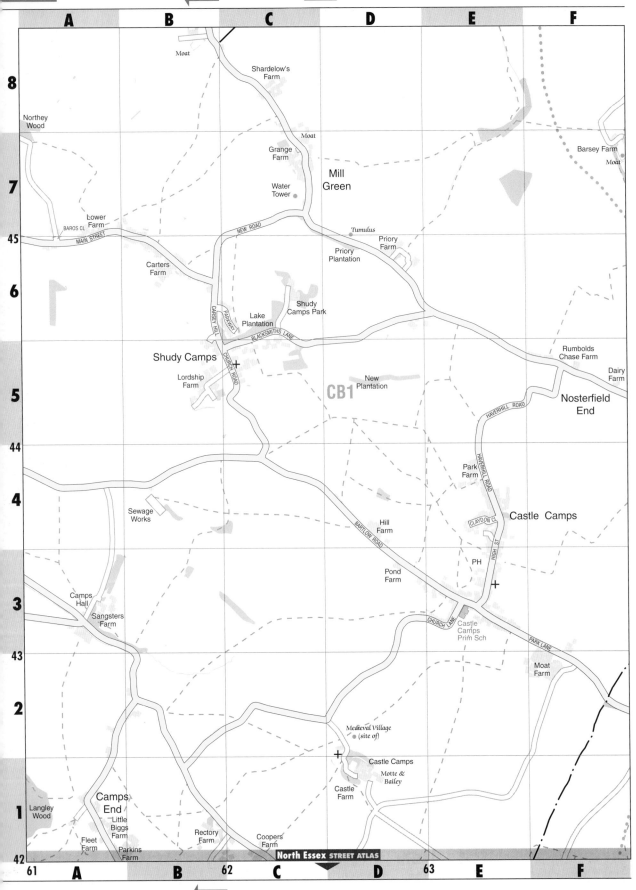

Moat

Shardelow's Farm

Northey Wood

Moat

Grange Farm

Mill Green

Barsey Farm

Moat

Water Tower

Lower Farm

BAROS CL

MAIN STREET

NEW ROAD

Tumulus

Priory Farm

Carters Farm

Priory Plantation

Shudy Camps Park

CARSEY HILL

PARKWAY

Lake Plantation

BLACKSMITHS LANE

Rumbolds Chase Farm

Dairy Farm

Shudy Camps

CHURCH ROAD

New Plantation

CB1

Nosterfield End

Lordship Farm

HAVERHILL ROAD

Park Farm

HAVERHILL ROAD

Sewage Works

BARTLOW ROAD

Hill Farm

CLAYDON CL

Castle Camps

PH

HIGH ST

Camps Hall

Sangsters Farm

Pond Farm

CHURCH LANE

Castle Camps Prim Sch

PARK LANE

Moat Farm

Medieval Village (site of)

Castle Camps

Motte & Bailey

Langley Wood

Camps End

Little Biggs Farm

Rectory Farm

Coopers Farm

Castle Farm

Fleet Farm

Parkins Farm

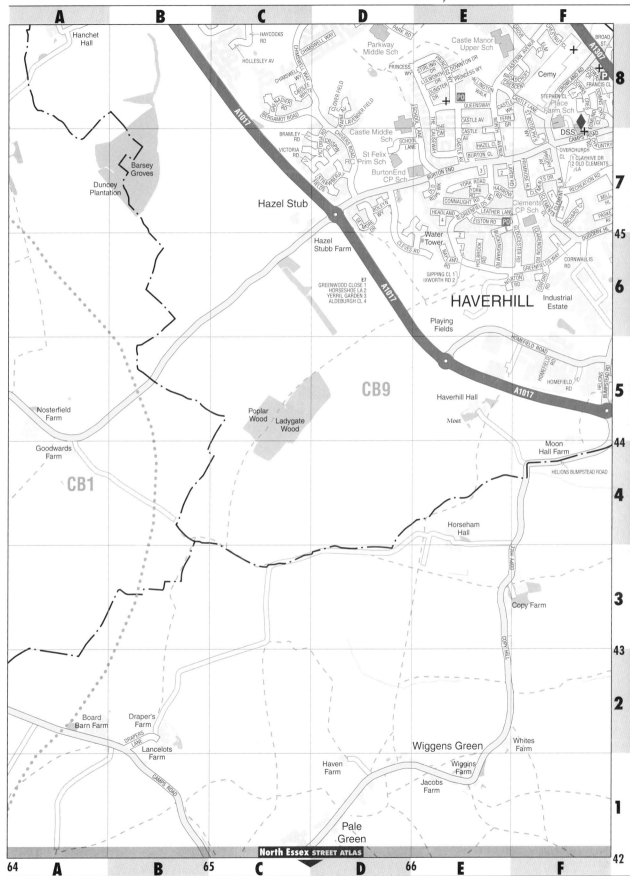

Hanchet Hall

HAYCOCKS RD
HOLLESLEY AV

CHIMSWELL WAY
CHIMSWELL WAY
Parkway Middle Sch
PARK RD
Castle Manor Upper Sch

CLOVER FIELD
PRINCESS WY

CROWN LA
EASTERN AVENUE
ELM
CHESTNUT CL.

BROAD ST.
A1307
P

PRINCESS WY
STIRLING DR
LULWORTH DR
DUNSTER DR
PRINCESS DR
DOWNTON DR
BROADCROFT
CASTLE WK
DOWNS CRES
DOWNS
CROWLAND RD
FRANCIS CL

Cemy

P

8

Barsey Groves

Duncey Plantation

GRENADIER RD
BERGAMOT ROAD
PAINE AV
LAVENDER FIELD

PRINCESS CRESCENT
WALLINGTON WALK
QUEENSWAY
CASTLE LANE
CASTLE AV
FERN GR

Stephen's Place Farm Sch

DSS
CAMPS ROAD

COUNTRY

BRAMLEY RD
VICTORIA RD
VICTORIA RD
CRISPIN
CHIVERS ROAD
Castle Middle Sch
St Felix RC Prim Sch
SCHOOL LANE
THE CW
SCHOOL LANE
CASTLE AV
THE CW
HAZEL CL.
CASTLE AV
BURTON CL

OVERCHURCH CL.
CLAYHIVE DR
OLD CLEMENTS LA
1
2

7

STRAWBERRY FIELDS
BurtonEnd CP Sch
BURTON END
LAYER RD
PRIMROSE HL
CLEMENTS LA
RECREATION RD
MILL HL

Hazel Stub

SYCAMORE DR
BOLEYN WY
YORK ROAD
YORK WK
HARROW WY
HEADLAND AV
GREENFIELDS WY
LEATHER LANE
ELSTON RD
PO
BUCKINGHAM RD
GLOUCESTER RD
CLARENDON RD
GREENFIELDS WAY
ORFORD RD
ORCHARD CL
DUDDERY HL
PASKE AV

45

Hazel Stubb Farm

ROPE WK
CONNAUGHT RD
Water Tower

HOLBROOK
NORTON RD

CORNWALLIS RD

E7
GREENWOOD CLOSE 1
HORSESHOE LA 2
YERRIL GARDEN 3
ALDEBURGH CL 4

GIPPING CL 1
IXWORTH RD 2

HAVERHILL
Industrial Estate

6

CB9

A1017

Playing Fields

HOMEFIELD ROAD
HOMEFIELD RD
HOMEFIELD RD

HELIONS BUMPSTEAD RD

5

Nosterfield Farm

Poplar Wood
Ladygate Wood

Haverhill Hall
Moat

A1017

Moon Hall Farm

44

Goodwards Farm

CB1

HELIONS BUMPSTEAD ROAD

Horseham Hall

4

COPY HILL

Copy Farm

3

43

Board Barn Farm
Draper's Farm
DRAPERS LANE
Lancelots Farm

Wiggens Green
Wiggins Farm
Whites Farm

2

CAMPS ROAD

Haven Farm
Jacobs Farm

1

Pale Green

64   A   B   65   C   D   66   E   F   42

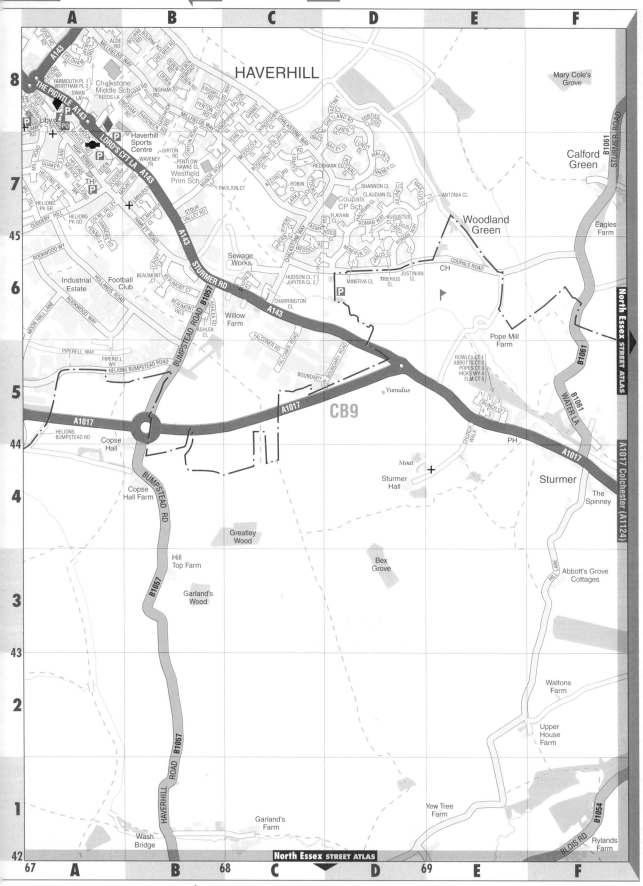

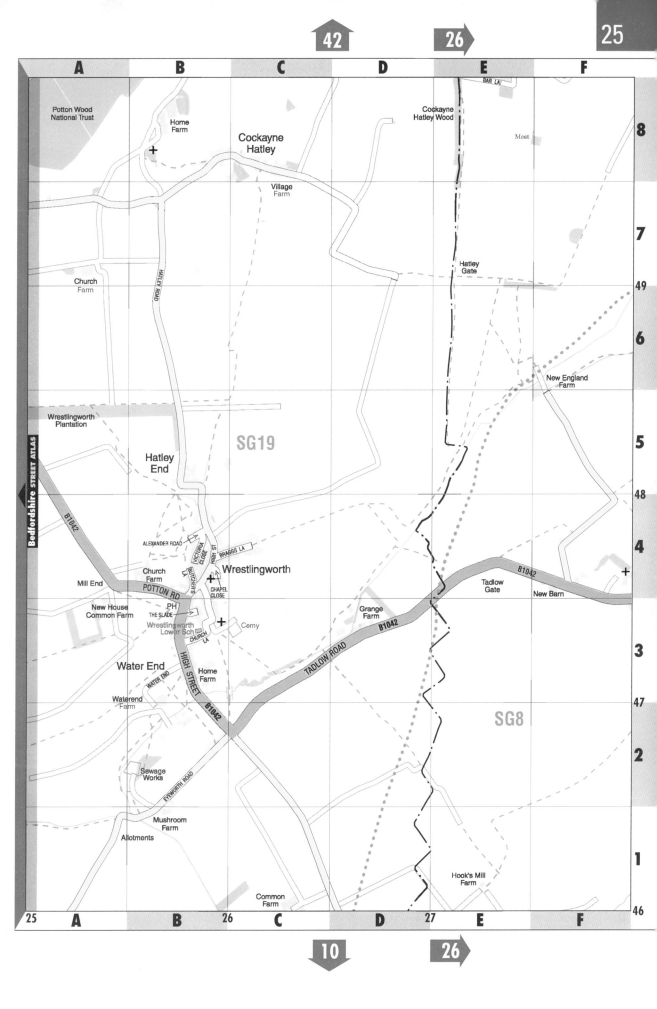

A B C D E F

Potton Wood
National Trust

Home
Farm

Cockayne
Hatley

Cockayne
Hatley Wood

BAR LA

Moat

8

Village
Farm

Church
Farm

HATLEY ROAD

Hatley
Gate

7

49

6

New England
Farm

Wrestlingworth
Plantation

SG19

Hatley
End

5

48

Bedfordshire STREET ATLAS

B1042

4

Mill End

ALEXANDER ROAD

VICTORIA CLOSE

HIGH ST

BRAGGS LA

Wrestlingworth

B1042

Tadlow
Gate

New Barn

Church
Farm

BUTCHER'S LA

CHAPEL
CLOSE

POTTON RD

New House
Common Farm

PH
THE SLADE
Wrestlingworth
Lower Sch

CHURCH LA

Cemy

Grange
Farm

B1042

TADLOW ROAD

3

Water End

HIGH STREET

WATER END

Home
Farm

SG8

Waterend
Farm

B1042

47

2

Sewage
Works

EYEWORTH ROAD

Mushroom
Farm

Allotments

Hook's Mill
Farm

1

Common
Farm

46

25 A B 26 C D 27 E F

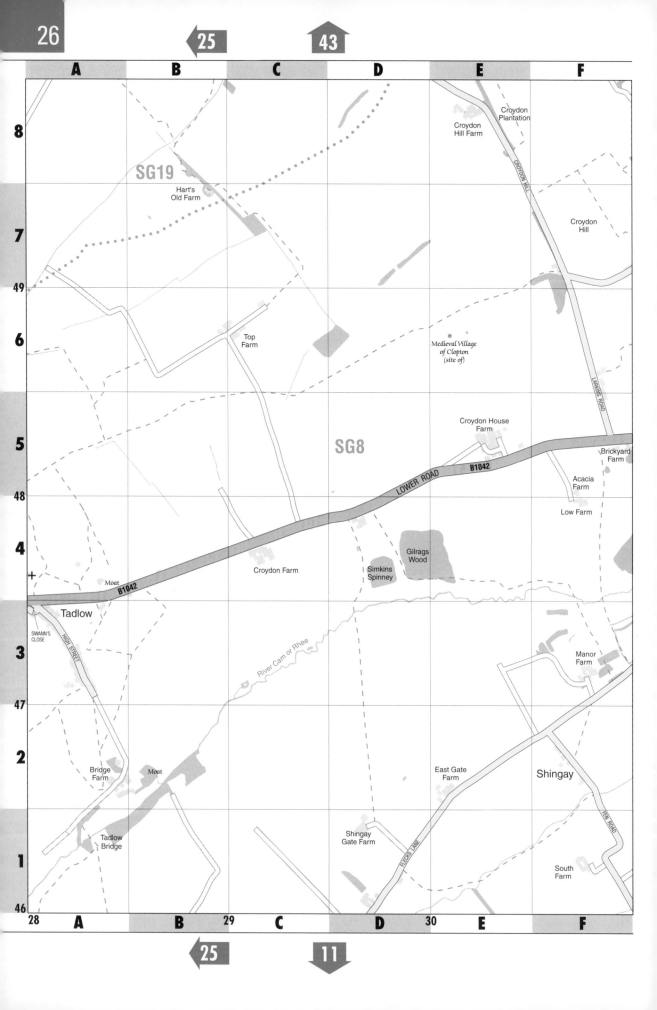

A B C D E F

8

SG19

Hart's
Old Farm

Croydon
Hill Farm

Croydon
Plantation

CROYDON HILL

7

Croydon
Hill

49

6

Top
Farm

Medieval Village
of Clopton
(site of)

LARKINS ROAD

5

SG8

Croydon House
Farm

Brickyard
Farm

LOWER ROAD B1042

Acacia
Farm

48

Low Farm

4

Croydon Farm

Simkins
Spinney

Gilrags
Wood

+

Moat B1042

Tadlow

SWANN'S
CLOSE

HIGH STREET

River Cam or Rhee

Manor
Farm

3

47

2

Bridge
Farm

Moat

East Gate
Farm

Shingay

FEN ROAD

FLECKS LANE

1

Tadlow
Bridge

Shingay
Gate Farm

South
Farm

46

A B C D E F

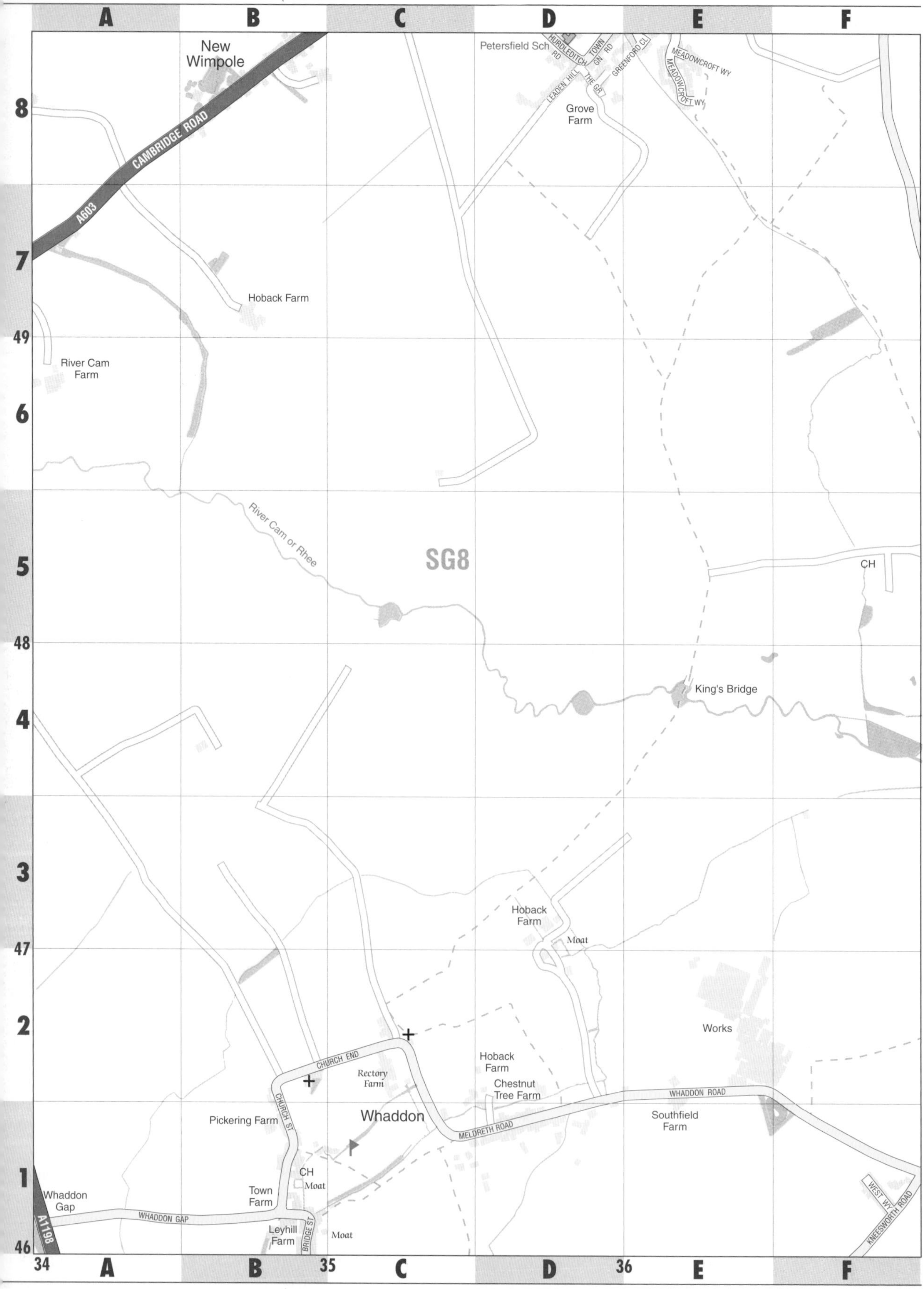

8

New Wimpole

CAMBRIDGE ROAD

A603

Petersfield Sch

Grove Farm

HURDLEDITCH RD
LEADEN HILL
THE GET
TOWN GN RD
GREENFORD CL

MEADOWCROFT WY
MEADOWCROFT WY

7

Hoback Farm

49

River Cam Farm

6

River Cam or Rhee

SG8

CH

5

48

King's Bridge

4

3

Hoback Farm

Moat

47

2

Works

Church End

Rectory Farm

Hoback Farm

Chestnut Tree Farm

WHADDON ROAD

CHURCH ST

Whaddon

MELDRETH ROAD

Southfield Farm

Pickering Farm

WEST WY

KNEESWORTH ROAD

1

Whaddon Gap

CH
Moat

Town Farm

A1198

WHADDON GAP

BRIDGE ST

Leyhill Farm

Moat

46

34 A B 35 C D 36 E F

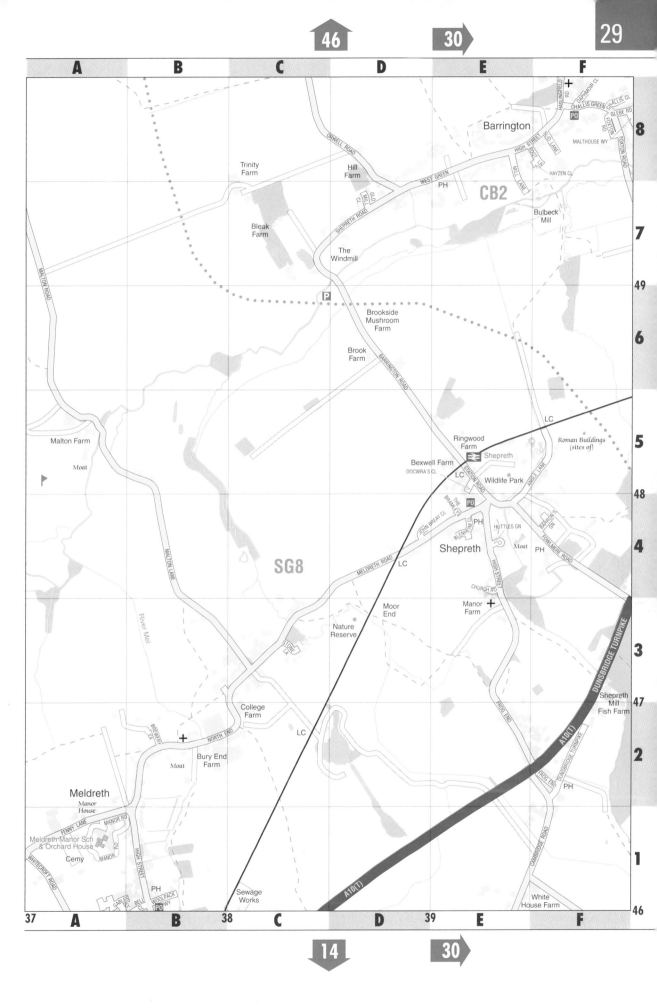

29
47

A
B
C
D
E
F
8
7
49
6
5
48
4
3
47
2
1
46
40
41
42
BENDYSHE WY
GLEBE ROAD
MALTHOUSE WY
River Cam or Rhee
Hoffers Brook Farm
ROYSTON RD
Hoffer Bridge
Manor Farm
Strip Lynchets
Rowley's Hill
FOXTON ROAD
LC
CAMBRIDGE ROAD
Sewage Plant &Works
College Farm
BARRINGTON ROAD
CB2
BARRINGTON RD
LC
Foxton
HALL CL
STATION ROAD
Bury Farm
Moat
Mortimer's Farm
Hoffer Brook
A10(T)
Foxton Prim Sch
BARONS LA
MORTIMERS LA
PH
ST LAURENCE RD
Windmill
HIGH STREET
PO
Foxton
ROYSTON ROAD
Beech Tree Farm
ILLINGWORTH WY
MALTING LANE
ROWLANDS CL
HILLFIELD
Hill Farm
THE GN
CAXTON LANE
Stocks Farm
WEST HL RD
SHEPRETH ROAD
West Hill
FOWLMERE ROAD
CAMBRIDGE ROAD
SHEPRETH ROAD
SG8
Field Farm
Rushmoor Plantation
Cemy
North Farm
The Cottage Lower Farm
LONG LANE
B1368
Lower Farm
Works
RAYNER'S CL
RECTORY LA
Home Farm
THRIPLOW ROAD
Fowlmere

29
15

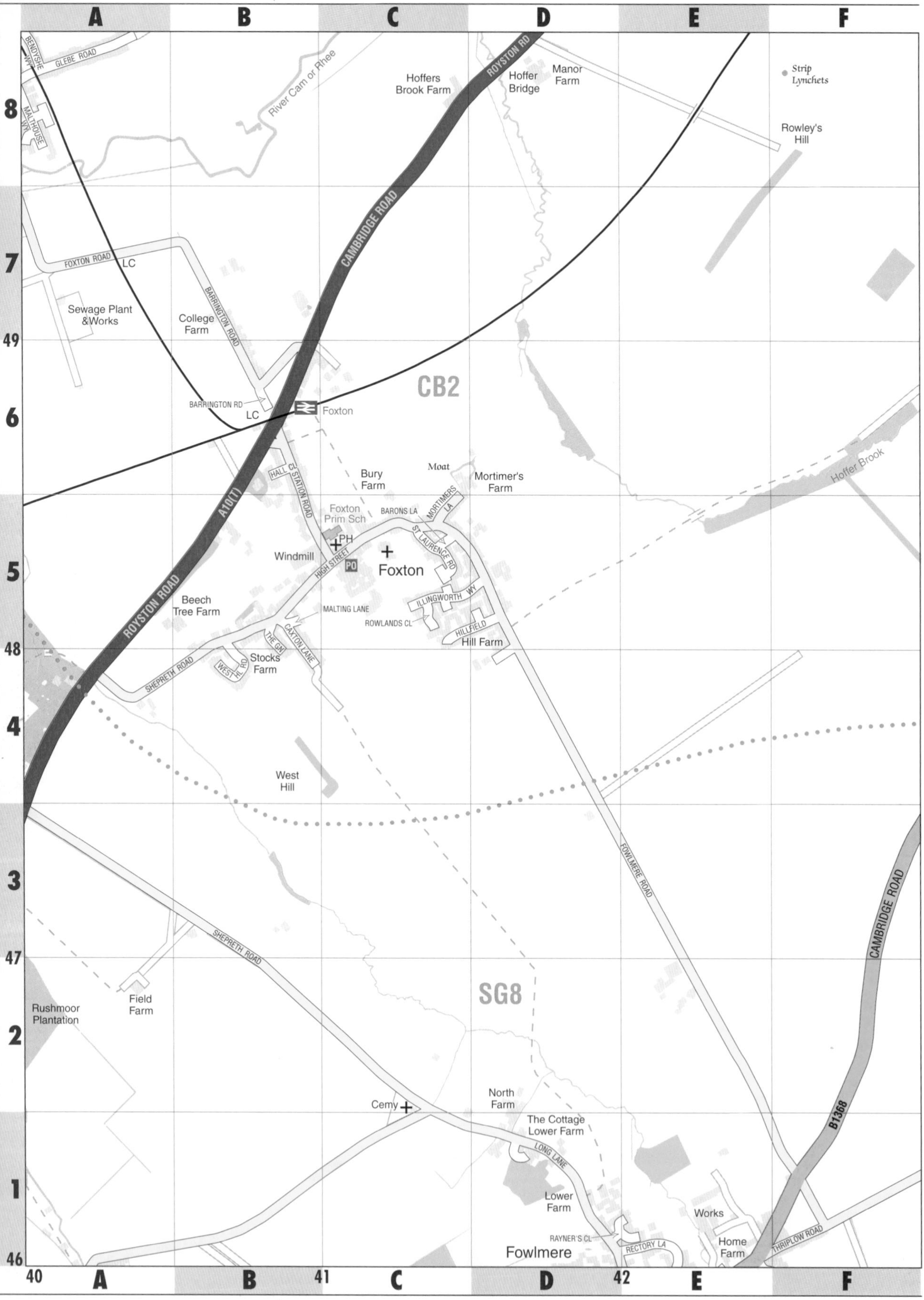

A B C D E F

8

7

49

6

5

48

4

3

47

2

1

46

Newton Hill
Poultry Farm

NEWTON ROAD

HARSTON ROAD

B1368 CAMBRIDGE ROAD

New Farm

Clunch
Pit Hill

Cockle
Hill

Newton

PO

KIDMANS CL

COCKLE CL

ORTS LEA

Top
Farm

Newton
Hall

COACH HO LA

TOWN STREET

PH

Newton
Manor

WHITTLESFORD ROAD

Kidman's
Plantation

New Farm

Fosters
Farm

NEWTON ROAD

M11

Reservoir

Hall
Farm

FOWLMERE ROAD

BROOK RD

B1368

CB2

Stanmoor Hall

Spinney
Hill Farm

BROOK ROAD

Fern
Wood

Squires
Plantation

SG8

Gate House
Thriplow Farm

Thriplow
CE Prim Sch

SCHOOL LANE

PIGEONS CL

CHURCH STREET

FOREMAN'S RD

SHERLD'S CFT LA

PO

FOWLMERE ROAD

PH

THE BAULK

Thriplow

Granary

LODGE ROAD

LOWER ST

Bassetts

Moat

Manor
Farm

FARM LANE

MIDDLE STREET

GRAVEL PIT HILL

CHURCH STREET

Newditch
Plantation

Heathfield

Duxford Camp

WHITEHALL GDNS

KINGSWAY

KINGSWAY

PEPPERS LA

WOBURN PL

LEDO ROAD

A505

Imperial
War
Museum

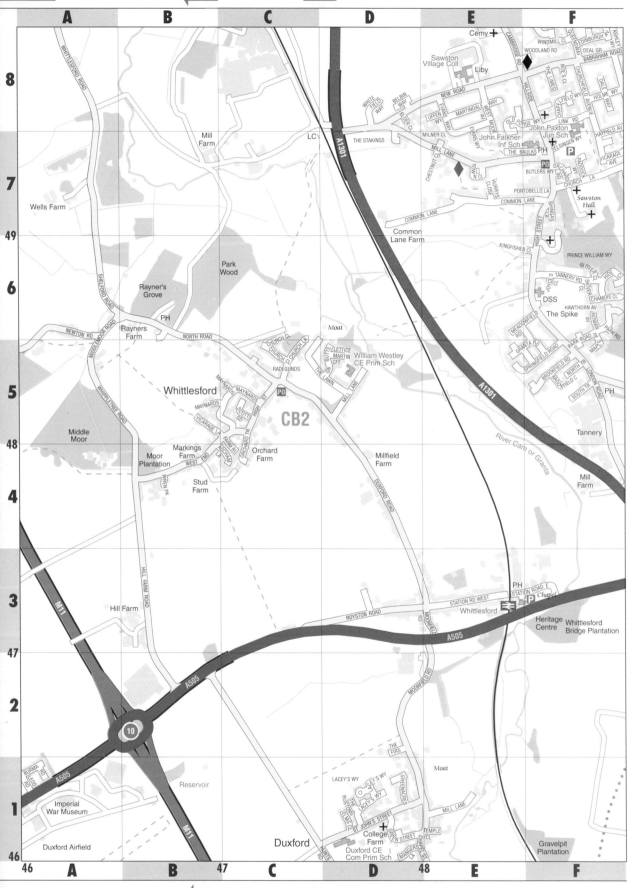

Mill
Hole

Sawston

GOSLING WY
WAKELIN AV
GROVE RD
LYNTON WY
TOWER RD
HUNTINGDON ROAD
SAFFRON RD
FALKNER RD
SUNDERLAND AVE
SAINFOIN CL
THE GREEN
HENRY MORRIS ROAD
PLANTATION RD
Icknield CP Sch
HALL CR
HUDDLESTON WAY
ST MARY'S ROAD

SAWSTON ROAD
HIGH ST

Hayfield
Plantation

49

West Green
Plantation

Dickman's
Grove

Creek's
Plantation

College
Farm

Moat

PH

Pampisford

BEECH LANE

Moat

CB2

Pampisford
Hall

NORTH ROAD

BREWERY ROAD

HAMMOND
HIGH ST
CHURCH LANE
CAUSEWAY
TOWN LA
GLEBE CR
PH

A505

Hanley
Hill

48

SOUTH ROAD

CB1

Railway
Plantation

A11(T)

47

A1301

Hinxton
Grange

Round
Plantation

CB10

Ash
Plantation

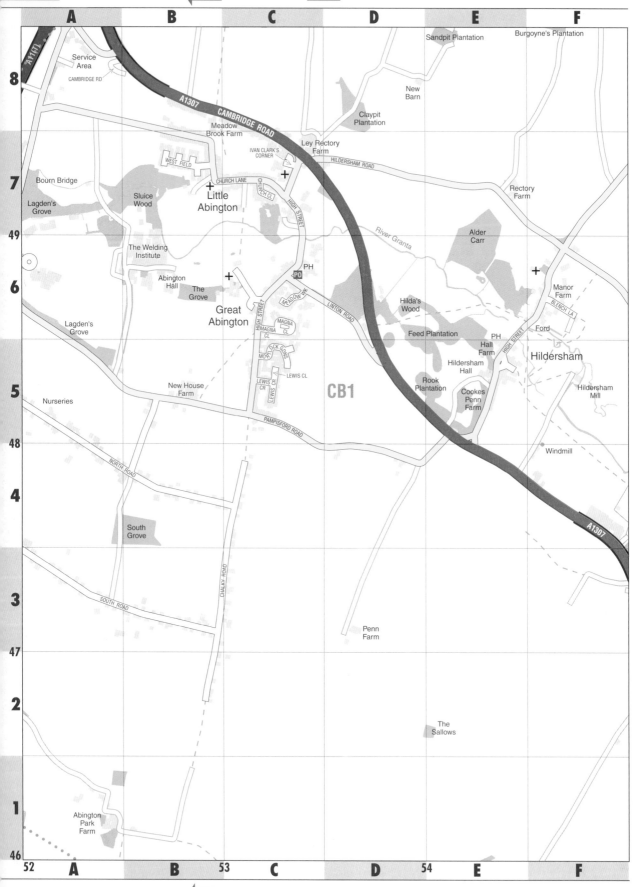

A   B   C   D   E   F

8

A11(T)

Service Area

CAMBRIDGE RD

A1307 CAMBRIDGE ROAD

Sandpit Plantation

Burgoyne's Plantation

New Barn

Claypit Plantation

Meadow Brook Farm

Ley Rectory Farm

HILDERSHAM ROAD

7

WEST FIELD

IVAN CLARK'S CORNER

CHURCH LANE

Bourn Bridge

Little Abington

CHURCH CL

CHURCH CL

HIGH STREET

Rectory Farm

Lagden's Grove

Sluice Wood

49

River Granta

Alder Carr

The Welding Institute

PH

PO

Manor Farm

BLENCH LA

6

Abington Hall

The Grove

Great Abington

MEADOW WK

LINTON ROAD

Hilda's Wood

Ford

Lagden's Grove

HIGH STREET

MAGNA CL

MAGNA CL

Feed Plantation

PH Hall Farm

HIGH STREET

Hildersham

MORTLOCK GDNS

Hildersham Hall

Hildersham Mill

LEWIS CL

LEWIS CL

LEWIS CR

Rook Plantation

5

New House Farm

CB1

Cookes Penn Farm

Nurseries

PAMPISFORD ROAD

48

NORTH. ROAD

Windmill

4

South Grove

A1307

3

CHALKY ROAD

SOUTH ROAD

Penn Farm

47

2

The Sallows

1

Abington Park Farm

46

52   A   B   53   C   D   54   E   F

A   B   C   D   E   F

8

Yole Farm

7

Green
Farm

49

Furze
Hill

6

Chilford Hall
Vineyard

Borley
Wood

Sand
Hill

B1052

CB1

5

Rivey
Hill

Greenditch Farm

48

Water
Tower

Square
Plantation

Little
Chilfords

Sewage
Works

Rivey
Wood

Borley
Wood

4

Cow Gallery
Wood

Fish
Ponds

THE WOODLANDS

Moat

THE WOODS

1 BALINGDON LA
2 PEMBROKE LA
3 DOLPHIN CL
4 MILLERS CL
5 CLOVER CT
6 RHUGARVE GDNS

CHERRY CL

BALSHAM ROAD

CRABTREE CROFT

CHALKLANDS

CHALKLANDS

TOWER VIEW

Linton

3

Little Linton

GIANT'S
LEYS

THE GROVE

PALMERS
CL

ST EDMONDS LANE

BACK ROAD

FLAXFIELDS

THE FURRELLS

RIVEY WAY

B1052

WHEAT
CFT

WHINBRINKMAN
RD

BAWTREE CR

HOLLYBUSH WY

CAMBRIDGE ROAD

Recreation Centre

HILLWAY

COLES LANE

Cemy

Liby

BARLEY
WAY

FAIRFIELD

Linton Heights
Jun Sch 3

47

Linton
Village Coll

MEADOW
LA

MARKET LA

FIELD
CL

JOINER'S RD

JOINER'S
CT

B1052

HORN LA

HIGH ST

GREEN
LA

MILL LA

PARSONAGE WY

HIGH ST

GRANTA
VALE

GRANTA
VALE

HORSEHEATH ROAD

GIBSON'S CL

BAKERS
LA

LONSDALE

MARTINS
LA

Harefield Rise

KENWOOD GDNS

THE RIDGEWAY

2

STATION RD

THE GRIP

HADSTOCK ROAD

PH

Linton CE
Inf Sch

BEECH WAY

Mill

CROSSWAYS

BARTLOW ROAD

PINCHAM'S
CLOSE

PINCHAM'S
CL

Linton Zoo
& Gardens

B1052

LONG LANE

A1307

Barham
Hall

1

The Windmill

55   A   56   B   C   57   D   E   F   46

A B C D E F

8

Water
Tower

Balsham
Wood

Icknield Way Path

MILL ROAD

Bottle
Hall

7

Chalk
Pit (dis)

49

6

Sewage
Works

Borley
Wood

WEBB'S ROAD

Mark's Grave

Ford

CB1

Streetly
Hall

5

48

Borley
Wood

Horseheath
Lodge

4

Heath
Farm

A1307

LINTON RD
PH

3

A1307

47

A1307

Crofts
Wood

2

A1307

Point to Point
Racecourse

1

46

37
55

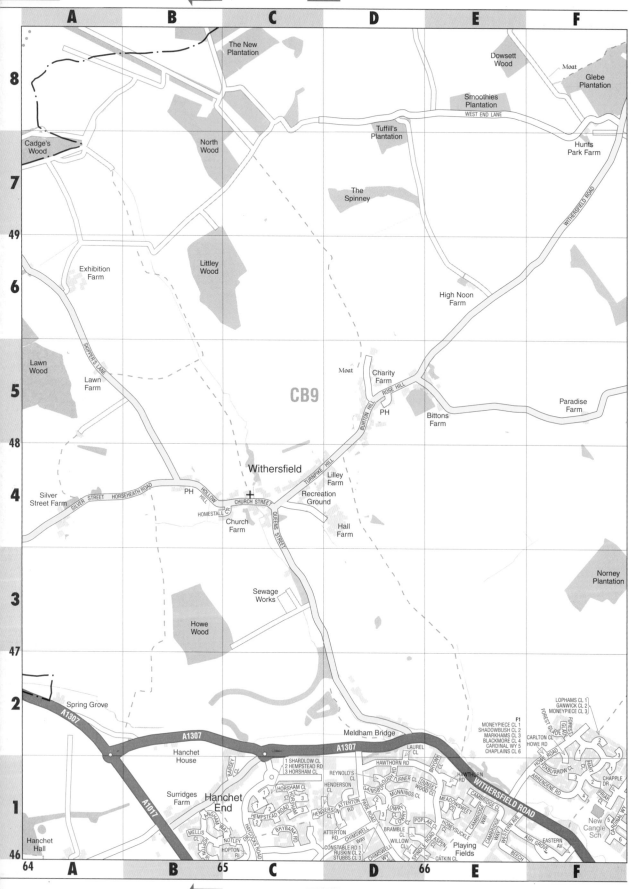

The New Plantation

Dowsett Wood

Moat

Glebe Plantation

Smoothies Plantation

WEST END LANE

Cadge's Wood

North Wood

Tuffill's Plantation

Hunts Park Farm

WITHERSFIELD ROAD

The Spinney

Exhibition Farm

Littley Wood

High Noon Farm

SKIPPER'S LANE

Lawn Wood

Lawn Farm

CB9

Moat

Charity Farm

ROSE HILL

PH

Bittons Farm

Paradise Farm

BURTON HILL

Silver Street Farm

SILVER STREET

HORSEHEATH ROAD

PH

HOLLOW HILL

CHURCH STREET

Withersfield

TURNPIKE HILL

Lilley Farm

Recreation Ground

HOMESTALL CL

Church Farm

QUEENS STREET

Hall Farm

Norney Plantation

Sewage Works

Howe Wood

Spring Grove

A1307

Meldham Bridge

A1307

F1
MONEYPIECE CL 1
SHADOWBUSH CL 2
MARKHAMS CL 3
BLACKMORE CL 4
CARDINAL WY 5
CHAPLAINS CL 6

LOPHAMS CL 1
GANWICK CL 2
MONEYPIECE CL 3

FOREST GLADE

CARLTON CL
HOWE RD

Hanchet House

LAUREL CL

BIXTON CL

HAWTHORN RD

Surridges Farm

Hanchet End

1 SHARDLOW CL
2 HEMPSTEAD RD
3 HORSHAM CL

HORSHAM CL

REYNOLD'S CL

HENDERSON CL

GAINSBOROUGH CL

TURNER RD

DINSEY WOOD CL

MUNNINGS CL

HAWTHORN RD

CAMBRIDGE CL

WITHERSFIELD ROAD

HOWE RD
FOXBUR/BROW CL

ARBENDENE RD

CHAPPLE DR

FRIAR CL

A1017

BARSEY CL

HEMPSTEAD ROAD

HANCROOKS ROAD

ANGHAM WAY

NOTLEY

HOPTON RI

BRYBANK RD

HENDERSON CL

ATTERTON RD

PARK ROAD

LOWRY CL

CHIMSWELL WAY

POPLAR CL

HONEYSUCKLE

MEADOWSWEET

CAMBRIDGE CL

WESTERN AV

New Cangle Sch

CARDINAL WY

MELLIS CL

ATTERTON RD

CONSTABLE RD 1
RUSKIN CL 2
STUBBS CL 3

CHIMSWELL WY

BRAMBLE CL

WILLOW

SPINDLE CL

ASPEN CL

SPINDLE ROAD

CATKIN CL

Playing Fields

ASH GROVE

BEECH

EASTERN AV

Hanchet Hall

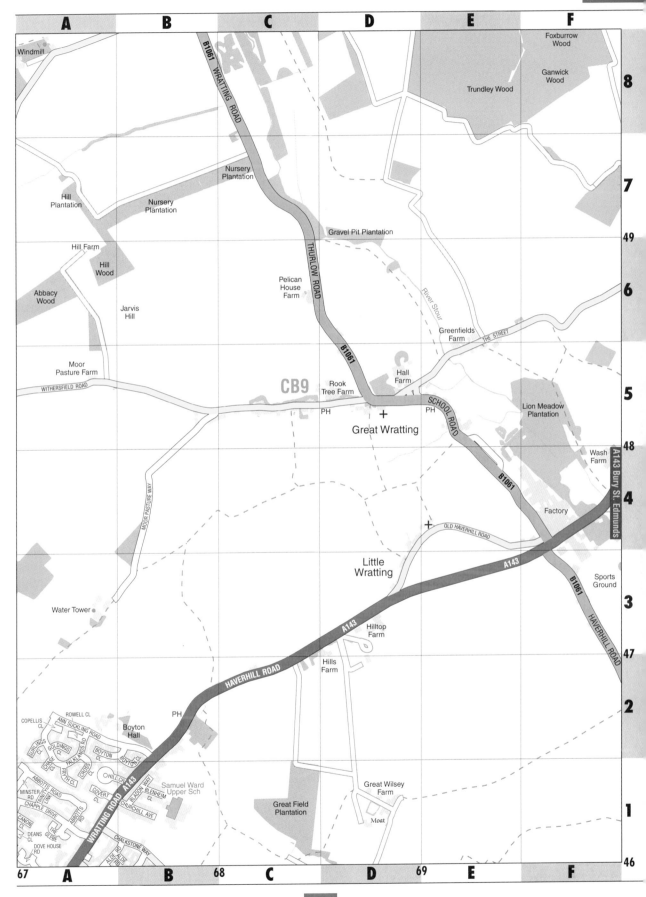

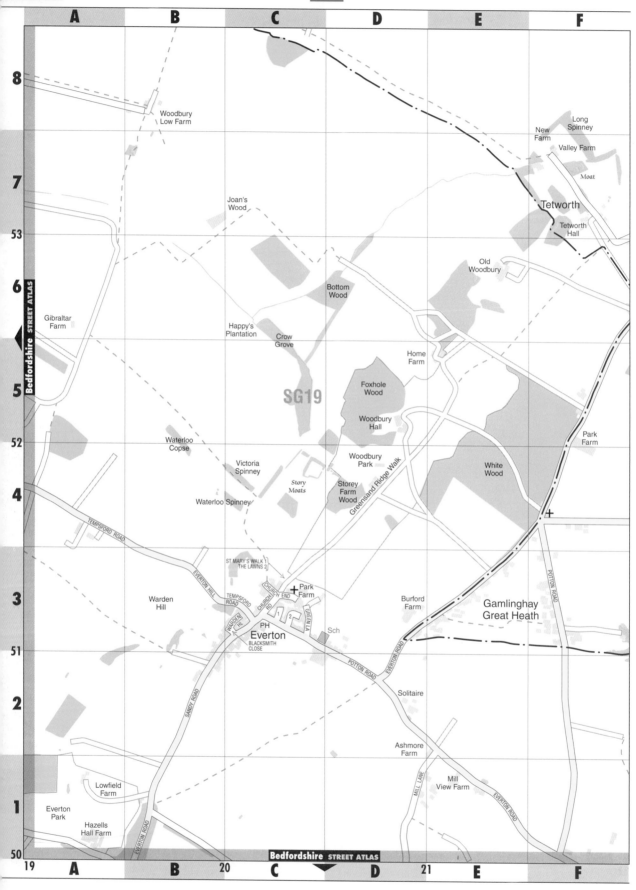

Bedfordshire STREET ATLAS

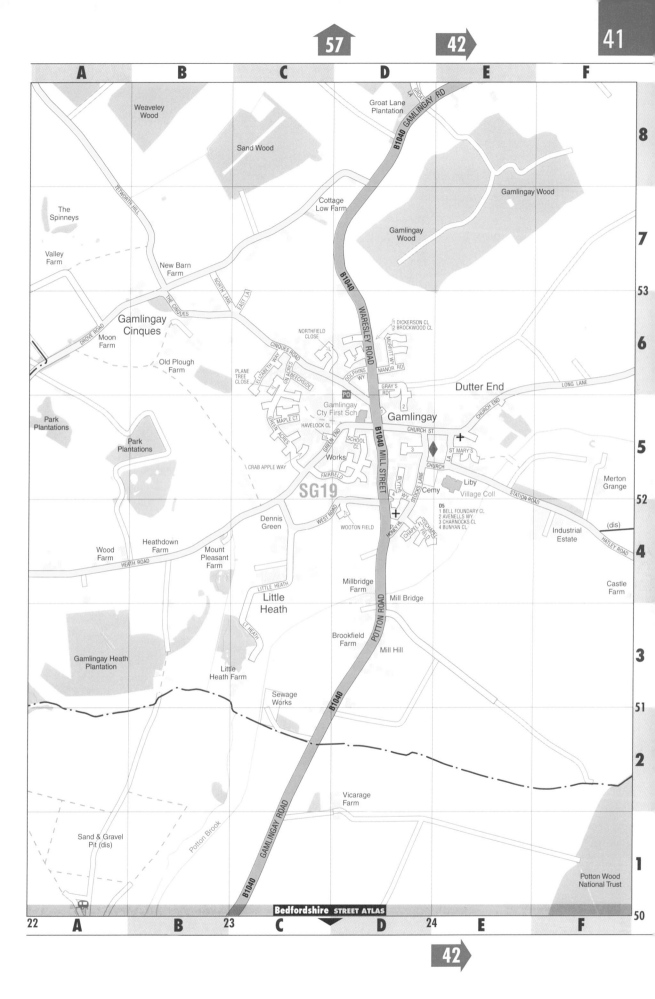

A B C D E F

8

Weaveley
Wood

Groat Lane
Plantation

B1040 GAMLINGAY RD

Sand Wood

Gamlingay Wood

7

The
Spinneys

Cottage
Low Farm

Gamlingay
Wood

53

Valley
Farm

New Barn
Farm

TETWORTH HILL

NORTH LANE

EAST LA

THE CINQUES

6

Gamlingay
Cinques

DROVE ROAD

Moon
Farm

Old Plough
Farm

CINQUES ROAD

NORTHFIELD
CLOSE

ELIZABETH WAY

DOLPHINS
WY

MANOR RD

MURITT WY

WARESLEY ROAD

B1040

1 DICKERSON CL
2 BROCKWOOD CL

1

2

GRAY'S
RD

Dutter End

LONG LANE

PLANE
TREE
CLOSE

THE ACRES

BEECHSIDE

PO

Gamlingay
Cty First Sch

2

Gamlingay

CHURCH END

Park
Plantations

GREEN END

MAPLE CT

HAVELOCK CL

SCHOOL
CL

3

CHURCH ST

ST MARY'S
CHURCH

5

Park
Plantations

GREEN ACRES

Works

FAIRFIELD

B1040 MILL STREET

BLYTHE WY

STOCKS LANE

CHURCH LA

Cemy

Liby
Village Coll

STATION ROAD

Merton
Grange

CRAB APPLE WAY

SG19

WEST ROAD

WOOTON FIELD

MONEY HL

CHAPEL FLD

RICHARD FIELD

D5
1 BELL FOUNDARY CL
2 AVENELLS WY
3 CHARNOCKS CL
4 BUNYAN CL

52

Wood
Farm

Heathdown
Farm

HEATH ROAD

Dennis
Green

Mount
Pleasant
Farm

LITTLE HEATH

Millbridge
Farm

Mill Bridge

Industrial
Estate

HATLEY ROAD

(dis)

4

Little
Heath

LT HEATH

Brookfield
Farm

POTTON ROAD

Mill Hill

Castle
Farm

Gamlingay Heath
Plantation

Little
Heath Farm

Sewage
Works

B1040

51

3

2

Potton Brook

GAMLINGAY ROAD

Vicarage
Farm

Sand & Gravel
Pit (dis)

B1040

1

Potton Wood
National Trust

50

22 A B 23 C D 24 E F

41
58

A B C D E F

8

7

53

6

Model
Farm

Fuller's
Hill Farm

Crooked Billet
Farm

LONG LANE

Allotments

SG19

5

52

4

Castle
Farm

HATLEY ROAD

Newlands
Buildings

BAULK LANE

Church
Farm

3

51

Dower
House

Hatley Park

BAR LANE

2

Wood
Farm

Cockayne Hatley
Wood

1

Potton Wood
National Trust

BAR LANE

BUFF LANE

50

25 A B 26 C D 27 E F

41
25

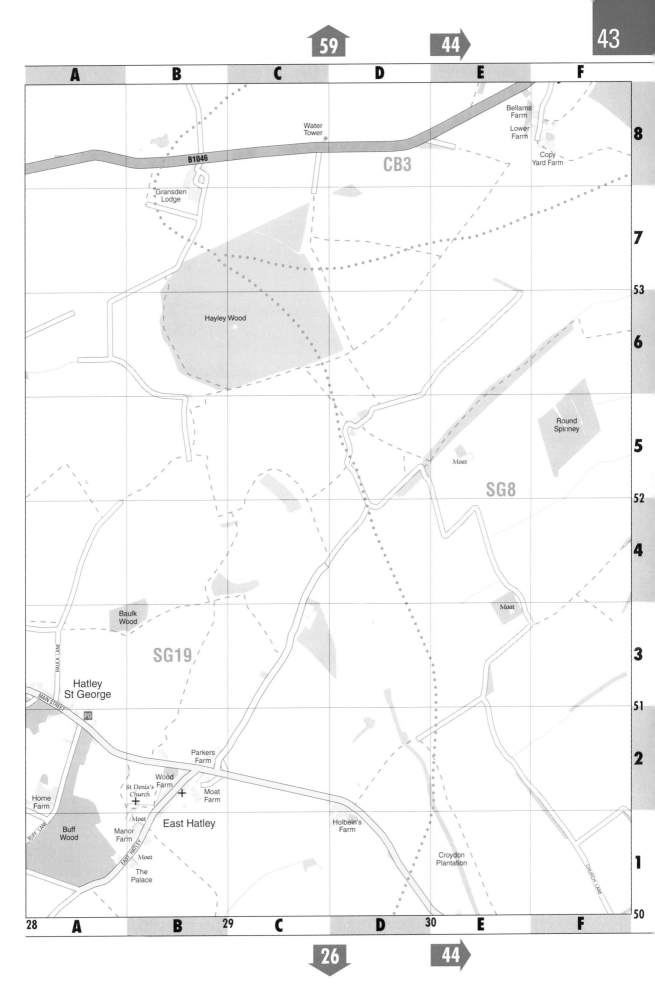

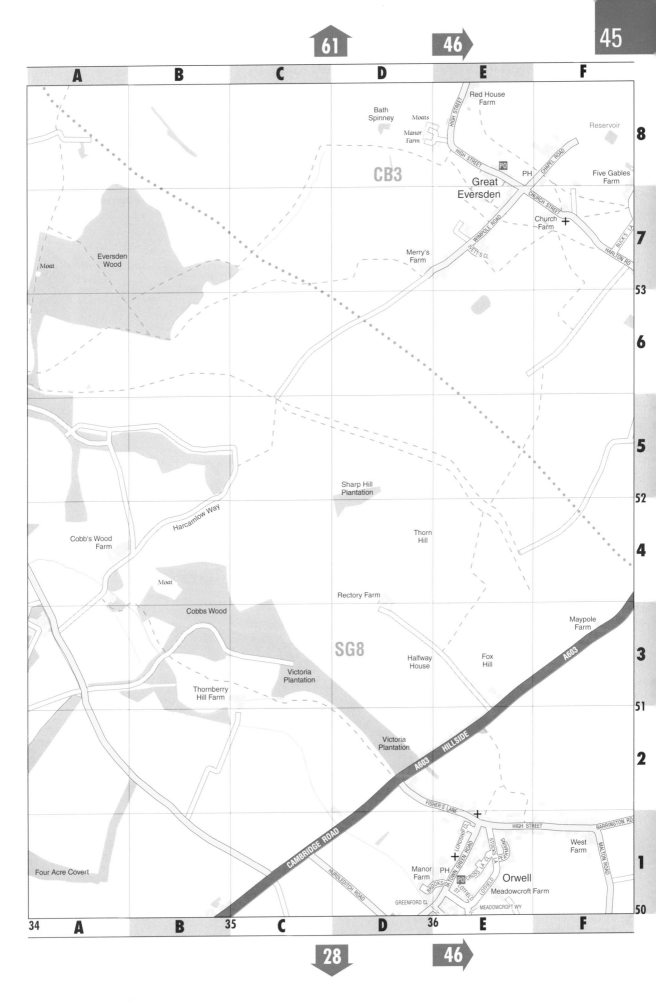

A B C D E F

8

Red House
Farm

Bath
Spinney   Moats   Reservoir

Manor
Farm

CB3   High Street   PO   Five Gables
Farm

Great
Eversden   PH

Church Street   Church
Farm   Bucks La
Harlton Rd

7

Wimpole Road   53

Merry's
Farm   Ayett's Cl

6

5

Harcamlow Way   Sharp Hill
Plantation   52

Thorn
Hill   4

Cobb's Wood
Farm

Moat

Cobbs Wood   Rectory Farm   Maypole
Farm   A603

SG8

Halfway
House   Fox
Hill   3

Victoria
Plantation   Hillside   A603   51

Thornberry
Hill Farm

Victoria
Plantation   A603   2

Fisher's Lane

Cambridge Road   High Street   Barrington Rd

Four Acre Covert   Lordship Cl   West
Farm   Malton Road   1

Hurdleditch Road   Manor
Farm   PH
PO   Stocks La   Cross La Cl   Orwell
Meadowcroft Farm

Greenford Cl   Brookside   Town Green Road   Lottield   Meadowcroft Wy   50

34   A   B   35   C   D   36   E   F

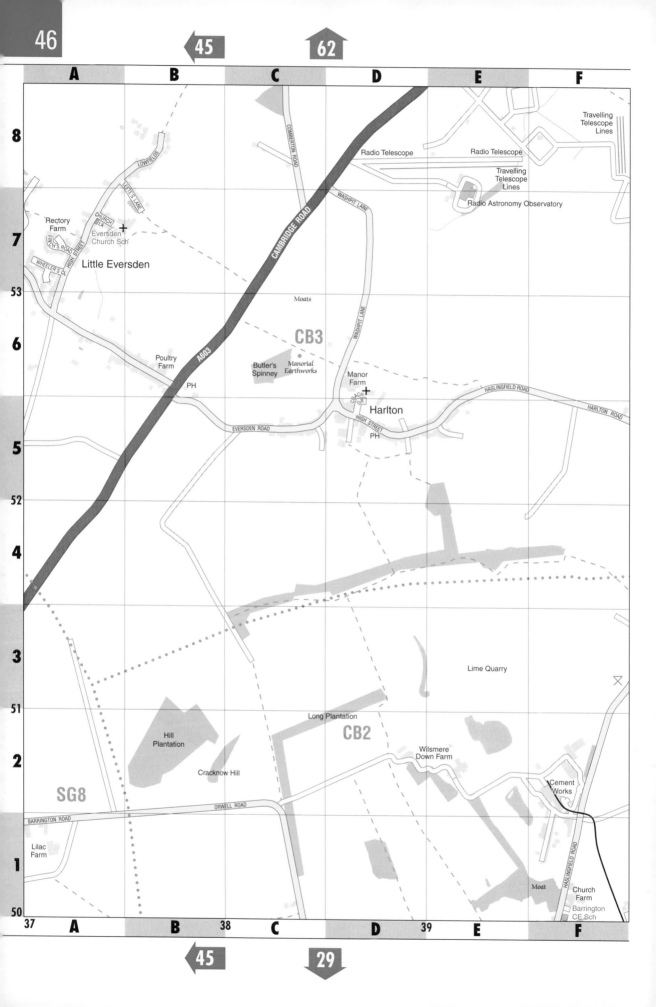

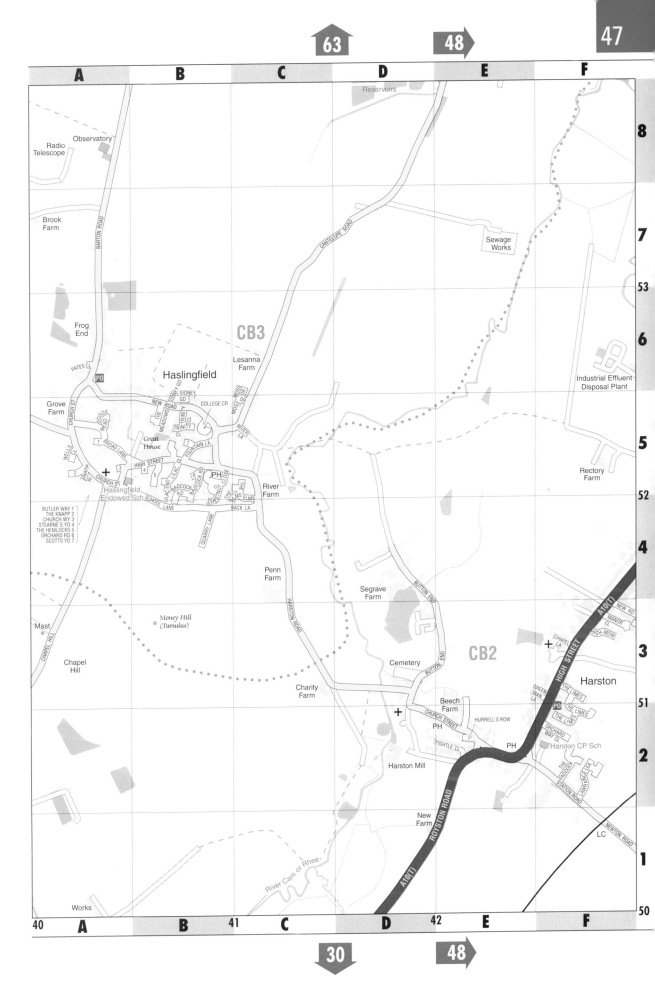

A   B   C   D   E   F

8

Reservoirs

Radio
Telescope
Observatory

7

Brook
Farm

BARTON ROAD

Sewage
Works

53

CANTELUPE ROAD

Frog
End

CB3

6

Lesanna
Farm

PATES CL

PO

Haslingfield

Industrial Effluent
Disposal Plant

Grove
Farm

CHURCH ST

SIDNEY GD
SIDNEY GD

NEW ROAD
THE MEADOWS
DUODS MEAD

COLLEGE CR

MOSS DR
MOSS DR

RIVER LA

5

TRINITY CL
TRINITY CL

Great
House

BROAD LANE

WELLS CL

HIGH STREET

FOUNTAIN LA

LILAC END

Rectory
Farm

KNAPP RD

2   +   3

CHURCH ST

4   5

BADCOCK RD
BADCOCK RD

6

PH

CHESTNUT CLOSE

THE ELMS
THE ELMS

52

River
Farm

Haslingfield
Endowed Sch

SCHOOL LANE

BACK LA

BUTLER WAY 1
THE KNAPP 2
CHURCH WY 3
STEARNE'S YD 4
THE HEMLOCKS 5
ORCHARD RD 6
SCOTTS YD 7

QUARRY LANE

4

Penn
Farm

HARSTON ROAD

Segrave
Farm

BUTTON END

A10(T)

NEW RD

MANOR CL

HIGH MDW

Mast

Money Hill
(Tumulus)

CHAPEL HILL

CHAPEL LA

+

HIGH STREET

3

Chapel
Hill

Cemetery

CB2

BUTTON END

Harston

THE LIMES

Charity
Farm

Beech
Farm

CHURCH STREET

GREEN MAN LA

PO

THE LIMES
THE LIMES
THE LIMES

51

PH

HURRELL'S ROW

ORCHARD WAY CL

+

PIGHTLE CL

PH

Harston CP Sch

Harston Mill

THE PADDOCK

LAWRANCE LEA

2

New
Farm

ROYSTON ROAD

STATION ROAD

NEWTON ROAD

LC

1

River Cam or Rhee

A10(T)

Works

50

47 64

A B C D E F

8

7

53

6

5

52

4

3

51

2

1

50

43 A B 44 C D 45 E F

M11

A1309

HAUXTON ROAD

SHELFORD RD

RED HL CL

CABBAGE MOOR

CAMBRIDGE RD

CAMBRIDGE ROAD

A1301

11

WESTFIELD ROAD

MARLEE

Mast

CHERRY TREES

THE HECTARE

Allotments

STONEHILL ROAD

WALDEN D

WY

MILL LA

M11

A10(T)

MORE'S MD

Cemy

BRIDGE CL

Hauxton Mill

Stone Hill

Works

River Cam or Granta

CHURCH ROAD

University Arms Farm

CB2

Great Shelford

JACKSON CL

BURSTEAD RD

HIGH STREET

PO

Great & Little Shelford CE Prim Sch

MOUNTFORD CL

Hauxton CP Sch

THE LANE

Manor Farm

Manor House

CHURCH ST

KINGS MILL LA

JOPLING

LEYS WK

HAWTHORN AV

WILLOW WAY

Hauxton

HAUXTON ROAD

MANOR RD

BRIDGE LANE

Moat

LC

CHURCH STREET

Shelford Mill

PH

HIGH ST

PH

THE CHESTNUTS

NEWTON ROAD

SD FIELDS

BEECH CL

HIGH STREET

COURTYARDS

QUEENS CL

NEW RD

QUEENS CL

MEADOW WY

Southcourts

PH

B1368

LONDON ROAD

Harston

Little Shelford

SHELFORD ROAD

Hall Farm

Moor Barn

The Spinney

WHITTLESFORD ROAD

Obelisk

B1368

Well Head Plantation

Sainsfoins

CAMBRIDGE ROAD

Harston Hill

Hill Farm

NEWTON ROAD

M11

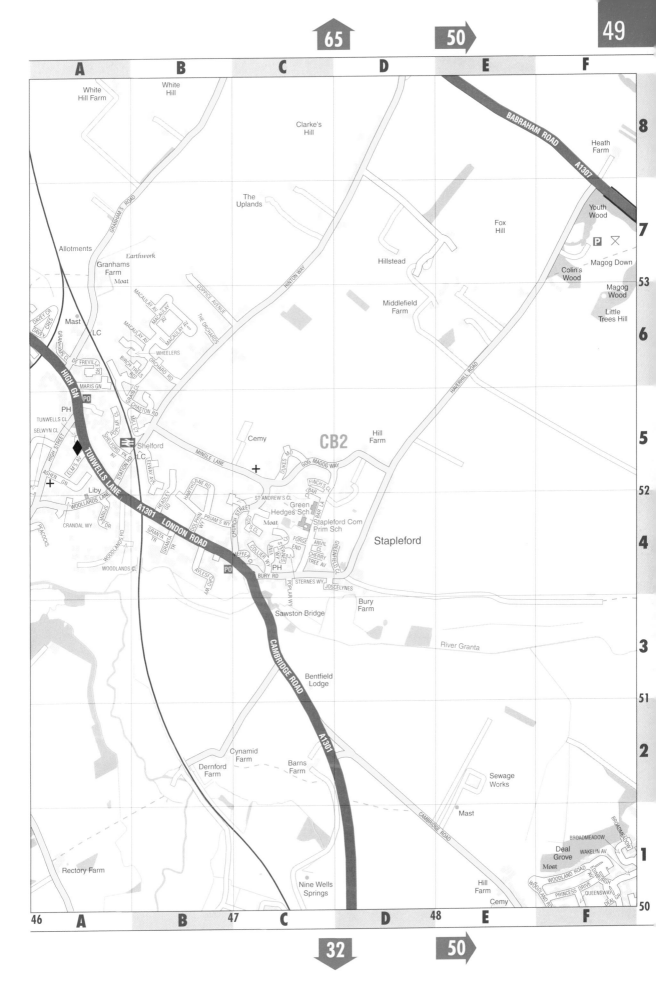

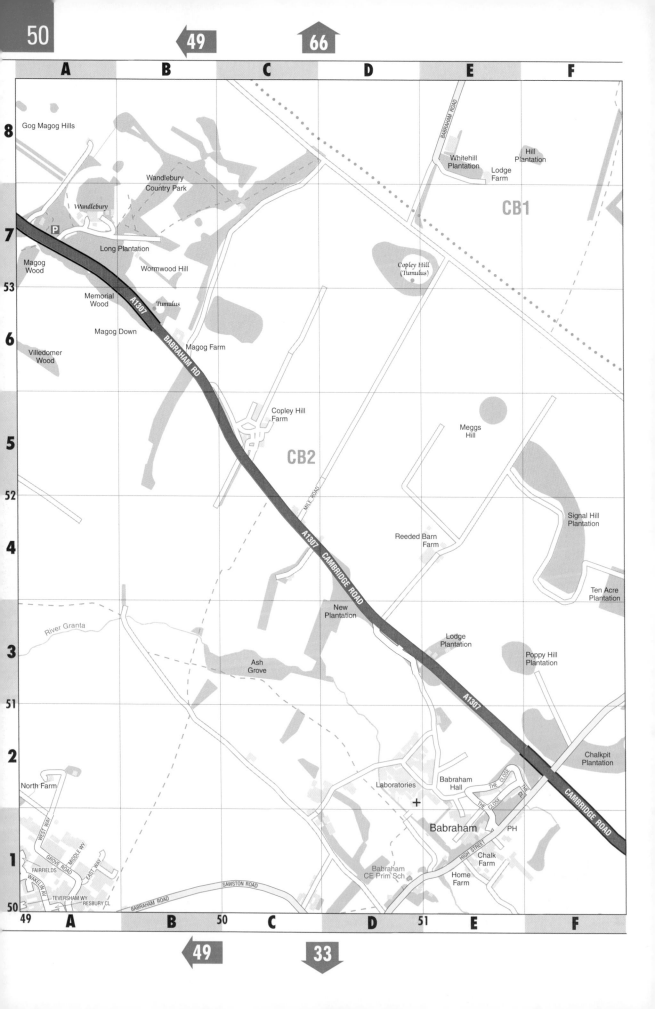

A   B   C   D   E   F

8 Gog Magog Hills

Wandlebury
Country Park

Wandlebury

7 P

Long Plantation

Magog
Wood

Wormwood Hill

53

Memorial
Wood

Tumulus

A1307

Magog Down

6 Magog Farm

BABRAHAM RD

Villedomer
Wood

Whitehill
Plantation

Hill
Plantation

Lodge
Farm

BABRAHAM ROAD

CB1

Copley Hill
(Tumulus)

Copley Hill
Farm

CB2

Meggs
Hill

5

MILE ROAD

52

Signal Hill
Plantation

A1307

Reeded Barn
Farm

4

CAMBRIDGE ROAD

Ten Acre
Plantation

River Granta

New
Plantation

Lodge
Plantation

Poppy Hill
Plantation

3 Ash
Grove

51

A1307

2

Chalkpit
Plantation

North Farm

Laboratories

Babraham
Hall

THE CLOSE

THE CLOSE

CAMBRIDGE ROAD

WEST WAY

GROVE ROAD

MIDDLE WY

EAST WAY

Babraham

PH

Chalk
Farm

1 FAIRFIELDS

WAKELIN AV

TEVERSHAM WY

RESBURY CL

Babraham
CE Prim Sch

HIGH STREET

Home
Farm

SAWSTON ROAD

50

BABRAHAM ROAD

49   A   B   50   C   D   51   E   F

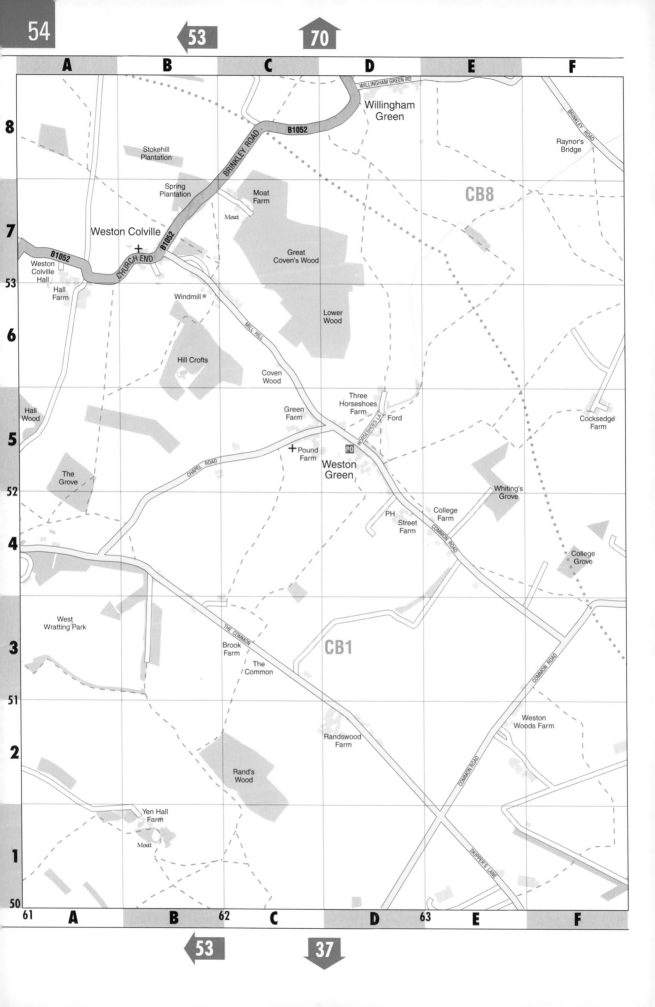

A B C D E F

8

7

53

6

5

52

4

3

51

2

1

50

Willingham Green Rd

Willingham
Green

CB8

Raynor's
Bridge

BRINKLEY ROAD

Stokehill
Plantation

Spring
Plantation

B1052

Moat
Farm

Moat

Weston Colville

B1052
B1052

CHURCH END

Weston
Colville
Hall

Hall
Farm

Windmill

Great
Coven's Wood

Lower
Wood

MILL HILL

Hill Crofts

Coven
Wood

Hall
Wood

Green
Farm

Three
Horseshoes
Farm

HORSESHOES LA

Ford

Cocksedge
Farm

The
Grove

CHAPEL ROAD

Pound
Farm

Weston
Green

PO

Whiting's
Grove

PH

Street
Farm

College
Farm

COMMON ROAD

College
Grove

West
Wratting Park

THE COMMON

Brook
Farm

The
Common

CB1

Randswood
Farm

Weston
Woods Farm

COMMON ROAD

Rand's
Wood

Yen Hall
Farm

Moat

SKIPPER'S LANE

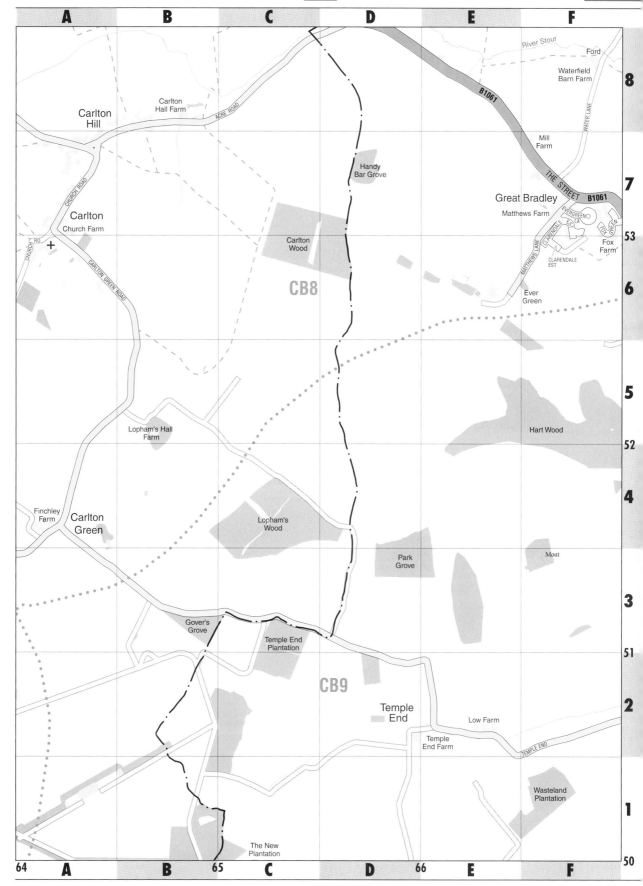

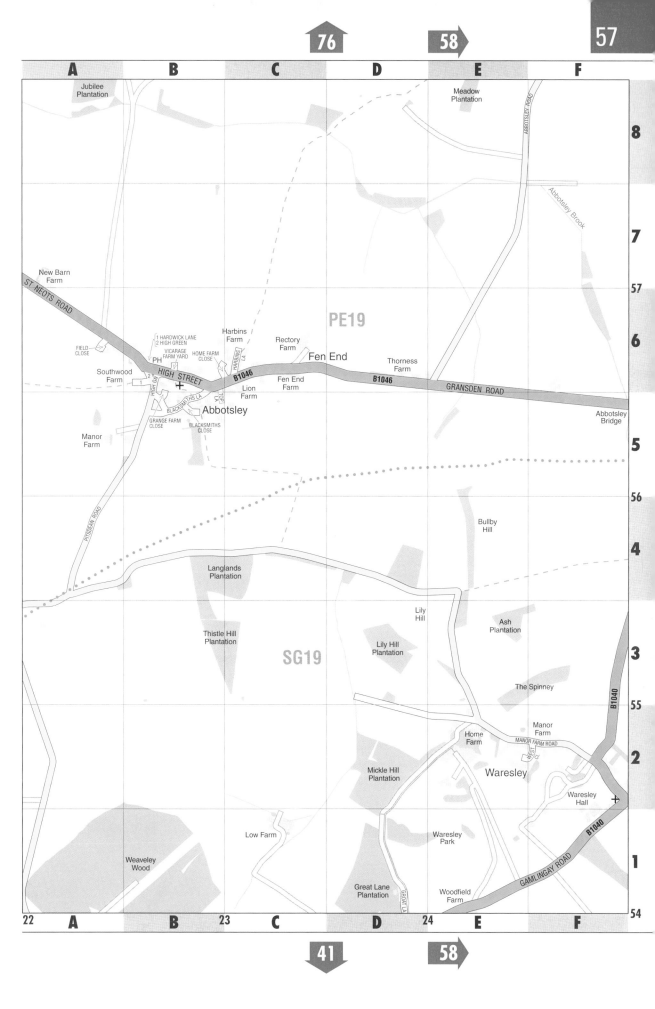

A B C D E F

8

7

PE19

57

6

B1040

Moor
Farm

B1046

Works

5

B1046

MEADOW ROAD

Kiln
Farm

SG19

Woodhams
Farm

Great
Gransden

56

Leycourt
Farm

ELTISLEY ROAD

HARDWICKE ROAD

Tower
Farm

Water Tower

Playing
Field

WINCHFIELD

CAXTON ROAD

Industrial
Estate

SAND ROAD

AUDLEY CL

PO

WEST STREET

FOX'S ST

AUDL CL

North
Farm

4

HALL FM LA

POPLAR
CL

MANOR LA

B1046

BALDWINS
MANOR

WEBBS MD

Barnabas Oley
CE Prim Sch

EAST ST

Moat

CROW TREE ST

CROW
TREE
ST

2
PH

MIDDLE ST

CHURCH ST

MANDENE GD

MANDENE GD

1 LITTLE LA
2 WHITTETS CL

Mandean Bridge

MILL ROAD

Great
Gransden
Windmill

3

WARESLEY ROAD

Sewage
Works

Gransden
Wood

LITTLE GRANSDEN LANE

MAIN RD

Rectory
Farm

Little
Gransden

CHURCH ST

PH

B1046

Primrose Hill

WINDMILL
CLOSE

Sewage
Works

55

Waresley
Wood

CHURCH WK

THE LEYS

2

PH

VICARAGE ROAD

Vicarage
Farm

Cemy

Wood
Farm

Elm
Farm

MAIN ROAD

Hill
Farm

1

Moat

Chase
Farm

54

25

A

B

26

C

D

27

E

F

A B C D E F

8

7

57

6

BOURN ROAD

Firs
Farm

Church
Farm

Vine
Farm

ST PETER'S ST

GRANSDEN ROAD

Redwood
Farm

Hardwicke
Farm

HARDWICKE ROAD

A1198

ROYSTON ROAD

A1198

Common
Farm

SG19

CB3

Home
Farm

Home
Wood

Ox
Grove

5

56

4

Longstowe
Park

Wilderness
Spinney

Pond
Plantation

Longstowe
Hall

Gashouse
Spinney

PARK LA

B1046

3

RUSHBROOK
CLOSE

Longstowe

55

Airfield
(dis)

PH

Middle
Farm

HIGH STREET

2

1

Broad Close
Spinney

B1046

54

28 A B 29 C 30 D E F

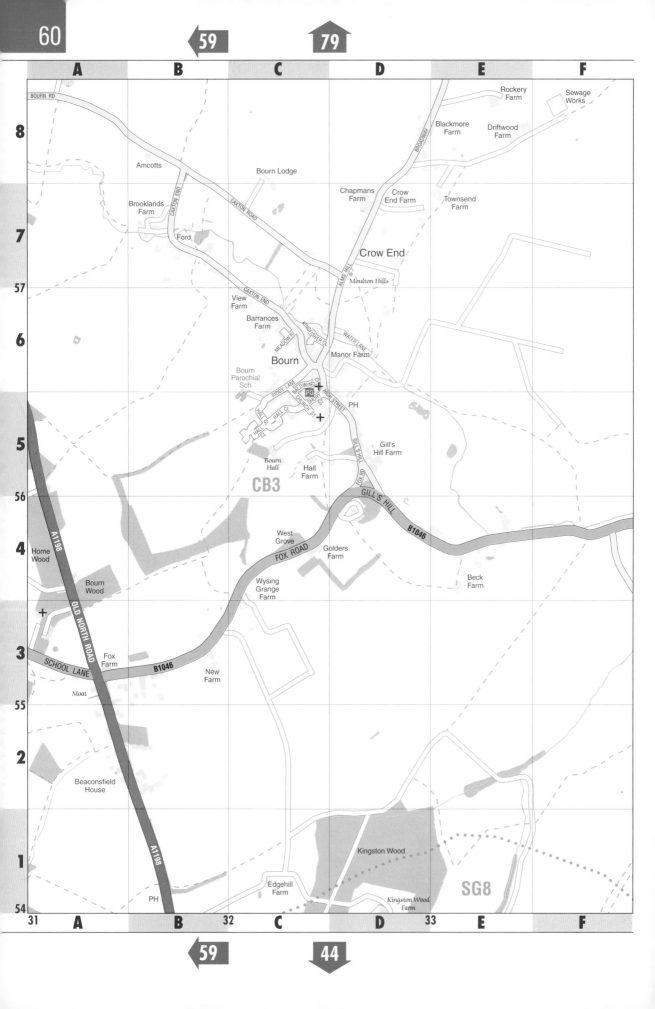

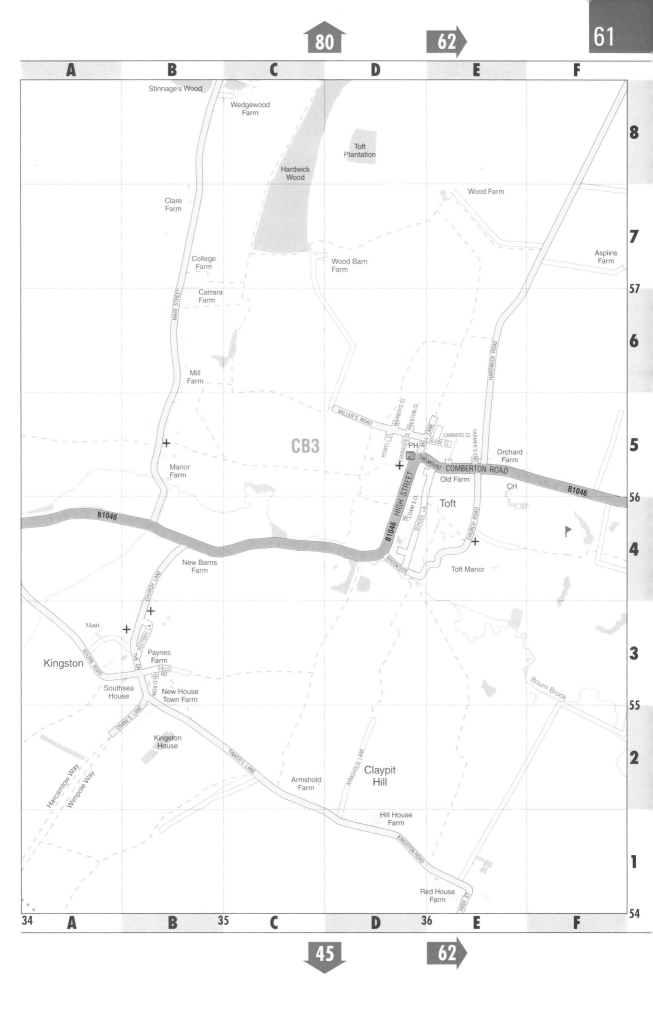

Stinnage's Wood
Wedgewood Farm
Toft Plantation
Hardwick Wood
Wood Farm
Clare Farm
College Farm
Asplins Farm
Carrara Farm
MAIN STREET
Wood Barn Farm
Mill Farm
HARDWICK ROAD
MILLER'S ROAD
CB3
WARBOYS CL
PRESTON CL
MILL LANE
CANNERS CL
GLEBE CL
FARMER'S END
POWELL CL
PH
RIVERSDENE CL
PO
Orchard Farm
THE MOUNT
COMBERTON ROAD
Manor Farm
HIGH STREET
Old Farm
CH
B1046
Toft
ADAM'S CL
SCHOOL LA
B1046
B1046
CHURCH ROAD
New Barns Farm
BROOKSIDE
Toft Manor
CHURCH LANE
Moat
RECTORY LA
Paynes Farm
Kingston
BOURN ROAD
THE GN
FIELD RD
FIELD ROW
New House Town Farm
Southsea House
CRANE'S LANE
Bourn Brook
Kingston House
TINKER'S LANE
Harcamlow Way
Wimpole Way
ARMSHOLD LANE
Armshold Farm
Claypit Hill
Hill House Farm
KINGSTON ROAD
Red House Farm
HIGH ST

8
7
57
6
5
56
4
3
55
2
1

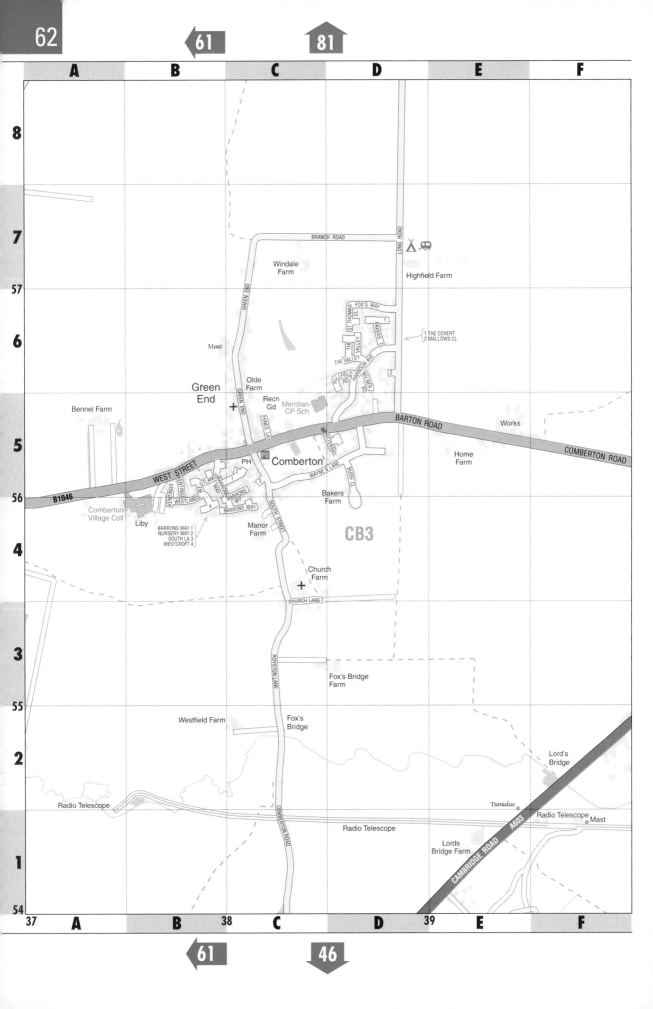

61

81

A   B   C   D   E   F

8

7

57

6

Windale Farm

Highfield Farm

BRANCH ROAD

LONG ROAD

FOX'S WAY

ST THOMAS CL

BAKERS CL

THE VALLEY

THE VALLEY

HARBOUR AVE

MILNER RD

HILLFIELD RD

1 THE COVERT
2 MALLOWS CL

Moat

Green End

Olde Farm

Recn Gd

Meridian CP Sch

BARTON ROAD

Works

COMBERTON ROAD

Bennel Farm

HINES LA

WROTTEN SQ

Home Farm

5

WEST STREET

KENTINGS

WESTLANDS

BARRONS WY

WAYNE'S LANE

BUSH CL

PH

PO

Comberton

56

B1046

Comberton Village Coll

Liby

BARRONS WAY

BARRONS WAY 1
NURSERY WAY 2
SOUTH LA 3
WESTCROFT 4

SOUTH STREET

Manor Farm

Bakers Farm

CB3

4

Church Farm

CHURCH LANE

3

ROYSTON LANE

Fox's Bridge Farm

55

Westfield Farm

Fox's Bridge

Lord's Bridge

2

Radio Telescope

COMBERTON ROAD

Radio Telescope

Tumulus

CAMBRIDGE ROAD

A603

Radio Telescope   Mast

Lords Bridge Farm

1

54

37   A   B   38   C   D   39   E   F

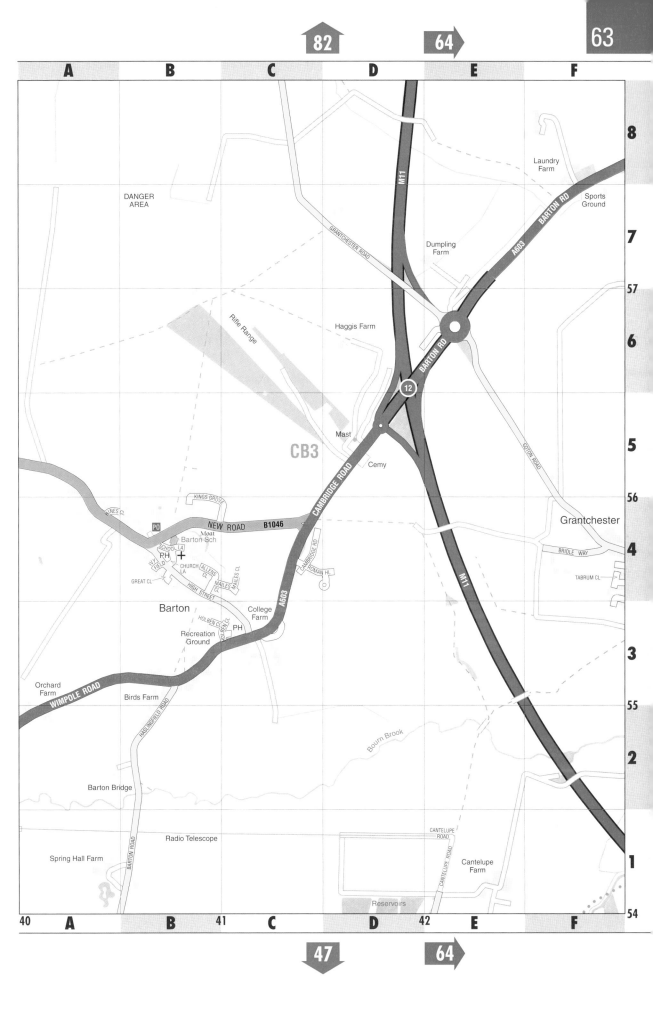

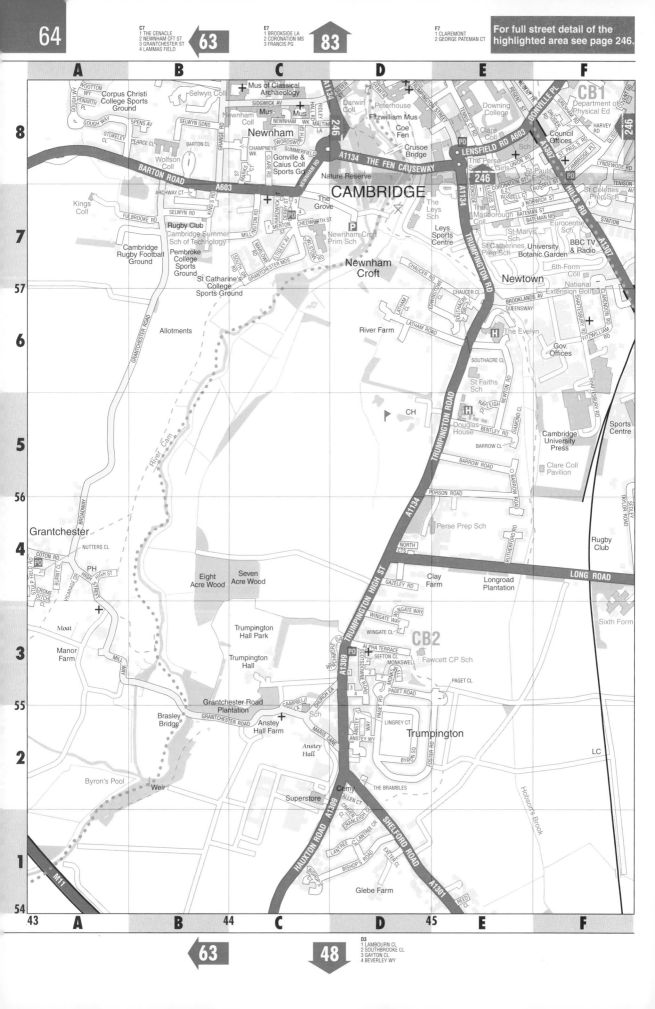

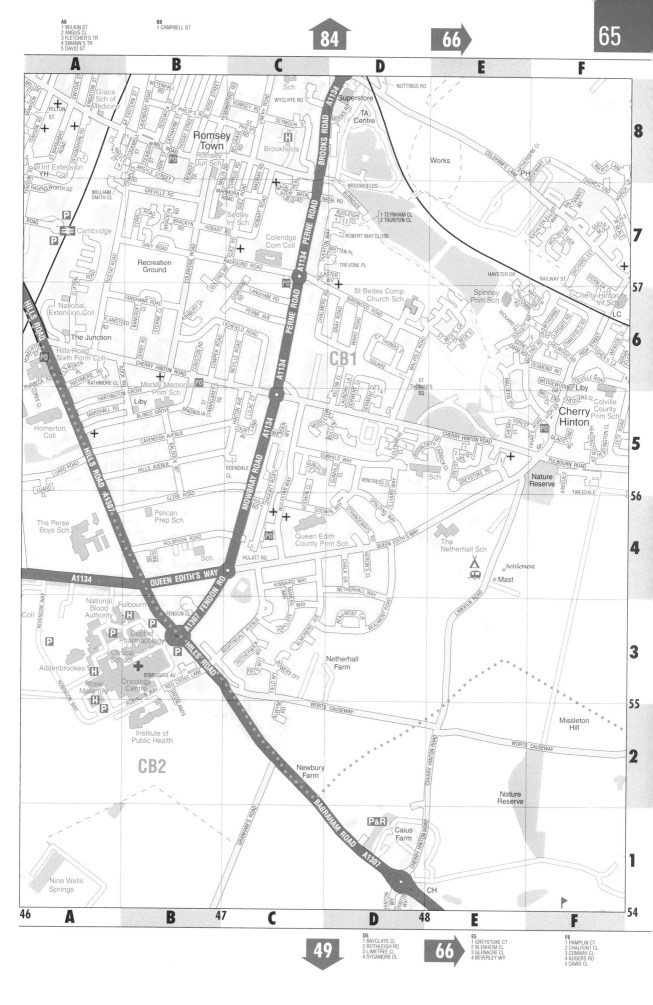

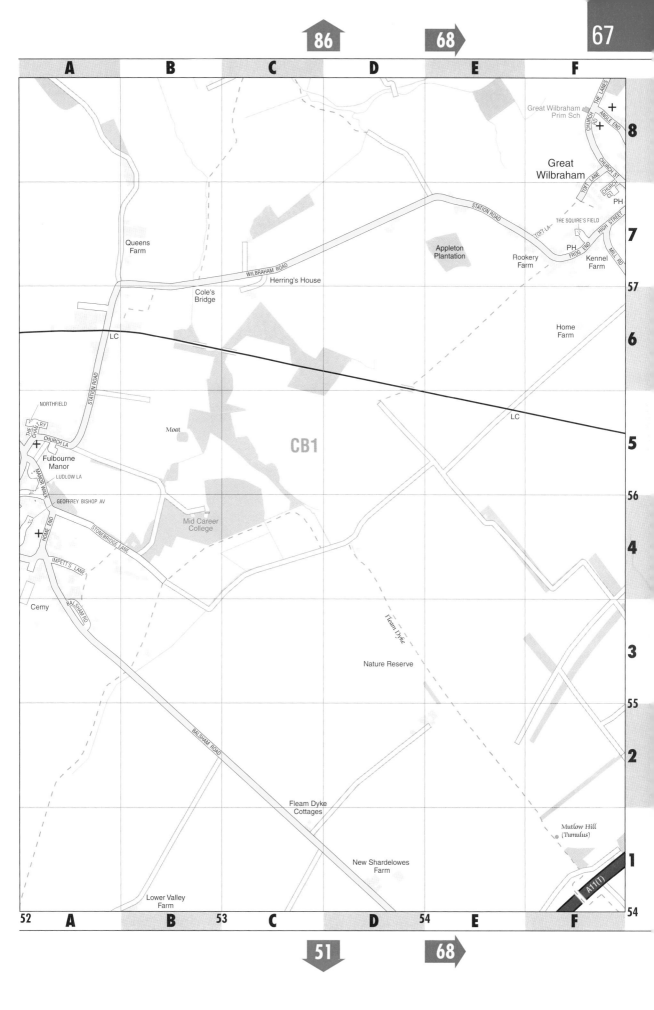

A B C D E F

8
7
57
6
5
56
4
3
55
2
1
54

Great Wilbraham Prim Sch
Great Wilbraham
STATION ROAD
Appleton Plantation
Rookery Farm
Kennel Farm
Home Farm
THE LANES
ANGLE END
CHURCH RD
CHURCH ST
TOFT LANE
CHURCH CL
PH
THE SQUIRE'S FIELD
PH
FROG END
TOFT LA
HIGH STREET
MILL RD

Queens Farm
WILBRAHAM ROAD
Herring's House
Cole's Bridge
LC
STATION ROAD

NORTHFIELD
THE CHANTRY
CHURCH LA
Fulbourne Manor
LUDLOW LA
MANOR WALK
GEOFFREY BISHOP AV
HOME END
Moat
CB1
LC

Mid Career College
STONEBRIDGE LANE
IMPETT S. LANE

Cemy
BALSHAM RD

Fleam Dyke
Nature Reserve

BALSHAM ROAD

Fleam Dyke Cottages

Mutlow Hill (Tumulus)

New Shardelowes Farm

A11(T)

Lower Valley Farm

A B C D E F

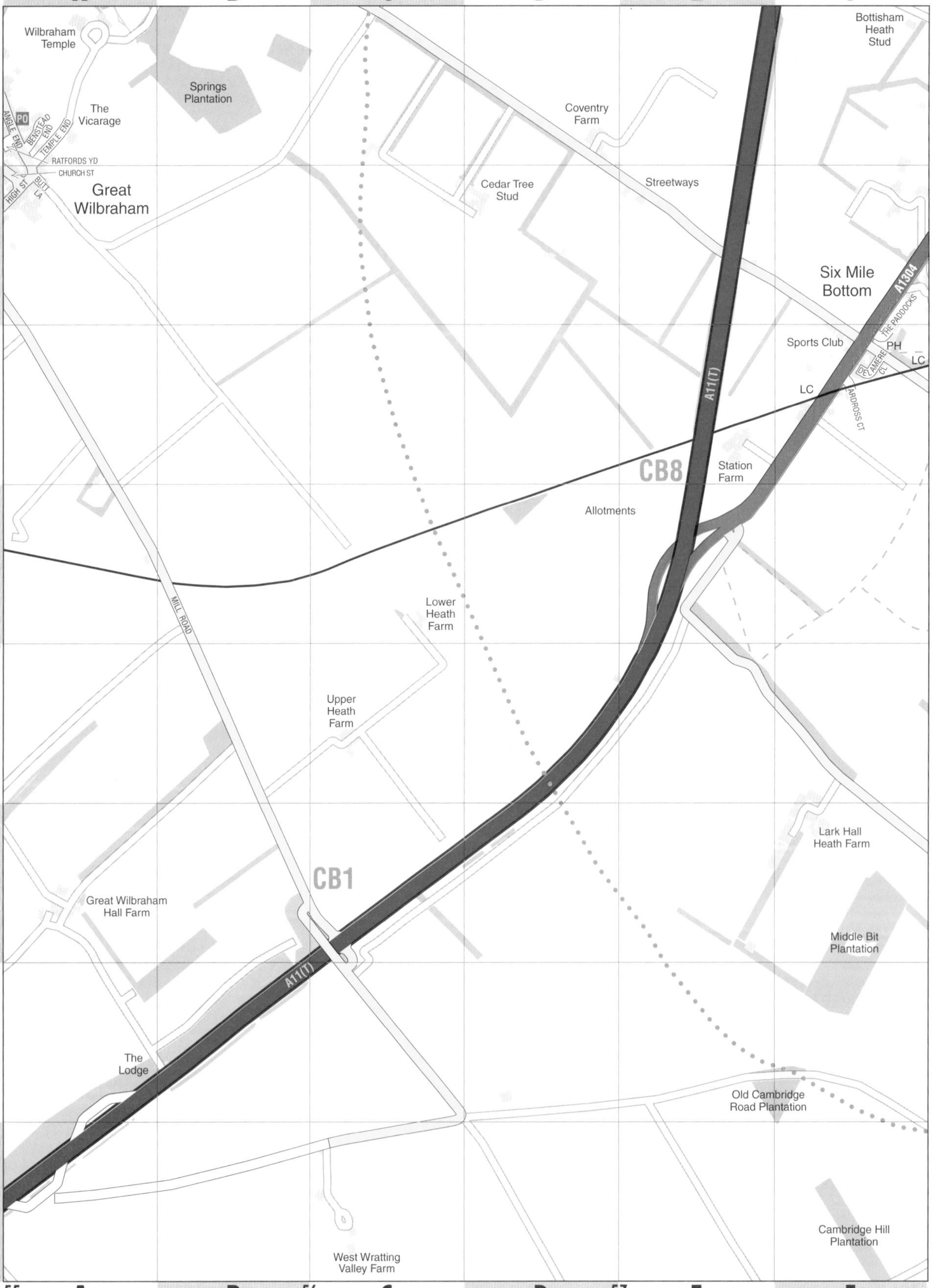

8

Wilbraham
Temple

Springs
Plantation

The
Vicarage

Coventry
Farm

Bottisham
Heath
Stud

PO

RATFORDS YD

CHURCH ST

Cedar Tree
Stud

Streetways

Great
Wilbraham

7

Six Mile
Bottom

A1304

57

Sports Club

PH

LC

6

A11(T)

LC

CARDROSS CT

CB8

Station
Farm

THE PADDOCKS

Allotments

5

MILL ROAD

Lower
Heath
Farm

56

Upper
Heath
Farm

4

Lark Hall
Heath Farm

3

CB1

Great Wilbraham
Hall Farm

Middle Bit
Plantation

55

A11(T)

2

The
Lodge

Old Cambridge
Road Plantation

1

Cambridge Hill
Plantation

54

West Wratting
Valley Farm

55 A B 56 C D 57 E F

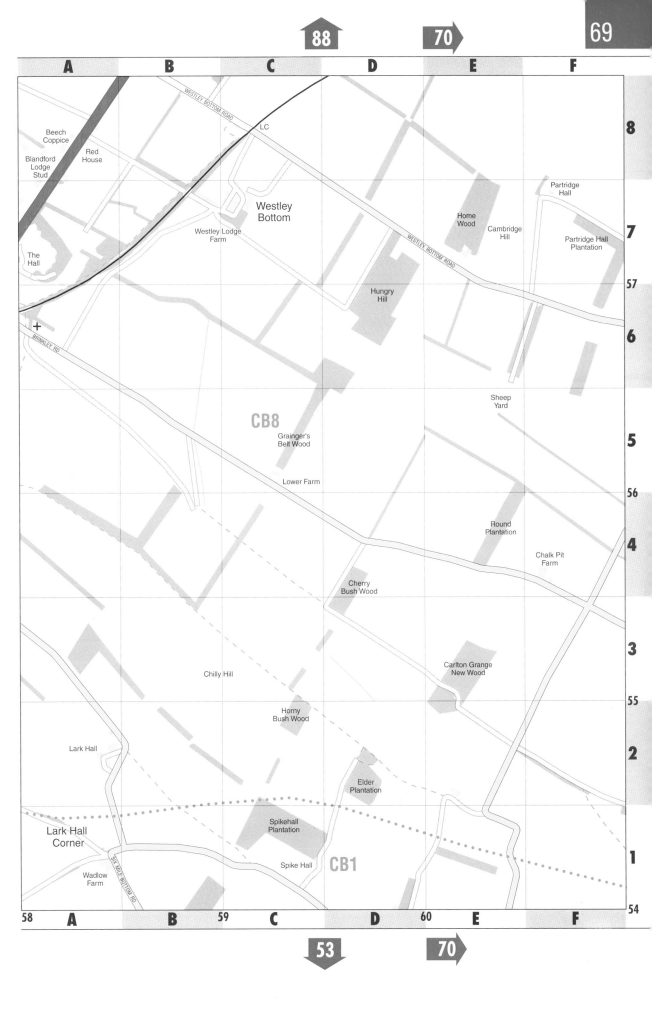

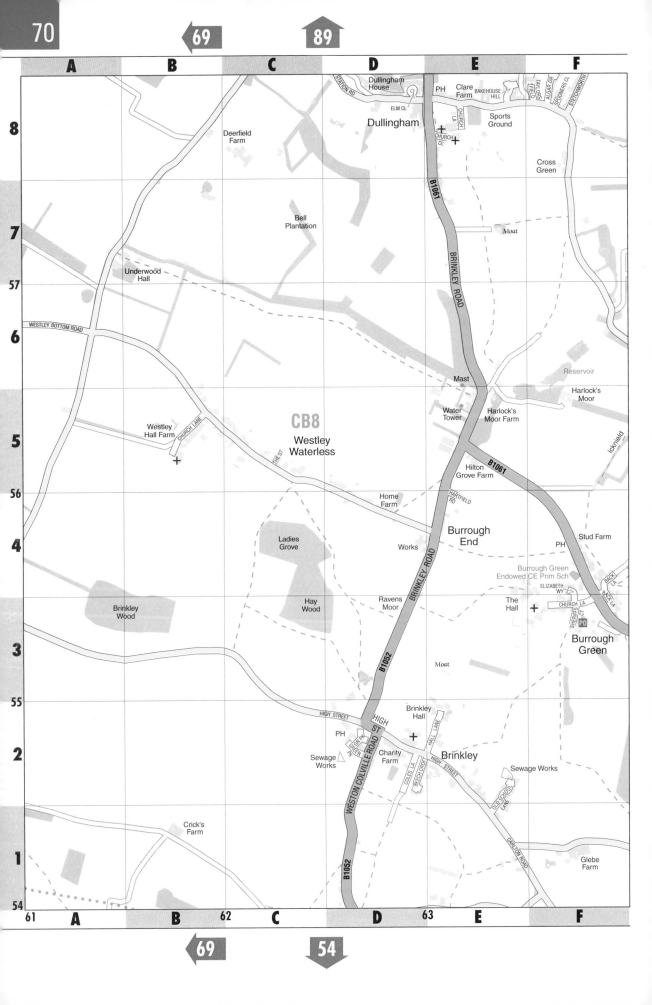

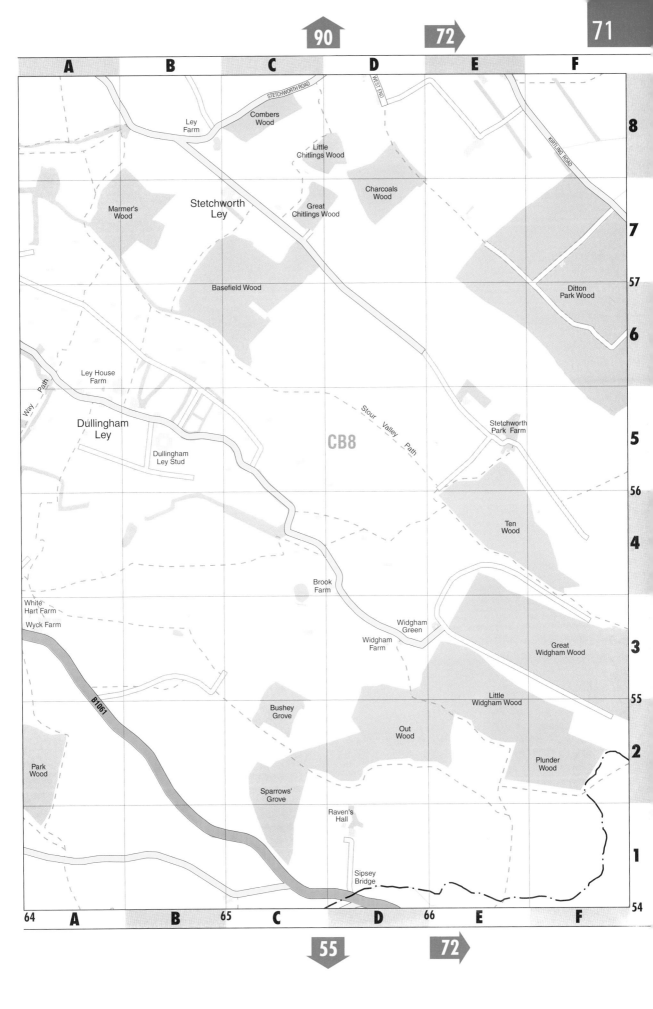

A B C D E F

8

Sixpenny
Wood

Hall
Farm

Chalkpit
Plantation

Place
Farm

Moat

Kirtling
Towers

Prince of Wales
Wood

7

Park
Cottage

Toilyard
Plantation

PH

57

Sewage
Works

Kirtling Road

Lucy
Wood

Kirtling

6

Ditton
Park Wood

Allotments

Kirtling Road

The Street

Parsonage
Farm

Jamies
Wood

Oak
Farm

Horn Lane

Chapel La.

5

Wootditton Road

Yew Tree
Farm

The Green

CB8

PO

PH

Mill Road

Mill
End

56

Batchelor's
Hall Farm

Dianas
Wood

4

Kirtling
Green

Whybrows
Farm

Malting End

Pratts
Green
Farm

Pear
Tree
Farm

Sascombe
Vineyard

Bradley Road

3

Great
Widgham
Wood

Thrift
Farm

55

College
Grove

Bradley Rd

2

Freedom
Farm Stud

Bases Wood

Bradley Road

1

Bradley Park
Wood

54

Street Farm
Cowlinge Corner
THE STREET
Suffolk House
B1063
PH Lidgate
THE STREET
Harvey Farm
BURY LANE
BURY LANE
HILL VIEW
Fetches Plantation

Pippin Park

B1063

Redhouse Farm

57

Vicarage Farm

Gallops

THE BELT

Kespar

Poundhouse Plantation

7

6

CB8

Shardelows Farm
Moat

Bridgelands Farm

Bloomfield's Farm

Bridges Farm

Caters Farm

5

The Thickets

Bloomfield's Wood

NEWMARKET ROAD

56

Branches Park

Long Black Belt

4

Banstead's Farm

The Hall

Pond Plantation

Jonathans Farm

3

Great Wood

Dowells Farm

Erratts Farm

NEWMARKET ROAD

Moat

Eleven Acre Wood

55

Parsonage Farm

Island Wood

2

Beeton's Plantation
Moat

Hobbles Green Farm

BRADLEY ROAD

PO

QUEEN ST

Rosalie Farm

TILLBROOKS HL

Cowlinge

Fairstead Farm
Moat

PH

KENNETSIDE

ERRATTS HILL

RED DOCK LA

1

54

Newmarket Road

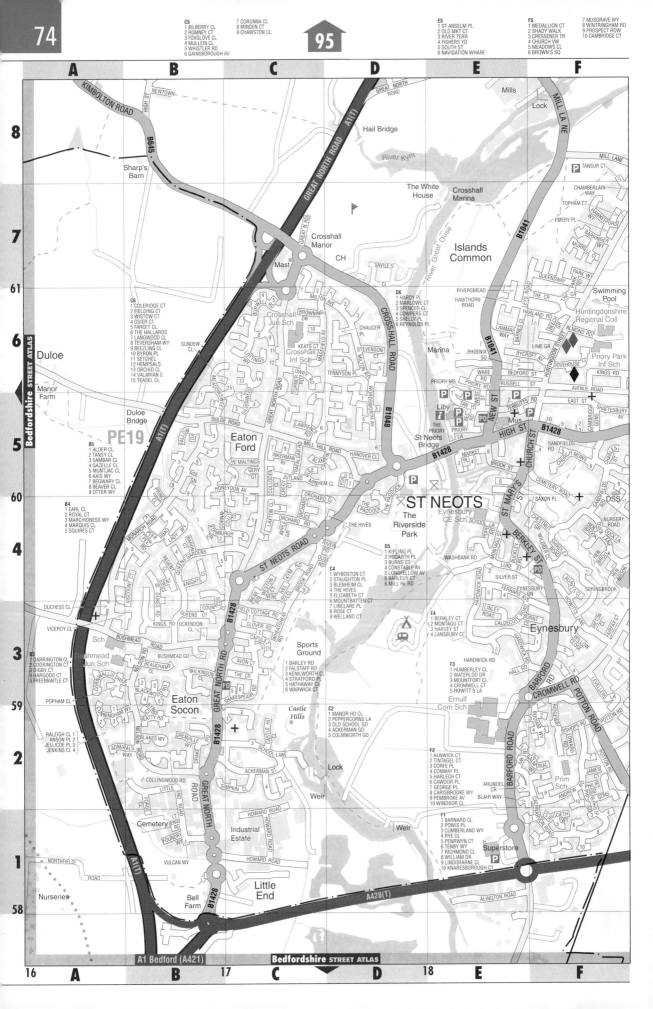

95

CS
1 BILBERRY CL
2 ROMNEY CT
3 FOXGLOVE CL
4 MULLEIN CL
5 WHISTLER RD
6 GAINSBOROUGH AV
7 CORUNNA CL
8 MINDEN CT
9 CHAWSTON CL

E5
1 ST ANSELM PL
2 OLD MKT CT
3 RIVER TERR
4 FISHERS YD
5 SOUTH ST
6 NAVIGATION WHARF

F5
1 MEDALLION CT
2 SHADY WALK
3 CRESSENER TR
4 CHURCH VW
5 MEADOWS CL
6 BROWN'S SQ
7 MUSGRAVE WY
8 WINTRINGHAM RD
9 PROSPECT ROW
10 CAMBRIDGE CT

C6
1 COLERIDGE CT
2 FIELDING CT
3 WISTOW CT
4 OSIER CT
5 FARCET CL
6 THE HALLARDS
7 LANGWOOD CL
8 TEVERSHAM WY
9 BEEZLING CL
10 BYRON PL
11 SETCHEL
12 HEMPSALS
13 ORCHID CL
14 VALARIAN C
15 TEASEL CL

D6
1 HARDY PL
2 MARLOWE CL
3 SPENCER CL
4 COWPERS CT
5 SHELLY PL
6 REYNOLDS PL

B5
1 ALDER CL
2 TANSY CL
3 SAMBAR CL
4 GAZELLE CL
5 MUNTJAC CL
6 AXIS WY
7 BEGWARY CL
8 BEAVER CL
9 OTTER WY

B4
1 EARL CL
2 ROYAL CT
3 MARCHIONESS WY
4 MARQUIS CL
5 SQUIRES CT

D5
1 KIPLING PL
2 HOGARTH PL
3 BURNS CT
4 CONSTABLE AV
5 LONGFELLOW AV
6 BARLEUY CL

C4
1 WYBOSTON CT
2 STAUGHTON PL
3 BLENHEIM CL
4 THE HIVES
5 ELIZABETH CT
6 MOUNTBATTEN CT
7 LINCLARE PL
8 ROSE CT
9 WELLAND CT

E4
1 BERKLEY CT
2 MONTAGU CT
3 HARVEY ST
4 LANSBURY CL

B3
1 DARRINGTON CL
2 CODRINGTON CT
3 DIGBY CT
4 HARGOOD CT
5 FREEMANTLE CT

B1
1 BARLEY RD
2 FALSTAFF RD
3 KENILWORTH CL
4 STRATFORD PL
5 HATHAWAY CL
6 WARWICK CT

F3
1 HUMBERLEY CL
2 WATERLOO DR
3 MOUNTFORT CL
4 CROMWELL CL
5 HOWITT'S LA

C2
1 MANOR HO CL
2 PEPPERCORNS LA
3 OLD SCHOOL GD
4 ACKERMAN GD
5 COLMWORTH GD

F2
1 ALNWICK CT
2 TINTAGEL CT
3 CORFE PL
4 CONWAY PL
5 HARLECH CT
6 CAWDOR PL
7 GEORGE PL
8 CARISBROOKE WY
9 PEMBROKE AV
10 WINDSOR CL

F1
1 BARNARD CL
2 POWIS PL
3 CUMBERLAND WY
4 RYE CL
5 PENRWYN CT
6 TENBY WY
7 RICHMOND CL
8 WILLIAM DR
9 LINDISFARNE CL
10 KNARESBOROUGH CL

Bedfordshire STREET ATLAS

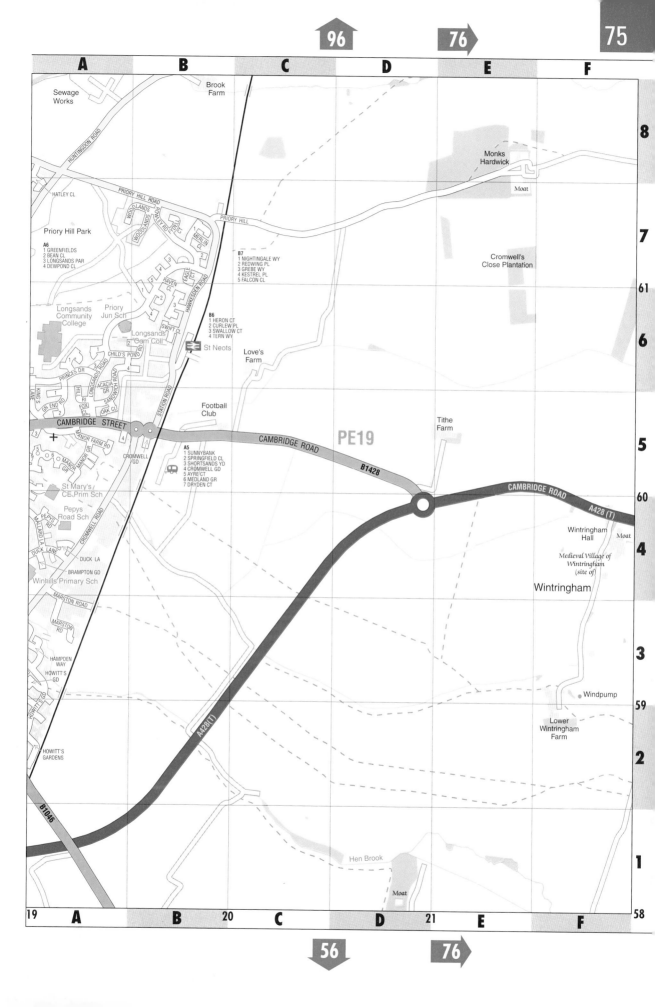

A B C D E F

Sewage Works

Brook Farm

8

Monks Hardwick

Moat

HATLEY CL

PRIORY HILL ROAD

Priory Hill Park

PRIORY HILL

7

Cromwell's Close Plantation

61

A6
1 GREENFIELDS
2 BEAN CL
3 LONGSANDS PAR
4 DEWPOND CL

B7
1 NIGHTINGALE WY
2 REDWING PL
3 GREBE WY
4 KESTREL PL
5 FALCON CL

Longsands Community College

Priory Jun Sch

B6
1 HERON CT
2 CURLEW PL
3 SWALLOW CT
4 TERN WY

6

Longsands Com Coll

CHILD'S POND

St Neots

Love's Farm

Football Club

Tithe Farm

PRINCES DR

KING'S LANE

CAMBRIDGE STREET

CAMBRIDGE ROAD

PE19

5

A5
1 SUNNYBANK
2 SPRINGFIELD CL
3 SHORTSANDS YD
4 CROMWELL GD
5 AYRE CT
6 MEDLAND GR
7 DRYDEN CT

B1428

CROMWELL GD

St Mary's CE Prim Sch

Pepys Road Sch

CAMBRIDGE ROAD

A428 (T)

60

Wintringham Hall

Moat

DUCK LANE

DUCK LA

BRAMPTON GD

Winhills Primary Sch

Medieval Village of Wintringham (site of)

Wintringham

4

MARSTON ROAD

MARSTON RD

A428 (T)

3

HAMPDEN WAY

HOWITT'S GD

Windpump

59

HOWITT'S GDS

HOWITT'S GARDENS

Lower Wintringham Farm

2

B1046

Hen Brook

1

Moat

58

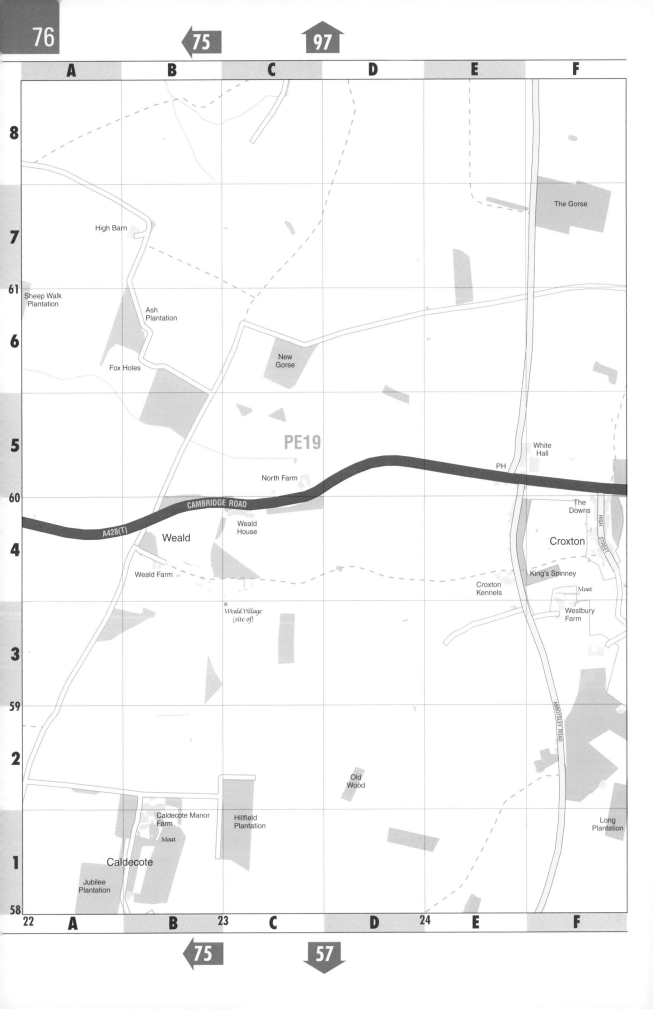

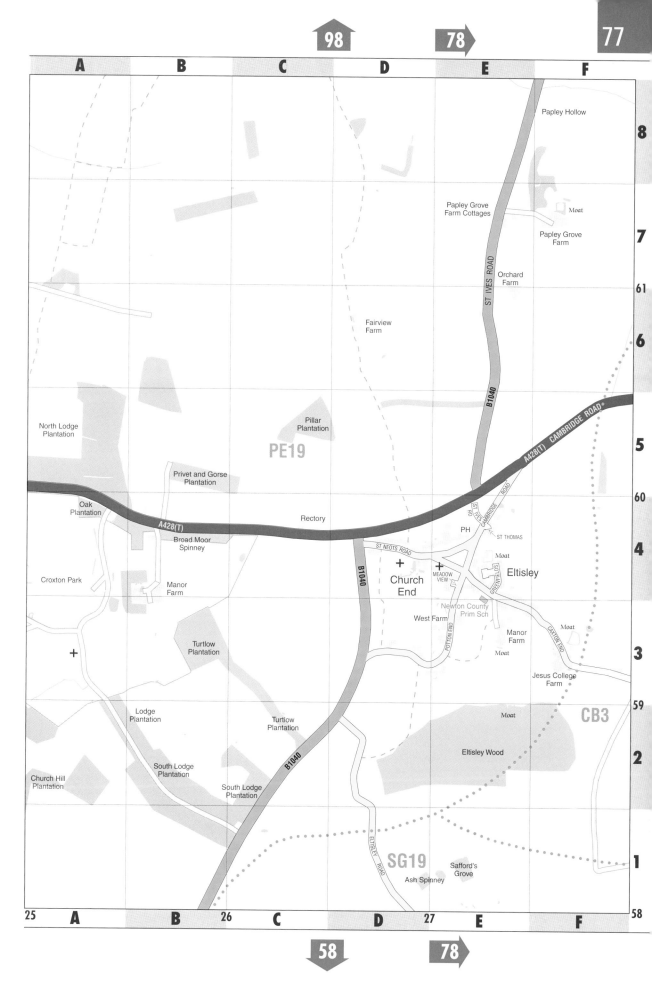

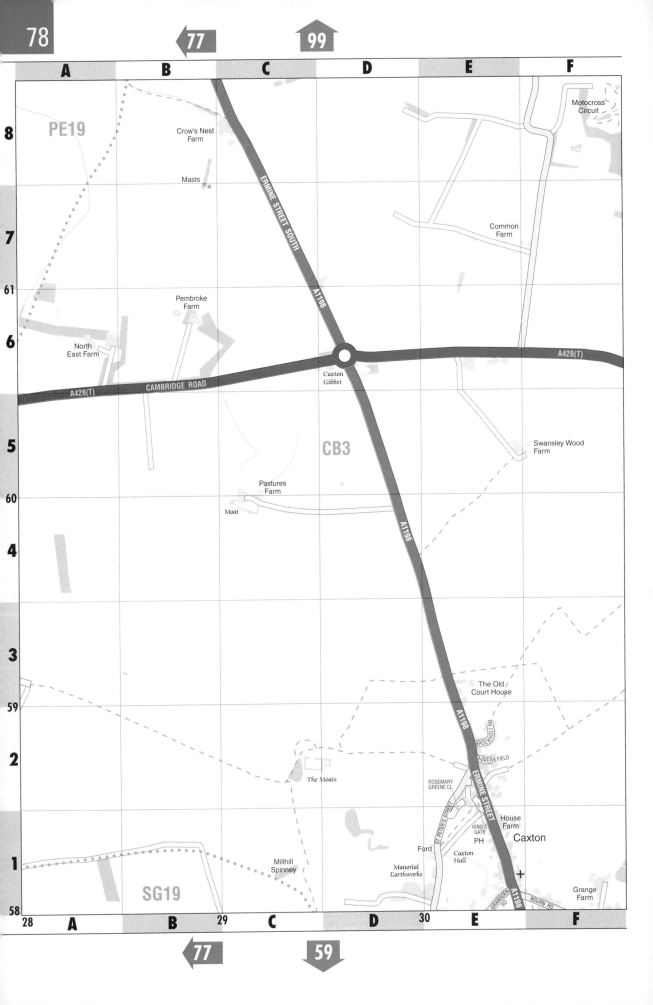

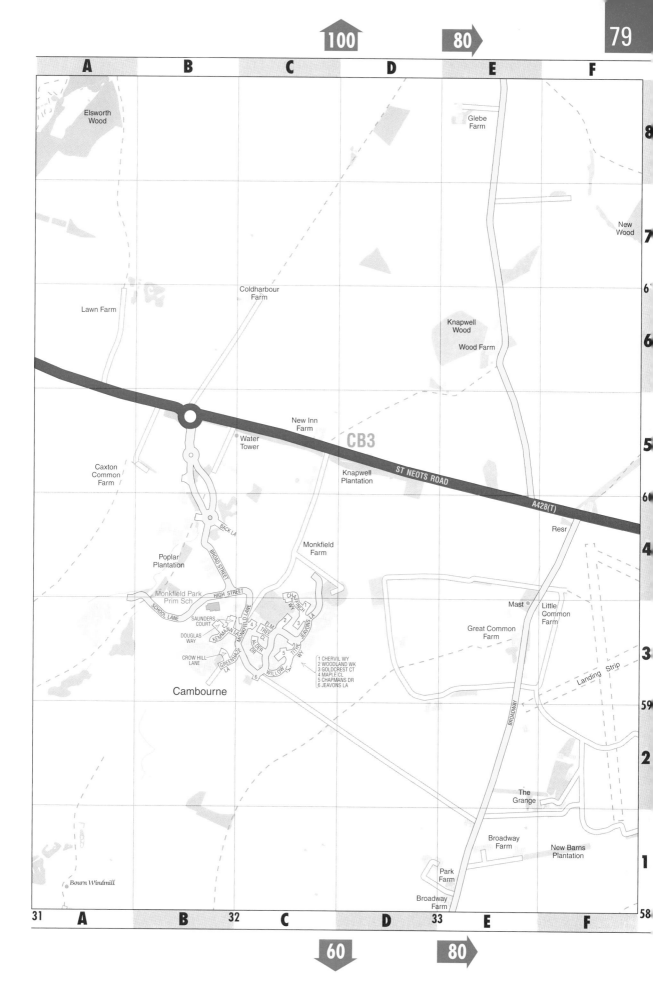

A B C D E F

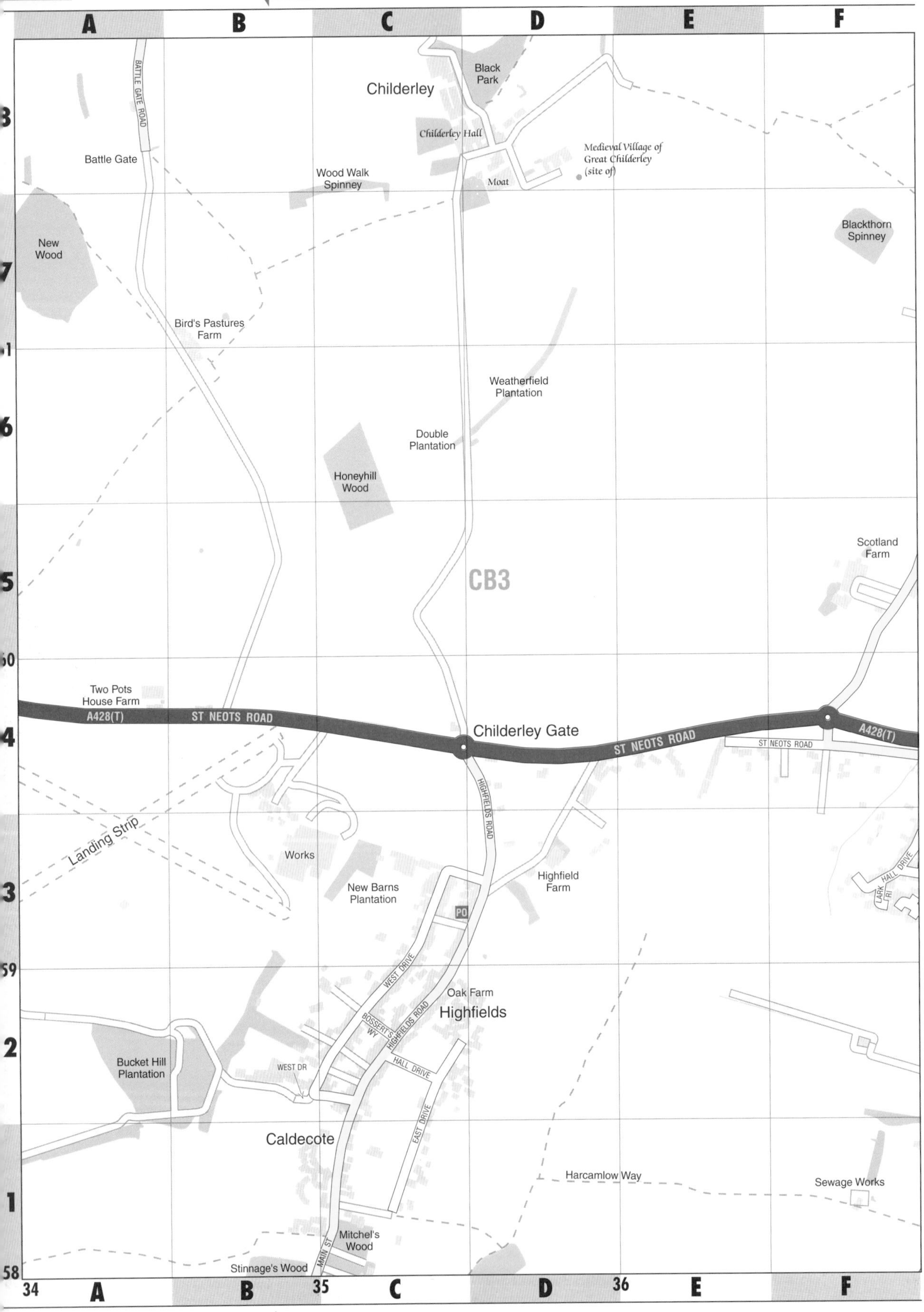

8

Childerley

Black Park

Childerley Hall

BATTLE GATE ROAD

Battle Gate

Wood Walk Spinney

Medieval Village of Great Childerley (site of)

Moat

Blackthorn Spinney

New Wood

Bird's Pastures Farm

Weatherfield Plantation

Double Plantation

Honeyhill Wood

CB3

Scotland Farm

Two Pots House Farm

A428(T) ST NEOTS ROAD

Childerley Gate ST NEOTS ROAD A428(T)

ST NEOTS ROAD

Landing Strip

HIGHFIELDS ROAD

LARK RI HALL DRIVE

Works

New Barns Plantation

Highfield Farm

PO

WEST DRIVE

BOSSEL'S WT

HIGHFIELDS ROAD

Oak Farm

Highfields

Bucket Hill Plantation

WEST DR

HALL DRIVE

EAST DRIVE

Caldecote

Harcamlow Way

Sewage Works

MAIN ST

Mitchel's Wood

Stinnage's Wood

34 A 35 B C 36 D E F

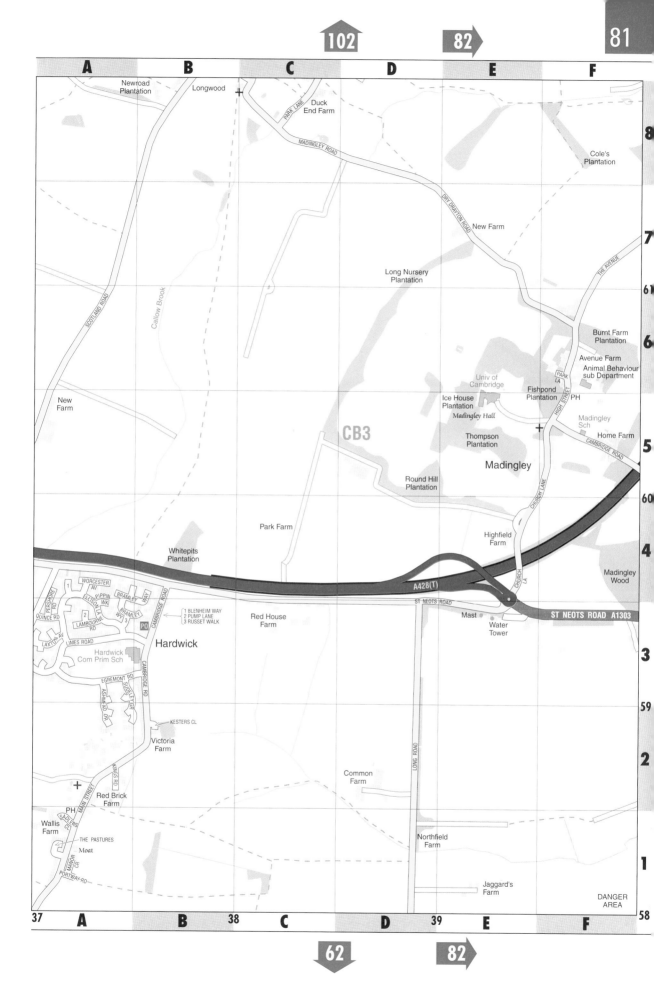

A B C D E F

Newroad Plantation
Longwood
Duck End Farm
PARK LANE
MADINGLEY ROAD
DRY DRAYTON ROAD
New Farm
Cole's Plantation
8
7
6
Long Nursery Plantation
THE AVENUE
Burnt Farm Plantation
Avenue Farm
Animal Behaviour sub Department
PARK LA
SCOTLAND ROAD
Callow Brook
New Farm
CB3
Univ of Cambridge
Ice House Plantation
Madingley Hall
Fishpond Plantation
HIGH STREET
PH
Madingley Sch
Home Farm
CAMBRIDGE ROAD
5
Thompson Plantation
Madingley
Round Hill Plantation
60
Park Farm
Highfield Farm
CHURCH LANE
4
Whitepits Plantation
Madingley Wood
A428(T)
ST NEOTS ROAD
CHURCH LA
CAMBRIDGE ROAD
WORCESTER AV
PIPPIN WK
BRAMLEY WAY
PERSHORE RD
ELLISON LA
1
BRAMLEY WY
QUINCE RD
2
LAMBOURNE RD
3
PO
1 BLENHEIM WAY
2 PUMP LANE
3 RUSSET WALK
Red House Farm
Mast
Water Tower
ST NEOTS ROAD A1303
LAXTON AV
LIMES ROAD
Hardwick
Hardwick Com Prim Sch
3
EGREMONT RD
ASHMEAD DV
SUDELEY CR
59
KESTERS CL
2
Victoria Farm
Common Farm
LONG ROAD
KINGS RD
Red Brick Farm
PH
MAIN STREET
SAZIERS CL
Wallis Farm
THE PASTURES
Moat
Northfield Farm
MANOR CR
PORTWAY RD
1
Jaggard's Farm
DANGER AREA

37 A B 38 C D 39 E F 58

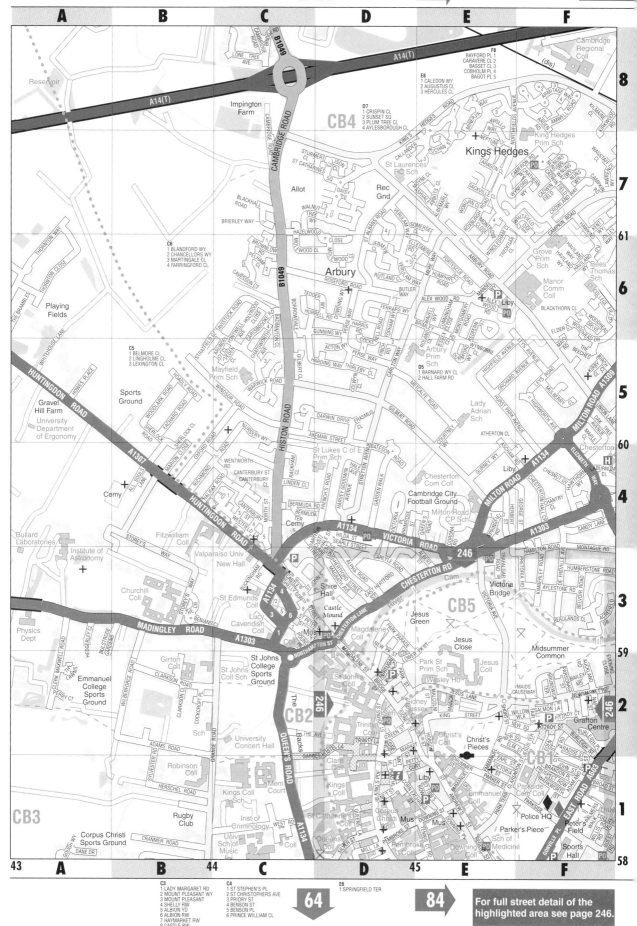

D6
1 FORDWICH CL
2 NORTHUMBERLAND CL
3 BRACKLEY CL

E7
1 MONCRIEFF CL
2 BANFF CL
3 JEDBURGH CL
4 ENNISDALE CL

F8
BAYFORD PL 1
CARAVERE CL 2
BASSET CL 3
COBHOLM PL 4
BAGOT PL 5

E8
1 CALEDON WY
2 AUGUSTUS CL
3 HERCULES CL

D7
1 CRISPIN CL
2 SUNSET SQ
3 PLUM TREE CL
4 AYLESBOROUGH CL

CB4

C6
1 BLANDFORD WY
2 CHANCELLORS WY
3 MARTINGALE CL
4 FARRINGFORD CL

C5
1 BELMORE CL
2 LINGHOLME CL
3 LEXINGTON CL

D5
1 BARNARD WY CL
2 HALL FARM RD

Kings Hedges

Arbury

CB5

CB2

CB3

CB1

C3
1 LADY MARGARET RD
2 MOUNT PLEASANT WY
3 MOUNT PLEASANT
4 SHELLY RW
5 ALBION YD
6 ALBION RW
7 HAYMARKET RW
8 CASTLE RW
9 HONEY HL

C4
1 ST STEPHEN'S PL
2 ST CHRISTOPHERS AVE
3 PRIORY RD
4 BENSON ST
5 BENSON PL
6 PRINCE WILLIAM CL

E6
1 SPRINGFIELD TER

64   84 ▶

For full street detail of the highlighted area see page 246.

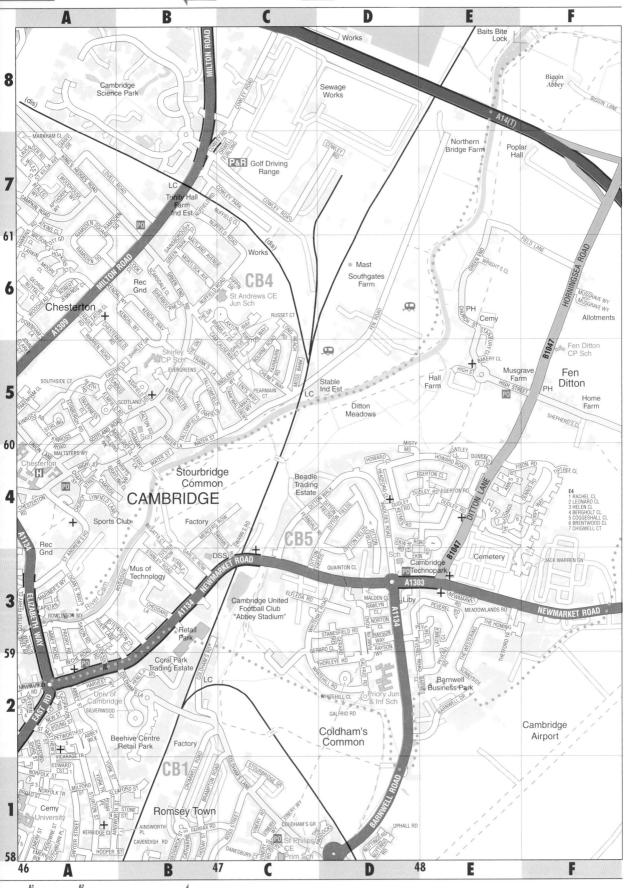

A1
1 UPR GWYDIR ST
2 FLOWER ST
3 BLOSSOM ST
4 AINSWORTH CT
5 MACKENZIE RD

A2
1 SUN ST
2 PARKER'S TR
3 WELLINGTON CT
4 WELLINGTON ST
5 ST MATTHEW'S CT

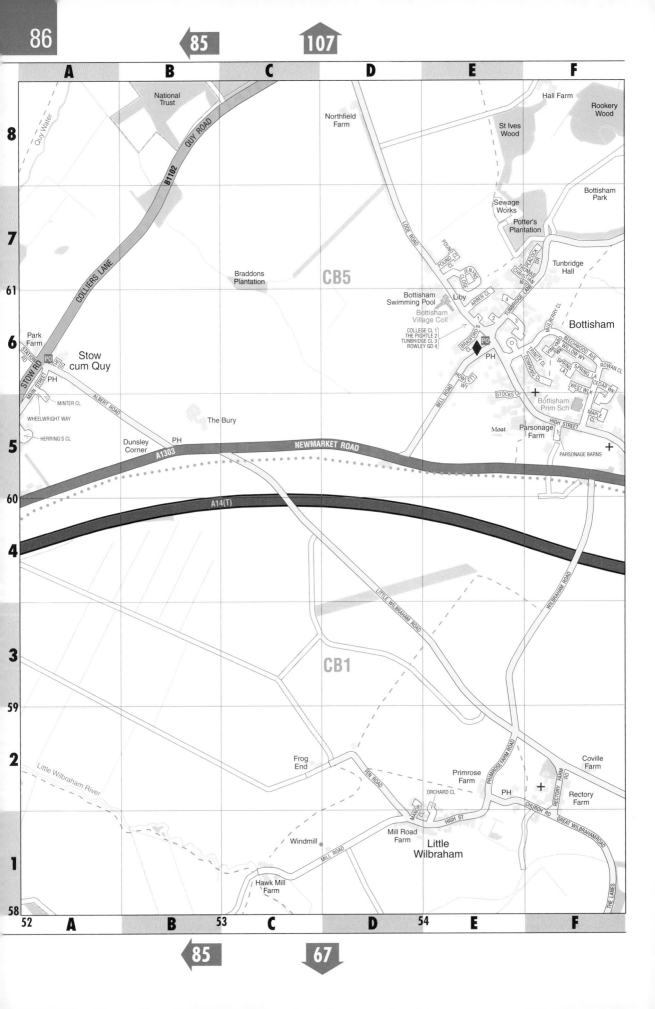

A B C D E F

Quy Water

National Trust

QUY ROAD

B1102

COLLIERS LANE

Hall Farm

Rookery Wood

Northfield Farm

St Ives Wood

Bottisham Park

Sewage Works

Potter's Plantation

CB5

Braddons Plantation

LODE ROAD

POUND HILL
POUND CL

JENKINS CLOSE

THOMAS CHRISTIAN WY
PEACOCK DR

Tunbridge Hall

TUNBRIDGE CL

Bottisham Swimming Pool

Liby

ARBER CL

Bottisham

Bottisham Village Coll

COLLEGE CL 1
THE PIGHTLE 2
TUNBRIDGE CL 3
ROWLEY GD 4

1 2 3

BRADFORDS CL

PO

MULBERRY CL

BEECHWOOD AVE

WILLOW WY

ROWAN CL

Park Farm

PO

STATION RD

STOW RD

Stow cum Quy

PH

MAIN STREET

MINTER CL

WHEELWRIGHT WAY

HERRING'S CL

ALBERT ROAD

The Bury

Dunsley Corner

A1303

PH

NEWMARKET ROAD

PH

BELL ROAD

HOWLETT WY

TRINITY CL

DOWNING CL

VINEYARD
SPRING CL
SPRING LA

CEDAR WK

WEST WLK

MAPLE CL

STOCKS CL

Bottisham Prim Sch

Moat

Parsonage Farm

HIGH STREET

PARSONAGE BARNS

A14(T)

LITTLE WILBRAHAM ROAD

WILBRAHAM ROAD

CB1

Little Wilbraham River

Frog End

FEN ROAD

Primrose Farm

PRIMROSE FARM ROAD

Coville Farm

PH

RECTORY FARM RD

Rectory Farm

ORCHARD CL

MANOR CL

HIGH ST

CHURCH RD

GREAT WILBRAHAM ROAD

Windmill

MILL ROAD

Mill Road Farm

Little Wilbraham

Hawk Mill Farm

THE LANES

8 7 61 6 5 60 4 3 59 2 1 58

52 53 54

Middle Hill
Plantations

SWAFFHAM HEATH ROAD

8

Park
End

Stone Bridge
Farm

Bottisham
Hall

7

Stone Bridge

Howe
Plantation

CB5

61

Bushmeadow
Wood

6

Chalk
Farm

5

PH

The Grange

A1303

60

Spring Hall

A14(T)

HEATH ROAD

4

CB1

3

A11(T)

59

CB8

2

Council
Farm

1

Bottisham
Heath Farm

A B C D E F

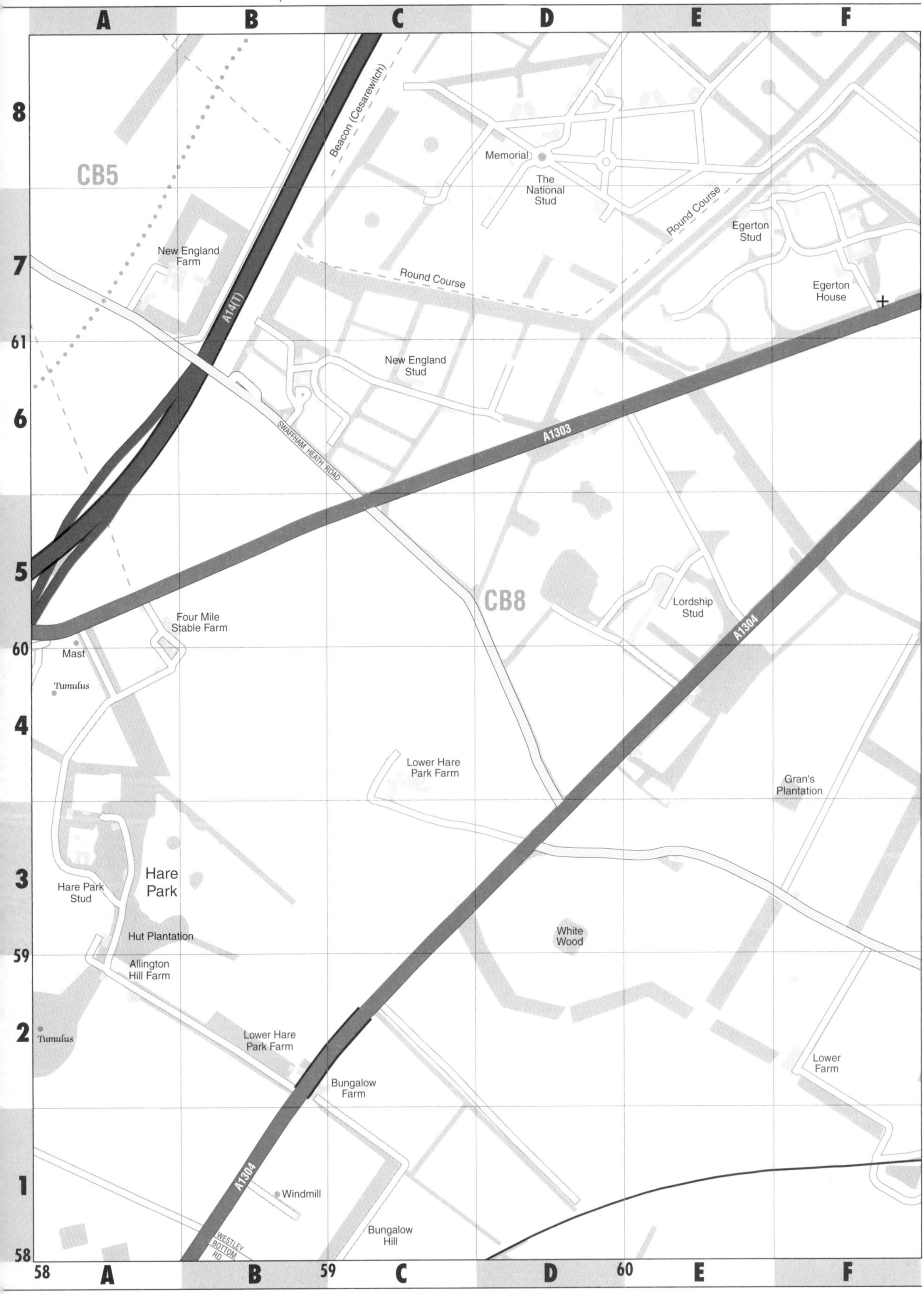

8

CB5

Beacon (Cesarewitch)

Memorial

The National Stud

Round Course

7

New England Farm

Egerton Stud

Round Course

Egerton House

A14(T)

61

New England Stud

SWAFFHAM HEATH ROAD

6

A1303

5

Four Mile Stable Farm

CB8

Lordship Stud

A1304

60

Mast

Tumulus

4

Lower Hare Park Farm

Gran's Plantation

3

Hare Park Stud

Hare Park

White Wood

Hut Plantation

59

Allington Hill Farm

2

Tumulus

Lower Hare Park Farm

Lower Farm

Bungalow Farm

1

A1304

Windmill

Bungalow Hill

58

WESTLEY BOTTOM RD

58 A B 59 C D 60 E F

A B C D E F

8
61
7
6
61
5
60
4
3
59
2
1
58

New Heath

The Clubhouse

Tumulus

BARBARA STRADBROKE AVENUE

A1304

CH

THE LINKS

Dullingham Road LC

B1061

The Links

Lower Links Covert

Stour Valley Path

Nature Reserve

Lingay Hill

LC

B1061

Four Gates Hall Farm

CB8

Hall Farm

Sidehill Plantation

Rook Plantation

Kidney Plantation

Stetchworth Park

Half Rounds Plantation

Sewage Works

DULLINGHAM ROAD

LC

Hill House Farm

Hill Farm

Sewage Works

Eagle Lane Farm

The Girls Grove

Dullingham LC

STATION ROAD

Lady's Plantation

VICARAGE CL

EAGLE LANE

B1061

Millfields

MILL LANE

PH

Allotments

Stetchworth

Sch

TEA KETTLE LANE

KETTLEFIELDS ROAD

THE CRESCENT

Tilbrook Farm

Dullingham

Dullingham House Park

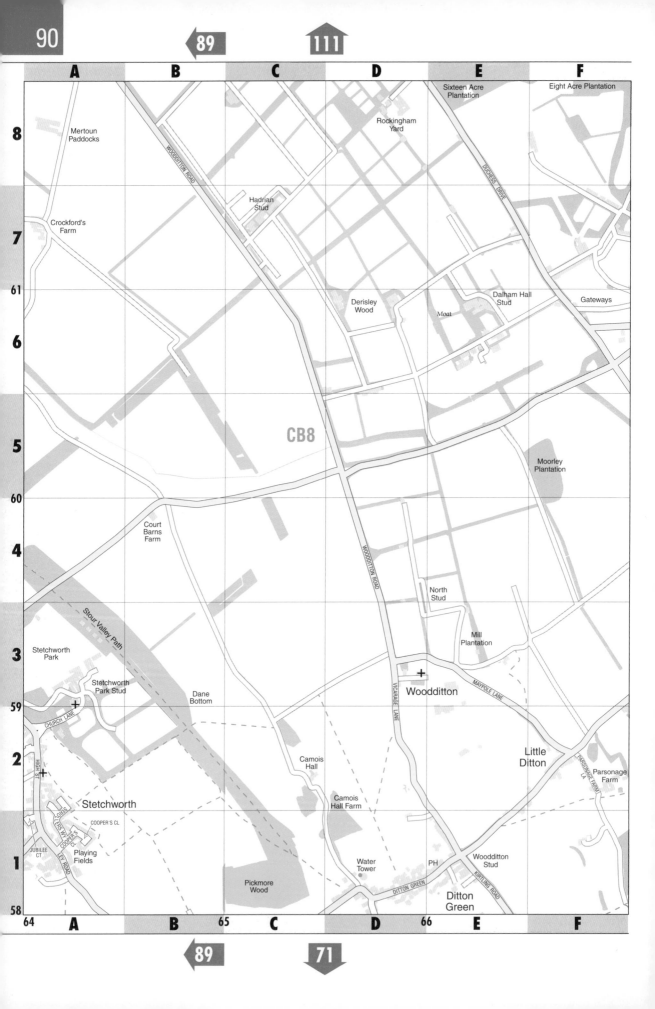

89
111

A   B   C   D   E   F

8   Mertoun
     Paddocks

     Rockingham
     Yard

     Sixteen Acre
     Plantation

     Eight Acre Plantation

     Hadrian
     Stud

7   Crockford's
     Farm

61   Derisley   Dalham Hall
                            Wood   Moat   Stud   Gateways

6

                                                               Moorley
5   CB8   Plantation

60   Court
4   Barns
                            Farm
                                              WOODDITTON ROAD
                                                       North
                                                       Stud

                                                            Mill
3   Stetchworth   Plantation
     Park
          Stetchworth   Dane
          Park Stud   Bottom   +
                                              Woodditton

59   CHURCH LANE   MAYPOLE LANE
                                                                          Little
2   HIGH ST   Camois   Ditton
     +   Hall
          Stetchworth   Parsonage
                                      Camois   Farm
                                      Hall Farm
     COOPER'S CL
1   JUBILEE   Woodditton
     CT   Playing   Pickmore   Water   PH   Stud
              Fields   Wood   Tower
                                                     DITTON GREEN   Ditton
58   Green
     64   A   B   65   C   D   66   E   F

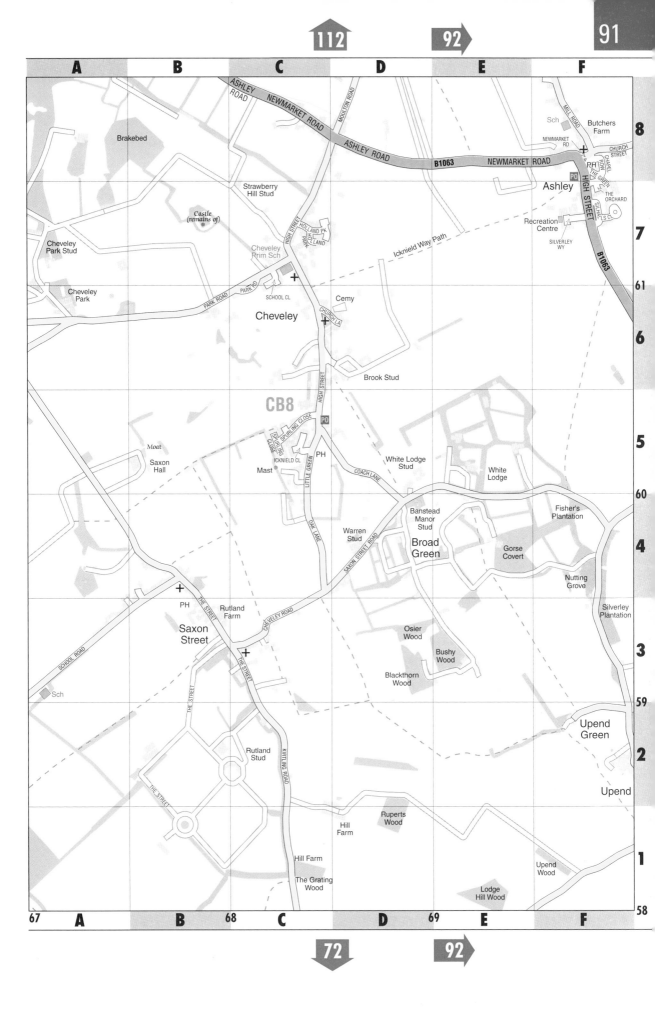

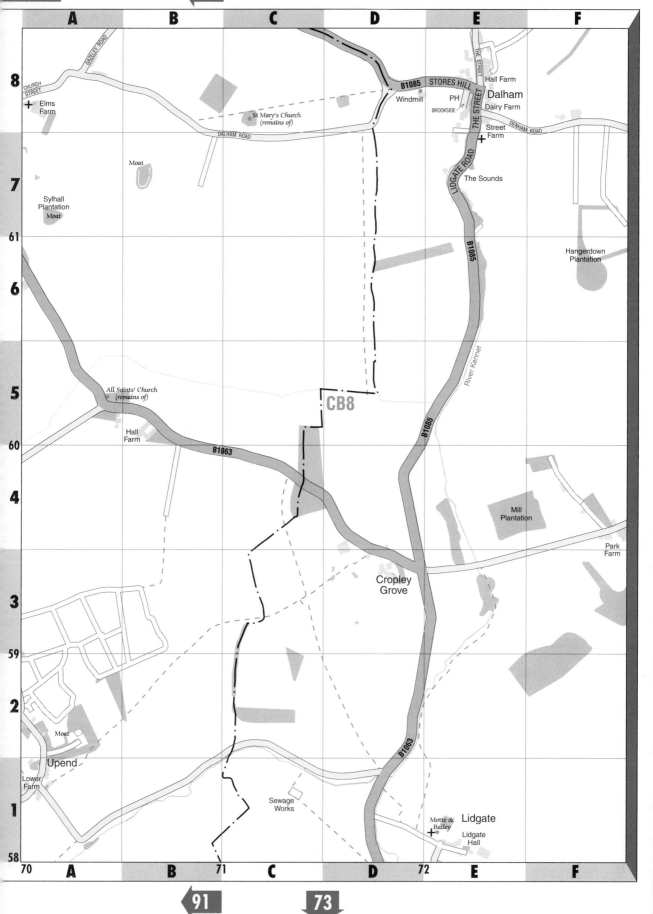

A   B   C   D   E   F

8

7

61

6

5

CB8

60

4

3

59

2

1

58

70   A   71   B   C   72   D   E   F

Church Street
Gazeley Road
Elms Farm
St Mary's Church (remains of)
Dalham Road
Moat
Sylhall Plantation
Moat
B1085
Stores Hill
Windmill
PH
BROOKSIDE
Dalham
Hall Farm
Dairy Farm
The Street
Street Farm
Denham Road
Lidgate Road
The Sounds
B1085
Hangerdown Plantation
River Kennet
All Saints' Church (remains of)
Hall Farm
B1063
B1085
Mill Plantation
Park Farm
Cropley Grove
Moat
Upend
Lower Farm
Sewage Works
B1063
Motte & Bailey
Lidgate
Lidgate Hall

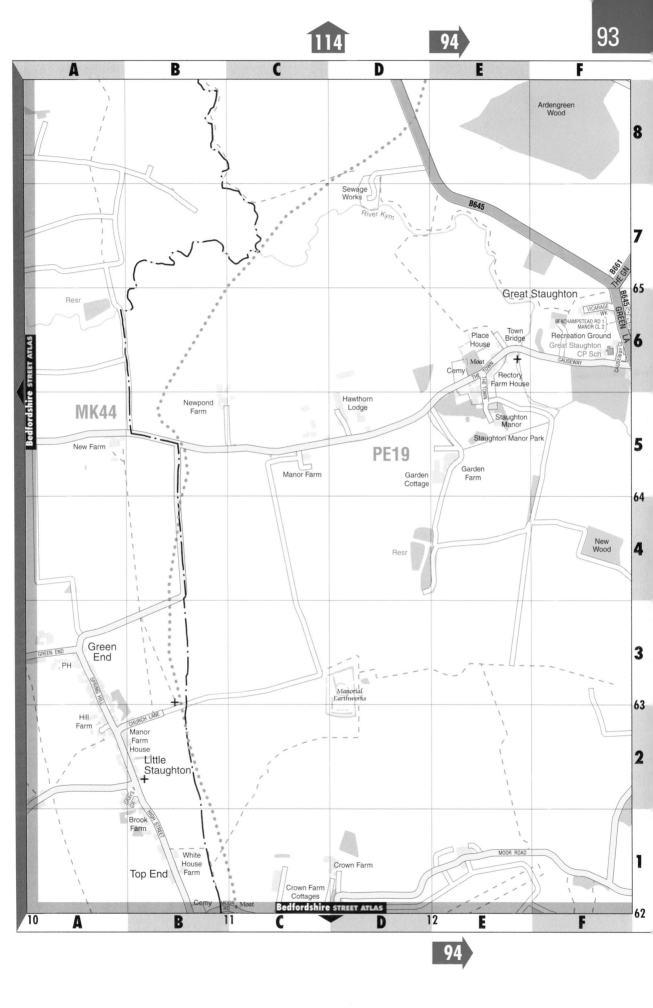

A B C D E F

Ardengreen
Wood

8

Sewage
Works

B645

River Kym

7

65

Great Staughton

VICARAGE
WK

BEACHAMPSTEAD RD 1
MANOR CL 2

B645

GREEN LA

B661
THE GN

Place
House

Town
Bridge

Recreation Ground

Great Staughton
CP Sch

6

Moat

CAUSEWAY

BLAXHAMS GR

Cemy

Rectory
Farm House

MK44

Newpond
Farm

Hawthorn
Lodge

THE TOWN

Staughton
Manor

New Farm

PE19

Staughton Manor Park

5

Manor Farm

Garden
Cottage

Garden
Farm

64

Resr

New
Wood

4

Green
End

GREEN END

PH

SPRING HILL

Manorial
Earthworks

3

Hill
Farm

CHURCH LANE

63

Manor Farm
House

Little
Staughton

2

GRAYS GR

HIGH STREET

Brook
Farm

MOOR ROAD

White
House
Farm

Top End

Crown Farm

1

Cemy

MOOR RD

Moat

Crown Farm
Cottages

62

10 A B 11 C D 12 E F

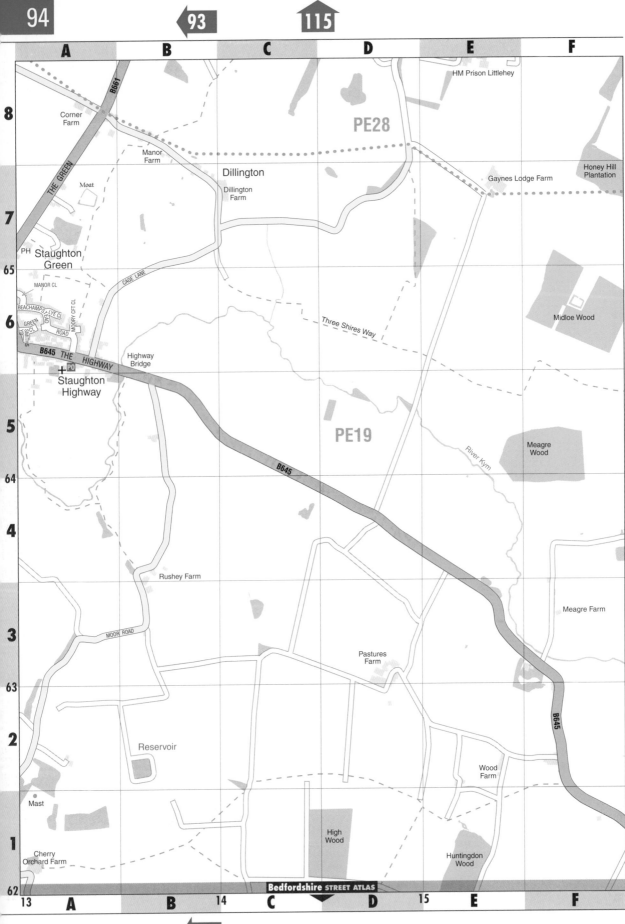

A B C D E F

8 Corner Farm

B661

Manor Farm

Dillington

PE28

HM Prison Littlehey

Honey Hill Plantation

Gaynes Lodge Farm

7 Moat

Dillington Farm

THE GREEN

65 PH Staughton Green

MANOR CL

CAGE LANE

Three Shires Way

Midloe Wood

6 BEACHAMPS LYE CL
GREEN
SMITHS CL
MOORY CFT CL
ROAD

B645 THE HIGHWAY

Highway Bridge

PO

Staughton Highway

River Kym

Meagre Wood

5 PE19

B645

64

Meagre Farm

4

Rushey Farm

3 MOOR ROAD

Pastures Farm

63

B645

2 Reservoir

Wood Farm

Mast

1 High Wood

Huntingdon Wood

Cherry Orchard Farm

62

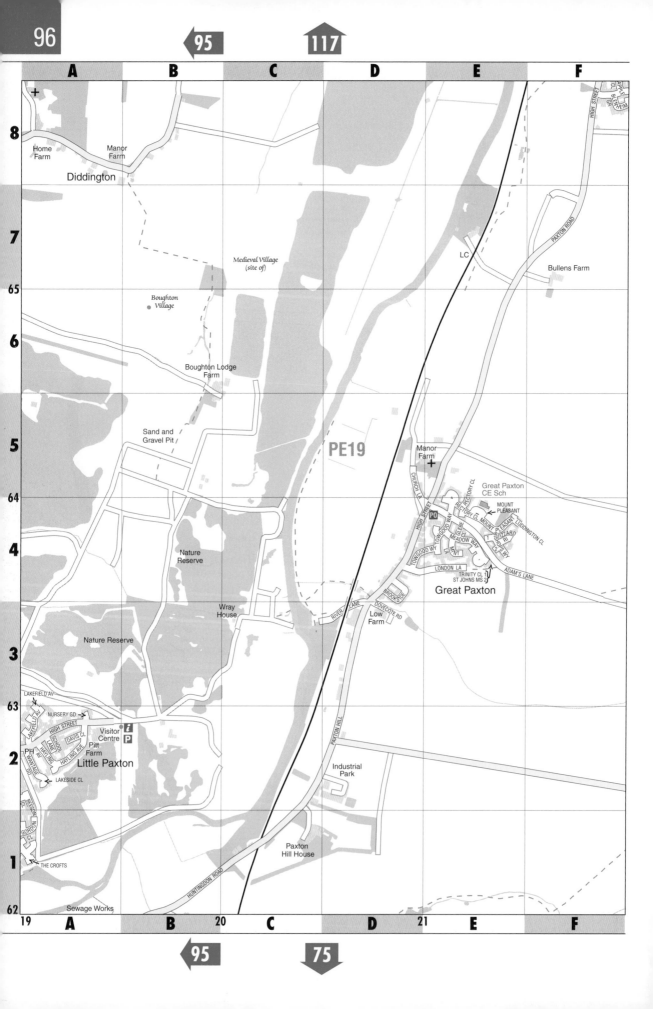

A   **B**   **C**   **D**   **E**   **F**

8

Home
Farm

Manor
Farm

Diddington

7

Medieval Village
(site of)

65

Boughton
Village

LC

Bullens Farm

6

Boughton Lodge
Farm

5

Sand and
Gravel Pit

PE19

Manor
Farm

Great Paxton
CE Sch

64

MOUNT
PLEASANT

PO

4

Nature
Reserve

MEADOW WAY

LONDON LA

TRINITY CL
ST JOHNS MS

Great Paxton

ADAM'S LANE

Wray
House

RIVER LANE

BROOK RD

DOVECOTE RD

Low
Farm

3

Nature Reserve

63

LAKEFIELD AV

NURSERY GD

LAMEFIELD AV

High Street

DAVIS CL

SCHOOL LANE

Visitor
Centre

Pitt
Farm

PAXTON HILL

2

PH

HAYLING AVE

WANTAGE RD

LAKESIDE CL

Little Paxton

Industrial
Park

GORDON CL

NORRIS CL

BELSON CL

1

THE CROFTS

Paxton
Hill House

62

Sewage Works

HUNTINGDON ROAD

A   19   **B**   20   **C**   **D**   21   **E**   **F**

PAXTON ROAD

APPLE CL
BLENHEIM GR
HIGH STREET

CHURCH LA

HIGH STREET

RECTORY CL
MOUNT PLEASANT
BUZZARD
GLEBE CL
BISHOP'S WY
TOWGOOD WY
MNT
TUDDINGTON CL

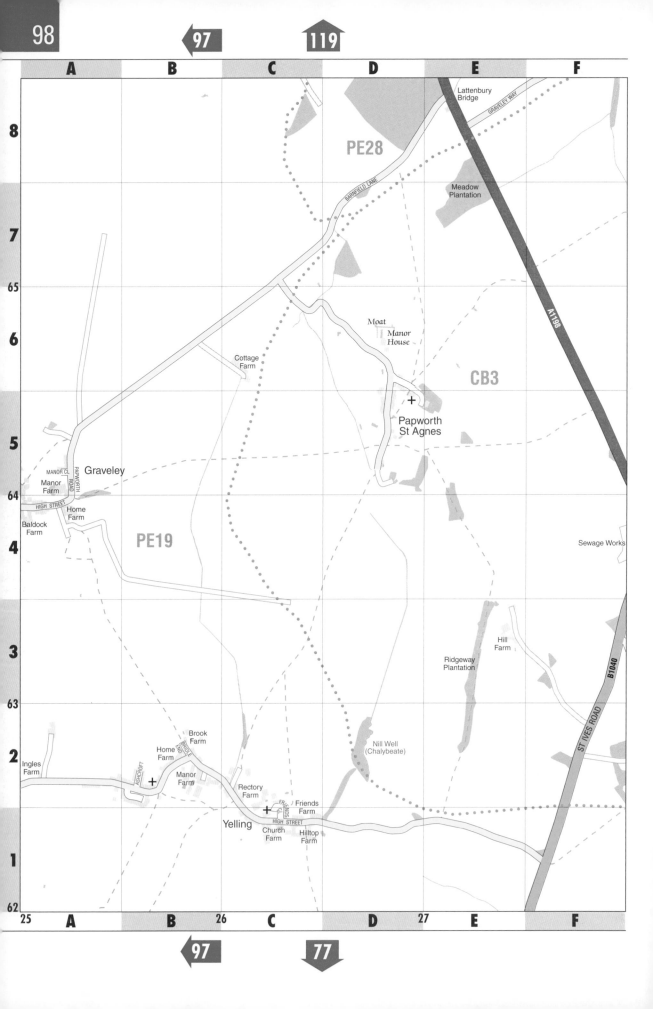

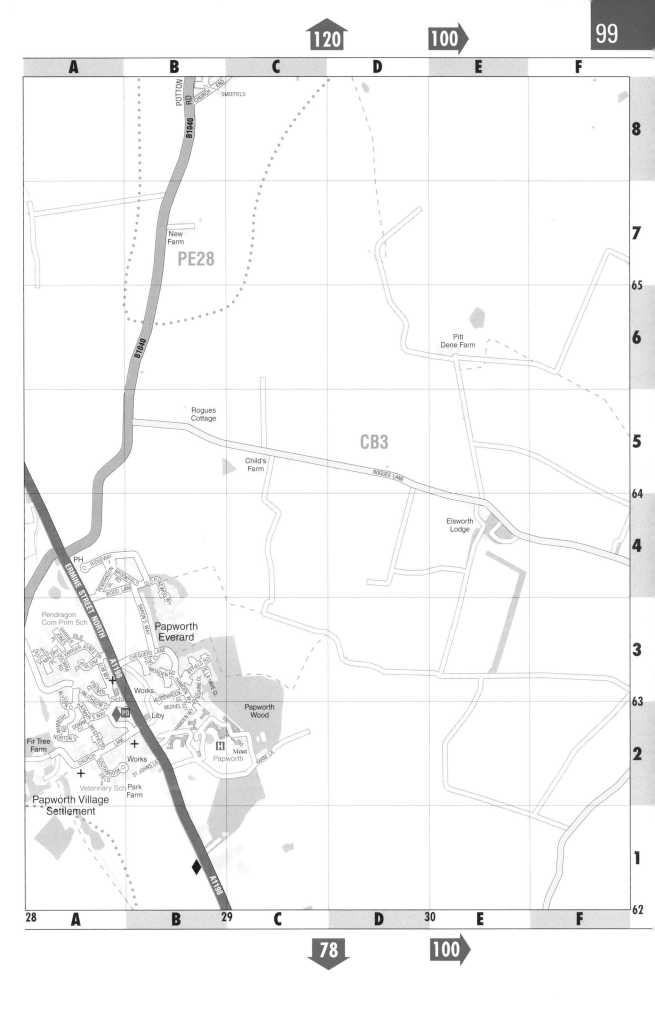

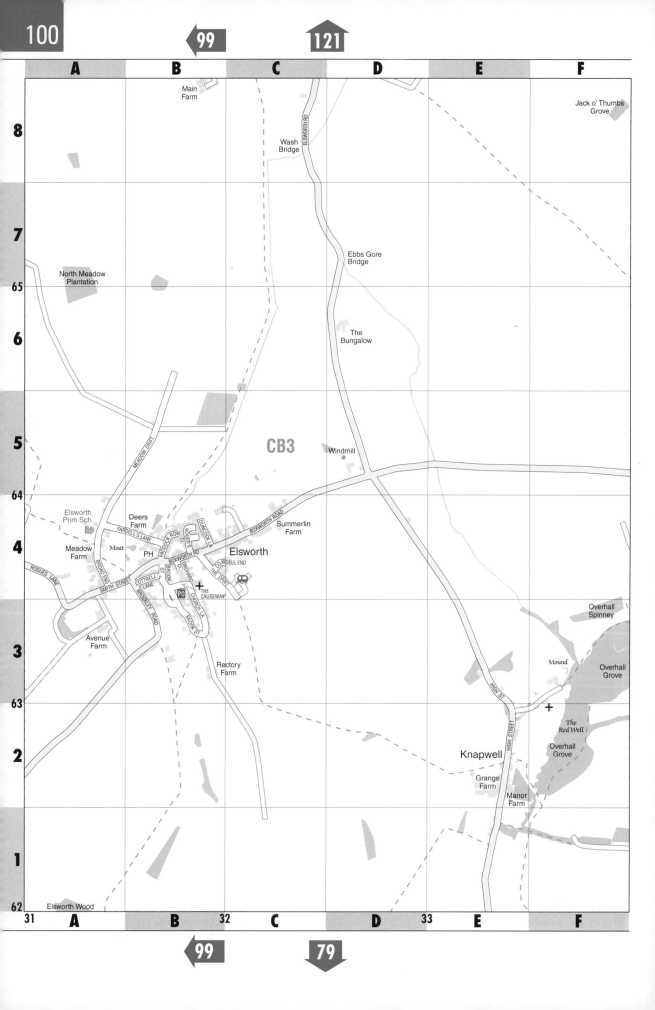

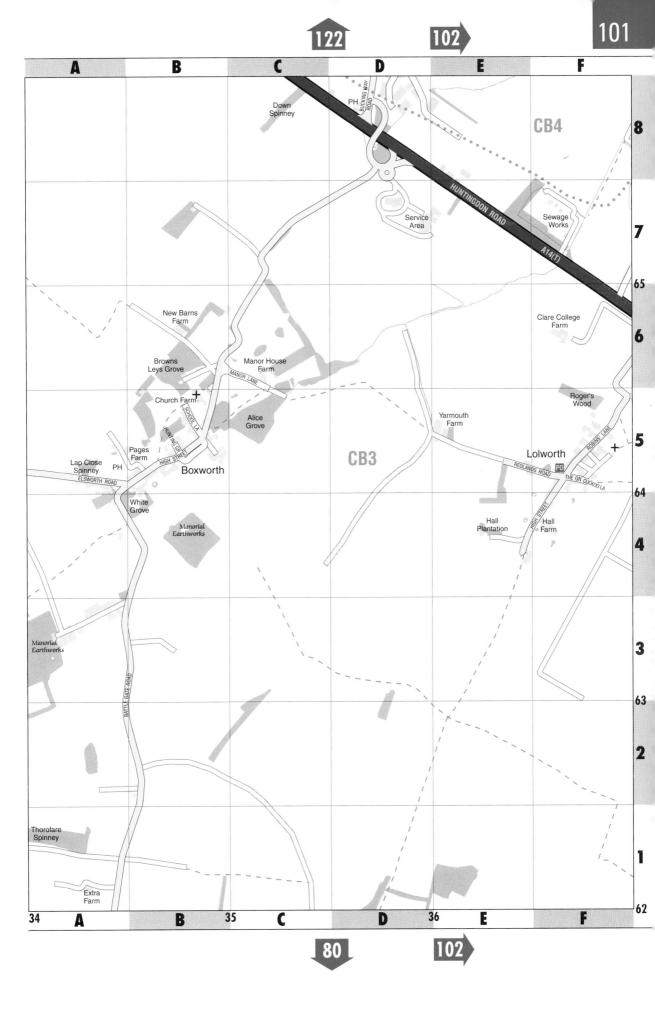

A B C D E F

8

7

65

6

5

64

4

3

63

2

1

62

CB4

Down
Spinney

PH

BUCKING WAY ROAD

HUNTINGDON ROAD

A14(T)

Service
Area

Sewage
Works

Clare College
Farm

New Barns
Farm

Browns
Leys Grove

Manor House
Farm

MANOR LANE

Roger's
Wood

ROBINS LANE

Church Farm

SCHOOL LA

Alice
Grove

Yarmouth
Farm

CB3

Lolworth

PO

Pages
Farm

HUNTING GR

HIGH STREET

Lap Close
Spinney

PH

Boxworth

ELSWORTH ROAD

REDLANDS ROAD

THE GN CUCKOO LA

White
Grove

Manorial
Earthworks

HIGH STREET

Hall
Plantation

Hall
Farm

Manorial
Earthworks

BATTLE GATE ROAD

Thorofare
Spinney

Extra
Farm

34 A B 35 C D 36 E F

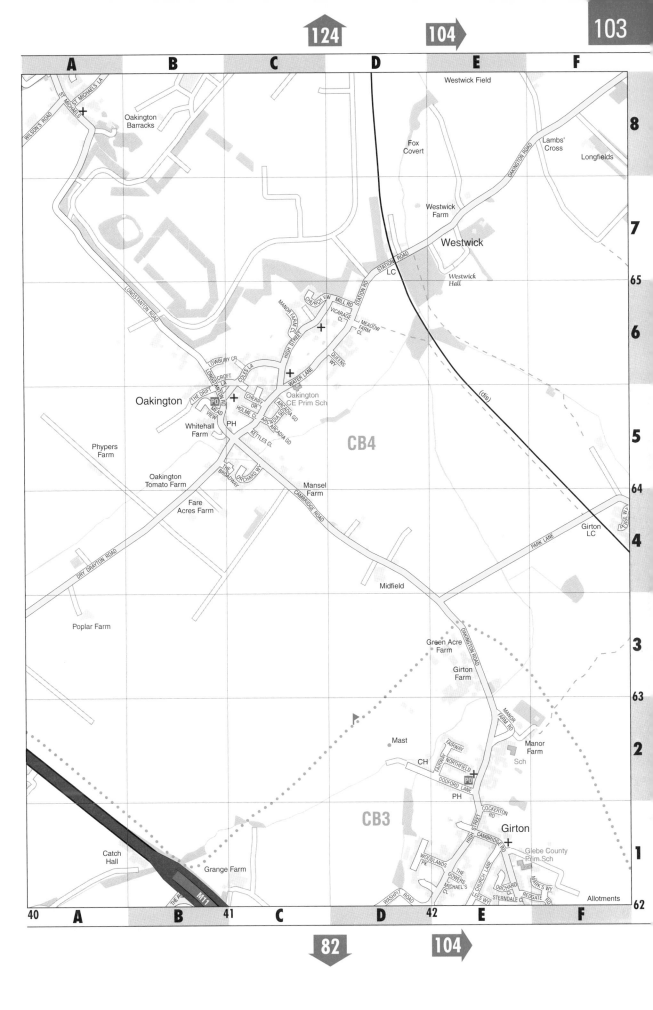

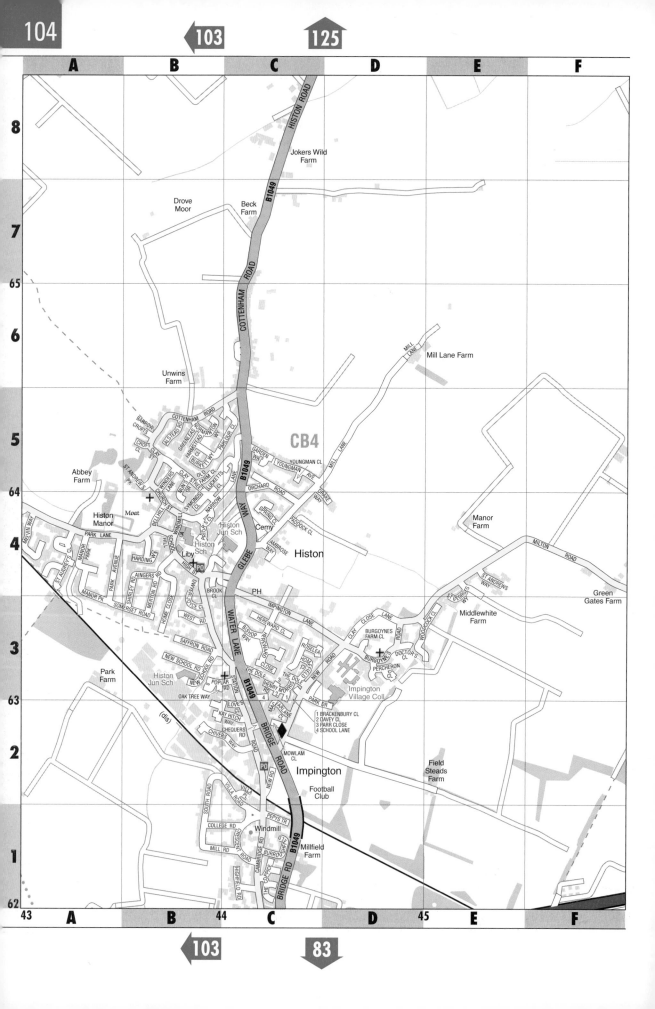

A B C D E F

8

HISTON ROAD

Jokers Wild
Farm

7

65

Drove
Moor

Beck
Farm

B1049

COTTENHAM ROAD

MILL
LANE

Mill Lane Farm

6

Unwins
Farm

CB4

5

BARROW
CROFTS

COTTENHAM ROAD

ALSTEAD RD
GREENLEAS
NORMANTON
WY

FARMSTEAD CL

BURKETT WY

PARLOUR CL

B1049

GARDEN
WY

YOUNGMAN CL

YOUNGMAN
AVE

MILL LANE

Abbey
Farm

CROFT
CLAY ST
CL

ST ANDREW'S
PK

CHURCH
LANE
WINDRUSH

CLAY ST
OLD
NUN'S
WY

FARM CL
LUCKETTS

SWIMONDS

ORCHARD ROAD

DRAKE
WAY

Manor
Farm

64

Histon
Manor

Moat

BELLHILL CL

SCHOOL HILL

SWINDMILL
MARROW

Histon
Jun Sch

Histon
Sch

CEMY

SPRING CL

PADDOCK CL

MANOR
PARK

PARK LANE

PATSY'S CL

GLEBE WAY

AMBROSE
WAY

Histon

MELVIN WAY

4

ST AUDREY'S CL

PARK AVENUE

HARDING

KEYS

Liby

High St

PO

MILTON ROAD

Green
Gates Farm

MANOR PK

SHIRLEY RD

AINGERS RD

MERTON RD

SOMERSET ROAD

HOME CLOSE

LAWRENCE CL

WEST
RD

BROOK
CL

WATER LANE

PH

IMPINGTON LANE

BISHOPS
WAY

HEREWARD CL

HEREWARD

ROSE LEA

CLAY CLOSE LANE

ST ANDREWS
WAY

ST GEORGE'S
WY

WOODROCK CL

Middlewhite
Farm

3

Park
Farm

SAFFRON ROAD

NEW SCHOOL RD

NEW SCHOOL RD

Histon
Jun Sch

NEW
POPLAR

THE DOLE

CLOSE

HOM CL

NEW
ROAD

Burgoynes
Farm CL

PERCHERON

DOCTOR'S
CL

BURGOYNES

B1049

STATION RD

MACFARLANE

HENRY MORRIS
RD

4

PARK DR

Impington
Village Coll

63

OAK TREE WAY

LOVE'S
CL

KAY HITCH
WAY

CHEQUERS
RD

CHIVERS WAY

BRIDGE ROAD

(dis)

1 BRACKENBURY CL
2 DAVEY CL
3 PARR CLOSE
4 SCHOOL LANE

Field
Steads
Farm

2

MOWLAM
CL

PO

Impington

Football
Club

SOUTH ROAD

VILLA ROAD

VILLA RD

NEW RD
OLD

PEPYS TR

COLLEGE RD

CRESCENT ROAD

CAMBRIDGE RD

THE OFFICE

BURROW

B1049

Windmill

Millfield
Farm

1

MILL RD

HIGHFIELD RD

THE BRIDGE RD

62

43 A B 44 C D 45 E F

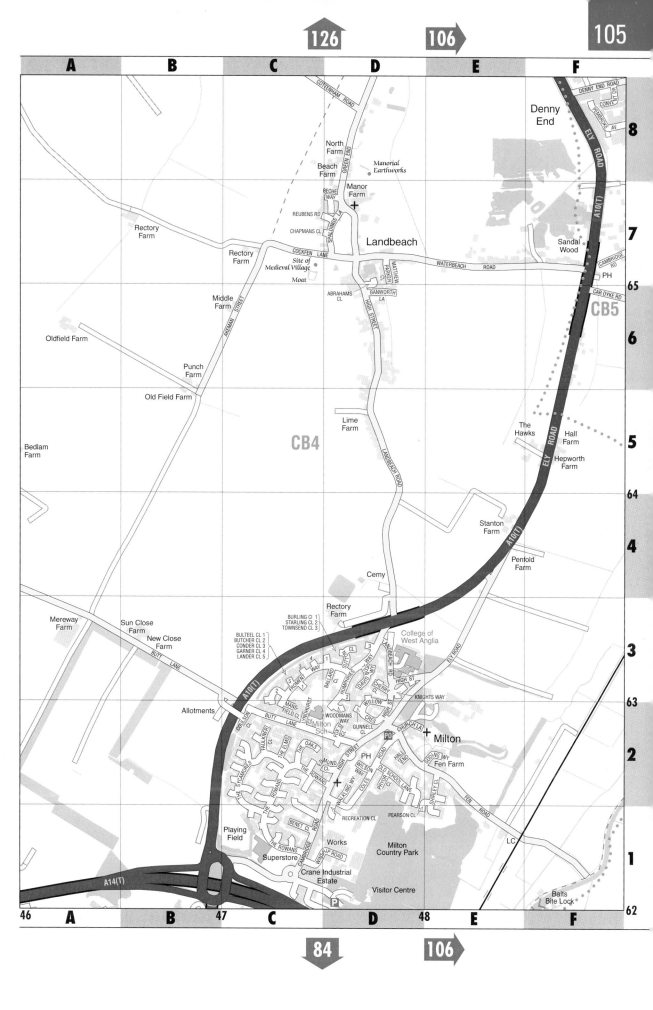

A B C D E F

Denny End
PEMBROKE AVE
WINFOLD ROAD
DENNY END RD
LEE CL
CLOAK
WADDELOW RD
BANNOLD CT
CODY RD
FENLEIGH CL
Waterbeach CP Sch
Liby
WILES CL
PRIMROSE LA
DEN CL
VICARAGE DR
PO
Cattell's La
BARKER CL
CAMPS CL
GREEN SIDE
HIGH STREET
SPURGEONS AV
PARK CR
JOSIAH CT
BANNOLD ROAD
Midlode Farm
Long Drove
Lock Farm
BANNOLD RD
LC

Bottisham Lock

HARDING CL 1
POORSFIELD RD 2
SAXON WAY 3
MILL
GLEBE ROAD
CORO-NATION CL
CAMBRIDGE ROAD
CHAPEL ROAD
GIBSON CL
CHAPEL HILL
ST ANDREWS
WELLINGTON
PIECES TR
PIECES LA
HARTLEY CL
WATERBEACH
Todds Farm
Hall Crest Farm
BURGESS'S DROVE
Frolic Farm
Hatley's Farm
LUG FEN DROVEWAY

Old Sunday Sch
St John's Cl
STATION ROAD
ROSEMARY RD
BURGESS ROAD
LODE AV
PAYTON
ADAMS CT
LC
Northfields Farm
Vicarage Farm

CAR DYKE ROAD
WHITMORE WAY
LC
Waterbeach
Clayhithe Road

River Cam
Clayhithe Road
Clayhithe
Clayhithe Farm
CB5
Queen's Fen

Queens Farm

Grange Farm

Eye Hall Farm

CB4

Roman Pottery Kilns (site of)

Clayhithe Road

Harcamlow Way

Manor Farm
DOCK LANE
ST JOHN'S LA
Northgate Farm
CHURCH END
PH
HIGH STREET
Kings Farm

Stow cum Quy Fen

ABBOTS WY
PRIORY RD
HORNINGSEA ROAD
Horningsea

Allicky Farm
STATION RD

Allotments

49 A B 50 C D 51 E F

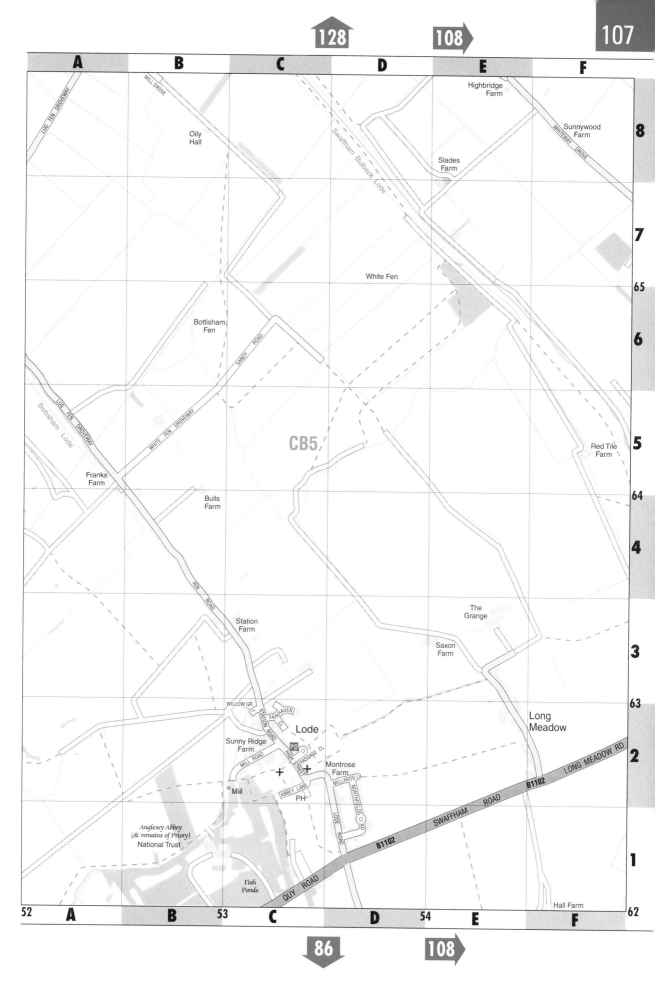

A B C D E F

LUG FEN DROVEWAY

MILL DROVE

Oily Hall

Swaffham Bulbeck Lode

Highbridge Farm

Sunnywood Farm

WHITEWAY DROVE

Slades Farm

White Fen

Bottisham Fen

SANDY ROAD

Bottisham Lode

LUG FEN DROVEWAY

WHITE FEN DROVEWAY

CB5

Red Tile Farm

Franks Farm

Bulls Farm

FEN ROAD

Station Farm

The Grange

Saxon Farm

Long Meadow

WILLOW GR

STATION ROAD

FAIRHAVEN CL

Lode

Sunny Ridge Farm

MILL ROAD

PO

HIGH STREET

PASSAGE CL

Montrose Farm

MILLARDS LA

LONG MEADOW RD

B1102

NORTHFIELDS RD

ABBEY LANE

PH

LODE ROAD

SWAFFHAM ROAD

B1102

Mill

Anglesey Abbey (& remains of Priory) National Trust

Fish Ponds

QUY ROAD

Hall Farm

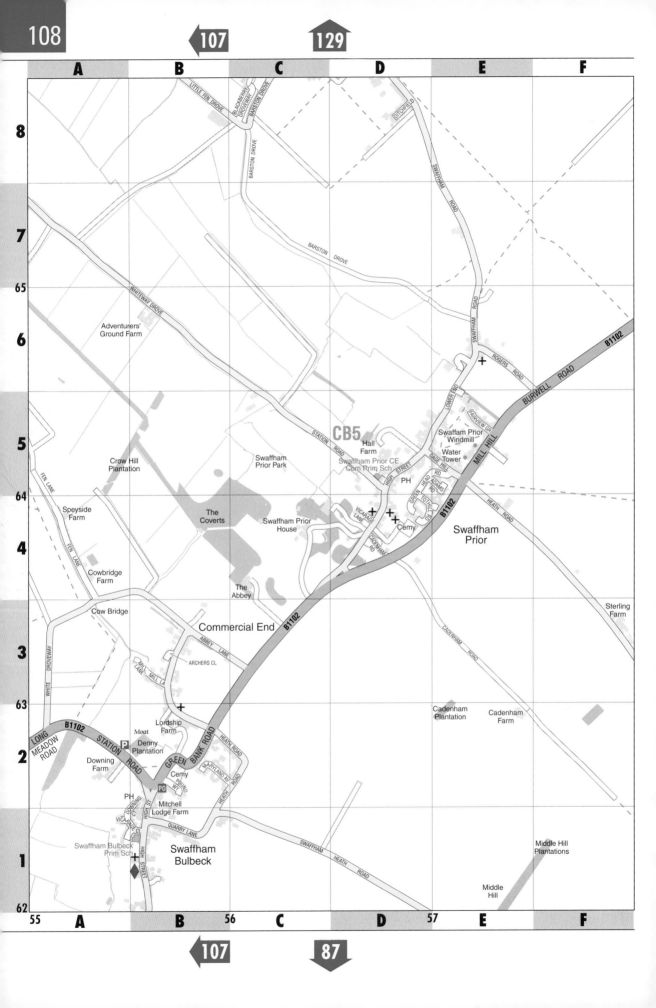

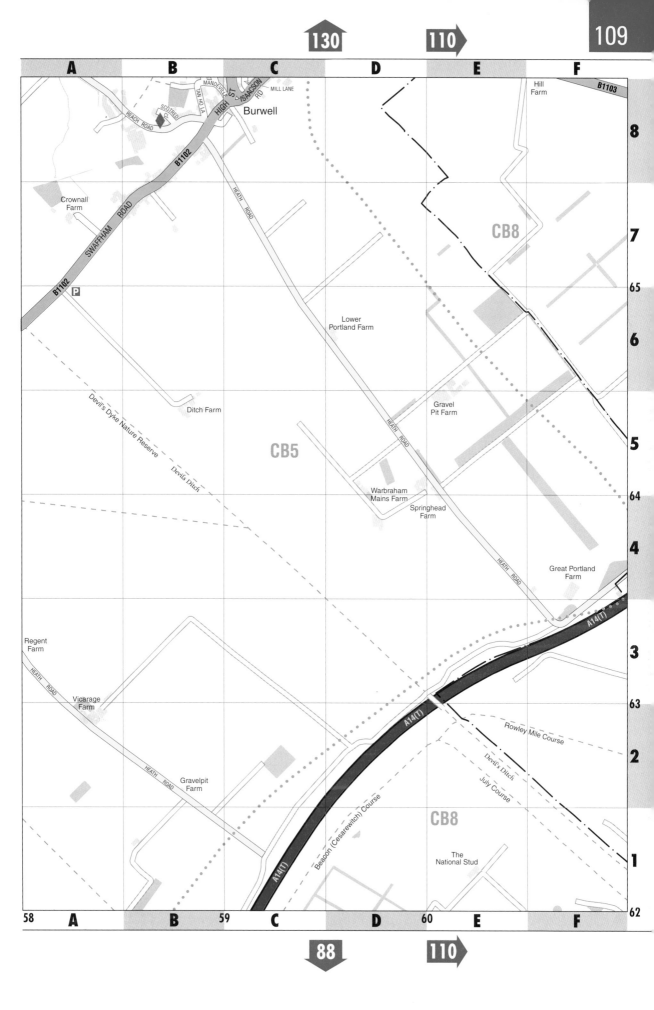

A B C D E F

8

7

65

6

5

64

4

3

63

2

1

62

61 A 62 B 62 C 62 D 63 E F

B1103 BURWELL ROAD
THE DRIFT
Orchard Farm
NEW RD
NORTH RD
MILL LA
QUEENS VIEW
ACRE WY
KING GEORGE AV
QUEENSWAY
Exning
OXFORD ST
SWAN LA
B1103
ANNE'S CL
Exning CP Sch
PO
CHURCH CL
SWAN GR
RIVER GN
BROOKSIDE
CHAPEL Church
WENDRED'S WAY
ST MARY'S WY
DUCK'S LANE
BROOMFIELD
LACEY'S LANE
Harraton Stud
Allotments
HEATH ROAD
COTTON END
Park
GEORGE GIBSON CLOSE
WINDMILL HILL
SAXON CL
THE HIGHLANDS
PH
BEECH WOOD CL
Exeter Stud
CHURCH ST
Cemy
ROYAL PALACE CLOSE
Brickfield Stud
B1103
EXNING ROAD
Studlands Park Business Centre
A14(T)
Industrial Estate
Studlands Park Ind Estate
Laureate CP Sch
Factory
HAMMOND CL
AUGATE SCHOOL RD
LAUREATE PADDOCKS
LAUREATE GDNS
CRAVEN WY
GUBNER'S
DEPOT RD
FEILDEN WAY
ROSEBERY WAY
Hamilton Road
Hamilton Stud
E5
ANDREW RD 1
BARTONS PL 2
COLLINGS PL 3
DURHAM WAY 5
Seven Springs
CB8
Southfield Farm
SEFTON WAY
DERBY WY
ROCHFORT
HALIFAX
NORFOLK AVE
CHURCHILL AVE
ELIZABETH WAY
FAIRHAVEN
KING EDWARD VII RD
Equine Pool
Hamilton Road
DRINKWATER CL
EDINBURGH
WINDSOR
MANGERSTON RD
PRINCESS WY
CHARLES CL
PORTLAND RD
VALLEY WAY
HILL RD
MANGERSTON RD
PHILIPS ROAD
Paddocks CP Sch
Pool
LEADER'S WAY
SUFFOLK WAY
STIRLING GO
ST FABIANS CL
PHILIPS ROAD
SHELROSS
CHAPEL ROW
Newmarket Upper Sch
1 BAHRAM CL
2 SOUTHFIELDS CL
ADASTRAL CLOSE
KINGSWAY
Playing Field
ROWLEY DR
Scaltback Middle Sch
B1103
PO
CORSICAN PINE CL
GREVILLE STARKEY AV 1
TOM JENNINGS CL 2
CROFT ROAD
GEORGE LAMBTON AVE
FIELD TR RD
HEASMAN AVE
WESTON WY
MURLESS RD
Sports Ctr
DSS
SOUTH ST
ST FABIANS DRIVE
TANNERSFIELD WAY
MILLBANK
FRESHFIELDS
EXNING ROAD
H
Newmarket Swimming Pool
HIGH ST
LOWTHER ST
BLACK BEAR LANE
FALMOUTH
THE ROWS
ROWLEY
THE BEECHES
FALMOUTH AV
Government Offices
THE HAMILTONS
Cooper Memorial Fountain
Cemetery
B1061
FAIRLAWNS RD 1
HALLWYCK GDNS 2
Holdsworth Valley CP Sch
Newmarket Heath
Rowley Mile Course
The Millennium Grandstand
Cambridge Hill
BARBARA STRADBROKE AVENUE
DULLINGHAM ROAD
Racecourses
Devil's Ditch
A1304
Wyck Hall Stud
B1061
FORDHAM RD
A142
Studlands Park
A14(T)
NIMBUS WAY
AUREOLE WK
AUREOLE WALK
PARKERS WALK
TULAR WALK
NIMBUS WAY
HYPERION WAY
PERSIMMON WAY
PINZA CL
HYPERION
WATER CL
MILES
BRICKFIELDS AVE
BOLDEN CLOSE
MILLER CLOSE
PETINGO
PARKERS WAY
HETHERSETT WAY
STUDLANDS
STUDLANDS PARK AVENUE
Sports Club
VICTORIA WAY
STUDLANDS PARK RD
WILLIE SMITH RD
Works
Works
OAKS DRIVE
Playing Fields
St Felix CE VC Middle Sch
DOUG SMITH CL 1
GORDON RICHARDS CL 2
LESTER PIGGOTT WAY 3
MATT DAWSON CL 4
A142

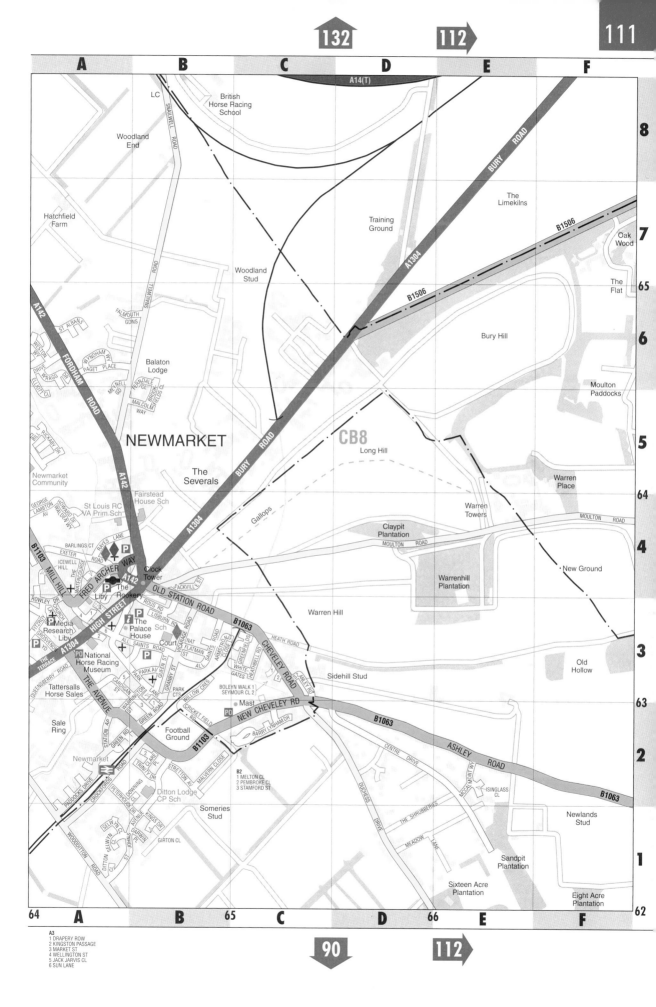

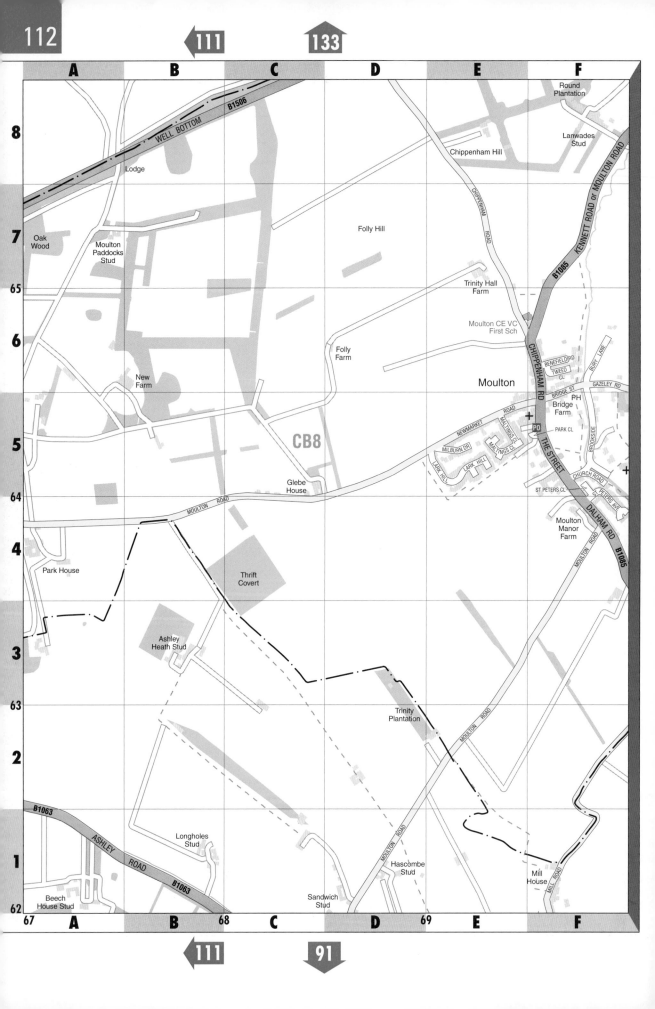

A B C D E F

8

7

65

6

5

64

4

3

63

2

1

62

67 A B 68 C D 69 E F

WELL BOTTOM B1506

Lodge

Oak Wood

Moulton Paddocks Stud

New Farm

Folly Hill

Folly Farm

Round Plantation

Lanwades Stud

Chippenham Hill

CHIPPENHAM ROAD

Trinity Hall Farm

Moulton CE VC First Sch

B1085

KENNETT ROAD or MOULTON ROAD

Moulton

CHIPPENHAM RD

BENEFIELD RD

TWEED CL

BRIDGE ST

PH

Bridge Farm

PARK CL

BURY LANE

GAZELEY RD

BROOKSIDE

CB8

Glebe House

MOULTON ROAD

NEWMARKET ROAD

MILBURN DR

LARK HILL

MALTINGS CL

MALTINGS CL

PO

THE STREET

CHURCH ROAD

ST PETERS CL

PETERS AVE

Moulton Manor Farm

DALHAM RD

B1085

Park House

Thrift Covert

Ashley Heath Stud

Trinity Plantation

MOULTON ROAD

B1063

ASHLEY ROAD

B1063

Longholes Stud

MOULTON ROAD

Hascombe Stud

Mill House

MILL ROAD

Beech House Stud

Sandwich Stud

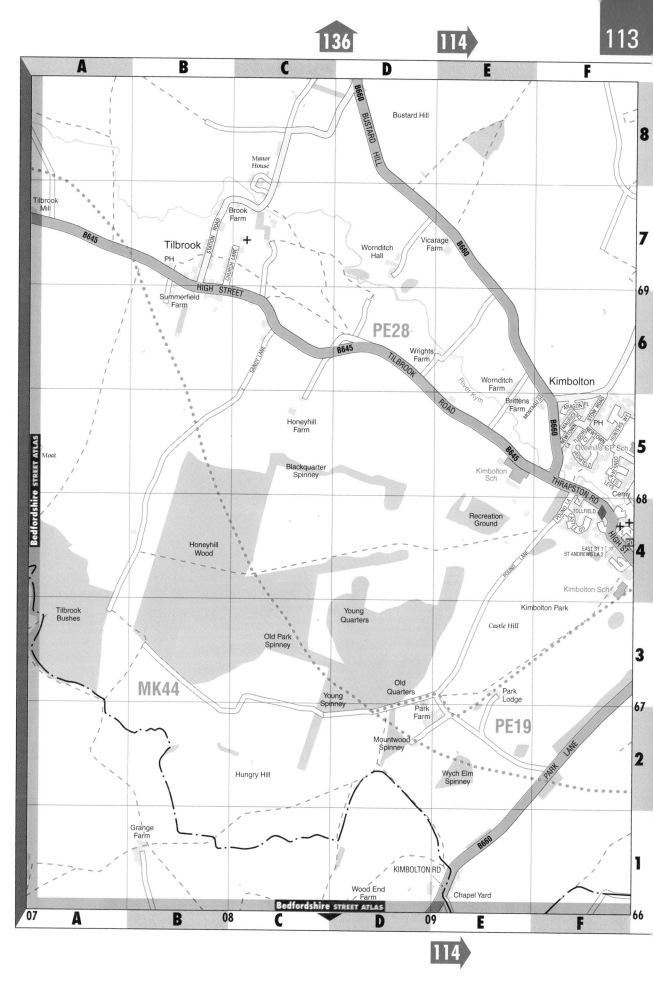

A   **B**   **C**   **D**   **E**   **F**

Airfield (disused)

Airfield (disused)

8

Magpie Farm

GROVEMERE CT

AVENUE

RIVER RD

KING ST

CLOSE

BROOK RD

Bicton Industrial Estate

Mast

Mast

STOCKING LANE

PE28

7

High Park Farm

BIGRAM'S LANE

69

Lowen Wood

6

Bigram's Farm

Warren Hill

EASTON ROAD

Warren Spinney

Newtown

5

Overhills CP Sch

Priory Farm

Three Shires Way

Dudney Wood

Cemy

68

PE19

Kimbolton

4

EAST ST

LONDON RD

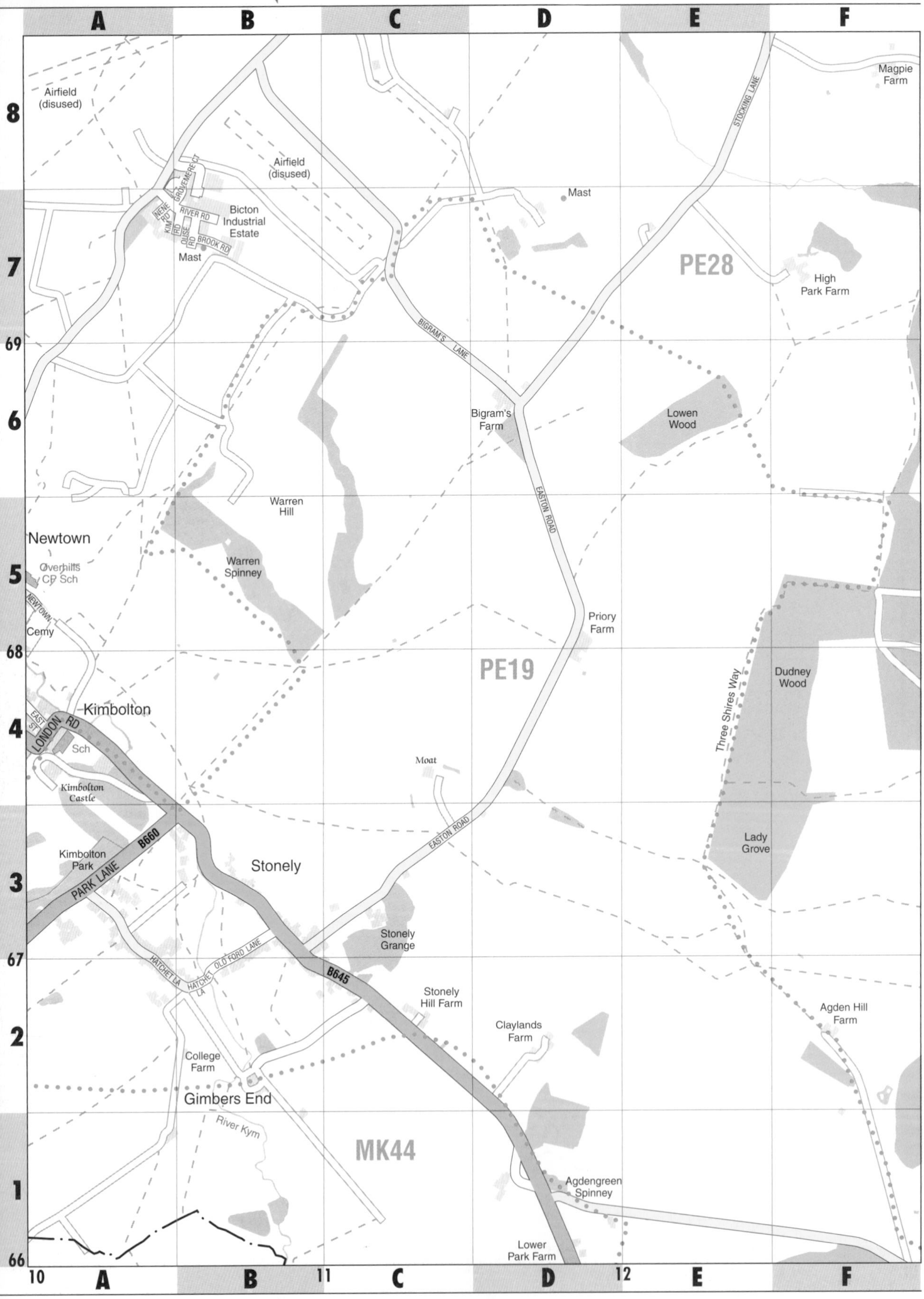

Sch

Moat

Kimbolton Castle

EASTON ROAD

Lady Grove

Kimbolton Park

3

B660

PARK LANE

Stonely

Stonely Grange

67

HATCHET LA

HATCHET LA

OLD FORD LANE

B645

Stonely Hill Farm

Agden Hill Farm

2

Claylands Farm

College Farm

Gimbers End

River Kym

MK44

Agdengreen Spinney

1

Lower Park Farm

66

10   **A**   **B**   **11**   **C**   **D**   **12**   **E**   **F**

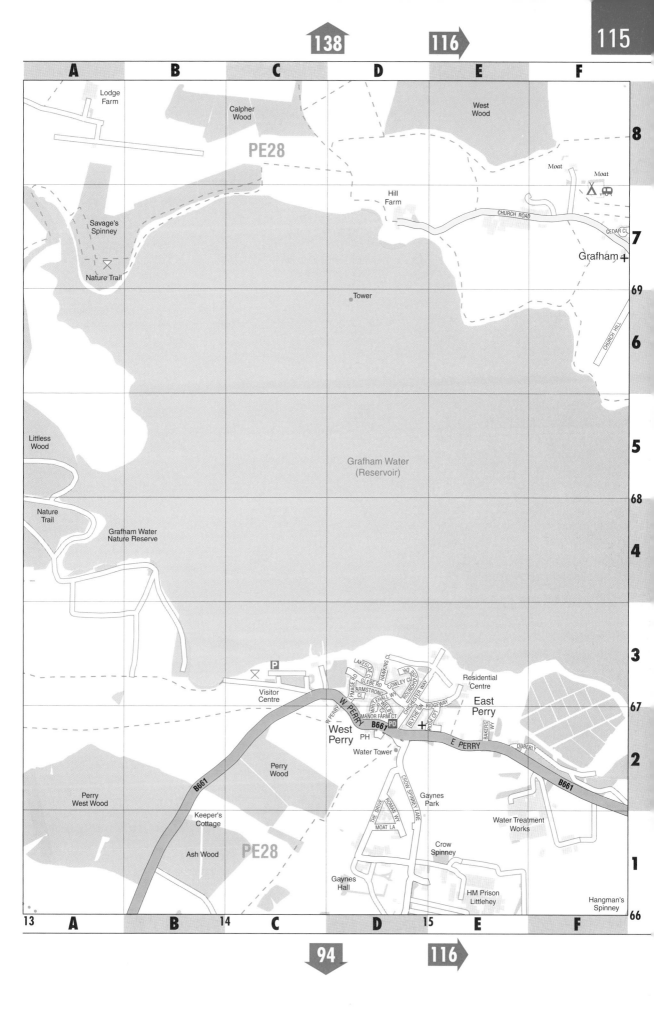

A B C D E F

8
7
69
6
5
68
4
3
67
2
1
66

Lodge
Farm

Calpher
Wood

West
Wood

PE28

Moat
Moat

Hill
Farm

CHURCH ROAD

CEDAR CL

Savage's
Spinney

Grafham ✛

Nature Trail

Tower

CHURCH HILL

Littless
Wood

Grafham Water
(Reservoir)

Nature
Trail

Grafham Water
Nature Reserve

Residential
Centre

LAKESIDE CL
HAWKINS CL
GLEBE RD
COWLEY CL
ROUNDHOOD
CHICHESTER WK

East
Perry

P
Visitor
Centre

PARSONAGE RD
ARMSTRONG CL
MANOR FARM CT
WHITEHALL WY
WEIR
CL
BLYTHE CW
RIDGEWAY
ROSE CT

W PERRY

B661
P
PH

BAKERS WY

West
Perry

E PERRY

DUBERLY

Water Tower

B661

B661

Perry
Wood

CROW SPINNEY LANE

Gaynes
Park

Water Treatment
Works

Perry
West Wood

Keeper's
Cottage

THE DRIVE
ROMAN WY
MOAT LA

Crow
Spinney

Ash Wood

PE28

Gaynes
Hall

HM Prison
Littlehey

Hangman's
Spinney

A   B   C   D   E   F

8
Sparrow's Spinney

Brampton Wood Nature Reserve

P

7
BREACH ROAD
MEADOWBOROUGH
CEDAR CL
VANDYKEMANS WY
NY_CRAFT CL
ALSYKE FIELD
HARTHAM CL
BRAMPTON RD
Moat
Playing Fields

69
CHURCH HILL
CHURCH RD
INHAMS WY
THE PIGHTLE
CHESTNUT CL
HOME CL
Grafham
Water Tower
BUCKDEN ROAD

Thistle Hill

6

Moat

5
PE28
PE19
Hardonian Farm
TAYLORS LANE
Paddock Farm

68
P
Grafham Water Exhibition Centre

4
Model Farm
Buckden Wood
Wood Farm

3
Grafham Water (Reservoir)
Tower
Moat
Shooter's Hollow
PERRY ROAD B661
Westfield Farm

67
B661

2
Diddington Wood

1
P
Highfield Farm
Diddington Wood
Jubilee Copse
Coronation Wood
Diddington Brook
GREAT NORTH ROAD
A1(T)

66
Lodge Farm
Paxton Road Farm

16   A   B   17   C   D   18   E   F

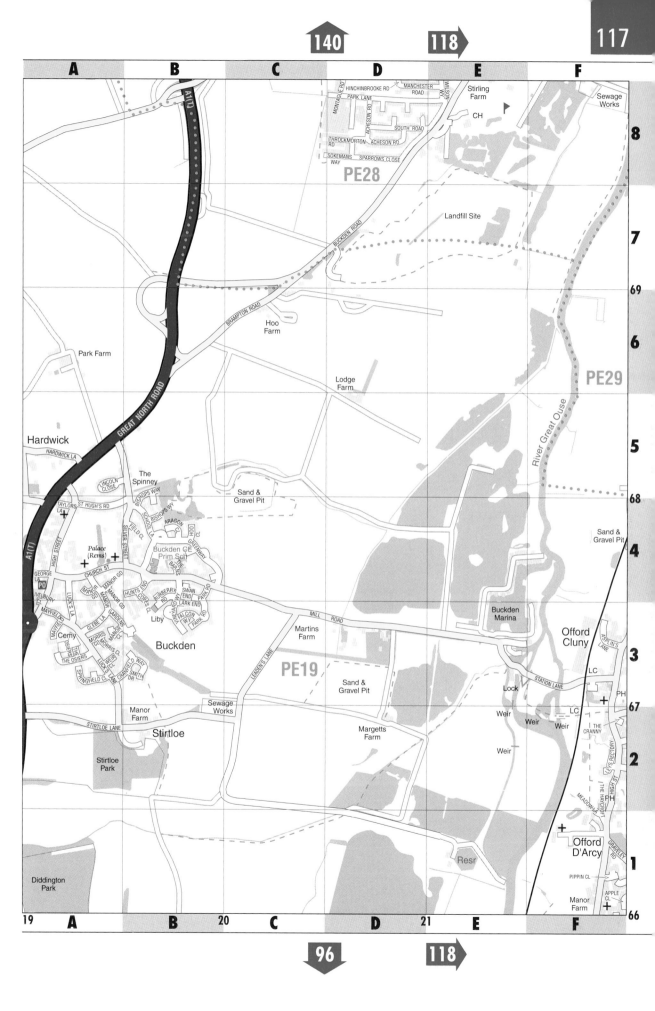

A B C D E F

8

7

69

6

5

68

4

67

3

2

1

66

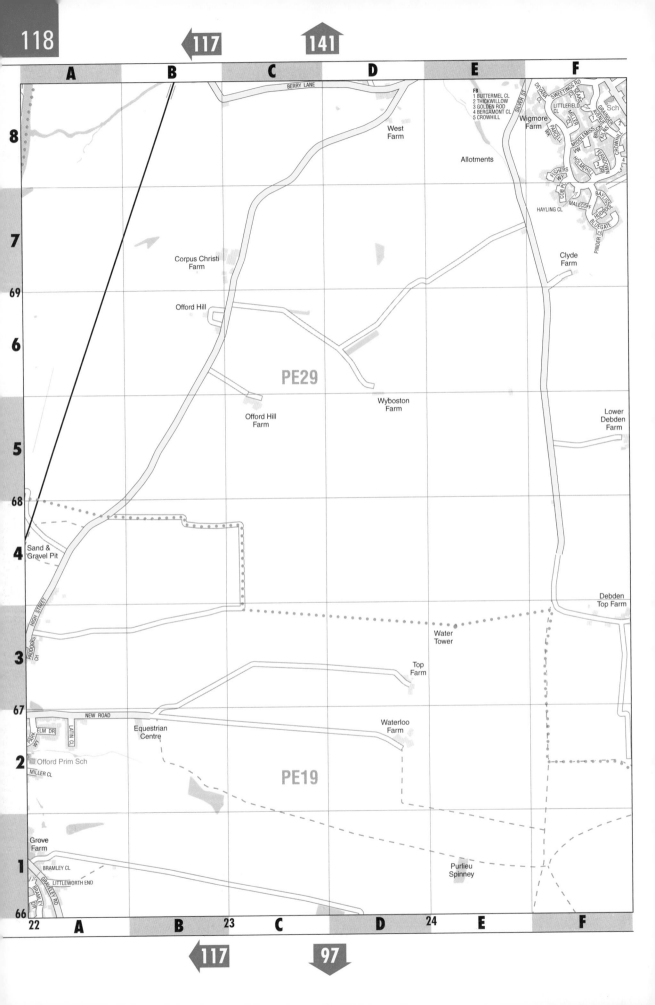

A   B   C   D   E   F

8

7

69

6

PE29

5

68

4

3

67

2

PE19

1

66

BERRY LANE

West Farm

Allotments

F8
1 BUTTERMEL CL
2 THICKWILLOW
3 GOLDEN ROD
4 BERGAMONT CL
5 CROWHILL

Wigmore Farm

Corpus Christi Farm

Offord Hill

Offord Hill Farm

Wyboston Farm

Clyde Farm

Lower Debden Farm

Sand & Gravel Pit

HIGH STREET

PADDOCK CH

Water Tower

Debden Top Farm

Top Farm

NEW ROAD

Equestrian Centre

Waterloo Farm

ELM DR

PARK WY

LATIN CL

Offord Prim Sch

MILLER CL

Grove Farm

BRAMLEY CL

LITTLEWORTH END

BRAMLEY DR

GRAVELEY RD

Purlieu Spinney

HAYLING CL

FISHERS WY

COB PL

MALECOFF

BAYLISS

HUDSON

BLUEGATE

PINDER CL

SILVER ST

DE-VANE CL

PURCELL INK

SWEETINGS RD

LITTLEFIELD CL

MILLER

BRICK KILNS

GRANGER AVENUE

CROWHILL

Sch

MIDDLEMISS

VERNON

HOLLYHILL

VW

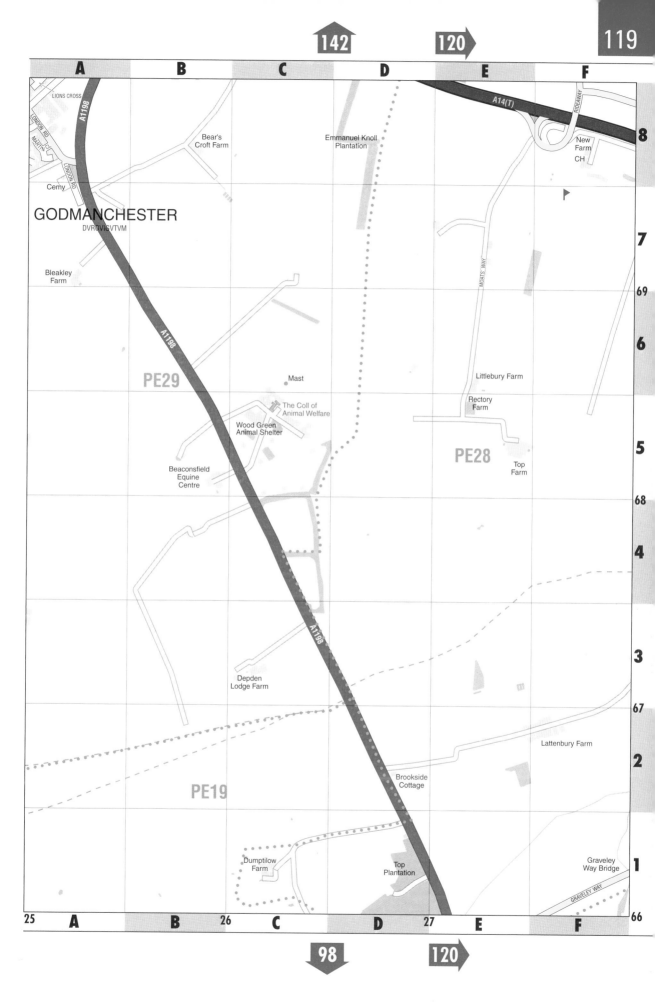

A B C D E F

8

7

69

6

A14(T)

RIDGEWAY

New Farm
CH

Emmanuel Knoll
Plantation

MOATS WAY

LIONS CROSS

A1198

LONDON RD

MARTIN ST

Cemy

GODMANCHESTER
DVROVIGVTVM

Bleakley
Farm

Bear's
Croft Farm

PE29

A1198

Mast

The Coll of
Animal Welfare

Wood Green
Animal Shelter

Beaconsfield
Equine
Centre

Littlebury Farm

Rectory
Farm

PE28

Top
Farm

5

68

4

67

3

A1198

Depden
Lodge Farm

Lattenbury Farm

2

PE19

Brookside
Cottage

Dumptilow
Farm

Top
Plantation

Graveley
Way Bridge

GRAVELEY WAY

1

66

25 A B 26 C D 27 E F

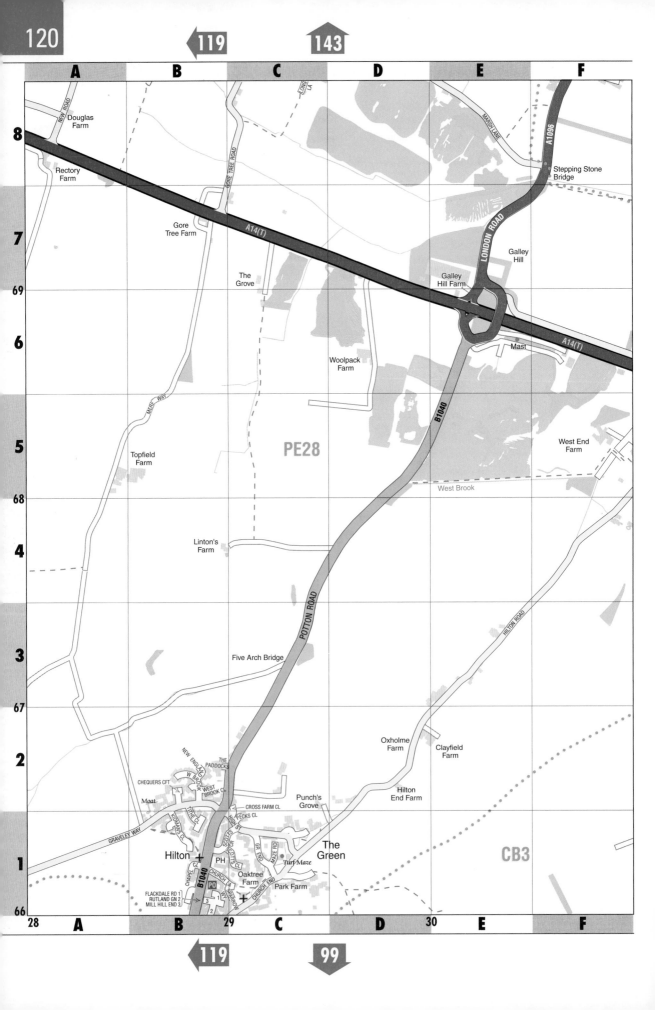

119
143

A   B   C   D   E   F

NEW ROAD

Douglas Farm

LONG LA

GORE TREE ROAD

A1096

8

Rectory Farm

Stepping Stone Bridge

MARSH LANE

LONDON ROAD

7

Gore Tree Farm

A14(T)

Galley Hill

69

The Grove

Galley Hill Farm

6

Woolpack Farm

Mast

A14(T)

MERE WAY

B1040

5

Topfield Farm

PE28

West End Farm

68

West Brook

4

Linton's Farm

HILTON ROAD

POTTON ROAD

3

Five Arch Bridge

67

Oxholme Farm

Clayfield Farm

2

NEW ENGLAND

THE PADDOCKS

CHEQUERS CFT

W BROOK

WEST BROOK CL

Punch's Grove

Moat

CROSS FARM CL

Hilton End Farm

CB3

GRAVELEY WAY

THE CL

KIDMANS CL

PECKS CL

1

Hilton

PH

SCOTTS CL

GR END

Turf Maze

The Green

CHAPEL CL

B1040

CHURCH LA

SPARROW

MAZE RD

Oaktree Farm

Park Farm

FLACKDALE RD 1
RUTLAND GN 2
MILL HILL END 3

PO

CHURCH END

28   A   B   29   C   D   30   E   F

119
99

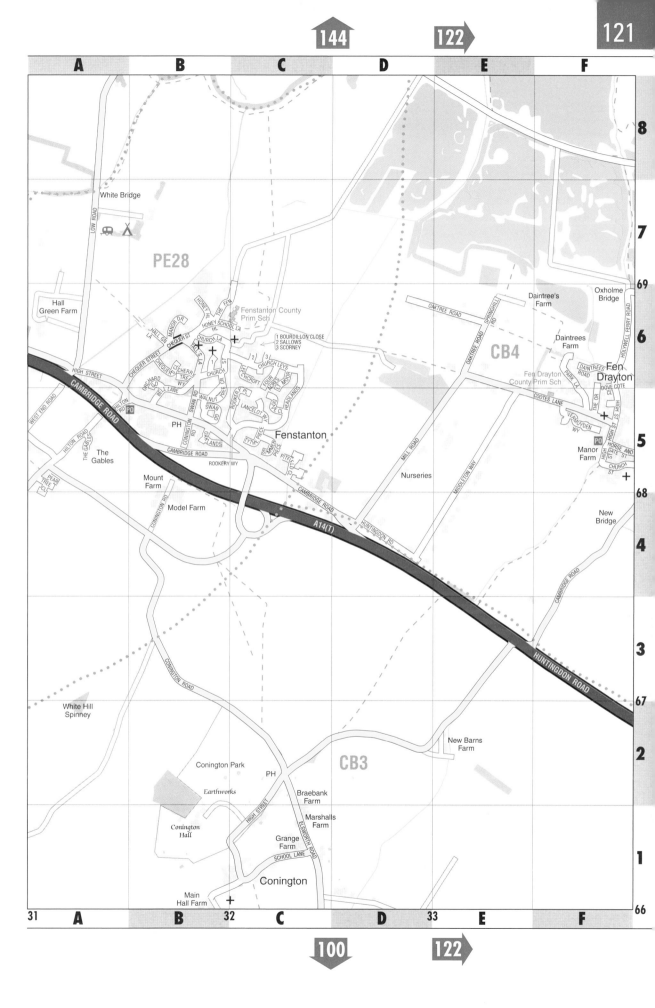

A **B** **C** **D** **E** **F**

Sand & Gravel Works

Church Farm

8

Covells Bridge

Mare Fen

Brownsfield Farm

High Causeway Bridge

(dis) LC

Cloverfield Farm

HOLYWELL FERRY ROAD

JOYER ROAD

STATION ROAD

LC

7

Church Bridge

STATION RD

Church End

69

TAYLOR'S LA

Friesland Farm

MILL WAY

Eathworks

PO

Market St

COW FEN ROAD

PH

BLACK CL

6

Windmill

WHITEGATE CL

MOAT WY

CHANTRY CL

HORSE LA

MOAT WY

HIGH STREET

HOBBLEDODDS CL

GREENSIDE CL

WAL MN'S LA

Swavesey

Swavesey County Prim Sch

THISTLE GN

SCHOOL LA

5

CHURCH ST

PH

HORSE AND GATE ST

HONEY HILL

High Causeway Bridge

CB4

FEN DRAYTON ROAD

CARTER'S WY

PRIORY AVE

GIBRALTER LANE

Swavesey Village Coll

Liby

MIDDLE WATCH

WHITTON CL

Mill Farm

68

CAMBRIDGE RD

WHITTON CL

4

SWAVESEY ROAD

St John's College Farm

Dairy Farm

Bancroft Bridge

ROSE AND CROWN ROAD

PINE GROVE

3

Works

BOXWORTH END

Boxworth End

67

Boxworth End Farm

A14(T)

2

HUNTINGDON ROAD

TIPPLERS ROAD

BUCKING WAY ROAD

Thorpes Farm

CB3

1

Friesland Farm

66

34 **A** **B** 35 **C** **D** 36 **E** **F**

A B C D E F

WEST ST
JENKIN'S LA
KING ST
WHINE'S LA
HADEN WY

Meadow
Mouse Farm

Nursery

Cold Harbour
Farm

Nursery

Sandpit
Pond Farm

MUSTILL'S LANE

Nursery

NORMAN WY

LONGSTANTON ROAD

Water Tower

Hill Farm

(dis)

Windmill

Mast

Stanton
Farm

GRAVEL BRIDGE ROAD

CB4

Mill
View Farm

(dis)

B1050

Cow Fen

Gravel Bridge

Redlands
Farm

LC

STATION ROAD

RAMPER ROAD

Striplands
Farm

CH

Old
Farm

BREWERS CL

Highfield
Farm

DYER ROAD

Home
Farm

HIGH STREET

LADY WALK

BROOKFIELD DR

Greenend
Farm

Longstanton
CP Sch

BROOKSIDE

Trinity
College Farm

Longstanton

B1050

SPRIGGOTS

PREST CL

HATTON'S PK

COLESFIELD

THORNHILL PL

MAGDALENE

HADDON'S CL

HIGH ST

THE CL

RECTORY CT

NETHER CL

RAMPTON RD

HATTON'S ROAD

PH

PO

STOKES CL

WOODSIDE

B1050

SCHOOL LANE

THATCHERS WOOD

37 38 39

A B C D E F

8 7 69 6 5 68 4 3 67 2 1 66

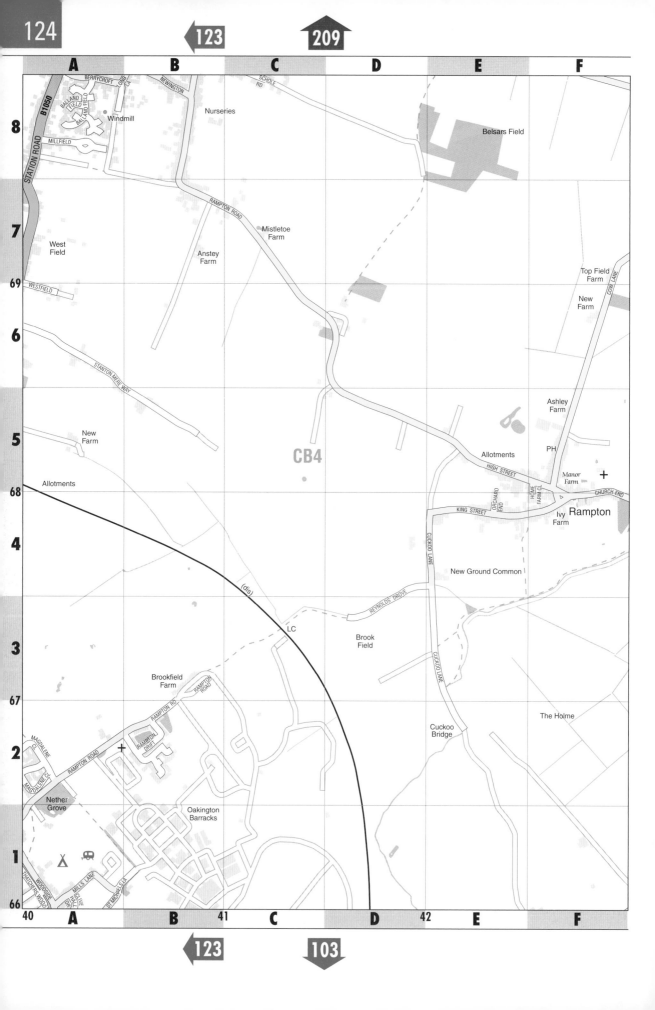

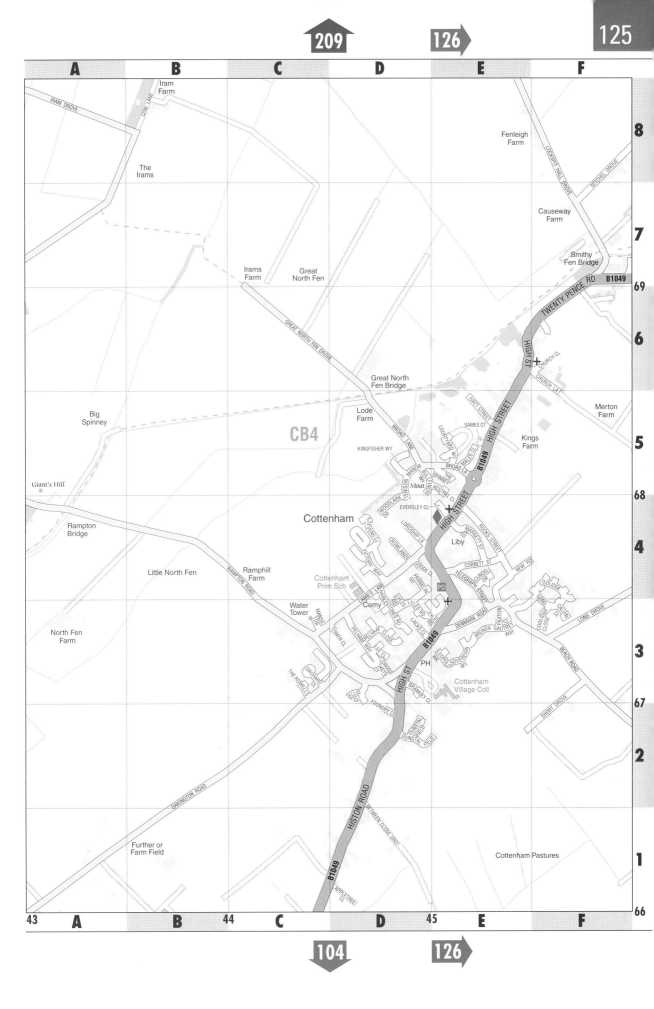

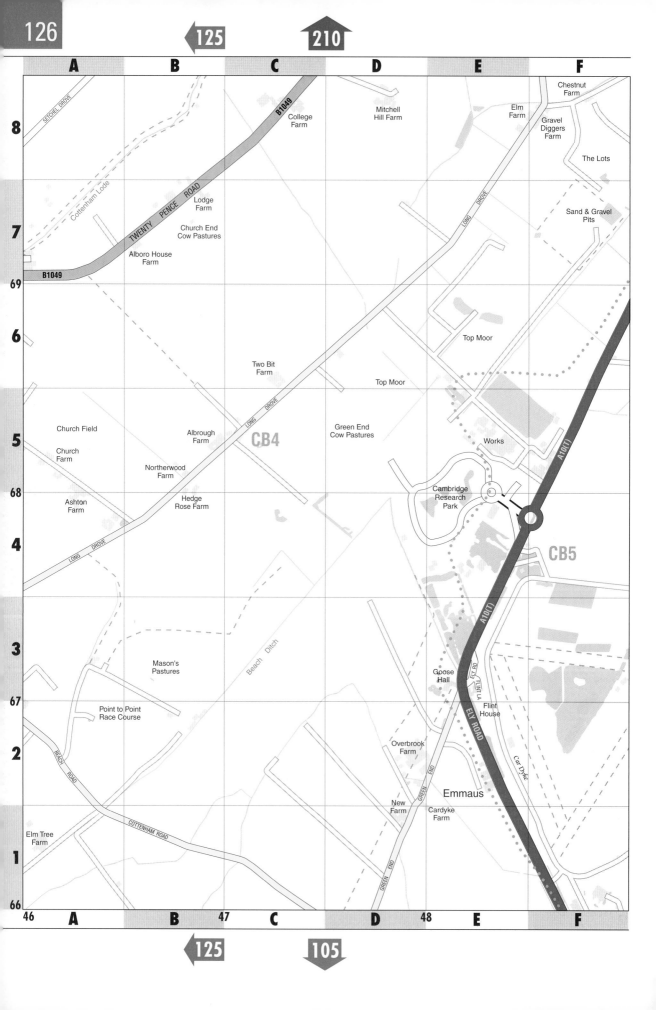

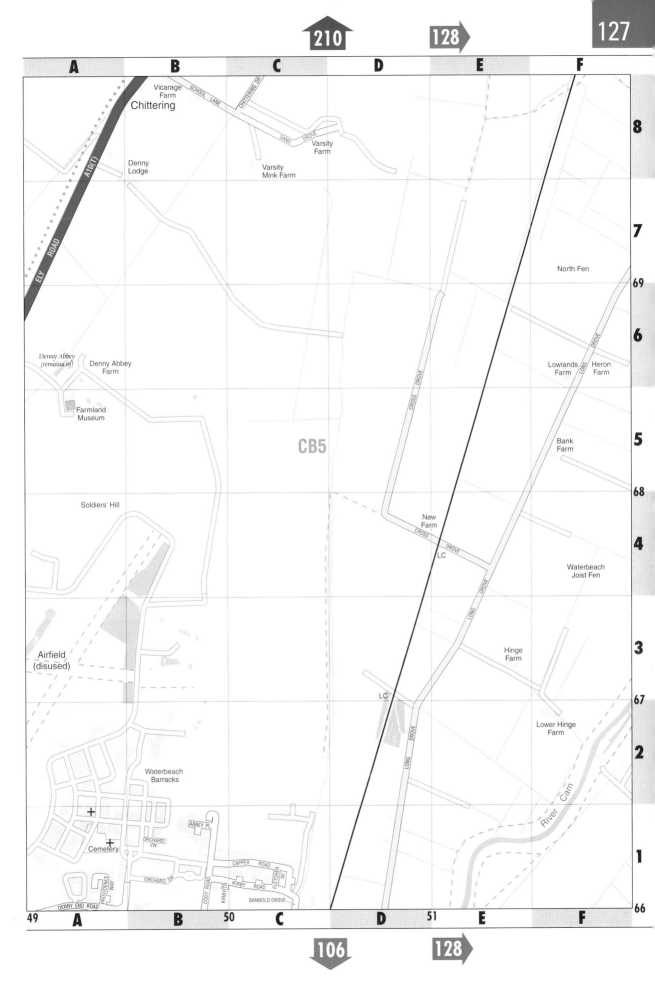

127
211

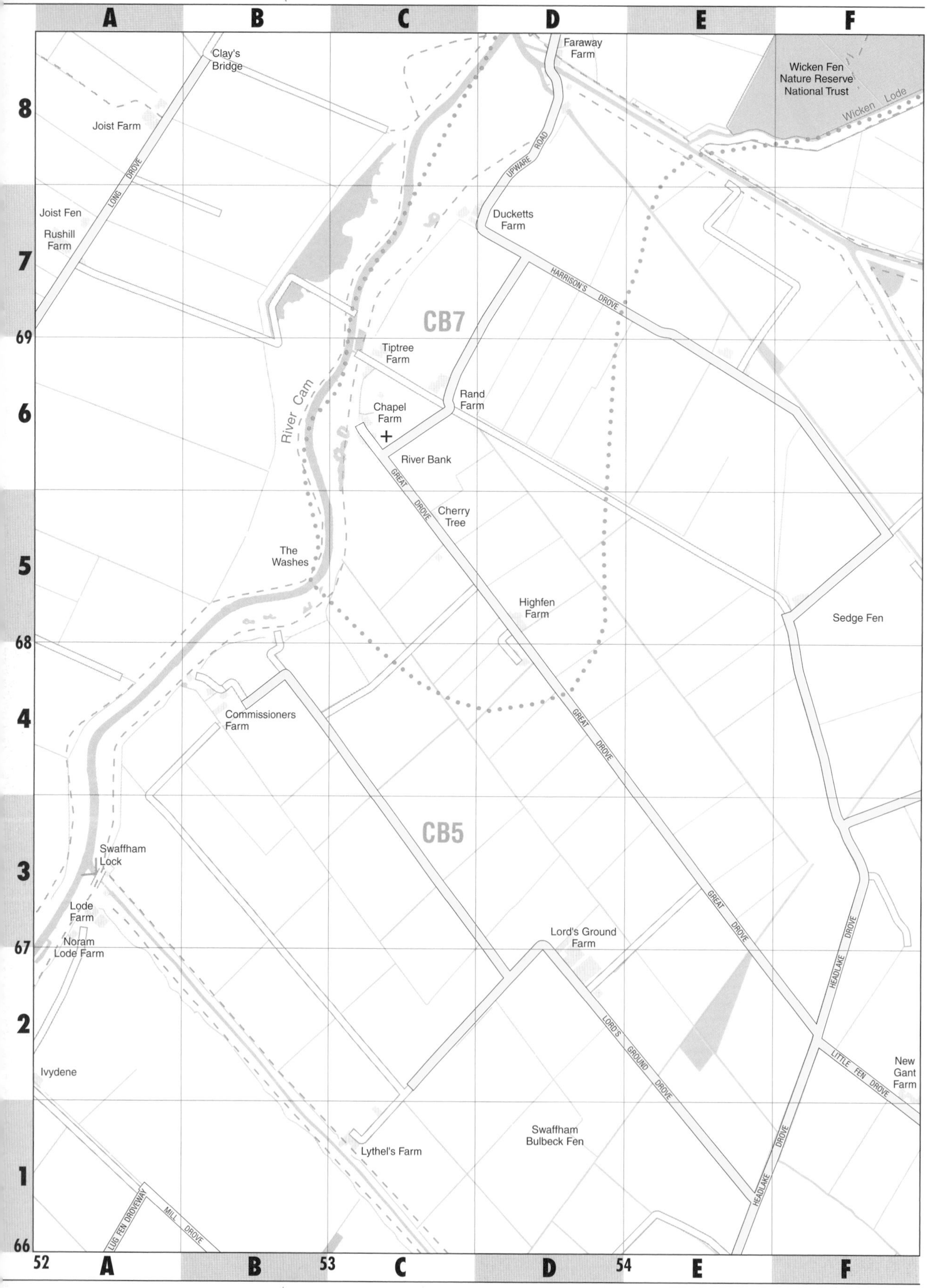

A B C D E F

8

7

69

6

5

68

4

3

67

2

1

66

Clay's Bridge

Joist Farm

Joist Fen
Rushill Farm

LONG DROVE

River Cam

The Washes

Swaffham Lock

Lode Farm

Noram Lode Farm

Ivydene

TUG FEN DROVEWAY

MILL DROVE

Commissioners Farm

Lythel's Farm

Faraway Farm

UPWARE ROAD

Ducketts Farm

HARRISON'S DROVE

CB7

Tiptree Farm

Rand Farm

Chapel Farm

River Bank

GREAT DROVE

Cherry Tree

Highfen Farm

CB5

GREAT DROVE

Lord's Ground Farm

LORD'S GROUND DROVE

Swaffham Bulbeck Fen

Wicken Fen Nature Reserve National Trust

Wicken Lode

Sedge Fen

HEADLAKE DROVE

LITTLE FEN DROVE

New Gant Farm

HEADLAKE DROVE

52 A B 53 C D 54 E F

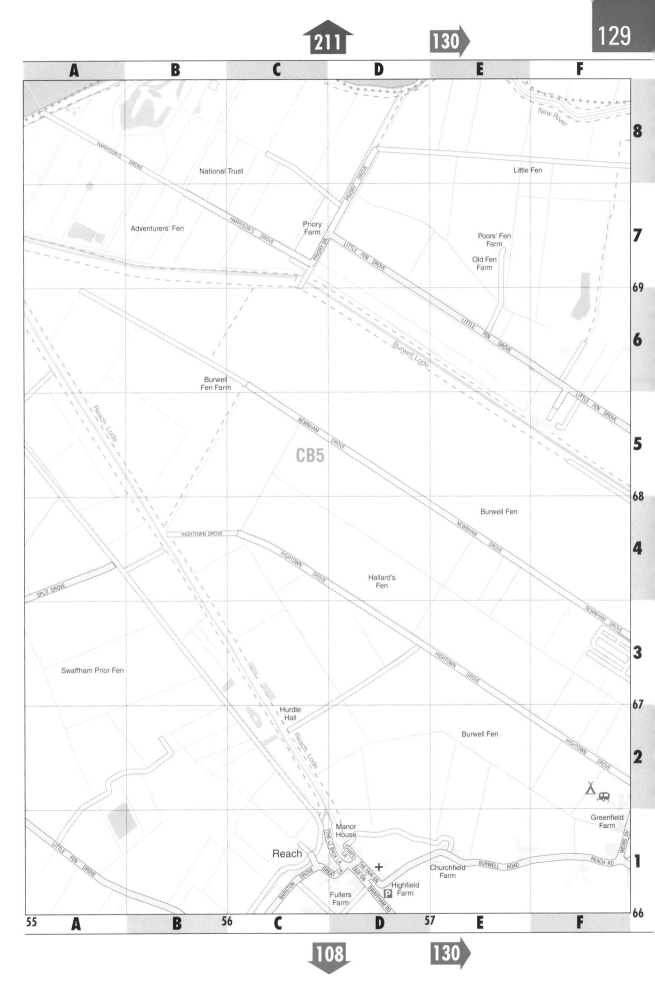

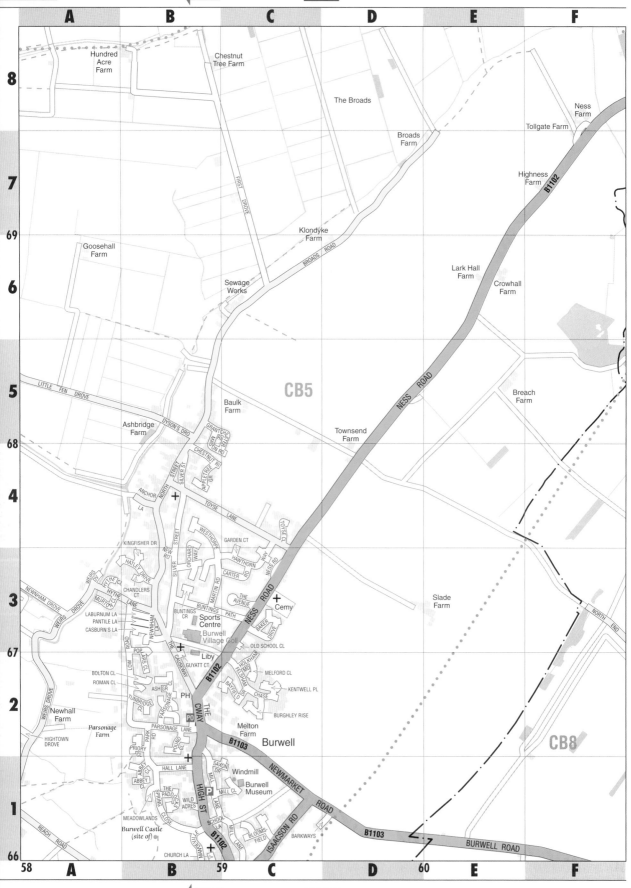

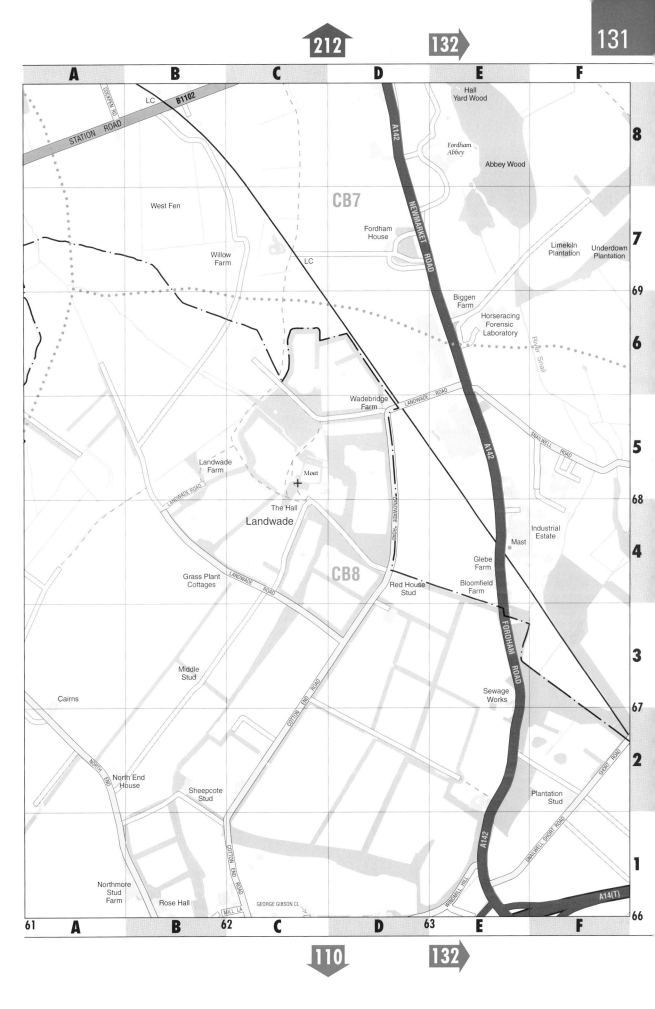

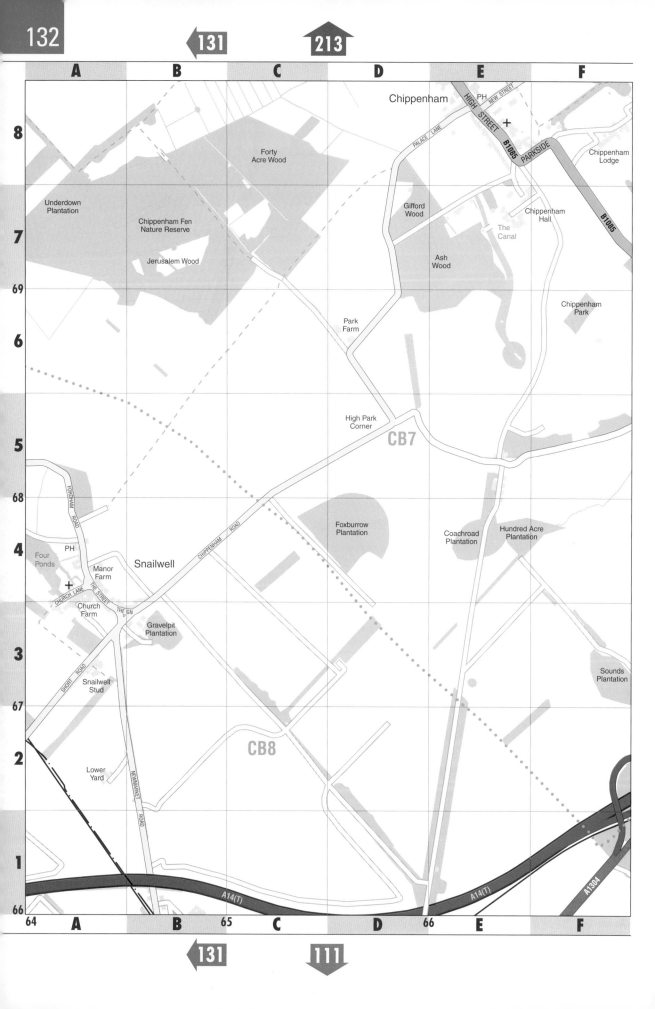

131
213

Chippenham

PH

NEW STREET

HIGH STREET

PALACE LANE

B1085

PARKSIDE

Chippenham
Lodge

Forty
Acre Wood

Underdown
Plantation

Gifford
Wood

Chippenham
Hall

Chippenham Fen
Nature Reserve

The
Canal

B1085

Chippenham
Park

Jerusalem Wood

Ash
Wood

Park
Farm

High Park
Corner

CB7

FORDHAM ROAD

Foxburrow
Plantation

Coachroad
Plantation

Hundred Acre
Plantation

PH

Four
Ponds

Manor
Farm

Snailwell

CHIPPENHAM ROAD

Church
Farm

CHURCH LANE

THE STREET

THE GN

Gravelpit
Plantation

Sounds
Plantation

SHORT ROAD

Snailwell
Stud

67

CB8

Lower
Yard

NEWMARKET ROAD

A14(T)

A14(T)

A1304

131
111

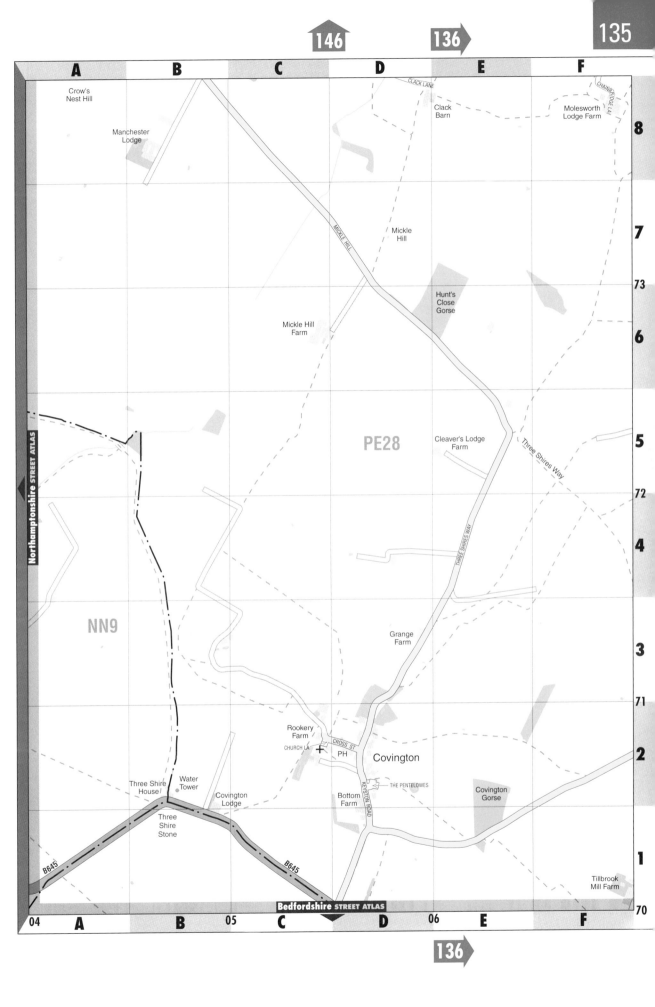

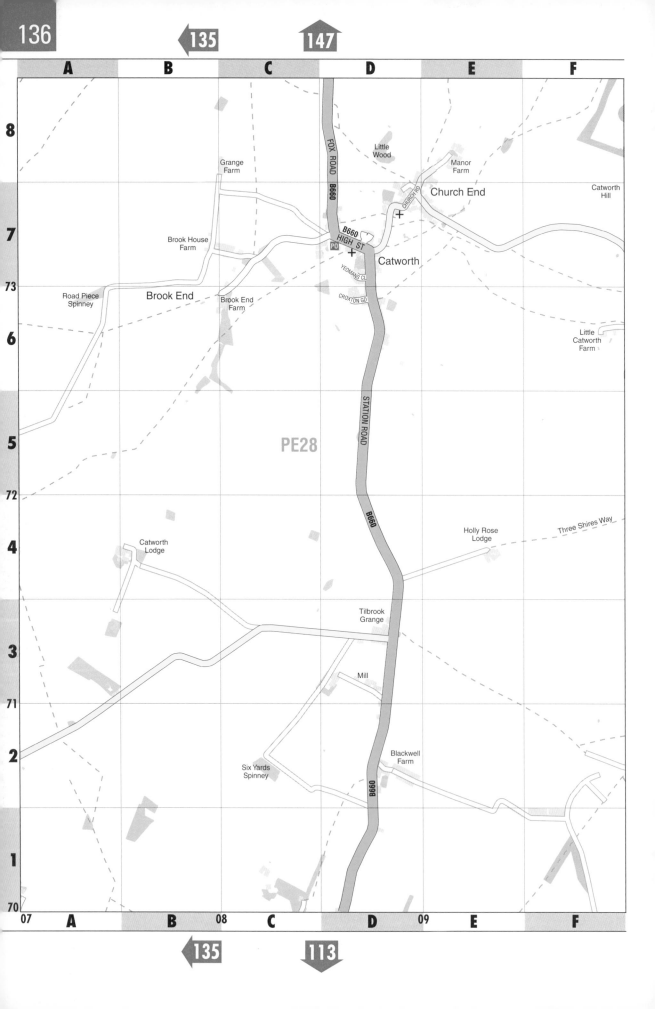

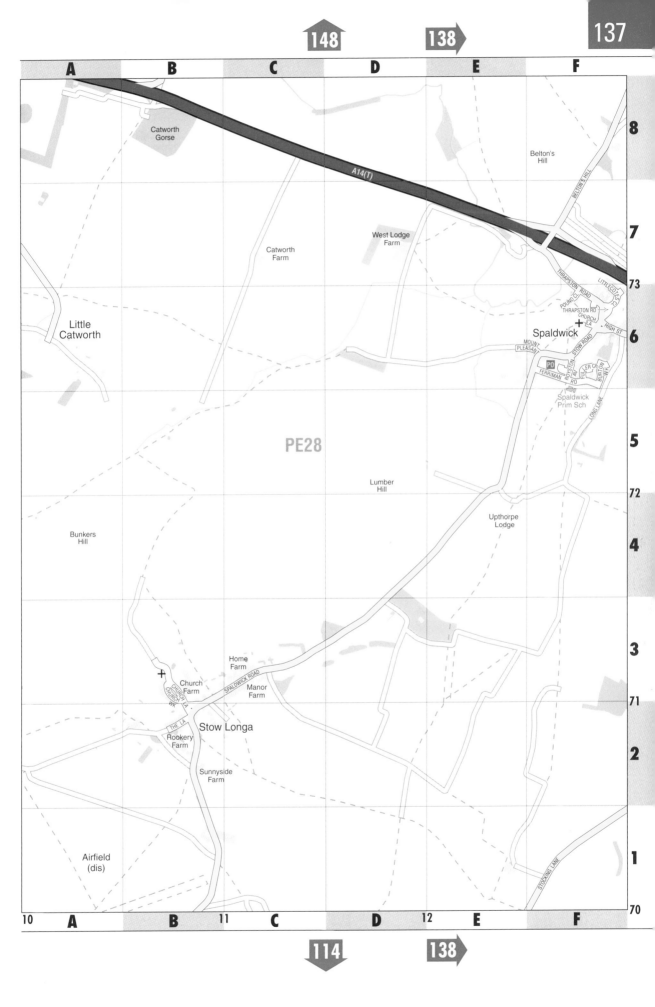

A B C D E F

8

Catworth
Gorse

A14(T)

Belton's
Hill

West Lodge
Farm

7

73

BELTON'S HILL

Catworth
Farm

Little
Catworth

THRAPSTON ROAD

LITTLECOTE

POUND CL
THRAPSTON RD
CHURCH LA

HIGH ST

Spaldwick

6

MOUNT
PLEASANT

STOW ROAD

PO

FERRIMAN
RD

RYSTON

FULLER CR
STOW ROAD
BURTON WY

LONG LANE

Spaldwick
Prim Sch

PE28

Lumber
Hill

5

72

Upthorpe
Lodge

Bunkers
Hill

4

3

Home
Farm

SPALDWICK ROAD

Church
Farm

CHURCH LA
CHURCH WK

Manor
Farm

71

THE LA

Stow Longa

Rookery
Farm

2

Sunnyside
Farm

Airfield
(dis)

STOCKING LANE

1

70

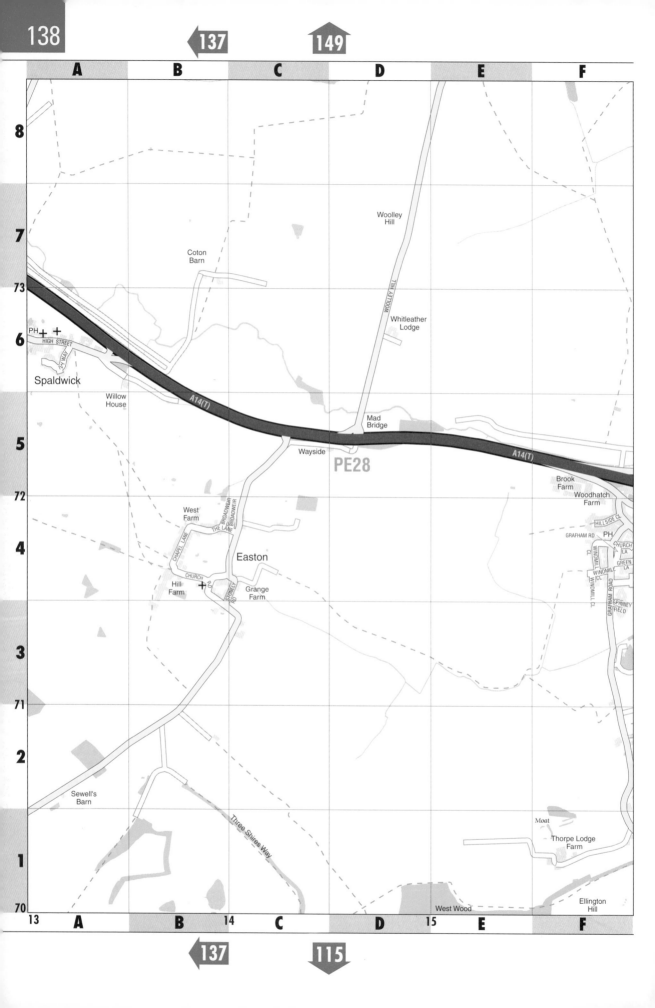

A   B   C   D   E   F

8

7

73

6

Spaldwick

PH

HIGH STREET

IVY WAY

Willow House

Coton Barn

A14(T)

Woolley Hill

WOOLLEY HILL

Whitleather Lodge

Mad Bridge

Wayside

PE28

A14(T)

5

72

West Farm

BROADWAY

BROADWEIR

THE LANE

CHAPEL LANE

Easton

CHURCH

STONELY RD

Hill Farm

Grange Farm

Brook Farm

Woodhatch Farm

HILLSIDE CL

GRAFHAM RD

PH

CHURCH LA

GREEN LA

WINDMILL CL

WINDMILL CL

WINDMILL CL

GRAFHAM ROAD

SPINNEY FIELD

4

3

71

2

Sewell's Barn

Three Shires Way

Moat

Thorpe Lodge Farm

1

70

West Wood

Ellington Hill

13   A   B   14   C   D   15   E   F

A   B   C   D   E   F

8

Moat

Weybridge
Lodge Farm

7

73

Weybridge
Farm

6

PE28

5

Grove
Bridge

Sand &
Gravel Pit

72

A14(T)

Moat
Manor Farm

Woodhatch
Farm

4

BLACKSMITHS LA
MALTING LA
HIGH ST
ST PETER'S WY
PETER'S WY

Ellington

PARSON'S DR

Low
Harthay

Church
Farm

High
Harthay

3

71

Ellington
Thorpe

2

Moat

Underlands
Wood

Red
Wood

Redwood
Lodge

Brampton Wood
Nature Reserve

Madders
Hill

1

PE19

Sparrow's
Spinney

70

139
151

A B C D E F

8
7
73
6
5
72
4
3
71
2
1
70

Alconbury Brook

Lodge Farm

LOW ROAD

LOW ROAD

Waterloo Farm

Brookfield Farm

Landing Strip

A14(T)

FLAMSTEED POND

PE28

Sand & Gravel Pit

Race Course

PE29

A14(T)

Long Plantation

Hinchingbrooke Country Park

Bobs

A14(T)

Rectory Farm

A14(T)

THRAPSTON ROAD

Weir

A14(T)

A1(T)

WOOD VW
LAWS CR
OAK DR
CRANE WK
THRAPSTON ROAD
B1514

C3
1 WESTBROOK CL
2 BRAMBLE CT
3 PAGES WY

DORLING WY
LOMAX DR
CARTER CLOSE
WOOLLEY CL

1 WATERLOO CL
2 SPINNEY CL
3 HANOVER CT

Poplar Farm

HANSELL RD
BELLE ISLE
WILLIAMS CL
CRESCENT
MILLER WY

MANDEVILLE RD
OLIVIA RD
BEAUMARD RD
EVANS CL
EVANS CL
MILLER WY
GROVE LA
ORCH LA

B1514 THRAPSTON ROAD

FIELD BELL

HANSELL RD
BELLE ISLE
BURNABY CL
CHARCOAL LA
WEST END

THE GREEN

KNOWLES CL

PEPYS RD

CROOTS CL
ELIZABETH WY
CLINT
ABBOTT
STEWART CL
CENTENARY WY
RIDDIFORD CR
WILLOW CL
PARK ROAD

Brampton County Jun Sch

GN LA
GN LA
CRANFIELD WAY
KYLE CR
KYLE CR
CROFT CL
HIGH STREET
RECTORY CL
MAN RUDGE CL

PEPYS House

Brampton County Inf Sch

LAYTON CR
LENTON WAY
HORSESHOES WAY
HAWKES END

PO

Cemy

Brampton

West Farm

West Farm

ALLEN S DR
BUCKDEN ROAD
FORSTER RD

PH

SANDWICH ROAD
NORTH ROAD
NORTH RD
DAULES RD
ST GEORGES CL

Park Farm

GLOUCESTER RD
CENTRAL AVE
FARNDON RD
FORSTER RD
FORSTER RD
BUCKDEN ROAD
RIVER LANE

Brampton Lodge

Brampton Park

MONTAGUE RD
HINCHINBROOKE RD

19 A B 20 C D 21 E F

139
117

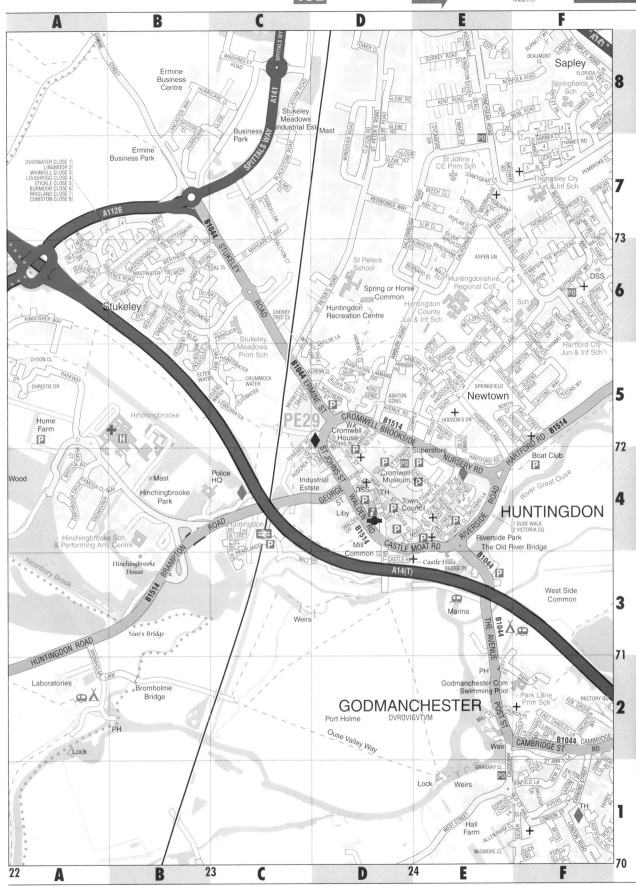

152   142   141

F8
ARMSTRONG CT
BEALE CT
JUDSON CT
GODEBY CT

F7
COTTON CT
SELBY CT
ST BARNABAS CT
LAVENDER CT
GIMBER CT

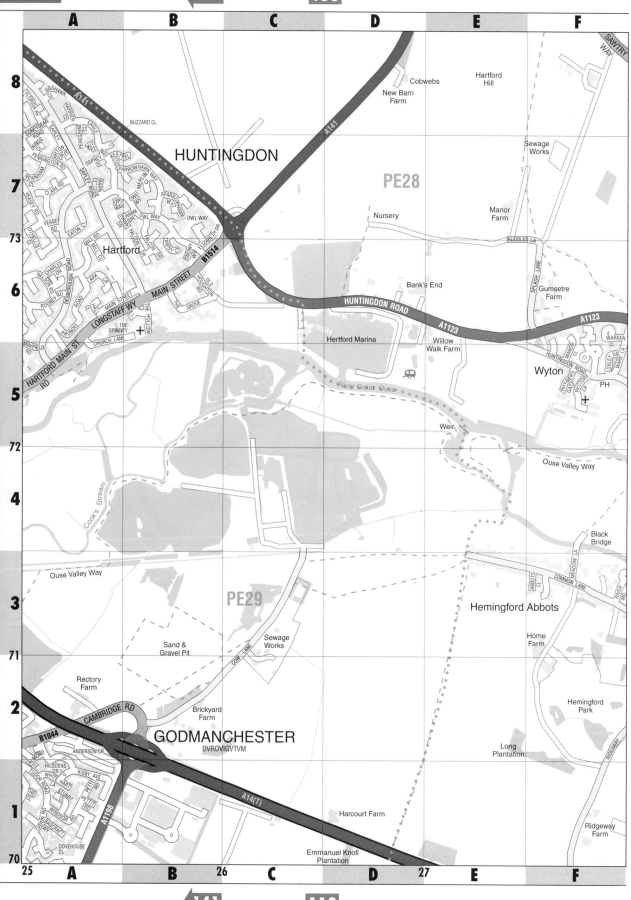

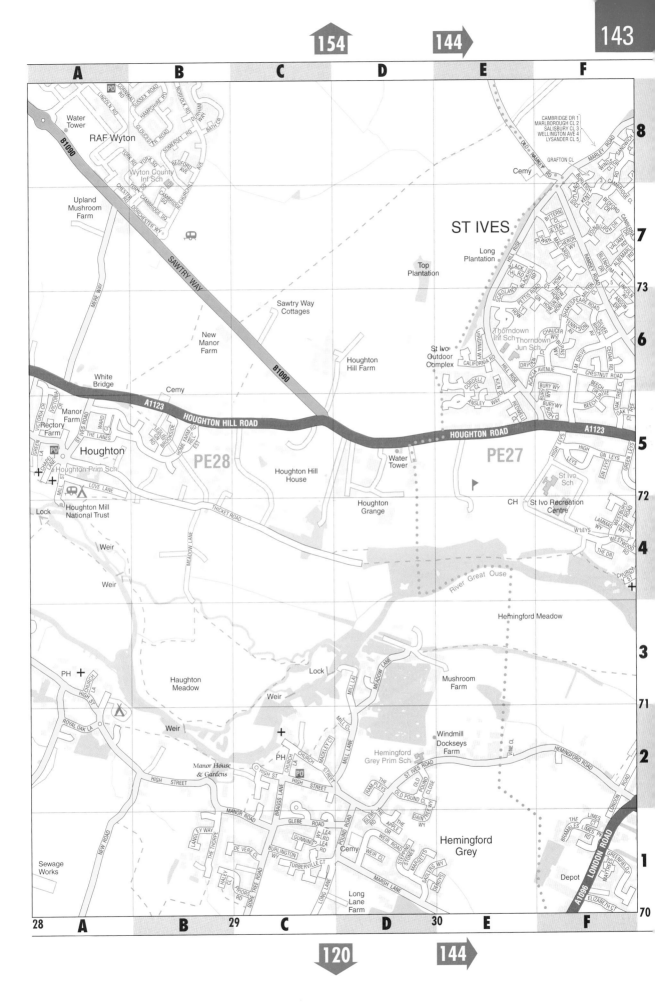

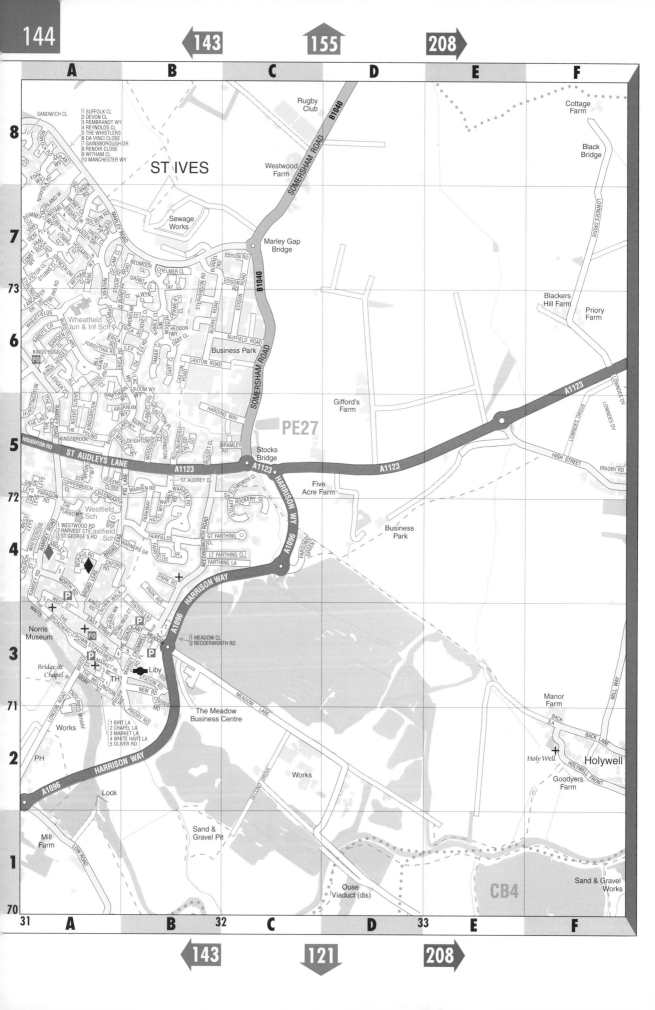

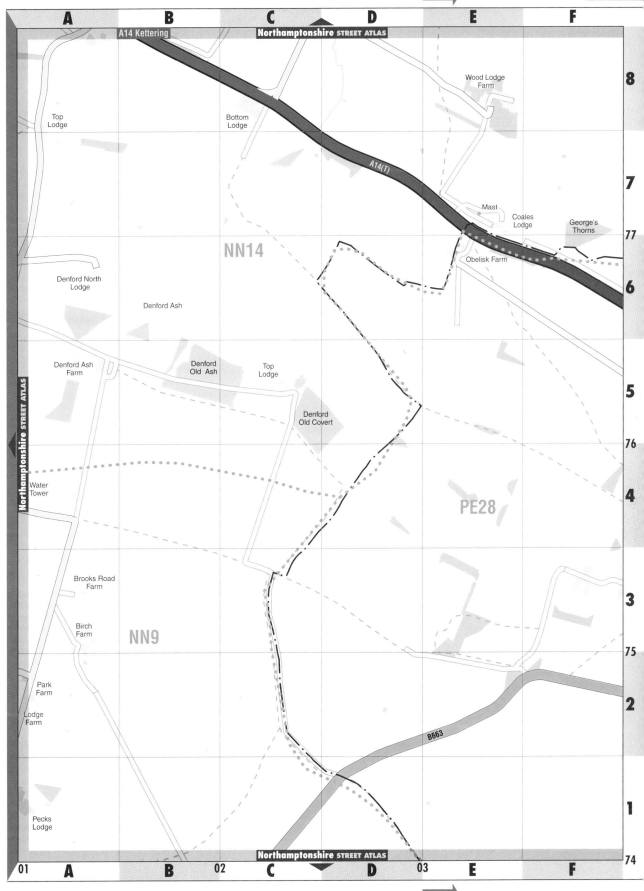

A14 Kettering

Top Lodge

Bottom Lodge

Wood Lodge Farm

A14(T)

Mast

Coales Lodge

George's Thorns

NN14

Denford North Lodge

Denford Ash

77

Obelisk Farm

6

Denford Ash Farm

Denford Old Ash

Top Lodge

5

Denford Old Covert

76

Water Tower

PE28

4

Brooks Road Farm

Birch Farm

NN9

3

75

Park Farm

Lodge Farm

B663

2

1

Pecks Lodge

74

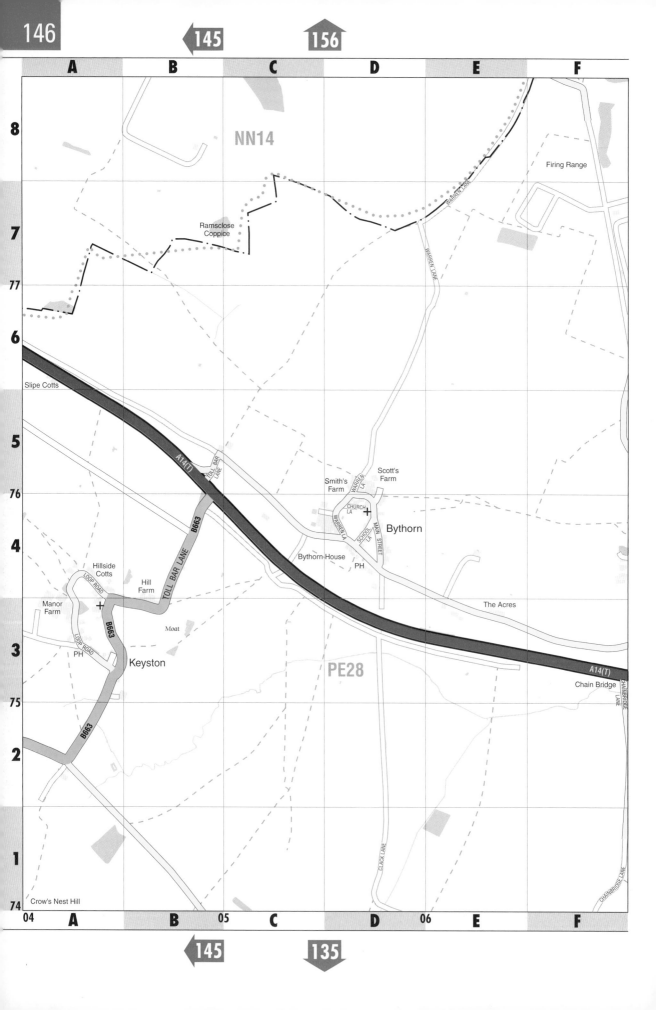

NN14

Firing Range

Ramsclose
Coppice

WARREN LANE

WARREN LANE

Slipe Cotts

A14(T)

TOLL BAR LANE

B663

Smith's
Farm

Scott's
Farm

WARREN LA

CHURCH
LA

SCHOOL
LA

MAIN STREET

Bythorn

Bythorn House

PH

The Acres

Hillside
Cotts

LOOP ROAD

Hill
Farm

TOLL BAR LANE

Manor
Farm

B663

Moat

LOOP ROAD

PH

Keyston

PE28

A14(T)

Chain Bridge

CHAINBRIDGE LANE

CHAINBRIDGE LANE

75

B663

CLACK LANE

Crow's Nest Hill

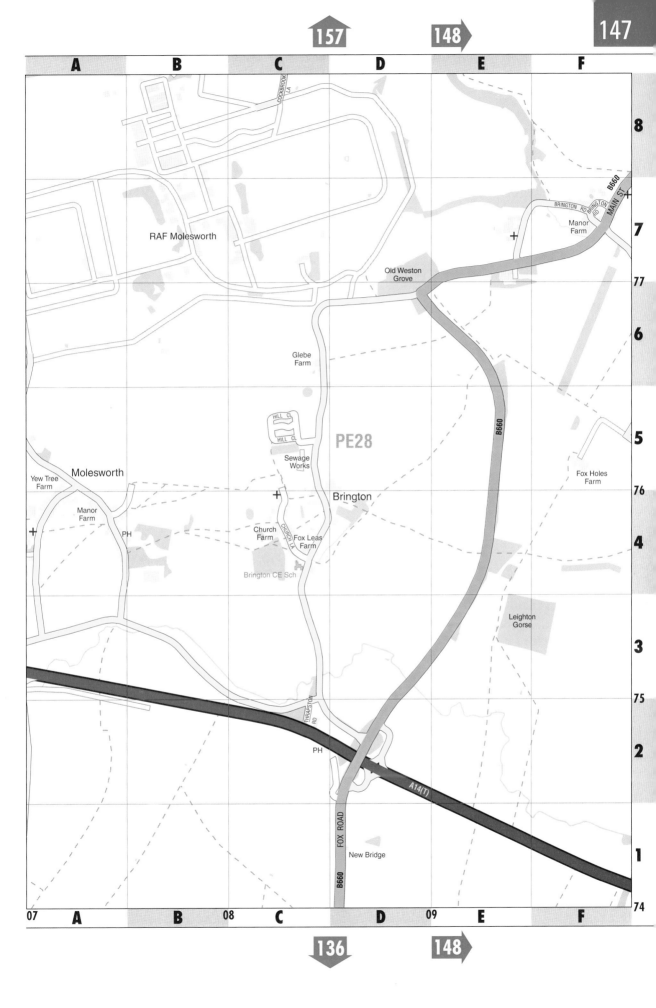

A   B   C   D   E   F

8

B660

BRINGTON RD BRINGTON RD

MAIN ST

7

Manor
Farm

RAF Molesworth

Old Weston
Grove

77

6

Glebe
Farm

B660

HILL CL

HILL CL

PE28

5

Fox Holes
Farm

Sewage
Works

Molesworth

Yew Tree
Farm

Brington

76

Manor
Farm

PH

Church
Farm

CHURCH LA

Fox Leas
Farm

4

Bringotn CE Sch

Leighton
Gorse

3

THRAPSTON RD

75

PH

A14(T)

2

FOX ROAD

B660

New Bridge

1

74

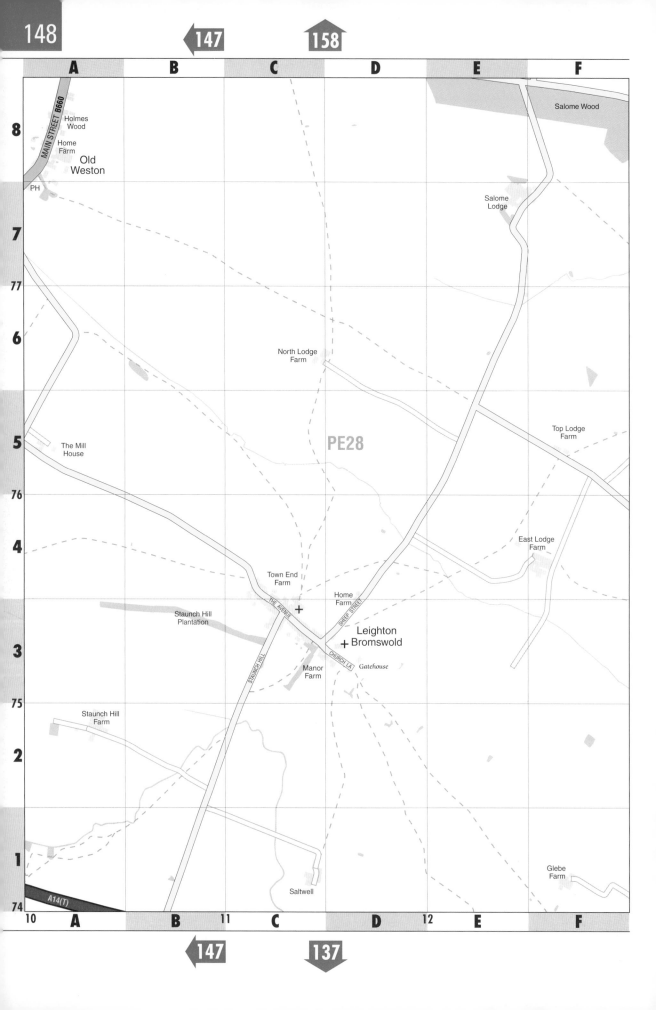

8

Salome Wood

MAIN STREET B660

Holmes
Wood

Home
Farm

Old
Weston

PH

Salome
Lodge

7

77

6

North Lodge
Farm

PE28

Top Lodge
Farm

5

The Mill
House

76

4

East Lodge
Farm

Town End
Farm

Home
Farm

THE AVENUE

SHEEP STREET

Staunch Hill
Plantation

Leighton
Bromswold

3

STAUNCH HILL

Manor
Farm

CHURCH LA

Gatehouse

75

Staunch Hill
Farm

2

1

Glebe
Farm

Saltwell

74

A14(T)

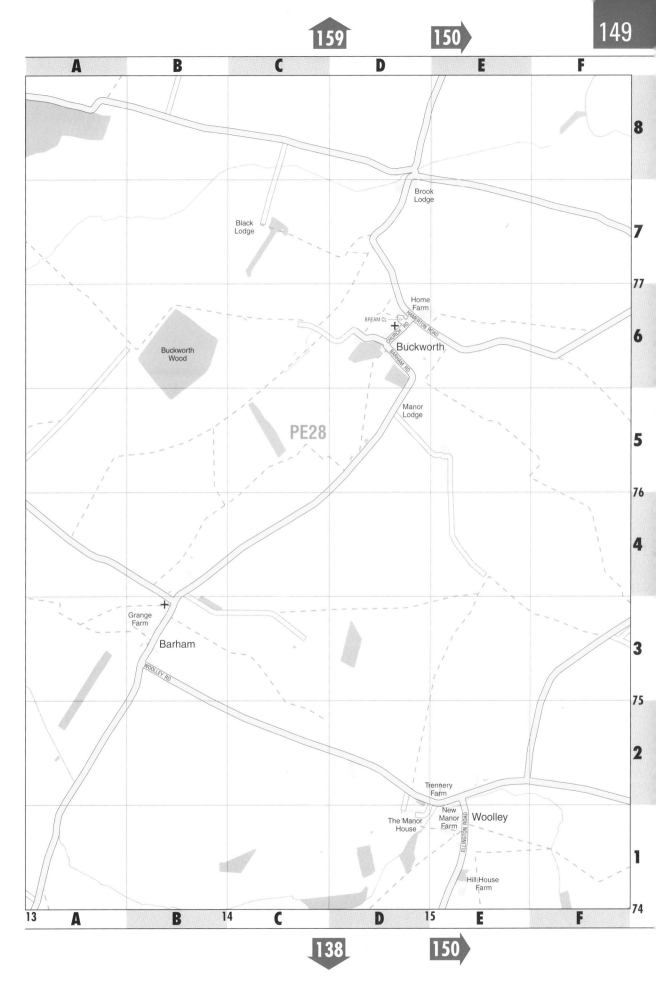

159
150

A B C D E F

8

7

77

6

Brook
Lodge

Black
Lodge

Home
Farm

BREAM CL

CHURCH RD

HAMERTON ROAD

Buckworth

Buckworth
Wood

BARHAM RD

Manor
Lodge

PE28

5

76

4

3

Grange
Farm

Barham

WOOLLEY RD

75

2

Trennery
Farm

New
Manor
Farm

Woolley

The Manor
House

ELLINGTON ROAD

1

Hill House
Farm

74

138
150

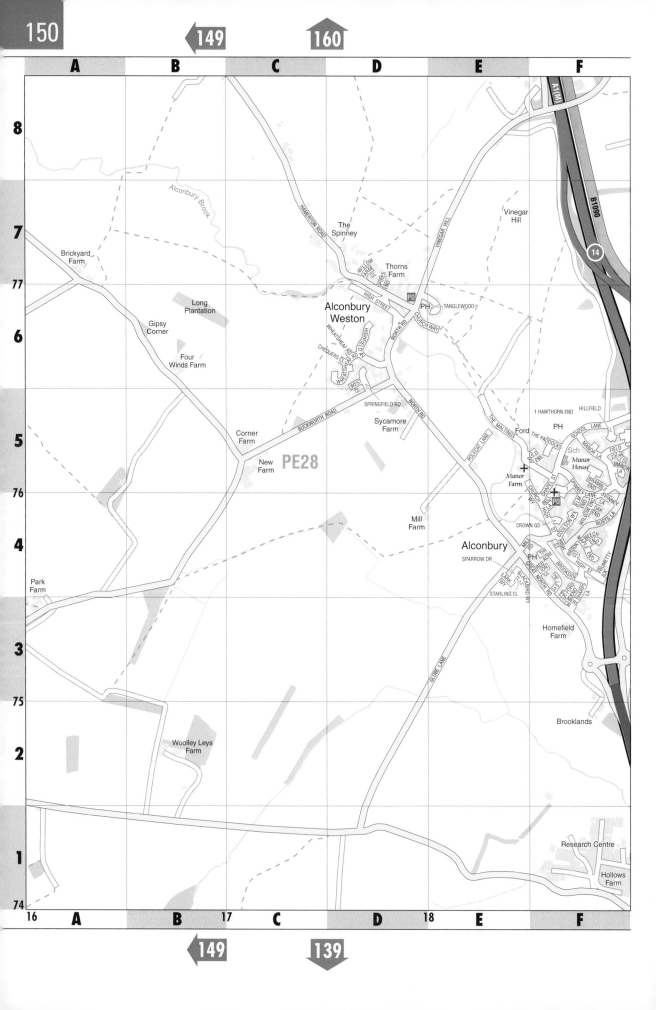

8

7

77

6

5

76

4

3

75

2

1

74

Alconbury Brook

Brickyard Farm

Hamerton Road

The Spinney

Vinegar Hill

Vinegar Hill

A1(M)

B1090

14

Long Plantation

Gipsy Corner

Four Winds Farm

WILLOW FARM CL

SPIRES END

Thorns Farm

High Street

Alconbury Weston

HIGHFIELD RD

WHEATSHEAF RD

CHEQUERS CL

WEST CL

NORTH RD

CHURCH WAY

PO

PH

Tanglewood

Corner Farm

Buckworth Road

New Farm

PE28

Springfield Rd

Sycamore Farm

NORTH RD

1 HAWTHORN END   HILLFIELD

THE MALTINGS

Ford

PH

THE PADDOCKS

SCHOOL LANE

Sch

FIELD END   MANOR LA

BRAMBLE END

SPINNEY LANE

MANOR LA

Manor House

Park Farm

Mill Farm

POLECAT LANE

Manor Farm

CHURCH HIGH ST

OLD GLEBE

GLEBE

DUPRE ST

ELM END   OAK END

WILLOW END

SPINNEY LA

RUSTS LA

+

+

PO

CROWN GD

Alconbury

PH

SPARROW DR

MILL LA

STARLING CL

BLACKBIRD WY

LARK WY

GREAT NORTH RD

THE ACRE

FIELD END

THE CL

FORD   PALMERS

BROOKSIDE

HIGH ST

BRONZE CL

BEECH END

HELMETH

Homefield Farm

Globe Lane

Brooklands

Woolley Leys Farm

Research Centre

Hollows Farm

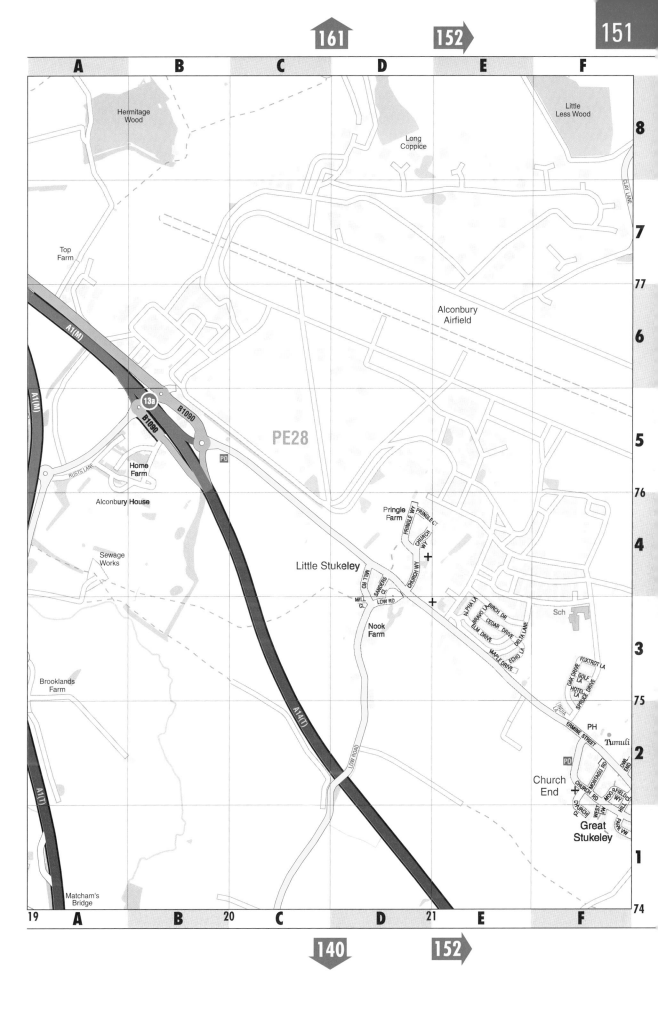

A B C D E F

8

7

77

6

5

76

4

3

75

2

1

74

Hermitage Wood

Little Less Wood

Long Coppice

CLAY LANE

Top Farm

Alconbury Airfield

A1(M)

A1(M)

13a

B1090

B1090

PO

PE28

Home Farm

RUSTS LANE

Alconbury House

Sewage Works

Pringle Farm

PRINGLE WY

PRINGLE CT

CHURCH WY

Little Stukeley

MILL RD

SANDERS CL

CHURCH WY

MILL CL

LOW RD

Nook Farm

ALPHA LA

BIRCH DR

BRAVO

CEDAR DRIVE

ELM DRIVE

DELTA LANE

MAPLE DRIVE

ECHO LA

Sch

A14(T)

FOXTROT LA

OAK DRIVE

GOLF LA

HOTEL LA

SPRUCE DRIVE

INDIA LA

ERMINE STREET

PH

Tumuli

PO

MONTAGU RD

Church End

CHURCH RD

WEST WY

MOOR FIELD CL

HILL

PARK VW

WEST WY

CHURCH CL

CHURCH HILL

A1(T)

LOW ROAD

Brooklands Farm

Matcham's Bridge

Great Stukeley

19 A 20 B C 20 D 21 E F 74

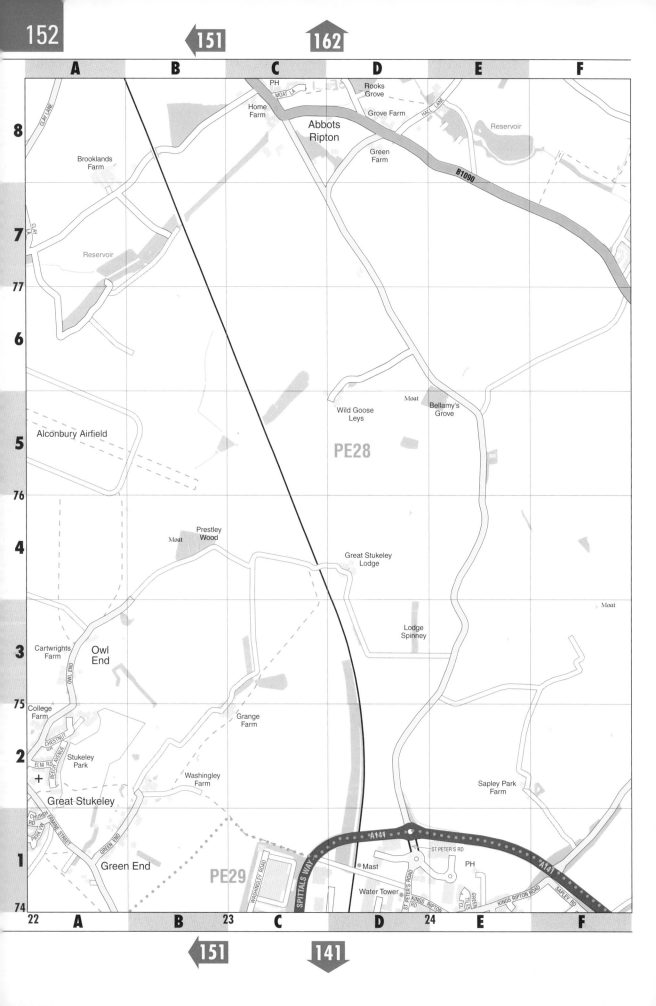

CLAY LANE

Brooklands
Farm

CLAY
LA

Reservoir

Home
Farm

PH

MOAT LA

Abbots
Ripton

Rooks
Grove

Grove Farm

HALL LANE

Reservoir

Green
Farm

B1090

Wild Goose
Leys

Moat

Bellamy's
Grove

PE28

Alconbury Airfield

Moat

Prestley
Wood

Great Stukeley
Lodge

Moat

Lodge
Spinney

Owl
End

OWL END

Cartwrights
Farm

College
Farm

CHESTNUT
GN

ELM RD

BEECH AVENUE

Stukeley
Park

Grange
Farm

Washingley
Farm

Sapley Park
Farm

Great Stukeley

CHURCH
RD

PERRY VW

ERMINE STREET

GREEN END

Green End

PE29

WASHINGLEY ROAD

SPITTALS WAY

A141

Mast

Water Tower

ST PETER'S ROAD

ST KINGS RIPTON
RD

St PETER'S RD

KINGS RIPTON ROAD

PH

GREEN
TILES
CL

A141

SAPLEY RD

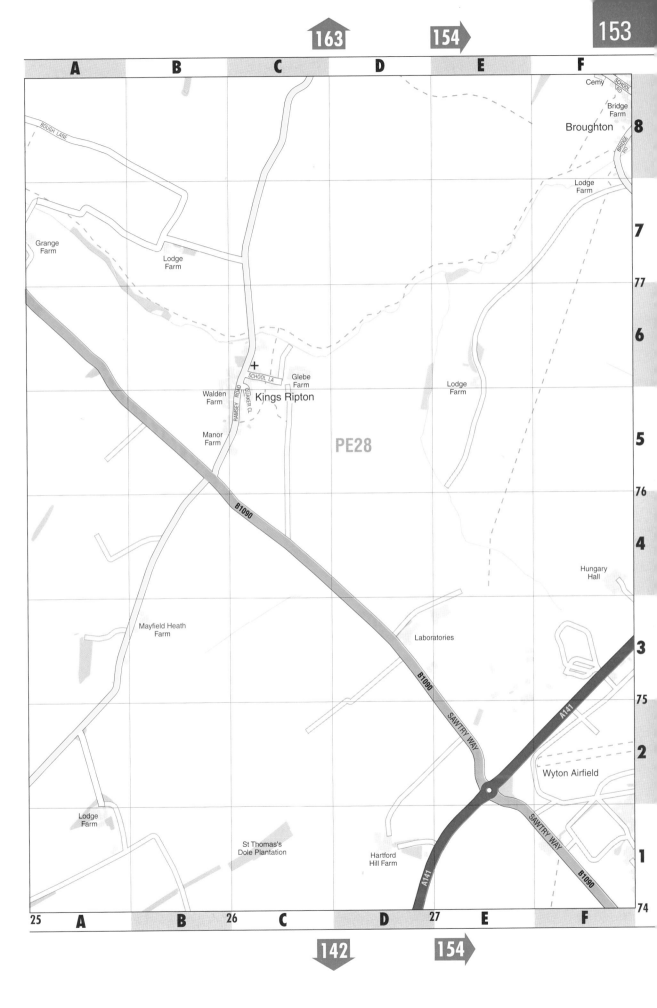

163
154

A B C D E F

Cemy

Bridge
Farm

Broughton

8

Lodge
Farm

7

77

Grange
Farm

BOUGH LANE

Lodge
Farm

6

SCHOOL RD

BRIDGE RD

Glebe
Farm

SCHOOL LA

Walden
Farm

RAMSEY ROAD

QUAKER CL

Kings Ripton

Lodge
Farm

5

Manor
Farm

PE28

76

B1090

4

Hungary
Hall

Mayfield Heath
Farm

Laboratories

3

B1090

SAWTRY WAY

A141

75

Lodge
Farm

Wyton Airfield

2

St Thomas's
Dole Plantation

Hartford
Hill Farm

SAWTRY WAY

A141

B1090

1

74

25   A   B   26   C   D   27   E   F

142
154

8 Bridge Rd
Causeway Road
Causeway Road
PO
+ White Hall Farm
PH
Broughton Lane
Sewage Works
Works
Old Hurst Grove

Church Farm
Moat
+

7 Mill Barn Farm
Ramsey Rd
CHURCH STREET
THE GRANARY
Manor Farms
THE LANE
WELLINGTON CL.

77 Ramsey Rd
PH
St Ives Rd
Old Hurst
Marsh Farm
Lancaster Cl

6

A141

5 PE28

76

4 • Mast

3

75

2 Wyton Airfield
Hiam Farm

Old Ramsey Rd

1 RAF Wyton
Devon Rd
Durham Wy
Pineview Kennels
PE27

Wiltshire Rd
Norfolk Rd

74

28 A B 29 C D 30 E F

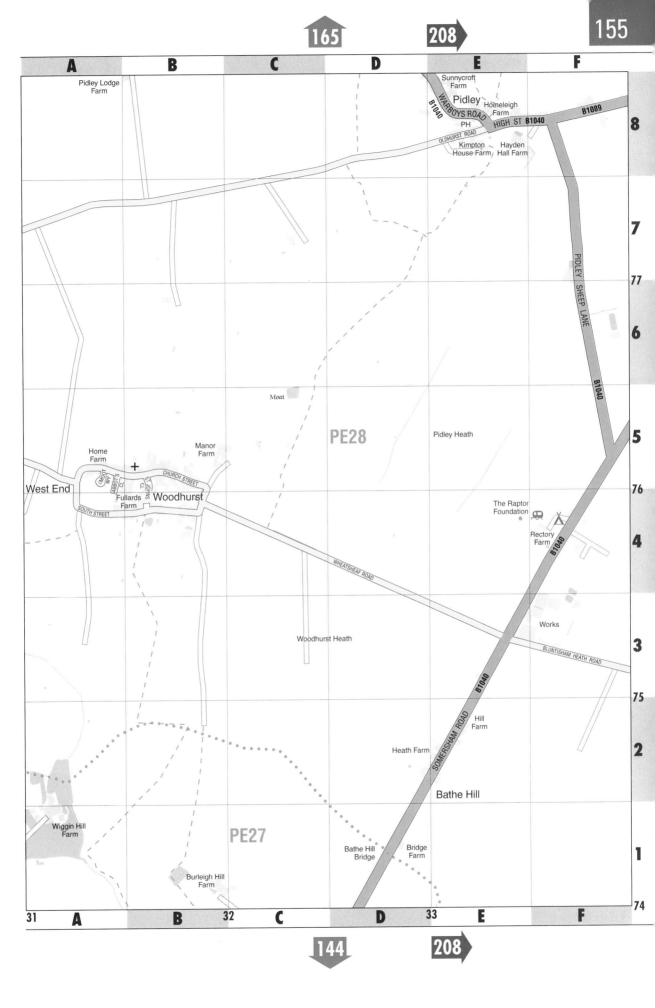

A B C D E F

8

7

77

6

5

76

4

3

75

2

1

74

Pidley Lodge Farm

Sunnycroft Farm

Pidley

Homeleigh Farm

B1040

WARBOYS ROAD

PH

HIGH ST B1040

B1089

OLDHURST ROAD

Kimpton House Farm

Hayden Hall Farm

PIDLEY SHEEP LANE

B1040

Moat

PE28

Pidley Heath

Home Farm

Manor Farm

CHURCH STREET

West End

MOOT WY
ABBOTS CL
ST JOHNS ST

Woodhurst

Fullards Farm

SOUTH STREET

The Raptor Foundation

Rectory Farm

B1040

WHEATSHEAF ROAD

Woodhurst Heath

Works

BLUNTISHAM HEATH ROAD

B1040

SOMERSHAM ROAD

Hill Farm

Heath Farm

Bathe Hill

Wiggin Hill Farm

PE27

Bathe Hill Bridge

Bridge Farm

Burleigh Hill Farm

31 A B 32 C D 33 E F

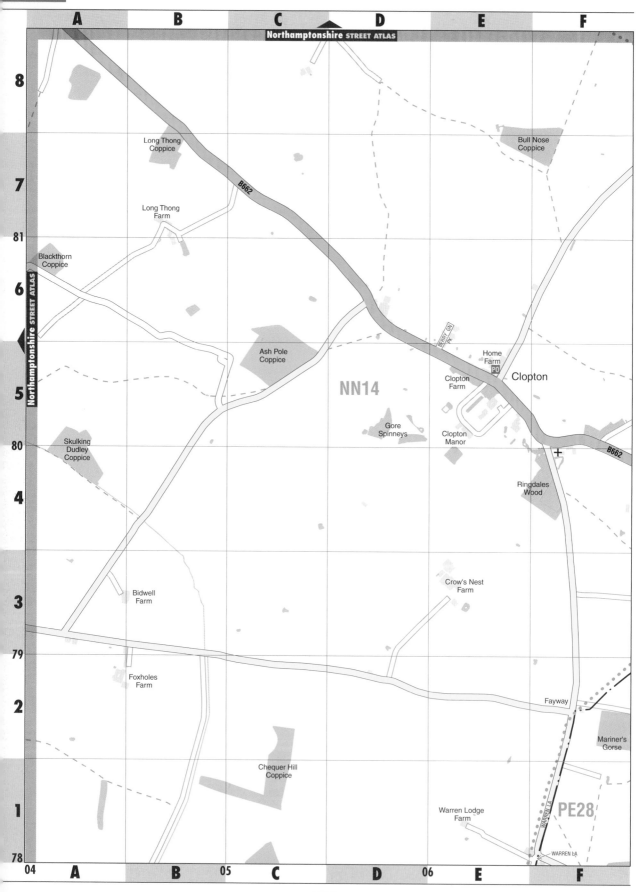

Northamptonshire STREET ATLAS

Long Thong
Coppice

Bull Nose
Coppice

B662

Long Thong
Farm

Blackthorn
Coppice

Ash Pole
Coppice

NN14

BERRY GN
PK

Home
Farm
PO

Clopton

Clopton
Farm

Gore
Spinneys

Clopton
Manor

Skulking
Dudley
Coppice

B662

Ringdales
Wood

Bidwell
Farm

Crow's Nest
Farm

Foxholes
Farm

Fayway

Mariner's
Gorse

Chequer Hill
Coppice

WARREN LA

PE28

Warren Lodge
Farm

WARREN LA

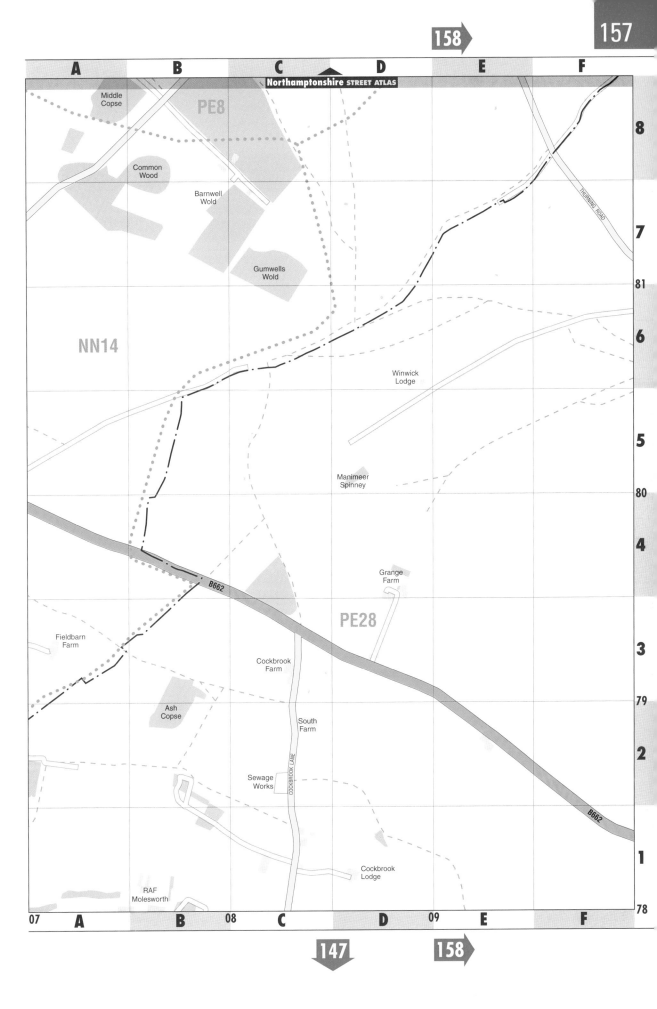

A | B | C | D | E | F

Northamptonshire STREET ATLAS

PE8

Middle Copse

Common Wood

Barnwell Wold

Gumwells Wold

THURNING ROAD

NN14

Winwick Lodge

Manimeer Spinney

B662

Grange Farm

PE28

Fieldbarn Farm

Cockbrook Farm

South Farm

Ash Copse

COCKBROOK LANE

Sewage Works

Cockbrook Lodge

B662

RAF Molesworth

8

7

81

6

5

80

4

3

79

2

1

78

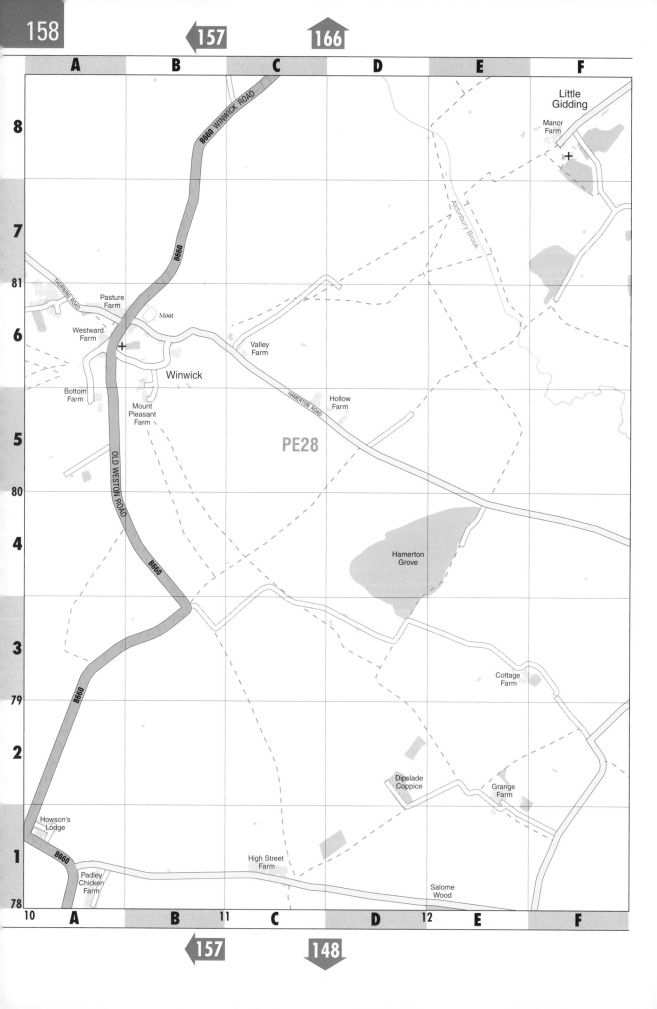

A B C D E F

8

7

81

6

5

80

4

3

79

2

1

78

Little Gidding

Manor Farm

Alconbury Brook

B660 WINWICK ROAD

B660

HORNING ROAD

Pasture Farm

Moat

Westward Farm

Winwick

Valley Farm

HAMERTON ROAD

Hollow Farm

Bottom Farm

Mount Pleasant Farm

OLD WESTON ROAD

PE28

Hamerton Grove

B660

Cottage Farm

Dipslade Coppice

Grange Farm

Howson's Lodge

B660

Padley Chicken Farm

High Street Farm

Salome Wood

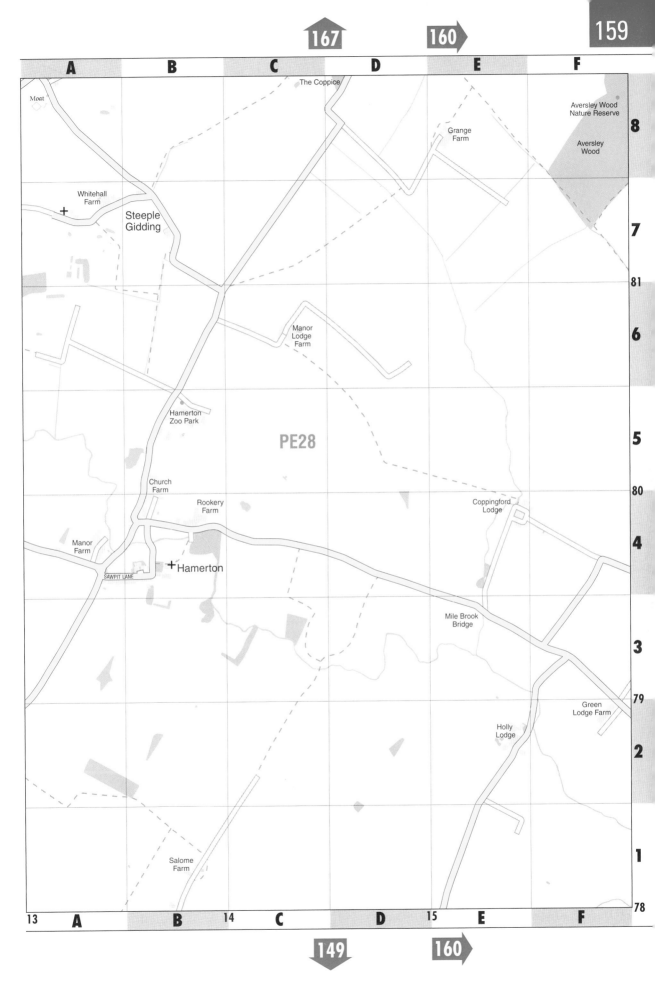

167
160

Moat

The Coppice

Aversley Wood
Nature Reserve

Grange
Farm

Aversley
Wood

Whitehall
Farm

Steeple
Gidding

Manor
Lodge
Farm

Hamerton
Zoo Park

PE28

Church
Farm

Rookery
Farm

Coppingford
Lodge

Manor
Farm

SAWPIT LANE

Hamerton

Mile Brook
Bridge

Green
Lodge Farm

Holly
Lodge

Salome
Farm

149
160

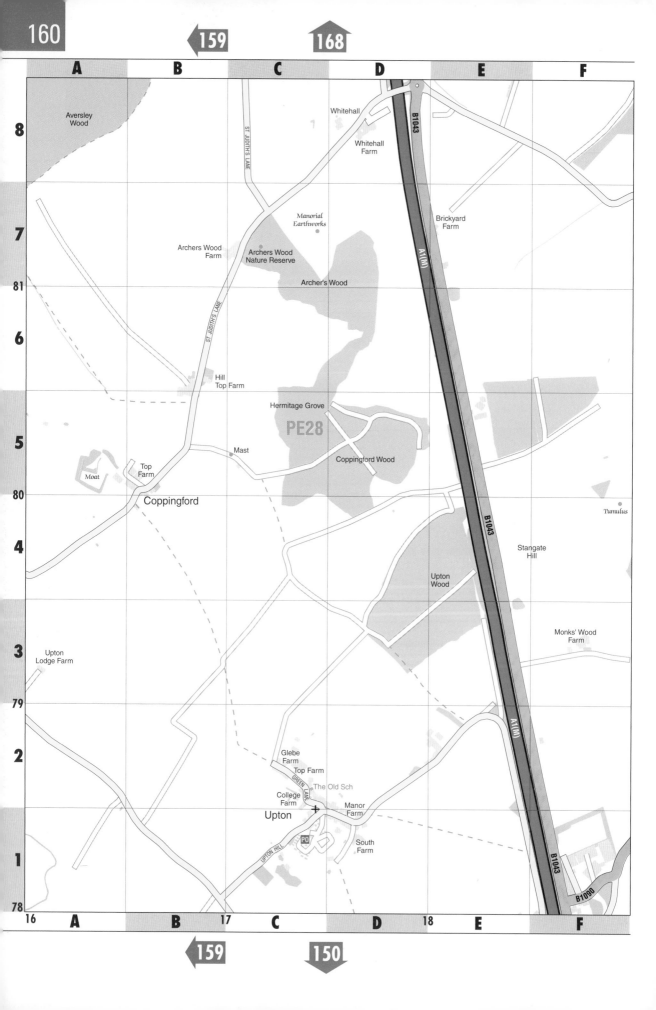

A B C D E F

8

7

81

6

5

80

4

3

79

2

1

78

16 A B 17 C D 18 E F

Aversley
Wood

St Judith's Lane

Whitehall

Whitehall
Farm

B1043

A1(M)

Brickyard
Farm

Manorial
Earthworks

Archers Wood
Farm

Archers Wood
Nature Reserve

Archer's Wood

Hill
Top Farm

Hermitage Grove

PE28

Mast

Top
Farm

Moat

Coppingford

Coppingford Wood

B1043

Tumulus

Stangate
Hill

Upton
Wood

Monks' Wood
Farm

Upton
Lodge Farm

A1(M)

Glebe
Farm

Top Farm

Green Lane

The Old Sch

College
Farm

Manor
Farm

Upton

PO

Upton Hill

South
Farm

B1043

B1090

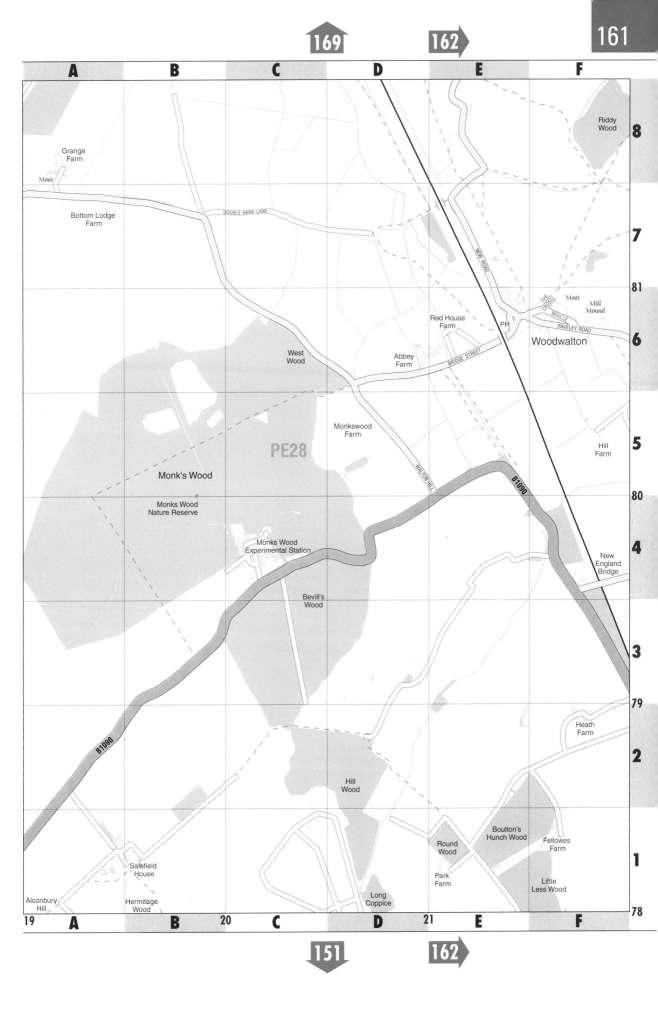

A B C D E F

8

7

81

6

5

80

4

3

79

2

1

78

Riddy
Wood

Grange
Farm

Moat

Bottom Lodge
Farm

DOUBLE BANK LANE

NEW ROAD

THE CROSS

Moat

Mill
Mound

BEVILLE

RAVELEY ROAD

PH

Woodwalton

Red House
Farm

West
Wood

Abbey
Farm

BRIDGE STREET

Monkswood
Farm

Hill
Farm

PE28

Monk's Wood

WALTON HILL

B1090

Monks Wood
Nature Reserve

Monks Wood
Experimental Station

New
England
Bridge

Bevill's
Wood

Hill
Wood

B1090

Heath
Farm

Round
Wood

Boulton's
Hunch Wood

Fellowes
Farm

Park
Farm

Little
Less Wood

Alconbury
Hill

Safefield
House

Hermitage
Wood

Long
Coppice

19 A B 20 C D 21 E F 78

161
170

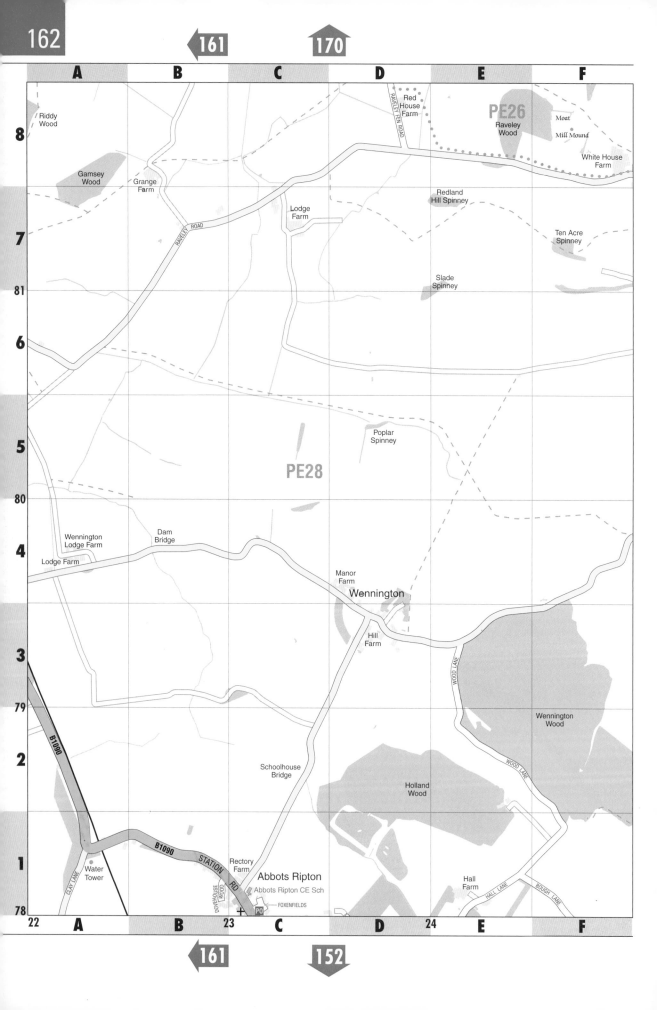

161
152

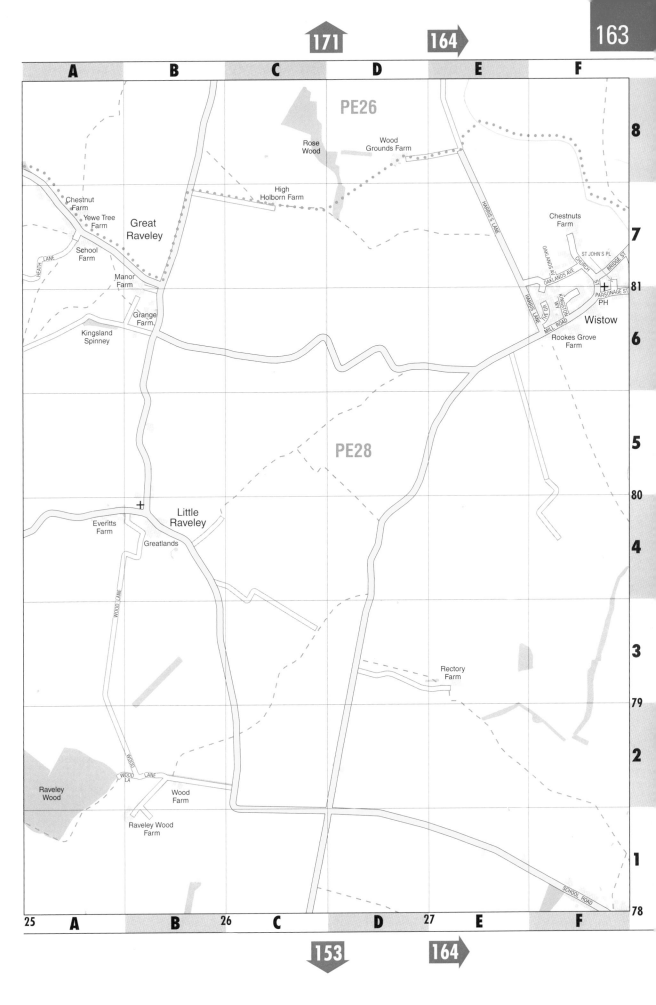

A B C D E F

PE26

Rose Wood

Wood Grounds Farm

High Holborn Farm

Chestnut Farm

Yewe Tree Farm

Great Raveley

School Farm

HEATH LANE

Manor Farm

Grange Farm

Kingsland Spinney

HARRIS'S LANE

Chestnuts Farm

St JOHN'S PL
ST JOHN'S ST
OAKLANDS AVE
CHURCH ST
BRIDGE ST
PARSONAGE ST
PH

HARRIS'S LANE
WEST ST
KINGSTON WAY
MILL ROAD

Wistow

Rookes Grove Farm

PE28

Everitts Farm

Little Raveley

Greatlands

WOOD LANE

Rectory Farm

Raveley Wood

WOOD LA
WOOD LANE

Wood Farm

Raveley Wood Farm

SCHOOL ROAD

25 26 27

8 7 81 6 5 80 4 3 79 2 1 78

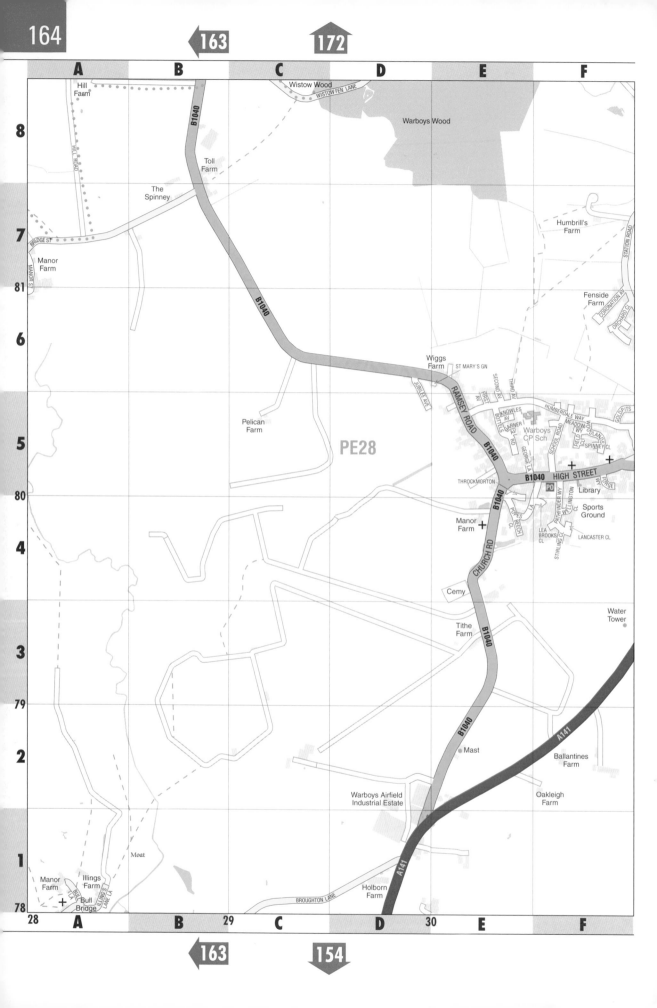

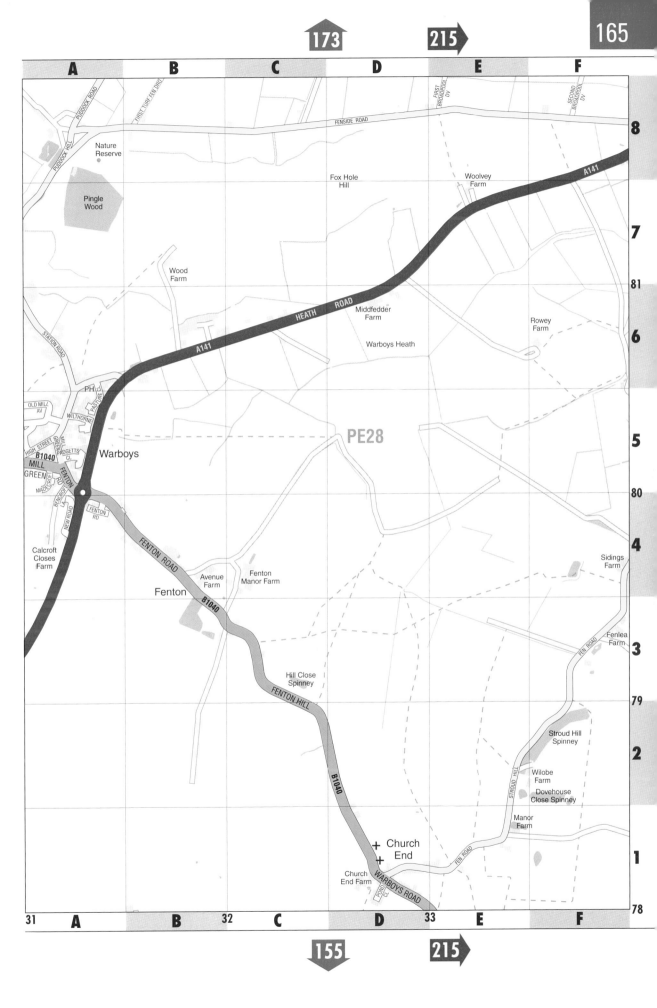

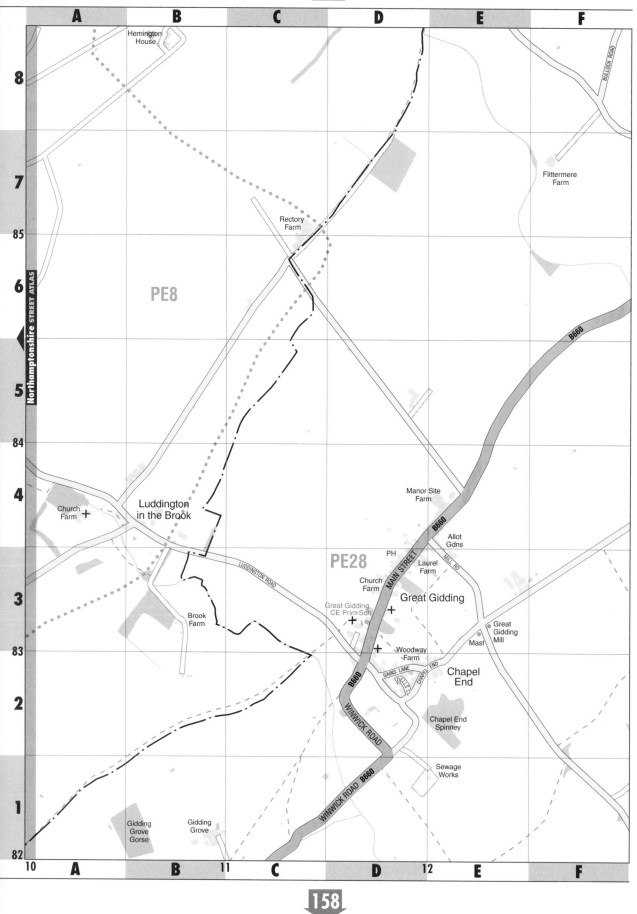

Hemington House

Flittermere Farm

BULLOCK ROAD

Rectory Farm

PE8

Northamptonshire STREET ATLAS

B660

Manor Site Farm

Luddington in the Brook

Church Farm

B660

Allot Gdns

PH

PE28

Laurel Farm

MILL RD

LUDDINGTON ROAD

Church Farm

MAIN STREET

Great Gidding

Great Gidding CE Prim Sch

Woodway Farm

Great Gidding Mill

Mast

Brook Farm

GAINS LANE

DELLS CL

CHAPEL END

Chapel End

B660

WINWICK ROAD

Chapel End Spinney

Sewage Works

WINWICK ROAD B660

Gidding Grove Gorse

Gidding Grove

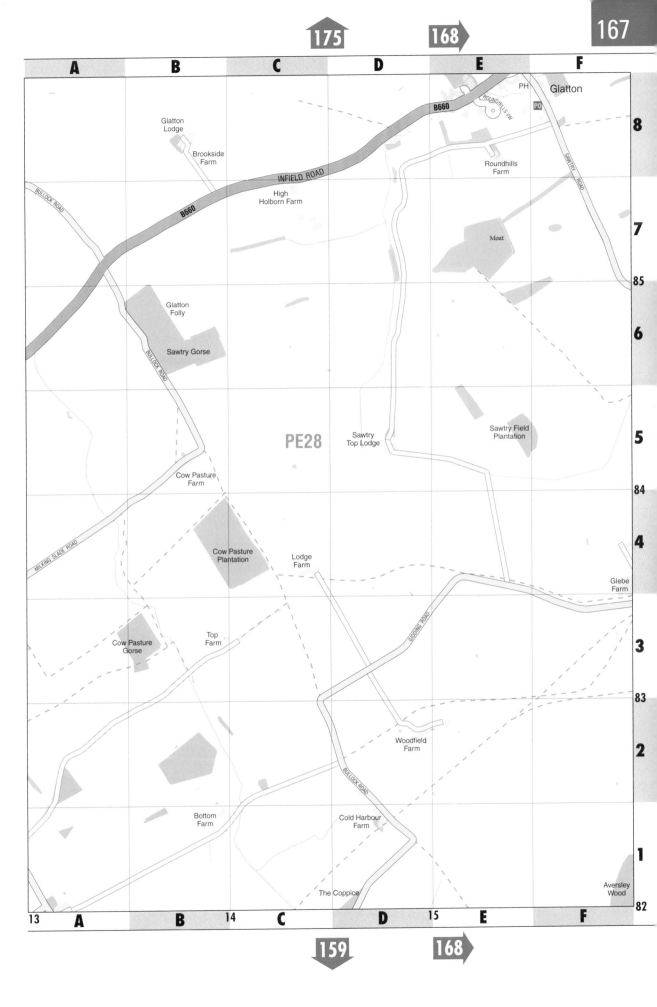

A B C D E F

8

7

85

6

5

84

4

3

83

2

1

82

Yew Tree Farm

CONINGTON LANE

Conington

COTTON CL

BRUCES LA

CHURCH ROAD

CHURCH LA

Palmer's Grove

PE7

Spot's Grove

High Fen

Duckpit Fen

A1(M)

B1043

15

Castle Grove

Bruce's Castle Farm

Moat

CREASE ROAD

COOKS LANE

Little Common Farm

Little Common

1 BLOOMFIELD WY
2 THE GRANARY
3 ALL SAINTS WY
4 ST DAVID'S WY
5 HUNTINGS DR

B1043

Middlemarsh Farm

SAWTRY RD

GLATTON ROAD

BROOKSIDE

BROOKSIDE

WESTERMAN CL

SALTERS WY

FAIRFIELD

GROUNDS RD

WELLS RD

WARREN CT

CHURCH STREET

PARK RD

CHESTNUT CL

RECTORY CL

TORT HL

WHITEHOUSE RD

SHAWLEY ROAD

DEERPARK

COPPINS CL

GLEBE RD

HATFIELD CL

ABBEY CL

BELGRAVE

MILL VW

HIGH ST

ANNESLEY CL

CHURCH CW

TINKERS LANE

NEWTON RD

MANOR DR

CHAPEL END

ST ANDREWS WAY

FEN LANE

Manor Farm

Glebe Farm

GIDDING ROAD

PH

PAPYRUS WY

MALTINGS CL

GREEN LANE

Sawtry Com Coll

Liby

Sawtry Sports Centre

WOODFIELD DR

WESTFIELD RD

CAVENDISH

MOYNE RD

YELVEYS

Black Horse Farm

OLD NORTH ROAD

STRAIGHT DROVE

ASHDALE CL 1
OAKLEY DR 2
HUNTERS WY 3
HAWTHORN WY 4
WINDSOR RD 5
DEVONSHIRE CL 6

WINDSOR RD

MIDDLEFIELD ROAD

THE BRIARS

CRABAPPLE

COLLEGE WY

COLITHE

MOYNE RD

BEAUMARIS RD

ERYNE WAY

STANCH HL

Great Common

PE28

Sawtry

LAUREL CL

MAPLE CL

ELM CL

BRAMBLE

GREEN END ROAD

PINCHBECK CL

APPOSTGATE

BLINDS

CROMWELL WY

MOINS

PH

BEDFORD WY

DOUGLAS RD

DURHAM CL

SAXON CL

Stanch-hill Bridge

A1(M)

Common Barn Farm

Sawtry Roughs

Wood End Farm

High Holborn Hill

GRANGE

ST JUDITHS LANE

Green End

ELWYN CL

ST GUTHLACS

HOLBURN WY

SCOTNEY WY

PO

CHESHAM RD

CHESHAM RD

BLOCKMARSH WY

CARDINAL

AVERSLEY RD

GRANGE

P

Manor House Farm

C2
1 EWINGSWOOD
2 WHEATSHEAVES
3 STANEGATE
4 STUMPCROSS
5 COTTON CL

15

B1043

A1(M)

Aversley Wood

16 A B 17 C D 18 E F

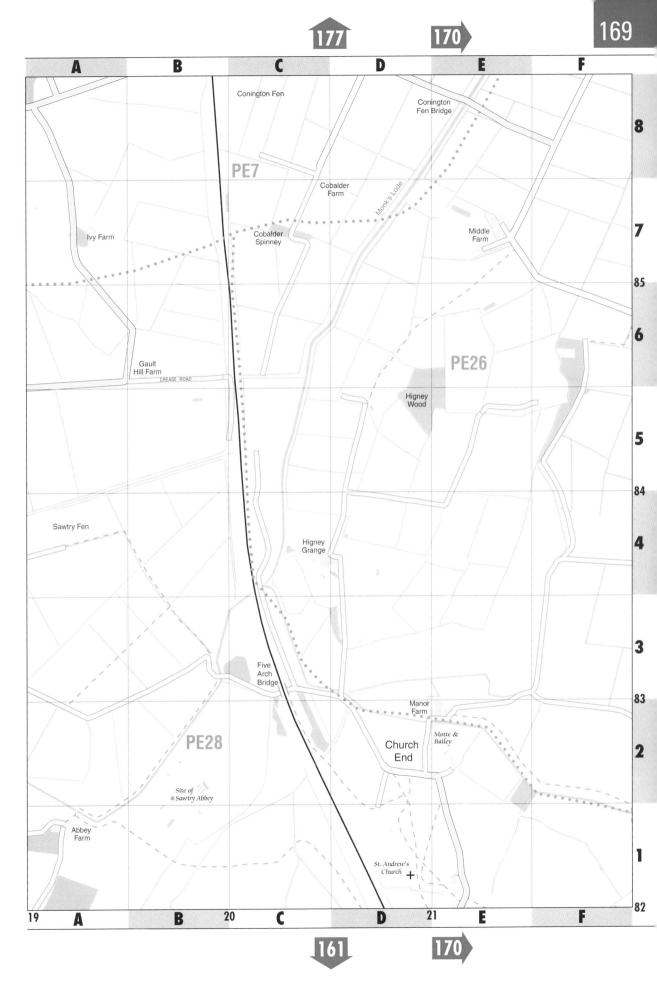

A B C D E F

8

7

85

6

5

84

4

83

3

2

1

82

RAY'S DROVE

Lotting
Fen

HARPER'S DROVE

HEIGHTS DROVE ROAD

HEIGHTS DROVE ROAD

Woodwalton Fen

Woodwalton Fen
Nature Reserve

Common
Farm

PE26

Wheatley's Drain

Great
Raveley Fen

Great Raveley Drain

Turf
Fen

TURF FEN ROAD

RAVELEY FEN ROAD

Lady's
Wood

PE28

Moat
Farm

RAVELEY
FEN RD.

22 A B 23 C D 24 E F

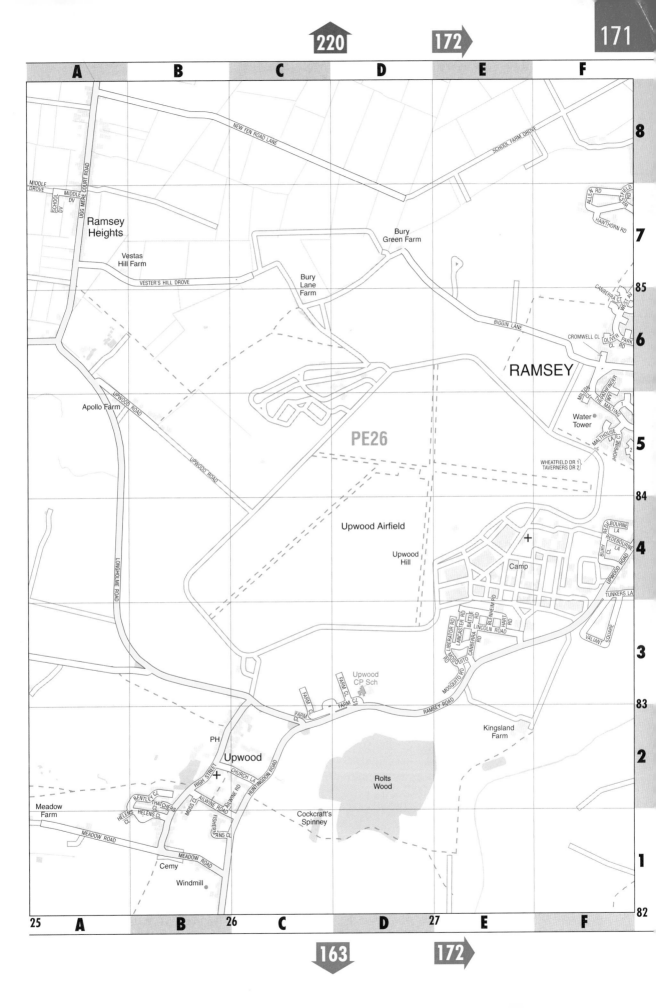

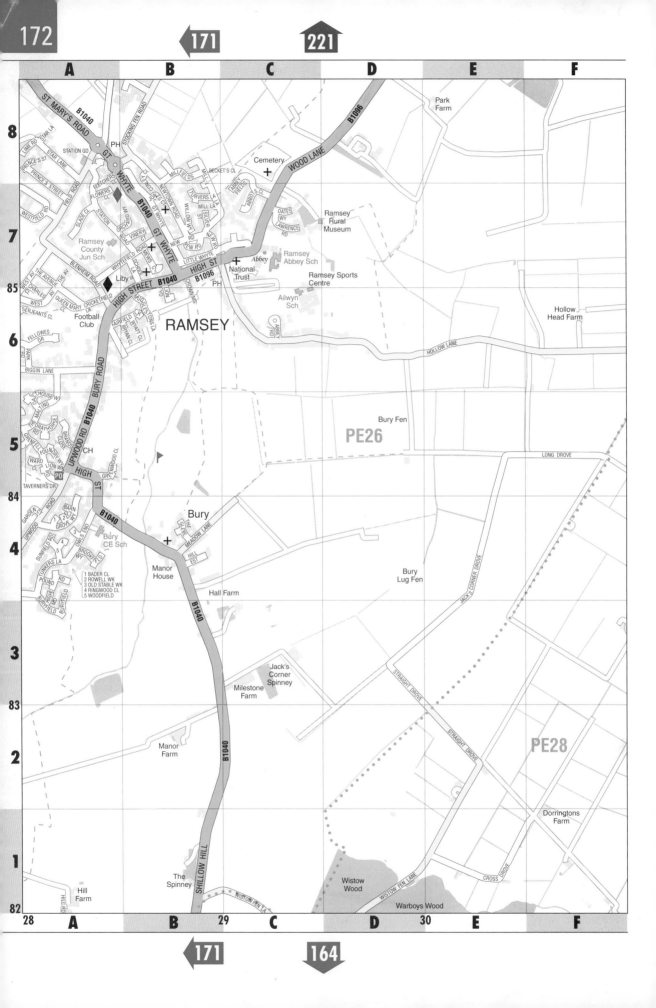

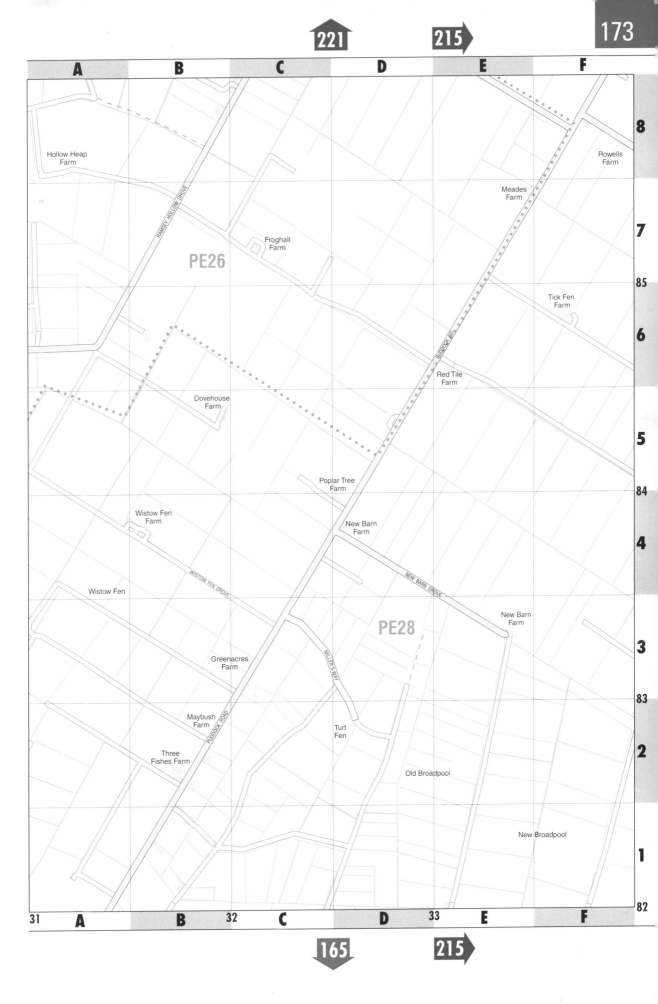

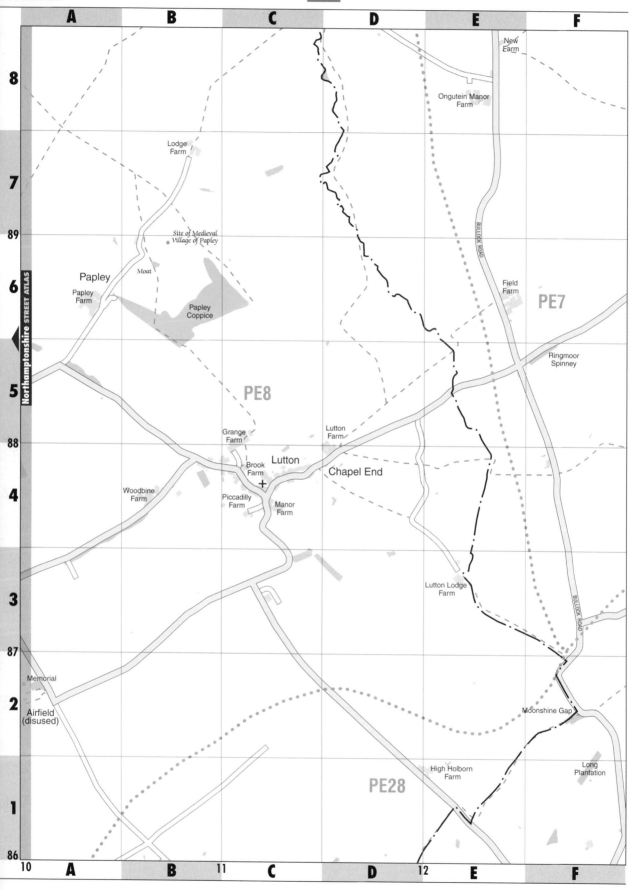

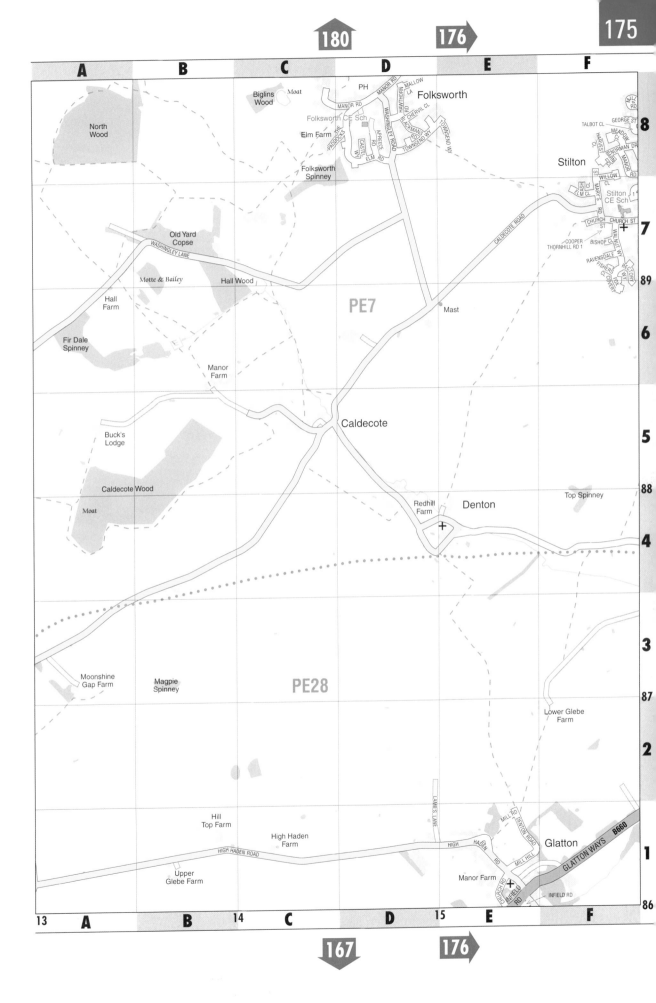

A B C D E F

North
Wood

Biglins
Wood Moat PH MANOR RD MALLOW Folksworth
MANOR RD HIGHLIANN CHERVIL CL
Folksworth CE Sch APREECE RD BLACKMANS TOWNSEND WY
Elm Farm PADDOCKS WASHINGLEY ROAD TOWNSEND WY
CASTEL WY ELM RD
Folksworth
Spinney

MILL RD
TALBOT CL GEORGE ST 8
MEADOW
HARVEST CL
CL B NORMAN DR
MANOR
WILLOW RD
CL
ELM CL Stilton Stilton
MARY'S RD CE Sch 1
CHURCH CHURCH ST
ST BISHOP CL
COOPER WALNUT WY
THORNHILL RD 1
RAVENSDALE RECTORY WY
FISHERS CL 89
COVERT

Old Yard
Copse PE7 Caldecote Road 7
WASHINGLEY LANE

Motte & Bailey Hall Wood Stilton

Hall Farm Mast 6

Fir Dale
Spinney

Manor
Farm

Buck's
Lodge Caldecote 5

Caldecote Wood Redhill Denton Top Spinney 88
Farm
Moat + 4

PE28

Moonshine
Gap Farm Magpie 87
Spinney Lower Glebe
Farm 2

Hill
Top Farm LAMBS LANE
High Haden MILL RD B660
Farm DENTON ROAD Glatton GLATTON WAYS 1
HIGH HADEN ROAD HIGH HADEN MILL HILL
RD
Upper Manor Farm +
Glebe Farm CHURCH RD INFIELD RD 86
INFIELD RD

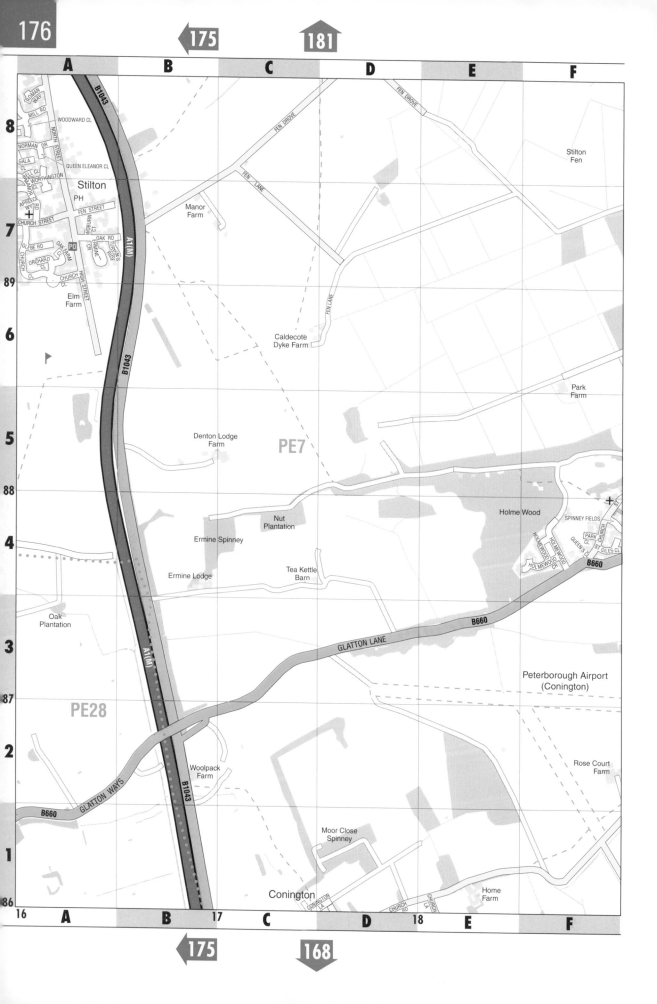

A B C D E F

8

7

89

6

5

88

4

3

87

2

1

86

16 A B 17 C D 18 E F

ROMAN WAY
MILL RD
WOODWARD CL
NORTH STREET
NORMAN DR
GALA CL
BELL CL
WORTHINGTON
APREECE WY RD
CHURCH STREET
QUEEN ELEANOR CL
Stilton
PH
FEN STREET
OAK RD
ERMINE
NYBROW
DUROINE RIDE
PO
GLEBE RD
OAK FARM CR
CHURCH CL
ORCHARD CL
CHURCH CL
HIGH STREET
Elm Farm
B1043

Manor Farm
FEN DROVE
FEN LANE
FEN DROVE
Stilton Fen
FEN LANE
Caldecote Dyke Farm
A1(M)
B1043

PE7

Park Farm

Denton Lodge Farm

Nut Plantation

Ermine Spinney

Holme Wood
SPINNEY FIELDS
HOLMEWOOD
HOLMEWOOD CR
PARK CL
QUEEN'S CL
ST GILES CL
ST CHURCH
B660

Ermine Lodge

Tea Kettle Barn

Oak Plantation

B660

GLATTON LANE

A1(M)

PE28

Peterborough Airport (Conington)

87

Woolpack Farm

Rose Court Farm

B1043

GLATTON WAYS

B660

Moor Close Spinney

Conington
CONINGTON LA
CHURCH RD
CHURCH LA
Home Farm

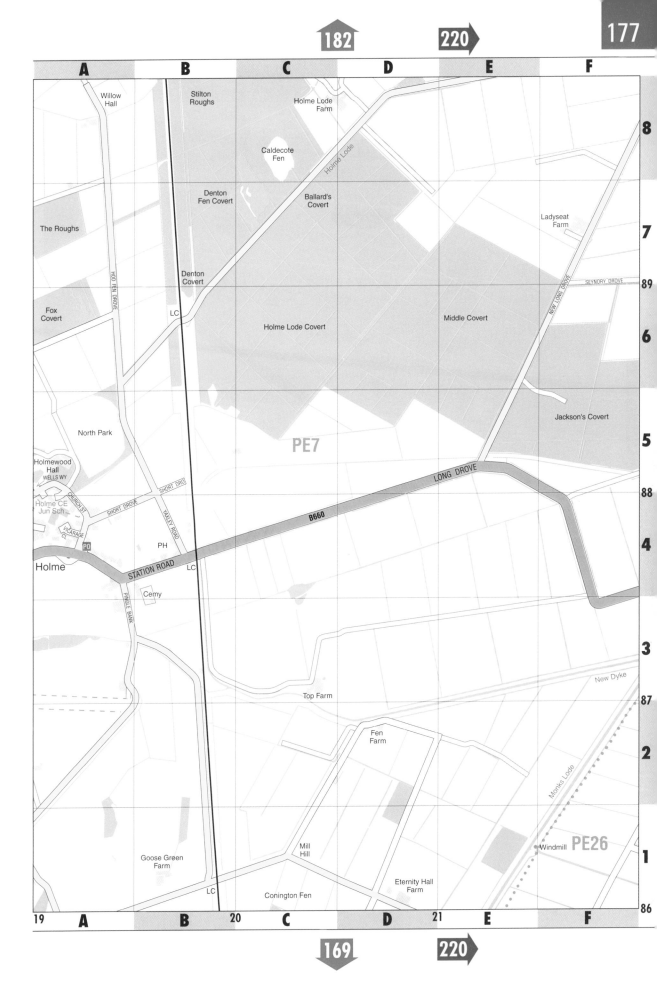

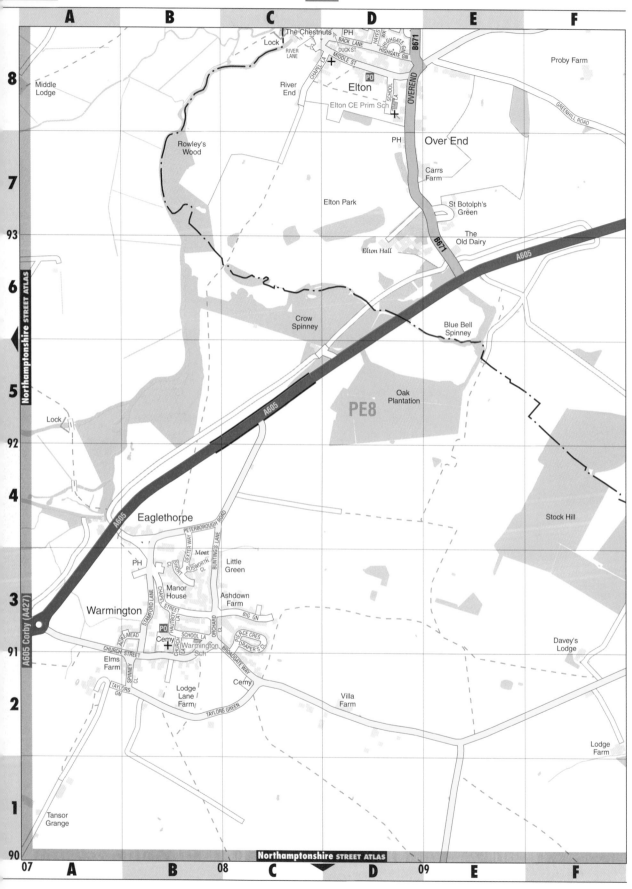

Northamptonshire STREET ATLAS

A B 08 C D 09 E F

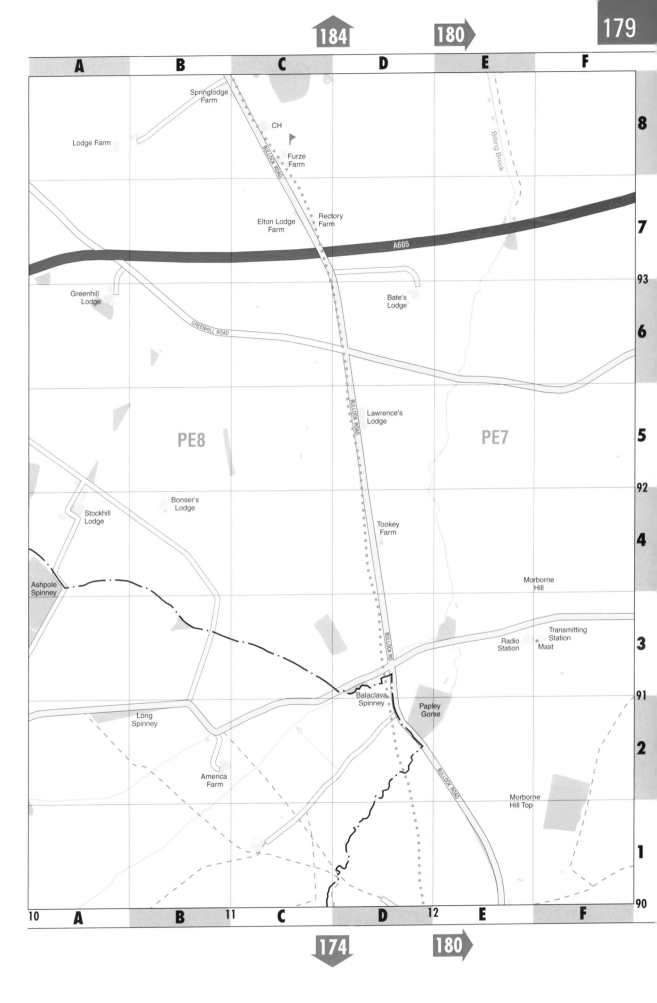

A   B   C   D   E   F

8

Springlodge
Farm

CH

Lodge Farm

Furze
Farm

BULLOCK ROAD

Elton Lodge
Farm

Rectory
Farm

Billing Brook

A605

7

93

Greenhill
Lodge

GREENHILL ROAD

Bate's
Lodge

6

BULLOCK ROAD

Lawrence's
Lodge

PE8

PE7

5

92

Bonser's
Lodge

Stockhill
Lodge

Tookey
Farm

4

Morborne
Hill

Ashpole
Spinney

Transmitting
Station

Radio
Station

Mast

3

91

Balaclava
Spinney

Papley
Gorse

Long
Spinney

BULLOCK RD

BULLOCK ROAD

2

America
Farm

Morborne
Hill Top

1

90

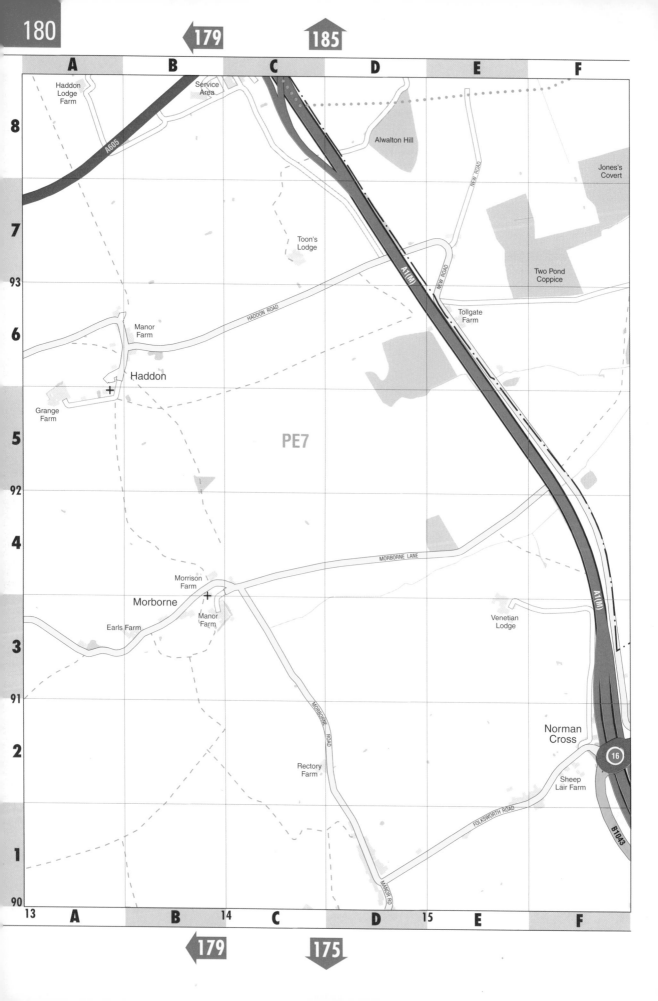

A B C D E F

8

7

93

6

5

92

4

3

91

2

1

90

Orton Brick Works

Pit
(dis)

Madam
White's
Covert

A15

LONDON ROAD

LONDON RD

FULLY CL

LONDON RD

Spendelows
Farm

LONDON RD

DOVECOTE LANE

PROBY

Cemy

WATERSLADE RD

Yaxley
Lodge Farm

Heye's Farm

A15

PE7

Manor
Farm

VICARAGE WY

VICARAGE WAY

WISTERIA

CHURCH STREET

LAUREL CL

LEE

WYKES
RD

WYKES
RD

WABROD WY

WEST END
WY

COCKSON
CLOSE

HOLME ROAD

LEADING DRIVE

Yards End Dyke

LEADING DRIVE

FEN DROVE

PART RIDGE CL
BRUNEL DR
OWL
END
KINGFISHER
COCK CLOSE RD
PHEASANT
WY
NIGHTINGALE DR
THE
ROOKERY
GREEN
SWAN
PODLEY WY

B1091

BROADWAY

MIDDLETONS ROAD

MANOR CL

CHAPEL ST
WESTFIELD RD
I FIELD
BEFIELD
STONEHOUSE
BEAUVOIR

MOUNTBATTEN
AV

BLENHEIM
WY
BLENHEIM WY
BLENHEIM
WY

HILLCREST AV

PH
THE GN
BACK LA

MAIN STREET

ASKEW'S LANE

BECKONS

MAIN STREET

Fourfields
Prim Sch

QUEEN STREET

CRANE AVE
SPEECHLEY RD

Yaxley
Jun Sch

PO
Liby

PARK
LANSDOWNE RD
VIXEN CL

LITCHFIELD CL

MARLBOROUGH CL

LIMETREE CL
CROCUS
QUEEN STREET
ORCHID
JASMINE WY
PRIM ROSE
ELM
MAPLE
LABURNUM AV

LANCASTER
CT
WINDSOR ROAD
LANCASTER WY

HAWTHORN RD
SPRING RD
SOUTHDOWN RD
BADGER
CL
MAIN ROAD

Yaxley

MERE DROVE

Hod
Fen

HOD FEN DROVE

North Street

B1043

16 17 18

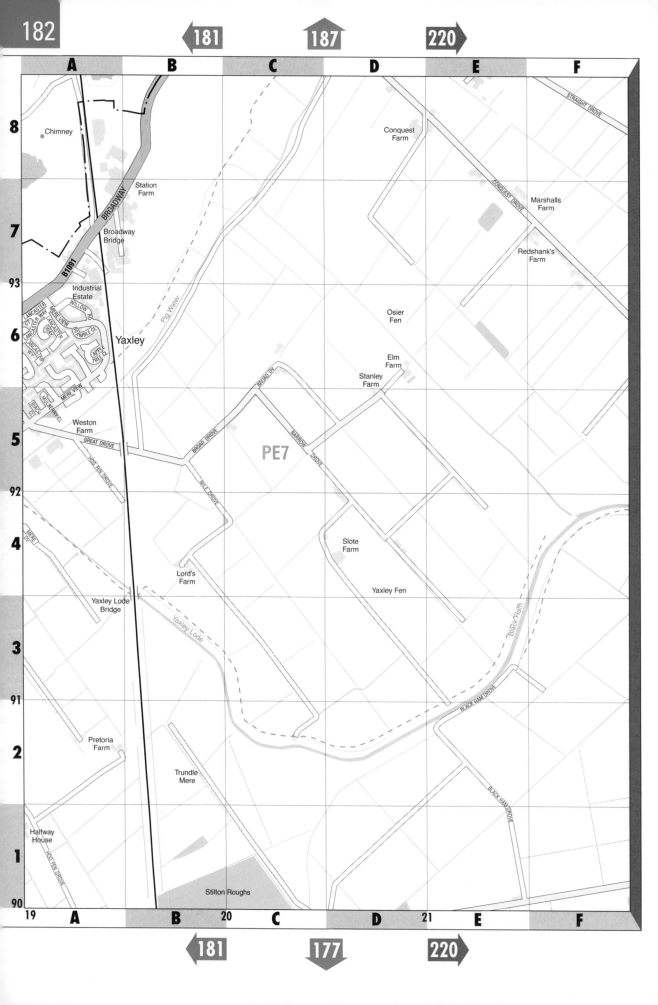

A B C D E F

8 Chimney

Conquest Farm

STRAIGHT DROVE

Station Farm

Marshalls Farm

7 Broadway Bridge

CONQUEST DROVE

Redshank's Farm

93

Industrial Estate

Osier Fen

6 Yaxley

Elm Farm

Stanley Farm

BROAD DV

Weston Farm

NARROW DROVE

5 GREAT DROVE

PE7

HOG FEN DROVE

BROAD DROVE

MILE DROVE

92

MERE DV

4 Slote Farm

Lord's Farm

Yaxley Fen

Yaxley Lode Bridge

Yaxley Lode

BLACK HAM

3

91

BLACK HAM DROVE

2 Pretoria Farm

Trundle Mere

BLACK HAM DROVE

Halfway House

1

ROO FEN DROVE

90

Stilton Roughs

19 A 20 B C 21 D E F

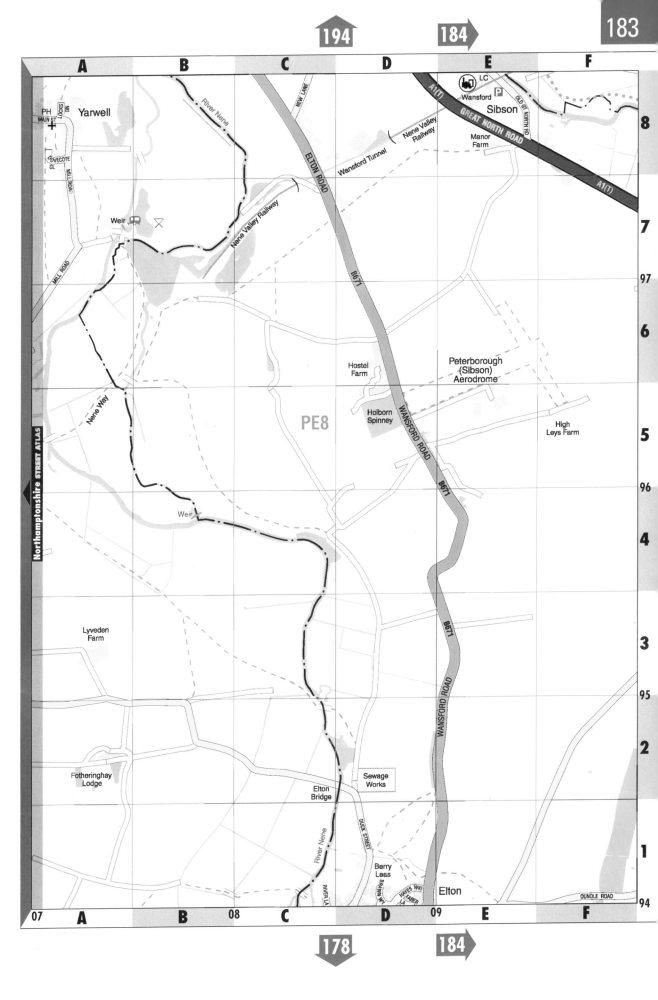

A B C D E F

Northamptonshire STREET ATLAS

8
7
97
6
5
96
4
3
95
2
1
94

Yarwell
PH
MAIN ST
LOCKS RD
DOVECOTE CL
MILL ROAD
River Nene
NEW LANE
ELTON ROAD
Wansford Tunnel
Nene Valley Railway
A1(T)
GREAT NORTH ROAD
OLD GT NORTH RD
Wansford
Sibson
LC
P
Manor Farm
A1(T)
Weir
Nene Valley Railway
B671
Nene Way
PE8
Hostel Farm
Holborn Spinney
Wansford Road
Peterborough (Sibson) Aerodrome
High Leys Farm
B671
Weir
Lyveden Farm
Fotheringhay Lodge
Elton Bridge
River Nene
RIVER LA
DUCK STREET
Sewage Works
Berry Leas
BRAMW...
HAYES WK
FABER LA
Elton
WANSFORD ROAD
B671
OUNDLE ROAD

07 08 09

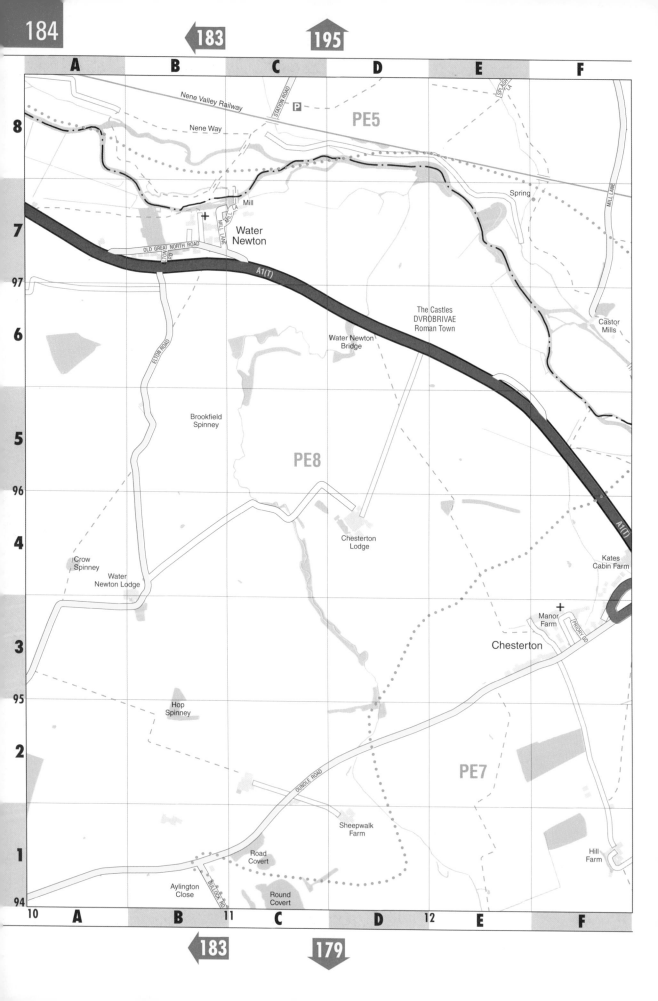

183
195

A B C D E F

8

Nene Valley Railway

Nene Way

STATION ROAD

P

PE5

Spring

MILL LANE

Mill

MILL LA

7

Water
Newton

OLD GREAT NORTH ROAD

ELTON RD

A1(T)

97

The Castles
DVROBRIVAE
Roman Town

Castor
Mills

SPLASH LA

6

ELTON ROAD

Water Newton
Bridge

5

Brookfield
Spinney

PE8

96

A1(T)

4

Crow
Spinney

Chesterton
Lodge

Kates
Cabin Farm

Water
Newton Lodge

3

Manor
Farm

Chesterton

PRIORY RD

95

Hop
Spinney

2

DUNDLE ROAD

PE7

Sheepwalk
Farm

Hill
Farm

1

Road
Covert

Aylington
Close

BULLOCK RD

Round
Covert

94

10 A B 11 C D 12 E F

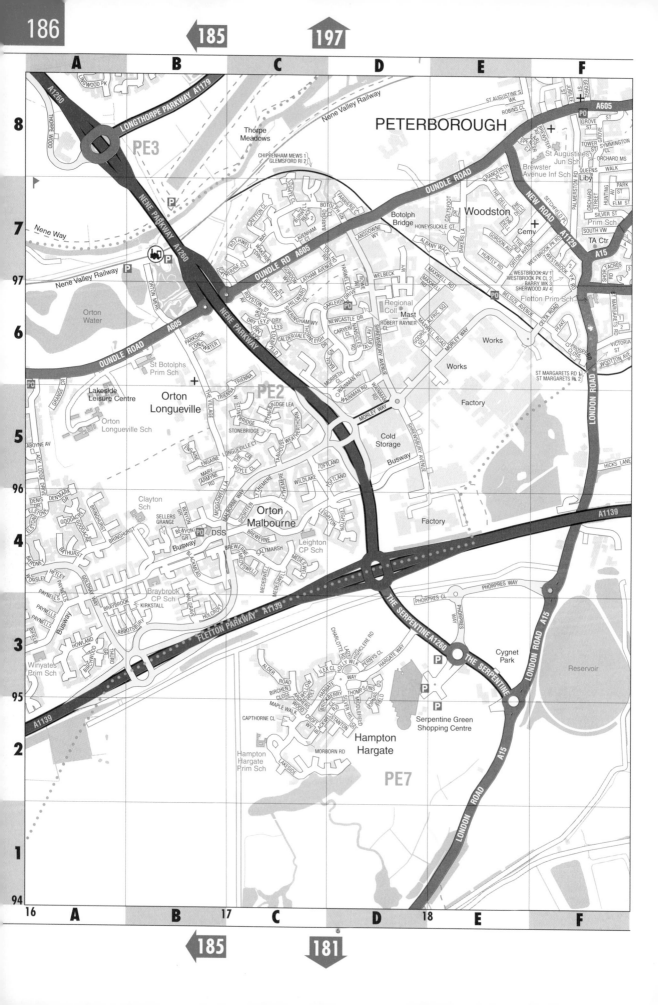

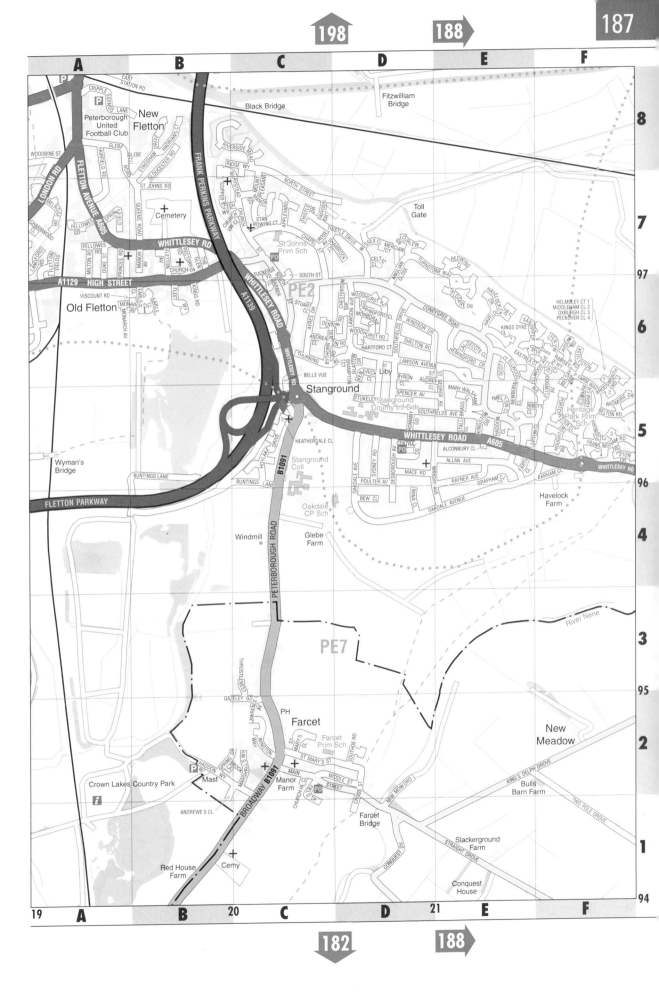

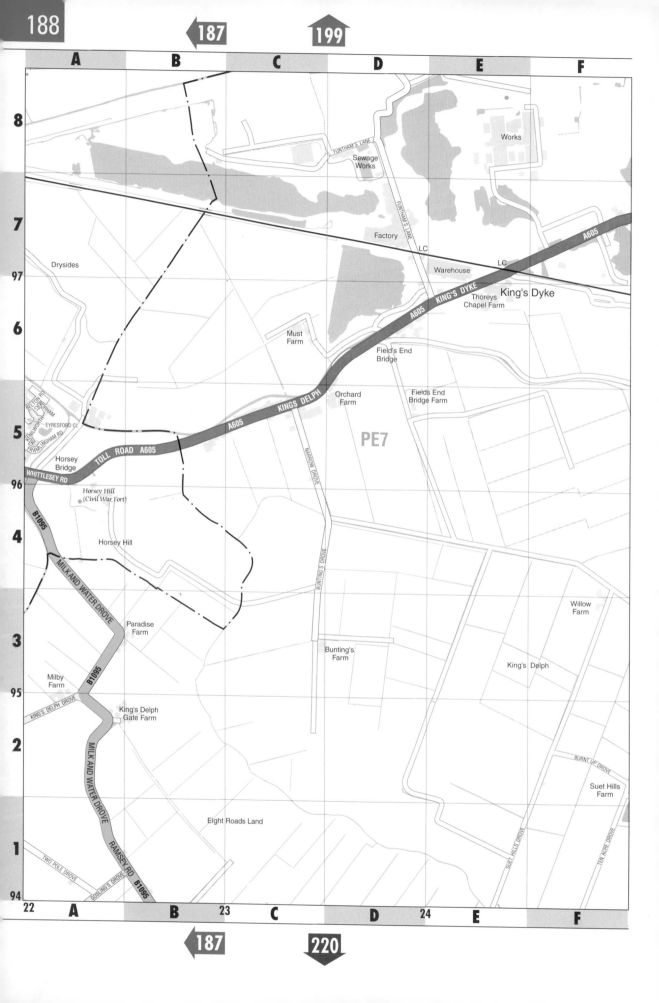

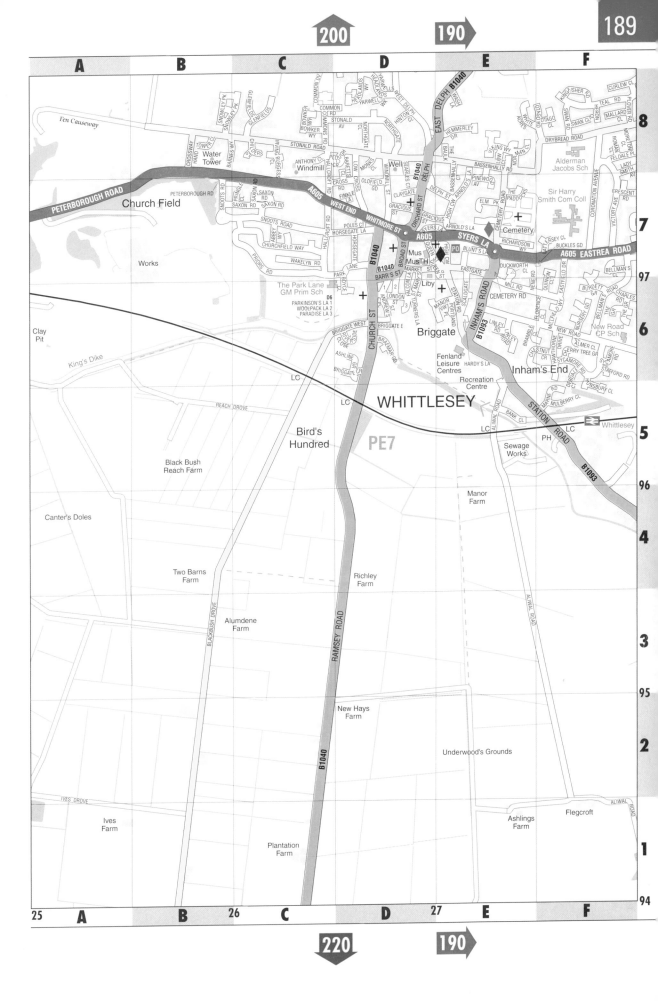

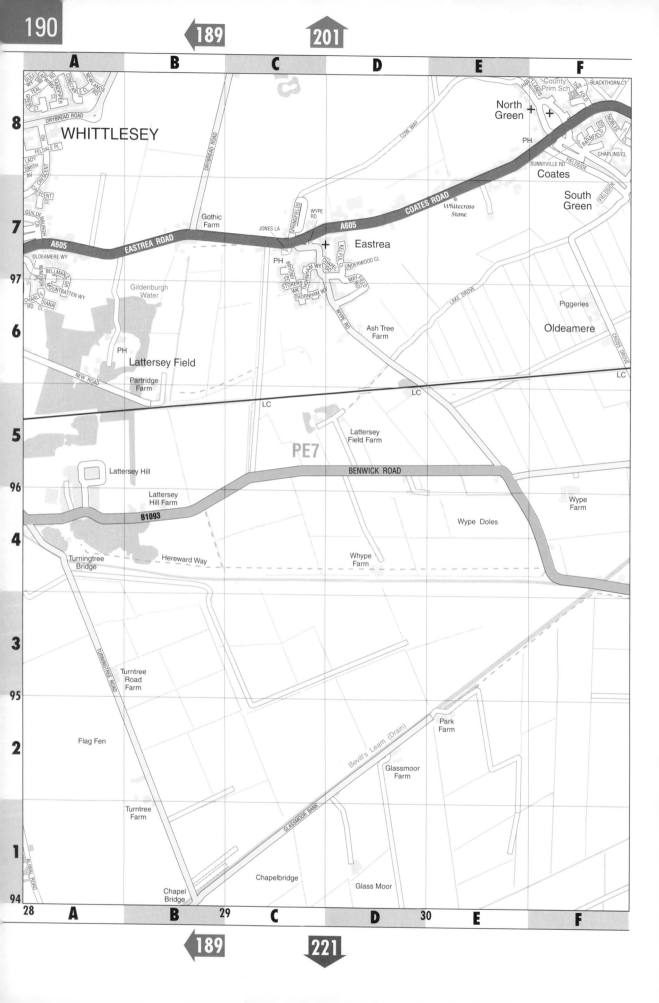

189

201

A B C D E F

8

WHITTLESEY

DRYBREAD ROAD

North Green

Coates

Whitecross Stone

South Green

7

Gothic Farm

Jones La

SPRINGFIELDS

WYPE RD

A605 EASTREA ROAD

COATES ROAD

A605

Eastrea

KELFUL CL

UNDERWOOD CL

OLDEAMERE WY

PH

BRYONY CL

STORERS WK

THORNHAM WY

CHAPEL GD

MAY FIELD RD

97

WINDSOR GR

BELLMANS GR

MOUNTBATTEN WY

CHARLES RD

DIANA CL

Gildenburgh Water

THORNHAM WY

WYPE RD

Ash Tree Farm

LAKE DROVE

Piggeries

Oldeamere

CROSS DRIVE

6

PH

Lattersey Field

NEW ROAD

Partridge Farm

LC

LC

LC

LC

5

Lattersey Field Farm

PE7

Lattersey Hill

Lattersey Hill Farm

BENWICK ROAD

Wype Farm

96

B1093

Wype Doles

4

Turningtree Bridge

Hereward Way

Whype Farm

TURNINGTREE ROAD

3

Turntree Road Farm

95

Park Farm

Bevill's Leam (Drain)

2

Flag Fen

Glassmoor Farm

GLASSMOOR BANK

Turntree Farm

1

ALWALTON ROAD

94

Chapel Bridge

Chapelbridge

Glass Moor

28 A 29 B C D 30 E F

189

221

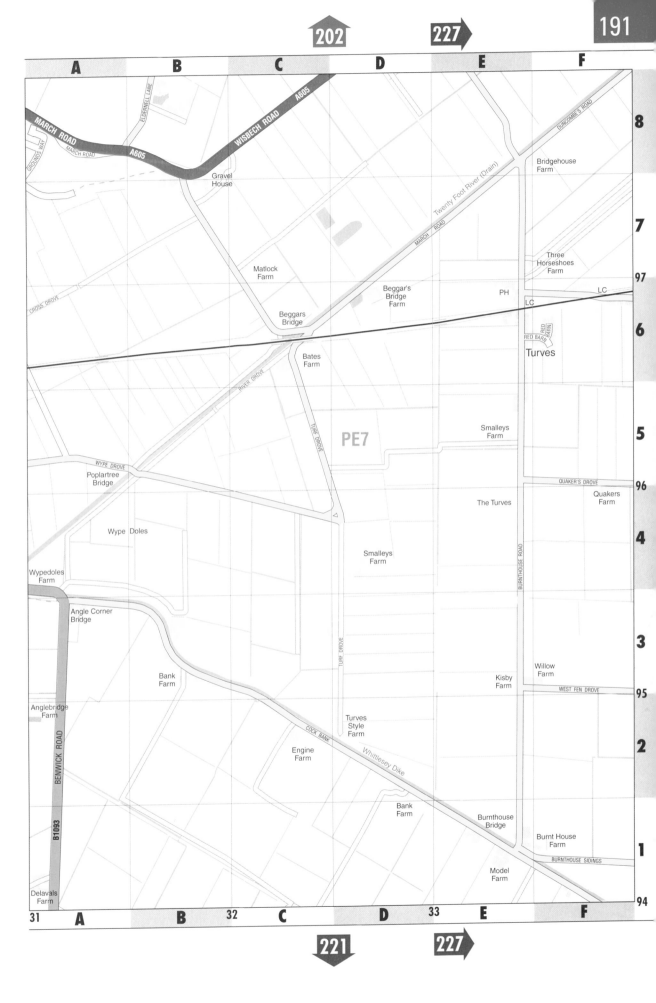

A   B   C   D   E   F

MARCH ROAD

A605

WISBECH ROAD

A605

ELDERNELL LANE

GROUNDS WAY

MARCH ROAD

8

Gravel House

Bridgehouse Farm

DUNCOMBE'S ROAD

7

Twenty Foot River (Drain)

MARCH ROAD

Three Horseshoes Farm

97

CROSS DROVE

Matlock Farm

Beggar's Bridge Farm

PH

LC

LC

6

Beggars Bridge

RED BARN

RED BARN

RIVER DROVE

Bates Farm

Turves

TURF DROVE

PE7

Smalleys Farm

5

WYPE DROVE

QUAKER'S DROVE

96

Poplartree Bridge

The Turves

Quakers Farm

Wype Doles

Smalleys Farm

BURNTHOUSE ROAD

4

Wypedoles Farm

Angle Corner Bridge

TURF DROVE

3

Bank Farm

Kisby Farm

Willow Farm

Anglebridge Farm

WEST FEN DROVE

95

BENWICK ROAD

Turves Style Farm

COCK BANK

Whittlesey Dike

2

Engine Farm

B1093

Bank Farm

Burnthouse Bridge

Burnt House Farm

1

BURNTHOUSE SIDINGS

Model Farm

Delavals Farm

94

PE9

A47 Leicester

7

01

COLLYWESTON
CROSS ROADS

6

A47(T)

A47(T)

Wittering
Lodge

Leicestershire STREET ATLAS

Collyweston
Great Wood

Easton
Hornstocks

5

Wittering
Coppice

00

Cross
Leys Farm

Westhay
Farm

4

3

Westhay
Lodge

PE8

99

St John's
Wood Farm

Windpump

2

Law's
Lawn

1

98

Memorial

Vigo
Wood

8

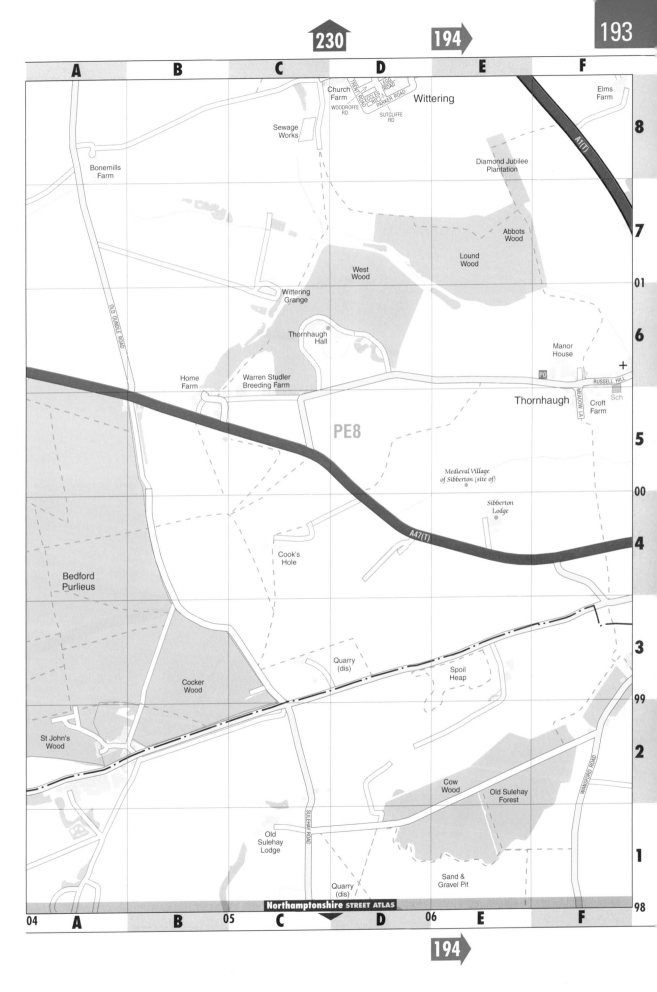

Elms Farm

Church Farm

WOODROFFE RD

Wittering

TRENT ROAD

ECCLES RD

LEGG ROAD

PARKER ROAD

SUTCLIFFE RD

Sewage Works

Diamond Jubilee Plantation

A1(T)

Bonemills Farm

Abbots Wood

Lound Wood

West Wood

Wittering Grange

OLD OUNDLE ROAD

Thornhaugh Hall

Manor House

PO

RUSSELL HILL

Sch

MEADOW LA

Home Farm

Warren Studler Breeding Farm

Thornhaugh

Croft Farm

PE8

Medieval Village of Sibberton (site of)

Sibberton Lodge

A47(T)

Bedford Purlieus

Cook's Hole

Quarry (dis)

Spoil Heap

Cocker Wood

St John's Wood

Cow Wood

Old Sulehay Forest

WANSFORD ROAD

SULEHAY ROAD

Old Sulehay Lodge

Sand & Gravel Pit

Quarry (dis)

8
7
01
6
5
00
4
3
99
2
1
98

04   A   B   05   C   D   06   E   F

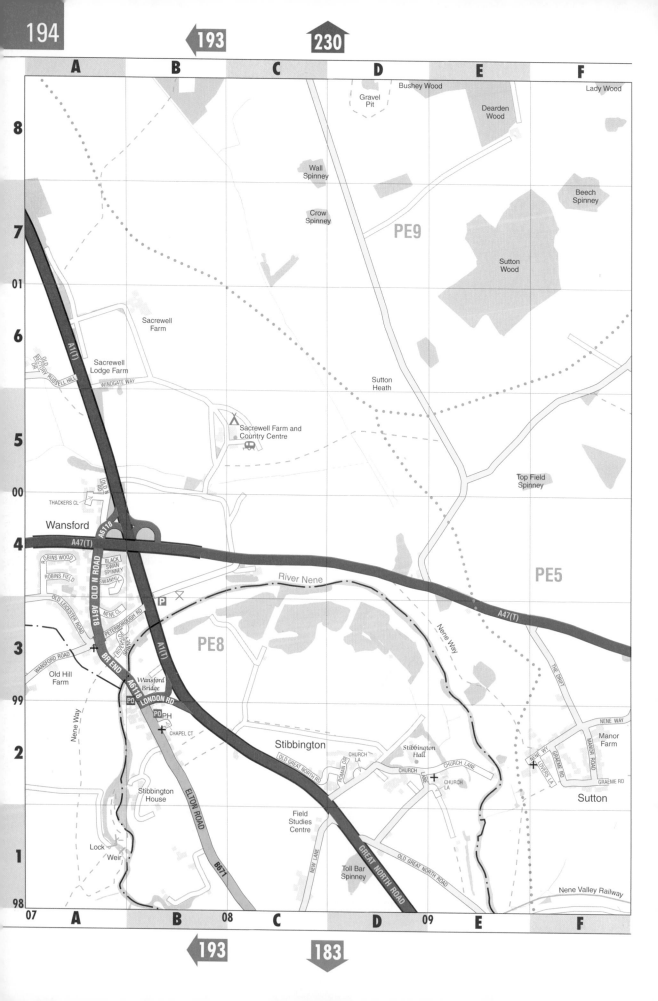

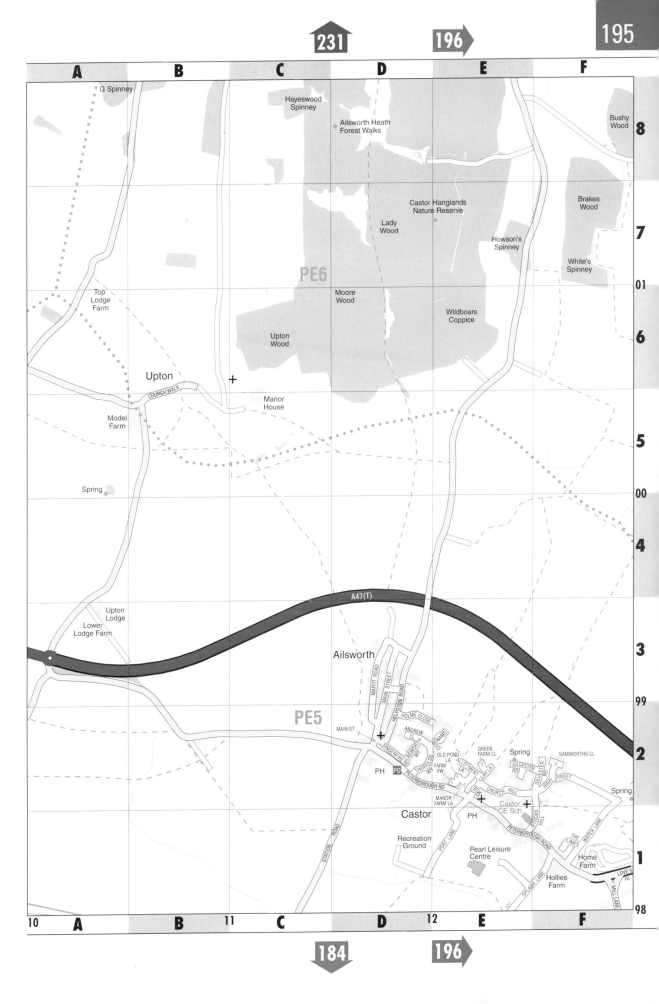

A   B   C   D   E   F

G Spinney

Hayeswood
Spinney

Bushy
Wood

8

Ailsworth Heath
Forest Walks

Castor Hanglands
Nature Reserve

Brakes
Wood

7

Lady
Wood

Howson's
Spinney

PE6

White's
Spinney

01

Moore
Wood

Wildboars
Coppice

6

Top
Lodge
Farm

Upton
Wood

Upton

CHURCH WALK

Manor
House

Model
Farm

5

Spring

00

4

A47(T)

Upton
Lodge

Ailsworth

3

Lower
Lodge Farm

MAFFIT ROAD

MAIN STREET

HELPSTON ROAD

99

PE5

MAIN ST

HOLME CLOSE

ANDREW
CL

BENMANS
CL

GREEN
FARM CL

Spring

SAMWORTHS CL

2

SINGERFIELD RD

AILSWORTH
VW

THOROLDS

OLD POND
LA

FARM
VW

ALLOTMENT
LA

CLAY LA

SILVESTER
RD

SILVESTER RD

HIGH STREET

Spring

PH

PO

PETERBOROUGH RD

MANOR
FARM LA

THE STOCKS

CHURCH HILL

Castor

Castor
CE Sch

Castor

PH

PORT LANE

PETERBOROUGH ROAD

THE STOCKS HILL

THE
LIMES

WATER LANE

Recreation
Ground

Pearl Leisure
Centre

Home
Farm

LOVE'S
HL

1

STATION ROAD

SPLASH LANE

Hollies
Farm

MILL LANE

98

10   A   B   11   C   D   12   E   F

A B C D E F

8

7

01

6

5

00

4

3

99

2

1

98

13 A B 14 C D 15 E F

Foster's Coppice

Bushy Wood

Home Farm

Burmer Wood

Marholm Lodges

GULLYMORE

Mucklands Wood

PE3

DURSBERRY

GULLYMORE

H.HOLMES

HY.HOLMES

WESTHAWE

BRETTON WAY

Spring

Spring

PARK FARM ROAD

WESTHAWE

WESTHAWE

Popple's Coppice

Belsize Farm

CASTOR ROAD

Grimeshaw Wood

Belsize Wood

Little Thistlemoor Wood

Thistlemoor Wood

Park Farm

PE6

Oldfield Pond

Stamford Plantations

Stamford Lodge

STAMFORD LODGE ROAD

PARK FARM ROAD

New Park Farm

Deer Park

Ten Acre Plantation

New Plantation

Salter's Wood

Milton Hall

STAMFORD LODGE ROAD

KENNELS ROAD

NICHOLAS TAYLOR GD 1
STAMPER ST 2
BRAILSFORD CL 3
JOROSE ST 4
TEANBY CT 5
CARTERS CL 6
THOMAS CL 7
GOODWOOD RD 8
BARNARD WY 9
HARRISON CL 10
LONGTHORPE HOUSE MEWS 11

MUSKHAM

MUSKHAM

SPRIGNAL

Recreation Ground

MARHOLM ROAD

Milton Park

WALKERS WY

RINGWOOD

Crickety Park

Sheep Park

HUNTSMANS GATE

LITTLE JOHNS CL

STRAIGHTS WY

MILTON WAY

ROBIN WOOD CL

BRETTON WAY

FERRY DRIVE

PETERBOROUGH DRIVE

Fitzwilliam

H

EGAR WY

HOLYWELL

PELHAM

PE3

Ferry House

MARHOLM ROAD

PE5

Heronry Drive

PEACOCK WY

LOSE AVENUE

PETERBOROUGH DR

Ferryhill Plantation

CH

A47(T)

River Nene

Bluebell Walk Plantation

P

Police HQ

VIRGINIA CL 1
CYPRESS CL 2
LONGTHORPE CL 3

Love's Hill

FERRY HILL

Little John

LOVE'S HILL

Robin Hood

P

Playing Fields

Mast

Thorpe Wood

NENE PARKWAY A1260

THORPE WOOD

PE2

Gunwade Lake

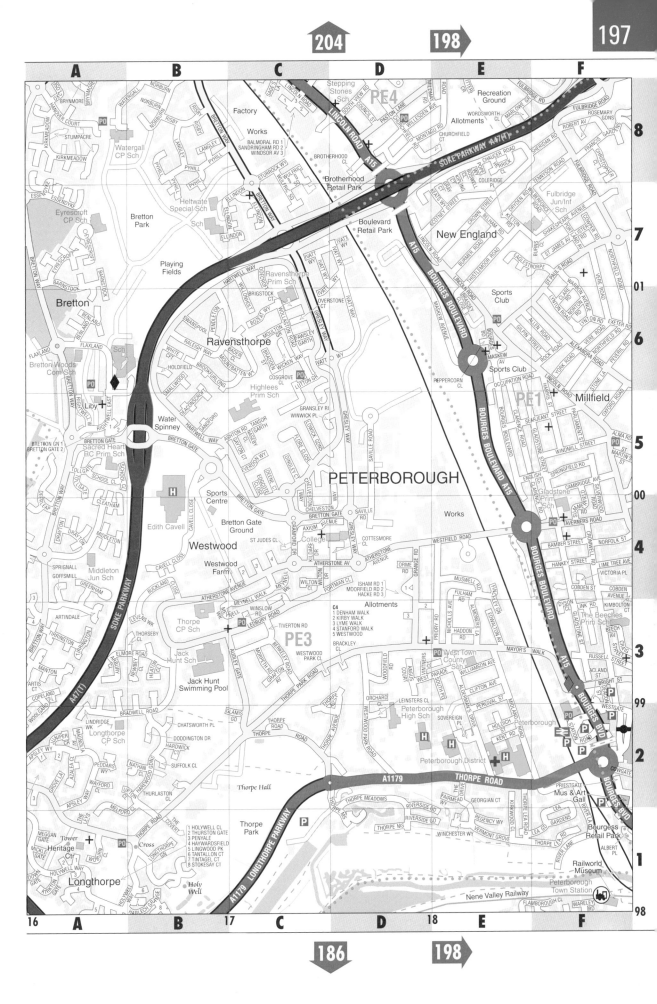

197
205

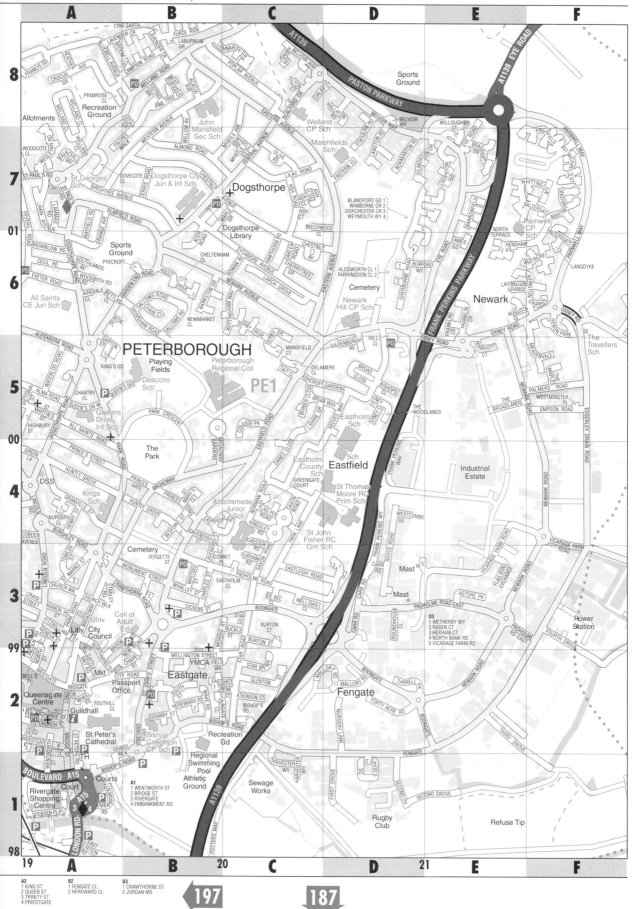

197
187

A2
1 KING ST
2 QUEEN ST
3 TRINITY ST
4 PRIESTGATE

B2
1 FENGATE CL
2 HEREWARD CL

B3
1 CRAWTHORNE ST
2 JORDAN MS

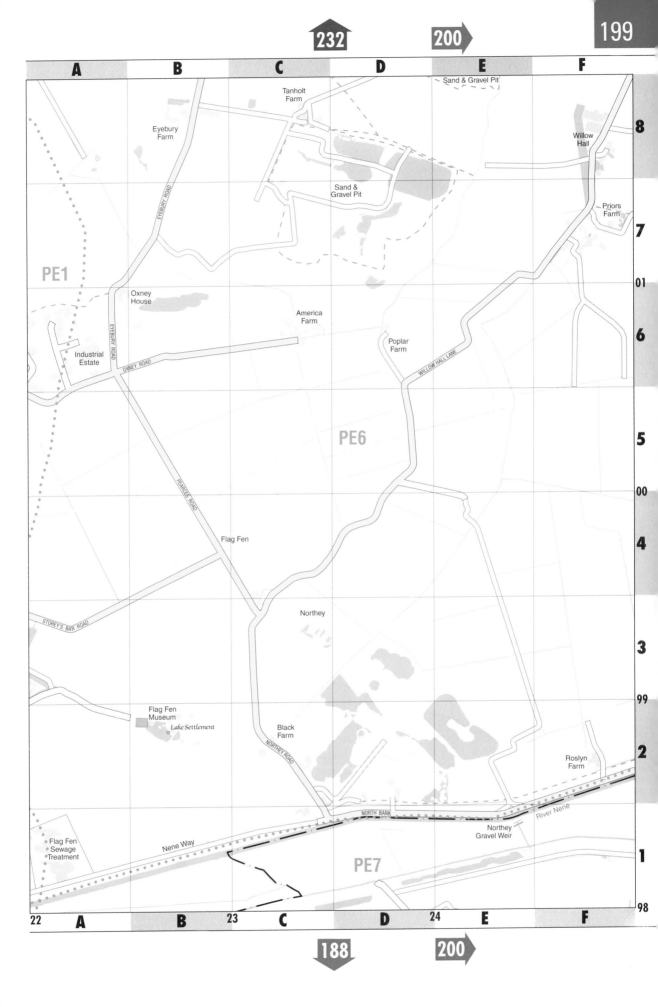

A **B** **C** **D** **E** **F**

Sand & Gravel Pit

Tanholt
Farm

Eyebury
Farm

Willow
Hall

8

Sand &
Gravel Pit

Priors
Farm

7

PE1

01

Oxney
House

America
Farm

6

Poplar
Farm

WILLOW HALL LANE

EYEBURY ROAD

OXNEY ROAD

Industrial
Estate

PE6

5

00

PEARCES ROAD

Flag Fen

4

STOREY'S BAR ROAD

Northey

3

99

Flag Fen
Museum

Lake Settlement

Black
Farm

NORTHEY ROAD

Roslyn
Farm

2

NORTH BANK

River Nene

Northey
Gravel Weir

Flag Fen
Sewage
Treatment

Nene Way

PE7

1

98

A **B** **C** **D** **E** **F**

22   23   24

199
232

A　B　C　D　E　F

8

The Gores

Gores Farm

THE CHASE

WHITTLESEY ROAD

7

Stone Bridge Corner

01

Stone Bridge

6

B1040

Prior's Fen

PE6

Teakettle Hall Farm

Teakettle Hall Bridge

5

NORTH SIDE

00

Priors Fen Farm

GREEN DROVE

4

Bank Farm

North Fen

LEVITT'S DROVE

Dog-in-a-Doublet Farm

North Side

Dog-in-a-Doublet Bridge

PH

Nature Reserve

3

Lock

Nene Way

LONG DROVE

The Wash

99

Gull Farm

NORTH BANK

Plum Tree Farm

Delph Dike

B1040

2

River Nene

Little Bridge

PE7

Morton's Leam

EAST DELPH

1

COMMON DV

Spring

YARWELLS HEADLANDS

98

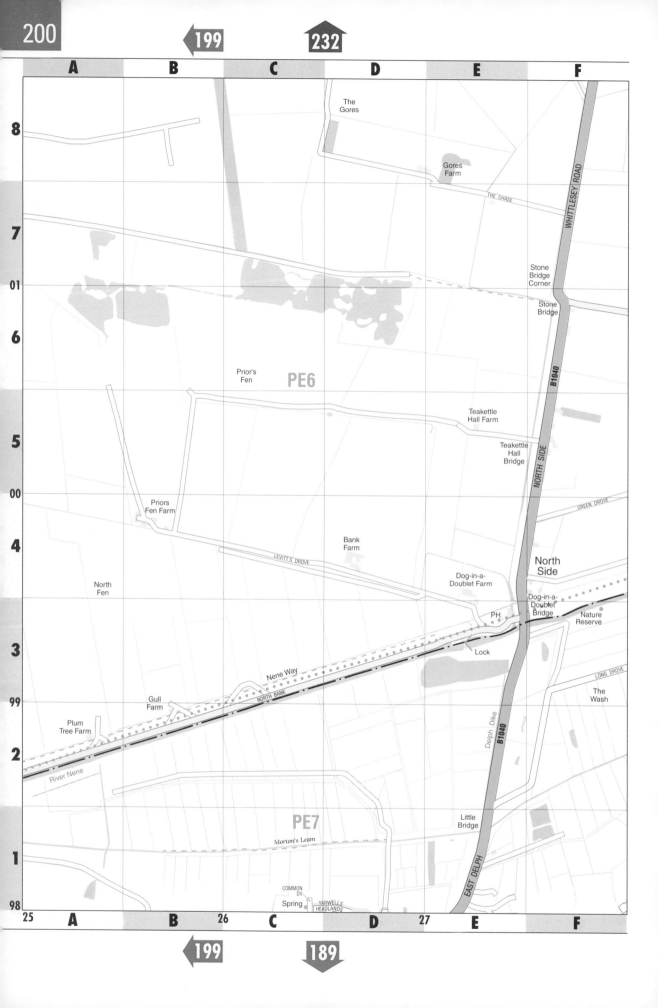

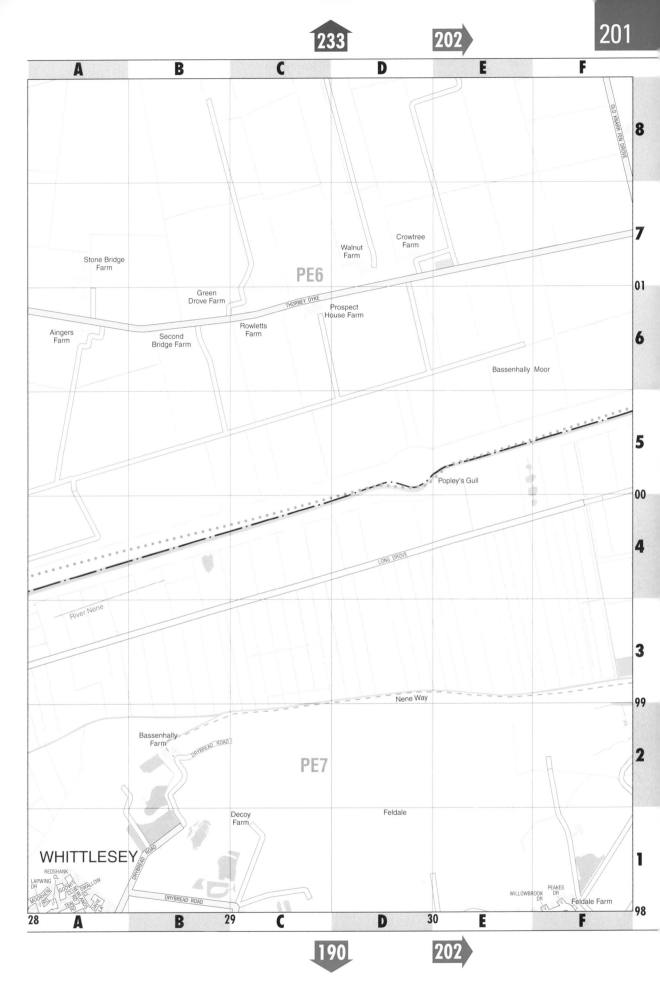

A B C D E F

8

7

01

6

5

00

4

3

99

2

1

98

Old Knarr Fen Drive

Crowtree
Farm

Walnut
Farm

Stone Bridge
Farm

PE6

Green
Drove Farm

THORNEY DYKE

Prospect
House Farm

Rowletts
Farm

Aingers
Farm

Second
Bridge Farm

Bassenhally Moor

Popley's Gull

LONG DROVE

River Nene

Nene Way

Bassenhally
Farm

DRYBREAD ROAD

PE7

Decoy
Farm

Feldale

WHITTLESEY

REDSHANK
CL
LAPWING
DR
MOORHEN
RD
GODWIT
CL
TEAL
RD
SWALLOW
CL
CURLEWLANDS
RD
LAPWING
LANE

DRYBREAD ROAD

DRYBREAD ROAD

WILLOWBROOK
DR

PEAKES
DR

Feldale Farm

28 A B 29 C D 30 E F

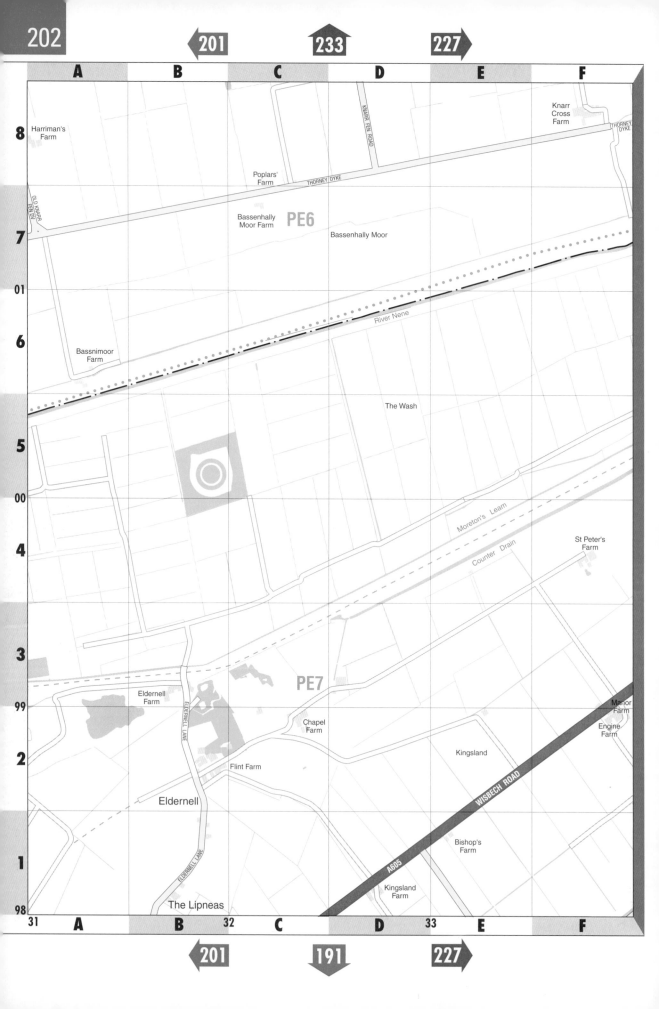

201
233
227

A B C D E F

8 Harriman's Farm

Knarr Cross Farm

THORNEY DYKE

Poplars' Farm

THORNEY DYKE

KNARR FEN ROAD

Bassenhally Moor Farm

PE6

Bassenhally Moor

7

OLD KNARR FEN DV

01

River Nene

6 Bassnimoor Farm

The Wash

5

Moreton's Leam

00

Counter Drain

St Peter's Farm

4

3

Eldernell Farm

PE7

99 Manor Farm

Chapel Farm

Engine Farm

Kingsland

2 Flint Farm

WISBECH ROAD

Eldernell

ELDERNELL LANE

A605

Bishop's Farm

1 Kingsland Farm

98 The Lipneas

31 A B 32 C D 33 E F

201
191
227

A B C D E F

8 7 05 6 5 04 4 3 03 2 1 02

The Elms

Helpston LC

GLINTON ROAD B1443

HELPSTON ROAD B1443

Howe Farm

MAIN ROAD

A15

OAK RD
CHESTNUT CL
ELM CR
BEECH RD
LINCOLN RD
NORTH FEN RD
HIGH ST PO

HELPSTON ROAD

WESTBOURNE DRIVE

RECTORY LA

Peakirk cum Glinton CE Prim Sch

PH

Websters Farm

PEAKIRK ROAD

B1443

Arthur Mellows Village Coll

Glinton

SCHOOL LA
RECTORY GD
SADDLERS
WEBSTERS CL

PEMBROKE GR
CLARENDON WY
THE WILLOWS

LINCOLN ROAD

ST BENEDICT'S CL

SCOTTS RD
WALKER RD
ASHBURN CL
HOLMES RD

VERGETTE RD
WILMORE ROAD

NEAVERSON RD

B1443

A15

A15

Coal Yard

Woodcroft LC

WOODCROFT ROAD

College Cott

PE6

Pasture Farm

WATERWORKS LANE

WERRINGTON PARKWAY

A15

LINCOLN ROAD

Cannon's Barn Farm

GASCOIGNE

OLD TOWN RD

LINCOLN RD

DAVID'S CLOSE

MAXHAM'S GREEN ROAD

Maxham Farm

Woodcroft Castle

Woodcroft Lodge

Steeping Wood

Marholm LC

Gate House Farm

HURN ROAD

PAPYRUS ROAD

Pellett Hall

WOODCROFT ROAD

Hayes Wood

Belham Wood

Ramshill Cottages

STAMFORD ROAD

Poplar Farm

Marholm Farm

Pocock's Wood

Peterborough Crematorium

STAXTON CL

Manor Farm

WATER END

Marholm

WALTON ROAD

Mucklands Wood

MOWBRAY RD

PH

CASTOR RD

DUNSBERRY

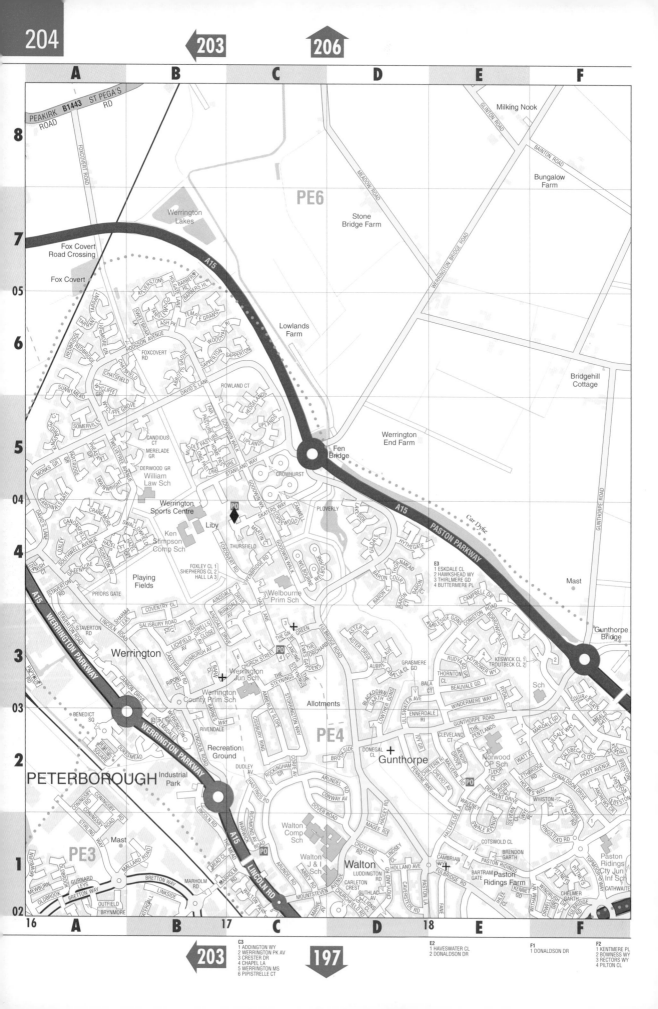

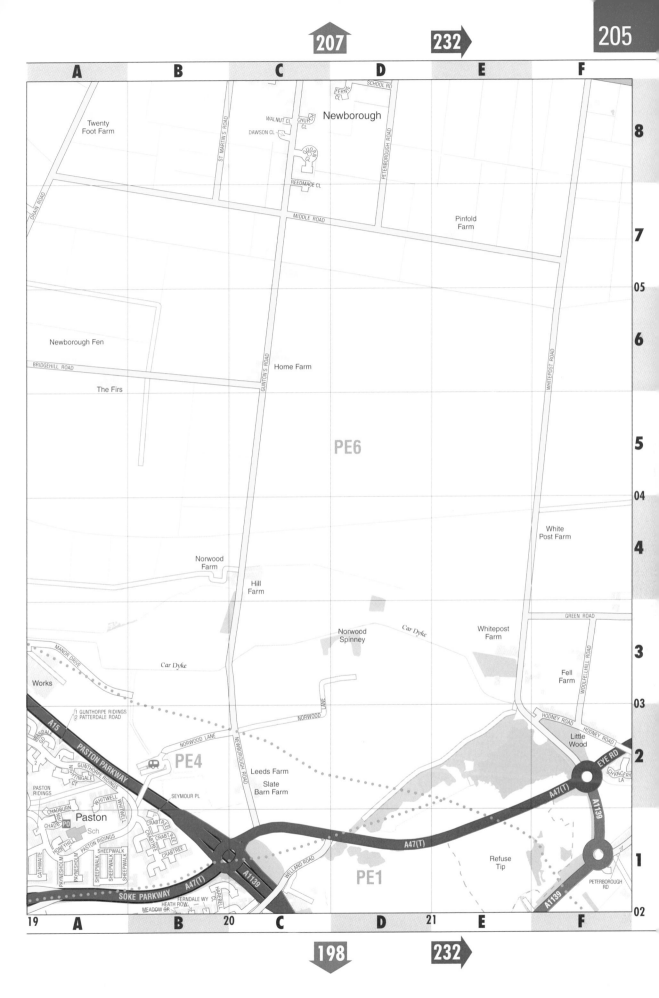

A B C D E F

8
7
05
6
5
04
4
3
03
2
1
02

Twenty
Foot Farm

Newborough

SCHOOL RD
FERN CL
WALNUT CL
CHURCH CL
DAWSON CL
CHURCH CL
REEDMACE CL

ST MARTIN'S ROAD

PETERBOROUGH ROAD

MIDDLE ROAD

Pinfold
Farm

DRAIN ROAD

Newborough Fen

BRIDGEHILL ROAD

The Firs

GUNTON'S ROAD

Home Farm

WHITEPOST ROAD

PE6

White
Post Farm

Norwood
Farm

Hill
Farm

Norwood
Spinney

Car Dyke

Whitepost
Farm

GREEN ROAD

WOOLFELL HILL ROAD

Fell
Farm

Car Dyke

MANOR DRIVE

Car Dyke

NORWOOD LANE

HODNEY ROAD

HODNEY ROAD

Little
Wood

EYE RD

CHANCERY LA

Works

1 Gunthorpe Ridings
2 Patterdale Road

NORWOOD LANE

NORWOOD ROAD

A15

PASTON PARKWAY

PE4

Leeds Farm

Slate
Barn Farm

SEYMOUR PL

A47(T)

A1139

PASTON
RIDINGS
GUNTHORPE RIDINGS
NIGHTINGALE CT
WHITWELL
CHADBURN
CHADS PD
HONEYHILL
PAYNESHOLM
CATHWAITE
PAYNESHOLM
WHITWELL
CRABTREE
CRABTREE
CRABTREE
CRABTREE
Paston
Sch
SHEEPWALK
SHEEPWALK
SHEEPWALK
SHEEPWALK
PASTON RIDINGS

SOKE PARKWAY

A47(T)

A1139

WELLAND ROAD

FERNDALE WY
HAREBELL CL
HEATH ROW
MEADOW GR

PE1

Refuse
Tip

A47(T)

A1139

PETERBOROUGH
RD

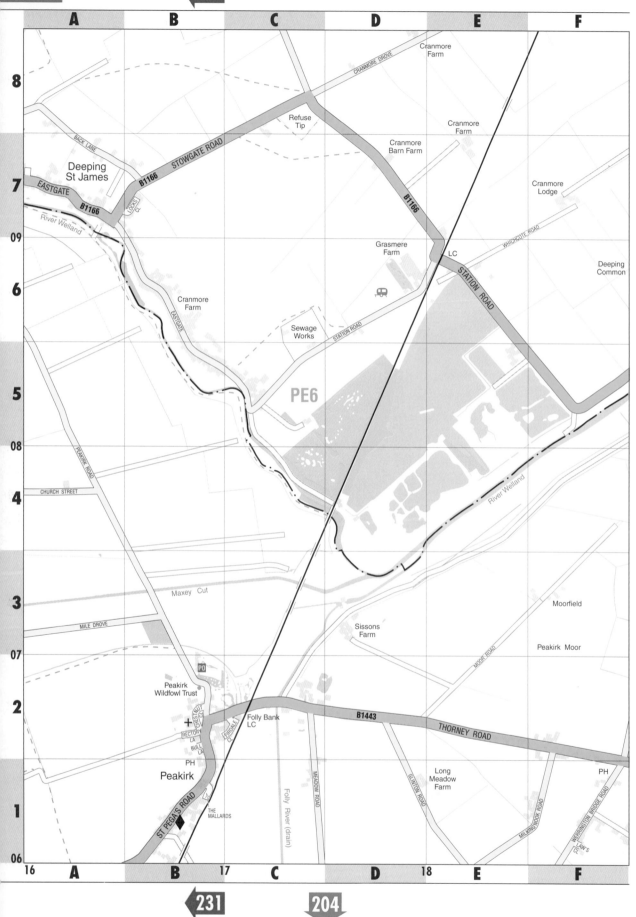

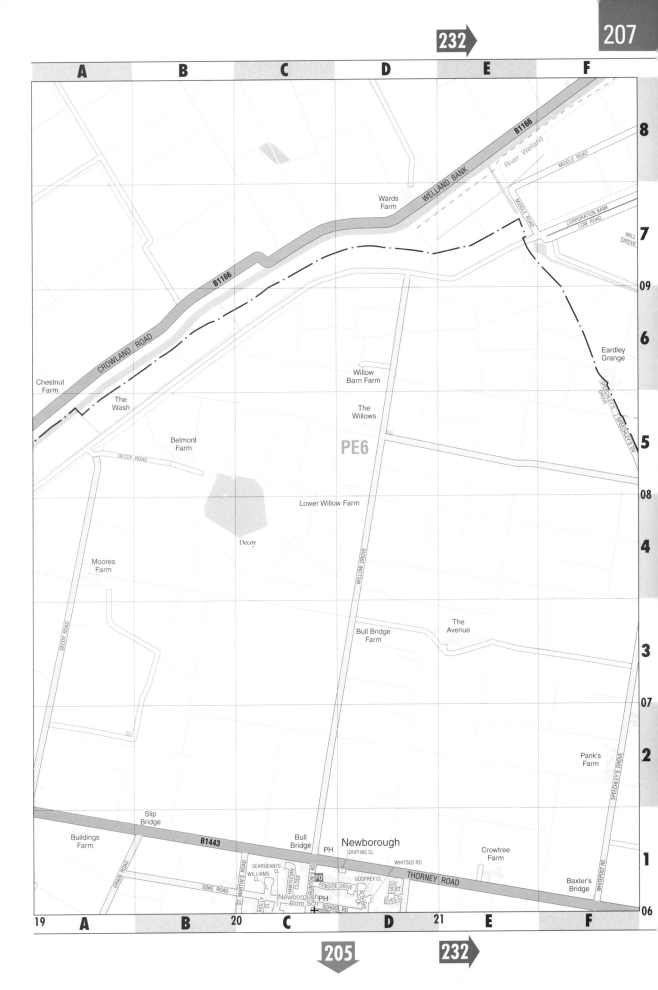

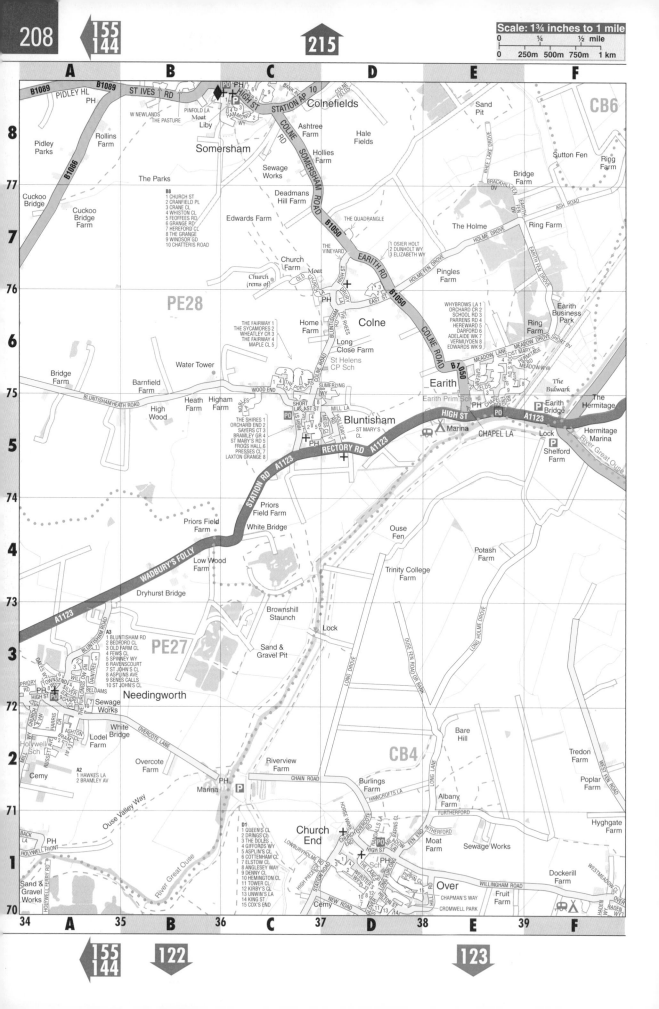

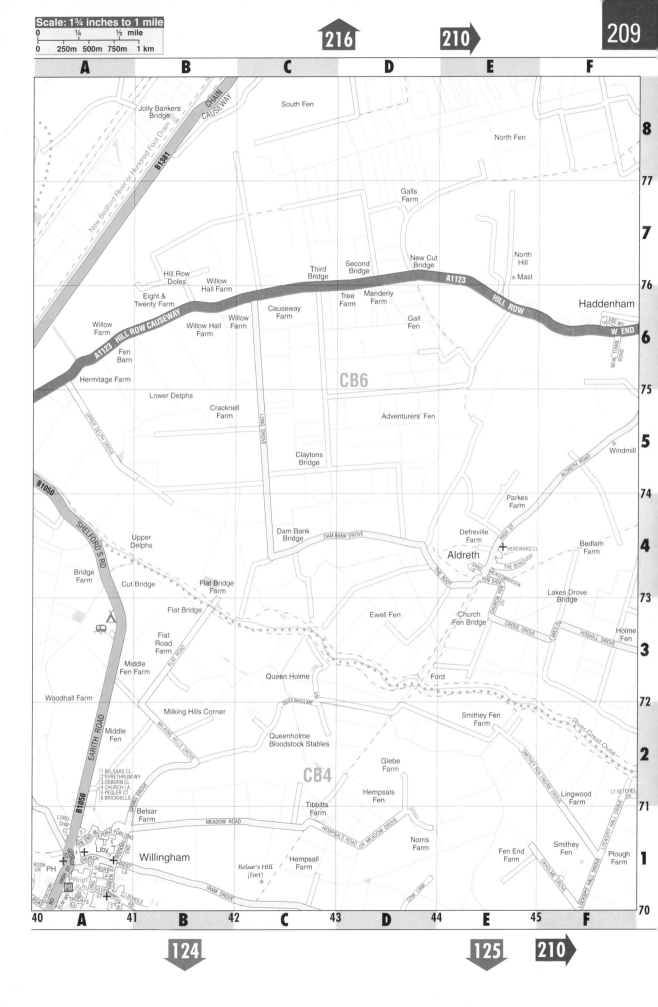

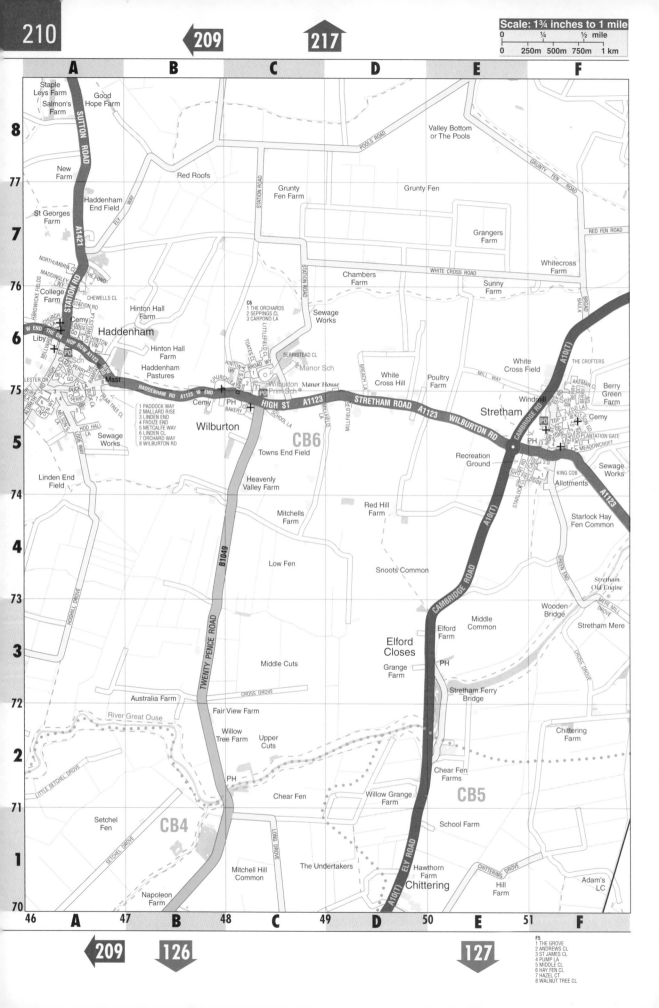

Scale: 1¾ inches to 1 mile

0   ¼   ½ mile
0   250m 500m 750m 1 km

A B C D E F

8 Staple
Leys Farm
Salmon's Farm
Good Hope Farm
SUTTON ROAD
New Farm
Valley Bottom or The Pools
GRUNTY FEN ROAD

77 Red Roofs
Station Road
Grunty Fen Farm
Grunty Fen
RED FEN ROAD

7 St Georges Farm
Haddenham End Field
ELY WAY
A1421
Grangers Farm
Whitecross Farm
A10(T)

76 College Farm
Station Rd
Hinton Hall Farm
STATION RD
CHEWELLS CL
White Cross Road
Chambers Farm
Sewage Works
Sunny Farm
BROAD BAULK

6 Haddenham
Liby
THE GN
Hinton Hall Farm
Haddenham Pastures
C6
1 THE ORCHARDS
2 SEPPINGS CL
3 CARPOND LA
LITTLEFIELD CL
BROAD WY
Berristead Cl
Manor Sch
BREACH LA
White Cross Field
THE CROFTERS
AKEMAN CL
Berry Green Farm
Windmill
MILL WAY

75 Mast
HADDENHAM RD A1123 W END
Cemy
PH
BAKERY
Wilburton Manor House
PO Prim Sch
HIGH ST A1123
STRETHAM ROAD A1123
White Cross Hill
Poultry Farm
WILBURTON RD
Stretham
CAMBRIDGE RD
PO
PH
PLANTATION GATE
MEADOWCROFT
Cemy

5 Sewage Works
Wilburton
CB6
Towns End Field
Heavenly Valley Farm
Recreation Ground
KING COB
Allotments
Sewage Works
A1123

74 Linden End Field
Mitchells Farm
Red Hill Farm
GREEN END
Starlock Hay Fen Common

4 HIGHHILL DROVE
B1049
Low Fen
Snoots Common
CAMBRIDGE ROAD
A10(T)
Stretham Old Engine
Wooden Bridge
MERE MILL DROVE
Stretham Mere

73 TWENTY PENCE ROAD
Middle Cuts
Middle Common
Elford Farm
CROSS DROVE
Stretham Mere

3 Australia Farm
CROSS DROVE
Elford Closes
PH
Grange Farm
Chittering Farm

72 River Great Ouse
Fair View Farm
Willow Tree Farm
Upper Cuts
Stretham Ferry Bridge

2 LITTLE SETCHEL DROVE
PH
Chear Fen
Willow Grange Farm
Chear Fen Farms
CB5

71 Setchel Fen
CB4
Chear Fen
LONG DROVE
School Farm
CHITTERING DROVE

1 SETCHEL DROVE
Mitchell Hill Common
The Undertakers
ELY ROAD
Hawthorn Farm
Chittering
Hill Farm
Adam's LC

70 Napoleon Farm
A10(T)

46 A 47 B 48 C 49 D 50 E 51 F

F5
1 THE GROVE
2 ANDREWS CL
3 ST JAMES CL
4 PUMP LA
5 MIDDLE CL
6 HAY FEN CL
7 HAZEL CT
8 WALNUT TREE CL

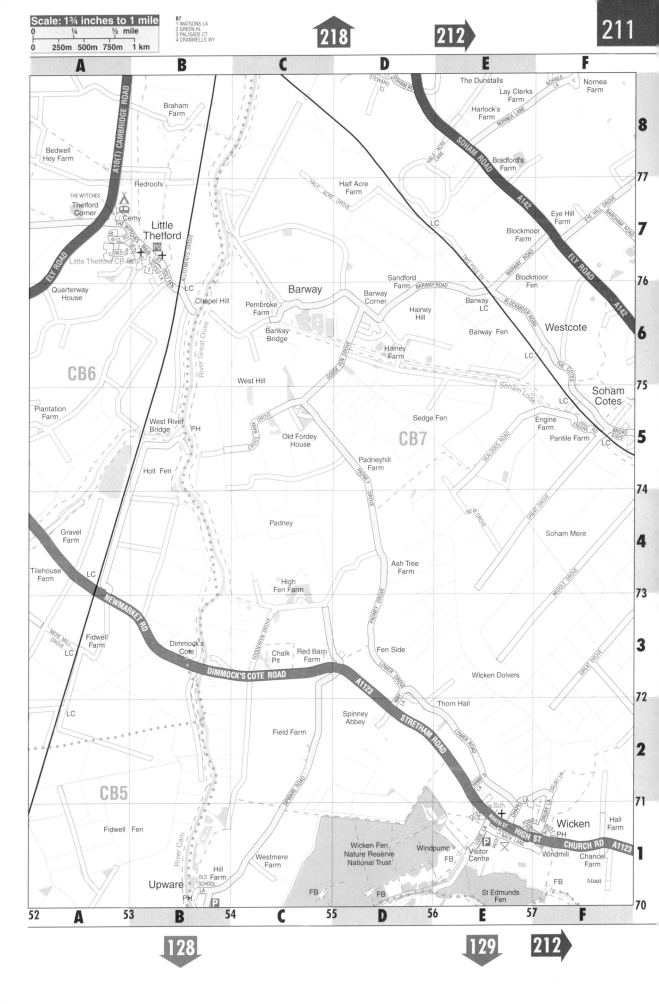

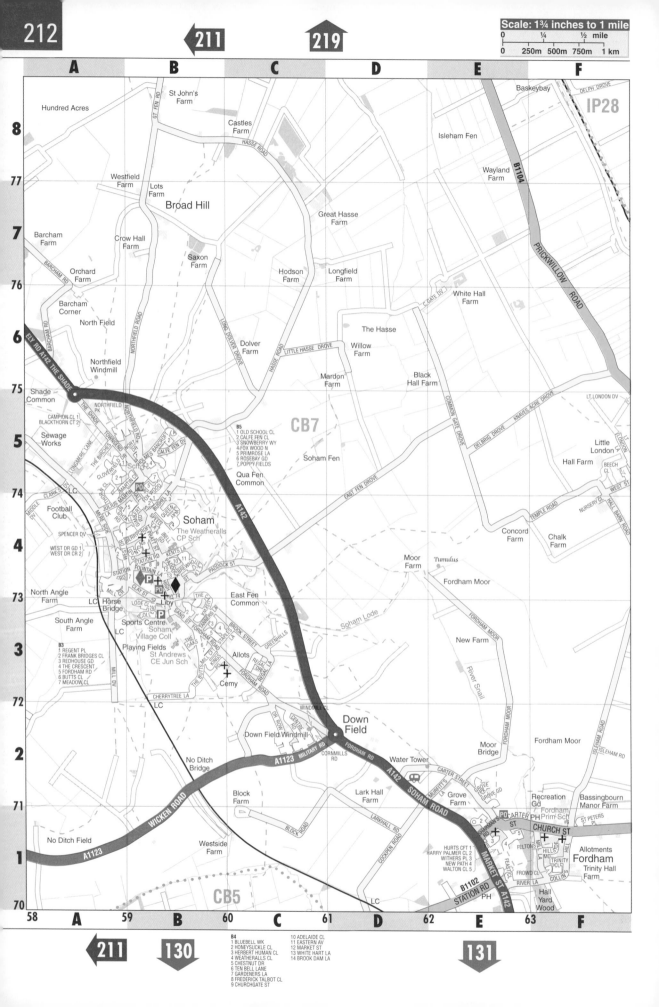

211
219

Scale: 1¾ inches to 1 mile

0   ¼   ½   mile
0   250m 500m 750m 1 km

A   B   C   D   E   F

IP28
DELPH DROVE

Baskeybay

8

Hundred Acres

St John's Farm

Castles Farm

Isleham Fen

77

Westfield Farm

Lots Farm

Broad Hill

Wayland Farm

HASSE ROAD

B1104

7

Barcham Farm

Crow Hall Farm

Great Hasse Farm

Saxon Farm

PRICKWILLOW ROAD

76

Orchard Farm

Hodson Farm

Longfield Farm

White Hall Farm

BARCHAM RD

Barcham Corner

North Field

C.GATE DV

The Hasse

NORTHFIELD ROAD

6

ELY RD A142 THE SHADE

Northfield Windmill

Dolver Farm

LONG DOLVER DROVE

Willow Farm

Black Hall Farm

Shade Common

75

LITTLE HASSE DROVE

HASSE ROAD

Mardon Farm

LT. LONDON DV

COMMON GATE DROVE

Campion CL 1
Blackthorn Ct 2

NORTHFIELD PK

CB7

KNAVES ACRE DROVE

BELBRIG DROVE

Little London

5

Sewage Works

THE SHADE

B5
1 OLD SCHOOL CL
2 CALFE FEN CL
3 SNOWBERRY WY
4 FOX WOOD N
5 PRIMROSE LA
6 ROSEBAY GD
7 POPPY FIELDS

Soham Fen

Hall Farm

BEECH CL

WEST ST

LONGMERE LANE

THE BIRCHES

CALFE FEN DV

LT LONDON RD

CLARK'S ST

LC

Qua Fen Common

EAST FEN DROVE

74

Football Club

Scholmes

TEMPLE ROAD

NURSERY CL

HALL BARN ROAD

MIDDLE DV

Soham

The Weatheralls CP Sch

Concord Farm

Chalk Farm

4

WEST DR GD 1
WEST DR CR 2

SPENCER DV

STATION RD

Moor Farm

Tumulus

KENTS LA

FOUNTAIN

Fordham Moor

73

North Angle Farm

LC Horse Bridge

Liby

East Fen Common

FORDHAM MOOR

MILL DR

South Angle Farm

Sports Centre

Soham Village Coll

Soham Lode

New Farm

River Snail

3

B3
1 REGENT PL
2 FRANK BRIDGES CL
3 REDHOUSE GD
4 THE CRESCENT
5 FORDHAM RD
6 BUTTS CL
7 MEADOW CL

Playing Fields

St Andrews CE Jun Sch

Allots

BROOK STREET

GREENHILLS

REGAL DR

KINGS

THE OAKS

FORDHAM ROAD

Cemy

FORDHAM MOOR

ISLEHAM ROAD

Fordham Moor

CHERRYTREE LA

LC

2

WICKEN ROAD

A1123

No Ditch Bridge

Down Field Windmill

WINDMILL CL

CORNMILLS RD

MILITARY RD

A1123

Down Field

Water Tower

A142 SOHAM ROAD

CARTER STREET

Moor Bridge

Fordham Moor

GROVE DROVE

71

Block Farm

Lark Hall Farm

Grove Farm

Recreation Gd

GROVE CL

GROVE GD

Fordham Prim Sch

Bassingbourn Manor Farm

ST PETERS PL

CARTER PH

PO

CHURCH ST

1

No Ditch Field

A1123

Westside Farm

BLOCK RD

LARKHALL RD

COOPER RD

HURTS CFT 1
HARRY PALMER CL 2
WITHERS PL 3
NEW PATH 4
WALTON CL 5

FELTONS

HILLS

Allotments

Fordham

Trinity Hall Farm

FROWD CL

River LA

COLLINS

Hall Yard Wood

CB5

B1102

STATION RD

MARKET ST A142

70

58   A   59   B   60   C   61   D   62   E   63   F

211
130
131

B4
1 BLUEBELL WK
2 HONEYSUCKLE CL
3 HERBERT HUMAN CL
4 WEATHERALLS CL
5 CHESTNUT DR
6 TEN BELL LANE
7 GARDENERS LA
8 FREDERICK TALBOT CL
9 CHURCHGATE ST
10 ADELAIDE CL
11 EASTERN AV
12 MARKET ST
13 WHITE HART LA
14 BROOK DAM LA

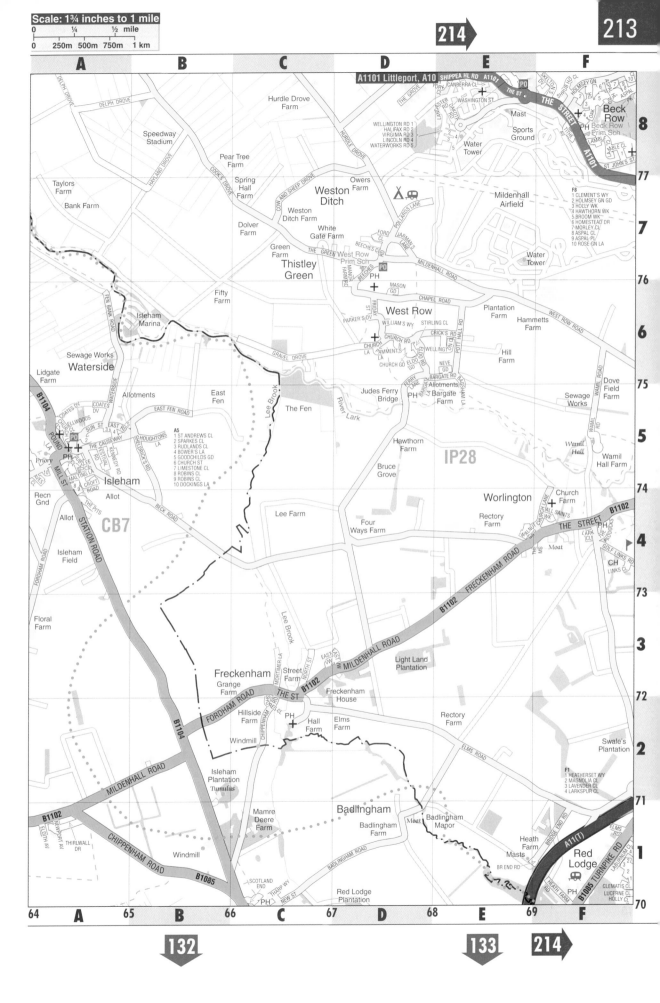

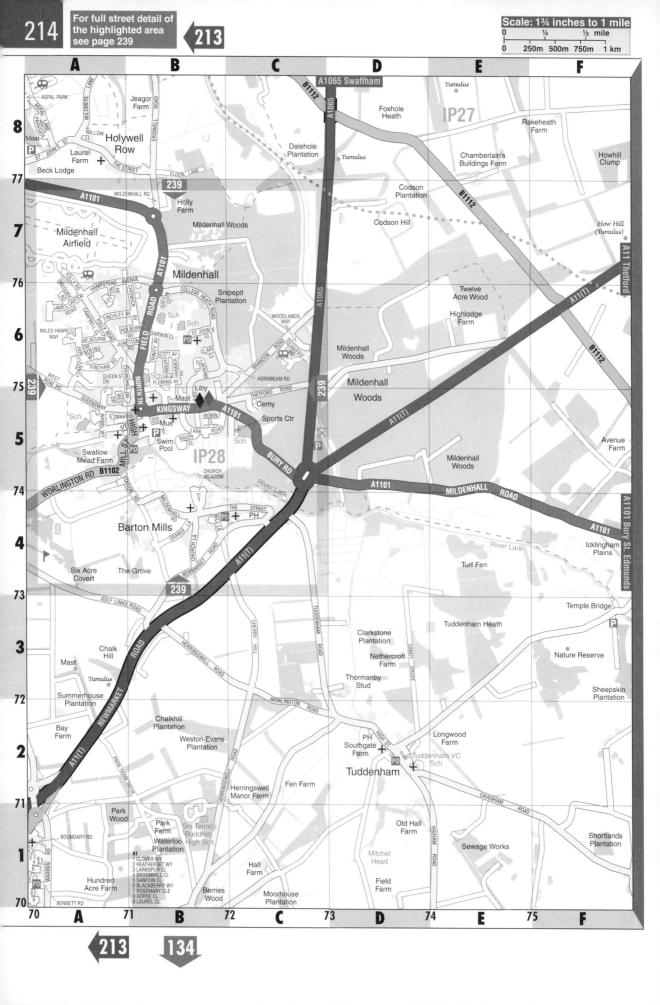

214

For full street detail of
the highlighted area
see page 239

213

Scale: 1¾ inches to 1 mile

0   ¼   ½   mile
0 250m 500m 750m 1 km

A   B   C   D   E   F

8

↙ ASPAL PARK
Moat
P
St John's St
Laurel Farm
Beck Lodge

WILDMERE LANE
WILLOW CL
Holywell Row
THE STREET

Jeagor Farm

ERISWELL ROAD
ELDON LANE

239

Dalehole Plantation

B1112

A1065 Swaffham

A1065

Foxhole Heath

Tumulus

IP27

Rakeheath Farm

Howhill Clump

77

A1101
MILDENHALL RD

Holly Farm

Tumulus

Codson Plantation

Chamberlain's Buildings Farm

B1112

How Hill ('Tumulus')

A11 Thetford

7

Mildenhall Airfield

Mildenhall Woods

Mildenhall

Codson Hill

76

FOLLY RD
GREGORY
JAMES CARTER ROAD
MILES HAWK WAY

HAMPSTEAD AVENUE
CHISWICK
FINCHLEY AV
HOLBORN AV
MELBOURNE
BOEING WY
DR
FINCHAM RD

FIELD ROAD
A1101

GIRTON
COLLEGE HEATH ROAD
Snipepit Plantation

Sch
Sch

DARWIN CL
TRINITY AV
SCOTT AV
HAMMER
FLEMING AV

ST JOHN'S CL
PO
CLARE CL

DOWNING CL

BRANDON ROAD
WOODLANDS WAY

QUAKERS
HORNBEAM RD

Twelve Acre Wood

Highlodge Farm

A1065

A11(T)

B1112

6

75

WEST ROW RD
239

QUEENSWAY
WARW WY
Sch

COMET DR
QUEEN'S DR

NORTH TR
HIGH ST
MILL ST
Cross
PO
Swallow Mead Farm

KINGSWAY
Mast
Liby
Mus
P
Swim. Pool
ROBIN CL
LARK CL
RAVEN CL

A1101
Cemy
Sports Ctr
Sch

THETFORD ROAD

Mildenhall Woods

P

Mildenhall Woods

Avenue Farm

5

WORLINGTON RD
B1102

STATION RD
MILDENHALL RD

IP28
CHURCH MEADOW
River Lark

BURY RD

A1101   MILDENHALL   ROAD

A1101

74

Barton Mills

NEWMARKET
A11(T)

CHURCH LA
GRANGE LA
BELL LA
PO
THE STREET
PH

A11(T)

River Lark

Icklingham Plains

A1101 Bury St. Edmunds

4

Six Acre Covert

The Grove

239

GOLF LINKS ROAD

Turf Fen

73

3

Mast

Chalk Hill

Tumulus

Summerhouse Plantation

Bay Farm

ROAD
NEWMARKET
A11(T)

HERRINGSWELL ROAD

CHERRY HILL

TUDDENHAM ROAD

Clarkstone Plantation

Nethercroft Farm

Thormanby Stud

SANDY DROVE

Tuddenham Heath

Nature Reserve

Temple Bridge
P

Sheepskin Plantation

72

Chalkhill Plantation

Weston-Evans Plantation

Herringswell Manor Farm

Fen Farm

WORLINGTON   ROAD

PH
Southgate Farm
PO
Tuddenham

HIGH ST

Tuddenham VC Sch

Longwood Farm

CAVENHAM   ROAD

HIGHAM ROAD

2

Park Wood

Park Farm

Waterloo Plantation

Shi Tennoji Buddhist High Sch

A1
1 CLOVER WY
2 HEATHERSET WY
3 LARKSPUR CL
4 BROOMHILL CL
5 SANFOIN CL
6 BLACKBERRY WY
7 ROSEMARY CLE
8 GORSE CL
9 LAUREL CL

Hall Farm

Moorhouse Plantation

Mitchel Head

Field Farm

Old Hall Farm

Sewage Works

Shortlands Plantation

1

BOUNDARY RD

WARREN RD

Hundred Acre Farm

BENNETT RD

PO

Berries Wood

70

70   A   71   B   72   C   73   D   74   E   75   F

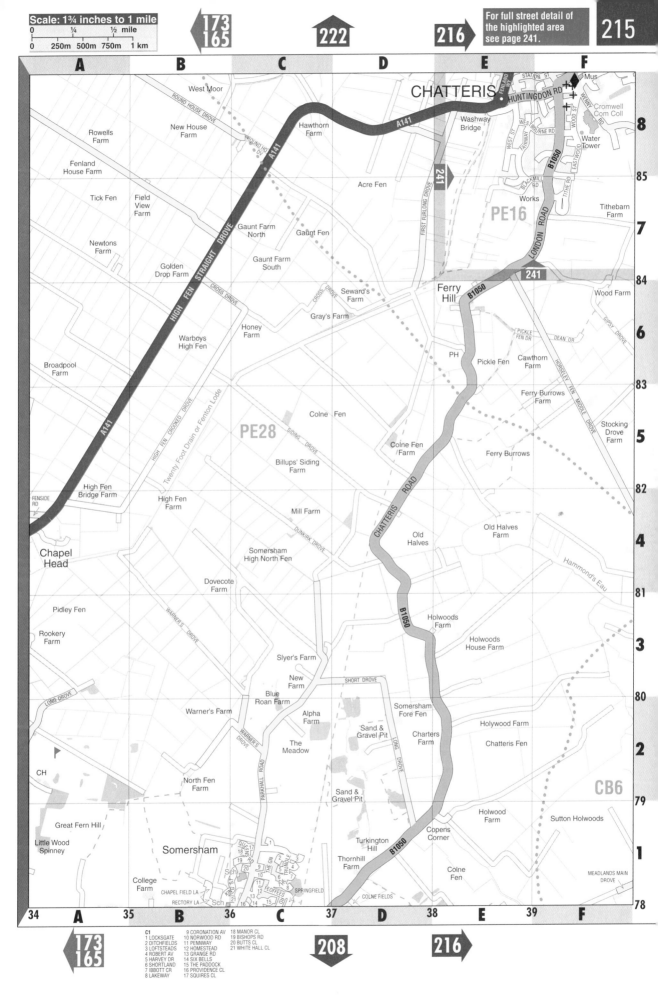

Scale: 1¾ inches to 1 mile

0 ¼ ½ mile
0 250m 500m 750m 1 km

173 165

222

216

For full street detail of the highlighted area see page 241.

215

CHATTERIS

West Moor

ROUND HOUSE DROVE

ROUND HO

New House Farm

Hawthorn Farm

A141

STATION ST
FENLAND HWY
HUNTINGDON RD

Mus

Cromwell Com Coll

Washway Bridge

WEST ST
WEST BOURNE RD
FAIRWAY

WOOD ST
WENNY RD
EASTWOOD

Water Tower

B1050

PE16

Works

BLACKMILL RD
TITHE RD

Rowells Farm

Fenland House Farm

Tick Fen

Field View Farm

Acre Fen

241

85

Tithebarn Farm

Newtons Farm

Gaunt Farm North

Gaunt Fen

Gaunt Farm South

7

Golden Drop Farm

HIGH FEN STRAIGHT DROVE

A141

CROSS DROVE

Seward's Farm

84

Ferry Hill

LONDON ROAD

241

B1050

Wood Farm

Honey Farm

Gray's Farm

CROSS DROVE

PH

GIPSY DROVE

Warboys High Fen

6

Pickle Fen

PICKLE FEN DR
DEAN DR

Cawthorn Farm

HORSELEY FEN MIDDLE DR

Broadpool Farm

A141

HIGH FEN CROOKED DROVE

Twenty Foot Drain or Fenton Lode

PE28

Colne Fen

SIDING DROVE

83

Ferry Burrows Farm

Stocking Drove Farm

5

Colne Fen Farm

Ferry Burrows

FENSIDE RD

High Fen Bridge Farm

High Fen Farm

Billups' Siding Farm

CHATTERIS ROAD

82

Old Halves

Old Halves Farm

4

Mill Farm

DUNKIRK DROVE

Somersham High North Fen

Hammond's Eau

81

Chapel Head

Dovecote Farm

Holwoods Farm

B1050

Pidley Fen

WARNER'S DROVE

Holwoods House Farm

3

Rookery Farm

Slyer's Farm

New Farm

SHORT DROVE

Somersham Fore Fen

LONG DROVE

Holywood Farm

80

CH

Warner's Farm

WARNER'S DROVE

Blue Roan Farm

Alpha Farm

Sand & Gravel Pit

Charters Farm

Chatteris Fen

2

North Fen Farm

PARKHALL ROAD

The Meadow

Sand & Gravel Pit

CB6

79

Great Fern Hill

Somersham

QUEEN... ST

Springfield

Turkington Hill

Copens Corner

B1050

Holwood Farm

Sutton Holwoods

1

Little Wood Spinney

College Farm

CHAPEL FIELD LA
RECTORY LA
KING ST
Sch
FEOFFEES CL

Thornhill Farm

Colne Fen

COLNE FIELDS

MEADLANDS MAIN DROVE

78

C1
1 LOCKSGATE
2 DITCHFIELDS
3 LOFTSTEADS
4 ROBERT AV
5 HARVEY DR
6 SHORTLAND
7 IBBOTT CR
8 LAKEWAY
9 CORONATION AV
10 NORWOOD RD
11 PENNWAY
12 HOMESTEAD
13 GRANGE RD
14 SIX BELLS
15 THE PADDOCK
16 PROVIDENCE CL
17 SQUIRES CL
18 MANOR CL
19 BISHOPS RD
20 BUTTS CL
21 WHITE HALL CL

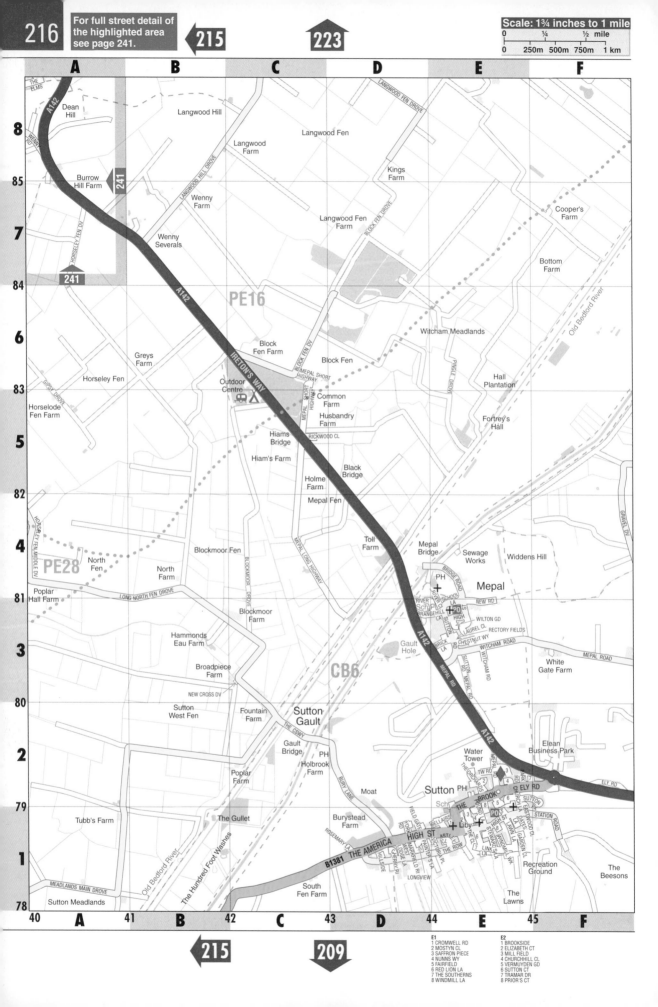

216

For full street detail of the highlighted area see page 241.

← 215

↑ 223

Scale: 1¾ inches to 1 mile
0   ¼   ½ mile
0   250m 500m 750m 1 km

A   B   C   D   E   F

THE ELMS

A142

Dean Hill

8

Burrow Hill Farm

← 241

Langwood Hill

Langwood Farm

Langwood Fen

Kings Farm

Cooper's Farm

85

HORSELEY FEN DV

241

Wenny Farm

Langwood Fen Farm

Langwood Fen Farm

BLOCK FEN DRIVE

Bottom Farm

7

Wenny Severals

LANGWOOD HILL DRIVE

A142

84

PE16

IRETON'S WAY

Witcham Meadlands

Old Bedford River

6

Greys Farm

Block Fen Farm

Block Fen

BLOCK FEN DV

Hall Plantation

PINGLE DROVE

GIPSY DROVE

Horseley Fen

Outdoor Centre

MEPAL SHORT HIGHWAY

Common Farm

Fortrey's Hall

83

Horselode Fen Farm

Hiams Bridge

RICKWOOD CL

Husbandry Farm

5

Hiam's Farm

Holme Farm

Black Bridge

82

Mepal Fen

MEPAL LONG HIGHWAY

HORSELEY FEN MIDDLE DV

Toll Farm

Mepal Bridge

Sewage Works

Widdens Hill

4

PE28

North Fen

North Farm

Blockmoor Fen

BLOCKMOOR DROVE

PH

Mepal

GRAVEL DV

81

Poplar Hall Farm

LONG NORTH FEN DROVE

Blockmoor Farm

River Sch

BRIDGE ROAD

NEW RD

BRANGEHILL LA

PO

HIGH

WILTON GD

SCHOOL LA

LAUREL CL

RECTORY FIELDS

3

Hammonds Eau Farm

Broadpiece Farm

NEW CROSS DV

Gault Hole

CB6

BRICK LA

CHESTNUT WY

SUTTON RD

MERAL RD

WITCHAM RD

White Gate Farm

MEPAL ROAD

WITCHAM ROAD

80

Sutton West Fen

Fountain Farm

Sutton Gault

THE CSWY

MEPAL RD

A142

2

Gault Bridge

PH Holbrook Farm

BURY LANE

Water Tower

THE CROSSWAYS

TW RD

PARK RD

Elean Business Park

ELY RD

79

Poplar Farm

Moat

Sutton PH

FIELD GATE RD

BELLAIRS

THE BROOK

Sch

Lby

CHURCH LA

SUTTON

STATION ROAD

1

Tubb's Farm

The Gullet

Burystead Farm

ROSEMARY LA

HIGH ST

HILLSIDE

MARKFIELD RD

CHERRY RD

PAUNTLEY STA

THE ROW

PO

STEWARTS LA

WOODE LA

GARDEN CL

LAWN LA

LINKS LA

Recreation Ground

The Beesons

78

Sutton Meadlands

MEADLANDS MAIN DROVE

Old Bedford River

The Hundred Foot Washes

THE AMERICA

B1381

South Fen Farm

LONGVIEW

The Lawns

40   A   41   B   42   C   43   D   44   E   45   F

E1
1 CROMWELL RD
2 MOSTYN CL
3 SAFFRON PIECE
4 NUNNS WY
5 FAIRFIELD
6 RED LION LA
7 THE SOUTHERNS
8 WINDMILL LA

E2
1 BROOKSIDE
2 ELIZABETH CT
3 MILL FIELD
4 CHURCHHILL CL
5 VERMUYDEN GD
6 SUTTON CT
7 TRAMAR DR
8 PRIOR'S CT

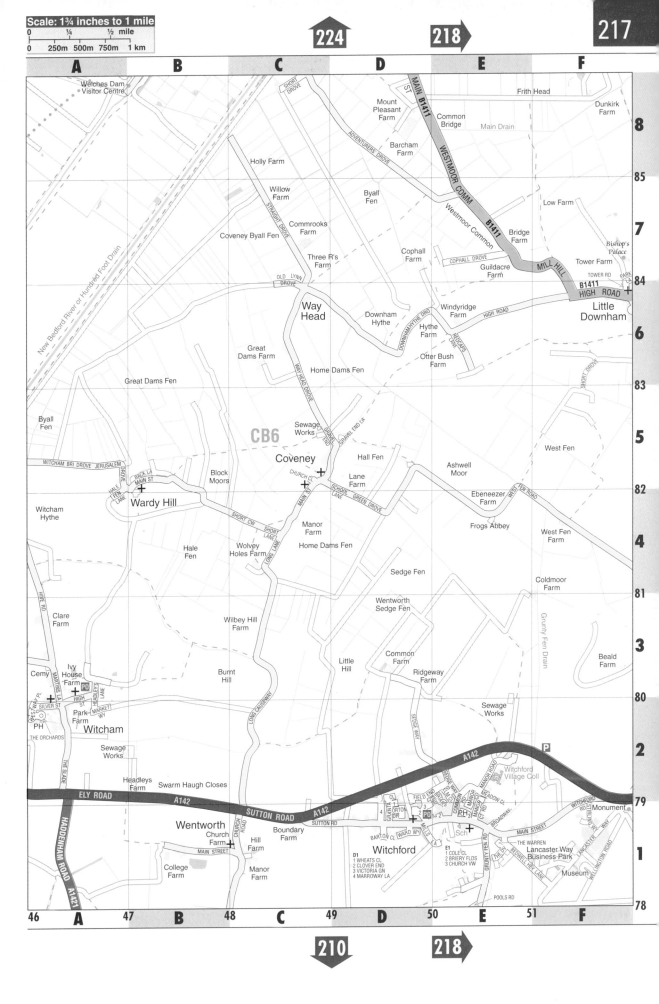

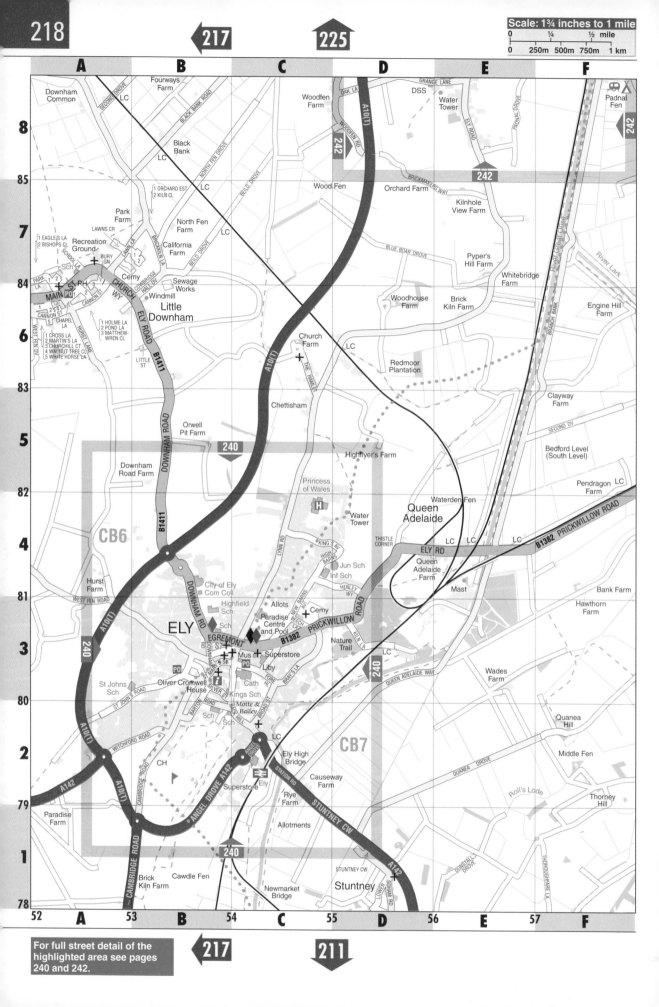

Scale: 1¾ inches to 1 mile

0   ¼   ½ mile
0 250m 500m 750m 1 km

Top border: A B C D E F

Left numbers: 8 85 7 84 6 83 5 82 4 81 3 80 2 79 1 78

Downham Common
Fourways Farm
Black Bank Road
Black Bank
LC
1 ORCHARD EST
2 KILN CL
North Fen Farm
California Farm
Park Farm
LAWNS CR
Recreation Ground
1 EAGLE'S LA
2 BISHOPS CL
Cemy
BURY GN
PH
MAIN ST
PO
CHURCH WY
ELY ROAD
Windmill
Little Downham
Sewage Works
1 CROSS LA
2 MARTIN'S LA
3 CHURCHILL CT
4 WALNUT TREE CL
5 WHITE HORSE LA
1 HOLME LA
2 POND LA
3 MATTHEW-WREN CL
LITTLE ST
B1411
WEST FEN DV
CHAPEL LA
CANNON ST
SCH LA
LAWN LA
BRICKKILN LA
COMBRIDGE HALL DV
HURST LANE
PARK LA

Woodfen Farm
OAK LA
DSS
Water Tower
PADNAL D DRIVE
Padnal Fen
242
WOODFEN RD
242
A10(T)
GRANGE LANE
ELY ROAD
Wood Fen
Brickmakers Way
242
Orchard Farm
Kilnhole View Farm
BLUE BOAR DROVE
Pyper's Hill Farm
Whitebridge Farm
River Lark
River Great Ouse
Engine Hill Farm
Church Farm
LC
THE HAMLET
Woodhouse Farm
Brick Kiln Farm
BRANCH BANK
Redmoor Plantation
Chettisham
Clayway Farm
SECOND DV
Bedford Level (South Level)
Orwell Pit Farm
240
Pendragon Farm
LC
Downham Road Farm
Highflyer's Farm
Waterden Fen
Queen Adelaide
B1382 PRICKWILLOW ROAD
Princess of Wales
H
Water Tower
THISTLE CORNER
ELY RD
LC LC LC
CB6
B1411
DOWNHAM ROAD
LYNN RD
KING'S AV
HIGH BARNS
Jun Sch
Inf Sch
Queen Adelaide Farm
Mast
Bank Farm
Hurst Farm
WEST FEN ROAD
City of Ely Com Coll
Highfield Sch
Allots
NEW BARNS
HENLEY WY
BEECH
PRICKWILLOW ROAD
Hawthorn Farm
ELY
EGREMONT ST
Paradise Centre and Pool
Cemy
Superstore
Nature Trail
KILN LA
LC
Wades Farm
A10(T)
240
Mus
Liby
PO
Superstore
BRAY'S LA
B1382
Sch
St Johns Sch
Oliver Cromwell House
Cath
Kings Sch
FORE HL
240
QUEEN ADELAIDE WAY
Quanea Hill
PO
OLIVER ST
BARTON ROAD
Motte & Bailey
BROAD ST
HILL
Sch Sch
ST JOHN'S RD
WITCHFORD ROAD
CAMBRIDGE ROAD
LC
CB7
Ely High Bridge
QUANEA DROVE
Middle Fen
CH
A142
ANGEL DROVE
Superstore
Ely
STATION RD
Causeway Farm
Roll's Lode
Thorney Hill
A10(T)
Paradise Farm
Rye Farm
STUNTNEY CW
DUNSTALL'S DROVE
THOROUGHFARE LA
Brick Kiln Farm
Cawdle Fen
240
Allotments
A142
SOHAM RD
Newmarket Bridge
Stuntney CW
Stuntney

Bottom border: 52 A 53 B 54 C 55 D 56 E 57 F

For full street detail of the highlighted area see pages 240 and 242.

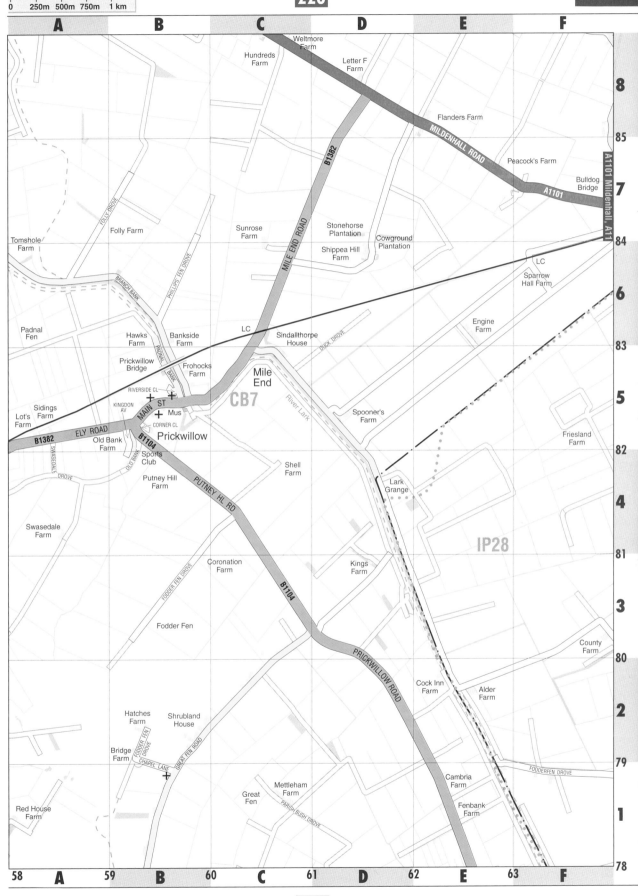

A   B   C   D   E   F

8

85

7

84

6

83

5

82

4

81

3

80

2

79

1

78

MILDENHALL ROAD

A1101

A1101 Mildenhall, A11

Weltmore Farm

Hundreds Farm

Letter F Farm

Flanders Farm

Peacock's Farm

Bulldog Bridge

B1382

MILE END ROAD

FOLLY DROVE

PHILLIPS FEN DROVE

BRANCH BANK

Folly Farm

Tomshole Farm

Sunrose Farm

Stonehorse Plantation

Shippea Hill Farm

Cowground Plantation

LC

Sparrow Hall Farm

Engine Farm

Padnal Fen

Hawks Farm

Bankside Farm

LC

Sindallthorpe House

DUCK DROVE

Prickwillow Bridge

Frohocks Farm

Mile End

PADNAL BANK

Sidings Farm

Lot's Farm

Hatches Farm

RIVERSIDE CL

KINGDON AV

MAIN ST

Mus

CORNER CL

CB7

River Lark

Spooner's Farm

Friesland Farm

B1382

ELY ROAD

Old Bank Farm

B1104

Prickwillow

OLD BANK

SWASEDALE DROVE

Sports Club

Putney Hill Farm

PUTNEY HL RD

Shell Farm

Lark Grange

IP28

Swasedale Farm

FODDER FEN DROVE

Coronation Farm

Kings Farm

Fodder Fen

B1104

PRICKWILLOW ROAD

County Farm

Cock Inn Farm

Alder Farm

FODDER FEN DROVE

CHAPEL LANE

GREAT FEN ROAD

Shrubland House

Bridge Farm

Cambria Farm

FODDERFEN DROVE

Red House Farm

Great Fen

Mettleham Farm

PARISH BUSH DROVE

Fenbank Farm

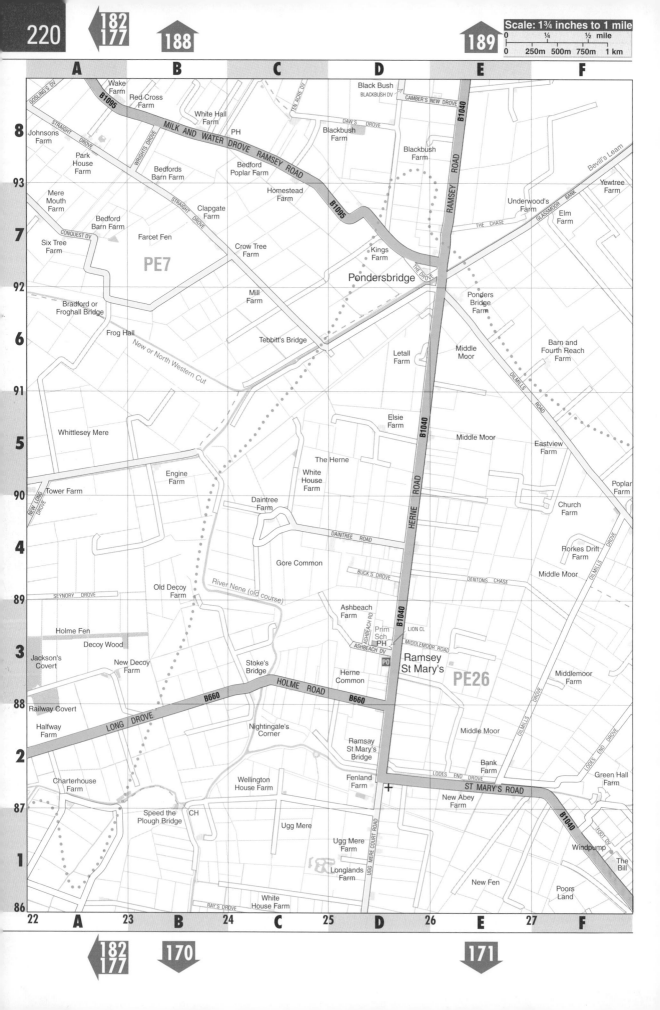

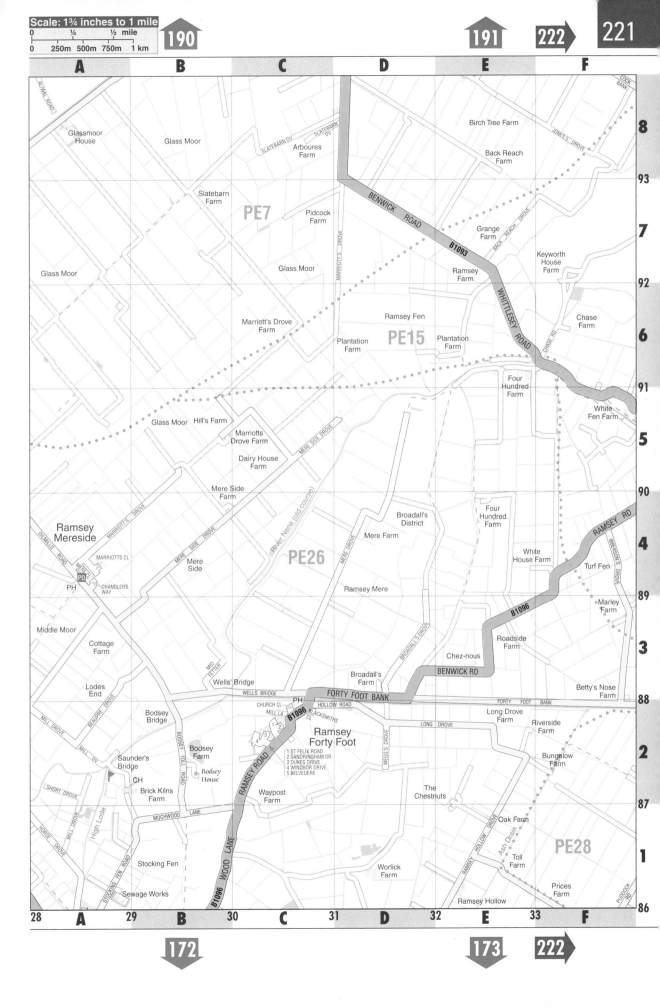

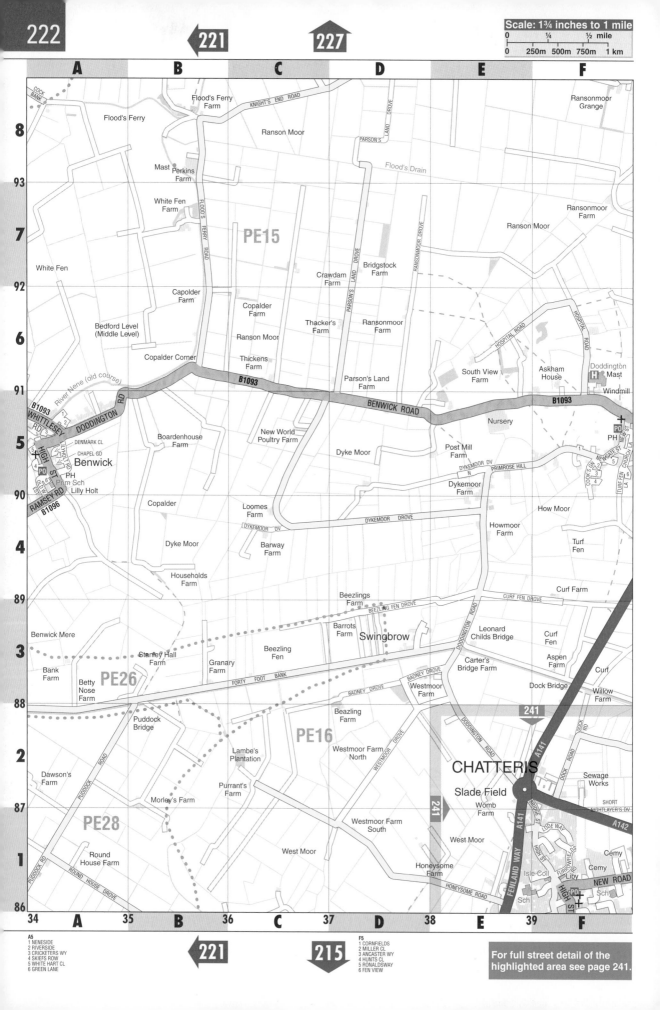

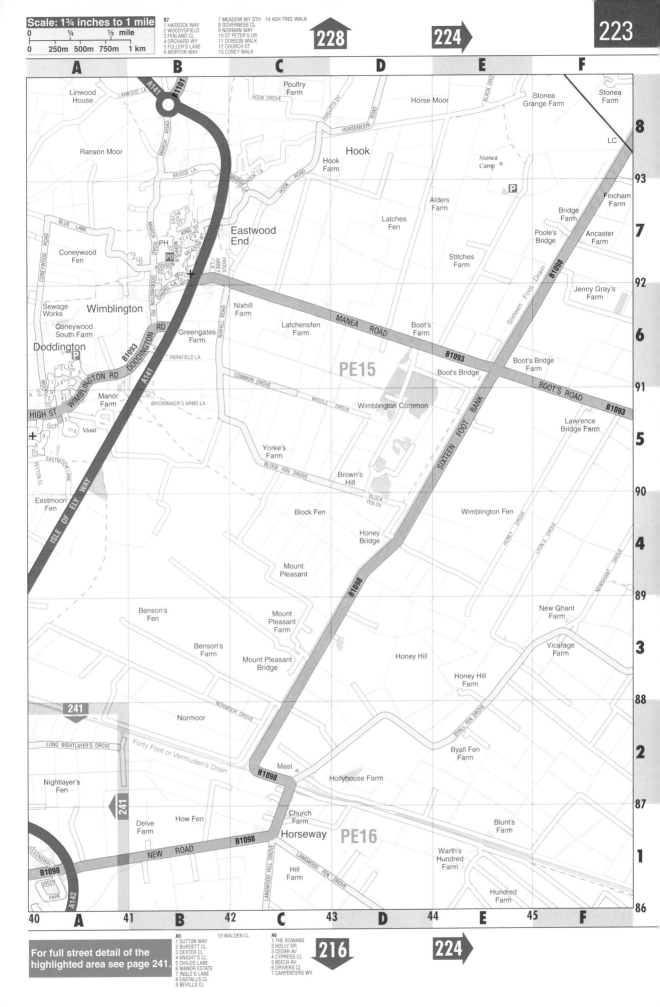

Scale: 1¾ inches to 1 mile
0   ¼   ½ mile
0   250m 500m 750m 1 km

B7
1 HASSOCK WAY
2 WOODYSFIELD
3 FENLAND CL
4 ORCHARD WY
5 FULLER'S LANE
6 MORTON WAY
7 MEADOW WY STH
8 GOVERNESS CL
9 NORMAN WAY
10 ST PETER'S DR
11 DOBSON WALK
12 CHURCH ST
13 CONEY WALK
14 ASH TREE WALK

228   224

A   B   C   D   E   F

Linwood House
Ranson Moor
Coneywood Fen
Blue Lane
Coneywood South Farm
Sewage Works
Wimblington
Doddington
Manor Farm
Moat
Sch
Eastmoor Lane
Eastmoon Fen
Peyton Cl
High St
Brickmaker's Arms La
Isle of Ely Way

Poultry Farm
Hook Drove
Hook
Hook Farm
Eastwood End
Hook La
Bridge La
King St
Eaton
Norfolk
Addison Rd
Chapel La
Rhogs Abbey La
Nixhill Rd
Nixhill Farm
Greengates Farm
Parkfield La
Common Drove
Middle Drove
Yorke's Farm
Block Fen Drove
Block Fen
Mount Pleasant
Block Fen Dv
Brown's Hill
Honey Bridge

Horse Moor
Horsemoor Road
Latches Fen
Alders Farm
Stitches Farm
Manea Road
Boot's Farm
B1093
Boot's Bridge
Wimblington Common
PE15
Sixteen Foot Bank

Stonea Grange Farm
Stonea Farm
LC
Stonea Camp
P
Fincham Farm
Bridge Farm
Poole's Bridge
Ancaster Farm
Sixteen Foot Drain
B1098
Jenny Gray's Farm
Boot's Bridge Farm
Boot's Road
Lawrence Bridge Farm
B1093

Benson's Fen
Benson's Farm
Mount Pleasant Farm
Mount Pleasant Bridge
Normoor
Normoor Drove
241
Long Nightlayer's Drove
Forty Foot or Vermuden's Drain
Nightlayer's Fen
241
Delve Farm
How Fen
New Road
B1098
Horseway
B1098
Church Farm
Hill Farm
Langwood Hill Drove
Langwood Fen Drove
PE16
Mast
Hollyhouse Farm

Honey Drove
Lyon's Drove
Newghant Drove
New Ghant Farm
Vicarage Farm
Honey Hill
Honey Hill Farm
Byall Fen Drove
Byall Fen Farm
Blunt's Farm
Warth's Hundred Farm
Hundred Farm

Queensway
B1098
Green Park
A142

8   93   7   92   6   91   5   90   4   89   3   88   2   87   1   86

40   A   41   B   42   C   43   D   44   E   45   F

For full street detail of the highlighted area see page 241.

A5
1 SUTTON WAY
2 BURDETT CL
3 DEXTER CL
4 KNIGHT'S CL
5 CHILDS LANE
6 MANOR ESTATE
7 INGLE'S LANE
8 EASTALLS CL
9 BEVILLS CL
10 WALDEN CL

A6
1 THE ROWANS
2 HOLLY DR
3 CEDAR AV
4 CYPRESS CL
5 BEECH AV
6 DRIVERS CL
7 CARPENTERS WY

216   224

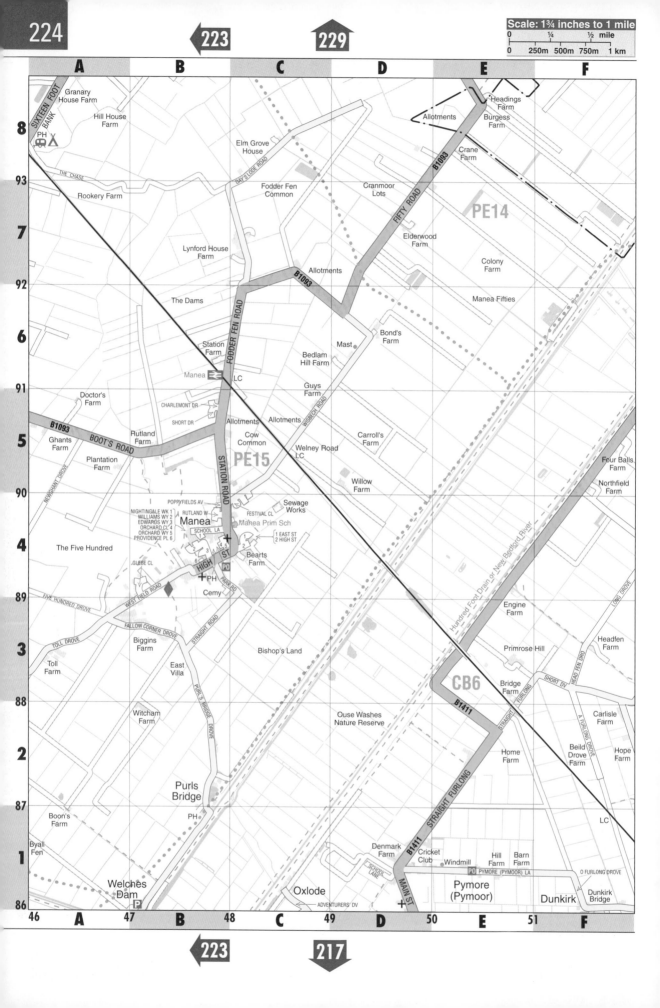

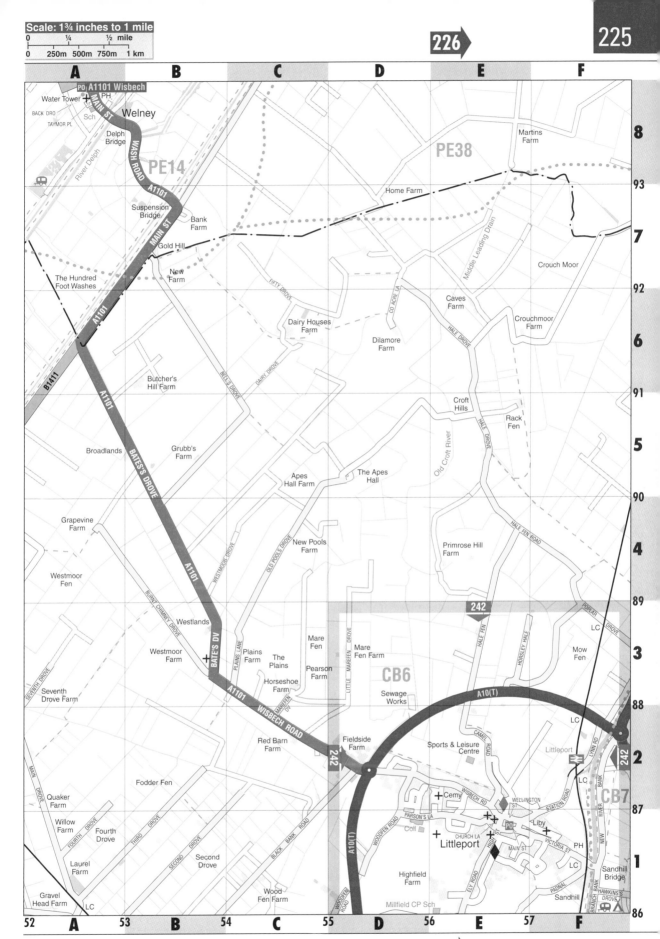

A   B   C   D   E   F

8

93

7

92

6

91

5

90

4

89

3

88

2

87

1

86

PO A1101 Wisbech
Water Tower
PH
BACK DRO
Welney
TAYMOR PL
Sch
Delph Bridge
River Delph
PE14
WASH ROAD
A1101
MAIN ST
Suspension Bridge
Bank Farm
Gold Hill
New Farm
The Hundred Foot Washes
A1101
B1411
FIFTY DROVE
Dairy Houses Farm
CO ACRE LA
Caves Farm
Crouch Moor
Crouchmoor Farm
HALF DROVE
Dilamore Farm
PE38
Home Farm
Martins Farm
Middle Leading Drain

Butcher's Hill Farm
BELL'S DROVE
DAIRY DROVE
Croft Hills
Rack Fen
HALF DROVE

Broadlands
Grubb's Farm
Apes Hall Farm
The Apes Hall
Old Croft River

Grapevine Farm
WESTMOOR DROVE
OLD POOL'S DROVE
New Pools Farm
Primrose Hill Farm
HALF FEN ROAD
POPLAR DROVE
LC

Westmoor Fen
BATE'S DROVE
A1101
BURNT CHIMNEY DROVE
Westlands
HALF FEN
HORSLEY HALE
Mow Fen
LC

Westmoor Farm
BATE'S DV
PLAINS LANE
Plains Farm
The Plains
Mare Fen
LITTLE MAREFEN DROVE
Mare Fen Farm
CB6
242
A10(T)

SEVENTH DROVE
Seventh Drove Farm
A1101
Pearson Farm
Horseshoe Farm
MAREFEN DV
WISBECH ROAD
Red Barn Farm
242
Fieldside Farm
Sewage Works
Sports & Leisure Centre
CAMEL ROAD
WISBECH RD
WELLINGTON ST
Littleport
STATION ROAD
LYNN RD
LC
242
CB7

MAIN DROVE
Quaker Farm
Fodder Fen
FOURTH DROVE
THIRD DROVE
SECOND DROVE
BLACK BANK ROAD
A10(T)
WOODFEN ROAD
PARSON'S LA
Coll
PO
Cemy
CHURCH LA
MAIN ST
Littleport
ELY ROAD
VICTORIA ST
Liby
PH
LC
RIVER BANK
NEW BANK

Willow Farm
Laurel Farm
Fourth Drove
Second Drove
Wood Fen Farm
Highfield Farm
Millfield CP Sch
WOODFEN ROAD
PADNAL
Sandhill
Sandhill Bridge
HAWKINS'S DROVE
BRANCH BANK

Gravel Head Farm
LC

52   **53**   **54**   **55**   **56**   **57**

A   B   C   D   E   F

218

226

For full street detail of the highlighted area see page 242.

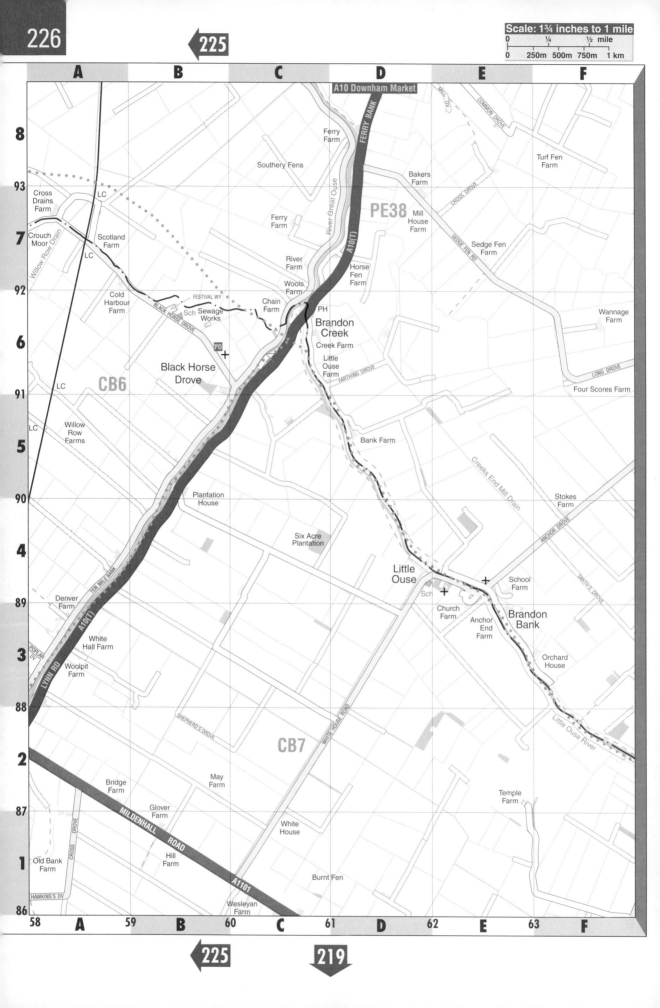

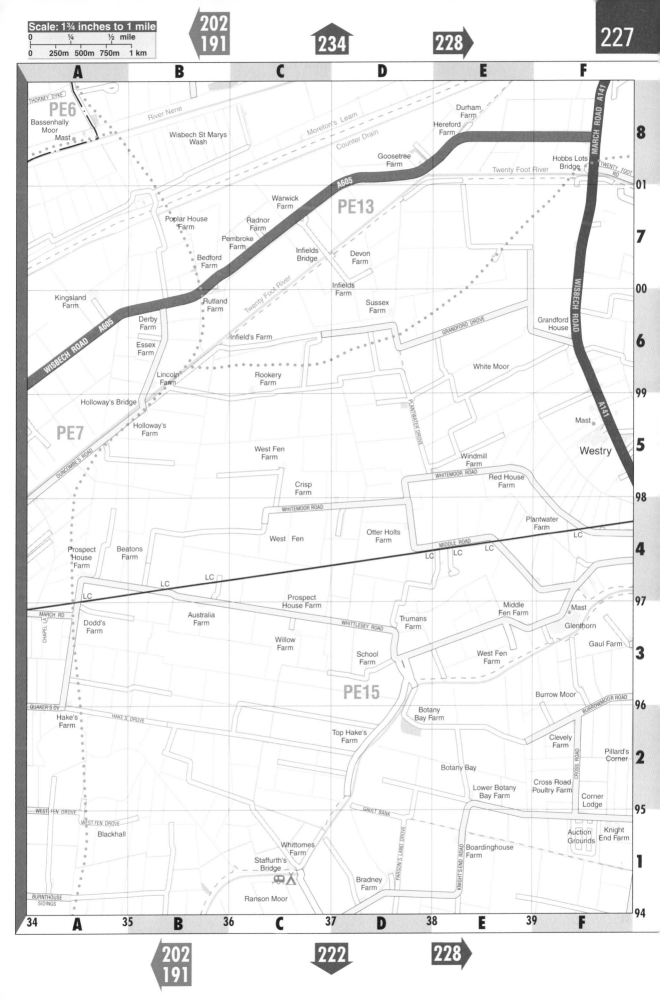

Scale: 1¾ inches to 1 mile

0   ¼   ½   mile
0 250m 500m 750m 1 km

202
191

234

228

227

A   B   C   D   E   F

THORNEY DYKE

PE6

Bassenhally Moor Mast

River Nene

Moreton's Leam

Counter Drain

Wisbech St Marys Wash

Durham Farm

Hereford Farm

Goosetree Farm

Twenty Foot River

Hobbs Lots Bridge

TWENTY FOOT RD

MARCH ROAD A141

8

01

A605

PE13

Warwick Farm

Poplar House Farm

Radnor Farm

Pembroke Farm

Bedford Farm

Infields Bridge

Devon Farm

7

Infields Farm

Kingsland Farm

A605 WISBECH ROAD

Rutland Farm

Twenty Foot River

Sussex Farm

Grandford House

Grandford Drive

WISBECH ROAD

00

6

Derby Farm

Essex Farm

Infield's Farm

White Moor

Lincoln Farm

Rookery Farm

99

Holloway's Bridge

PE7

Holloway's Farm

DUNCOMBE'S ROAD

Mast

A141

Westry

5

West Fen Farm

Windmill Farm

Red House Farm

98

Crisp Farm

WHITEMOOR ROAD

Plantwater Farm

LC

Prospect House Farm

Beatons Farm

WHITEMOOR ROAD

West Fen

Otter Holts Farm

PLANTWATER DROVE

MIDDLE ROAD

LC

LC

LC

LC

4

LC

LC

March Rd

Chapel La

Dodd's Farm

Australia Farm

Prospect House Farm

WHITTLESEY ROAD

Trumans Farm

Middle Fen Farm

Mast

Glenthorn

Gaul Farm

97

Willow Farm

School Farm

West Fen Farm

3

PE15

QUAKER'S DV

Hake's Farm

HAKE'S DROVE

Top Hake's Farm

Botany Bay Farm

Burrow Moor

BURROWMOOR ROAD

96

Clevely Farm

CROSS ROAD

Pillard's Corner

2

Botany Bay

Cross Road Poultry Farm

Corner Lodge

WEST FEN DROVE

WEST FEN DROVE

Blackhall

Lower Botany Bay Farm

95

GAULT BANK

PARSON'S LAND DROVE

KNIGHT'S END ROAD

Boardinghouse Farm

Auction Grounds

Knight End Farm

1

Whittomes Farm

Staffurth's Bridge

Bradney Farm

BURNTHOUSE SIDINGS

Ranson Moor

94

34   A   35   B   36   C   37   D   38   E   39   F

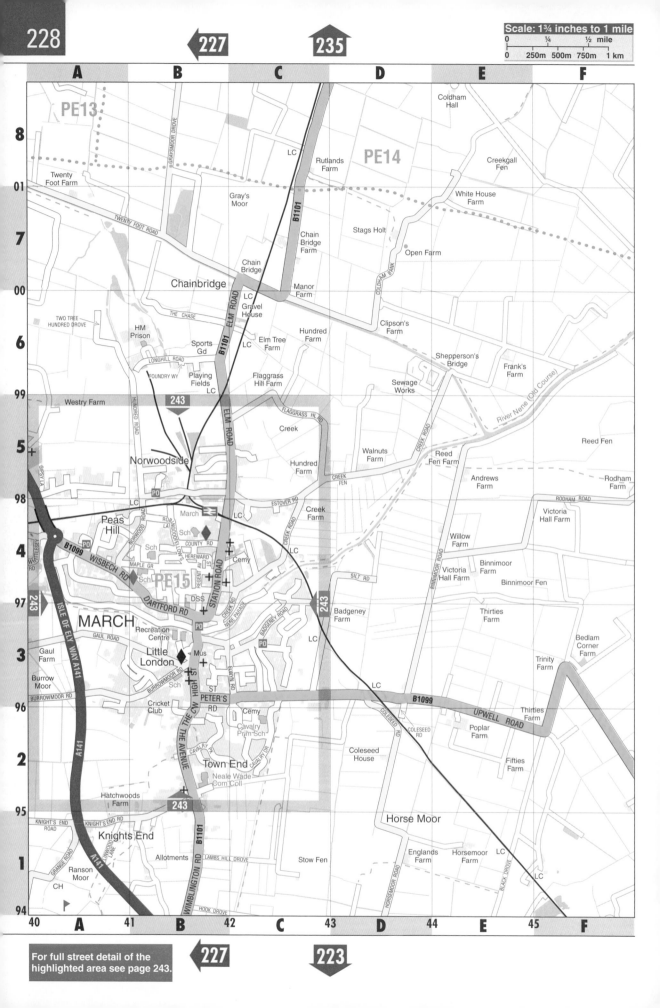

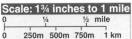

236

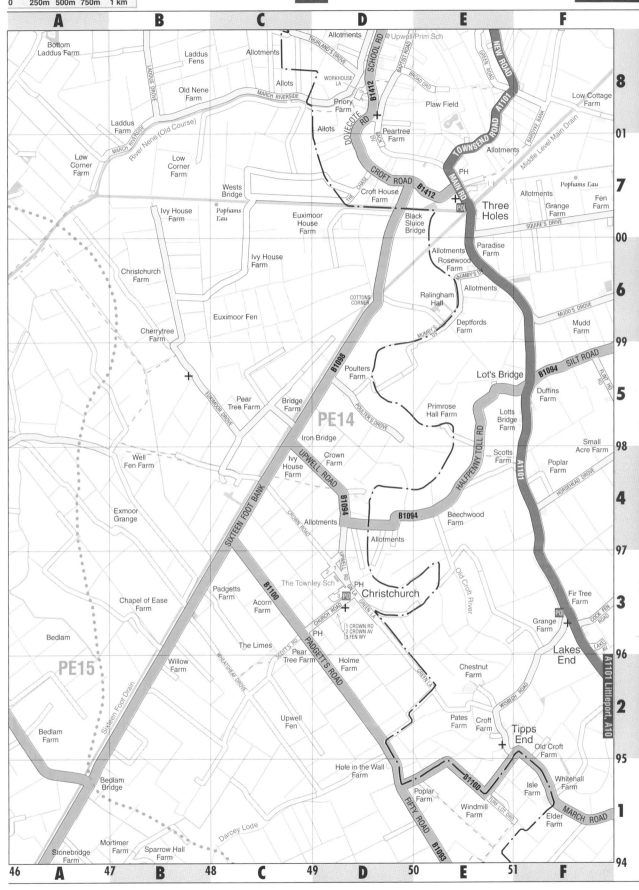

Scale: 1¾ inches to 1 mile

0   ¼   ½ mile
0 250m 500m 750m 1 km

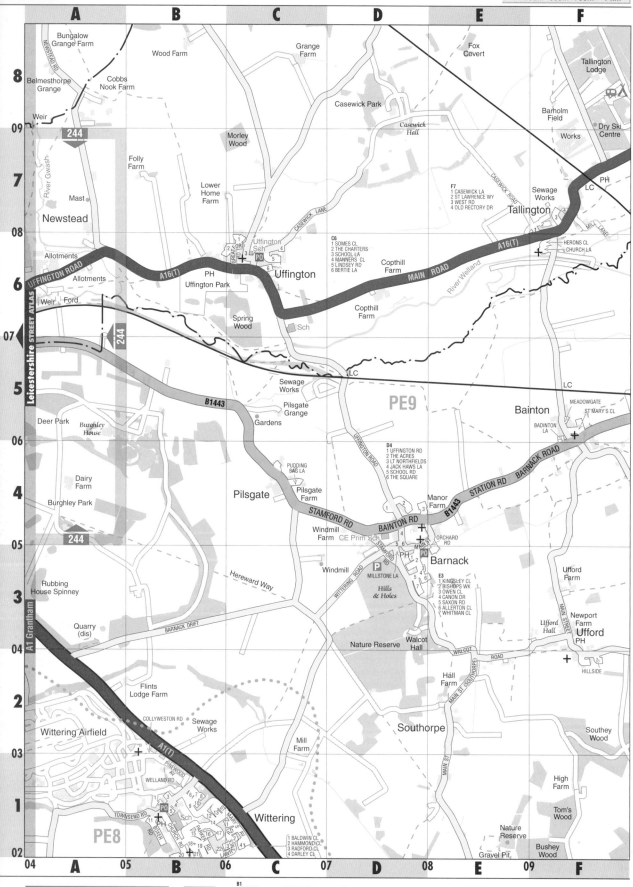

A16(T)

B1443

PE9

PE8

Newstead

Uffington

Tallington

Bainton

Pilsgate

Barnack

Ufford

Southorpe

Wittering

Wittering Airfield

Leicestershire STREET ATLAS

Bungalow Grange Farm
Belmesthorpe Grange
Weir
244
Mast
Allotments
Uffington Road
Allotments
Weir Ford
244
A1 Grantham
A1(T)
Rubbing House Spinney
Quarry (dis)
Dairy Farm
Burghley Park
Deer Park
Burghley House
244
Flints Lodge Farm
Collyweston Rd
Sewage Works
Pinewood
Welland Rd
Townsend Rd
PO
PH
Sch

Wood Farm
Cobbs Nook Farm
Folly Farm
Lower Home Farm
PH
Uffington Park
Spring Wood
Sch
B1443
Pilsgate Grange
Gardens
Pudding Bag La
Pilsgate Farm
Stamford Rd
Barnack Drift
Hereward Way
Windmill Farm
CE Prim Sch
Windmill
Millstone La
P
Wittering Road
Nature Reserve
Mill Farm

Grange Farm
Casewick Park
Morley Wood
Casewick Hall
Casewick Lane
ORD
Uffington Sch
PO
Sewage Works
LC
Copthill Farm
Copthill Farm
Bainton Rd
Manor Farm
Hills & Holes
Walcot Hall
Nature Reserve

Fox Covert
Tallington Lodge
Barholm Field
Works
Dry Ski Centre
PH
LC
Sewage Works
Casewick Road
Main Road
River Welland
HERONS CL
CHURCH LA
Meadowgate
ST MARY'S CL
Badinton La
Station Rd
Barnack Road
Orchard Rd
Ufford Farm
Manor Farm
PO
PH
Ufford Hall
Newport Farm
Ufford
PH
HILLSIDE
Walcot Road
Hall Farm
Main St Southorpe
Southey Wood
High Farm
Tom's Wood
Nature Reserve
Gravel Pit
Bushey Wood

River Gwash

Uffington Road
A16(T)
Ford

River Welland

Uffington Road

F7
1 CASEWICK LA
2 ST LAWRENCE WY
3 WEST RD
4 OLD RECTORY DR

C6
1 SOMES CL
2 THE CHARTERS
3 SCHOOL LA
4 MANNERS CL
5 LINDSEY RD
6 BERTIE LA

D4
1 UFFINGTON RD
2 THE ACRES
3 LT NORTHFIELDS
4 JACK HAWS LA
5 SCHOOL RD
6 THE SQUARE

E3
1 KINGSLEY CL
2 BISHOPS WK
3 OWEN CL
4 CANON DR
5 SAXON RD
6 ALLERTON CL
7 WHITMAN CL

For full street detail of the highlighted area see page 244.

193

194

B1
1 GLEN RD
2 NENE CL
3 CHATER RD
4 HARVEY CL
5 THE LIMES
6 BROWNES RD
7 EXETER RD
8 THE HOLT
9 BURGHLEY AV
10 FREEMANS CL
11 MANOR CL
12 ST MICHAEL'S RD
13 ST JOHN S RD
14 ST GEORGE'S RD
15 BROADHURST RD
16 NEWMAN CL
17 MALTBY CL
18 CARNEGIE RD
19 EMBRY RD
20 HALL LA
21 LEGG RD
22 JEFFERSON CL

Wittering
1 BALDWIN CL
2 HAMMOND CL
3 RADFORD CL
4 DARLEY CL

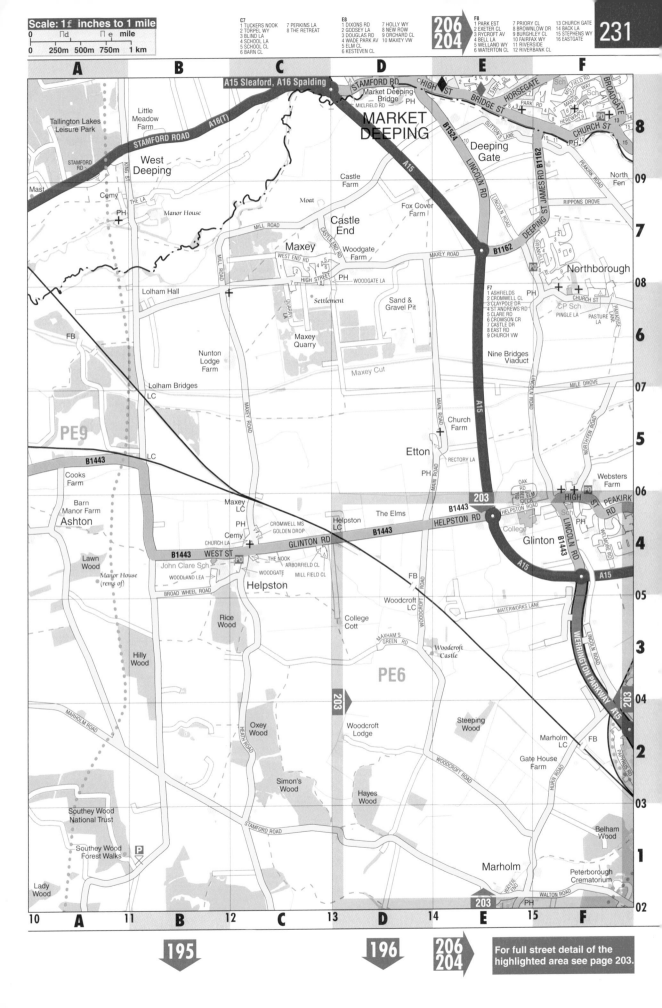

207
205

Scale: 1¾ inches to 1 mile

0   ¼   ½ mile
0   250m 500m 750m 1 km

A   B   C   D   E   F

8
09
7
08
6
07
5
06
4
05
3
04
2
03
1
02

Crowland
Crowland High Wash
Middle Rd
Corporation Bank
Low Rd
Plank Drive
Crease Drove
Harvester Way
Alderlands
Broadway
Low Rd
Sch
Peterborough Road
Barbers Drove
A1073 Spalding
A1073

Ashley's Barn
Harrington Dr
Carrington's Drove
Greenbank Farm
Green Drove
Sheppard's Drove
Empsons Farm
Old South Eau

Kennulph's Farm
Poplar Farm
Wright's Drove
Eardley Grange Farm
Vine House Farm
B1040
South Eau Farm
Falls Bridge
Empsons Farm
Fall's Drove
Blue Bell Farm

Toll House Farm
Hundreds Farm
Hundreds Road
Nene Terrace
St Vincent's Cross
St Vincent's Cross Farm
French Drove
Old Hall Farm
Blue Bell Bridge
Bell Drove

Old Farm
Pepper Lake Farm
Horseshoe Bridge
Singlesole Farm
St Vincent's Cross
Bennett's Pieces
Hangman's Corner

Moor's Farm
Gray's Farm
Cross
B1040
Singlecote Farm
Crowland Road
Lodge Farm

Olympia Farm
Hill Farm
Steam House Farm
PE6
Cat's Water Plantation
Little Tower's Fen

Flood Farm
B1443 Thorney Road
Mason's Bridge
Thorney Road
Powder Blue Farm
B1443
Bukehorn Road
Buke Horn Farm
B1443

Hill Farm
Fletchers Farm
Hurn Farm
Cat's Water
The Beaches
Bedford Level (North Level)
Rose Farm
Buke Horn Plantation
ASH CL 1
LAUREL DR 2
BERBERIS CL 3
ORCHARD CT 4

Turves Farm
Elm Tree Farm
Oakhurst Farm
Crowland Rd
A1073
Northolm Farm
Cat's Water Plantation
Middle West Farm
Great Towers Fen
Hightrees Farm
Windmill
Abbey House

Eye Green
Northham Cl
Newstead Cl
Turves Road
Northolme Coppice
Nipcot Road
Catwater Farm
Causeway Toll Farm
A47(T)
The Causeway
Pode Hole Farm
Guys Fen

PH
Green Rd
Eye Green Industries
Crowland Rd
Thorney Road
A47(T)
Pasture House Farm
Willow Hall Lane
Toneham Farm
Toneham Lane

A47(T) Eye Road
PO
PH
High St
Back Lane
Cemy Liby
Fountains Pl
Eye CE Sch
Eye
Hayne's Farm
Bar Pastures
Bar Pasture Farm
Barlees Fen
Chicell's Hurst
Thorney River
Hill Farm
Whittlesey Rd

Peterborough Rd
Eyebury Rd
Lindisfarne Rd
Little Cl
Sand & Gravel Pit

207
205
199
200

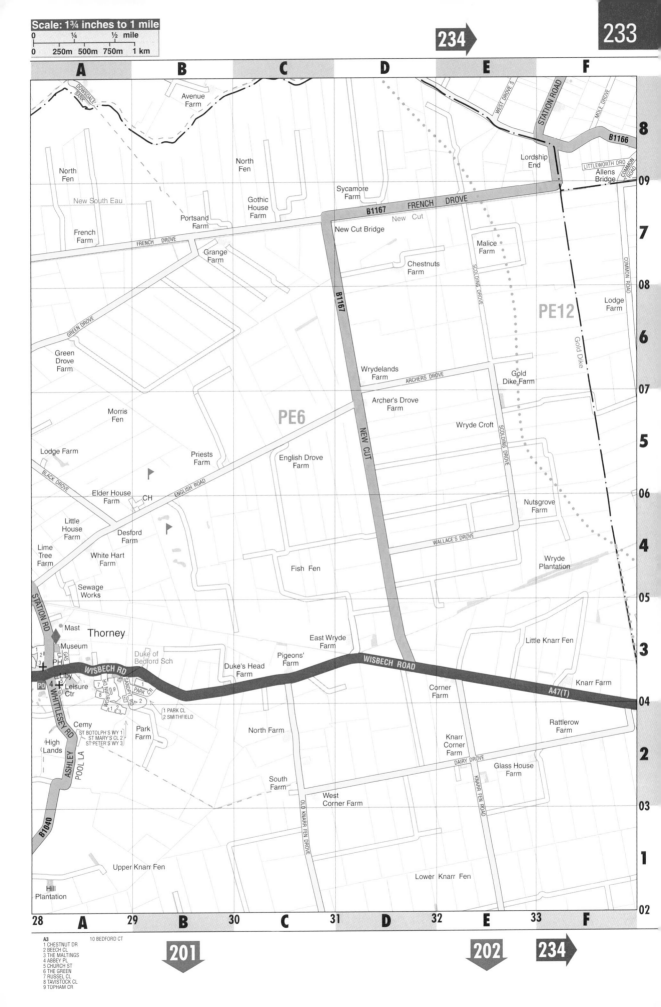

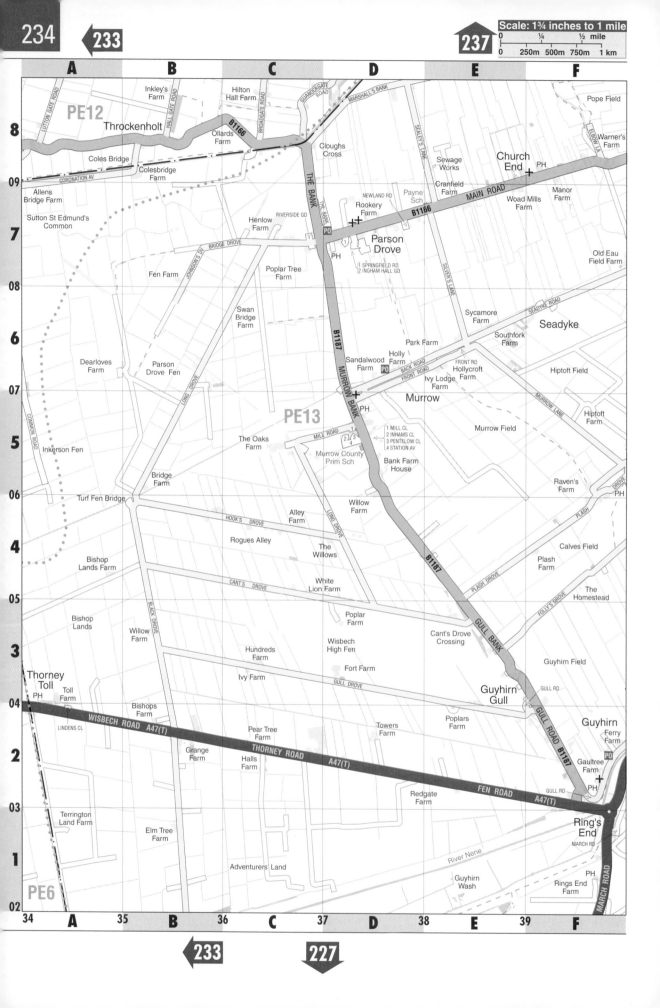

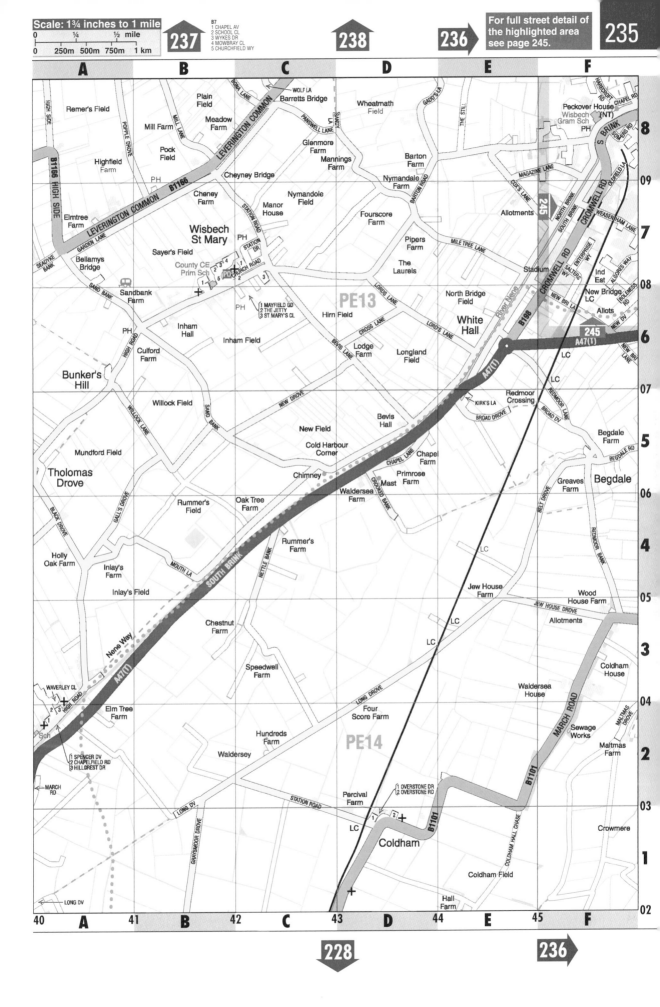

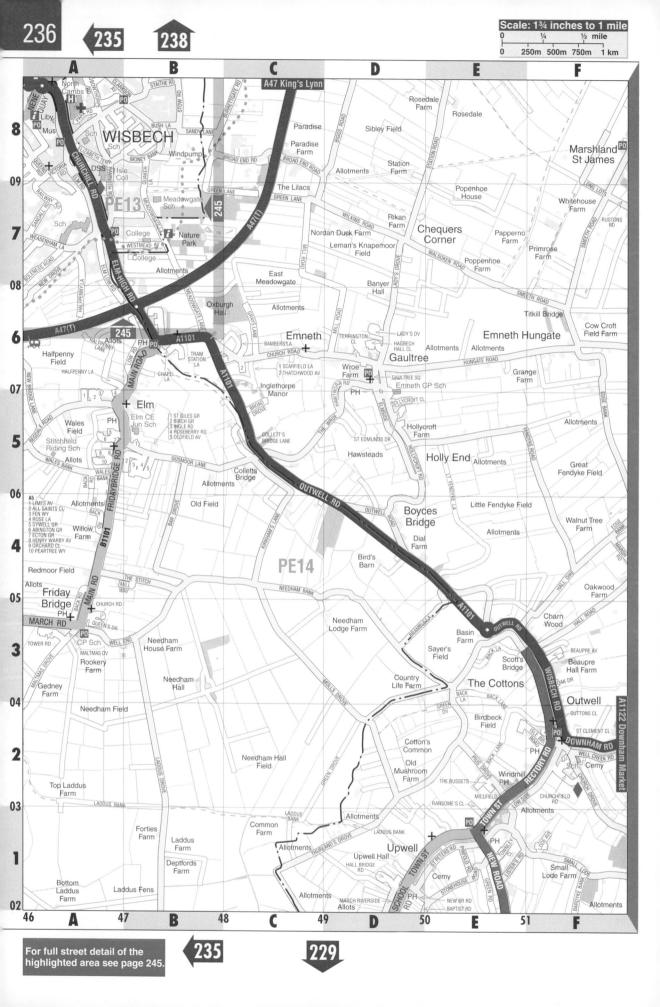

Scale: 1¾ inches to 1 mile
0   ¼   ½   mile
0   250m   500m   750m   1 km

A   B   C   D   E   F

A47 King's Lynn

8

WISBECH

PE13

North Cambs
NENE QUAY
Liby
Mus
DSS

Clarkson Rd
Staithe Rd
Stow Rd
Sandy Lane
Bush La
Money Bank

Windpump
Meadowgate Sch

Green Lane

Paradise
Paradise Farm

Rosedale Farm
Rosedale

Sibley Field

Station Farm

Marshland St James

Whitehouse Farm

Long Lots

09

The Lilacs

Green Lane

Allotments

Popenhoe House

Rustons Rd

7

Churchill Rd
Elm Rd
Victoria Rd
Railway Rd
Queens Rd
Weasenham La

College
Westmead Av
College
Sch

Nature Park

A47(T)

Wilkins Road
Nordan Duck Farm
Leman's Knapemoor Field

Rikan Farm

Chequers Corner

Papperno Farm

Poppenhoe Farm

Primrose Farm

Smeeth Rd

08

New Drove
Boleness Road
Halfpenny La

Elm High Rd
Allotments

Oxburgh Hall

East Meadowgate

Allotments

Mill Road

Lady's Drove
Walsoken Road

Banyer Hall

Smeeth Road

Titkill Bridge

Cow Croft Field Farm

6

A47(T)
Halfpenny Field
Halfpenny La
Halfpenny Lane

Main Road
Low Rd
245
PH
A1101
TRAM STATION LA
CHAPEL LA

A1101

Bambers La
Church Road

Grays Lane

Emneth

1 Scarfield La
2 Thatchwood Av

Terrington CL
Hagbech Hall CL
Lady's DV

Gaultree

Emneth Hungate

Allotments   Allotments

Hungate Road

Grange Farm

Edge Bank

07

New Bridge Lane
Begdale Road

Wales Field
PH
Stitchfield Riding Sch

Elm

Fridaybridge Rd

1 St Giles Gr
2 Birch Gr
3 Ingle Rd
4 Roseberry Rd
5 Oldfield Av

Gosmoor Lane

Colletts Bridge Lane
Broad Drove

Inglethorpe Manor

The Wroe

Hanthorn Rd

Wroe Farm

PH
Gaultree Sq
Emneth CP Sch

Elmside

Hollycroft CL

Hollycroft Farm

St Edmunds Dr

Holly End

Hawsteads

Allotments

Fendyke Road

Lt Fendyke La

Allotments

Great Fendyke Field

5

Elm CE Jun Sch

Allots
Wales Bank
Wales Bank
Back

B1101
Bar Drove
Back

Colletts Bridge

Allotments

Old Field

Outwell Rd

Boyces Bridge

Dial Farm

Outwell Rd

Little Fendyke Field

Allotments

Walnut Tree Farm

Edge Bank

06

A5
1 LIMES AV
2 ALL SAINTS CL
3 FEN WY
4 ROSE LA
5 SYWELL GR
6 ABINGTON GR
7 ECTON GR
8 HENRY WARBY AV
9 ORCHARD CL
10 PEARTREE WY

Allotments

Willow Farm

Redmoor Field

Kirkham's Lane

PE14

Bird's Barn

A1101

Oakwood Farm

Hall Drive

Marsh Rd

4

Allots
Friday Bridge
PH
MARCH RD

Main Rd
Back Rd
Church Rd
THE STITCH
MILL WAY
Queen's Dr

Needham Bank

Needham Lodge Farm

Sayer's Field

Basin Farm

Brambly La

Scott's Bridge

Charn Wood

Hall Rd

Beaupre Av
Beaupre Hall Farm

05

Tower Rd
Maltmas Drove
Gedney Farm

CP Sch
MALTMAS DV
Rookery Farm

Needham House Farm

Needham Hall

Molls Drove

Country Life Farm

Green DV

The Cottons

Back La
Back Lane

Birdbeck Field

Oak Dr

Wisbech Rd

Outwell

Suttons CL
St Clement CL

A1122 Downham Market

04

Needham Field

Laddus Drove

Needham Hall Field

Green Drove

Cotton's Common

Plus Drove
Back Lane

Rectory Rd
Isle Br Road

PH
Well Creek Rd

Downham Rd

Sch
Church Drove
Cemy

03

Top Laddus Farm

Laddus Bank

Laddus Bank

Common Farm

Thurland's Drove

Laddus Bank

Allotments

Old Mushroom Farm

THE RUSSETS

Ransome's CL
Millfield

Town St
Windmill PH

Low Side

Churchfield Rd

Allotments

Edge Ave

02

Bottom Laddus Farm

Laddus Fens

Forties Farm

Laddus Farm

Deptfords Farm

Allotments

Allotments

Upwell Hall

HALL BRIDGE RD

Upwell

St Peters Rd

Cemy

Stonehouse

School Rd

Town St
New Road

MARCH RIVERSIDE
Allots
PH
NEW BR RD
Baptist Rd

Green Rd
LISTER'S RD
PINFOLD RD

Small Lode Farm

Small Lode

Bardyke Bank

Allotments

46   A   47   B   48   C   49   D   50   E   51   F

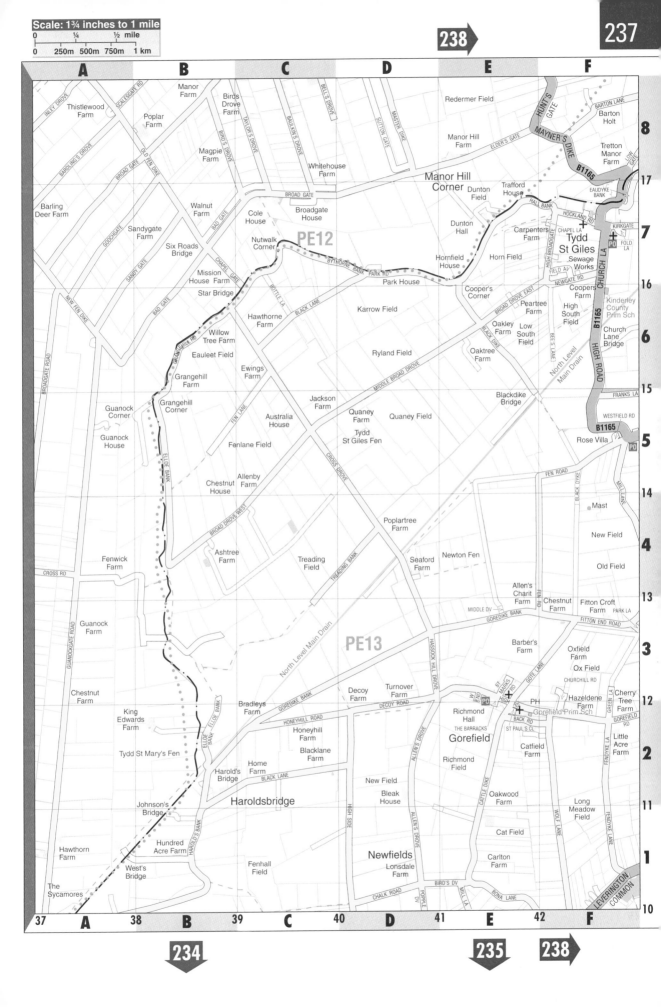

Scale: 1¾ inches to 1 mile

0   ¼   ½ mile
0   250m 500m 750m 1 km

A **B** **C** **D** **E** **F**

Inley Drove
Thistlewood Farm
Scalesgate Rd
Poplar Farm
Manor Farm
Birds Drove Farm
Bell's Drove
Redermer Field
Hunt's Gate
Barton Lane
Barton Holt
Mayner's Dike
B1165
Tretton Manor Farm
Low Gate

8

Bardling's Drove
Old Fen Dike
Broad Gate
Magpie Farm
Taylor's Drove
Bird's Drove
Baulkin's Drove
Whitehouse Farm
Sutton Gate
Master Dike
Elder's Gate
Manor Hill Farm
Manor Hill Corner
Trafford House
Dunton Field
Hall Bank
Hockland Rd
Eaudyke Bank
Kirkgate

17

Barling Deer Farm
Goochgate
Sandygate Farm
Walnut Farm
Bad Gate
Cole House
Broad Gate
Broadgate House
Dunton Hall
Carpenters Farm
Chapel La
High Broadgate
Tydd St Giles
PO
Fold La

7

Sandy Gate
Six Roads Bridge
Chapel Gate
Nutwalk Corner
PE12
Bythorne Bank
Park Rd
Park House
Hornfield House
Horn Field
Sewage Works
Field Av
Newgate Rd
Church La

New Fen Dike
Bad Gate
Mission House Farm
Star Bridge
Hawthorne Farm
Bottle La
Black Lane
Karrow Field
Cooper's Corner
Broad Drove East
Peartree Farm
High South Field
B1165
Kinderley County Prim Sch
Church Lane Bridge

16

Willow Tree Farm
Eauleet Field
Grangehill Rd
Ewings Farm
Ryland Field
Black Dyke
Oakley Farm
Low South Field
Oaktree Farm
Bee's Lane
North Level Main Drain
High Road
Franks La

6

Grangehill Farm
Grangehill Corner
Fen Lane
Australia House
Jackson Farm
Middle Broad Drove
Quaney Farm
Quaney Field
Blackdike Bridge
Westfield Rd
B1165
Rose Villa
PO

15

Guanock Corner
Guanock House
Elloe Bank
Fenlane Field
Cross Drove
Tydd St Giles Fen
Fen Road
Black Dyke
Mill Lane

5

Chestnut House
Allenby Farm
Broad Drove West
Mast

14

Fenwick Farm
Cross Rd
Ashtree Farm
Treading Field
Treading Bank
Poplartree Farm
Seaford Farm
Newton Fen
New Field
Old Field

4

Guanock Road
Guanock Farm
North Level Main Drain
Allen's Charit Farm
Middle Dv
Goredike Bank
Chestnut Farm
Fen Rd
Fitton Croft Farm
Park La
Fitton End Road

13

Chestnut Farm
PE13
Hassock Hill Drove
Barber's Farm
Oxfield Farm
Ox Field
Churchill Rd
Gote Lane
Green La
Gorefield Rd

3

King Edwards Farm
Bradleys Farm
Goredike Bank
Decoy Farm
Turnover Farm
Decoy Road
Richmond Hall
St Mark's
High Rd
PH
Gorefield Prim Sch
Back Rd
Hazeldene Farm
Cherry Tree Farm
Little Acre Farm

12

Tydd St Mary's Fen
Elloe Bank
Honeyhill Road
Honeyhill Farm
Blacklane Farm
Allen's Drove
St Paul's Cl
The Barracks
Gorefield
Richmond Field
Catfield Farm
Fendyke La

2

Harold's Bridge
Home Farm
Black Lane
New Field
Bleak House
Oakwood Farm
Wolf Lane
Long Meadow Field

Johnson's Bridge
Haroldsbridge
High Side
Cat Field
Carlton Farm

11

Hawthorn Farm
Hundred Acre Farm
Harold's Bank
Fenhall Field
Newfields
Lonsdale Farm
Bird's Dv
Cattle Dike
Bona Lane
Mill La
Leverington Common

1

West's Bridge
The Sycamores
Chalk Road
Popple Dv

10

37   **A** 38   **B** 39   **C** 40   **D** 41   **E** 42   **F**

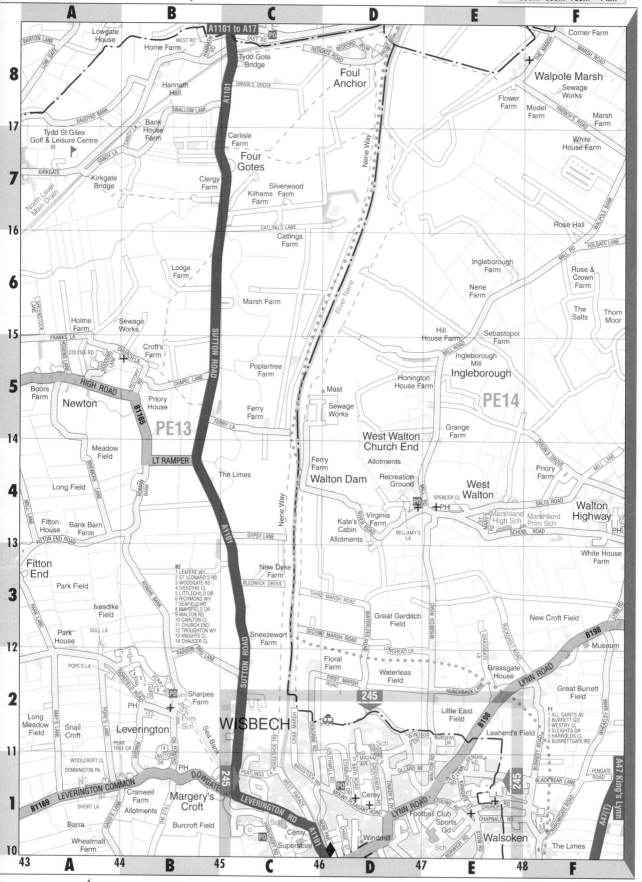

Scale: 1¾ inches to 1 mile
0   ¼   ½   mile
0 250m 500m 750m 1 km

A · B · C · D · E · F

Barton Lane
Low Gate
Lowgate House
Home Farm
WEST RD
A1101 to A17
EAST RD
PO
Tydd Gote Bridge
REDGATE ROAD
BEDFORD ROW
POINT RD
Corner Farm
MARSH ROAD

8

Foul Anchor
Walpole Marsh
Sewage Works
THE MARSH
Flower Farm
Model Farm
FRENCH'S RD
Marsh Farm

EAUDYKE BANK
Tydd St Giles Golf & Leisure Centre
Hannath Hall
SWALLOW LANE
Carlisle Farm
Nene Way

17

White House Farm

KIRKGATE
Kirkgate Bridge
Bank House Farm
SANDY LA
A1101
Four Gotes
Clergy Farm
Silverwood Farm
Kilhams Farm

7

Rose Hall

North Level Main Drain
Lodge Farm
CATLING'S LANE
Catlings Farm
MILL RD
FOLGATE LANE

16

Rose & Crown Farm

GREENSTOCK LANE
Holme Farm
Sewage Works
Croft's Farm
Marsh Farm
River Nene
Ingleborough Farm
Nene Farm
The Salts
Thorn Moor

15

FRANKS LA
COLVILLE RD
CHURCH LA
RECTORY LA
CHAPEL LANE
SUTTON ROAD
Poplartree Farm
Hill House Farm
MILL ROAD
Sebastopol Farm
Ingleborough Mill

Boors Farm
HIGH ROAD
Newton
Priory House
PE13
Ferry Farm
Mast
Sewage Works
Honington House Farm
Ingleborough
PE14
Grange Farm

5

B1165

Meadow Field
FERRY LA
The Limes
West Walton Church End
Allotments
Priory Farm
MILL LANE
Walton Highway

14

LT RAMPER
Ferry Farm
Walton Dam
Recreation Ground
PO
SPENCER CL
PH
West Walton
SALTS ROAD

Long Field
BREWERS LANE
ROMAN BANK
Kate's Cabin Allotments
Virginia Farm
ST MARY'S RD
Marshland High Sch
Marshland Prim Sch
SCHOOL ROAD
PH

4

Fitton House
Bank Barn Farm
A1101
GYPSY LANE
BELLAMY'S LA
WISBECH ROAD
White House Farm
MILL LANE

13

FITTON END ROAD
Fitton End
B2
1 LEAFERE WY
2 ST LEONARD'S RD
3 WOODGATE RD
4 IVESDYKE CL
5 LITTLECHILD DR
6 RICHMOND WY
7 SEAFIELD RD
8 MAYSFIELD DR
9 WALTON RD
10 CARLTON CL
11 CHURCH END
12 TROUGHTON WY
13 KNIGHTS CL
14 CHAUCER CL
New Dyke Farm
BLEDWICK DROVE
THIRD MARSH ROAD
Great Garditch Field
New Croft Field
B198

Park Field
Ivesdike Field
ROMAN BANK
WATERLEES ROAD
LONGHEAD LA
BUCKSHEIT ROAD
GRASSGATE
Museum
LYNN RD

3

Park House
GULL LA
PARSON DROVE LANE
Sneezewort Farm
SECOND MARSH ROAD
Waterleas Field
Grassgate House
Great Burrett Field

12

POPE'S LA
Floral Farm
FIRST MARSH ROAD
HUNCHBACK LANE
F1
1 ALL SAINTS AV
2 BURRETT GD
3 WESTRY CL
4 SLEIGHTS DR
5 HARROLDS CL
6 BURRETTGATE RD

Long Meadow Field
DOWGATE ROAD
PO
Sharpes Farm
PH
Prim Sch
WISBECH
245
Little East Field
B198
FENGATE ROAD
A47 King's Lynn

2

MAY'S LA
Snail Croft
Leverington
PEAR TREE CR
CHURCH DR
SEA BANK
CRAB MARSH
HORSESHOE TER
Sch
WINDSOR DR
NURSERY DR
Leaherd's Field
BURRETT ROAD
BLACK BEAR LANE
WHEATLEY BANK
SPARROWGATE ROAD

11

WOOLCROFT CL
DONNINGTON PK
RIBER
PH
BRIGSTOCK RD
WEST PARADE
PEATLINGS LA
SOUTHWELL RD
EDINBURGH DR
ST MICHAEL AVE
BATH RD
GROSVENOR
OLLARD AV
TINKER'S DV
WALTON ROAD
OLD LYNN RD
KIRGATE RD
PENDULA RD
Church

B1169
LEVERINGTON COMMON
Cranwell Farm Allotments
THE STILL
GADD'S LANE
Margery's Croft
245
LEVERINGTON RD
NENE PAR
PO
MOUNT PLEASANT ROAD
Cemy
Football Club
Sports Gd
CHAPNALL RD
Walsoken

1

Barra
Wheatmalt Farm
Burcroft Field
Superstore
Cemy
Superstore
A1101
CHASE ST
NORWICH RD
Windmill
Sch
245
The Limes

10

43 · A · 44 · B · 45 · C · 46 · D · 47 · E · 48 · F

For full street detail of the highlighted area see page 245.

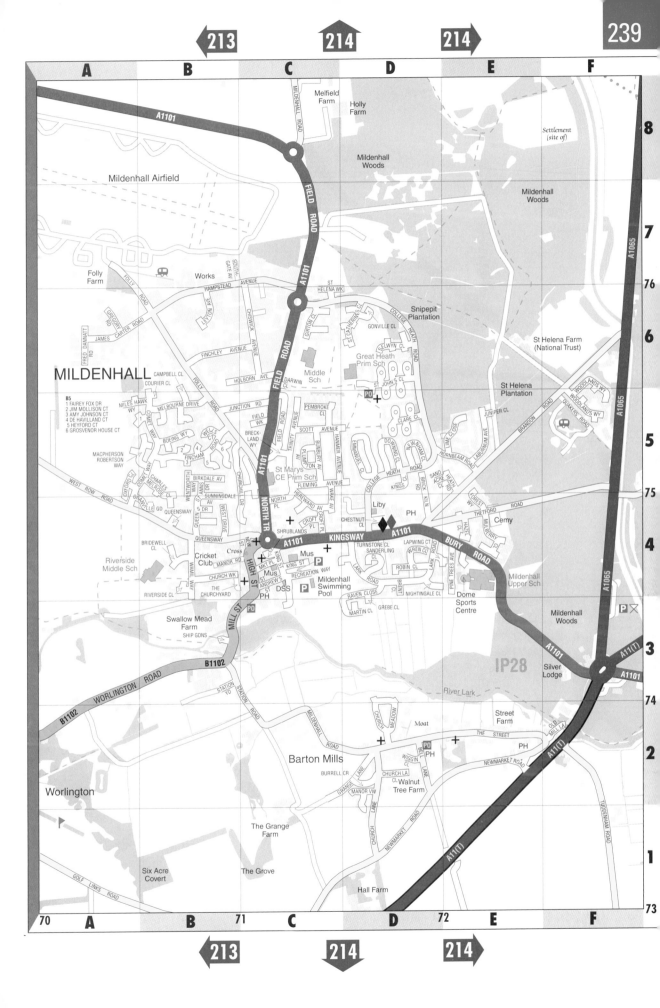

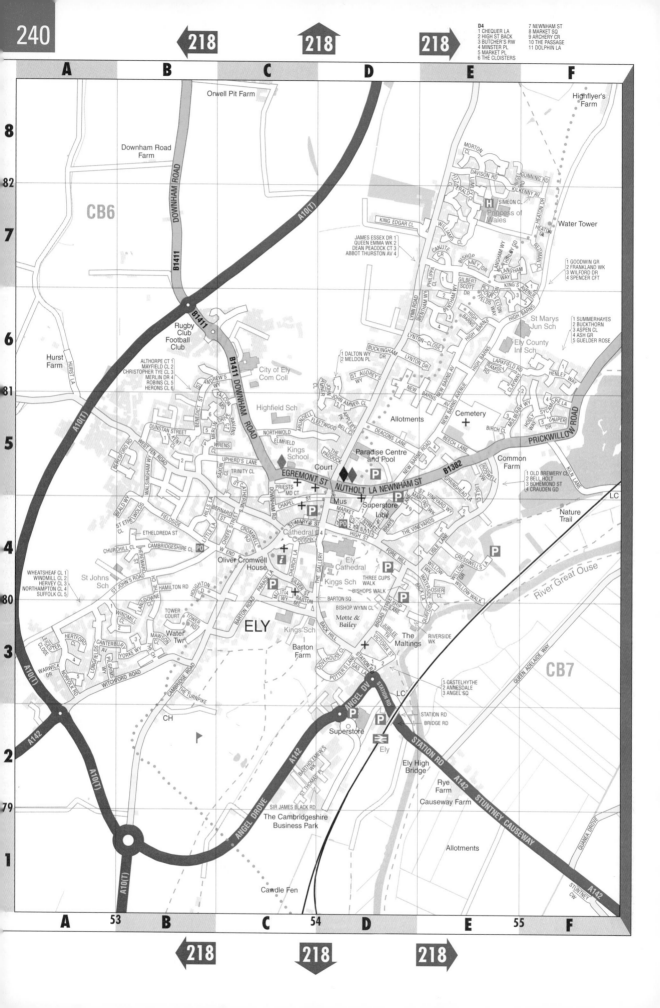

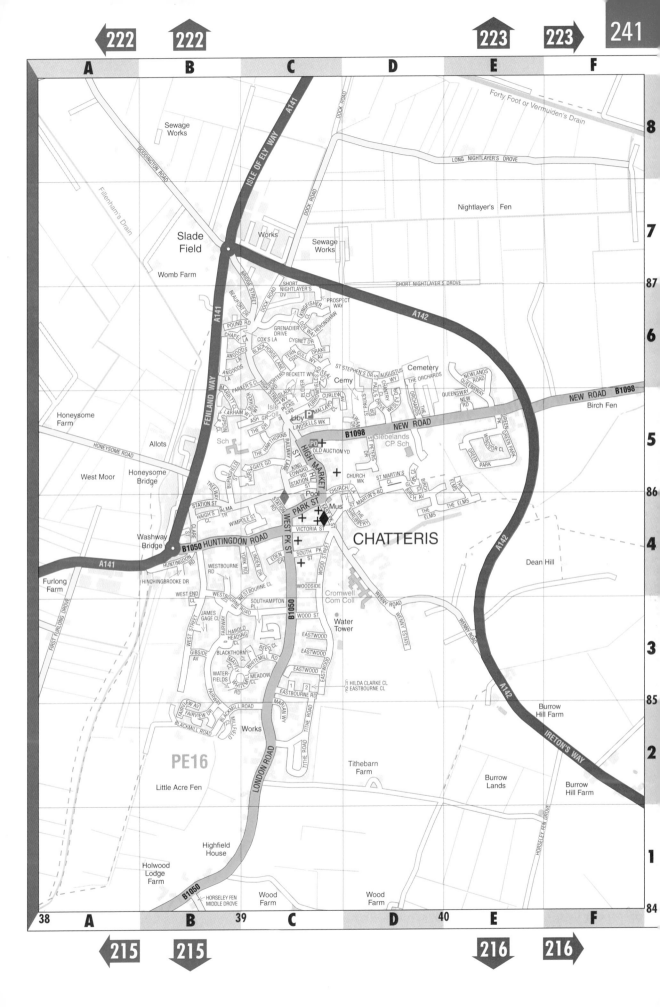

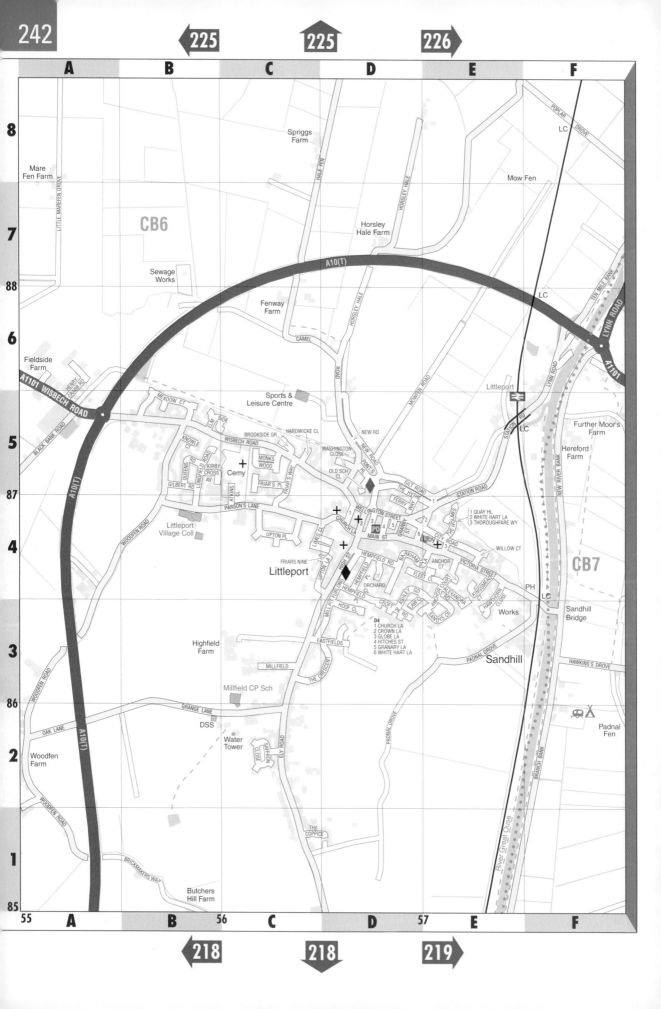

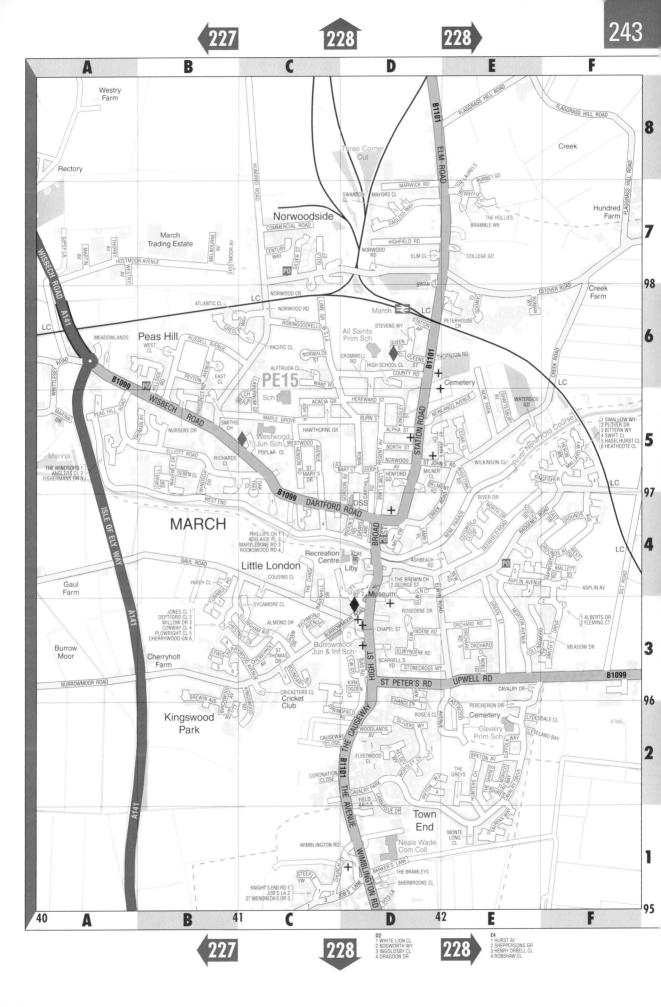

A B C D E F

8
7
98
6
5
97
4
3
96
2
1
95

Westry Farm
Rectory

March Trading Estate
Norwoodside
COMMERCIAL ROAD

Three Corner Cut

B1101 ELM ROAD

FLAGGRASS HILL ROAD
Creek
Hundred Farm
FLAGGRASS HILL ROAD

GIPSY LA
MARTIN AV
THORBY AV
MELBOURNE AV
HOSTMOOR AVENUE
WESTRY AV

SWANTON CL
MAYORS CL
MARWICK RD
THE LAURELS
BURNET GD
BERRYFIELD
THE HOLLIES
BRAMBLE WK
ESTOVER ROAD
Creek Farm

WISBECH ROAD A141
LC

MEADOWLANDS
Peas Hill

CENTURY WAY
SILVER ST
OTGO ST
PO
NORWOOD CR
ATLANTIC CL
NORWOOD RD
LIME GR
HIGHFIELD RD
NORWOOD RD
ELM CL
COLLEGE GD
SWAN CT
CAWOOD
PETERHOUSE CR
ROMAN WY

LC
WEST CL
RUSSELL AVENUE
GRESLEY
ROBINGOODFELLOW LA
PACIFIC CL
NORWALDE ST

March
STEVENS WY
STATION AP
LC

B1099 PO
HILLSIDE RD
PEYTON AVENUE
EAST CL
PROSPECT RD
LABURNUM GR
ALFTRUDA CL
WAKE RD
PE15 Sch
CROMWELL ST
HIGH SCHOOL CL
QUEEN ST
QUEENS
COUNTY RD
B1101
THORNTON RD
Cemetery
NEW PARK
SHAFTESBURY
WATERSIDE GD
CREEK ROAD
LC

All Saints Prim Sch

MARINA DR
WHITTLESEY ROAD
Peas Hill Road
PRIMAN AV
NURSERY DR
WISBECH ROAD
BEECH RD
SMITHS CH
MAPLE GROVE
ACACIA GR
HEREWARD ST
ASH GR
HAWTHORNE GR
BURN ST
KINGSLEY
ALPHA ST
NEWLANDS AVENUE
CEDAR GR
ST JOHN'S RD
WILKINSON CL
KINGFISHER
River Nene (Old Course)
HELEN WY
MALLARD WY
1 SWALLOW WY
2 PLOVER DR
3 BITTERN WY
4 SWIFT CL
5 HASELHURST CL
6 HEATHCOTE CL
LC

Marina
1 THE WINDSORS
2 ANGLERS CL
3 FISHERMANS DR
ELLIOTT ROAD
WINDSOR DR
RICHARDS CL
Westwood Jun Sch
WESTWOOD AVENUE
POPLAR CL
HENSON RD
ST MARY'S DR
NORTH ST
ROBIN
NORWOOD CL
REGENT AV
ST MOT
HENFORD
MILNER CL
BELMONT
RIVER DR
NORTH DR
COTSWOLD CLOSE
BADGENEY ROAD
DEERFIELD ROAD
GROUNDS
GROUNDS AV
PAPWORTH CL
MALLETT CL
SILT ROAD
LC

ORWELL DR
DEBEN CL
WAVENEY DR
OAK TREE CL
B1099
WEST END
DARTFORD ROAD
BART CT
GOODFE
GORDON RD
OARTHILL
DSS
BROOKS RD
GRAYS LANE
NENE PARADE
CREEK RD
B1099

MARCH
GAUL ROAD
Little London
Recreation Centre
Liby
PHILLIPS CH 1
ADELAIDE PL 2
MARYLEBONE RD 3
ROOKSWOOD RD 4
ACRE RD
BROAD ST
POST
ASHBEACH RD
ELWYN ROAD
PO
ASPLIN AVENUE
ASPLIN AV
1 ALBERTS DR
2 FLEMING CT

Gaul Farm
YARDY CL
COUSINS CL
THE CHASE
TRAVELHILL DR
RICHMOND AVENUE
Museum
1 THE BREWIN CH
2 GEORGE ST
ROSEDENE CL
ELWYNDENE RD
ORCHARD RD
ORCHARD RD S
MORTON AVENUE
MEADOW DR

TURNBULL RD
SYCAMORE CL
ALMOND DR
SHAW DR
ST THOMAS DR
BURROWMOOR ROAD
CHAPEL ST
ELWYNDENE RD
COLLINGWOOD
SMITH'S DRIVE

Burrow Moor
JONES CL 1
DEPTFORD CL 2
WILLOW DR 3
CONWAY CL 4
PLOWRIGHT CL 5
CHERRYWOOD GN 6
ELLINGHAM AVE
CHESTNUT CR
CHERRYWOOD AVENUE
LEWIS CR
BOUNDARY CL
Burrowmoor Jun & Inf Sch
SCARGELL'S YD
STONECROSS WY

Cherryholt Farm
BURROWMOOR ROAD
CRICKETERS CL
Cricket Club
KIRK OGDEN CL
HIGH ST
ST PETER'S RD
UPWELL RD
B1099
CAVALRY DR
Cemetery
PERCHERON DR
CLYDESDALE CL
CLEVELAND BAY

Kingswood Park
BIRCHWOOD RD
KINGSWOOD RD
BREWIN AVE
BUTT AV
RINGFIELD CL
CHANDLER WY
ROSE'S CL
OLIVERS WY
Cavalry Prim Sch
SUFFOLK WY

THE CAUSEWAY B1101
WOODLANDS AV
KELSEY CL
WORSLEY CL
AVENUE
BRETON AV
BRETON WY
THE GREYS
THE SHIRES
NORFOLK BAY
THE SHIRES
HUNTERS CH
CAVALRY DRIVE

CAUSEWAY CLOSE
FLEETWOOD CL
CORONATION CLOSE
CAVALRY PARK
THE AVENUE
FIELD BAULK
CAMARGUE DR
Town End
MONTE LONG CL
FAIRFAX WY

WIMBLINGTON RD
Neale Wade Com Coll
WIMBLINGTON RD

STEEP LE VW
CHURCH ST
JOB'S LANE
BARKER'S LANE
PITS LA
THE BRAMLEYS
SHERBROOKE CL
KNIGHT'S END RD 1
JOB'S LA 2
ST WENDREDA'S DR 3

40 A B 41 C D 42 E F

D2
1 WHITE LION CL
2 BOSWORTH WY
3 INGOLDSBY CL
4 DRAGOON DR

E4
1 HURST AV
2 SHEPPERSONS GR
3 HENRY ORBELL CL
4 ROBSHAW CL

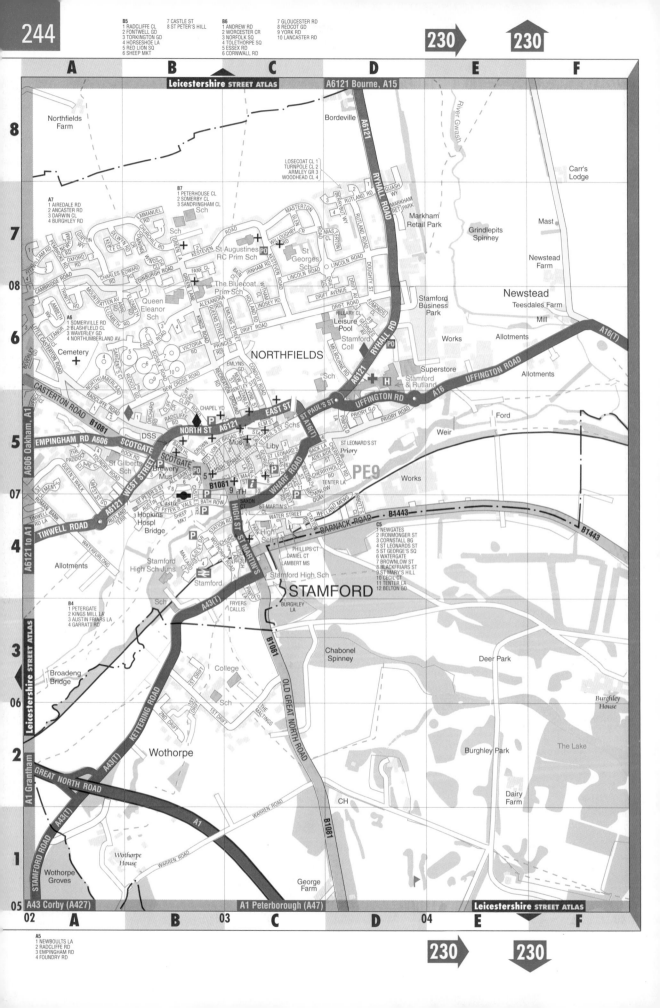

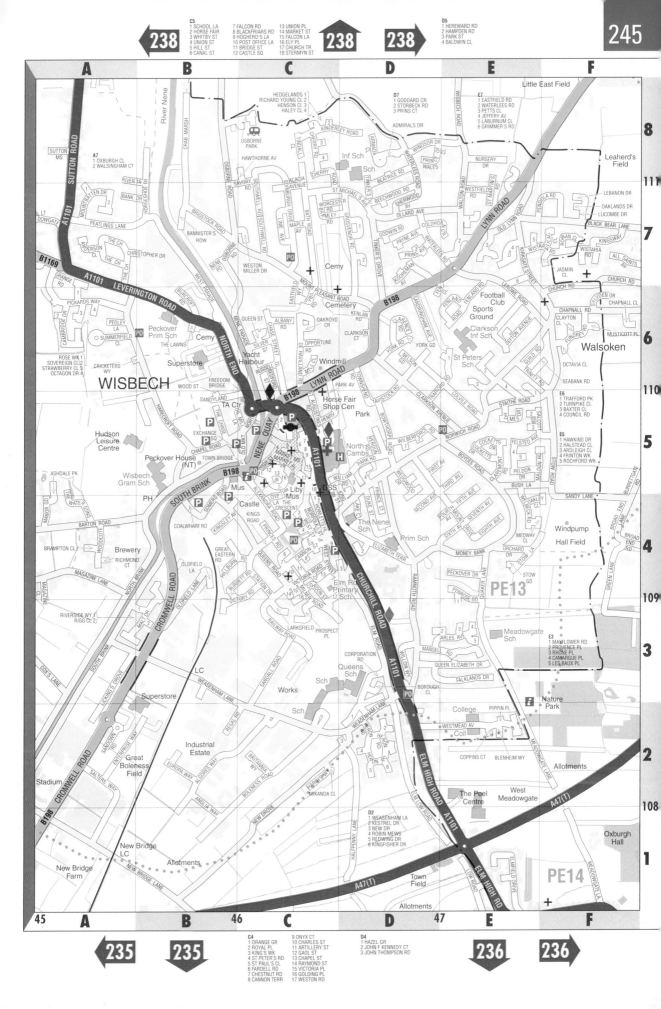

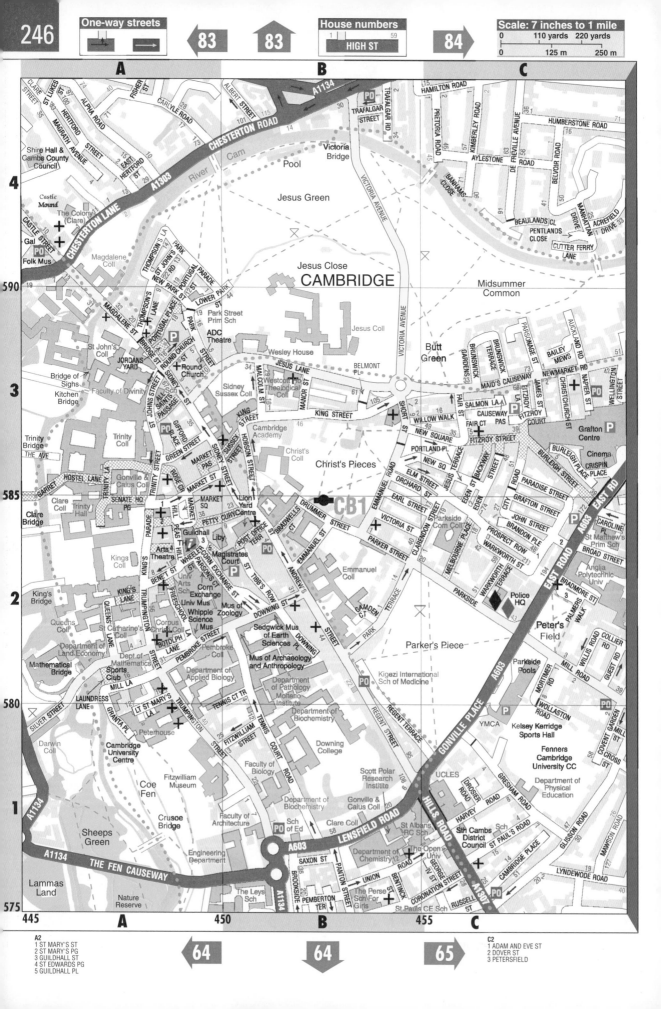

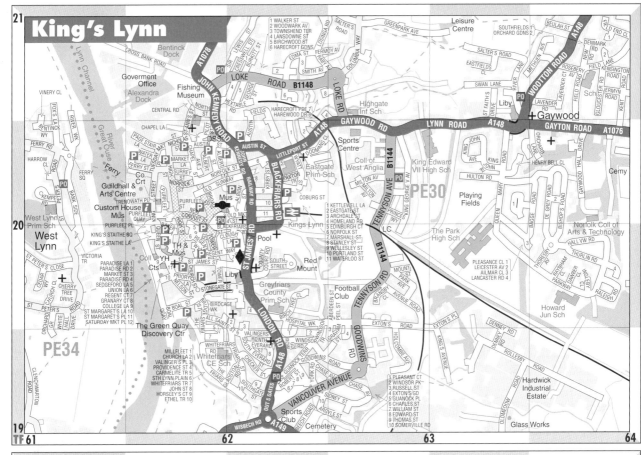

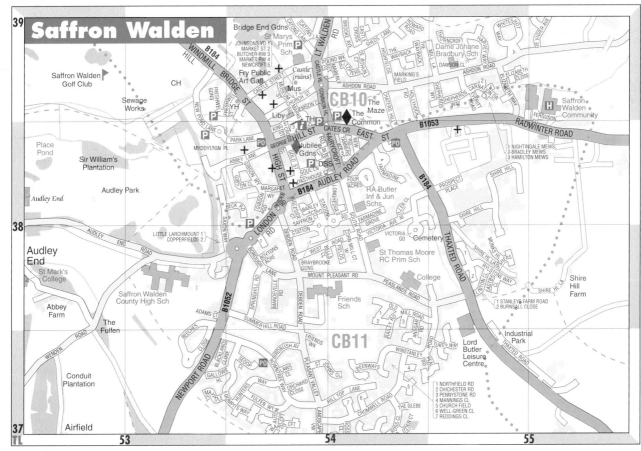

Index

Church Rd 6 Beckenham BR2..........**53** C6

Place name	Location number	Locality, town or village	Postcode district	Page and grid square
May be abbreviated on the map	Present when a number indicates the place's position in a crowded area of mapping	Shown when more than one place has the same name	District for the indexed place	Page number and grid reference for the standard mapping

Public and commercial buildings are highlighted in magenta   **Places of interest** are highlighted in blue with a star★

Abbreviations used in the index

Acad	**Academy**	Comm	**Common**	Gd	**Ground**	L	**Leisure**	Prom	**Prom**
App	**Approach**	Cott	**Cottage**	Gdn	**Garden**	La	**Lane**	Rd	**Road**
Arc	**Arcade**	Cres	**Crescent**	Gn	**Green**	Liby	**Library**	Recn	**Recreation**
Ave	**Avenue**	Cswy	**Causeway**	Gr	**Grove**	Mdw	**Meadow**	Ret	**Retail**
Bglw	**Bungalow**	Ct	**Court**	H	**Hall**	Meml	**Memorial**	Sh	**Shopping**
Bldg	**Building**	Ctr	**Centre**	Ho	**House**	Mkt	**Market**	Sq	**Square**
Bsns, Bus	**Business**	Ctry	**Country**	Hospl	**Hospital**	Mus	**Museum**	St	**Street**
Bvd	**Boulevard**	Cty	**County**	HQ	**Headquarters**	Orch	**Orchard**	Sta	**Station**
Cath	**Cathedral**	Dr	**Drive**	Hts	**Heights**	Pal	**Palace**	Terr	**Terrace**
Cir	**Circus**	Dro	**Drove**	Ind	**Industrial**	Par	**Parade**	TH	**Town Hall**
Cl	**Close**	Ed	**Education**	Inst	**Institute**	Pas	**Passage**	Univ	**University**
Cnr	**Corner**	Emb	**Embankment**	Int	**International**	Pk	**Park**	Wk, Wlk	**Walk**
Coll	**College**	Est	**Estate**	Intc	**Interchange**	Pl	**Place**	Wr	**Water**
Com	**Community**	Ex	**Exhibition**	Junc	**Junction**	Prec	**Precinct**	Yd	**Yard**

Index of localities, towns and villages

A

Abbots Ripton 162 C1
Abbotsley 57 C5
Abington Piggots 11 E5
Ailsworth 195 D3
Alconbury 150 E4
Alconbury Weston 150 D6
Aldreth 209 E4
Alwalton 185 B4
Arbury 83 D6
Arrington 44 C1
Ashdon 21 B1
Ashley 91 F7
Ashton 231 A4
Ashwell 2 E4
Ashwell End 2 A5

B

Babraham 50 E1
Badlingham 213 D1
Bainton 230 F5
Balsham 53 A2
Bar Hill 102 C3
Barham 149 B3
Barley 6 F2
Barnack 230 E3
Barrington 29 E8
Bartlow 21 A7
Barton 63 B3

Barton Mills 239 C2
Barway 211 C6
Bassingbourn 12 F4
Beck Row 213 F8
Begdale 235 F5
Benwick 222 A5
Bird's Hundred 189 C5
Black Horse
Drove 226 B6
Blackhall 227 A1
Bluntisham 208 D5
Bottisham 86 F6
Bourn 60 C6
Boxworth 101 B5
Boyces Bridge 236 D4
Brampton 140 C2
Brampton Park 140 D1
Brandon Bank 226 E3
Brandon Creek 226 D6
Bretton 197 A6
Briggate 189 E6
Brington 147 D4
Brinkley 70 E2
Broad Green 8 C3
Broad Green 91 D4
Brook End 136 B6
Broughton 153 F8
Buckden 117 B3
Buckworth 149 E6
Bunker's Hill 235 A6
Burrough End 70 E4
Burrough Green 70 F3
Burton End 37 C8
Burwell 130 C2

Bury 172 B4
Bythorn 146 D4

C

Caldecote 80 B1
Caldecote 76 B1
Caldecote 175 D5
Calford Green 24 F7
Cambridge 246 B4
Camps End 22 A1
Cardinal's Green 37 B1
Carlton 55 A7
Carlton Green 55 A4
Carlton Hill 55 A8
Castle Camps 22 F4
Castle End 231 D7
Castor 195 D1
Catworth 136 D7
Caxton 78 F1
Chainbridge 228 B7
Chapel End 174 D4
Chatteris 241 D4
Cherry Hinton 65 F5
Chesterton 84 A6
Chesterton 184 E3
Cheveley 91 C6
Childerley 80 C8
Childerley Gate 80 D4
Chippenham 132 E8
Chittering 127 B8
Chrishall 8 D4

Christchurch 229 D3
Church End 77 D4
Church End 169 D2
Church End 165 D1
Church End 151 F2
Church End 136 E7
Church End 122 E7
Church End 208 C1
Church Field 189 B7
Clayhithe 106 D5
Claypit Hill 61 D2
Clopton 156 E5
Coates 190 F8
Cockayne Hatley 25 C8
Coldham 235 D1
Coldham's Common 84 D2
Colne 208 D6
Colnefields 208 D8
Comberton 62 C5
Commercial End 108 C3
Conington 168 C8
Conington 121 C1
Coton 82 B2
Cottenham 125 D4
Coveney 217 C5
Covington 135 D2
Cowlinge 73 D1
Crawley End 8 D5
Cropley Grove 92 D3
Crow End 60 D7
Crowland 232 B8
Croxton 76 F4
Croydon 27 A7

D

Dalham 92 E8
Deeping Gate 231 E8
Deeping St James 206 A7
Denny End 105 F8
Denton 175 E4
Diddington 96 A8
Dillington 94 C7
Ditton Green 90 E1
Doddington 223 A6
Dogsthorpe 198 C7
Down Field 212 D2
Dry Drayton 102 C1
Duck End 97 F5
Dullingham 70 D8
Dullingham Ley 71 A5
Duloe 74 A6
Dunkirk 224 F1
Duxford 32 C1
Dyer's Green 13 C8

E

Eaglethorpe 178 B4
Earith 208 E6
East Hatley 43 B1
East Perry 115 E3
Eastfield 198 C4
Eastgate 198 B2
Easton 138 C4

Eastrea 190 D7
Eaton Ford 74 C5
Eaton Socon 74 B3
Eldernell 202 B2
Ellington 139 A4
Ellington Thorpe 139 A2
Elm 236 B5
Elmdon 9 A4
Elsworth 100 C4
Eltisley 77 E4
Elton 178 D8
Ely 240 C3
Emmaus 126 E2
Emneth 236 C6
Emneth Hungate 236 E6
Etton 231 D5
Everton 40 C3
Exning 110 A8
Eye 232 B1
Eye Green 232 B2
Eynesbury 74 F3

F

Farcet 187 C2
Fen Ditton 84 F5
Fen Drayton 121 F6
Fen End 57 D6
Fengate 198 D2
Fenstanton 122 C5
Fenton 165 B4
Fitton End 238 A3
Flint Cross 15 B2
Folksworth 175 D8
Fordham 212 F1
Fowlmere 15 D8
Foxton 30 C5
Freckenham 213 C3
Friday Bridge 236 A4
Fulbourn 66 F4

G

Gamlingay 41 D5
Gamlingay Cinques 41 B6
Gamlinghay Great Heath 40 E3
Gaultree 236 D6
Gimbers End 114 B2
Girton 82 F8
Glatton 175 F1
Glinton 203 E8
Godmanchester 141 E2
Gorefield 237 E2
Grafham 116 A7
Grantchester 64 A4
Graveley 97 F4
Great Abington 34 C6
Great Bradley 55 F7
Great Chesterford 18 D2
Great Chishill 7 F2
Great Eversden 45 E8
Great Gidding 166 E3
Great Gransden 58 D5
Great Paxton 96 E4
Great Raveley 163 B7
Great Shelford 48 F5
Great Staughton 93 F6
Great Stukeley 152 A2
Great Wilbraham 68 A7
Great Wratting 39 D5
Green End 93 A3
Green End 62 B6
Green End 152 A1
Guilden Morden 10 E4
Gunthorpe 204 D2
Guyhirn 234 F2

H

Haddenham 210 B6
Haddon 180 B6
Hadstock 20 C6
Hail Weston 95 B1
Hamerton 159 B4
Hampton Hargate 186 D2
Hanchet End 38 C1
Hardwick 81 B3
Hardwick 117 A5
Hare Park 88 A3
Harlton 46 D5
Haroldsbridge 237 C2
Harston 48 A3
Hartford 142 A6
Haslingfield 47 B6
Hatley End 25 B5
Hatley St George 43 A3
Hauxton 48 B4

Haverhill 24 C8
Hazel Stub 23 C7
Helpston 231 C4
Hemingford Abbots 142 E3
Hemingford Grey 143 E1
Herringswell 134 E8
Heydon 8 A5
High Cross 82 E2
Highfields 80 D2
Hildersham 34 F5
Hilton 121 B1
Hinxton 18 A7
Histon 104 C4
Holly End 236 E5
Holme 177 A4
Holywell 144 F2
Holywell Row 214 A8
Hook 223 D8
Horningsea 106 A1
Horse Moor 228 D1
Horseheath 37 A3
Houghton 143 A5
Huntingdon 141 F4

I

Ickleton 18 A4
Ickleton 9 A8
Impington 104 C2
Ingleborough 238 E5
Inham's End 189 F6
Islands Common 74 E7
Isleham 213 A5

K

Kennett 133 F5
Kennett End 134 A2
Kentford 134 B2
Keyston 146 B3
Kimbolton 113 F6
King's Dyke 188 E6
Kings Hedges 83 E7
Kings Ripton 153 C5
Kingston 61 A3
Kingswood Park 243 B2
Kirtling 72 E6
Kirtling Green 72 C4
Kirtling Towers 72 D7
Knapwell 100 E2
Kneesworth 13 A6
Knights End 228 A1

L

Lakes End 229 F3
Landbeach 105 D7
Landwade 131 C4
Lark Hall Corner 69 A1
Lattersea Field 190 B6
Leighton Bromswold 148 D3
Leverington 238 B2
Lidgate 73 E8
Linton 35 E3
Litlington 12 B2
Little Abington 34 B7
Little Catworth 137 A6
Little Chishill 1 C7
Little Ditton 90 F2
Little Downham 218 B6
Little End 74 C1
Little Eversden 46 A7
Little Gidding 158 F8
Little Gransden 58 D3
Little Heath 41 C4
Little Linton 35 B3
Little London 243 C4
Little Ouse 226 D4
Little Paxton 96 B2
Little Raveley 163 B4
Little Shelford 48 E3
Little Staughton 93 B6
Little Stukeley 151 C4
Little Thetford 211 B7
Little Wilbraham 86 E1
Little Wratting 39 D3
Littlebury Green 9 F2
Littleport 242 C4
Lode 107 C2
Lolworth 101 F5
Long Meadow 107 F2
Longstanton 123 E2
Longstowe 59 F3
Longthorpe 197 A1
Luddington in
  the Brook 166 B4
Lutton 174 C4

M

Madingley 81 E5
Manea 224 B4
March 243 B4
Margery's Croft 238 B1
Marholm 203 E1
Market Deeping 231 D8
Marshland
  St James 236 F8
Maxey 231 C7
Melbourn 14 C5
Meldreth 29 A2
Mepal 216 E4
Mildenhall 239 A6
Mile End 219 C5
Mill End 72 E5
Mill Green 22 D7
Millfield 197 F5
Milton 105 E2
Molesworth 147 A5
Morborne 180 B3
Morden Green 11 C1
Moulton 112 E6
Murrow 234 D5

N

Needingworth 208 B3
Nene Terrace 232 D6
New England 197 E7
New Fletton 187 B8
New Meadow 187 F2
Newark 198 E6
New Wimpole 28 B8
Newborough 207 D1
Newfields 237 D1
Newham 64 C8
Newnham
  Croft 64 D7
Newstead 244 E6
Newton 31 C8
Newton 238 A5
Newtown 64 E7
Newtown 141 E5
Newtown 114 A5
Norman Cross 180 F2
North Green 190 E8
North Side 200 F4
Northborough 231 F7
Northfields 244 C6
Norwoodside 243 C7
Nosterfield End 22 F5

O

Oakington 103 B5
Odsey 3 C1
Offord Cluny 117 F3
Offord D'Arcy 117 F1
Old Fletton 187 A6
Old Hurst 154 E7
Old Weston 148 A8
Old Wimpole 44 F3
Orton Brimbles 185 D5
Orton Goldhay 185 F3
Orton Longueville 186 B5
Orton Malbourne 186 C4
Orton Southgate 185 C2
Orton Waterville 185 E4
Orton Wistow 185 C6
Orwell 45 E1
Outwell 236 F3
Over 208 E1
Over End 178 E7
Owl End 152 A3
Oxlode 224 C1

P

Pale Green 23 D1
Pampisford 33 B5
Papley 174 A6
Papworth Everard 99 B3
Papworth St Agnes 98 D5
Parson Drove 234 D7
Paston 205 A1
Peakirk 206 B1
Peas Hill 243 B6
Peterborough 197 D5
Pidley 155 E8
Pilsgate 230 C4
Pondersbridge 220 D7
Prickwillow 219 B5
Pymore (Pymoor) 224 E1

Q

Queen Adelaide 218 D4

R

Rampton 124 F4
Ramsey 172 B6
Ramsey Forty Foot 221 C2
Ramsey Heights 171 A7
Ramsey Mereside 221 A4
Ramsey St Mary's 220 D3
Ravensthorpe 197 C6
Reach 129 C1
Red Lodge 213 F1
Ring's End 234 F1
Romsey Town 65 B8
Royston 5 B6

S

St Ives 143 E7
St Neots 74 E4
Sandhill 242 E3
Sapley 141 F8
Sawston 33 A7
Sawtry 168 A3
Saxon Street 91 B3
Seadyke 234 F6
Shepreth 29 E4
Shingay 26 F2
Shudy Camps 22 B5
Sibson 183 E8
Six Mile Bottom 68 F7
Slade Field 241 B7
Snailwell 132 B4
Soham 212 B4
Soham Cotes 211 F5
Somersham 215 B1
South Green 190 F7
Southoe 95 E5
Southorpe 230 D2
Spaldwick 137 F6
Stamford 244 D4
Stanground 187 C5
Stapleford 49 D4
Staughton Green 94 A7
Staughton Highway 94 A5
Steeple Gidding 159 B7
Steeple Morden 11 B2
Stetchworth 90 A2
Stetchworth Ley 71 B7
Steventon End 21 C2
Stibbington 194 C2
Stilton 176 A7
Stirtloe 117 B2
Stonely 114 B3
Stourbridge Common 84 B4
Stow Cum Quy 86 A6
Stow Longa 137 C2
Streetly End 37 A5
Strethall 9 F4
Stretham 210 E5
Studlands Park 110 F8
Stukeley 141 B6
Stuntney 218 D1
Sturmer 24 F4
Sutton 216 E2
Sutton 194 E7
Sutton Gault 216 C2
Swaffham Bulbeck 108 B1
Swaffham Prior 108 A4
Swavesey 122 E6
Swingbrow 222 D3

T

Tadlow 26 A3
Tallington 230 E7
Temple End 55 D2
Tetworth 40 F7
Teversham 85 C1
The Cottons 236 E3
The Green 122 D1
The Lipneas 202 B1
Thistley Green 213 C7
Tholomas Drove 235 A5
Thorney 233 A3
Thorney Toll 234 A3
Thornhaugh 193 F5
Three Holes 229 C2
Thriplow 31 C2
Throckenholt 234 B8
Tilbrook 113 B7
Tipps End 229 F2
Toft 61 E4

W

Top End 93 B1
Toseland 97 E2
Town End 243 D1
Trumpington 64 E2
Tuddenham 214 D2
Turves 191 F6
Tydd St Giles 237 F7

U

Uffington 230 C6
Ufford 230 F3
Upend 92 A1
Upend Green 91 F2
Upton 160 C1
Upton 195 B6
Upware 211 B1
Upwell 236 D1
Upwood 171 C2

W

Walpole Marsh 238 F8
Walsoken 245 F6
Walton 204 D1
Walton Dam 238 D4
Walton Highway 238 F4
Wansford 194 A4
Warboys 165 A5
Wardy Hill 217 B4
Waresley 57 E2
Warmington 178 A3
Water End 25 B3
Water Newton 184 C7
Waterbeach 106 C7
Waterside 213 A6
Way Head 217 C6
Weald 76 B4
Welches Dam 224 A1
Welney 225 B8
Wendy 27 C4
Wennington 162 D4
Wentworth 217 B1
Werrington 204 B3
West Deeping 231 B8
West End 155 A5
West Perry 115 D2
West Row 213 D6
West Walton 238 E4
West Walton
  Church End 238 D5
West Wickham 37 B7
West Wratting 53 E5
Westcote 211 F6
Westley Bottom 69 C7
Westley Waterless 70 C5
Weston Colville 54 B7
Weston Ditch 213 C7
Weston Green 54 D5
Westry 227 F5
Westwick 103 E7
Westwood 197 B4
Whaddon 28 C1
White Hall 235 E6
Whittlesey 189 D5
Whittlesford 32 B5
Wicken 211 F1
Wiggens Green 23 E2
Wilburton 210 B5
Willingham 209 B1
Willingham Green 54 D8
Wimblington 223 A6
Wintringham 75 F4
Winwick 158 B6
Wisbech 245 A6
Wisbech St Mary 235 B7
Wistow 163 F6
Witcham 217 A2
Witchford 217 D1
Withersfield 38 C4
Wittering 230 C4
Woodditton 90 E3
Woodhurst 155 B4
Woodland Green 24 E7
Woodston 186 E7
Woodwalton 161 F6
Woolley 149 E1
Worlington 213 E4
Wothorpe 244 B2
Wrestlingworth 25 C4
Wyton 142 F5

Y

Yarwell 183 A8
Yaxley 181 F4
Yelling 98 C1

A

A Furlong Dro CB6 224 F2
Abbey Cl Burwell CB5 130 B1
Sawtry PE28 168 B4
Abbey Fields PE26 172 C7
Abbey La Lode CB5 107 C2
Swaffham Bulbeck CB5 108 B3
Abbey Pl 4 Thorney PE6 233 A3
Waterbeach CB5 127 B1
Abbey Rd Cambridge CB5 84 A3
Peterborough PE4 204 C1
Ramsey PE26 172 C6
Abbey St Cambridge CB1 84 A2
Ickleton CB10 17 F3
Abbey Way PE7 189 C7
Abbey Wlk CB1 84 A2
Abbot Thurston Ave 4 CB6 240 E6
Abbot Way PE7 181 D4
Abbot's Cl PE28 155 A5
Abbots Cl Cambridge CB4 83 E7
Hemingford Abbots PE28 142 F3
Ramsey PE26 172 C7
Abbots Cres PE27 144 A6
Abbots Dr 1 PE6 232 B8
Abbots Ripton CE Sch PE28 162 C1
Abbots Way CB5 106 A1
Abbotsbury PE2 186 A3
Abbotsley Rd PE19 57 E8
Abbotsmede Jun Sch PE1 198 C4
Abbott Cl PE28 140 C3
Abbott's Cl PE9 244 D4
Abbott's Grove Cotts CB9 24 F3
Abbotts Cl SG8 12 A2
Abbotts Ct 2 CB9 24 E5
Abbotts Gr PE4 204 B6
Abbotts Rd CB9 39 A1
Abington Gr 6 PE14 236 A5
Abington H CB1 34 B6
Abington Rd SG8 11 F2
Aboyne Ave PE2 185 F5
Abrahams Cl CB4 105 D6
Abram's La SG8 8 C4
Acacia Ave
Peterborough PE1 198 B8
St Ives PE27 143 E6
Wisbech PE13 245 C8
Acacia Gr March PE15 243 C5
St Neots PE19 75 A6
Acer Rd PE1 198 B6
Acheson Rd PE28 117 D8
Ackerman Gdns 4 PE19 74 C2
Ackerman St PE19 74 C2
Ackroyd Rd 2 SG8 5 E8
Acland St PE1 197 F3
Acorn Ave CB3 102 C4
Acre Rd Carlton CB8 55 B8
March PE15 243 D4
Acre The PE28 150 F4
Acrefield Dr CB4 246 C4
Acremead PE8 178 A3
Acres The 2 PE9 230 D4
Acton Way CB4 83 D5
Adam & Eve St 1 CB1 246 C1
Adam's La PE19 96 E4
Adams Ct CB5 106 C7
Adams Rd Cambridge CB3 83 B2
Swaffham Prior CB5 108 D5
Adastral Cl CB8 110 E4
Addenbrookes Hospl CB2 65 A3
Addington Way 1 PE4 204 C3
Addison Rd PE15 223 B7
Adelaide Cl 10 CB7 212 B4
Adelaide Pl 2 PE15 243 C4
Adelaide St PE9 244 C5
Adelaide Wlk 7 PE28 208 E6
Admirals Dr PE13 245 D8
Admirals Way PE19 74 A2
Adventurers' Dro CB6 224 C1
Ailwine Rd PE26 171 B2
Ailwyn Sch PE26 172 C6
Aingers Rd CB4 104 B4
Ainsdale CB1 65 F5
Ainsdale Dr PE4 204 B4
Ainsworth Ct 4 CB1 84 A1
Ainsworth Pl CB1 84 B1
Ainsworth St CB1 84 A1
Aintree Rd SG8 5 F6
Airedale Cl PE1 198 A6
Airedale Rd 1 PE9 244 A7
Airport Way CB1 85 B2
Akeman Cl CB6 210 F6
Akeman St Cambridge CB4 83 C5
Landbeach CB4 105 C6
Alamein Ct PE19 74 C5
Albany Rd PE13 245 C6
Albany Wlk PE2 186 D7
Albemarle Rd PE27 143 F7
Albemarle Way CB4 83 E7
Albert Pl PE3 197 F1
Albert Rd Stamford PE9 244 C5
Stow cum Quy CB5 86 A5
Albert St CB4 246 B4
Alberta Cres PE29 141 E5
Albert's Dr 1 PE15 243 F3
Albion Row 6 CB3 83 C3
Albion Yd 5 CB3 83 C3
Alconbury Airfield PE28 151 E6
Alconbury CE Sch PE28 150 F5
Alconbury Cl PE2 187 E5
Alde Rd CB9 39 A1
Aldeburgh Cl 4 CB9 23 E7
Alder Cl 1 PE19 74 B5
Alder Dr Bourn CB3 79 C3
Huntingdon PE29 141 D5
Alder Rd PE7 186 C3
Alderlands Cl 6 PE6 232 B8
Alderman Jacobs Sch PE7 189 F8
Alderman's Dr PE3 197 E3
Aldreth Rd CB6 209 F5
Aldsworth Cl 1 PE1 198 D6
Alec Rolph Cl CB1 66 D5
Alex Wood Rd CB4 83 E6
Alexander Rd SG19 25 B4
Alexandra Rd
Littleport CB6 242 E4
Peterborough PE1 197 F6
Stamford PE9 244 B6
Wisbech PE13 245 C5
Alfric Sq PE2 186 D6
Alftruda Cl PE15 243 C6
Algar Dr CB8 70 F8
Algores Way PE13 245 B2
Alington Rd PE19 74 E1
Aliwal Rd PE7 189 F1
All Saints Ave
1 Leverington PE13 238 F1
Leverington PE13 245 F7
All Saints CE Jun Sch PE1 198 A6
All Saints Cl
St Ives PE27 144 A6
2 Wisbech PE14 236 A5
All Saints Gn PE27 144 A6
All Saints Pas CB2 246 A3
All Saints Prim Sch
March PE15 243 D6
Newmarket CB8 111 B3
All Saints Rd Fulbourn CB1 66 F5
Newmarket CB8 111 A3
All Saints' Rd PE1 198 A5
All Saints' St PE9 244 B5
All Saints Way 3 PE28 168 C4
All Saints Wlk IP28 213 F4
All Souls La CB3 83 B4
Allan Ave PE2 187 E5
Allen Ct CB2 64 D2
Allen Farm Cl PE29 141 E1
Allen Rd
Peterborough PE1 197 E6
Ramsey PE26 171 F7
Allen's Dro PE13 237 D1
Allen's Orch PE28 140 E1
Allens Cl CB3 63 B4
Allerton Cl 6 PE9 230 D3
Allerton Garth PE7 185 A4
Allington Wlk CB9 23 E8
Allotment La PE5 195 E2
Allotments Dro CB6 211 B7
Alma Rd PE1 197 F5
Alma Terr PE16 241 B4
Almond Cl PE29 142 A1
Almond Dr PE15 243 C3
Almond Gr CB3 102 C4
Almond Rd
Peterborough PE1 198 B7
St Neots PE19 74 F6
Almoners' Ave CB1 65 C3
Almoners La PE3 197 E3
Alms Cl PE29 141 C7
Alms Hill CB3 60 D7
Alms La 3 SG7 2 D4
Alnwick Ct 1 PE19 74 F2
Alpha La PE28 151 E3
Alpha Rd CB4 246 A4
Alpha St PE15 243 D5
Alpha Terr CB2 64 D3
Alstead Rd CB4 104 B5
Alsyke Cl PE28 116 A7
Althorpe Ct 1 CB6 240 B5
Alwin Cl PE28 168 B3
Alwyn Cl PE27 144 B6
Alwyne Rd CB1 65 C2
Amberley Slope PE4 204 C3
Ambleside Gdns PE4 204 D3
Ambrose Way CB4 104 C4
Ambury Hill PE29 141 E5
Ambury Rd PE29 141 D5
Ambury Rd S PE29 141 D5
America The CB6 216 D1
American Air Mus* CB2 16 F8
American La PE29 141 E5
Amwell Rd CB4 83 F8
Amy Johnson Ct 3 IP28 239 B5
Ancaster Rd 2 PE9 244 A7
Ancaster Way
Cambridge CB1 65 C7
3 Doddington/Wimblington PE15 222 F5
Anchor Ct CB6 242 E3
Anchor Dro PE38 226 F4
Anchor La CB5 130 B4
Anderson Cl PE13 245 A7
Anderson Cres PE29 142 A2
Andrea Cl PE2 187 C6
Andrew Cl PE5 195 D2
Andrew Rd
1 Newmarket CB8 110 E5
St Neots PE19 74 F2
1 Stamford PE9 244 B6
Andrewe's Cl PE7 187 B1
Andrews Cl 2 CB6 210 F5
Andrews Cres PE4 204 F2
Angel Dro CB7 240 D2
Angel Sq 3 CB7 240 D3
Angell's Mdw SG7 2 D4
Angle End CB1 67 F8
Angle La SG8 29 E5
Anglers Cl 2 PE15 243 A5
Anglers Way CB4 84 C5
Anglesey Way 8 CB4 208 D1
Anglia Polytechnic Univ CB1 246 C2
Anglia Way PE13 245 B2
Anglian Bsns Pk SG8 5 B7
Anglian Cl PE2 187 D6
Angoods La PE16 241 B6
Angus Cl 2 CB1 65 A8
Angus Ct PE3 197 D3
Animal Health Trust CB8 133 F1
Ann Suckling Rd CB9 39 A2
Anne Rd PE9 244 A6
Anne's Cl CB8 110 B8
Annesdale 2 CB7 240 D3
Annesley Cl PE28 168 B4
Annington Cres SG8 13 A8
Ann's Rd CB5 84 E4
Ansley Way PE27 143 E5
Anson Dr PE27 143 F6
Anson Pl 2 PE19 74 A2
Anstey H* CB2 64 C2
Anstey Way CB2 64 D2
Antelope Way 2 CB1 66 A7
Anthony Cl PE7 189 C8
Antonia Cl CB9 24 E7
Anvil Ave SG8 12 A2
Anvil Cl CB2 49 C4
Apollo Way CB4 83 E8
Apple Cl PE19 96 F8
Apple Gr PE19 74 C4
Apple Orch The PE28 143 D2
Apple Tree Cl PE7 182 A6
Appleby Pk CB6 240 D5
Appletree Cl CB4 125 D1
Appletree Gr CB5 130 B4
Appletrees CB3 102 C3
Appleyard PE2 187 C7
Apreece Rd PE7 175 D8
Apreece Way PE7 176 A7
Apsley Way PE3 197 A2
Apthorpe St CB1 66 F6
Apthorpe Way CB4 84 A7
Aragon Cl Buckden PE19 117 B4
Cambridge CB4 83 E7
Aragon Pl PE28 113 F5
Arber Cl CB5 86 E6
Arborfield Cl PE6 231 C4
Arbury Cl PE3 197 A3
Arbury Prim Sch CB4 83 E5
Arbury Rd CB4 83 E6
Arcadia Gdns CB4 103 C5
Archers Cl CB5 108 B3
Archers Dro PE6 233 D6
Archers Wood PE7 186 C3
Archers Wood Nature Reserve* PE28 160 C7
Archery Cres 9 CB7 240 D4
Archway Ct CB3 64 B7
Arden Rd CB4 83 F8
Ardleigh Cl 3 PE13 245 E5
Ardross Ct CB8 68 F6
Argyle St CB1 65 B8
Arles Ave PE13 245 E3
Armada Cl PE13 245 D8
Armingford Cres SG8 14 E7
Armitage Way CB4 83 F8
Armley Gr 3 PE9 244 D7
Armshold La CB3 61 D2
Armstrong Cl
Newmarket CB8 111 B3
Perry PE28 115 D3
Armstrong Ct 1 PE29 141 F8
Arnhem Cl PE19 74 C5
Arnold's La PE7 189 E7
Arran Cl CB1 65 F6
Arran Way PE27 144 A8
Arrendene Rd CB9 38 F1
Arthur Mellows Village Coll PE6 203 D8
Arthur St CB4 83 C4
Artillery St 11 PE13 245 C4
Artindale PE3 197 A3
Artis Ct PE3 197 A3
Arundel Cl CB4 83 C5
Arundel Cres PE19 74 E2
Arundel Rd
Huntingdon PE29 142 A6
Peterborough PE4 204 C1
Arundell CB6 240 C5
Ascham La CB2 32 B4
Ascham Rd CB4 83 E4
Ascot Dr PE1 198 B6
Ascot Rd SG8 5 F6
Ash Cl Huntingdon PE29 141 E7
Peterborough PE1 198 C7
Stilton PE7 175 F7
1 Thorney PE6 232 F3
Ash Ct Brampton PE28 140 C3
Peterborough PE1 198 C7
Ash Gn CB10 18 D1
Ash Gr Burwell CB5 130 B2
Chatteris PE16 241 C5
4 Ely CB7 240 F5
Haverhill CB9 38 E1
March PE15 243 C5
Melbourn SG8 14 C5
Ash Pk PE4 204 B6
Ash Rd Earith PE28 208 F7
Peterborough PE1 198 C7
Ash Tree Cl 14 PE15 223 B7
Ashbeach Dro PE26 220 D3
Ashbeach Prim Sch The PE26 220 D3
Ashbeach Rd
March PE15 243 D4
Ramsey PE26 220 D3
Ashburn Cl PE6 203 F7
Ashbury Cl CB1 65 B6
Ashcroft PE19 98 B2
Ashcroft Gdns PE1 198 C5
Ashdale Cl 1 PE28 168 B3
Ashdale Pk PE13 245 A5
Ashdon CP Sch CB10 21 B1
Ashen Gn CB2 49 A5
Ashfield PE28 113 F5
Ashfield Rd CB4 84 B5
Ashfields 1 PE6 231 F7
Ashlea Cl CB9 24 B6
Ashlea Rd CB9 24 B6
Ashleigh PE2 185 C6
Ashley Gdns CB6 242 D3
Ashley Pool La PE6 233 A2
Ashley Rd Cheveley CB8 112 A1
Newmarket CB8 111 E2
Ashley Way CB2 32 F8
Ashline Gr PE7 189 D6
Ashmead Dr CB3 81 A3
Ashton Cl PE27 208 A2
Ashton Gdns PE29 141 D5
Ashton Rd PE3 197 B5
Ashvale CB4 83 D7
Ashwell & Morden Sta SG7 3 D2
Ashwell Rd
Guilden Morden SG8 10 F2
Newnham SG7 2 A1
Ashwell St Ashwell SG7 2 D3
Bassingbourn cum Kneesworth SG8 13 A3
Askers Field CB3 78 E2
Askew's La PE7 181 E4
Aspal Cl 8 IP28 213 F8
Aspal Hall Rd IP28 213 F8
Aspal La IP28 214 A8
Aspal Pk
"Beck Row, Holywell Row & Kenny Hill" IP28 214 A8
Mildenhall IP28 213 F8
Aspal Pl 9 IP28 213 F8
Aspen Cl 3 Ely CB7 240 E5
Haverhill CB9 38 E1
Aspen Gn PE29 141 E6
Asplin Ave PE15 243 E4
Asplin's Cl 5 CB4 208 D1
Asplin's La PE19 117 F3
Asplins Ave 8 PE27 208 A3
Aster Dr PE4 204 D3
Astilbe La PE29 141 D5
Astley Cl CB6 216 E1
Astore Pk PE1 198 E3
Atherstone Ave PE3 197 B4
Atherton Cl CB4 83 E5
Athlone Cl CB3 99 A3
Atkins Cl Cambridge CB4 84 A7
Littleport CB6 242 C5
Atkinson St PE1 198 C2
Atlantic Cl PE15 243 B6
Atterton Rd CB9 38 D1
Aubretia Ave PE4 204 D3
Auckland Rd CB5 246 C3
Audley Cl SG19 58 E4
Audley Gate PE3 197 C3
Audley Way CB1 37 A3
Augers Rd 4 CB1 65 F6
Augusta Cl PE1 198 E6
Augustus Cl
2 Cambridge CB4 83 E8
Haverhill CB9 24 D7
Augustus Way PE16 241 D6
Aureole Wlk CB8 110 E8
Austin Friars La 3 PE9 244 B4
Austin St PE9 244 B4
Avenells Way 2 SG19 41 D5
Avenue Rd
Huntingdon PE29 141 D5
St Neots PE19 74 F6
Avenue The Burwell CB5 130 C3
Cambridge CB3 246 A3
Girton CB3 103 B1
Godmanchester PE29 141 E3
Leighton PE28 148 C3
Madingley CB3 81 F7
March PE15 243 D2
Newmarket CB8 111 A3
Ramsey PE26 172 A7
Aversley Rd PE28 168 C2
Aversley Wood Nature Reserve* PE28 159 F8
Aves Cl CB7 213 A5
Avon Ct Eaton Socon PE19 74 C3
Peterborough PE4 204 E2
Axiom Ave PE3 197 C4
Axis Way 6 PE19 74 B5
Aydon Rd PE7 187 F6
Aylesborough Cl 4 CB4 83 D7
Aylesford Way CB2 49 B4
Aylestone Rd CB4 246 C4
Ayre Ct 5 PE19 75 A5
Ayres Dr PE2 187 C6
Azalea Cl PE3 197 A2

B

Babraham CE Prim Sch CB2 50 D1
Babraham Rd
Babraham CB2 50 B1
Cambridge CB2 65 C2
Babraham Rd *continued*
Fulbourn CB1 50 E8
Great Shelford CB2 49 E8
Sawston CB2 32 F8
Stapleford CB2 50 B6
Back Dro Upwell PE14 229 D8
Welney PE14 225 A8
Back Hill Ely CB7 240 D3
Hadstock CB1 20 B6
Back La Bourn CB3 79 B4
Burrough Green CB8 70 F4
Coveney CB6 217 B5
14 Deeping St James PE6 231 F8
Elton PE8 178 D8
Ely CB7 240 D4
Eye PE6 232 A1
Haslingfield CB3 47 B4
Holywell-cum-Needingworth PE27 144 F2
Ickleton CB10 18 A3
Market Deeping PE6 206 A7
Melbourn SG8 14 C4
Outwell PE14 236 E3
Stamford PE9 244 C5
Wicken CB7 211 E1
Yaxley PE7 181 E5
Back Rd Elm PE14 236 A5
Gorefield PE13 237 E2
Linton CB1 35 C3
Murrow PE13 234 D6
Wisbech PE14 236 A3
Back Reach Dro PE15 221 E7
Back St SG7 2 D3
Bacon's Yd SG7 2 D4
Bad Gate PE12 237 B7
Badcock Rd CB3 47 B5
Bader Cl
Peterborough PE3 197 B6
1 Ramsey PE26 172 A4
Badgeney Rd PE15 243 E4
Badger Cl PE7 181 F5
Badinton La PE9 230 F5
Badlingham Rd CB7 213 C1
Badminton Cl CB4 83 C6
Badney Dro PE16 222 D3
Bagot Pl 5 CB4 83 F8
Bagsham La IP28 213 E6
Bahram Cl 1 CB8 110 E4
Bailey Cl CB9 24 D7
Bailey Mews CB5 246 C3
Bain Cl PE9 244 C7
Bainton Rd Barnack PE9 230 D4
Newborough PE6 204 F8
Bakehouse Hill CB8 70 E8
Baker Dr CB5 130 C3
Bakers Cl CB3 62 D6
Bakers La Barley SG8 6 F3
Linton CB1 35 D2
Peterborough PE2 186 E7
Bakers Way PE28 115 E2
Bakery Cl Fen Ditton CB5 84 E5
Wilburton CB6 210 C5
Bakewell Rd PE2 185 C2
Bala Ct PE4 204 E3
Baldock Rd SG8 4 C4
Baldock St SG8 5 D6
Baldock Way CB1 65 B5
Baldwin Cl
1 Wisbech PE13 245 D5
1 Wittering PE8 230 C1
Baldwins Cl CB3 60 C5
Baldwins Manor SG19 58 D4
Balingdon La 1 CB1 35 D3
Balintore Rise PE2 185 D4
Balland Field CB4 124 A8
Ballard Cl CB4 105 D3
Balmoral Rd 1 PE4 197 C8
Balmoral Way PE19 74 E2
Balsham Rd Fulbourn CB1 67 B2
Linton CB1 35 D3
Bamber St PE1 197 F4
Bambers La PE14 236 C6
Bancroft Cl CB1 65 B6
Bancroft La CB7 212 B5
Bandon Rd CB3 82 F6
Banff Cl 2 CB4 83 E7
Banhams Cl CB4 246 C4
Bank Ave PE28 208 C8
Bank Cl PE7 189 E5
Bank Dr PE13 245 A7
Bank The PE13 234 C7
Bannister's Row PE13 245 B7
Bannold Ct CB5 106 B8
Bannold Dro CB5 106 C8
Bannold Rd CB5 106 D8
Banworth La CB4 105 D6
Baptist Rd PE14 229 D8
Bar Cl CB2 49 C5
Bar Dro PE14 236 B4
Bar La Hatley SG19 42 E2
Stapleford CB2 49 C4
Tadlow SG19 25 E8
Barbara Stradbroke Ave CB8 89 B7
Barber Cl PE2 187 C7
Barbers Dro PE6 232 C8
Barbers Hill PE4 204 B7
Barcham Rd CB7 211 F7
Bardling's Dro PE12 237 A8
Bardney PE2 186 A4
Bardyke Bank PE14 229 F7
Baretts Cl PE7 189 D8
Barford Cl PE2 186 C7
Barford Rd PE19 74 E2
Bargate La IP28 213 D5
Bargate Rd IP28 213 D6
Barham Cl PE2 187 F5
Barham Ct SG8 14 D6

Barham Rd PE28 ....149 D6
Barker Cl
  Hail Weston PE19 ....95 A1
  Waterbeach CB5 ....106 B8
Barker's La CB6 ....243 D1
Barkham's La CB6 .....242 D4
Barkston Dr PE1 ....198 B6
Barkway Rd SG8 ....5 E5
Barkway St SG8 ....5 D5
Barkways CB5 ....130 C1
Barleuy Ct 6 PE19 .....74 D5
Barley Rd
  1 Eaton Socon PE19 ...74 C3
  Great & Little Chishill SG8 ...7 A7
Barley VP Sch SG8 ....7 A2
Barley Way CB1 ....35 D2
Barlings Ct CB8 ....111 A4
Barn Cl Huntingdon PE29 .142 A7
  6 Maxey PE6 ....231 C7
  Peterborough PE4 .....204 B3
  Ramsey PE26 ....172 A4
  Stilton PE7 ....175 F8
Barn Hill PE9 ....244 B5
Barnabas Oley CE Prim Sch
  SG19 ....58 E4
Barnack CE Prim Sch
  PE9 ....230 D4
Barnack Drift PE9 .....230 B3
Barnack Rd Bainton PE9 .230 E4
  St Martin's Without PE9 .244 C4
Barnard Cl 1 PE19 .....74 F1
Barnard Way
  1 Cambridge CB4 ......83 D5
  9 Peterborough PE3 ..196 F3
Barnes Cl Cambridge CB5 .84 D2
  St Neots PE19 ....74 E6
Barnes Way
  Peterborough PE4 .....204 B3
  Whittlesey PE7 ....189 B8
Barnfield Gdns PE7 ....190 F8
Barnfield La PE28 ....98 D7
Barns Cl CB4 ....208 D1
Barns The PE19 ....117 B4
Barnstock PE3 ....197 A7
Barnwell Dr CB1 ....84 E2
Barnwell Rd CB1 ....84 D1
Baron Ct Eaton Socon PE19 74 B4
  Peterborough PE4 .....204 D4
Baron's Way CB3 ....99 B3
Barons La CB2 ....30 C5
Baros Cl CB1 ....22 A7
Barracks The PE13 .....237 E2
Barringer Way PE19 ....74 F7
Barrington CE Sch CB2 ..46 F1
  Shepreth SG8 ....29 D6
Barrington Rd Orwell SG8 45 F1
Barron's Gn SG8 ....29 F4
Barrons Way 1 CB3 ....62 C5
Barrow Cl CB2 ....64 E5
Barrow Rd CB2 ....64 E5
Barrowcrofts CB4 .....104 B5
Barrowfield PE1 ....198 E4
Barr's St PE7 ....189 D7
Barry Lynham Dr CB8 ..111 C2
Barry Wlk 8 PE2 ......186 F7
Barsey Cl CB9 ....38 C1
Barston Dro CB5 ......108 C7
Bartholemew's Wlk CB7 240 C2
Bartholomew Cl CB10 ...18 E2
Bartlow Rd
  Castle Camps CB1 ......22 D4
  Hadstock CB1 ....20 D7
  Linton CB1 ....35 E2
Barton Cl Cambridge CB3 .64 B8
  Witchford CB6 ....217 D1
Barton La PE13 ....237 F8
Barton Mews CB7 ....240 C4
Barton Rd Cambridge CB3 .64 B8
  Comberton CB3 ....62 D5
  Ely CB7 ....240 C3
  Haslingfield CB3 ......47 A7
  Wisbech PE13 ....245 A4
Barton Sch CB3 ....63 B4
Barton Sq CB7 ....240 D4
Bartons Cl CB1 ....53 B2
Bartons Pl 2 CB8 .....110 E5
Bartram Gate PE4 .....204 E1
Barway Rd CB7 ....211 E7
Bascraft Way PE29 ....142 A1
Basil Gn PE2 ....186 D6
Bassenhally Ct PE7 ...189 E7
Bassenhally Rd PE7 ...189 E8
Bassenthwaite PE29 ...141 B6
Basset Cl 3 CB4 ....83 F8
Bassingbourn Cty Prim Sch
  SG8 ....12 D4
Bassingbourn Rd SG8 ..12 B3
Bassingbourn Village Coll
  SG8 ....12 E4
Bateman Mews CB2 ....64 E7
Bateman St CB2 ....64 E7
Bate's Dro CB6 ....225 B3
Bateson Rd CB4 ....83 D4
Bates's Dro CB6 ......225 B5
Bath Cres PE28 ....143 B8
Bath Rd PE13 ....245 C4
Bath Row PE9 ....244 B4
Bathurst PE2 ....186 A4
Battle Gate Rd CB3 ....80 A8
Battle Rd PE26 ....171 E3
Baulk La SG19 ....43 A3
Baulk The Thriplow SG8 ..31 B2
  Whittlesey PE7 ....189 E8
Baulkin's Dro PE12 ...237 C8
Baulks The CB2 ....32 C7
Bawtree Cres CB1 ......35 E3
Baxter Cl 3 PE13 .....245 E6
Baycliffe Cl 1 CB1 ....65 D5

Bayfield Dr CB5 ....130 C2
Bayford Pl 1 CB4 ......83 F8
Bayliss PE7 ....118 F7
Beach Rd CB4 ....125 F3
Beachampstead Rd 1
  PE19 ....93 F6
Beacon Cl PE29 ....141 A6
Beald Way CB6 ....240 A6
Beale Ct 2 PE29 ......141 F8
Beales Way CB4 ....84 A7
Bean Cl 2 PE19 ....75 A6
Bear La SG7 ....2 D4
Beatrice Rd PE13 .....245 D7
Beatty Rd PE19 ....74 B2
Beauchamp Cl PE29 ....74 B3
Beaufort Dr PE16 .....241 B6
Beaulands Cl CB4 .....246 C4
Beaulieu Ct 1 PE6 ....232 A1
Beaumaris Rd CB4 ....168 C3
Beaumont Cl PE29 .....141 F8
Beaumont Cres CB1 ....65 D3
Beaumont Ct CB9 ....24 B6
Beaumont Rd CB1 ......65 D3
Beaumont Vale CB9 ....24 B6
Beaupre Ave PE14 ....236 F3
Beaupre Dro PE26 ....221 A2
Beauvale Gdns PE4 ...204 E3
Beauvoir Pl PE7 ......181 E5
Beaver Ct 8 PE19 .....74 B5
Bec Rd PE19 ....74 E5
Beccelm Dr 9 PE6 ....232 B8
Beche Rd CB5 ....84 A2
Beche Way CB4 ....105 C7
Beck Rd CB7 ....213 B4
Beck Row Prim Sch
  IP28 ....213 F8
Becket's Cl PE26 .....172 B8
Beckett Rd PE16 .....241 C6
Beckingham PE2 ......185 F3
Bede Pl PE1 ....198 A6
Bedford Ave PE28 ....143 B8
Bedford Cl
  2 Needingworth PE27 .208 A3
  St Ives PE27 ....143 F7
Bedford Ct 10 PE6 ...233 A3
Bedford Row PE13 ....238 D8
Bedford St
  Peterborough PE1 ....198 B4
  St Neots PE19 ....74 E6
  Wisbech PE13 ....245 C6
Bedford Way CB4 .....168 C3
Bedwell Hey La CB6 ..217 C1
Beech Ave
  7 Doddington/Wimblington
    PE15 ....223 A6
  Little Stukeley PE28 ..152 A2
  Peterborough PE1 ....197 F3
Beech Cl
  Great Shelford CB2 ....48 E3
  Huntingdon PE29 .....141 E7
  Isleham CB7 ....212 F5
  2 Thorney PE6 ....233 A4
  Warboys PE28 ....164 E4
Beech Croft CB8 ....70 D2
Beech Dr PE27 ....143 F5
Beech End PE28 ......150 F4
Beech Gr Haverhill CB9 ..23 E8
  March PE15 ....243 C5
  St Neots PE19 ....74 F6
Beech La Ely CB7 ....240 E5
Beech Rd Ely CB7 ....240 E5
  Pampisford CB2 ....33 B5
Beech Rd PE6 ....203 D8
Beech Way CB1 ....35 C2
Beeches Prim Sch The
  PE1 ....197 F3
Beeches IP28 ....213 D7
Beeches The CB4 ......83 F5
Beechside SG19 ....41 C6
Beechwood Ave
  Bottisham CB5 ....86 F6
  Melbourn SG8 ....14 C5
Beechwood Cl
  Exning CB8 ....110 C8
  Peterborough PE1 ....198 C7
Beechwood Rd PE13 ..245 D7
Beehive Centre Ret Pk
  CB1 ....84 B2
Bee's La PE13 ....237 F6
Beeson Cl PE19 ....95 F2
Beeston Dr PE7 ......187 F5
Beeton Cl SG8 ....14 C6
Beetons Ct PE7 ......181 E5
Beezling Cl 9 PE19 ...74 C6
Beezling Fen Dro PE26 222 D3
Begdale Rd PE14 .....235 F5
Begwary Cl 7 PE19 ....74 B5
Beild Dro CB7 ....218 B7
Belbin Way CB2 ....32 D8
Beldam Ave CB5 ....5 E5
Beldam's Cl CB3 ....61 D4
Beldams PE27 ....208 A3
Belgrave Rd CB1 ......65 C8
Belgrave Sq PE28 ....168 B4
Belham Rd PE1 ....197 E7
Bell Cl Ely CB6 ......240 D5
  Meldreth SG8 ....14 A8
  Stilton PE7 ....176 A7
Bell Dro PE6 ....232 F6
Bell Foundry Cl 1 SG19 .41 D5
Bell Gdns
  Haddenham CB6 ......210 A6
  Soham CB7 ....212 B4
Bell Hill CB4 ....104 B4
Bell Holt 2 CB7 ......240 E4
Bell La Alconbury PE17 .150 F4
  Barton Mills IP28 ....239 D2

Bell La continued
  Fenstanton PE28 .....121 B5
  4 Market Deeping PE6 .231 F8
  Nuthampstead SG8 .....1 A2
  Southoe & Midloe PE19 ..95 E6
Bell Rd CB5 ....86 E5
Bellairs CB6 ....216 E1
Bellamy's La PE14 ...238 D4
Belle Isle PE28 ......140 B3
Belle Isle Cres PE28 .140 B3
Belle Vue PE2 ....187 C6
Bellman's Cl PE7 ....189 F7
Bellman's Rd PE7 ....189 F6
Bellmans Dr PE7 .....189 F7
Bell's Dro Littleport CB6 .225 B6
  Sutton St James PE12 .237 C8
Bell's Pl PE1 ....198 A2
Bells Mdw SG8 ....11 A5
Belmont PE15 ....246 B3
Belmont Rd PE15 ....243 D5
Belmore Cl 1 CB4 .....83 C5
Belsars Cl 1 CB4 ....209 A1
Belsay Dr PE1 ....187 F5
Belsize Ave PE2 .....186 E6
Belt Dro PE14 ....235 F4
Belt The CB8 ....73 D8
Belton Rd PE7 ....187 F5
Belton St PE9 ....244 C5
Belton's Hill PE28 ...137 F7
Belvedere 5 PE26 ...221 C2
Belvoir Rd CB4 ......246 C4
Belvoir Way PE1 .....198 C8
Benams CI PE5 ....195 E2
Bencroft La PE28 ....165 A4
Bendyshe Way CB2 ....30 A8
Benedict Sq PE4 .....204 A2
Benedict St CB6 .....240 B5
Benefield Rd CB8 ....112 F6
Benet Cl CB4 ....105 C1
Bene't St CB2 ....246 A2
Benians Ct CB3 ....83 B3
Benland PE3 ....197 A6
Bennett Rd IP28 ....214 A1
Benny's Way CB3 ......82 B2
Benson Pl 6 CB4 .....83 C4
Benson St 4 CB4 .....83 C4
Benstead End CB8 .....68 A8
Bentham Way CB6 ....240 E6
Bentinck St CB2 .....246 B1
Bentley Cl PE26 .....171 B2
Bentley Rd CB2 ....64 E5
Bentley St PE9 ......244 C5
Benwick Prim Sch PE15 222 A5
Benwick Rd
  Doddington PE15 .....222 D5
  Ramsey PE26 ....221 E3
  Whittlesey PE7 ......221 D7
Benyon Gr PE2 ....186 B4
Berberis Cl 3 PE6 ...232 F3
Beresford Rd CB6 ....240 A5
Bergamont Cl 5 PE29 .118 F8
Bergamot Rd CB9 ......23 C8
Bergholt Cl 4 CB5 ....84 E4
Berkeley Rd PE3 .....197 C3
Berkley Ct 1 PE19 ....74 E4
Berkley St PE19 ......74 E4
Bermuda Rd CB4 ......83 C4
Bermuda Terr CB4 ....83 C4
Bernard Cl PE29 .....141 D6
Bernard Rd PE28 ....140 D3
Bernard St CB6 .....240 C4
Berristead Cl CB6 ...210 C6
Berry Cl CB6 ....210 F5
Berry Gn CB6 ....210 F5
Berry Green Pk NN14 .156 E5
Berry La PE29 ....118 C8
Berrybut Way PE9 ...244 D7
Berrycroft Soham CB7 .212 B4
  Willingham CB4 ......124 A8
Berryfield PE15 .....243 E7
Bertie La 6 PE9 .....230 C6
Betjamin Rd SG8 ......5 D8
Betjeman Rd SG8 .....13 D1
Betony Vale SG8 ....5 E5
Bettles Cl PE1 ......198 A6
Betts Cl PE1 ....141 F1
Between Close Dro
  CB4 ....125 D2
Bevan Cl PE29 ....141 E6
Beverley Cl SG8 ......5 B8
Beverley Gdns PE29 .244 A6
Beverley Way 4 CB2 ..64 D3
Beverstone PE2 .....185 D5
Beville PE28 ....161 F6
Bevills Ct 16 PE15 ..223 A5
Bevis La CB4 ....235 C6
Bew Cl PE2 ....187 D4
Bicton Ind Est PE28 .114 B7
Bifield PE2 ....185 F3
Big Gn PE5 ....178 C3
Biggen The CB2 ......17 E8
Biggin Abbey* CB5 ...84 F8
Biggin La Fen Ditton CB5 .84 F8
  Ramsey PE26 ....171 E6
Biggs Rd PE14 ......236 D8
Bigram's La PE19 ....114 C7
Bilberry Cl 1 PE19 ...74 C5
Bilberry End CB1 .....20 C7
Bill Rickaby Dr CB8 ..111 A5
Binnimoor Rd PE15 ..228 E4
Birch Ave PE16 .....241 D5
Birch Cl Cambridge CB4 .83 F5
  Chatteris PE16 ......241 D5
  Yaxley PE7 ....182 A5
Birch Dr PE28 ....151 E3
Birch Gr 2 PE14 ....236 B5
Birch Trees Rd CB2 ..49 A6

Birchen Cl PE7 ......186 C3
Birches The CB7 .....212 A5
Birchtree Ave PE1 ...198 A7
Birchwood PE2 ......186 A3
Birchwood Ave PE15 .243 B2
Bird Farm Rd CB1 ....66 E5
Bird La PE19 ....95 A1
Bird's Dro Gorefield PE13 237 D1
  Sutton St James PE12 .237 B8
Birds Cl CB10 ....18 A3
Birdwood Rd CB1 .....65 D6
Birkdale Ave
  Mildenhall IP28 .....239 B5
  Peterborough PE4 ...204 B3
Birt La 1 PE27 .....144 A3
Biscay Cl CB9 ....24 C7
Bishop Cl PE7 ......175 F7
Bishop Creighton CP Sch
  PE1 ....198 B2
Bishop Laney Dr CB6 .240 C3
Bishop Way CB4 ....104 C3
Bishop Wynn Cl CB7 ..240 D3
Bishop's Ct CB2 .....64 C1
Bishop's Pal* CB6 ...217 F7
Bishop's Rd
  Cambridge CB2 ....64 D1
  Peterborough PE1 ...198 A1
Bishops Cl
  2 Little Downham CB6 .218 A4
  Peterborough PE1 ...198 D5
Bishops Rd St Neots PE19 74 F2
  19 Somersham PE28 ..215 C1
Bishops Way
  Buckden PE19 ....117 B4
  Great Paxton PE19 ....96 E4
Bishops Wlk
  2 Barnack PE9 ......230 D3
  Ely CB7 ....240 D4
Bittern Cl PE7 ......143 F7
Bittern Way 3 PE13 .243 F5
Black Bank Rd CB6 ..218 B8
Black Bear La
  Leverington PE13 ...245 F4
  Newmarket CB8 ......110 F3
  Walsoken PE13 ......238 F1
Black Dike PE13 ....237 E6
Black Dro March PE15 .223 E8
  Thorney PE6 ....233 A5
  Wisbech St Mary PE13 .234 B3
Black Dyke PE13 ....237 F4
Black Ham Dro PE7 ..182 E2
Black Hill Rd PE27 .143 C6
Black Horse Dro CB6 226 B6
Black Horse La
  Chatteris PE16 .....241 C6
  Swavesey CB4 ....122 C6
Black La Gorefield PE13 237 C2
  Tydd St Giles PE13 ..237 C6
Black Swan Spinney
  PE8 ....194 A4
Blackberry Droveway
  CB5 ....108 C8
Blackberry Way 6 IP28 214 A1
Blackbird Way CB4 ..150 E4
Blackbush Dro PE7 ..220 D8
Blackdown Garth PE4 .204 A3
Blackfriars 8 CB3 ..245 C5
Blackfriars St 8 PE9 244 C5
Blackhall Rd CB4 .....83 C7
Blackmans Rd PE7 ..175 D8
Blackmead PE2 .....186 B4
Blackmill Rd PE16 ..241 B2
Blackmore Cl 4 CB9 ..38 C1
Blacksmith Cl SG19 ..40 C3
Blacksmiths
  Abbotsley PE19 ....57 B5
  Ramsey Forty Foot PE26 .221 C2
Blacksmiths La
  Abbotsley PE19 ....57 B5
  Ellington PE28 .....139 A4
  Shudy Camps CB1 ....22 C5
Blackstone Rd PE29 .141 C7
Blackthorn Cl
  Cambridge CB4 ......83 F6
  Chatteris PE16 ....241 C6
Blackthorn Ct
  Coates/Eastrea PE7 .190 F8
  2 Soham CB7 ....212 A5
Blackwell Rd PE7 ...186 C2
Blackwood Rd PE19 ..74 B3
Bladon Way CB9 ......39 B1
Blair Way PE19 ....74 E2
Blake Cl SG8 ....13 D1
Blakeland Hill CB2 ...17 D8
Blakes Way PE19 .....74 B2
Blandford Gdns 1 PE1 198 E4
Blandford Wlk 1 CB4 ..83 C6
Blashfield Cl 2 PE9 .244 A6
Blea Wr PE29 ....141 B6
Bledwick Dro PE13 ..238 C3
Blench La CB1 ....34 F6
Blenheim Cl
  2 Cambridge CB1 ....65 E5
  3 Eaton Socon PE19 .74 C4
  Haverhill CB9 ....39 B1
  Shepreth SG8 ....29 E4
Blenheim Dr PE27 ...143 F7
Blenheim Gr PE19 ....96 F8
Blenheim Rd PE26 ..171 E3
Blenheim Way
  Emneth PE14 ....245 E2
  1 Hardwick CB3 .....81 A4
  Yaxley PE7 ....181 E5
Blethan Dr PE29 ....141 A6
Blinco Gr CB1 ....65 B5
Blind La 3 Maxey PE6 .231 C7
  Sawtry PE28 ....168 C3
Bliss Way CB1 ....66 A6

Bar – Bra 251

Block Fen Dro
  Chatteris PE16 .....216 C6
  Wimblington PE15 ..223 C5
Block Rd PE13 ......212 C1
Blockmoor Dro CB6 .216 C6
Blockmoor Rd CB7 ..211 E6
Blois Rd CB9 ....24 F1
Bloomfield Cl PE19 ..95 E1
Bloomfield Way 1
  PE28 ....168 C4
Bloomsfield CB5 ....130 C1
Blossom St 3 CB1 ...84 A1
Blue Boar Dro CB6 .218 D2
Blue La PE15 ....223 A7
Bluebell Ave PE1 ...198 A8
Bluebell Wlk 1 CB7 .212 B4
Bluecoat Prim Sch The
  PE9 ....244 B6
Bluegate PE29 ......118 F7
Bluntisham Heath Rd
  PE28 ....155 F3
Bluntisham Rd
  Bluntisham/Colne PE28 .208 D6
  1 Needingworth PE27 .208 A3
Blunt's La PE7 .....189 E7
Blythe Gn PE28 ....115 D2
Blythe Way SG19 ....41 D5
Blyton Cl CB3 ....99 A3
Boardman Cl PE19 ...95 F2
Bodiam Way PE19 ....74 F2
Bodsey Ho* PE26 ..221 B2
Bodsey Toll Rd PE26 221 B2
Boeing Way IP28 ...239 B5
Bogmoor Rd SG8 .....7 C1
Bogs Gap La SG8 ....11 B3
Bohemond St 3 CB7 .240 E5
Boleness Rd PE13 ..245 C2
Boleyn Way CB9 .....23 D7
Boleyn Wlk 1 CB8 ..111 C3
Bolton Cl CB5 ....130 A2
Bona La PE13 ......235 B8
Boongate PE1 ......198 C3
Boot La CB2 ....29 E8
Boot The CB6 ......209 D4
Booth Way PE19 .....95 F1
Boot's Rd PE15 ....223 F6
Boretree Way PE29 .141 A7
Borough Cl PE13 ...245 D3
Borough The CB6 ...209 E4
Borrowdale CB4 .....83 C6
Borrowdale Cl PE4 .204 E3
Borthwick Pl PE2 ..185 D6
Bossert's Way CB3 ..80 C2
Boswell Cl PE1 ....197 E8
Bosworth Cl PE8 ...178 B3
Bosworth Rd CB1 ....65 D5
Bosworth Way 2 PE15 243 D2
Botolph Gn PE2 ....186 C7
Botolph La CB2 ....246 A2
Bottels Rd PE28 ...164 E5
Bottisham H* CB5 ...87 A8
Bottisham Park* CB6 ..86 F7
Bottisham Prim Sch CB5 .86 F5
Bottisham Swimming Pool
  CB5 ....86 E6
Bottisham Village Coll
  CB5 ....86 E6
Bottle La PE13 ....237 C7
Bough La PE28 ....162 F1
Boulevard Ret Pk PE1 .197 D7
Boundary Dr PE15 ..243 C3
Boundary Rd
  Haverhill CB9 ....24 D5
  Red Lodge IP28 ....214 A1
Bourdillon Cl 1 PE28 .121 B6
Bourges Bvd PE1 ...197 F1
Bourgess Ret Pk PE3 .197 F1
Bourn H* CB3 ....60 C5
Bourn Parochial Sch
  CB3 ....60 C6
Bourn Rd CB3 ....59 F8
Bourn Windmill* CB3 .79 A1
Bourne Rd Cambridge CB4 84 C5
  Haverhill CB9 ....24 B8
Bower Cl PE1 ......198 C5
Bower's La 4 CB7 ..213 A5
Bowers Croft CB1 ...65 C3
Bowker Way PE7 ...189 C8
Bowlings Ct PE27 ..144 A3
Bowness Way 2 PE4 .204 F2
Bowsers La CB10 ....20 B2
Bowthorpe Rd PE13 .245 D5
Boxer Rd PE8 ......230 B1
Boxgrove Cl 14 PE6 .232 A1
Boxworth End CB4 ..122 C4
Boxworth Rd CB3 ...100 C4
Boyce Cl PE7 ......189 D7
Boyces Rd PE13 ...245 E5
Boyton Cl CB9 ....39 A2
Bozeat Way PE3 ...197 C6
Brackenbury Cl 1 CB4 104 C3
Brackhill Fen Dro PE28 208 E8
Brackley Cl
  3 Cambridge CB4 ....83 D6
  Peterborough PE3 ..197 D3
Brackwood PE2 .....185 D6
Brackyn Rd CB1 .....65 B7
Bradden St PE3 ....197 C6
Bradegate Dr PE1 ..198 E7
Bradford's Cl CB5 ..86 E6
Bradley Rd Cowlinge CB8 72 F1
  Kirtling CB8 ....72 F3
Bradmore St CB1 ..246 C2
Bradshaw Cl PE29 ..141 E6
Bradwell Rd PE3 ...197 A2

Bradwells Ct CB1 . . . . . .246 B2
Braemar Gdns PE7 . . . . .189 D6
Braggs La
  Hemingford Grey PE28 . . .143 C1
  Wrestlingworth SG19 . . . . .25 B4
Brailsford Cl **3** PE3 . . . .197 A4
Bramble Cl Haverhill CB9 .38 D1
  Whittlesey PE7 . . . . .189 E6
  Yaxley PE7 . . . . .182 A6
Bramble Ct **2** PE28 . . . .140 C3
Bramble End
  Alconbury PE28 . . . . .150 F5
  Sawtry PE28 . . . . .168 B3
Bramble La PE14 . . . . . . .236 D3
Bramble Wlk PE15 . . . . . .243 E7
Brambles The
  Balsham CB1 . . . . .53 C1
  Bar Hill CB3 . . . . .102 D3
  Cambridge CB2 . . . . .64 D2
  Girton CB3 . . . . .83 A6
  Hemingford Grey PE27 . . .143 F1
  3 Royston SG8 . . . . .5 E5
Bramley Ave
  Melbourn SG8 . . . . .14 D1
  2 Needingworth PE27 . . .208 A2
Bramley Cl
  Cottenham CB4 . . . . .125 D3
  Offord Cluny PE19 . . . . . .118 A1
Bramley Ct CB4 . . . . .84 B6
Bramley Dr PE19 . . . . . . .118 A1
Bramley Gr **4** PE28 . . . .208 C5
Bramley Rd Haverhill CB9 .23 C7
  St Ives PE27 . . . . .144 B5
  Wisbech PE13 . . . . .245 C7
Bramley Way CB3 . . . . . . .81 A4
Bramleys The
  March PE15 . . . . .243 D1
  Shepreth SG8 . . . . .29 E4
Brampton Cl PE13 . . . . . .245 A4
Brampton Ct PE2 . . . . . . .187 C6
Brampton Cty Inf Sch
  PE28 . . . . .140 C2
Brampton Cty Jun Sch
  PE28 . . . . .140 C2
Brampton Gdns PE19 . . . .75 A4
Brampton Rd
  Buckden PE19 . . . . .117 C6
  Cambridge CB1 . . . . .84 B1
  Grafham PE28 . . . . .116 B7
  Huntingdon PE29 . . . . . . .141 B3
  Royston SG8 . . . . .5 F6
Brampton Wood Nature
  Reserve★ PE19 . . . . . . .139 D1
Brancepeth Pl PE2 . . . . . .186 E7
Branch Bank Ely CB7 . . . .218 F6
  Littleport CB7 . . . . .242 F2
Branch Rd CB3 . . . . .62 C7
Brandon Pl CB1 . . . . .246 C2
Brandon Rd IP28 . . . . . . .239 C5
Brands Cl PE26 . . . . .172 A5
Brangehill La CB6 . . . . . . .216 D3
Brassey Cl PE2 . . . . .197 E6
Bravo La PE2 . . . . .151 E3
Brawn Way PE8 . . . . .183 D1
Braybrook PE2 . . . . .186 A3
Braybrook CP Sch PE2 . . .186 B4
Brays La CB7 . . . . .240 D4
Breach La CB6 . . . . .210 D6
Breach Rd PE28 . . . . .116 A7
Bream Cl PE28 . . . . .149 D6
Breckenwood Rd CB1 . . . .66 E6
Breckland Way IP28 . . . . .239 C5
Brecon Way PE29 . . . . . . .141 A4
Brenda Gautrey Way
  CB4 . . . . .125 E3
Brendon Garth PE4 . . . . .204 E1
Brent Cl PE3 . . . . .239 D4
Brentwood Cl **6** CB5 . . . .84 E4
Breton Ave PE15 . . . . . . .243 E2
Bretton Gate **2** PE3 . . . .197 A5
Bretton Gn **1** PE3 . . . . .197 A5
Bretton Way Bretton PE3 .197 A4
  Peterborough PE3 . . . . . .196 F2
Bretton Woods Com Sch
  PE3 . . . . .197 A6
Brewerne PE2 . . . . .186 C4
Brewers Cl CB4 . . . . .123 F5
Brewers La PE13 . . . . . . .238 A4
Brewery La SG8 . . . . .29 B2
Brewery Mus★ PE9 . . . . .244 B5
Brewery Rd CB2 . . . . .33 A5
Brewhouse La CB7 . . . . . .212 B4
Brewin Ave PE15 . . . . . . .243 B3
Brewin Chase The **1**
  PE15 . . . . .243 D4
Brewster Ave PE2 . . . . . .186 F8
Brewster Avenue Inf Sch
  PE2 . . . . .186 E8
Briar Way PE1 . . . . .198 C5
Briars End CB6 . . . . .217 E2
Briars The PE28 . . . . .168 B3
Briary La SG8 . . . . .5 C5
Brick Kiln Rd IP28 . . . . . .239 D5
Brick Kilns PE29 . . . . . . .118 F8
Brick La CB6 . . . . .216 E3
Brick Row SG8 . . . . .8 D3
Brickberry Cl PE7 . . . . . .186 C2
Brickfields Ave CB8 . . . . .110 D7
Brickhills CB8 . . . . .209 A1
Brickkiln La CB6 . . . . . . .218 B4
Brickmaker's Arms La
  PE15 . . . . .223 B5
Brickmakers Way CB6 . . .242 B1
Bridewell Cl IP28 . . . . . . .239 B4
Bridewell Rd CB1 . . . . . . .66 A5

Bridge Cl CB2 . . . . .48 F6
Bridge Dro PE13 . . . . . . .234 B7
Bridge End Earith PE28 . .208 E5
  Wansford PE8 . . . . .194 A3
Bridge End Rd
  Freckenham IP28 . . . . . .213 E1
  Red Lodge IP28 . . . . . . .213 F1
Bridge La
  Great Shelford CB2 . . . . . .48 E4
  Wimblington PE15 . . . . . .223 B8
Bridge of Sighs★ CB3 . . .246 A3
Bridge Pl PE29 . . . . .141 E3
Bridge Rd
  Broughton PE28 . . . . . . .153 F8
  Ely CB7 . . . . .240 E2
  Histon CB4 . . . . .104 C2
  Impington CB4 . . . . .83 C8
  Mepal CB6 . . . . .216 E4
Bridge St Cambridge CB2 .246 A3
  Chatteris PE16 . . . . .241 B7
  Market Deeping PE6 . . . .231 E8
  Moulton CB8 . . . . .112 F5
  St Ives PE27 . . . . .144 A3
  Whaddon SG8 . . . . .13 B8
  11 Wisbech PE13 . . . . . .245 C5
  Wistow PE28 . . . . .163 F7
  Wood Walton PE28 . . . . .161 E6
Bridgehill Rd PE6 . . . . . .205 A6
Bridle End PE19 . . . . .98 B2
Bridle Way CB3 . . . . .63 F4
Brierley Wlk CB4 . . . . .83 C7
Briery Fields **2** CB6 . . . .217 E1
Briggate Cres PE7 . . . . . .189 C6
Briggate E PE7 . . . . .189 D6
Briggate W PE7 . . . . .189 C6
Bright St PE1 . . . . .197 F3
Brigland Ct **7** PE2 . . . . .141 B6
Brigstock Ct PE3 . . . . . . .197 C6
Brigstock Rd PE13 . . . . . .245 B7
Brimbles Way PE2 . . . . . .185 E5
Brimley Rd CB4 . . . . .83 D6
Bringhurst PE2 . . . . .186 A4
Brington CE Sch PE28 . . .147 C4
Brington Rd PE28 . . . . . . .147 D3
Brinkley Rd Brinkley CB8 . .69 A6
  Carlton CB8 . . . . .54 F8
  Westley Waterless CB8 . . . .70 D3
  Weston Colville CB8 . . . . .54 C8
Brinkman Rd CB1 . . . . . . .35 D3
Bristol Ave PE4 . . . . .204 B3
Britannia Way PE13 . . . . .245 C2
Britannic Way CB1 . . . . . . .65 F7
British Horse Racing Sch
  CB8 . . . . .111 B8
Britten Pl CB1 . . . . .65 D7
Broad Baulk CB6 . . . . . . .210 F6
Broad Cl PE1 . . . . .198 D5
Broad Dro Emneth PE14 . .236 C5
  Upwell PE14 . . . . .229 D8
  Wisbech PE14 . . . . .235 F5
  Yaxley PE7 . . . . .182 B5
Broad Dro E PE13 . . . . . .237 E6
Broad Dro W PE13 . . . . . .237 B4
Broad End CB3 . . . . .100 A4
Broad End La PE13 . . . . . .245 F4
Broad End Rd PE14 . . . . .245 F4
Broad Gate PE12 . . . . . . .237 A8
Broad Leas PE27 . . . . . . .144 A4
Broad Piece CB7 . . . . . . .211 F5
Broad St Bourn CB3 . . . . . .79 B4
  Cambridge CB1 . . . . .246 C2
  Ely CB7 . . . . .240 D3
  Haverhill CB9 . . . . .23 F8
  March PE15 . . . . .243 D4
  Stamford PE9 . . . . .244 B5
  Whittlesey PE7 . . . . .189 D7
Broad Way CB6 . . . . .210 C6
Broad Wheel Rd PE6 . . . .231 B4
Broadall's Dro PE14 . . . . .221 D3
Broadcroft Cres CB9 . . . . .23 E8
Broadgate La PE6 . . . . . . .231 F8
Broadgate Rd PE12 . . . . .234 C8
Broadgate Way PE8 . . . . .178 B3
Broadhurst Rd **15** PE8 . . .230 A1
Broadlands The PE1 . . . . .198 E5
Broadmeadow CB2 . . . . . .49 F1
Broads Rd CB5 . . . . .130 C6
Broadway Bourn CB3 . . . . .60 D8
  Crowland PE6 . . . . .232 B8
  Farcet PE7 . . . . .187 C1
  Grantchester CB3 . . . . . . .64 A4
  Witchford CB6 . . . . .217 D1
  Yaxley PE7 . . . . .181 E5
Broadway Gdns PE1 . . . . .198 B5
Broadway The
  Oakington/Longstanton
  CB4 . . . . .103 B5
  St Ives PE27 . . . . .144 A4
Broadweir PE28 . . . . .138 C4
Brockholt Rd CB3 . . . . . . .78 E2
Brockley Rd CB3 . . . . . . .100 B4
Brockwood Cl **2** SG19 . . . .41 D6
Brodsworth Rd PE7 . . . . .187 F5
Bromholme La PE28 . . . . .141 A3
Brook Cl Alconbury PE28 . .150 F4
  Histon CB4 . . . . .104 B4
Brook Dam La **14** CB6 . . . .212 B4
Brook End SG8 . . . . .11 C3
Brook La Coton CB3 . . . . . .82 C2
  Farcet PE7 . . . . .187 B2
  Stretham CB6 . . . . .210 F5
Brook Rd
  Bassingbourn cum Kneesworth
  SG8 . . . . .12 D4
  Eaton Socon PE19 . . . . . . .74 C4

Brook Rd continued
  Kimbolton PE28 . . . . . . .114 B7
  Newton CB2 . . . . .31 B6
  Thriplow SG8 . . . . .31 B4
Brook Service Rd CB9 . . . .24 A8
Brook St Elsworth CB3 . . .100 B3
  Peterborough PE1 . . . . . .198 A2
  St Neots PE19 . . . . .74 E5
  Soham CB7 . . . . .212 C3
Brook The CB6 . . . . .216 E1
Brookdale CB3 . . . . .102 C3
Brooke Rd SG8 . . . . .5 D8
Brookfield Cl CB2 . . . . .32 F5
Brookfield Dr CB4 . . . . . .123 F3
Brookfield Rd Coton CB3 . .82 B2
  Papworth Everard CB3 . . . .99 A4
  Sawston CB2 . . . . .32 F5
Brookfield Way PE26 . . . .172 A4
Brookfields CB1 . . . . .65 D7
Brookfields Cl CB8 . . . . . .111 B5
Brookfields Hospl CB1 . . . .65 C8
Brookfurlong PE3 . . . . . . .197 B6
Brookhampton St CB10 . . .18 A5
Brooklands Ave CB2 . . . . . .64 E6
Brook's Rd PE15 . . . . . . .243 D4
Brooks Rd CB1 . . . . .65 D8
Brookside
  Alconbury PE28 . . . . .150 F4
  Cambridge CB2 . . . . .246 B1
  Dalham CB8 . . . . .92 E8
  Exning CB8 . . . . .110 C8
  Great Paxton PE19 . . . . . .96 D4
  Huntingdon PE29 . . . . . . .141 D5
  Moulton CB8 . . . . .112 F5
  Oakington/Longstanton
  CB4 . . . . .123 F7
  Orwell SG8 . . . . .45 D1
  Peterborough PE4 . . . . . .204 D2
  St Ives PE28 . . . . .143 B5
  Sawtry PE28 . . . . .168 B5
  1 Sutton CB6 . . . . .216 E2
  Toft CB3 . . . . .61 D4
Brookside Gr CB6 . . . . . . .242 C5
Brookside La **1** CB2 . . . . .64 E7
Broom Cl PE1 . . . . .198 A8
Broom Way PE27 . . . . . . .144 B5
Broom Wlk **5** IP28 . . . . .213 F8
Broomhill Cl **4** IP28 . . . .214 A1
Brotherhood CP PE4 . . . .197 D8
Brotherhood Ret Pk
  PE4 . . . . .197 D8
Broughton La PE28 . . . . . .154 B8
Brownes Rd **6** PE8 . . . . .230 B1
Browning Dr PE9 . . . . .74 C6
Brownlow Dr **8** PE6 . . . . .231 F8
Brownlow Quay PE9 . . . . .244 C5
Brownlow Rd
  Cambridge CB4 . . . . .83 C6
  Peterborough PE1 . . . . . .198 A6
Brownlow St **7** PE9 . . . . .244 A6
Brown's Sq **6** PE9 . . . . . .74 F5
Broxbourne Cl **4** CB1 . . . .66 A7
Bruces Cl PE7 . . . . .168 D8
Brudenell PE2 . . . . .185 E2
Brunel Dr PE7 . . . . .181 D6
Brunswick Ct CB1 . . . . . . .66 E5
Brunswick Gdns CB5 . . . .246 C3
Brunswick Terr CB5 . . . . .246 C3
Bryan Cl PE26 . . . . .172 B6
Brybank Rd CB9 . . . . .38 C1
Brynmore PE3 . . . . .204 A1
Bryony Cl
  Coates/Eastrea PE7 . . . . .190 C7
  Haverhill CB9 . . . . .38 E1
Buchan St CB4 . . . . .83 E7
Buckden CE Prim Sch
  PE19 . . . . .117 B4
Buckden Rd
  Brampton PE28 . . . . .117 D7
  Grafham PE28 . . . . .116 A6
Bucking Way Rd CB3 . . . .101 D8
Buckingham Dr CB6 . . . . .240 D6
Buckingham Rd
  Cambridge CB3 . . . . .83 C3
  Haverhill CB9 . . . . .23 E7
Buckingham Way PE28 . . .168 C2
Buckland Cl PE3 . . . . .197 B4
Buckle St PE1 . . . . .198 C3
Buckles Gdns PE7 . . . . . .189 F7
Buckley Rd PE19 . . . . .74 E4
Buck's Dro PE26 . . . . . . .220 D4
Buck's La CB3 . . . . .45 F7
Bucksholt Rd PE14 . . . . . .238 E3
Buckthorn **2** CB7 . . . . . .240 F6
Buckworth Rd PE28 . . . . .150 C5
Budge CP PE28 . . . . .138 E2
Budleigh Cl CB1 . . . . .65 D7
Buff La SG19 . . . . .43 A1
Buffalo Way CB1 . . . . .66 A7
Building End Rd SG8 . . . . . .1 F7
Bukehorn Rd PE6 . . . . . . .232 D4
Bull La Broughton PE28 . . .164 A1
  Langley CB11 . . . . .1 F2
  Peakirk PE6 . . . . .206 B2
  West Wratting CB1 . . . . . .53 F6
Bullard Laboratories
  CB3 . . . . .83 A4
Bullen Cl CB1 . . . . .65 D5
Bullfinch Way CB4 . . . . . .125 D5
Bullock Rd Elton PE8 . . . .184 B1
  Folksworth & Washingley
  PE7 . . . . .174 C7
  Great Gidding PE28 . . . . .167 B6
  Little Gidding PE28 . . . . .167 D2
Bulstrode Gdns CB3 . . . . . .83 A2
Bulteel Cl **1** CB4 . . . . . . .105 C3
Bumpstead Rd
  Haverhill CB9 . . . . .24 B5

Bumpstead Rd continued
  Helions Bumpstead CB9 . . .24 B4
Bunbury Ave IP28 . . . . . . .239 C5
Bunting's Dro PE7 . . . . . .188 C4
Bunting's La PE8 . . . . . . .178 B3
Buntings Cres CB5 . . . . . .130 B3
Buntings La PE7 . . . . .187 B5
Buntings Path CB5 . . . . . .130 B3
Bunyan Cl **4** SG19 . . . . . .41 D5
Burberry Rd PE19 . . . . . .117 B3
Burcroft Rd PE13 . . . . . . .245 B6
Burdett Cl **3** PE15 . . . . . .223 A5
Burdett Gr PE7 . . . . .189 F6
Burdett Rd PE13 . . . . . . .245 B4
Bure Cl PE27 . . . . .144 B6
Burford Way PE1 . . . . . . .198 D6
Burgess Rd CB5 . . . . .106 B7
Burgess's Dro CB5 . . . . . .106 C7
Burghley Ave **9** PE8 . . . .230 B1
Burghley Cl **9** PE6 . . . . .231 F8
Burghley Ho★ PE9 . . . . . .244 F3
Burghley Rd
  1 Peterborough PE1 . . .198 A3
  4 Stamford PE9 . . . . . .244 A7
Burghley Rise CB5 . . . . . .130 C2
Burghley Sq **2** PE1 . . . . .198 A3
Burgoyne's Rd CB4 . . . . . .104 D3
Burgoynes Farm Cl CB4 . .104 D3
Buristead Rd CB2 . . . . .48 F5
Burkett Way CB4 . . . . . . .104 B5
Burleigh Pl CB1 . . . . .246 C3
Burleigh Rd PE27 . . . . . . .143 F8
Burleigh St CB1 . . . . .246 C3
Burling Wlk **1** CB4 . . . . .105 D3
Burlington Way PE28 . . . .143 C1
Burma Rd CB2 . . . . .32 A1
Burmer Rd PE1 . . . . .197 E2
Burmoor Cl **6** PE29 . . . . .141 B6
Burn St PE15 . . . . .243 D5
Burnaby Cl PE28 . . . . . . .140 C3
Burnet Gdns PE15 . . . . . .243 E7
Burnett Way PE29 . . . . . .141 F8
Burnham Cl CB1 . . . . .66 A6
Burns Cl PE1 . . . . .197 F7
Burns Ct **3** PE19 . . . . . . .74 D5
Burns Rd SG8 . . . . .5 C8
Burns Way PE27 . . . . . . .143 F6
Burnsfield Inf Sch PE16 . .241 B5
Burnsfield St PE16 . . . . . .241 B5
Burnside CB1 . . . . .65 D7
Burnt Chy Dro CB6 . . . . .225 B4
Burnt Cl Grantchester CB3 .64 A4
  St Neots PE19 . . . . .74 E3
Burnt Up Dro PE7 . . . . . .188 F2
Burnthouse Rd PE7 . . . . .191 E4
Burnthouse Sidings
  PE7 . . . . .191 F1
Burrel Rd PE27 . . . . .144 B6
Burrell Cres IP28 . . . . . . .239 C2
Burrell Way CB1 . . . . .53 B2
Burrett Gdns **2** PE13 . . .238 F1
Burrett Rd PE13 . . . . .238 F1
Burrettgate Rd
  6 Leverington PE13 . . . .238 F1
  Walsoken PE13 . . . . .245 F5
Burrough Field CB4 . . . . .104 C1
Burrough Green Endowed CE
  Prim Sch CB8 . . . . .70 F4
Burrowmoor Jun & Inf Sch
  PE15 . . . . .243 C3
Burrowmoor Rd PE15 . . . .243 C3
Burstellars PE27 . . . . . . .144 A6
Burswood PE2 . . . . .185 F2
Burton Cl CB9 . . . . .23 E7
Burton Ct PE1 . . . . .198 C3
Burton End Haverhill CB9 . .23 E7
  West Wickham CB1 . . . . . .37 C8
Burton End CP Sch CB9 . . .23 D7
Burton Hill CB9 . . . . .38 D5
Burton St PE1 . . . . .198 C3
Burton Way PE26 . . . . . . .137 F6
Burwell Mus★ CB5 . . . . . .130 C1
Burwell Rd
  Eaton Socon PE19 . . . . . .74 C6
  Exning CB8 . . . . .110 A8
  Reach CB5 . . . . .129 E1
  Swaffham Prior CB5 . . . . .108 E5
Burwell Reach PE2 . . . . . .186 C7
Burwell Village Coll
  CB5 . . . . .130 B3
Bury CE Sch PE26 . . . . . .172 A4
Bury Cl Ramsey PE26 . . . .171 F4
  St Ives PE27 . . . . .143 F5
Bury Gn CB6 . . . . .218 A7
Bury La Chrishall SG8 . . . . .8 D1
  Haddenham CB6 . . . . . . .210 A5
  Lidgate CB8 . . . . .73 F8
  Meldreth SG8 . . . . .14 A5
  Moulton CB8 . . . . .112 F6
  Sutton CB6 . . . . .216 D2
Bury Rd
  Great Shelford CB2 . . . . . .49 C4
  Kentford CB8 . . . . .134 B2
  Mildenhall IP28 . . . . .239 E4
  Newmarket CB8 . . . . . . .111 C5
  Ramsey PE26 . . . . .172 A5
  Snailwell CB8 . . . . .111 E8
Bury Way PE27 . . . . .143 F5
Buryfield PE26 . . . . .172 A4
Burystead PE2 . . . . .187 B8
Bush Cl CB3 . . . . .62 D5
Bush La PE13 . . . . .245 E5
Bushel La CB7 . . . . .212 B4
Bushfield Com Coll PE2 . .185 E3
Bushfield Sports Ctr
  PE2 . . . . .185 E4

Bushmead Jun Sch PE19 . .74 A3
Bushmead Rd PE19 . . . . . .74 A3
Bustard Hill PE28 . . . . . . .113 D8
Bustler's Rise CB2 . . . . . . .17 D8
Butcher Cl **2** CB4 . . . . . .105 C3
Butcher's Hill CB10 . . . . . .18 A4
Butcher's La SG19 . . . . . . .25 B4
Butcher's Row **3** CB7 . . .240 C4
Butler Way
  Cambridge CB3 . . . . .83 D6
  1 Haslingfield CB3 . . . . .47 A5
Butlers Way CB2 . . . . .32 F7
Butt Ave PE15 . . . . .243 B2
Butt La
  Great Wilbraham CB1 . . . .68 A7
  Milton CB4 . . . . .105 B3
Buttermel Cl **1** PE29 . . . .118 F8
Buttermere PE29 . . . . . . .141 B6
Buttermere Pl **4** PE4 . . . .204 E3
Button End CB2 . . . . .47 D4
Butt's La CB7 . . . . .211 F1
Butts Cl **6** Soham CB7 . . .212 B3
  20 Somersham PE28 . . .215 C1
Butts The Fowlmere SG8 . .15 D8
  Soham CB7 . . . . .212 B3
Buttsgrove Way PE29 . . . .141 F7
Buxtons La SG8 . . . . .10 F3
Buzzard Cl PE28 . . . . .142 B8
Byall Fen Dro PE15 . . . . .223 E2
Bydand La PE19 . . . . .95 F2
Byfield Rd CB3 . . . . .99 B3
Byng Cl PE19 . . . . .74 B2
Byron Cl Huntingdon PE29 .141 F6
  Peterborough PE2 . . . . . .187 D6
Byron Pl **10** PE19 . . . . . . .74 C6
Byron Rd **4** SG8 . . . . .5 E8
Byron Sq CB2 . . . . .64 D2
Bythorn Rd PE28 . . . . . . .187 C6
Bythorne Bank PE13 . . . .237 C7

Cabbage Moor CB2 . . . . . .48 E8
Cadenham Rd CB5 . . . . . .108 E3
Cadwin Field CB4 . . . . .83 F7
Caernarvon Rd PE19 . . . . .74 F2
Cage Hill CB5 . . . . .108 D5
Cage La
  Great Staughton PE19 . . . .94 B6
  Stretham CB6 . . . . .210 F5
Caldbeck Cl PE4 . . . . .204 F2
Caldecote Cl PE2 . . . . . . .187 E6
Caldecote Rd
  St Neots PE19 . . . . .74 E3
  Stilton PE7 . . . . .175 E7
Caldervale PE2 . . . . .186 C6
Caledon Way **1** CB4 . . . . .83 E8
Calfe Fen Cl **2** CB7 . . . . .212 B5
Calfe Fen Dro CB7 . . . . . .212 B5
California Rd
  Huntingdon PE29 . . . . . . .141 E6
  St Ives PE27 . . . . .143 E6
Callander Cl CB4 . . . . .83 D7
Calvin Cl CB4 . . . . .125 F3
Cam Cl PE27 . . . . .144 A7
Cam Cswy CB4 . . . . .84 B6
Camargue Dr PE15 . . . . .243 D2
Camargue Pl **4** PE13 . . . .245 E3
Camber's New Dro PE7 . .220 D8
Cambrian Way PE4 . . . . . .204 E1
Cambridge & Cty Folk Mus★
  CB3 . . . . .246 A4
Cambridge Acad CB1 . . . .246 B3
Cambridge Airport CB1 . . . .84 F2
Cambridge Ave PE1 . . . . .197 F5
Cambridge Cl
  Haverhill CB9 . . . . .38 E1
  St Ives PE27 . . . . .143 F8
Cambridge Cres SG8 . . . . .13 A8
Cambridge Ct **10** PE19 . . .74 F5
Cambridge Dr
  1 St Ives PE27 . . . . . . .143 F8
  Wisbech PE13 . . . . .245 A6
Cambridge Gdns PE19 . . . .74 F5
Cambridge Pl CB1 . . . . . .246 C1
Cambridge Rd
  Babraham CB2 . . . . .50 D4
  Balsham CB1 . . . . .52 F2
  Barley SG8 . . . . .7 A3
  Barton CB3 . . . . .62 E1
  Ely CB7 . . . . .240 B3
  Eynesbury Hardwicke PE19 .76 B4
  Fenstanton PE28 . . . . . . .121 A6
  Foxton CB2 . . . . .30 C7
  Fulbourn CB1 . . . . .66 A5
  Girton CB3 . . . . .82 E8
  Godmanchester PE29 . . . .141 F2
  Great Shelford CB2 . . . . . .48 F7
  Hardwick CB3 . . . . .81 B3
  Hauxton CB2 . . . . .48 A5
  Histon CB4 . . . . .83 C8
  Madingley CB3 . . . . .81 F5
  Melbourn SG8 . . . . .14 E7
  Milton CB4 . . . . .105 C1
  Newton CB2 . . . . .31 B8
  Oakington/Longstanton
  CB4 . . . . .103 C4
  Orwell SG8 . . . . .45 C1
  St Neots Rural PE19 . . . . .75 C5
  Sawston CB2 . . . . .32 E8
  Stamford PE9 . . . . .244 A6
  Stretham CB6 . . . . .210 E3
  Thetford CB6 . . . . .211 A8
  Thriplow SG8 . . . . .30 F3
  Waterbeach CB5 . . . . . . .105 F7
  Wimpole SG8 . . . . .27 F6

Cambridge Regional Coll
CB4 . . . . .83 F8
Cambridge Science Pk
CB4 . . . . .84 B8
Cambridge Sq PE28 . . . .143 B7
Cambridge St
Godmanchester PE29 . . .141 F2
St Neots PE19 . . . . .75 A5
Cambridge Sta CB1 . . . . .65 A7
Cambridge Summer Sch of
Tech CB3 . . . . .64 B7
Cambridge Univ Ctr
CB2 . . . . .246 A1
Cambridge Way CB9 . . . . .38 E1
Cambridgeshire Cl CB6 .240 B4
Camden Ct CB1 . . . . .246 B2
Camel Rd CB6 . . . . .242 C6
Camelia Cl PE4 . . . . .204 D3
Cameron Rd CB4 . . . . .83 E7
Campbell Cl IP28 . . . . . . .239 B6
Campbell Dr PE4 . . . . . . .204 E4
Campbell La CB2 . . . . .64 C2
Campbell St ■ CB1 . . . . . .65 B8
Camping Cl CB6 . . . . .210 A6
Campion Cl ■ CB7 . . . . . .212 A5
Campion Rd PE1 . . . . . . .198 B8
Campion Way SG8 . . . . . . .5 E5
Campkin Rd CB4 . . . . .83 F7
Camps Cl CB5 . . . . .106 B7
Camps Rd Bartlow CB1 . . .21 B7
Haverhill CB9 . . . . .23 F7
Helions Bumpstead CB9 . .23 B1
Camside CB4 . . . . .84 A4
Canal St ■ PE13 . . . . . . .245 C5
Canberra Cl
Bassingbourn SG8 . . . . . .13 B5
Mildenhall IP28 . . . . .213 E8
Canberra Ct PE26 . . . . . .171 F7
Canberra Dr PE27 . . . . . .143 F7
Canberra Rd PE26 . . . . . .171 E3
Candidus Ct PE4 . . . . . . .204 B5
Canmore Rd PE28 . . . . . .168 C2
Canners Cl CB3 . . . . .61 E5
Cannon St
Little Downham CB6 . . . . .218 A6
Wisbech PE13 . . . . .245 C4
Cannon Terr ■ PE13 . . . .245 C4
Cannon's Cl SG8 . . . . .10 F5
Canon Cl CB9 . . . . .39 A1
Canon Dr ■ PE9 . . . . . . .230 D3
Canonsfield PE4 . . . . . . .204 A4
Cantelupe Rd CB3 . . . . . . .47 C7
Canterbury Ave CB6 . . . .240 C4
Canterbury Cl CB4 . . . . . .83 C4
Canterbury Rd PE4 . . . . .204 B4
Canterbury St CB4 . . . . . .83 C4
Cant's Dro PE13 . . . . . . .234 C4
Canute Cres CB6 . . . . . . .240 C4
Canwell PE4 . . . . .204 C4
Capper Rd CB5 . . . . .127 C1
Capstan Cl CB4 . . . . .84 A3
Capthorne Cl PE7 . . . . . .186 C2
Capulet Cl PE19 . . . . .74 C3
Car Dyke Rd
Landbeach CB5 . . . . .105 F6
Waterbeach CB5 . . . . . . .106 A6
Caravere Cl ■ CB4 . . . . . .83 F8
Caraway Rd CB1 . . . . .66 E5
Cardiff Pl SG8 . . . . .13 A8
Cardigan St CB4 . . . . .111 A3
Cardinal Way ■ CB9 . . . . .38 F1
Caribou Way CB1 . . . . . . .66 A7
Cardinals Gate PE4 . . . . .204 A5
Carisbrooke Rd CB4 . . . . .83 C5
Carisbrooke Way ■
PE19 . . . . .74 F2
Carleton Crest PE4 . . . . .204 D1
Carlton Cl Haverhill CB9 . .38 F2
■ Leverington PE13 . . . .238 B2
Carlton Green Rd CB8 . . .55 A6
Carlton Cl CB8 . . . . .70 E1
Carlton Rise SG8 . . . . . . .14 D5
Carlton Way CB4 . . . . .83 D5
Carlyle Rd CB4 . . . . .246 A4
Carmel St CB10 . . . . .18 D2
Carmen St CB10 . . . . .18 D3
Carnation Way IP28 . . . . .133 F8
Carnegie Rd ■ PE8 . . . . .230 B1
Caroline Pl CB1 . . . . .246 C2
Carpenters Way ■
PE15 . . . . .223 A6
Carpond La ■ CB6 . . . . . .210 C6
Carr Rd PE1 . . . . .198 D3
Carradale PE2 . . . . .185 D5
Carrick Cl CB1 . . . . .65 E5
Carrington's Dro PE6 . . .232 B8
Carron Dr PE4 . . . . .204 A3
Carrops The CB8 . . . . . . .134 A6
Carsey Hill CB1 . . . . .22 B6
Carter Cl Brampton PE28 .140 C3
Duxford CB2 . . . . .17 E8
Carter Rd CB5 . . . . .130 C3
Carter St CB7 . . . . .212 E1
Carter's Way CB4 . . . . . .122 E5
Carters Cl ■ PE3 . . . . . . .196 F3
Carters Croft CB10 . . . . . .21 B1
Cartmel Way ■ PE6 . . . .232 A1
Cartwright Rd ■ SG8 . . . . .5 D5
Caryer Cl PE2 . . . . .186 D6
Casburn's La CB3 . . . . . . .130 A3
Casewick H★ PE9 . . . . . .230 D8
Casewick La ■ PE9 . . . . .230 F7
Casewick Rd PE9 . . . . . . .230 E7
Castel Way PE7 . . . . .175 D8
Castelhythe ■ CB7 . . . . .240 D3
Casterton Rd PE9 . . . . . .244 A6
Castle Ave CB9 . . . . .23 E7

Castle Camps Prim Sch
CB1 . . . . .22 E3
Castle Dr ■ PE6 . . . . . . .231 F7
Castle Dyke PE9 . . . . . . .244 B5
Castle End Rd PE6 . . . . . .231 C7
Castle Gdns PE28 . . . . . .113 F4
Castle Hill PE29 . . . . .141 D3
Castle Hill Cl PE19 . . . . . .74 C2
Castle La CB9 . . . . .23 E8
Castle Manor Upper Sch
CB9 . . . . .23 E8
Castle Mid Sch CB9 . . . . .23 D7
Castle Moat Rd PE29 . . .141 D4
Castle Mound★ CB4 . . . .246 A4
Castle Row ■ CB3 . . . . . . .83 C3
Castle Sq ■ PE13 . . . . . .245 C5
Castle St Cambridge CB3 .246 A4
■ Stamford PE9 . . . . . . .244 B5
Castle Wlk CB9 . . . . .23 E8
Castor CE Sch PE5 . . . . .195 E2
Castor Hanglands Nature
Reserve★ PE6 . . . . .195 E7
Castor Rd Castor PE6 . . .196 C6
Marholm PE6 . . . . .203 D1
Casworth Way PE5 . . . . .195 D2
Catharine St CB1 . . . . .65 B8
Catherine Cl PE2 . . . . . . .186 B7
Cathwaite PE4 . . . . .204 F1
Catkin Cl PE9 . . . . .38 E1
Catling's La PE13 . . . . . . .238 C2
Cattell's La CB5 . . . . .106 B8
Cattle Dike PE13 . . . . . . .237 E2
Cattle Mkt Rd PE1 . . . . . .198 A2
Causeway
Godmanchester PE29 . . .141 E4
Great Staughton PE19 . . .93 F6
Pampisford CB2 . . . . .33 C5
Causeway Cl
Great Staughton PE19 . . .93 F6
March PE15 . . . . .243 C2
Causeway Gdns PE15 . . .243 D4
Causeway Pas CB1 . . . . .246 C3
Causeway PE28 . . . . .154 A8
Causeway The
Bassingbourn SG8 . . . . . .13 A5
Burwell CB5 . . . . .130 A4
Elsworth CB3 . . . . .100 B4
Haverhill CB9 . . . . .23 E8
Isleham CB7 . . . . .213 A5
March PE15 . . . . .243 D2
Soham CB7 . . . . .212 B4
Sutton CB6 . . . . .216 C2
Thorney PE6 . . . . .232 E4
West Wratting CB1 . . . . . .53 E5
Cavalry Dr PE15 . . . . . . .243 E4
Cavalry Pk PE15 . . . . . . .243 D2
Cavalry Prim Sch PE15 .243 E2
Cavell Cl CB1 . . . . .65 B5
Cavendish Cl PE28 . . . . .168 C3
Cavendish Rd CB1 . . . . . .84 B1
Cavendish St PE1 . . . . . .198 B4
Cavenham Rd IP28 . . . . .214 E2
Caverstede Rd PE4 . . . . .204 D1
Caville White CB9 . . . . . . .23 C8
Cawdor Pl ■ PE19 . . . . . .74 F2
Cawood Cl PE15 . . . . . . .243 E6
Caxton End Bourn CB3 . . .60 B7
Eltisley PE19 . . . . .77 F3
Duxford CB2 . . . . .32 D1
Exning CB8 . . . . .110 B8
Caxton Gibbet★ CB3 . . . .78 D6
Caxton H★ CB3 . . . . .78 E1
Caxton La CB2 . . . . .30 B5
Caxton Rd Bourn CB3 . . . .60 C7
Great Gransden SG19 . . . .58 E5
St Ives PE27 . . . . .144 B4
Cecil Ct ■ PE19 . . . . . . .244 C5
Cecil Lodge Cl CB8 . . . . .110 F3
Cecil Rd PE1 . . . . .198 A6
Cedar Ave CB5 . . . . .223 A6
Cedar Cl Grafham PE28 . .115 F7
March PE15 . . . . .243 E5
Melbourn SG8 . . . . .14 C5
Cedar Cres SG8 . . . . .5 B6
Cedar Dr PE28 . . . . .151 E3
Cedar Gr PE1 . . . . .198 B8
Cedar Rd PE27 . . . . .143 F6
Cedar Wlk CB5 . . . . .86 F6
Celta Rd PE2 . . . . .186 F6
Celtic Pl PE2 . . . . .187 D7
Cemetery Rd
St Neots PE19 . . . . .74 F5
Whittlesey PE7 . . . . .189 E6
Cenacle The ■ CB3 . . . . .64 C7
Centenary Way PE28 . . .140 C2
Central Ave
Brampton PE28 . . . . .140 D1
Peterborough PE1 . . . . . .198 C7
Central Sq PE2 . . . . .187 D5
Centre Dr CB8 . . . . .111 D2
Centre Rd CB7 . . . . .212 C2
Century Way PE15 . . . . . .243 C7
Cerris Rd PE1 . . . . .198 B7
Chadburn PE4 . . . . .205 A1
Chadley La PE29 . . . . . . .141 F2
Chaffinch Way CB3 . . . . . .79 C4
Chain Cl PE1 . . . . .198 B6
Chain Cswy CB6 . . . . . . .209 B8
Chain Rd CB4 . . . . .208 C2
Chainbridge La PE28 . . . .135 F8
Chalfont Cl ■ CB1 . . . . . .65 F6
Chalk Gr CB1 . . . . .65 D4
Chalk Rd PE13 . . . . .237 D1
Chalklands CB1 . . . . .35 C3
Chalkstone Way CB9 . . . . .39 A1
Chalky La SG8 . . . . .8 D2
Chalky Rd CB1 . . . . .34 C3

Challis Cl CB2 . . . . .29 F8
Challis Gn CB2 . . . . .29 F8
Chalmers Rd CB1 . . . . . . .65 C6
Chamberlain Way PE19 . .74 F7
Chamois Cl CB2 . . . . .32 F6
Champions Cl ■ SG8 . . . .15 E8
Champneys Wlk CB3 . . . . .64 C8
Chancellor Cl PE29 . . . . .141 C7
Chancellors Wlk ■ CB4 . .83 C6
Chancery La ■ PE6 . . . . .232 A1
Chandler's Way PE15 . . .243 D2
Chandlers PE2 . . . . .185 E5
Chandlers Ct CB5 . . . . . .130 B3
Chandlers Way PE26 . . . .221 A4
Chantry Cl Cambridge CB4 .83 F4
Chatteris PE16 . . . . .241 D6
Peterborough PE1 . . . . . .198 A5
Swavesey CB4 . . . . .122 E6
Chantry The CB1 . . . . .67 A5
Chapel Ave ■ PE13 . . . . .235 B7
Chapel Cl Hilton PE28 . . .120 B1
Litlington SG8 . . . . .12 A2
Needingworth PE27 . . . . .208 A3
Waterbeach CB5 . . . . . . .106 B7
Wrestlingworth SG19 . . . .25 B4
Chapel Ct PE8 . . . . .194 B2
Chapel End
Great Gidding PE28 . . . . .166 D2
Sawtry PE28 . . . . .168 C4
Chapel Field SG19 . . . . . . .41 D4
Chapel Field La PE28 . . .215 B1
Chapel Gate PE12 . . . . . .237 B7
Chapel Gdns
Benwick PE15 . . . . .222 A5
Coates/Eastrea PE7 . . . .190 C7
Chapel La Chatteris PE16 241 B6
Downham PE28 . . . . .218 A6
Easton PE28 . . . . .138 B4
Elm PE14 . . . . .236 B6
Elton PE8 . . . . .178 C8
Fowlmere SG8 . . . . .15 E8
Harston CB2 . . . . .47 F3
Kirtling CB8 . . . . .72 C5
Melbourn SG8 . . . . .14 C6
Newton PE13 . . . . .238 B5
Peterborough PE2 . . . . . .185 F5
■ Peterborough PE4 . . . .204 C3
Reach CB5 . . . . .129 D1
St Ives PE28 . . . . .143 A5
■ St Ives PE27 . . . . .144 A3
Soham CB7 . . . . .219 B2
Tydd St Giles PE13 . . . . .237 F7
Whittlesey PE7 . . . . .227 A3
Wicken CB7 . . . . .211 E1
Willingham CB4 . . . . .208 C6
Wimblington PE15 . . . . . .223 B4
Wisbech PE14 . . . . .235 D5
Chapel Rd
"Beck Row, Holywell Row
& Kenny Hill" IP28 . . . . .213 D6
Earith PE28 . . . . .208 E5
Great Eversden CB3 . . . . .45 F8
Weston Colville CB1 . . . . .54 B5
Wisbech PE13 . . . . .245 B5
Chapel Row CB8 . . . . .91 F8
Chapel St Alconbury PE28 150 F4
Cambridge CB4 . . . . .84 A4
■ Crowland PE6 . . . . . . .232 B8
Duxford CB2 . . . . .32 D1
Ely CB6 . . . . .240 C4
Exning CB8 . . . . .110 B8
March PE15 . . . . .243 D3
Peterborough PE2 . . . . . .187 C7
Peterborough PE1 . . . . . .198 B2
Stretham CB6 . . . . .210 F5
Warmington PE8 . . . . . . .178 B3
Waterbeach CB5 . . . . . . .106 B7
■ Wisbech PE13 . . . . . . .245 C4
Yaxley PE7 . . . . .181 D5
Chapel Yd PE9 . . . . .244 C5
Chapelfield Rd ■ PE13 .235 A2
Chapelfield Way CB2 . . . . .32 F8
Chaplains Cl ■ CB9 . . . . .38 F1
Chaplin's Cl CB1 . . . . .66 F5
Chaplins Cl PE7 . . . . .190 F8
Chapman's Cl SG8 . . . . . .14 C6
Chapman's Way CB4 . . . .208 E1
Chapmans Cl CB4 . . . . . .105 C7
Chapmans Dr ■ CB3 . . . .79 C3
Chapnall Cl PE13 . . . . . . .245 F6
Chapnall Rd PE13 . . . . . .245 F6
Chapple Dr CB9 . . . . .38 F1
Charcoal La PE28 . . . . . .140 C3
Charlemont Dr PE15 . . . .224 B5
Charles Cl
Newmarket CB8 . . . . .110 E3
Ramsey PE26 . . . . .172 A7
Charles Cope Rd PE2 . . .185 F5
Charles Dr PE29 . . . . . . .142 A6
Charles Melrose Cl
IP28 . . . . .239 B5
Charles Rd Stamford PE9 244 A7
Whittlesey PE7 . . . . .189 F6
Charles St Cambridge CB1 .65 B7
Peterborough PE1 . . . . . .198 B3
Charles' St PE19 . . . . .74 F5
Charles St ■ PE13 . . . . . .245 C6
Charnocks Cl ■ SG19 . . . .41 D5
Charnwood Cl PE2 . . . . . .187 A7
Charrington Cl CB9 . . . . . .24 C6
Charters The ■ PE9 . . . .230 C6
Chartfield Rd CB1 . . . . . . .65 F6
Chase Cl CB9 . . . . .39 A1
Chase Rd PE15 . . . . .221 F6
Chase St PE13 . . . . .245 C6
Chase The Ely CB6 . . . . .240 B4
March PE15 . . . . .243 C4

Chase The continued
Thorney PE6 . . . . .200 E7
Upwell PE14 . . . . .229 D7
Whittlesey PE7 . . . . .220 E7
Wimblington PE15 . . . . . .224 A8
Wisbech PE13 . . . . .245 A7
Chaston Rd CB2 . . . . .49 A5
Chater Rd ■ PE8 . . . . . . .230 B1
Chatsfield PE4 . . . . .204 A6
Chatsworth Ave CB4 . . . .83 C5
Chatsworth Pl PE3 . . . . .197 B2
Chatteris Rd
Chatteris PE28 . . . . .215 D4
■ Somersham PE28 . . . .208 C8
Chaucer Cl Cambridge CB2 64 E6
■ Wisbech PE13 . . . . . . .238 B2
Chaucer Pl PE19 . . . . . . .74 D6
Chaucer Rd
Cambridge CB2 . . . . .64 D7
Peterborough PE1 . . . . . .197 C5
Royston SG8 . . . . .5 C8
Chaucer Way PE27 . . . . .143 F6
Chauntry Rd CB9 . . . . . . .23 F7
Chawston Cl ■ PE19 . . . .74 C5
Cheddars La CB5 . . . . .84 B3
Chedworth St CB3 . . . . . .64 C7
Chelmer PE27 . . . . .144 B7
Chelmer Garth PE4 . . . . .204 F1
Chelmer Rd PE29 . . . . . . .24 B8
Cheltenham Cl PE1 . . . . .198 B6
Chelveston Way PE3 . . . .197 C5
Chelwood Rd CB1 . . . . . .65 F6
Cheney Way CB4 . . . . . . .84 C5
Chequer La ■ CB7 . . . . . .240 D4
Chequer St PE28 . . . . . . .121 B6
Chequers
Alconbury Weston PE28 . .150 C6
Cambridge CB1 . . . . .65 F5
Fenstanton PE28 . . . . . . .121 B6
Chequers Croft PE28 . . .120 B2
Chequers La CB3 . . . . .99 B3
Chequers Rd CB4 . . . . . .104 C2
Chequers Way PE28 . . . .141 D4
Cherry Bounds Rd CB3 . .82 E8
Cherry Cl Cambridge CB1 .65 B5
Linton CB1 . . . . .35 B3
Milton CB4 . . . . .105 D3
Cherry Dr SG8 . . . . .5 E7
Cherry Hill IP28 . . . . .214 C3
Cherry Hinton Com Jun Sch
CB1 . . . . .66 A6
Cherry Hinton Inf Sch
CB1 . . . . .65 F6
Cherry Hinton Rd
Cambridge CB1 . . . . .65 B6
Great Shelford CB2 . . . . . .65 D1
Teversham CB1 . . . . .66 A8
Cherry Holt La PE9 . . . .244 D5
Cherry Orch Fulbourn CB1 66 D5
Haddenham CB6 . . . . . . .210 A5
Oakington/Longstanton
CB4 . . . . .103 C5
Cherry Orton Rd PE2 . . .185 F5
Cherry Rd PE13 . . . . .245 C8
Cherry Rise CB6 . . . . . . .216 D1
Cherry Tree Ave CB2 . . . . .49 C4
Cherry Tree Cl
Huntingdon PE29 . . . . . . .141 C6
Litlington SG8 . . . . .12 A1
Cherry Tree Gr PE7 . . . .189 F6
Cherry Tree Way PE21 . .121 B6
Cherry Trees CB2 . . . . . . .48 E7
Cherryfields PE2 . . . . . . .185 E6
Cherryholt Ave PE15 . . . .243 C3
Cherryholt Rd PE9 . . . . .244 D5
Cherrytree Gr PE1 . . . . .198 C6
Cherrytree La CB7 . . . . . .212 B3
Cherrywood Ave PE15 . . .243 B3
Cherrywood Gn ■ PE15 243 B3
Chervil Cl PE7 . . . . .175 D8
Chervil Way ■ CB3 . . . . . .79 C3
Chesham Rd PE28 . . . . . .168 C2
Chesnut Gr CB4 . . . . .83 F4
Chester Rd
Peterborough PE1 . . . . . .198 C3
Wyton Airfield PE28 . . . .143 B7
Chesterfield Rd CB4 . . . . .84 A6
Chesterton Com Coll
CB4 . . . . .83 E4
Chesterton Gr PE2 . . . . .187 D6
Chesterton Hall Cres
CB4 . . . . .83 F4
Chesterton Hospl CB4 . . .83 F4
Chesterton La CB4 . . . . .246 A4
Chesterton Rd CB4 . . . . .246 A4
Chestnut Ave PE1 . . . . . .198 C6
Chestnut Cl
Brampton PE28 . . . . .140 D2
Glinton PE6 . . . . .203 D8
Grafham PE28 . . . . .116 A7
Haslingfield CB3 . . . . .47 B4
Haverhill CB9 . . . . .23 F8
Huntingdon PE29 . . . . . . .141 E7
Mildenhall IP28 . . . . .239 D4
Peakirk PE6 . . . . .206 B2
Sawston CB2 . . . . .32 F7
Sawtry PE28 . . . . .168 B4
Chestnut Cres
March PE15 . . . . .243 B3
Whittlesey PE7 . . . . .189 E6
Chestnut Dr
■ Soham CB7 . . . . .212 B4
■ Thorney PE6 . . . . .233 A3
Chestnut Gr
Little Stukeley PE28 . . . .152 A2
St Neots PE19 . . . . .74 F4
Chestnut La SG8 . . . . .13 B6
Chestnut Rd St Ives PE27 143 F6

Chestnut Rd continued
■ Wisbech PE13 . . . . . . .245 C4
Chestnut Rise
Bar Hill CB3 . . . . .102 D3
Burwell CB5 . . . . .130 B4
Chestnut Way CB6 . . . . . .216 E3
Chestnut Wlk ■ SG8 . . . . .5 E5
Chestnuts The 48 A4
Cheveley Prim Sch CB8 .91 C7
Cheveley Rd
Newmarket CB8 . . . . .111 C3
Woodditton CB8 . . . . .91 C3
Cheviot Ave PE4 . . . . . . .204 E2
Chewells Cl CB6 . . . . . . .210 A6
Chewells La CB6 . . . . . . .210 A6
Cheyney Cl SG8 . . . . .11 B1
Cheyney St SG8 . . . . .11 B1
Chichester Way PE28 . . .115 D2
Chiefs St CB6 . . . . .240 C4
Chigwell Ct ■ CB5 . . . . . .84 E4
Chilcourt SG8 . . . . .5 C6
Childerley H★ CB3 . . . . . .80 D8
Childers St PE7 . . . . .189 C8
Child's Pond Rd PE19 . . .75 A4
Childs La ■ PE15 . . . . . . .223 A5
Chiltern Rise PE4 . . . . . . .204 D2
Chimsell Way CB9 . . . . . .23 C8
Chippenham Mews ■
PE2 . . . . .186 C7
Chippenham Rd
Chippenham CB7 . . . . . . .133 C2
Fordham CB7 . . . . .213 A1
Freckenham IP28 . . . . . . .213 C2
Moulton CB8 . . . . .133 D1
Chisenhale PE2 . . . . .185 E6
Chishill Rd Barley SG8 . . .7 A1
Great & Little Chishill SG8 . .7 F3
Heydon SG8 . . . . .8 A4
Chishill Windmill★ SG8 . .7 C7
Chiswick Ave PE28 . . . . .239 C6
Chiswick End SG8 . . . . . .14 A7
Chittering Dro CB5 . . . . .127 C8
Chivers Rd CB5 . . . . .23 D7
Chivers Way CB4 . . . . . . .104 B2
Chrishall Rd SG8 . . . . . . .15 F6
Christchurch St CB1 . . . .246 C3
Christie Dr PE29 . . . . . . .141 A5
Christopher Cl PE1 . . . . .197 F8
Christopher Dr PE13 . . . .245 A7
Christopher Tye Cl ■
CB6 . . . . .240 B5
Christ's Coll CB1 . . . . . . .246 B3
Church Cl
Bassingbourn SG8 . . . . . .12 E5
Cottenham CB4 . . . . .125 F6
Coveney CB6 . . . . .217 C5
Dullingham CB8 . . . . .70 E2
Exning CB8 . . . . .110 C8
Great & Little Abington CB1 34 C7
Great Wilbraham CB1 . . . .67 F7
Newborough PE6 . . . . . . .205 C8
Ramsey PE26 . . . . .221 C2
Stilton PE7 . . . . .176 A7
The Stukeleys PE28 . . . .151 F2
Whittlesford PE22 . . . . . . .32 C5
Church Cswy PE28 . . . . .168 C2
Church Dr PE2 . . . . .185 F5
Church Dro PE14 . . . . . . .236 F2
Church End Arrington SG8 44 D1
Barley SG8 . . . . .7 A1
Cambridge CB1 . . . . .65 F8
Coton CB3 . . . . .82 B2
Everton SG19 . . . . .40 C3
Gamlingay SG19 . . . . .41 E5
Hilton PE28 . . . . .99 B8
Horningsea CB5 . . . . .106 A2
■ Leverington PE13 . . . .238 B2
Over CB4 . . . . .208 D1
Rampton CB4 . . . . .124 F4
Weston Colville CB1 . . . . .54 A7
Whaddon SG8 . . . . .28 B2
Church Farm La SG8 . . . .11 B1
Church Fen Dro CB6 . . . .209 E3
Church Gate ■ PE6 . . . . .231 F8
Church Gdns IP28 . . . . . .213 D6
Church Gn CB10 . . . . .18 B7
Church Hill Castor PE5 . .195 E2
Grafham PE28 . . . . .115 F6
Church Hill Cl PE7 . . . . . .187 C1
Church La
Abington Pigotts SG8 . . . .11 F5
Arrington SG8 . . . . .44 D1
■ Ashwell SG7 . . . . .2 D4
■ Ashwell SG7 . . . . .2 D4
Balsham CB1 . . . . .53 B2
Barton CB3 . . . . .63 B4
Barton Mills IP28 . . . . . . .239 D1
"Beck Row, Holywell Row
& Kenny Hill" IP28 . . . . .213 D6
Brington & Molesworth
PE28 . . . . .147 C4
Burwell CB5 . . . . .130 B1
Cambridge CB2 . . . . .64 C2
Castle Camps CB1 . . . . . .22 E3
Chatteris PE16 . . . . .241 C4
Cheveley CB8 . . . . .91 C6
Comberton CB3 . . . . .62 C3
Conington PE7 . . . . .168 E8
Cottenham CB4 . . . . .125 F6
Covington PE28 . . . . .135 C2
Croydon SG8 . . . . .27 A8
Doddington/Wimblington
PE15 . . . . .222 F5
Ellington PE28 . . . . .138 F4
Elsworth CB3 . . . . .100 B4

Church La continued
Ely CB7 . . . . .240 C4
Exning CB8 . . . . .110 C8
Fenstanton PE28 . . . . . . .121 B6
Fulbourn CB1 . . . . .67 A5
Gamlingay SG19 . . . . .41 D5
Girton CB3 . . . . .82 E8
Graveley PE19 . . . . .97 F5
Great & Little Abington CB1 .34 B7
Great Paxton PE19 . . . . . . .96 D5
Guilden Morden SG8 . . . . .10 F5
Haddenham CB6 . . . . .210 A6
Helpston PE6 . . . . .231 B4
Hemingford Abbots PE28 . .143 A3
Hemingford Grey PE28 . . .143 C2
Hilton PE28 . . . . .120 B1
Huntingdon PE29 . . . . . . .142 A5
Isleham CB7 . . . . .213 A5
Kennett CB8 . . . . .133 F5
Kingston CB3 . . . . .61 B3
Leighton PE28 . . . . .148 D3
Linton CB1 . . . . .35 C2
Little Eversden CB3 . . . . . .46 A7
Little Staughton MK44 . . . .93 B2
☑ Littleport CB6 . . . . .242 D4
Madingley CB3 . . . . .81 E4
Milton CB4 . . . . .105 D2
Newmarket CB8 . . . . .111 A3
Newton PE13 . . . . .238 A5
Pampisford CB2 . . . . .33 B5
Papworth Everard CB3 . . . .99 A2
Peterborough PE2 . . . . . . .185 F5
Peterborough PE2 . . . . . . .187 B7
Ramsey PE26 . . . . .171 B2
Sawston CB2 . . . . .32 F7
Sibson cum Stibbington
PE8 . . . . .194 E2
Snailwell CB8 . . . . .132 A3
Spaldwick PE28 . . . . .137 F6
Stamford PE9 . . . . .244 C4
Stetchworth CB8 . . . . .90 A2
Stow Longa PE28 . . . . . . .137 B3
Sutton CB6 . . . . .216 E2
Tallington PE9 . . . . .230 F6
Tilbrook PE28 . . . . .113 B7
Tydd St Giles PE13 . . . . . .237 F6
Warmington PE8 . . . . .178 B2
Westley Waterless CB8 . . . .70 B5
Whittlesford CB2 . . . . .32 C5
Wilburton CB6 . . . . .210 B6
☑ Willingham CB4 . . . . . .209 A1
Worlington IP28 . . . . .213 F4
Wrestlingworth SG19 . . . . .25 B3
Church Lane Cl IP28 . . .239 D2
Church Leys PE28 . . . . . .121 C6
Church Mdw PE28 . . . . . .239 D2
Church Mdws PE19 . . . . .74 F5
Church Path CB1 . . . . . . .20 B6
Church Pl PE29 . . . . .141 E2
Church Rd
Brampton PE28 . . . . .140 E2
Buckworth PE28 . . . . . . .149 D6
Carlton CB8 . . . . .55 A6
Catworth PE28 . . . . .136 D7
Chrishall SG8 . . . . .8 D3
Christchurch PE14 . . . . . . .229 D3
Conington PE7 . . . . .168 D8
Easton PE28 . . . . .138 B4
Everton SG19 . . . . .40 C3
Glatton PE28 . . . . .175 E1
Grafham PE28 . . . . .115 E7
Great Wilbraham CB1 . . . . .67 F8
Hauxton CB2 . . . . .48 A5
Leverington PE13 . . . . . . .245 F7
Little Stukeley PE28 . . . . .151 F2
Little Wilbraham CB1 . . . . .86 F2
Moulton CB8 . . . . .112 F5
Shepreth SG8 . . . . .29 E4
Shudy Camps CB1 . . . . . . .22 C5
Stow cum Quy CB5 . . . . . .85 F4
Teversham CB1 . . . . .85 B2
Thistley Green IP28 . . . . . .213 D6
Toft CB3 . . . . .61 E4
Warboys PE28 . . . . .164 E4
Wentworth CB6 . . . . .217 C1
Wicken CB7 . . . . .211 F1
Wisbech PE14 . . . . .236 A3
Wisbech PE13 . . . . .238 B1
Wisbech St Mary PE13 . . .235 B7
Wittering PE8 . . . . .230 B1
Church St Ashley CB8 . . .91 F8
Bourn CB3 . . . . .60 C5
Buckden PE19 . . . . .117 A4
Cambridge CB1 . . . . .84 A4
☑ Doddington/Wimblington
PE15 . . . . .223 B7
Exning CB8 . . . . .110 C8
Fen Ditton CB5 . . . . .84 E6
Fen Drayton CB4 . . . . .121 F5
Fenstanton PE28 . . . . . . .121 B6
Fordham CB7 . . . . .212 F1
Gamlingay SG19 . . . . .41 D5
Great Chesterford CB10 . . .18 D2
Great Eversden CB3 . . . . . .45 E7
Great Gransden SG19 . . . .58 E4
Great Shelford CB2 . . . . . .48 E4
Great Shelford CB2 . . . . . .49 C4
Great Wilbraham CB1 . . . . .67 F8
Guilden Morden SG8 . . . . .10 F4
Harston CB2 . . . . .47 D2
Haslingfield CB3 . . . . .47 A5
Hemingford Grey PE28 . . .143 C2
Histon CB4 . . . . .104 B5
Holme PE7 . . . . .176 F4
Ickleton CB10 . . . . .18 A4

Church St continued
☑ Isleham CB7 . . . . .213 A5
Litlington SG8 . . . . .12 A2
Little Gransden SG19 . . . . .58 E3
March PE15 . . . . .243 C1
Market Deeping PE6 . . . . .231 F8
Needingworth PE27 . . . . .208 A2
Northborough PE6 . . . . . .206 A4
Northborough PE6 . . . . . .231 F6
Old Hurst PE28 . . . . .154 D7
Peterborough PE7 . . . . . . .185 A4
Peterborough PE2 . . . . . . .187 C7
Peterborough PE1 . . . . . . .198 A2
Peterborough PE4 . . . . . . .204 C3
St Ives PE27 . . . . .143 F4
St Ives PE27 . . . . .144 A4
St Neots PE19 . . . . .74 F5
Sawtry PE28 . . . . .168 B4
☑ Somersham PE28 . . . . .208 C8
Stamford PE9 . . . . .244 B4
Steeple Morden SG8 . . . . .11 B1
Stilton PE7 . . . . .175 F7
☑ Thorney PE6 . . . . .233 A3
Thriplow SG8 . . . . .31 C1
Warmington PE8 . . . . .178 A3
Whaddon SG8 . . . . .28 B2
Whittlesey PE7 . . . . .189 D6
Willingham CB4 . . . . .209 A1
Wistow PE28 . . . . .163 F7
Withersfield CB9 . . . . .38 C4
Woodhurst PE28 . . . . . . .155 B5
Yaxley PE7 . . . . .181 D4
Church Terr ☑ PE13 . . . .245 C5
Church View
☑ Northborough PE6 . . . .231 F7
Oakington/Longstanton
CB4 . . . . .103 C6
☑ St Neots PE19 . . . . .74 F5
☑ Witchford CB6 . . . . . . .217 E1
Church View Cl PE2 . . . .187 B7
Church Way
Alconbury PE28 . . . . .150 E5
Alconbury Weston PE28 . .150 D6
Downham PE28 . . . . .218 A7
☑ Haslingfield CB3 . . . . . .47 A5
Little Stukeley PE28 . . . . .151 D4
Church Wlk
Chatteris PE16 . . . . .241 D5
Little Gransden SG19 . . . . .58 E3
Mildenhall IP28 . . . . .239 B4
Peterborough PE1 . . . . . . .198 A3
Stow Longa PE28 . . . . . . .137 B3
Sturmer CB9 . . . . .24 E5
Upton PE6 . . . . .195 B5
Churchfield SG8 . . . . .7 A1
Churchfield Ave CB2 . . . .32 F8
Churchfield Ct PE4 . . . . .197 E8
Churchfield Rd
Peterborough PE4 . . . . . . .197 D8
Upwell PE14 . . . . .236 F2
Churchfield Way
Whittlesey PE7 . . . . .189 C7
☑ Wisbech St Mary PE13 .235 B7
Churchgate St ☑ CB7 . . .212 B4
Churchhill Cl ☑ CB6 . . . .216 E2
Churchill Ave
Haverhill CB9 . . . . .39 B1
Houghton & Wyton PE28 .143 B7
Newmarket CB8 . . . . .110 D5
Churchill Cl CB6 . . . . . . .240 A4
Churchill Coll CB3 . . . . . . .83 B3
Churchill Ct ☑ CB6 . . . . .218 A6
Churchill Dr IP28 . . . . . .239 B5
Churchill Rd
Gorefield PE13 . . . . .237 F3
Stamford PE9 . . . . .244 B7
Wisbech PE13 . . . . .245 D4
Churchyard The PE28 . . .239 B4
Cinques Rd SG19 . . . . . . .41 C6
Cinques The SG19 . . . . . .41 B6
Cissbury Ring PE4 . . . . . .204 C2
City of Ely Com Coll
CB6 . . . . .240 C6
City Rd Cambridge CB1 . .246 C2
Littleport CB6 . . . . .242 E4
March PE15 . . . . .243 D4
Peterborough PE1 . . . . . . .198 A2
Clack La PE28 . . . . .135 D8
Clare Cl Mildenhall IP28 .239 D5
Stamford PE9 . . . . .244 A5
Waterbeach CB5 . . . . .106 A8
Clare Coll CB2 . . . . .246 A2
Clare Coll Pavilion CB2 . . .64 F5
Clare Pl CB8 . . . . .111 B2
Clare Rd Cambridge CB3 . .64 C8
Huntingdon PE29 . . . . . . .142 A7
☑ Northborough PE6 . . . .231 F7
Peterborough PE1 . . . . . . .197 F6
Clare St Cambridge CB4 . .246 A4
Chatteris PE16 . . . . .241 B4
Claremont ☑ CB1 . . . . . . .64 F7
Claremont Rd PE13 . . . . .245 E5
Clarence Rd
Peterborough PE1 . . . . . . .197 E5
Wisbech PE13 . . . . .245 D6
Clarendale Est CB8 . . . . .55 F6
Clarendon Rd
Cambridge CB2 . . . . .64 F6
Haverhill CB9 . . . . .23 F7
Clarendon St CB1 . . . . . .246 B2
Clarendon Way PE6 . . . .203 F8
Clark Rd SG8 . . . . .5 D7
Clarke's La CB6 . . . . . . .210 C5
Clarkes Way SG8 . . . . . . .12 F5
Clark's Dro PE14 . . . . . . .212 A4
Clarkson Ave PE13 . . . . .245 D5
Clarkson Cl CB3 . . . . .83 B2
Clarkson Ct PE13 . . . . . .245 D6

Clarkson Inf Sch PE13 . .245 E6
Clarkson Rd CB3 . . . . . . .83 B2
Claudian Cl CB9 . . . . .24 D7
Clay Close La CB4 . . . . . .104 D3
Clay La
Abbots Ripton PE28 . . . . .162 A1
Castor PE5 . . . . .195 E2
Little Stukeley PE28 . . . . .151 F7
Soham CB7 . . . . .212 B4
Claybush Rd SG7 . . . . .2 D3
Claydon Cl CB1 . . . . .22 E4
Claygate PE7 . . . . .189 D7
Claygate Rd CB1 . . . . .65 F5
Clayhithe Rd
Horningsea CB5 . . . . .106 C5
Waterbeach CB5 . . . . .106 C6
Clayhive Dr ☑ CB9 . . . . . .23 F7
Claypole Dr ☑ PE6 . . . . .231 F7
Clayton Cl PE13 . . . . .245 F6
Clayton Sch PE2 . . . . . . .186 B4
Claytons Way PE29 . . . . .141 F5
Clayway CB7 . . . . .240 C6
Clear Cres SG8 . . . . .14 D5
Cleatham PE3 . . . . .197 A4
Clematis Cl IP28 . . . . . . .213 F1
Clement's La CB9 . . . . . . .23 F7
Clement's Way ☑ IP28 . .213 F8
Clements Cl CB9 . . . . .23 F7
Clements CP Sch CB9 . . .23 F7
Clements Dr CB9 . . . . . . .23 F7
Clerk Maxwell Rd CB3 . . .83 A2
Cleve Pl PE6 . . . . .232 A1
Cleveland Bay PE15 . . . . .243 E2
Cleveland Ct PE4 . . . . . . .204 E2
Cleves Rd CB9 . . . . .23 D6
Clifden Cl SG8 . . . . .44 D1
Cliff Cres PE9 . . . . .244 B5
Cliff Rd PE9 . . . . .244 B5
Clifton Ave PE3 . . . . .197 E3
Clifton Rd Cambridge CB1 .65 A6
Huntingdon PE29 . . . . . . .141 D7
Clive Hall Dr CB4 . . . . . .124 A1
Cliveden Cl CB4 . . . . .83 C5
Cloisters The ☑ CB7 . . . .240 D4
Close The Babraham CB2 . .50 E2
Godmanchester PE29 . . . .142 A1
Kennett CB8 . . . . .133 F5
Papworth Everard CB3 . . . .99 B3
Royston SG8 . . . . .5 F7
Sutton CB6 . . . . .216 E1
Clover Cl Cambridge CB1 . .66 A5
☑ Linton CB1 . . . . .35 D2
Clover End ☑ CB6 . . . . . .217 D1
Clover Field PE9 . . . . .23 D8
Clover Rd PE19 . . . . .74 C3
Clover Way ☑ IP28 . . . . .214 A1
Cloverfield Dr CB7 . . . . .212 A5
Clydesdale Cl PE15 . . . . .243 E2
Clydesdale Rd ☑ SG8 . . . . .5 E6
Coach Dr CB3 . . . . .46 D5
Coach House La CB2 . . . . .31 B7
Coach La CB8 . . . . .91 D5
Coalwharf Rd PE13 . . . . .245 B4
Coates Dro CB7 . . . . .213 A5
Coates Rd PE7 . . . . .190 D7
Cob Pl PE29 . . . . .118 F7
Cobbet Pl PE1 . . . . .198 B3
Cobden Ave PE1 . . . . . . .197 F4
Cobden St PE1 . . . . .197 F4
Cobholm Pl ☑ CB4 . . . . . .83 F8
Cock Bank
Whittlesey PE7 . . . . .191 C2
Whittlesey PE7 . . . . .221 F8
Cock Fen Rd PE14 . . . . . .229 F3
Cockbrook La
Brington & Molesworth
PE28 . . . . .147 C8
Old Weston PE28 . . . . . . .157 C2
Cockburn St CB1 . . . . . . .65 B8
Cockcroft Pl CB3 . . . . . . .83 B2
Cockerell Rd CB4 . . . . . . .83 D5
Cockerton Rd CB3 . . . . . .103 E1
Cocketts Dr PE13 . . . . . .245 E5
Cockfen La CB4 . . . . .105 C7
Cockhall Cl SG8 . . . . .12 A1
Cockhall La SG8 . . . . .12 A1
Cockle Cl CB2 . . . . .31 C7
Cockpen Rd CB7 . . . . . . .131 A8
Codrington Ct ☑ PE19 . . .74 B3
Cody Rd CB5 . . . . .127 B1
Coggeshall Cl ☑ CB5 . . . .84 E4
Colbron Cl SG7 . . . . .2 C1
Coldham Bank PE15 . . . .228 D6
Coldham Hall Chase
PE14 . . . . .235 E1
Coldham's Gr CB1 . . . . . .84 C1
Coldham's La CB1 . . . . . .84 C1
Coldham's Rd CB1 . . . . . .84 B2
Coldhams Cres PE29 . . . .141 F6
Coldhams N PE29 . . . . . .141 F6
Coldhams S PE29 . . . . . .141 F6
Coldhorn Cres PE13 . . . .245 D7
Cole Cl ☑ CB6 . . . . .217 D1
Coleridge Com Coll CB1 .65 C7
Coleridge Cl ☑ PE19 . . . .74 C6
Coleridge Pl PE1 . . . . . . .197 E8
Coleridge Rd CB1 . . . . . . .65 B6
Coles La Brinkley CB8 . . . .70 D2
Linton CB1 . . . . .35 C2
Oakington/Longstanton
CB4 . . . . .103 C6
Coles Rd CB4 . . . . .105 D2
Coleseed Rd PE15 . . . . . .228 D2
Colesfield CB4 . . . . .123 E2
Coll of Animal Welfare The
PE29 . . . . .119 C5

Coll of West Anglia
CB4 . . . . .105 D3
College Cl ☑ CB5 . . . . . . .86 E6
College Cres CB3 . . . . . . .47 B5
College Ct PE28 . . . . .168 C3
College Fields CB4 . . . . . .83 F6
College Gdns PE15 . . . . .243 E7
College Heath Rd IP28 . .239 D6
College Pk PE1 . . . . .198 C5
College Rd Histon CB4 . . .104 B1
Soham CB7 . . . . .212 B3
Collett's Bridge La PE14 .236 C5
Collier Cl CB1 . . . . .246 C2
Collier Way CB2 . . . . .49 C4
Colliers La CB5 . . . . .86 A6
Collingham PE2 . . . . .185 F3
Collings Pl ☑ CB8 . . . . . .110 E5
Collingwood Ave PE15 . .243 E3
Collingwood Ct SG8 . . . . . .5 E7
Collingwood Rd PE19 . . . .74 B2
Collin's Hill CB7 . . . . . . .212 F1
Collyweston Rd PE9 . . . .230 B2
Colmworth Gdns ☑ PE19 74 C2
Colne Fields Colne PE28 .215 D1
Somersham PE28 . . . . . . .208 D8
Colne Rd
Bluntisham PE28 . . . . . . .208 C6
Colne PE28 . . . . .208 C8
Earith PE28 . . . . .208 D6
Colne Valley Rd CB9 . . . . .24 A7
Colour Ct PE29 . . . . .141 D7
Colts Croft SG8 . . . . .7 E2
Coltsfoot Cl CB1 . . . . .66 A5
Coltsfoot Dr
Peterborough PE2 . . . . . . .186 E7
Royston SG8 . . . . .5 A6
Colvile Rd Newton PE13 .238 A5
Wisbech PE13 . . . . .245 E5
Colville Cty Prim Sch
CB1 . . . . .65 F5
Colville Rd CB1 . . . . .65 F6
Colwyn Cl CB4 . . . . .83 D5
Comberton Rd Barton CB3 .62 F5
Little Eversden CB3 . . . . . .46 C8
Toft CB3 . . . . .61 E5
Comberton Village Coll
CB3 . . . . .62 A4
Comet Way
Mildenhall IP28 . . . . .239 B5
St Ives PE27 . . . . .144 A7
Comfrey Ct CB1 . . . . .66 A5
Commercial Rd PE15 . . . .243 C7
Common Acre La CB6 . . .225 D6
Common Dro
Southery PE38 . . . . .226 E8
Whittlesey PE7 . . . . .189 C8
Wimblington PE15 . . . . . .223 C6
Common Gate Dro CB7 . .212 E6
Common La Ashwell SG7 . . .2 B6
Chrishall SG8 . . . . .1 F7
Hemingford Abbots PE28 .142 F3
Sawston CB2 . . . . .32 D7
Common Rd
Parson Drove PE12 . . . . . .233 F7
Sutton St Edmund PE12 . .233 F8
West Wratting CB1 . . . . . . .54 E2
Weston Colville CB1 . . . . . .54 E4
Whittlesey PE7 . . . . .189 C8
Witchford PE7 . . . . .217 E1
Common The
West Wratting CB1 . . . . . . .53 F4
West Wratting CB1 . . . . . . .54 C3
Commons Rd PE28 . . . . .189 C8
Compton Fields CB7 . . . .240 E7
Conder Cl ☑ CB4 . . . . . . .105 C3
Conduit Head Rd CB3 . . .82 F3
Conduit Rd PE9 . . . . .244 C6
Coneygear Ct PE29 . . . . .141 E7
Coneygear Rd PE29 . . . . .141 E8
Coneygree Rd PE7 . . . . . .187 D6
Coneywood Rd PE15 . . . .223 A7
Conifers The PE2 . . . . . . .185 F6
Coningsby Rd PE3 . . . . . .204 A2
Conington La PE7 . . . . . .168 C8
Conington Rd CB3 . . . . . .121 B3
Coniston Cl ☑ PE29 . . . .141 B6
Coniston Rd
Cambridge CB1 . . . . .65 B6
Peterborough PE4 . . . . . . .204 E3
Conley Cl PE26 . . . . .172 B7
Conner's Cl SG8 . . . . . . .110 F4
Conquest Dro PE7 . . . . . .187 D1
Constable Ave ☑ PE19 . . .74 D5
Constable Cl PE7 . . . . . . .190 A8
Constable Rd
☑ Haverhill CB9 . . . . .38 D1
St Ives PE27 . . . . .144 A7
Constables Leys CB8 . . . .113 F5
Convent Dr CB5 . . . . .105 F8
Conway Ave PE4 . . . . . . .204 C2
Conway Cl
☑ Cambridge CB1 . . . . . . .65 F6
☑ March PE15 . . . . .243 B3
Conway Pl ☑ PE19 . . . . . .74 F2
Cook Cl CB4 . . . . .84 B6
Cook Close Rd PE7 . . . . .181 D6
Cook's Dro
"Beck Row, Holywell Row
& Kenny Hill" IP28 . . . .213 B8
Earith PE28 . . . . .208 E6
Cook's Gn PE15 . . . . .222 F5
Cooks La PE28 . . . . .168 D5
Cookson Cl PE7 . . . . .181 D4
Coolidge Gdns CB4 . . . . .125 F4
Coombe Rd SG8 . . . . .4 A1
Coombelands Rd ☑ SG8 . . .5 E8

Cooper Thornhill Rd ☑
PE7 . . . . .175 F7
Cooper's Cl CB8 . . . . .90 A1
Cootes La CB4 . . . . .121 E5
Cootes Mdw PE27 . . . . . .144 B3
Copeland PE3 . . . . .197 A3
Copellis Cl CB9 . . . . .39 A2
Copes Cl PE19 . . . . .117 B4
Cophall Dro CB6 . . . . . . .217 E4
Coploe Rd CB10 . . . . .17 F3
Copper Beech Way PE2 . .187 B7
Copperbeech Cl PE27 . . .144 A5
Copperfields SG8 . . . . .5 B6
Coppice Ave CB2 . . . . . . .49 B6
Coppice The Histon CB4 .104 C1
Littleport CB6 . . . . .242 C1
Coppingford Cl PE2 . . . . .187 D6
Coppins Cl PE28 . . . . . . .168 A4
Coppins Ct PE14 . . . . . . .245 E2
Copsewood PE4 . . . . .204 C4
Copy Hill CB9 . . . . .23 E3
Coral Park Trading Est
CB1 . . . . .84 B2
Corbett St CB4 . . . . .125 E4
Cordell Cl PE27 . . . . .143 E6
Cordon St PE13 . . . . .245 C4
Coree Cl CB2 . . . . .65 A5
Corfe Ave PE4 . . . . .204 C2
Corfe Pl ☑ PE19 . . . . .74 F2
Cormas Cl SG8 . . . . .5 E8
Corn Exchange St CB2 . . .246 A2
Corner Cl CB7 . . . . .219 B5
Cornfields ☑ PE15 . . . . .222 F5
Cornish Cl CB1 . . . . .37 A3
Cornmills Rd CB7 . . . . . .212 D2
Cornstall Bldgs ☑ PE9 . .244 C5
Cornwall Ct PE19 . . . . . . .74 B4
Cornwall Rd
☑ Stamford PE9 . . . . . . .244 B6
Wyton Airfield PE28 . . . . .143 A8
Cornwallis Dr PE19 . . . . . .74 A3
Cornwallis Rd CB9 . . . . . .23 F6
Corona Rd CB4 . . . . .83 E4
Coronation Ave
☑ Crowland PE6 . . . . . . .232 B8
Huntingdon PE29 . . . . . . .141 E5
Parson Drove PE12 . . . . . .234 A7
Royston SG8 . . . . .5 C5
☑ Somersham PE28 . . . . .215 C1
Warboys PE28 . . . . .164 F6
Whittlesey PE7 . . . . .189 F7
Coronation Cl
March PE15 . . . . .243 C2
Waterbeach CB5 . . . . .106 A4
Coronation Mews ☑ CB2 64 E7
Coronation St CB2 . . . . . .246 B1
Corporation Bank PE6 . . .207 F7
Corporation Rd PE13 . . . .245 D3
Corpus Christi Coll CB2 . .246 A2
Corpus Christi La PE29 . .141 E1
Corrie Rd CB1 . . . . .65 B7
Corsican Pine Cl CB8 . . .110 F5
Corunna Cl ☑ PE19 . . . . .74 C5
Cosgrove Cl PE3 . . . . . . .197 C6
Cotes The CB7 . . . . .211 F6
Coton C of E Com Prim Sch
CB3 . . . . .82 B2
Coton Rd CB3 . . . . .63 E5
Cotswold Cl March PE15 .243 E4
Peterborough PE4 . . . . . . .204 E1
Cottenham Cl ☑ CB6 . . .208 D1
Cottenham Prim Sch
CB4 . . . . .125 D4
Cottenham Rd
Histon CB4 . . . . .104 B5
Landbeach CB4 . . . . .126 B1
Cottenham Village Coll
CB4 . . . . .125 E3
Cottesmore Cl PE3 . . . . .197 D4
Cotton Cl Conington PE7 .168 C8
☑ Sawtry PE28 . . . . .168 C2
Cotton Ct ☑ PE29 . . . . . .141 F7
Cotton End Rd CB8 . . . . .110 C8
Cotton La PE19 . . . . .97 C7
Cotton's Field CB3 . . . . . .102 B1
Cottrell's La CB9 . . . . . . .100 B4
Coulson Cl CB4 . . . . .105 C2
Coulson Way PE28 . . . . .150 F4
Council Rd ☑ PE13 . . . . .245 E6
Council St PE4 . . . . .197 D8
Countess Cl PE19 . . . . . . .74 B3
County Rd PE15 . . . . . . .243 D6
Coupals Cl CB9 . . . . .24 C6
Coupals CP Sch CB9 . . . . .24 D7
Coupals Rd CB9 . . . . .24 E6
Courier Cl IP28 . . . . .239 B6
Courtland Ave CB1 . . . . . .65 C5
Courtney Way CB4 . . . . . .83 E4
Courtyard Way CB4 . . . . .125 E5
Courtyards CB2 . . . . .48 F3
Cousins Cl PE15 . . . . . . .243 C4
Covent Gdn CB1 . . . . . . .246 C1
Coventry Cl PE4 . . . . . . .204 B3
Covert Cl CB9 . . . . .39 A1
Covert The
☑ Comberton CB3 . . . . . . .62 D6
Peterborough PE3 . . . . . . .197 B1
Cow & Sheep Dro IP28 . .213 C2
Cow Fen Rd CB4 . . . . . . .122 E6
Cow La Fulbourn CB1 . . . .66 E5
Godmanchester PE29 . . . .142 C2
Great Chesterford CB10 . . .19 A4
Rampton CB4 . . . . .124 F6
Cow Way PE7 . . . . .190 D8
Cowbridge Hall Dro
CB6 . . . . .218 B6
Cowdell End CB3 . . . . . . .100 B4
Cowgate PE1 . . . . .197 F2

Cowley Cl PE28 ......115 D3
Cowley Pk CB4 ......84 B7
Cowley Rd CB4 ......84 C7
Cowper Rd Cambridge CB1 65 B6
Huntingdon PE29 ......141 D5
Peterborough PE1 ......197 F7
Cowpers Ct 4 PE19 ......74 D6
Cowslip Cl 1 SG8 ......5 F5
Cowslip Dr CB6 ......211 A7
Coxons Cl PE29 ......141 E5
Cox's Cl CB2 ......49 C4
Cox's Dro CB1 ......66 F6
Cox's End 15 CB4 ......208 D1
Cox's La Chatteris PE16 ......241 C6
Wisbech PE13 ......245 A3
Crab Apple Way SG19 ......41 C5
Crab Marsh PE13 ......245 B8
Crabapple Cl PE28 ......168 B3
Crabtree PE4 ......205 B1
Crabtree Croft CB1 ......35 B3
Craft Way SG8 ......11 B2
Crafts Way CB3 ......102 C3
Craig St PE1 ......197 F3
Crandal Way CB2 ......49 A4
Crane Ave PE7 ......181 F6
Crane Cl 3 PE28 ......208 C8
Crane St PE28 ......140 C3
Cranemore PE4 ......204 A4
Crane's La CB3 ......61 A2
Cranfield Pl 2 PE28 ......208 C8
Cranfield Way
Brampton PE28 ......140 D2
Buckden PE19 ......117 A3
Cranford Dr PE3 ......197 C4
Cranleigh Cl CB2 ......64 D1
Cranmer Rd CB3 ......83 B1
Cranmore Dro PE6 ......206 D8
Cranny The PE19 ......117 F2
Cranwells Way 4 CB6 ......211 B7
Crathern Way CB4 ......83 F7
Crauden Gdns 4 CB7 ......240 E5
Craven Cl CB2 ......64 D2
Craven Way CB8 ......110 E6
Crawford Gdns 2 PE6 ......232 C8
Crawley End SG8 ......8 D4
Crawthorne Rd PE1 ......198 A3
Crawthorne St 1 PE1 ......198 B3
Crease Dro PE6 ......232 B8
Crease Rd
Conington PE28 ......168 F5
Sawtry PE28 ......169 B6
Crecy Ct PE19 ......74 C5
Creek Fen PE15 ......228 D5
Creek Rd PE15 ......243 D4
Crescent Cl PE7 ......190 A4
Crescent Rd Histon CB4 ......104 C1
Whittlesey PE7 ......189 F7
Crescent The
Cambridge CB3 ......83 B3
Dullingham CB8 ......89 C1
Eaton Socon PE19 ......74 C3
Eye PE6 ......232 A1
Littleport CB6 ......242 C3
Peterborough PE2 ......186 E7
St Ives PE27 ......144 A5
St Neots PE19 ......74 F6
4 Soham CB7 ......212 B3
Wicken CB7 ......211 E1
Wisbech PE13 ......245 C4
Cressener Terr 3 PE19 ......74 F3
Cresswells La CB7 ......240 E4
Crester Dr 3 PE4 ......204 C3
Criccieth Way PE19 ......74 F1
Cricket Field Rd CB8 ......111 B2
Cricketers Cl PE15 ......243 C3
Cricketers Way
3 Benwick PE15 ......222 A5
Wisbech PE13 ......245 A6
Cricketfield La PE26 ......172 A6
Crick's Rd IP28 ......213 D6
Cripple Sidings La PE2 ......187 A8
Crishall CE Prim Sch SG8 ......8 C3
Crispin Cl Haverhill CB9 ......23 D7
1 Impington CB4 ......83 D7
Crispin Pl CB1 ......246 C3
Crockfords Rd CB8 ......111 A2
Crocus Cl PE7 ......181 F6
Crocus Gr PE1 ......198 A8
Croft Cl Brampton PE28 ......140 D2
Histon CB4 ......104 B5
Croft La Haverhill CB9 ......24 B6
Oakington/Longstanton
CB4 ......103 B6
Croft Park Rd CB6 ......242 D3
Croft Pl IP28 ......239 C4
Croft Rd Isleham CB7 ......213 A5
Newmarket CB8 ......110 E5
Outwell PE14 ......229 D7
Croft The CB1 ......66 E5
Croft Way PE7 ......186 C2
Crofters The CB6 ......210 F6
Croftfield Rd PE29 ......141 F1
Crofts The PE19 ......95 F1
Crome Ditch Cl CB3 ......64 A4
Cromwell Cl
2 Northborough PE6 ......231 F7
Ramsey PE26 ......171 F6
Cromwell Com Coll
PE16 ......241 C4
Cromwell Ct 3 PE19 ......74 D5
Cromwell Gdns 4 PE19 ......75 A5
Cromwell Ho* PE29 ......141 D5
Cromwell Mews PE6 ......231 C4
Cromwell Mus* PE29 ......141 D4
Cromwell Pk PE28 ......208 E1
Cromwell Pl PE27 ......144 B3
Cromwell Rd
Cambridge CB1 ......84 B1

Cromwell Rd continued
Ely CB6 ......240 C4
March PE15 ......243 D6
Peterborough PE1 ......197 F4
St Neots PE19 ......74 F3
1 Sutton CB6 ......216 C1
Wisbech PE13 ......245 B3
Cromwell Way PE28 ......168 B3
Cromwell Wlk PE29 ......141 D5
Crooked Bank PE14 ......235 D5
Croots Cl PE28 ......140 B2
Cropston Rd PE1 ......198 E7
Cross Bank Dro CB7 ......211 C5
Cross Cl CB9 ......39 A1
Cross Dro
Haddenham CB6 ......209 E3
Littleport CB7 ......226 A1
Southery PE38 ......226 E7
Stretham CB6 ......210 F3
Tydd St Giles PE13 ......237 C5
Warboys PE28 ......215 C6
Waterbeach CB5 ......127 D4
Wilburton CB6 ......210 C3
Wistow PE28 ......172 E1
Cross Farm Cl PE28 ......120 C2
Cross Hall Rd PE19 ......74 D6
Cross Keys Ct CB4 ......125 D3
Cross La
1 Little Downham CB6 ......218 A6
Melbourn SG8 ......14 C6
Wisbech PE13 ......235 D6
Cross Lane Cl SG8 ......45 L1
Cross Rd March PE15 ......227 F2
Sutton St Edmund PE12 ......237 A4
Whittlesey PE7 ......189 C7
Cross St Cambridge CB1 ......246 C1
Covington PE28 ......135 D2
Farcet PE7 ......187 D1
Huntingdon PE29 ......141 E5
Peterborough PE1 ......198 A2
Cross The PE28 ......161 F6
Crosshall Inf Sch PE19 ......74 C6
Crosshall Jun Sch PE19 ......74 C6
Crosshall Marina* PE19 ......74 E7
Crosshall Rd PE19 ......74 D6
Crossroad Cotts CB10 ......17 E2
Crossway Hand PE7 ......189 B8
Crossways Barley SG8 ......6 F1
Linton CB1 ......35 D2
Crow Hill La CB3 ......79 B3
Crow Spinney La PE28 ......115 D2
Crow Tree St SG19 ......58 D4
Crowhill CB6 ......211 F4
Crowhill Rd PE29 ......118 F8
Crowhurst PE4 ......204 C5
Crowland Rd
Deeping St James PE6 ......207 A6
Eye PE6 ......232 A3
Haverhill CB9 ......23 F8
Newborough PE6 ......232 A2
Thorney PE6 ......232 E5
Crowland Way CB4 ......83 F7
Crowlands CB4 ......125 D4
Crown Ave 2 PE14 ......229 D3
Crown Cl PE19 ......95 A1
Crown Gdns PE28 ......150 E4
Crown La 2 CB6 ......242 D4
Crown Lakes Ctry Pk*
PE7 ......187 B2
Crown Mews PE26 ......172 B7
Crown Rd 1 PE14 ......229 D3
Crown St
Peterborough PE1 ......197 E7
St Ives PE27 ......144 A3
Stamford PE9 ......244 B5
Crown Wlk PE27 ......144 A3
Crowson Cres 6 PE6 ......231 F7
Crowthorne Cl 65 F6
Croxton Gdns PE28 ......136 D6
Croydon Hill SG8 ......26 E8
Croydon Rd Arrington SG8 ......44 C1
Croydon SG8 ......27 B8
Croyland Rd PE4 ......204 D1
Crummock Wr PE29 ......141 C5
Crunch Croft CB9 ......24 E5
Cuckoo La Lolworth CB3 ......101 F5
Rampton CB4 ......124 E3
Culloden Cl PE19 ......74 C5
Cumberland Way 3
PE19 ......74 F1
Cundell Dr CB4 ......125 E4
Cunningham Cl CB4 ......83 E6
Cunningham Way PE19 ......74 A2
Curf Fen Dro PE16 ......222 F4
Curlew Ave PE16 ......241 C5
Curlew Cl PE7 ......189 F8
Curlew Cres 6 SG8 ......5 E8
Curlew Gr PE2 ......187 D7
Curlew Pl 2 PE19 ......75 B6
Cutter Ferry Cl CB4 ......84 A3
Cutter Ferry La CB4 ......246 C4
Cygnet Dr PE16 ......241 C6
Cygnet Pk PE7 ......186 E3
Cypress Cl
6 Doddington PE15 ......223 A6
2 Peterborough PE3 ......197 A2
Cyprus Rd CB1 ......65 C7

D

Da Vinci Cl 6 PE27 ......144 A7
Dacre Gn SG8 ......5 F6
Daffodil Gr PE2 ......187 C7
Dagless Way PE15 ......243 D7
Daintree PE27 ......208 A3
Daintree Rd PE26 ......220 D4
Daintree Way PE28 ......143 D1

Daintrees Rd CB4 ......121 F6
Dairy Dro Littleport CB6 ......225 C6
Thorney PE6 ......233 E2
Daisy Cl CB4 ......83 D7
Dakota Rd IP28 ......213 E8
Dalby Ct PE1 ......198 C8
Dale Cl PE2 ......185 F5
Dale The CB4 ......123 F1
Dale Way CB2 ......32 F8
Dales Way PE7 ......208 A3
Dalham Rd Ashley CB8 ......92 B7
Moulton CB8 ......112 F4
Dalton Sq CB4 ......84 B5
Dalton Way 1 CB6 ......240 D6
Dam Bank Dro CB6 ......209 C4
Dane Dr CB3 ......83 A1
Dane Hill Rd CB8 ......133 D5
Danes Cl PE1 ......198 C4
Danesbury Ct CB1 ......84 C1
Daniel Ct PE9 ......244 C4
Danish Ct PE4 ......204 A4
Daphmoir Cl CB2 ......29 F8
Darford 6 PE28 ......208 E6
Darley Cl 4 PE8 ......230 C1
Darrington Cl 1 PE19 ......74 B3
Dart Cl PE27 ......144 B6
Dartford Rd PE15 ......243 A6
Darthill Rd PE15 ......243 D5
Dartmoor Dr PE29 ......141 A4
Darwin Cl
Mildenhall IP28 ......239 C6
3 Stamford PE9 ......244 A7
Darwin Coll CB3 ......246 A1
Darwin Dr CB4 ......83 D5
Darwin Pl CB8 ......111 B1
Daules Rd PE28 ......140 E1
Davey Cl 2 CB4 ......104 C3
Davey Cres CB2 ......49 A6
David Bull Way CB4 ......105 D3
David St 5 CB1 ......65 A8
David's Cl PE4 ......203 F4
David's La PE4 ......204 B6
Davie La PE7 ......201 A1
Davis Cl PE19 ......96 A2
Davison Rd CB6 ......240 E8
Davy Rd CB1 ......65 B7
Daws Cl 5 CB1 ......65 F6
Dawson Cl PE6 ......205 C8
Day's Cl SG8 ......5 C5
Day's Lode Rd PE15 ......224 C7
De Bec Cl PE1 ......198 C3
De Freville Ave CB4 ......246 C4
De Freville Rd CB2 ......44 A6
De Havilland Ct 4 IP28 239 B5
De Havilland Rd PE13 ......245 C6
De La Haye Cl CB3 ......99 B3
De Vere Cl PE28 ......143 B1
Deacon St PE1 ......197 F3
Deacons La CB7 ......240 D5
Deacons Sch PE1 ......198 B5
Deaconscroft PE3 ......197 B5
Deal Cl PE29 ......141 E8
Deal Gr CB2 ......32 F8
Dean Dr CB1 ......65 B4
Dean Dro PE16 ......215 F6
Dean Peacock Ct 3
CB6 ......240 E6
Dean Rd CB1 ......21 B8
Deans Cl PE19 ......39 A1
Debdale Ct PE7 ......189 F5
Deben Ave PE27 ......144 A7
Deben Cl PE15 ......243 B5
Deben Rd CB9 ......24 B8
Decoy Rd
Borough Fen PE6 ......207 A3
Gorefield PE13 ......237 D2
Deene Cl PE3 ......197 C5
Deeping St James CP Sch
PE6 ......231 F8
Deeping St James Rd
PE6 ......231 E7
Deepings Sch The PE6 ......231 F8
Deerfield Rd PE15 ......243 E4
Deerhurst Way 13 PE6 ......232 A1
Deerleap PE3 ......197 A5
Deerpark Rd PE28 ......168 A4
Degas Dr PE27 ......144 A7
Deighton Cl PE27 ......144 B5
Delamere Cl
Little Downham CB8 ......68 F6
Peterborough PE1 ......198 C5
Delapre St 9 PE6 ......232 A1
Delbrig Dro CB7 ......212 E5
Dell The
Peterborough PE2 ......186 E7
Royston SG8 ......5 C5
Dells Cl PE28 ......166 D2
Delph PE7 ......189 D7
Delph Ct PE7 ......187 F6
Delph Dro IP28 ......212 F8
Delph St PE7 ......189 D7
Delta La PE28 ......151 E3
Dendys PE28 ......143 D1
Dengaine Cl CB3 ......99 B2
Denham Rd CB8 ......92 E8
Denham Wlk 1 PE3 ......197 C4
Denis Dr PE2 ......186 A4
Denmark Cl PE15 ......222 A5
Denmark Dr PE2 ......186 A4
Denmark Rd CB4 ......125 E3
Dennis Rd CB5 ......84 F4
Denny Abbey* CB5 ......127 A6
Denny Cl 9 CB4 ......208 D1
Denny End Rd CB5 ......105 F8
Denson Cl CB5 ......106 A8
Denton Rd Glatton PE28 ......175 E1
Peterborough PE2 ......187 C6

Dentons Chase PE26 ......220 E4
Depot Rd CB8 ......110 E6
Deptford Cl 2 PE15 ......243 B3
Derby Dr PE1 ......198 C6
Derby Rd CB1 ......65 B6
Derby St CB3 ......64 C7
Derby Way CB8 ......110 D3
Derwent Cl
Cambridge CB1 ......65 D5
Huntingdon PE29 ......141 B5
St Ives PE27 ......144 B6
Derwent Dr PE4 ......204 E2
Derwood Gr PE4 ......204 B5
Desborough Ave PE2 ......187 D5
Desborough Rd PE29 ......142 A6
Desmond Ave CB1 ......65 F6
Devana Cl PE29 ......118 F8
Devoke Cl PE29 ......141 B6
Devon Cl 2 PE27 ......144 A8
Devon Rd PE28 ......154 A1
Devonshire Cl 6 PE28 ......168 B3
Devonshire Rd CB1 ......65 A8
Dewpond Cl 4 PE19 ......75 A6
Dexter Cl 10 PE15 ......223 A5
Dexter Way PE8 ......178 B3
Dial Cl PE19 ......95 F2
Diamond Cl CB2 ......64 E5
Diana Cl PE7 ......190 A6
Dickasons SG8 ......14 D7
Dickens St PE1 ......198 B3
Dickerson Cl 1 SG19 ......41 D6
Digby Ct 3 PE19 ......74 B3
Dimmock's Cote Rd
CB7 ......211 B3
Dingley Ct PE3 ......197 C5
Ditchburn Pl CB1 ......84 A1
Ditchfield CB5 ......108 D8
Ditchfields 2 PE28 ......215 C1
Ditton Cl CB8 ......111 A1
Ditton Fields CB5 ......84 C3
Ditton Gn CB8 ......90 D1
Ditton La CB5 ......84 E4
Ditton Lodge CP Sch
CB8 ......111 B2
Ditton Wlk CB5 ......84 C4
Dixies Cl SG7 ......2 D3
Dixon's Dro PE14 ......238 F5
Dixons Rd 1 PE6 ......231 E8
Dobson Wlk 11 PE15 ......223 B7
Dock La CB5 ......106 A2
Dock Rd PE16 ......241 C6
Dockings La 10 CB7 ......213 A5
Doctor's Cl CB4 ......104 D3
Docwra Rd CB3 ......99 A3
Docwra's Cl SG8 ......29 D5
Doddington Dr PE3 ......197 B2
Doddington Hospl PE15 222 F6
Doddington Rd
Benwick PE15 ......222 A5
Chatteris PE16 ......241 A8
Doddington/Wimblington
PE15 ......223 B6
Dodds Mead CB3 ......47 A5
Dodford La CB3 ......103 D2
Dog Kennel La SG8 ......5 D6
Dogget La PE14 ......66 F4
Doggett Rd CB1 ......65 E6
Dogsthorpe Cty Jun & Inf Sch
PE1 ......198 B7
Dogsthorpe Rd PE1 ......198 A5
Dole The CB4 ......104 C3
Doles The 3 CB4 ......208 D1
Dolls Cl CB1 ......53 C1
Dolphin Cl Cambridge CB1 66 A7
3 Linton CB1 ......35 D2
Dolphin La 11 Ely CB7 ......240 D4
Melbourn SG8 ......14 B6
Dolphin Way CB2 ......49 B4
Dolphins Way SG19 ......41 D6
Dome Sports Ctr IP28 ......239 E4
Donaldson Dr
2 Peterborough PE4 ......204 E2
1 Peterborough PE4 ......204 F1
Donegal Cl PE4 ......204 D2
Donne Cl SG8 ......5 C8
Donnington Pk PE13 ......238 A1
Dorchester Cres 3 PE1 198 D7
Dorchester Way PE28 ......143 B7
Doris St CB8 ......110 F3
Dorling Way PE28 ......140 B3
Dorvis La CB10 ......21 B1
Double Bank La PE28 ......161 B7
Doug Smith Cl 1 CB8 ......110 F6
Doughty St PE9 ......244 D7
Douglas House Hospl
CB2 ......64 E5
Douglas Rd 3 PE6 ......231 E8
Douglas Way CB3 ......79 B3
Dove Cl PE4 ......121 C5
Dove Cote Cl CB4 ......121 F5
Dove House Rd CB9 ......24 A8
Dovecote Cl
Peterborough PE1 ......198 A7
Yarwell PE8 ......183 A8
Dovecote La PE7 ......181 C5
Dovecote Rd
Great Paxton PE19 ......96 D3
Upwell PE14 ......229 D7
Dovehouse Cl Ely CB7 ......240 D3
Fowlmere SG8 ......15 E8
Godmanchester PE29 ......142 A1
St Neots PE19 ......74 F6
Dovehouse Wood PE28 ......162 B1
Dover Cl PE29 ......141 E8
Dover Rd PE4 ......204 C2
Dovey Cl PE27 ......144 B6
Dowding Way CB4 ......83 D6

Dowgate Rd PE13 ......238 B1
Down Gate PE3 ......197 A1
Downe Cl CB3 ......99 A2
Downham Feoffees Sch
CB6 ......218 A7
Downham Hythe Dro
CB6 ......217 D6
Downham Rd Ely CB6 ......240 B7
Outwell PE14 ......236 F2
Downham's La CB4 ......84 A6
Downing Cl Bottisham CB5 86 E6
Mildenhall IP28 ......239 D5
Newmarket CB8 ......111 A2
Downing Coll CB3 ......246 B1
Downing Cres PE9 ......244 A3
Downing Ct CB5 ......108 A1
Downing Pl 2 CB2 ......246 B2
Downing St CB2 ......246 B2
Downlands SG8 ......5 C6
Downs Cres CB9 ......23 F8
Downton Dr PE9 ......23 E8
Dowsdale Bank PE6 ......233 A8
Dragoon Dr 4 PE15 ......243 D2
Drain Rd PE6 ......205 A7
Drake Ave PE16 ......241 C6
Drake Cl PE29 ......141 F6
Drake Rd PE19 ......74 B2
Drake Way CB4 ......104 C5
Draper's Cl PE8 ......178 C3
Drapers La PE9 ......23 B2
Drapery Row 1 CB8 ......111 A3
Drayhorse Rd PE26 ......172 A5
Drayton PE3 ......197 A4
Drayton Cl CB1 ......66 A5
Drayton Rd CB1 ......66 A5
Drewels La PE19 ......56 D4
Drift Ave PE9 ......244 D7
Drift Gdns PE9 ......244 D6
Drift Rd PE9 ......244 C6
Drift The Elsworth CB3 ......100 B4
Exning CB8 ......110 A8
Oakington/Longstanton
CB4 ......103 B5
Sutton PE5 ......194 F3
Drings Cl 2 CB4 ......208 D1
Drinkwater Cl CB8 ......110 E4
Drive The Perry PE28 ......115 D1
Peterborough PE3 ......197 E2
St Ives PE27 ......143 F4
Drivers Ave PE29 ......141 E5
Drivers Cl 8 PE15 ......223 A6
Drosier Rd CB1 ......246 C1
Drove Rd SG19 ......41 A6
Drove The Farcet PE26 ......220 D7
Witchford CB6 ......217 E1
Drummer St PE1 ......246 B2
Drury La
Bluntisham/Colne PE28 ......208 D7
Melbourn SG8 ......14 D6
Wicken CB7 ......211 F2
Dry Drayton Prim Sch
CB3 ......102 C1
Dry Drayton Rd
Madingley CB3 ......81 D7
Oakington & Westwick
CB4 ......103 A4
Dry Leys PE2 ......186 C6
Drybread Rd PE7 ......189 F8
Dryden Cl PE27 ......143 E6
Dryden Ct 7 PE19 ......75 A5
Dryden Rd PE1 ......197 F2
Dubbs Knoll Rd SG8 ......10 F5
Duberly Ct PE28 ......115 E2
Duchess Cl PE19 ......74 A3
Duchess Dr
Newmarket CB8 ......111 D2
Woodditton CB8 ......90 E8
Duck Dro CB7 ......219 D5
Duck End Girton CB3 ......82 D8
Godmanchester PE29 ......141 F1
Duck La Haddenham CB6 ......210 A6
St Neots PE19 ......74 F4
Duck St PE8 ......178 D8
Ducks La CB8 ......110 C2
Duckworth Cl PE7 ......189 E7
Duddery Hill CB9 ......23 F6
Duddery Rd CB9 ......24 A7
Dudley Ave PE4 ......204 C2
Dudley Rd CB5 ......84 E4
Duke of Bedford Sch
PE6 ......233 B3
Duke St
Peterborough PE2 ......187 A7
Wisbech PE13 ......245 D4
Dukes Dr 3 PE26 ......221 C2
Dukes Mdw PE2 ......49 C5
Dukes Rd PE19 ......74 B4
Dukesmead PE4 ......204 A2
Dullingham Rd
Newmarket CB8 ......110 F1
Stetchworth CB8 ......89 D3
Woodditton CB8 ......89 F7
Dullingham Sta CB8 ......89 B2
Duloe Rd PE19 ......74 B5
Dunblane Dr PE2 ......185 D4
Duncan Way PE29 ......141 F7
Duncock La CB3 ......100 B4
Duncombe's Rd PE7 ......191 F8
Dundee Cl CB4 ......84 A5
Dungate La CB1 ......52 B6
Dunholt Way 2 PE28 ......208 D6
Dunkirk Dro PE28 ......215 C4
Dunmowe Way CB1 ......66 E5
Dunsberry Marholm PE3 ......203 F1
Peterborough PE3 ......196 F8

Dunsbridge Turnpike
SG8 29 F2
Dunsey Wood Cl CB9 38 E1
Dunsmore Cl CB5 84 E4
Dunstal Field CB4 125 D2
Dunstall's Dro CB7 218 E1
Dunstan St CB6 240 B5
Dunster Dr CB9 23 E8
Durham Cl PE28 168 C2
Durham Rd PE1 198 C3
Durham Way
4 Newmarket CB8 110 E5
Wyton Airfield PE28 143 B8
Durnford Way CB4 83 E5
Duxford Airfield CB2 17 A8
Duxford CE Com Prim Sch
CB2 32 D1
Duxford Rd Hinxton CB10 18 A7
Ickleton CB10 17 F5
Whittlesford CB2 32 D4
Dwyer-Joyce Cl CB4 104 B4
Dykemoor Dro PE15 222 C4
Dykemoor Dro N PE15 222 E5
Dyson Cl
Peterborough PE1 197 F3
The Stukeleys PE29 141 A5
Dyson's Dro CB5 130 B5

E

Eachard Rd CB3 83 B5
Eagle Ct PE19 75 B7
Eagle La CB8 89 D1
Eagle Way PE29 142 A8
Eagle's La 1 CB6 218 A7
Eaglesthorpe PE1 197 E7
Eames Gdns PE1 198 E6
Earith Bsns Pk PE28 208 F6
Earith Fen Dro PE28 208 F7
Earith Prim Sch PE28 208 E5
Earith Rd
Bluntisham/Colne PE28 208 D7
Willingham CB4 209 A2
Earl Cl 1 PE19 74 B4
Earl Spencer Ct PE2 186 E8
Earl St CB1 246 B2
Earls Cl PE2 187 B6
Earls Hill Gdns SG8 5 C6
Earlswood PE2 185 E5
Earning St PE29 141 F1
Earth Cl PE2 187 E5
East Chadley La PE29 141 F2
East Cl PE15 243 B6
East Delph PE7 189 E8
East Dr Caldecote CB3 80 C1
March PE15 243 F4
East Fen Dro CB7 212 D4
East Fen Rd CB7 213 B5
East Hatley SG19 43 A1
East Hertford St CB4 246 A4
East La SG19 41 C6
East of England
Showground* PE2 185 C4
East Park St PE16 241 C4
East Perry PE28 115 E2
East Rd Cambridge CB1 246 C2
Isleham CB7 213 A5
8 Northborough PE6 231 F8
Tydd St Mary PE13 238 C8
East St
Bluntisham/Colne PE28 208 C5
Great Gransden SG19 58 E4
Huntingdon PE29 141 F5
1 Kimbolton PE28 113 F4
1 Manea PE15 224 C4
St Ives PE27 144 A3
St Neots PE19 74 F5
Stamford PE9 244 C5
East Sta Rd PE2 187 A8
East View IP28 213 C3
East Way CB2 50 A1
Eastalls Cl 15 PE15 223 A5
Eastbourne Cl 2 PE16 241 C3
Eastbourne Rd PE16 241 C3
Eastern Ave Haverhill CB9 23 E8
Peterborough PE1 198 C8
11 Soham CB7 212 B4
Eastern Cl PE1 198 D7
Eastfield CB4 84 A5
Eastfield Dr PE7 189 F6
Eastfield Gr PE1 198 B4
Eastfield Rd
Peterborough PE1 198 C4
Royston SG8 5 E6
1 Wisbech PE13 245 E7
Eastfield Sch PE27 144 A4
Eastfield Way PE13 245 C6
Eastfields CB6 242 C3
Eastgate
Great Chesterford CB10 18 D2
Market Deeping PE6 206 B6
15 Market Deeping PE6 231 F8
Peterborough PE1 198 B2
Whittlesey PE7 189 E7
Eastholm Cl PE1 198 C3
Eastholm Cty Sch PE1 198 C4
Eastholm Sch PE1 198 D5
Eastleigh Rd PE1 198 C3
Eastmoor La PE15 223 A5
Easton Rd PE19 114 C3
Eastrea Ct PE2 187 E6
Eastrea Rd PE7 189 F7
Eastwood PE16 241 C3
Eastwood Ave PE15 243 E3
Eastwood Cl CB6 216 E2
Eaton Cl Cambridge CB4 84 A6
Huntingdon PE29 142 A7
Eaton Est PE15 223 B7
Eaudyke Bank PE13 237 F7
Eccles Rd PE8 193 D8
Echo Hill SG8 5 C5
Echo La PE28 151 E3
Ecton Gr 7 PE14 236 A5
Eden Cres PE16 241 C4
Eden Rd CB9 24 A7
Eden St CB1 246 C3
Eden Street Backway
CB1 246 C2
Edendale Cl CB1 65 C5
Edenfield PE2 186 C6
Edgcote Cl PE3 197 C5
Edge Bank PE14 236 F6
Edgeborough Cl CB8 134 A1
Edgerley Drain Rd PE1 198 F5
Edinburgh Ave
Peterborough PE4 204 B3
Sawston CB2 32 F8
Edinburgh Dr
Eaton Socon PE19 74 B4
St Ives PE27 143 F7
Wisbech PE13 245 C8
Edinburgh Rd
Cambridge CB4 84 A5
Newmarket CB8 110 E4
Stamford PE9 244 B7
Edison Rd PE27 144 C6
Edith Cavell Hospl PE3 197 B4
Edmonds Cl PE9 244 D6
Edmund Cl Haverhill CB9 23 F7
Milton CB4 105 C2
Edwalton Ave PE3 197 E3
Edward Rd St Neots PE19 74 F2
Stamford PE9 244 B7
Edward St CB1 84 A1
Edwards Way 3 PE15 224 B4
Edwards Wlk 9 PE28 208 E6
Edwinstowe Cl CB2 64 E6
Egar Way PE3 196 F2
Egerton Cl CB5 84 D4
Egerton Rd CB5 84 E4
Egremont Rd CB3 81 A3
Egremont St CB6 240 C5
Eighth Ave PE13 245 E4
Ekin Rd CB5 84 D4
Eland Way CB1 66 A7
Elbourn Way SG8 12 F5
Elbow La PE13 234 F8
Elder Cl Cambridge CB4 83 F6
Sawston CB2 32 D8
Eldernell La PE7 191 B8
Elder's Gate PE12 237 E8
Eldith Ave CB7 213 A1
Eldo Gdns IP28 213 D6
Eldo Rd IP28 213 D6
Eldon La IP28 214 B8
Elean Bsns Pk CB6 216 F2
Eleanor Cl PE9 244 A6
Elecks La SG8 11 D8
Elfleda Rd CB5 84 C3
Elin Way SG8 14 B8
Eliot Rd SG8 5 D8
Elizabeth Ave CB8 110 E5
Elizabeth Ct
5 Eaton Socon PE19 74 C4
Hemingford Grey PE27 143 F1
2 Sutton CB6 216 E2
Elizabeth Dr PE29 142 B6
Elizabeth Rd PE9 244 A6
Elizabeth Terr PE13 245 D4
Elizabeth Way
3 Bluntisham/Colne
PE28 208 D7
Burrough Green CB8 70 F4
Cambridge CB4 83 F4
Gamlingay SG19 41 C6
Elizabethan Way PE28 140 B2
Ellesmere Rd CB4 83 D6
Ellindon PE3 197 B7
Ellingham Ave PE15 243 C3
Ellington Rd PE28 149 E1
Elliot Ave PE3 196 F2
Elliott Cl CB8 111 A6
Elliott Rd PE15 243 B5
Ellis Cl CB4 125 D3
Ellison Cl CB4 83 D7
Ellison La CB3 81 A4
Elloe Bank Newton PE13 237 B2
Tydd St Giles PE13 237 B5
Ellwood Ave PE2 187 E5
Ellwoods Cl CB7 213 A5
Elm CE Jun Sch PE14 236 B5
Elm Cl Dullingham CB8 70 D8
Haverhill CB9 23 F8
Huntingdon PE29 141 E7
March PE15 243 D7
5 Market Deeping PE6 231 E8
Stilton PE7 175 F7
Witchford CB6 217 E2
Yaxley PE7 181 F7
Elm Cres PE6 203 D8
Elm Croft PE19 95 F3
Elm Ct Elmdon CB11 9 B4
3 Sturmer CB9 24 E5
Elm Dr
Little Stukeley PE28 151 E3
Offord Cluny PE19 118 A2
St Ives PE27 143 F6
Elm End PE28 150 F4
Elm High Rd PE14 245 E1
Elm Low Rd PE14 245 D2
Elm Pk PE7 189 E7
Elm Rd Folksworth PE7 175 D8
Elm Rd continued
Little Stukeley PE28 152 A2
March PE15 243 D8
Wisbech PE13 245 D3
Elm Road Prim Sch
PE13 245 D4
Elm Side CB6 242 B5
Elm St Cambridge CB1 246 B3
Peterborough PE2 186 F7
Stamford PE9 244 C5
Elm Tree Cl CB3 79 C3
Elm Tree Dr SG8 12 F4
Elm Way Melbourn SG8 14 C5
Papworth Everard CB3 99 A3
Sawtry PE28 168 B3
Willingham CB4 209 A1
Elm Wlk SG8 5 F7
Elmfield CB6 240 C5
Elmfield Dr PE14 245 E1
Elmfield Rd
Cambridge CB4 84 A5
Peterborough PE1 198 A7
Elmhurst Cl CB9 24 B7
Elmore Rd PE3 197 A3
Elm's Ave CB2 49 A5
Elms Cl CB2 32 D1
Elms Rd
Freckenham IP28 213 E2
Red Lodge IP28 213 F1
Elms The Chatteris PE16 241 E4
Great Chesterford CB10 18 E3
Haslingfield CB3 47 C5
Milton CB4 105 C2
Elmside PE14 236 D5
Elstone PE2 186 A4
Elstow Cl 7 CB4 208 D1
Elsworth Cl PE27 144 C5
Elsworth Pl CB1 65 A6
Elsworth Prim Sch CB3 100 A4
Elsworth Rd
Boxworth CB3 101 A5
Conington CB3 100 C8
Elter Wr PE29 141 B5
Eltisley Ave CB3 64 C7
Eltisley Rd SG19 58 E6
Elton CE Prim Sch PE8 178 D8
Elton H* PE8 178 D6
Elton Rd
Sibson cum Stibbington
PE8 183 C8
Water Newton PE8 184 B7
Elvedon Way CB8 110 E5
Elwyn Ct PE15 243 D3
Elwyn Rd PE15 243 D4
Elwyndene Rd PE15 243 D3
Ely Cath CB7 240 D4
Ely Cl PE4 204 B3
Ely Cty Inf Sch CB7 240 E6
Ely Mus* CB7 240 D4
Ely Pl 16 PE13 245 C5
Ely Rd Downham CB6 218 B6
Ely CB7 218 D4
Landbeach CB5 105 F8
Littleport CB6 242 C2
Milton CB4 105 E3
Soham CB7 211 F7
Stretham CB6 210 F5
Sutton CB6 216 F2
Waterbeach CB5 126 E3
Wentworth CB6 217 A2
Ely Way CB6 210 A7
Embankment Rd 4 PE1 198 A1
Embry Rd 18 PE8 230 B1
Emery Cl PE28 140 C3
Emery Pl PE19 74 F7
Emery Rd CB1 84 A1
Emery St CB1 84 A1
Emlyns Gdns PE9 244 C6
Emlyns St PE9 244 C6
Emmanuel Cl IP28 239 D5
Emmanuel Coll CB1 246 B2
Emmanuel Rd
Cambridge CB1 246 B2
Stamford PE9 244 B7
Emmanuel St CB1 246 B2
Emneth CP Sch PE14 236 D6
Empingham Rd 3 PE9 244 A5
Empress Swimming Pool
PE16 241 C4
Empson Rd PE1 198 F5
Emson's Cl CB1 35 D2
Enderbys Wharf PE27 144 A3
Engaine PE2 186 B5
Engine Rd CB7 211 F5
Engleric SG8 8 D4
English Rd PE6 233 B4
English St PE1 197 E5
Ennerdale Cl PE29 141 B6
Ennerdale Rise PE4 204 D2
Ennisdale Cl 4 CB4 83 E7
Enniskillen Rd CB4 84 B5
Enterprise Way PE13 245 A2
Erasmus Cl CB4 83 D5
Erica Rd PE27 144 A6
Eriswell Rd
"Beck Row, Holywell Row
& Kenny Hill" IP28 214 B8
Haverhill CB9 24 B8
Ermine Bsns Ctr PE29 141 B8
Ermine Bsns Pk PE29 141 B7
Ermine Cl SG8 5 D8
Ermine Cres PE27 176 A7
Ermine St Caxton CB3 78 E2
Huntingdon PE29 141 C5
Little Stukeley PE28 151 F2
The Stukeleys PE28 141 A8
Ermine St N CB3 99 A4
Ermine St S CB3 78 C8
Ermine Way Arrington SG8 44 C4
Sawtry PE28 168 C3
Ernulf Com Sch PE19 74 E3
Erratts Hill CB8 73 D1
Eskdale Cl 1 PE4 204 E3
Essendyke PE3 197 A7
Essex Cl CB4 83 E5
Essex Hill CB11 9 B2
Essex Rd
Huntingdon PE29 141 E8
5 Stamford PE9 244 B6
Estover Rd PE15 243 E6
Etheldreda St CB6 240 B4
Eurocentre Sch CB2 64 F7
Europa Way PE13 245 B2
Euston St PE29 141 E4
Euximoor Dro PE14 229 B5
Evans Cl PE28 140 D3
Evans Way CB2 32 E8
Evelyn Hospl The CB2 64 E6
Everdon Way PE3 197 C5
Evergreen La CB8 55 F7
Evergreens CB4 84 B5
Everingham PE2 185 D5
Eversden Church Sch
CB3 46 A7
Eversden Cl CB3 61 D5
Eversden Rd CB3 46 C5
Eversley Cl CB4 125 D4
Everton Hill SG19 40 B3
Everton Rd SG19 40 B1
Eves Cl PE6 207 D1
Ewingswood 1 PE28 168 C2
Exchange Sq PE13 245 B5
Exchange St PE1 198 A2
Exeter Cl Cambridge CB2 64 D1
2 Market Deeping PE6 231 F8
Exeter Rd
Newmarket CB8 111 A4
Peterborough PE1 197 F6
7 Wittering PE8 230 B1
Exmoor Cl PE29 141 A4
Exning CP Sch CB8 110 B8
Exning Rd CB8 110 D6
Eye CE Sch PE6 232 B1
Eye Hill Dro CB7 211 F7
Eye Rd PE1 198 E7
Eyebury Rd PE6 199 A6
Eyeworth Rd SG19 25 B2
Eynesbury CE Sch PE19 74 E4
Eynesbury Gn PE19 74 F4
Eyrescroft PE3 197 A7
Eyrescroft CP Sch PE3 197 A7
Eyresford Cl PE7 188 A5

F

Faber La PE8 183 D1
Fair Ct CB1 246 C3
Fair Green The CB5 129 D1
Fair St CB1 246 C3
Fairbairn Rd CB4 84 C5
Fairchild Way PE1 198 A7
Fairey Ave PE29 141 F1
Fairey Fox Dr 1 IP28 239 B5
Fairfax Ct PE19 74 F3
Fairfax Rd CB1 84 B1
Fairfax Way March PE15 243 E1
10 Market Deeping PE6 231 F8
Fairfield Gamlingay SG19 41 C5
5 Sutton CB6 216 E1
Fairfield Dr PE26 172 A6
Fairfield Rd PE2 187 A8
Fairfield Way CB1 35 D3
Fairfields St Ives PE27 144 B4
Sawston CB2 50 A1
Fairfields Cres PE27 144 B4
Fairhaven Cl CB5 107 C2
Fairhaven Way CB8 110 E5
Fairlawns Rd 1 CB8 110 F2
Fairmead Way PE3 197 E2
Fairstead Ho Sch CB8 111 B4
Fairview Ave PE16 241 B2
Fairview Dr PE16 241 B2
Fairview Gr CB5 108 E5
Fairway Chatteris PE16 241 B3
Girton CB3 103 E2
Fairway The Bar Hill CB3 102 D3
1 Bluntisham/Colne
PE28 208 C6
4 Bluntisham/Colne
PE28 208 C6
Falcon Cl Haverhill CB9 24 C8
5 St Neots PE19 75 B7
Falcon Dr PE29 142 B7
Falcon La Whittlesey PE7 189 D6
15 Wisbech PE13 245 C5
Falcon Mews CB6 240 B5
Falcon Rd 7 PE13 245 C5
Falcon Way PE19 117 B3
Falconer Rd CB9 24 C5
Falklands Dr PE13 245 E3
Falklands Rd CB9 39 A1
Falkner Rd CB2 33 A8
Fallodan Rd PE2 185 C3
Fallow Corner Dro
PE15 224 A3
Fallow Dr PE19 74 B5
Fallowfield Cambridge CB4 84 B5
Peterborough PE2 185 D5
Fall's Dro PE6 232 F7
Falmouth Ave CB8 110 F3
Falmouth Gdns CB8 111 A6
Falmouth St CB8 110 F3
Falstaff Rd 2 PE19 74 C3
Fane Cl PE9 244 B7
Fane Rd PE4 197 E8
Fanshawe Rd CB1 65 A6
Far Pasture PE4 204 B5
Farcet Cl 5 PE19 74 C6
Farcet Prim Sch PE7 187 C2
Fardell Rd 6 PE13 245 C4
Fardell's La CB3 100 A4
Farendon Rd PE28 140 E1
Farfield Cl PE28 168 A5
Farleigh Fields PE2 185 D7
Farm Cl Ramsey PE26 171 C3
Sawtry PE28 168 B4
Farm La
Papworth Everard CB3 99 C2
Thriplow SG8 31 B1
Farm Rise CB2 32 C5
Farm View PE5 195 E2
Farmer's End CB3 61 E5
Farmer's Row CB1 66 E4
Farmland Mus* CB5 127 A5
Farmstead Cl CB4 104 B5
Farriers Ct PE2 186 D7
Farringdon Cl 2 PE1 198 D6
Farringford Cl 4 CB4 83 C6
Farthing Dro PE38 226 D6
Farthing La PE27 144 B4
Fassage Cl CB5 107 C2
Fastnet Cl CB9 24 D8
Faulkner Cl CB4 105 C2
Fawcett CP Sch CB2 64 D3
Fawsley Garth PE3 197 C6
Feast Cl CB7 212 E1
Feilden Way CB8 110 E5
Feldale Pl PE7 189 F8
Fellowes Dr PE26 172 A6
Fellowes Gdns PE2 187 A7
Fellowes Rd PE2 187 A7
Felsham Chase CB5 130 C2
Felsted Ave PE13 245 E5
Felton St CB1 65 A8
Felton Way CB7 240 E6
Feltons CB7 212 E1
Fen Bank Rd CB7 213 A6
Fen Causeway* PE7 189 A8
Fen Causeway The CB3 246 A1
Fen Cl PE13 245 E6
Fen Ditton CP Sch CB5 84 F5
Fen Drayton Cty Prim Sch
CB4 121 F6
Fen Drayton Rd CB4 122 C5
Fen Dro PE7 176 C8
Fen End Over CB4 208 D1
Willingham CB4 209 A1
Fen La Sawtry PE28 168 C3
Stilton PE7 176 C8
Swaffham Bulbeck CB5 108 A4
Tydd St Giles PE13 237 B5
Fen Rd
Bassingbourn cum Kneesworth
SG8 12 B7
Little Wilbraham CB1 86 D2
Lode CB5 107 B4
Milton CB4 84 D6
Newton PE13 237 E4
Pidley cum Fenton PE28 165 E1
Shingay cum Wendy SG8 26 F1
Wisbech St Mary PE13 234 E2
Fen Side CB6 209 E4
Fen St PE7 176 A7
Fen The PE28 121 B6
Fen View
3 Christchurch PE14 229 D3
6 Doddington/Wimblington
PE15 222 F5
Peterborough PE2 187 F6
Fen Way 3 PE14 236 A5
Fenbridge Rd PE4 204 C4
Fendon Cl CB1 65 B3
Fendon Rd CB1 65 B3
Fendyke La PE13 237 F1
Fendyke Rd PE14 236 E5
Fengate PE1 198 D1
Fengate Cl 1 PE1 198 B2
Fengate Rd PE14 238 F1
Fenland Cl 3 PE15 223 B7
Fenland L Ctrs PE7 189 E6
Fenland Rd PE13 245 E6
Fenland Way PE16 241 B5
Fenleigh Cl CB5 106 B8
Fennec Cl CB1 66 B6
Fennels Cl CB9 24 A7
Fenny La SG8 29 A1
Fenside Dr PE6 207 C1
Fenside Rd PE28 165 D8
Fenstanton Cty Prim Sch
PE28 121 C6
Fenton Hill PE28 165 C3
Fenton Rd Haverhill CB9 24 B8
Warboys PE28 165 A4
Feoffees Rd 5 PE28 208 C8
Fern Gr CB9 23 E8
Ferndale CB1 66 C8
Ferndale Cl CB8 111 B5
Ferndale Rise CB5 84 C4
Ferndale Way PE1 205 B1
Ferndown Dr PE29 118 F8
Fernie Cl PE6 205 D8
Fernlea Cl CB1 65 F7
Ferrars Ave PE19 74 E4
Ferrars Rd PE29 141 D5
Ferrars Way CB4 83 D6
Ferriman Rd PE28 137 F6
Ferry Bank PE38 226 D8
Ferry Cutter La CB4 246 C4
Ferry Dr PE6 196 D3
Ferry Hill PE5 196 B1
Ferry La
"Beck Row, Holywell Row
& Kenny Hill" IP28 213 D5

Ferry La continued
Cambridge CB4 . . . . .84 B4
Newton PE13 . . . . .238 B5
Ferry Meadows Ctry Pk★
PE2 . . . . .185 D8
Ferry Way CB6 . . . . .242 D4
Ferryview PE2 . . . . .185 E6
Festival CI PE15 . . . . .224 C4
Festival Rd CB7 . . . . .213 A5
Festival Way CB6 . . . . . . .226 B6
Fews CI 4 PE27 . . . . .208 A3
Field Ave PE13 . . . . .237 F7
Field Baulk PE15 . . . . . . .243 D2
Field Bell PE2 . . . . .140 F3
Field CI Abbotsley PE19 . . . .57 A6
Alconbury PE28 . . . . .150 F5
Buckden PE19 . . . . .117 B4
Grafham PE28 . . . . .116 A7
Linton CB1 . . . . .35 B2
Little Paxton PE19 . . . . . . .95 F2
Warboys PE26 . . . . .164 F5
Field Cottage Rd PE19 . . . .74 C3
Field Cres SG8 . . . . .5 F7
Field End Balsham CB1 . . . .53 B2
Witchford CB6 . . . . .217 D2
Field Farm Cotts CB10 . . . .18 F7
Field Gate CB6 . . . . .216 D2
Field La CB5 . . . . .84 E6
Field Rd Kingston CB3 . . . . .61 B3
Mildenhall IP28 . . . . .239 C5
Ramsey PE26 . . . . .172 A7
Field Rise PE7 . . . . .181 D5
Field Row CB3 . . . . .61 B3
Field Studies Ctr★ PE8 194 C1
Field Terr PE7 . . . . .187 C2
Field Terrace Rd CB8 . . . .110 F5
Field View Bar Hill CB3 . . .102 B2
Harston CB2 . . . . .48 A4
Field Way CB1 . . . . .65 C3
Field Wlk Mildenhall IP28 239 C5
Peterborough PE1 . . . . . .198 B2
Fieldfare Dr PE2 . . . . .187 E6
Fieldfare Way 10 SG8 . . . . .5 E8
Fielding Ct 2 PE19 . . . . . .74 C6
Fielding Pl PE19 . . . . .97 F4
Fieldside Ely CB6 . . . . . . .240 B4
Stretham CB6 . . . . .210 E5
Whittlesey PE7 . . . . .190 F8
Fifth Ave CB1 . . . . .245 E4
Fifty Dro CB6 . . . . .225 C7
Fifty Rd
Christchurch PE14 . . . . . .229 D1
Manea PE14 . . . . .224 D7
Figtree Wlk PE1 . . . . .198 B8
Fillance The SG8 . . . . .12 D5
Finch Rd CB4 . . . . .83 D5
Fincham Rd IP28 . . . . . . .239 B5
Fincham's CI CB1 . . . . .35 D2
Finchfield PE1 . . . . .198 F7
Finchley Ave IP28 . . . . . . .239 B6
Finchley Gn PE3 . . . . .197 E4
Finch's CI CB2 . . . . .49 C5
Finch's Rd CB3 . . . . .46 A7
Finkle La PE7 . . . . .189 D7
Firdale CI PE6 . . . . .206 C2
Firelots Dro PE15 . . . . . . .223 C8
Firs The CB2 . . . . .32 D2
First Ave Warboys PE28 . . .164 E6
Wisbech PE13 . . . . .245 D5
First Broadpool Dro
PE28 . . . . .165 E8
First Drift PE9 . . . . .244 B2
First Dro Burwell CB5 . . . .130 C7
Peterborough PE1 . . . . . .198 D1
First Furlong Dro PE16 . . .241 A3
First Marsh Rd PE13 . . . . .238 D2
First Turf Fen Dro PE28 . .165 B8
Fish Hill SG8 . . . . .5 D6
Fisher CI CB9 . . . . .24 D7
Fisher St CB4 . . . . .246 A4
Fishermans CI PE26 . . . . .171 B1
Fishermans Dr 3 PE15 . . .243 A5
Fisher's La Cambridge CB1 65 F6
Orwell SG8 . . . . .45 D2
Fishers CI PE7 . . . . .175 F7
Fishers Way PE19 . . . . . . .118 F8
Fishers Yd 4 PE19 . . . . . . .74 E5
Fison Rd CB5 . . . . .84 E4
Fitton End Rd PE13 . . . . . .237 F3
Fitzgerald CI CB6 . . . . . . .240 E8
Fitzroy Ct CB1 . . . . .246 C3
Fitzroy La CB5 . . . . .246 C3
Fitzroy St Cambridge CB1 246 C3
Newmarket CB8 . . . . .111 A3
Fitzwilliam Coll CB3 . . . .83 B4
Fitzwilliam Hospl PE6 . .196 E2
Fitzwilliam Mus★ CB2 .246 A1
Fitzwilliam Rd
Cambridge CB2 . . . . .64 F6
Stamford PE9 . . . . .244 A7
Fitzwilliam St
Cambridge CB2 . . . . .246 B1
Peterborough PE1 . . . . . .198 A3
Five Arches PE2 . . . . .185 C6
Five Hundred Rd PE14 . . .224 A4
Flackdale Rd 1 PE28 . . . .120 B1
Flag Fen Mus★ PE6 . . . .199 B2
Flag Fen Rd PE1 . . . . .198 C4
Flaggrass Hill Rd PE15 . .243 D8
Flambards CI SG8 . . . . .14 B8
Flamborough CI PE2 . . . .197 E1
Flamsteed Dr PE29 . . . . . .140 F5
Flamsteed Rd CB1 . . . . . . .65 A6
Flat Rd CB4 . . . . .209 B3
Flavian CI CB9 . . . . .24 D7
Flaxfields CB1 . . . . .35 C3
Flaxland Castor PE5 . . . . .197 A6
Peterborough PE3 . . . . . .197 A6

Fleam Dyke Cotts CB1 . . .67 C2
Flecks La
Shingay cum Wendy SG8 . . .26 D1
Steeple Morden SG8 . . . . .11 D8
Fleet CI CB6 . . . . .242 D4
Fleet The SG8 . . . . .5 C6
Fleet Way PE2 . . . . .187 B6
Fleetwood CB6 . . . . .240 C5
Fleetwood CI PE15 . . . . . .243 D2
Fleming Ave IP28 . . . . . . .239 C5
Fleming Ct 2 PE15 . . . . . .243 F3
Fletcher Ave CB5 . . . . . . .127 C1
Fletcher's Terr 3 CB1 . . . .65 A8
Fletchers CI PE26 . . . . . . .172 A7
Fletton Ave PE2 . . . . .187 A4
Fletton Fields PE2 . . . . . .187 A7
Fletton Parkway PE2 . . . .185 F2
Fletton Prim Sch PE2 . . .186 F6
Flint CI PE28 . . . . .140 C2
Flint House Rd PE14 . . . . .229 F5
Flint La CB5 . . . . .126 E3
Flint Way PE19 . . . . .74 E2
Flood's Ferry Rd PE15 . . .222 B7
Flore CI PE3 . . . . .197 C5
Florence CI PE7 . . . . .189 F6
Florida Ave PE29 . . . . .141 F8
Flower St 2 CB1 . . . . .84 A1
Flowers CI PE26 . . . . .172 A7
Flowmere Rd SG8 . . . . .8 A5
Fodder Fen Dro CB7 . . . . .219 B3
Fodder Fen Rd PE15 . . . . .224 C6
Fodderfen Dro
"Beck Row, Holywell Row
& Kenny Hill" 219 F1
Wicken CB7 . . . . .211 C3
Fold La PE13 . . . . .237 F7
Fold The PE7 . . . . .190 F8
Folgate La PE14 . . . . .238 F6
Folksworth CE Sch PE7 175 D8
Folksworth Rd PE7 . . . . . .180 E1
Folly CI PE7 . . . . .181 C5
Folly Dro CB7 . . . . .219 A7
Folly Rd IP28 . . . . .239 B6
Folly's Dro PE13 . . . . .234 F3
Fontwell Ave CB4 . . . . .83 C5
Fontwell Gdns 2 PE9 . . . .244 B5
Foot Dro PE26 . . . . .220 F1
Footpath The CB3 . . . . .82 C2
Ford CI
"Beck Row, Holywell Row
& Kenny Hill" IP28 . . . . .213 D7
Eaton Socon PE19 . . . . . . .74 D5
Ford End Alconbury PE28 .150 F4
Hail Weston PE19 . . . . . . .95 B1
Fordham Abbey★ CB7 .131 E8
Fordham CI SG7 . . . . .2 D5
Fordham Moor CB7 . . . . .212 E3
Fordham Prim Sch CB7 212 F1
Fordham Rd Exning CB8 . .131 E3
Freckenham IP28 . . . . . . .213 B2
Isleham CB7 . . . . .213 A4
Newmarket CB8 . . . . .110 F8
5 Royston SG8 . . . . .5 E5
Snailwell CB8 . . . . .132 A5
5 Soham CB7 . . . . .212 B3
Fordham Way SG8 . . . . . . .14 D5
Fordwich CI 1 CB4 . . . . . . .83 D6
Fore Hill CB7 . . . . .240 D4
Foreman's Rd SG8 . . . . . . .31 B2
Forest End CB8 . . . . .134 A6
Forest Glade CB9 . . . . .38 F2
Forest Rd CB1 . . . . .65 E5
Forest Way PE19 . . . . .239 E4
Forge CI PE19 . . . . .74 B2
Forge End
Great Shelford CB2 . . . . . .49 C4
Peterborough PE7 . . . . . .185 A4
Forge Way PE6 . . . . .164 F5
Forster Rd CB8 . . . . .140 E1
Forsythia Rd PE27 . . . . . .144 A6
Fortescue Rd CB4 . . . . .83 E6
Forties CI CB9 . . . . .24 D8
Fortune Way SG8 . . . . .12 E5
Forty Acre Rd PE1 . . . . . .198 D2
Forty Foot Bank
Doddington PE26 . . . . . . .222 C3
Ramsey PE26 . . . . .221 E2
Ramsey Forty Foot PE26 . .221 C3
Foster Rd CB2 . . . . .64 D2
Foundry CI CB4 . . . . .125 D3
Foundry Rd 4 PE9 . . . . . .244 A5
Foundry Way
Eaton Socon PE19 . . . . . . .74 B1
March PE15 . . . . .228 B6
Ramsey PE26 . . . . .172 A5
Fountain La
Haslingfield CB3 . . . . .47 B5
Soham CB7 . . . . .212 B4
Fountains Pl PE6 . . . . .232 B1
Four Acres
Fenstanton PE28 . . . . . . .121 C6
Great Chesterford CB10 . . .18 D3
Fourfields Prim Sch
PE7 . . . . .181 E6
Fourth Ave PE13 . . . . .245 E4
Fourth Dro
Downham CB6 . . . . .225 A1
Peterborough PE1 . . . . . .198 D3
Fowlmere Cty Prim Sch
SG8 . . . . .15 D8
Fowlmere Nature Reserve★
SG8 . . . . .15 B8
Fowlmere Rd Foxton SG8 . .30 D1
Heydon SG8 . . . . .7 F8
Newton CB22 . . . . .31 B6
Shepreth SG8 . . . . .29 F4
Thriplow SG8 . . . . .31 A2
Fox CI PE19 . . . . .75 A5

Fox Cnr SG8 . . . . .10 F5
Fox Covert PE7 . . . . .175 F7
Fox Gn CB8 . . . . .55 F7
Fox Gr PE29 . . . . .141 F2
Fox Hill SG8 . . . . .11 A5
Fox Hill Rd SG8 . . . . .10 F5
Fox Hollow CB3 . . . . .102 C4
Fox Rd Balsham CB1 . . . . . .52 F3
Bourn CB3 . . . . .60 D5
Catworth PE28 . . . . .136 D8
Fox St SG19 . . . . .58 E5
Fox Wood N 4 CB7 . . . . . .212 B5
Fox Wood S CB7 . . . . .212 B4
Foxburrow CI CB9 . . . . .38 F1
Foxcovert Rd
Peakirk PE6 . . . . .204 A8
Peterborough PE6 . . . . . .204 B4
Foxenfields PE28 . . . . . . .162 C1
Foxglove Bank 2 SG8 . . . . .5 F5
Foxglove CI 3 PE19 . . . . . .74 C5
Foxley CI 1 PE4 . . . . .204 C4
Fox's CI CB3 . . . . .105 D2
Fox's Way CB3 . . . . .62 D6
Foxton Prim Sch SG8 . . . .30 C5
Foxton Rd Barrington CB2 . .29 F8
Foxton CB2 . . . . .30 A7
Foxton Sta CB2 . . . . .30 C6
Foxtrot La PE28 . . . . .151 F3
Framlingham Rd PE7 . . . . .187 F5
Francis CI CB9 . . . . .23 F8
Francis Gdns PE26 . . . . . .197 F8
Francis Pas 3 CB2 . . . . . . .64 E7
Frank Bridges CI 2
CB7 . . . . .212 B3
Frank Perkins Parkway
. . . . .187 B8
Frank Perkins Way PE1 198 D4
Frankland Wlk 2 CB7 . . . .240 F6
Franklin Cres PE1 . . . . . . .198 E6
Franklin Gdns CB4 . . . . . .125 D4
Frank's La CB4 . . . . .84 B5
Franks La PE13 . . . . .237 F5
Fraser Dr PE27 . . . . .144 A7
Fraser Rd CB4 . . . . .84 A6
Fraserburgh Way 2
PE2 . . . . .186 C4
Freckenham Rd IP28 . . . . .213 E3
Fred Archer Way CB8 . . . .111 A3
Fred Dannatt Rd IP28 . . . .239 A6
Frederick Talbot CI 8
CB7 . . . . .212 B4
Free Sch La CB2 . . . . .246 A2
Freedom Bridge PE13 . . . .245 B6
Freeman CI 10 PE6 . . . . . .232 E7
Freemantle Ct 5 PE19 . . . .74 B3
Freesia Way PE7 . . . . .181 F6
Freewood La CB11 . . . . .9 B3
French Dro PE6 . . . . .232 E7
French's Rd
Cambridge CB4 . . . . .83 D4
Walpole PE14 . . . . .238 F8
Freshfields CB8 . . . . .110 F4
Freston PE4 . . . . .204 F2
Friar CI CB9 . . . . .38 F1
Friar's CI CB6 . . . . .65 F5
Friar's Pl CB6 . . . . .242 C5
Friar's Way CB6 . . . . .242 C5
Friars Nine CB6 . . . . .242 C4
Friday St IP28 . . . . .213 D6
Fridaybridge CP Sch
PE14 . . . . .236 A3
Fridaybridge Rd PE14 . . .236 A4
Friends CI PE19 . . . . .98 C2
Frinton Way 4 PE13 . . . . .245 E5
Frobisher CI PE29 . . . . . . .141 F6
Frog End
Great Wilbraham CB1 . . . . .67 F7
Shepreth SG8 . . . . .29 F2
Frogge St CB10 . . . . .18 B3
Frogmore CB8 . . . . .110 B7
Frogs Abbey La PE15 . . . .223 B7
Frogs Hall 6 PE26 . . . . . .208 C5
Froize End 4 CB6 . . . . . . .210 A5
Froment Way CB4 . . . . . . .105 C3
Fromont CI CB1 . . . . .66 E4
Front Rd Murrow PE13 . . . .234 D6
Tydd St Giles PE13 . . . . . .238 D8
Frowd CI CB7 . . . . .212 E1
Frumetty La PE28 . . . . . . .150 F4
Fryers Callis PE9 . . . . .244 C3
Fryth CI CB9 . . . . .39 A1
Fulbourn CP Sch CB1 . . . .66 F5
Fulbourn Hospl
Cambridge CB2 . . . . .65 B3
Fulbourn CB1 . . . . .66 C5
Fulbourn Old Drift CB1 . .66 A6
Fulbourn Rd
Cambridge CB1 . . . . .65 F5
Fulbourn CB1 . . . . .66 D7
Fulbridge Jun & Inf Sch
PE1 . . . . .197 F7
Fulbridge Rd PE1 . . . . . . .197 F8
Fulbrooke Rd CB3 . . . . .64 A7
Fulham Rd PE3 . . . . .197 E4
Fuller CI PE28 . . . . .137 F6
Fuller's La 5 PE15 . . . . . .223 B7
Fundrey Rd PE13 . . . . .245 F6
Funtham's La PE7 . . . . . . .188 D7
Furlongs The PE27 . . . . . .208 A2
Furrells The CB1 . . . . .35 C3
Furrowfields Rd PE16 . . . .241 C5
Furrows The PE27 . . . . . . .144 A4
Furtherford CB4 . . . . .208 E1
Furze Gr SG8 . . . . .15 A7
Furze Ride PE1 . . . . .198 B8
Fydell Ct PE19 . . . . .75 B7

G

Gables CI SG8 . . . . .29 A1
Gables The PE28 . . . . .121 A5
Gadd's La PE13 . . . . .235 D8
Gage CI SG8 . . . . .5 D8
Gains La PE28 . . . . .166 D2
Gainsborough Ave 6
PE19 . . . . .74 C5
Gainsborough CI CB4 . . . . .84 B6
Gainsborough Dr 7
PE27 . . . . .144 A7
Gainsborough Rd CB9 . . . .38 D1
Gala CI PE7 . . . . .176 A3
Galfrid Rd CB5 . . . . .84 D2
Gall The CB7 . . . . .240 D4
Gallions CI PE4 . . . . .204 D1
Gall's Dro CB7 . . . . .235 A4
Gamlingay Cty Fst Sch
SG19 . . . . .41 D5
Gamlingay Rd
Gamlingay SG19 . . . . .41 D8
Potton SG19 . . . . .41 C1
Waresley SG19 . . . . .57 E1
Gannet CI CB9 . . . . .24 C8
Gannocks CI PE2 . . . . .185 F5
Gannocks The PE2 . . . . . .185 F5
Ganwick CI 2 CB9 . . . . . . .38 F2
Gaol St 12 PE13 . . . . .245 C4
Garden CI Royston SG8 . . . . .5 E7
St Ives PE27 . . . . .144 A6
Sutton CB6 . . . . .216 E1
Garden Ct Burwell CB5 . . .130 C4
Ramsey PE26 . . . . .172 A4
Garden End SG8 . . . . .14 D5
Garden End Rd PE1 . . . . .198 B6
Garden Fields CB2 . . . . . . .48 E3
Garden La Royston SG8 . . . . .5 D5
Wisbech St Mary PE13 . . .235 A7
Garden Wlk
Cambridge CB4 . . . . .83 D4
Histon CB4 . . . . .104 C5
Royston SG8 . . . . .5 E7
Gardeners La 7 CB7 . . . . .212 B4
Gardiners La SG7 . . . . .2 A4
Garlic Row CB5 . . . . .84 B3
Garner Ave PE28 . . . . .164 E5
Garner CI 4 CB4 . . . . .105 C3
Garner Ct PE29 . . . . .141 F7
Garratt Rd 4 PE9 . . . . . . .244 B4
Garret Hostel La CB2 . . . .246 A2
Garry Dr CB4 . . . . .84 A7
Garton St PE1 . . . . .198 A5
Gas La Ely CB7 . . . . .240 D3
Stamford PE9 . . . . .244 C5
Thorney PE6 . . . . .233 A3
Gas Rd PE15 . . . . .243 D3
Gas St PE9 . . . . .244 C5
Gascoigne PE6 . . . . .203 F5
Gaul Rd PE15 . . . . .243 B4
Gault Bank PE15 . . . . .227 D1
Gaultree Sq PE14 . . . . . . .236 D6
Gayton CI 3 CB2 . . . . .64 D3
Gayton Ct PE3 . . . . .197 C5
Gazeley Gdns 2 PE7 . . . . .187 B2
Gazeley Rd Ashley CB8 . . . .92 A8
Cambridge CB2 . . . . .64 D4
Kentford CB8 . . . . .134 C1
Moulton CB8 . . . . .112 F6
Gazelle CI 4 PE19 . . . . . . .74 B5
Gazelle Way CB1 . . . . .66 B7
Geneva St PE1 . . . . .198 A3
Geoffrey Bishop Ave CB1 67 A4
George Gibson CI CB8 . . .110 C8
George IV St CB2 . . . . . . .246 C1
George La Buckden PE19 117 A4
Royston SG8 . . . . .5 D5
Warboys PE28 . . . . .164 E5
George Lambton Ave
CB8 . . . . .110 F4
George Nuttall CI CB4 . . . .84 A6
George Pateman Ct 2
CB1 . . . . .64 F7
George Pl 7 PE19 . . . . .74 C5
George St Cambridge CB4 . .83 F4
Huntingdon PE29 . . . . . . .141 D4
2 March PE15 . . . . .243 D4
Peterborough PE2 . . . . . .186 F8
Stilton PE7 . . . . .175 F4
Willingham CB4 . . . . .209 A1
Georgian Ct PE3 . . . . .197 C2
Gerard CI CB2 . . . . .84 C2
Gerard Rd CB5 . . . . .84 D3
Gery Ct PE19 . . . . .74 C5
Gibralter La CB4 . . . . .122 E5
Gibside Ave PE16 . . . . . . .241 B3
Gibson CI CB5 . . . . .106 A7
Gidding Rd PE28 . . . . .167 D3
Giddings CI PE2 . . . . .185 F4
Gifford Pl CB2 . . . . .246 A3
Gifford's CI CB3 . . . . .82 E8
Giffords Way 4 CB4 . . . . .208 D1
Gilbert CI CB4 . . . . .83 C5
Gilbert Rd Cambridge CB4 .83 D5
Littleport CB6 . . . . .242 B5
Gilbert Scott Dr CB6 . . . .240 E7
Gildale PE4 . . . . .204 D4
Gill's Hill CB3 . . . . .60 D5
Gilmorton Dr PE1 . . . . . . .198 D7
Gilpin St PE1 . . . . .197 E6
Gilvan Ct PE19 . . . . .95 C1
Gimber CI 5 PE29 . . . . . . .141 F7
Gimbert Rd CB7 . . . . .212 B4
Gipping CI 1 CB9 . . . . .23 F8
Gipson CI PE16 . . . . .241 B5
Gipsy Dro PE16 . . . . .215 F6

Gipsy La PE15 . . . . .243 A7
Girton CI Mildenhall IP28 239 C6
Woodditton CB8 . . . . .111 B1
Girton Coll Cambridge CB3 83 B2
Girton CB3 . . . . .82 F6
Girton Cres PE29 . . . . .142 A7
Girton Rd Girton CB3 . . . . .82 F7
Haverhill CB9 . . . . .24 B7
Girton Way PE7 . . . . .244 A4
Gisborne Rd CB1 . . . . .65 C6
Gladeside CB3 . . . . .102 C4
Gladstone Prim Sch
PE1 . . . . .197 F5
Gladstone St PE1 . . . . . . .197 F5
Gladstone Way CB1 . . . . . .65 F5
Glamis Gdns PE3 . . . . . . .197 B2
Glassmoor Bank PE7 . . . .220 F7
Glastonbury CI 11 PE6 . . .232 A1
Glatton Dr PE2 . . . . .187 D6
Glatton La PE7 . . . . .176 D3
Glatton Rd PE28 . . . . .168 A6
Glatton Ways PE28 . . . . . .175 F4
Glebe Ave PE2 . . . . .185 E4
Glebe CI Chatteris PE16 . .241 D5
Great Paxton PE19 . . . . . . .96 E4
Toft CB3 . . . . .61 E5
Wimblington PE15 . . . . . .224 B4
Glebe Cres CB2 . . . . .33 B4
Glebe Ct PE2 . . . . .187 B4
Glebe City Prim Sch
CB3 . . . . .103 E1
Glebe Gdns 2 PE6 . . . . . .232 B8
Glebe La PE19 . . . . .117 B3
Glebe Rd Barrington CB2 . .29 F8
Brampton PE28 . . . . .140 E2
Cambridge CB1 . . . . .65 B4
Hemingford Grey PE28 . . .143 D1
Huntingdon PE29 . . . . . . .141 E9
Perry PE28 . . . . .115 D3
Peterborough PE2 . . . . . .187 B4
Sawtry PE28 . . . . .168 A4
Stilton PE7 . . . . .176 A7
Waterbeach CB5 . . . . . . .106 A7
Glebe The Haverhill CB9 . . .39 A1
Ramsey PE26 . . . . .172 B4
Glebe Way
Haddenham CB6 . . . . .209 F6
Histon CB4 . . . . .104 C4
Glebelands CP Sch
PE16 . . . . .241 D5
Glemsford Rise 2 PE2 . . .186 C7
Glen Cres PE9 . . . . .244 C7
Glen Rd 1 PE8 . . . . .230 B1
Glen The PE2 . . . . .187 B7
Glenacre CI 3 CB1 . . . . . . .65 E5
Glencoe Way PE2 . . . . . . .185 D3
Glendale PE2 . . . . .185 D6
Gleneagles PE2 . . . . .185 F6
Glenfields CI PE7 . . . . . . .189 C4
Glenmere CI CB1 . . . . .65 D5
Glenton St PE1 . . . . .198 C2
Glinton Rd Helpston PE6 . .203 A8
Newborough PE6 . . . . . . .204 E8
Glisson Rd CB1 . . . . .246 C1
Globe La Alconbury PE28 .150 E3
3 Littleport CB6 . . . . .242 C4
Gloucester Rd
Brampton PE28 . . . . .140 D1
Haverhill CB9 . . . . .23 F7
Peterborough PE2 . . . . . .187 B7
Sawtry PE28 . . . . .168 C3
7 Stamford PE9 . . . . .244 B6
Wyton Airfield PE28 . . . . .143 B8
Glover CI CB2 . . . . .32 F6
Glover St CB4 . . . . .208 D1
Goddard Cres 1 PE13 . . . .245 D7
Godeby Ct 4 PE29 . . . . . . .141 F8
Godesdone Rd CB5 . . . . . . .84 A3
Godfrey CI PE6 . . . . .207 D1
Goding Way CB4 . . . . .105 E2
Godmanchester Com
Swimming Pool PE29 . .141 E2
Godric Sq 2 PE6 . . . . .186 D6
Godsey La 2 PE6 . . . . .231 E8
Godwin CI CB1 . . . . .65 C4
Godwin Rd PE13 . . . . .245 D7
Godwin Way CB1 . . . . .65 C4
Goffin CI PE7 . . . . .201 A1
Goffsmill PE3 . . . . .197 A4
Gog Magog Way CB2 . . . . .49 C5
Gold St PE15 . . . . .243 C7
Goldcrest Ct 3 CB3 . . . . . .79 C3
Golden Drop PE6 . . . . .231 C4
Golden Miller CI CB8 . . . .110 D7
Golden Rod 3 PE29 . . . . . .118 F8
Goldhay Way PE2 . . . . . . .185 F2
Goldie La PE2 . . . . .185 F6
Golding Pl 15 PE15 . . . . . .245 C4
Golding Rd CB1 . . . . .65 B6
Goldings CI CB9 . . . . .39 A2
Goldpits PE28 . . . . .164 C5
Golf La PE28 . . . . .151 F3
Golf Links Rd
Barton Mills IP28 . . . . . . .214 A3
Worlington IP28 . . . . .239 A1
Gonville & Caius Coll
CB2 . . . . .246 B1
Gonville CI IP28 . . . . .239 D6
Gonville Pl CB1 . . . . .246 C1
Goochgate PE12 . . . . .237 A7
Goodacre PE2 . . . . .186 A4
Goodchilds Gdns 5
CB7 . . . . .213 A5
Goode CI CB4 . . . . .125 D4
Goodens La PE13 . . . . . . .238 A5

Goodliffe Ave CB1 . . . . .53 C2
Goodwin Gr 1 CB7 . . . . . .240 F7
Goodwin Wlk PE4 . . . . . .204 C4
Goodwood Rd
 8 Peterborough PE3 . . . .196 F3
 1 Royston SG8 . . . . .5 F6
Goose Fen Dro CB2 . . . . . .33 A8
Gordon Ave March PE15 .243 D4
 Peterborough PE2 . . . . . .186 E7
Gordon Cl PE19 . . . . .95 F1
Gordon Fendick Sch
 PE13 . . . . .245 D8
Gordon Rd PE19 . . . . . . .95 F1
Gordon Richards Cl 2
 CB8 . . . . .110 F6
Gordon Way PE2 . . . . . . .186 C7
Gore Tree Rd PE28 . . . . .120 C7
Goredike Bank PE13 . . . .237 E3
Gorefield Prim Sch
 PE13 . . . . .237 E2
Gorefield Rd PE13 . . . . . .237 F2
Gorse Cl 8 IP28 . . . . . . .214 A1
Gorse Way PE27 . . . . . . .144 B5
Goshawk Cl PE29 . . . . . .142 A8
Gosling Way CB2 . . . . . . .33 A8
Gosling's Dro PE27 . . . . .220 A8
Gosmoor La PE14 . . . . . .236 B5
Gosslan Cl PE27 . . . . . . .144 A6
Gostwick PE2 . . . . .185 D5
Gote La PE13 . . . . .237 E3
Gough Way CB3 . . . . .64 A8
Governess Cl 8 PE15 . .223 B7
Gower Rd SG8 . . . . .5 C7
Gowers The CB3 . . . . . . .103 E1
Grace Sch of Medicine
 CB1 . . . . .65 A8
Gracious St PE7 . . . . . . .189 D7
Graeme Rd PE5 . . . . . . .194 F2
Grafham Cl PE2 . . . . . . .187 E4
Grafham Rd PE28 . . . . . .138 F4
Grafham Water Ex Ctr
 PE28 . . . . .116 B5
Grafham Water Nature
 Reserve ★ PE28 . . . . . .115 A4
Grafton Ave PE3 . . . . . . .197 C3
Grafton Cl PE27 . . . . . . .143 F8
Grafton St CB1 . . . . .246 C2
Grain Cl CB2 . . . . .49 A5
Grainger Ave PE29 . . . . .118 F8
Granary Cl PE29 . . . . . . .141 E4
Granary La 5 CB6 . . . . . .242 D4
Granary The
 Old Hurst PE28 . . . . . . .154 D7
 2 Sawtry PE28 . . . . . . .168 B4
Granby St Littleport CB6 .242 C4
 Newmarket CB8 . . . . . .111 B3
 Peterborough PE1 . . . . . .198 B2
Grandford Dro PE15 . . . .227 E6
Grandridge Cl CB1 . . . . . .66 F4
Grange Ave PE1 . . . . . . .198 A6
Grange Bottom SG8 . . . . . .5 E5
Grange Cres PE2 . . . . . . .186 A5
Grange Dr CB3 . . . . .82 E7
Grange Farm Cl PE19 . . . .57 B5
Grange La
 Barton Mills IP28 . . . . . .239 C2
 Littleport CB6 . . . . .242 B2
Grange Rd Cambridge CB3 64 B8
 Duxford CB2 . . . . .17 A6
 Ickleton CB10 . . . . .9 A8
 March PE15 . . . . .228 A1
 Peterborough PE3 . . . . . .197 D4
 6 Somersham PE28 . . . .208 C8
 13 Somersham PE28 . . . .215 C1
 Wisbech PE13 . . . . .245 A4
Grange The Meldreth SG8 .14 B8
 8 Somersham PE28 . . . .208 C8
Grangehill Rd PE13 . . . . .237 B6
Granham's Rd
 Cambridge CB2 . . . . .65 C1
 Great Shelford CB2 . . . . .49 A7
Granhams Cl CB2 . . . . . . .49 A6
Gransden Rd
 Abbotsley PE19 . . . . . . .57 E6
 Caxton CB3 . . . . .59 D8
Gransley Rise PE3 . . . . . .197 C5
Granta Cl
 Great Chesterford CB10 . .18 D1
 St Ives PE27 . . . . .144 F4
 Witchford CB6 . . . . .217 D1
Granta Cotts CB10 . . . . . .18 C2
Granta Leys CB1 . . . . .35 B3
Granta Pl CB2 . . . . .246 A1
Granta Rd CB2 . . . . .32 E5
Granta Terr CB2 . . . . .49 B4
Granta Vale CB1 . . . . .35 C2
Grantchester Mdws CB3 .64 C7
Grantchester Rd
 Barton CB3 . . . . .63 D7
 Cambridge CB3 . . . . .64 B2
 Coton CB3 . . . . .82 C1
 Grantchester CB3 . . . . . .64 B6
Grantchester Rise CB5 .130 B4
Grantchester St 3 CB3 . .64 C7
Grantham Cl SG8 . . . . .5 B8
Granville Ave PE6 . . . . . .231 F7
Granville Gdns IP28 . . . .239 A4
Granville St PE1 . . . . . . .198 A4
Grasmere PE29 . . . . .141 B6
Grasmere Gdns PE4 . . . .204 D3
Grass Plant Cotts CB8 .131 B4
Grassgate La PE14 . . . . .238 E3
Gravel Bridge Rd CB4 . .123 C6

Gravel Dro
 "Beck Row, Holywell Row
 & Kenny Hill" IP28 . . . .213 C6
 Witcham CB6 . . . . .216 F4
Gravel End CB6 . . . . .217 C5
Gravel End La CB6 . . . . . .217 D5
Gravel Pit Hill SG8 . . . . . .16 C8
Gravel Wlk PE1 . . . . .198 A2
Graveley Rd PE19 . . . . . . .97 A8
Graveley Way PE28 . . . . . .98 E8
Gray Ct PE1 . . . . .197 E8
Gray Rd CB1 . . . . .65 D6
Grayling Cl CB4 . . . . .84 A4
Gray's Rd SG19 . . . . .41 D6
Grays Cl SG8 . . . . .5 C8
Grays Gr MK44 . . . . .93 B2
Grays La Emneth PE14 . . .236 C6
 March PE15 . . . . .243 D4
Graysmoor Dro PE14 . . .228 B3
Great & Little Shelford CE
 Prim Sch CB2 . . . . .48 F4
Great Chesterford Sta
 CB10 . . . . .18 C1
Great Cl CB3 . . . . .63 B4
Great Dro Soham CB7 . . .211 F3
 Swaffham Prior CB7 . . . .128 C6
 Yaxley PE7 . . . . .182 A5
Great Eastern Rd PE13 . .245 B8
Great Eastern St CB1 . . . .65 B8
Great Farthing Cl PE27 . .144 B4
Great Fen Rd CB7 . . . . . .212 A2
Great Gidding CE Prim Sch
 PE28 . . . . .166 D3
Great Heath Prim Sch
 IP28 . . . . .239 D6
Great Ho ★ CB3 . . . . .47 B5
Great How PE27 . . . . . . .143 F7
Great La CB5 . . . . .129 C1
Great North Fen Dro
 CB4 . . . . .125 C6
Great North Rd
 Alconbury PE28 . . . . . . .150 E4
 Buckden PE19 . . . . .117 A5
 Eaton Socon PE19 . . . . . .74 A5
 St Neots PE19 . . . . .74 C7
 Sibson cum Stibbington
 PE8 . . . . .183 E8
 Southoe & Midloe PE19 . . .95 F4
 Wothorpe PE9 . . . . .244 A2
Great Northern St PE1 141 D5
Great Paxton CE Sch
 PE19 . . . . .96 E5
Great Staughton CP Sch
 PE19 . . . . .93 F6
Great Whyte PE26 . . . . . .172 A8
Great Wilbraham Prim Sch
 CB1 . . . . .67 F8
Great Wilbraham Rd 86 F1
Greater Foxes CB1 . . . . . .66 F5
Greatford Rd PE9 . . . . . .230 C6
Grebe Cl IP28 . . . . .239 D3
Grebe Ct PE7 . . . . .190 A8
Grebe Way 3 PE19 . . . . . .75 B7
Green Acres SG19 . . . . . .41 C5
Green Bank Rd CB5 . . . .108 B2
Green Butts CB2 . . . . .32 D5
Green Cl PE19 . . . . .94 A6
Green Drift SG8 . . . . .5 B6
Green Dro Coveney CB6 . .217 D4
 Crowland PE6 . . . . .232 D8
 Elm PE14 . . . . .236 D2
 Outwell PE14 . . . . .236 E2
 Thorney PE6 . . . . .200 F4
 Thorney PE6 . . . . .233 A6
Green End Comberton CB3 62 C6
 Fen Ditton CB5 . . . . .84 E6
 Gamlingay SG19 . . . . . . .41 C5
 Landbeach CB4 . . . . . . .105 D8
 Little Staughton MK44 . . .93 A3
 Little Stukeley PE28 . . . .152 A1
 Stretham CB6 . . . . .210 F4
Green End Rd
 Cambridge CB4 . . . . .84 B6
 St Neots PE19 . . . . .75 A5
 Sawtry PE28 . . . . .168 B3
Green Farm Cl PE5 . . . . .195 E2
Green Head Rd CB5 . . . . .108 C4
Green Hedges Sch CB2 . .49 C4
Green Hill 3 CB6 . . . . . .211 B7
Green How PE27 . . . . . . .143 E6
Green La Ashwell SG7 . . . . .2 E5
 6 Benwick PE15 . . . . . .222 A5
 Brampton PE28 . . . . . . .140 D2
 Christchurch PE14 . . . . .229 D3
 Ellington PE28 . . . . .138 F4
 Everton SG19 . . . . .40 C3
 Great Staughton PE19 . . .93 F6
 Hail Weston PE19 . . . . . .95 A1
 Leverington PE13 . . . . . .237 F2
 Linton CB1 . . . . .35 C2
 Peterborough PE1 . . . . . .198 A4
 St Ives PE28 . . . . .143 A5
 Stamford PE9 . . . . .244 B7
 Upton & Coppingford PE28 160 C2
 Walsoken PE14 . . . . . . .245 F4
 Yaxley PE7 . . . . .181 D6
Green Leys PE27 . . . . . . .143 F5
Green Man La CB2 . . . . . . .47 B8
Green Pk Brinkley CB8 . . . .70 D2
 Cambridge CB4 . . . . .84 B6
 Chatteris PE16 . . . . . . .241 C6
Green Rd
 Newborough PE6 . . . . . .205 F3
 Newmarket CB8 . . . . . . .111 B2
 Upwell PE14 . . . . .229 E8
Green Rd The CB2 . . . . . . .33 A8
Green Side CB5 . . . . .106 B7
Green St Cambridge CB2 .246 A3

Green St continued
 Duxford CB2 . . . . .32 D1
 March PE15 . . . . .243 E3
 Royston SG8 . . . . .5 D8
 Willingham CB4 . . . . . . .209 A1
Green The Ashley CB8 . . . .91 F8
 "Beck Row, Holywell Row
 & Kenny Hill" IP28 . . . .213 C7
 Brampton PE28 . . . . . . .140 D2
 Cambridge CB4 . . . . .84 B5
 Castor PE5 . . . . .195 E2
 Foxton CB2 . . . . .30 B5
 Glinton PE6 . . . . .203 E8
 Great Staughton PE19 . . .93 F7
 Haddenham CB6 . . . . . .210 A6
 Kingston CB3 . . . . .61 B3
 Kirtling CB8 . . . . .72 C5
 Lolworth CB3 . . . . .101 F5
 Peterborough PE4 . . . . . .204 C3
 Royston SG8 . . . . .5 D6
 Snailwell CB8 . . . . .132 A3
 Somersham PE28 . . . . . .215 C1
 Steeple Morden SG8 . . . .11 C1
 6 Thorney PE6 . . . . . . .233 A3
 Yaxley PE7 . . . . .181 E5
Green Tiles CB7 . . . . . . .152 E1
Greenacres Duxford CB2 . .32 D1
 Peterborough PE4 . . . . . .204 A4
Greenbanks CB8 . . . . .14 C5
Greenbury Cl SG8 . . . . .6 F1
Greendale PE27 . . . . .141 A6
Greenfield SG8 . . . . .5 B7
Greenfield Cl CB2 . . . . . . .49 D4
Greenfields Earith PE28 . .208 E6
 Eltisley PE19 . . . . .77 E4
 Hemingford Grey PE27 . . .143 F1
 Newmarket CB8 . . . . . . .111 C3
 1 St Neots PE19 . . . . . .75 A6
 1 St Neots PE19 . . . . . .75 A6
Greenfields Way CB9 . . . . .23 F6
Greenford Cl SG8 . . . . . . .28 C8
Greengage Cl SG8 . . . . . .14 C4
Greengage Rise SG8 . . . . .14 C5
Greengarth PE27 . . . . . . .144 A5
Greengate Ct PE1 . . . . . .198 C4
Greenham PE3 . . . . .197 A4
Greenhaze La CB3 . . . . . . .79 B3
Greenhill Rd PE8 . . . . . . .178 F4
Greenhills CB7 . . . . .212 C3
Greenlands CB2 . . . . .65 B3
Greenleas CB4 . . . . .104 B5
Green's Rd CB4 . . . . .83 E4
Greenside Cl CB4 . . . . . .122 C6
Greenstock La PE13 . . . .238 A6
Greenway PE19 . . . . .117 B4
Greenwood Cl
 1 Haverhill CB9 . . . . . . .23 E7
 Ramsey PE26 . . . . .172 A5
Gregory Rd IP28 . . . . . . .239 A6
Grenadier Dr PE16 . . . . .241 C6
Grenadier Rd PE9 . . . . . . .23 C8
Greneway Sch The SG8 . . .5 E7
Grenfell Rd PE26 . . . . . . .172 A5
Grenville Way PE19 . . . . . .74 B2
Gresham Rd CB1 . . . . . . .246 C1
Gresley Dr PE19 . . . . .94 B4
Gresley Way March PE15 243 B6
 Peterborough PE3 . . . . . .197 C6
Gretton Cl PE2 . . . . .186 C7
Greville Rd CB1 . . . . .65 B7
Greville Starkey Ave 1
 CB8 . . . . .110 F5
Greys The PE15 . . . . . . .243 E2
Greystoke Ct 1 CB1 . . . . .65 C5
Greystoke Rd CB1 . . . . . .65 C5
Grieve Ct CB4 . . . . .84 C5
Griffins Cl PE6 . . . . .207 D1
Griffiths St PE2 . . . . .185 E5
Grimmer's Rd 6 PE13 . . .245 E7
Grimshaw Rd PE1 . . . . . .198 B6
Grip The CB1 . . . . .35 B1
Groat La SG19 . . . . .41 D8
Grosvenor House Ct 6
 IP28 . . . . .239 B5
Grosvenor Rd PE19 . . . . .245 D7
Grosvenor Yd CB8 . . . . . .111 A3
Grounds Ave PE15 . . . . . .243 F4
Grounds Way PE7 . . . . . .191 A8
Grove Ct PE19 . . . . .95 F2
Grove End PE28 . . . . . . .120 C1
Grove Gdns CB7 . . . . . . .212 E2
Grove La Brampton PE28 .140 D3
 Peterborough PE3 . . . . . .197 A2
Grove Pk CB7 . . . . .212 E2
Grove Prim Sch CB4 . . . . .83 F6
Grove Rd
 Little Paxton PE19 . . . . . .95 F2
 Sawston CB2 . . . . .33 A8
Grove St PE2 . . . . .186 F8
Grove The Cambridge CB4 .84 B6
 Chatteris PE16 . . . . . . .241 C5
 Huntingdon PE29 . . . . . .142 B6
 Linton CB1 . . . . .35 B3
 Mildenhall IP28 . . . . . . .213 D8
 Orwell SG8 . . . . .28 D8
 1 Stretham CB6 . . . . . .210 F5
 Whittlesey PE7 . . . . . . .189 F6
 Wistow PE28 . . . . .163 F6
Grove Way PE26 . . . . . . .172 A4
Grovemere Ct PE28 . . . . .114 B7
Grunty Fen Rd CB6 . . . . .210 F8
Guanockgate Rd PE12 . .234 C8
Guash Way PE9 . . . . .244 D7
Guelder Rose 5 CB7 . . . .240 F5
Guest Rd CB1 . . . . .246 C2
Guild Rd PE13 . . . . .245 E6
Guilden Morden Sch SG8 10 F5
Guildenburgh Cres PE7 190 A7

Guildhall Pl 5 CB1 . . . . .246 A2
Guildhall St 3 CB1 . . . . .246 A2
Guineas Cl CB8 . . . . .110 E6
Guise La SG8 . . . . .12 D6
Gull Bank PE13 . . . . .234 E3
Gull Dro PE13 . . . . .234 D3
Gull La PE13 . . . . .238 A3
Gull Rd PE13 . . . . .234 E3
Gull Way Chatteris PE16 .241 C6
 Whittlesey PE7 . . . . . . .190 A8
Gullymore PE3 . . . . .196 F8
Gunhild Cl CB1 . . . . .65 C5
Gunhild Ct CB1 . . . . .65 C5
Gunhild Way CB1 . . . . . . .65 C5
Gunnell Cl CB4 . . . . .105 D2
Gunning Rd CB6 . . . . . . .240 E8
Gunning Way CB4 . . . . . . .83 C6
Gunnings Way PE28 . . . . .143 C1
Gunthorpe Rd
 Newborough PE6 . . . . . .204 F4
 Peterborough PE4 . . . . . .204 E2
Gunthorpe Ridings 1
 PE4 . . . . .205 A2
Gunton's Rd PE6 . . . . . . .205 C6
Guntons Cl CB7 . . . . .212 B4
Guntons Cl CB9 . . . . .39 A2
Gurnard Leys PE3 . . . . . .204 A1
Gurney Way CB4 . . . . .83 E4
Guthlac Ave PE4 . . . . . . .204 D1
Guyatt Ct CB5 . . . . .130 B2
Guyhirn VC Sch PE13 . . .235 A2
Gwydir St CB1 . . . . .65 A8
Gypsy La PE13 . . . . .238 C4

H

Hacke Rd 3 PE3 . . . . . .197 D3
Haddenham Rd CB6 . . . .217 A1
Haddon Cl PE2 . . . . .187 E5
Haddon Rd Haddon PE7 . .180 C6
 Peterborough PE3 . . . . . .197 E3
Haddow Way PE7 . . . . . . .187 B2
Haddow's Cl CB4 . . . . . . .123 F2
Haden Way Over CB4 . . . .208 F1
 Willingham CB4 . . . . . . .123 F8
Hadley Rd PE4 . . . . .204 D1
Hadrian Cl CB9 . . . . .24 D7
Hadrians Ct PE2 . . . . . . .187 B8
Hadstock Rd CB1 . . . . . . .35 B1
Hagbech Hall Cl PE14 . . .236 D6
Hagger's Cl CB4 . . . . .14 D6
Haggis Gap CB1 . . . . .66 F5
Haigh's Cl PE16 . . . . .241 B4
Hake's Dro PE15 . . . . . . .227 A2
Halcyon Ct PE29 . . . . . . .141 C6
Hale Ave CB4 . . . . .83 D4
Hale Cl SG8 . . . . .14 D6
Hale Dro CB6 . . . . .225 E6
Hale Fen CB6 . . . . .242 C6
Hale Fen La CB6 . . . . . . .217 A4
Hale Fen Rd CB6 . . . . . . .225 E4
Haley Cl
 Hemingford Grey PE28 . . .143 B1
 4 Wisbech PE13 . . . . . .245 C8
Half Acre Dro CB7 . . . . . .211 C7
Half Acre La CB7 . . . . . . .211 D8
Halfpenny La PE14 . . . . .245 D1
Halfpenny Toll Rd PE14 .229 E4
Halifax Rd Cambridge CB4 .83 B4
 Mildenhall IP28 . . . . . . .213 E8
Halifax Way CB8 . . . . . . .110 E5
Hall Bank PE13 . . . . .237 E7
Hall Barn Rd CB7 . . . . . .212 F4
Hall Bridge Rd PE14 . . . .236 D1
Hall Cl Bourn CB3 . . . . . . .60 C5
 Foxton CB2 . . . . .30 B6
 Huntingdon PE29 . . . . . .142 A6
 Little Paxton PE19 . . . . . .95 F2
Hall Cres CB2 . . . . .33 A7
Hall Dike PE14 . . . . .236 F4
Hall Dr Hardwick CB3 . . . .80 F3
 Highfields CB3 . . . . .80 C2
Hall End CB4 . . . . .105 D2
Hall Farm La SG19 . . . . . .58 D4
Hall Farm Rd 2 CB4 . . . . .83 D5
Hall Gate Rd PE12 . . . . . .234 B8
Hall Green La PE28 . . . . .121 B6
Hall La
 Abbots Ripton PE28 . . . .152 D8
 Brinkley CB8 . . . . .70 E2
 Burwell CB5 . . . . .130 B1
 Great & Little Chishill SG8 . .7 F2
 3 Peterborough PE4 . . . .204 C4
 20 Wittering PE8 . . . . . .230 B1
Hall Rd Outwell PE14 . . . .236 F3
 St Neots PE19 . . . . .74 E3
Hall St CB7 . . . . .212 B5
Hallards The 6 PE19 . . . .74 C6
Hallaton Rd PE1 . . . . . . .198 D8
Hallcroft Rd PE7 . . . . . . .189 C8
Hallfields La PE4 . . . . . . .204 C1
Hallwyck Gdns 2 CB8 . . .110 F2
Halstead Cl 2 PE13 . . . . .245 E5
Ham La PE2 . . . . .185 E7
Ham Mere Bird Sanctuary ★
 PE2 . . . . .185 E7
Hamden Way CB3 . . . . . . .99 B3
Hamerton Rd
 Alconbury Weston PE28 . .150 C7
 Buckworth PE28 . . . . . .149 D6
 Winwick PE28 . . . . .158 C5
Hamerton Zoo Pk ★
 PE28 . . . . .159 B5
Hamilton Rd
 Cambridge CB4 . . . . . . .246 B4
 Ely CB6 . . . . .240 B4
 Newmarket CB8 . . . . . . .110 E3

Hamiltons The CB8 . . . . .110 E2
Hamlet Cl PE29 . . . . .141 F6
Hamlet Rd CB9 . . . . .24 B7
Hamlet The CB6 . . . . . . .218 C6
Hammond Cl
 Newmarket CB8 . . . . . . .110 E6
 Pampisford CB2 . . . . . . .33 B5
 2 Wittering PE8 . . . . . . .230 C1
Hammond Way PE28 . . . .208 C8
Hampden Rd 2 PE13 . . . .245 D5
Hampden Way PE19 . . . . .75 A3
Hampshire Rd PE28 . . . . .143 B8
Hampstead Ave IP28 . . . .239 B6
Hampton Hargate Prim Sch
 PE7 . . . . .186 C2
Hanaper Dr SG8 . . . . .6 F1
Hanbury PE2 . . . . .185 F3
Hankey St PE1 . . . . .197 F4
Hanmer Ave IP28 . . . . . .239 C5
Hannath Rd PE13 . . . . . .238 B8
Hanover Cl Bar Hill CB3 .102 B3
 Eaton Socon PE19 . . . . . .74 D5
Hanover Ct
 3 Brampton PE28 . . . . .140 D3
 Peterborough PE3 . . . . . .197 A8
Hansell Rd PE28 . . . . . . .140 B3
Harbins La PE19 . . . . .57 C6
Harbour Ave CB3 . . . . . . .62 D6
Harcombe Rd CB1 . . . . . . .65 E6
Harding Cl 1 CB5 . . . . . .106 A7
Harding Way
 Cambridge CB4 . . . . .83 C5
 Histon CB4 . . . . .104 B4
 St Ives PE27 . . . . .144 B5
Hardwick Com Prim Sch
 CB3 . . . . .81 A3
Hardwick Ct PE3 . . . . . . .197 B2
Hardwick La
 1 Abbotsley PE19 . . . . . .57 B6
 Buckden PE19 . . . . .117 A5
Hardwick Rd
 Haverhill CB9 . . . . .24 B8
 St Neots PE19 . . . . .74 E3
 Toft CB3 . . . . .61 E6
Hardwick St CB2 . . . . .64 C7
Hardwicke Cl CB6 . . . . . .242 C5
Hardwicke Fields CB6 . . .210 A6
Hardwicke Rd SG19 . . . . .58 F6
Hardy Cl PE29 . . . . .141 F6
Hardy Dr SG8 . . . . .5 D8
Hardy Pl 1 PE19 . . . . . . .74 D6
Hardy's La PE7 . . . . .189 E6
Harebell Cl
 Cambridge CB1 . . . . .66 A5
 Huntingdon PE29 . . . . . .141 D6
 Peterborough PE1 . . . . . .205 B1
Harecroft Rd PE13 . . . . . .245 B5
Harefield Rise CB1 . . . . . .35 E2
Harewood Gdns PE3 . . . .197 B2
Hargate Way PE7 . . . . . .186 D3
Hargood Ct 4 PE19 . . . . .74 B3
Hargrave Rd 6 SG8 . . . . . .5 D5
Harland Rd PE19 . . . . .74 E6
Harlech Ct 5 PE19 . . . . . .74 E6
Harlech Grange PE3 . . . .197 B1
Harlestones Rd CB4 . . . . .125 D4
Harlton Cl PE2 . . . . .187 E5
Harlton Rd
 Great Eversden CB3 . . . . .45 F7
 Haslingfield CB3 . . . . . . .46 F5
Harold Heading Cl PE16 241 B3
Harold's Bank PE13 . . . . .237 B1
Harper's Dro PE26 . . . . . .170 F7
Harrier Cl PE29 . . . . .142 A8
Harrington Dr PE6 . . . . . .232 C8
Harris Cres PE28 . . . . . . .208 A2
Harris La PE28 . . . . .163 E6
Harris Rd CB4 . . . . .83 D6
Harris St PE1 . . . . .197 F6
Harrison Cl 10 PE29 . . . .196 F3
Harrison Way PE27 . . . . .144 B3
Harrison's Dro
 Burwell CB5 . . . . .129 A8
 Swaffham Prior CB7 . . . .128 D7
Harris's La PE28 . . . . . . .163 E7
Harrolds Cl 5 PE13 . . . . .238 F1
Harrow Rd PE9 . . . . .23 E7
Harry Palmer Cl 2 PE28 212 E1
Harrys Way PE13 . . . . . .245 C2
Harston CP Sch CB2 . . . . .47 F2
Harston Rd
 Haslingfield CB3 . . . . . . .47 C4
 Newton CB2 . . . . .31 B8
Hart Cl CB9 . . . . .38 F1
Hart Rd PE26 . . . . .171 E3
Hartfield Rd CB8 . . . . .70 E4
Hartford Ct PE2 . . . . . . .187 D6
Hartford Cty Jun & Inf Sch
 PE29 . . . . .141 F5
Hartford Rd PE29 . . . . . .141 E4
Hartington Gr CB1 . . . . . .65 A5
Hartlands PE7 . . . . .190 E8
Hartley Cl CB5 . . . . .106 B8
Hartwell Way PE3 . . . . . .197 B5
Harvest Cl PE7 . . . . .175 F8
Harvest Ct 2 PE27 . . . . .144 A4
Harvest Way CB1 . . . . .84 A2
Harvester Way
 Crowland PE6 . . . . .232 B8
 Peterborough PE1 . . . . . .198 C1
Harvey Cl 4 PE8 . . . . . . .230 B1
Harvey Dr 5 PE15 . . . . . .215 C1
Harvey Goodwin Ave
 CB4 . . . . .83 D4
Harvey Rd CB1 . . . . .246 C1
Harvey St 3 PE19 . . . . . . .74 E4
Haselhurst Cl 5 PE15 . . .243 F4

Haslingfield Endowed Sch CB3 .47 A5
Haslingfield Rd
Barrington CB2 .29 F8
Barton CB3 .63 B2
Harlton CB3 .46 E6
Hasse Rd CB7 .212 C8
Hassock Hill Dro PE13 .237 D3
Hassock Way 1 PE15 .223 B7
Hastings Rd PE4 .204 C2
Hatchet La PE19 .114 B2
Hatfield Rd PE28 .168 A4
Hathaway Cl 5 PE19 .74 C3
Hatherdene Cl CB1 .65 E8
Hatley Cl PE19 .75 A7
Hatley Dr CB5 .130 B3
Hatley Park* SG19 .42 F2
Hatley Rd Gamlingay SG19 .41 F4
Wrestlingworth & Cockayne Hatley SG19 .25 B7
Hatton's Pk CB4 .123 F2
Hatton's Rd CB4 .102 D6
Hauston CP Sch CB2 .48 C4
Hautboy La PE8 .178 B3
Hauxton Industrial Effluent Disposal Plant CB2 .47 F6
Hauxton Rd
Cambridge CB2 .48 C8
Great Shelford CB2 .48 D4
Havelock Cl SG19 .41 C5
Havelock Dr PE2 .187 E6
Haven The CB1 .66 F5
Haverhill Rd
Castle Camps CB1 .22 E4
Horseheath CB1 .37 A3
Little Wratting CB9 .39 F3
Stapleford CB2 .49 E5
Steeple Bumpstead CB9 .24 B1
Haverhill Sports Ctr CB9 .24 B7
Haverhill TH CB9 .24 A7
Haveswater Cl 1 PE4 .204 E2
Haviland Way CB4 .83 F6
Hawcrofts La CB4 .208 D2
Hawe's La CB7 .211 E2
Haweswater PE29 .141 C5
Hawk Dr PE29 .142 B7
Hawkes End PE28 .140 E2
Hawkes La 1 PE27 .208 A2
Hawkesden Rd PE19 .75 B6
Hawkesford Way PE19 .74 F7
Hawkins Cl PE28 .115 D3
Hawkins Dr 1 PE13 .245 E5
Hawkins Rd CB4 .83 F7
Hawkins's Dro CB7 .242 F3
Hawkshead Way 2 PE4 204 E3
Hawthorn Ave
Hauxton CB2 .48 B4
Sawston CB2 .32 F6
Hawthorn Cl
Little Paxton PE19 .95 F2
Littleport CB6 .242 E3
Newborough PE6 .207 C1
Royston SG8 .5 F7
Hawthorn Dr PE29 .141 D5
Hawthorn End 1 PE28 .150 F5
Hawthorn Rd
Emneth PE14 .236 D5
Folksworth PE7 .175 D8
Haverhill CB9 .38 D1
Peterborough PE1 .198 C6
Ramsey PE26 .171 F7
St Neots PE19 .74 E6
Yaxley PE7 .181 F5
Hawthorn Way
Burwell CB5 .130 C3
Cambridge CB4 .83 F4
Royston SG8 .5 F7
St Ives PE27 .144 A5
4 Sawtry PE28 .168 B3
Hawthorn Wlk 4 IP28 .213 F8
Hawthorne Ave PE13 .245 C8
Hawthorne Dr PE7 .189 F6
Hawthorne Gr PE15 .243 C5
Hawthorne Rd CB2 .49 B4
Hawthorns The PE16 .241 C5
Hay Cl CB1 .53 B1
Hay Fen Cl 6 CB6 .210 F5
Hay St SG8 .11 B2
Haycocks Rd CB9 .23 C8
Haycraft Cl PE28 .116 A7
Haycroft The PE19 .117 F2
Haydock Rd 2 SG8 .5 F6
Hayes Wlk PE8 .178 D8
Hayfield Ave CB2 .32 F7
Hayland Dro IP28 .213 B7
Hayling Ave PE19 .96 A2
Hayling Cl 4 PE29 .118 F7
Hayman's Way CB3 .99 A2
Haymarket Rd 7 CB3 .83 C3
Hayster Dr CB1 .65 E6
Hayter Cl CB1 .53 F4
Haywardsfield 4 PE3 .197 A1
Haywoods La SG8 .5 E7
Hayzen Cl CB2 .29 F8
Hazel Cl Haverhill CB9 .23 E7
Mildenhall IP28 .239 E4
Hazel Croft PE4 .204 A4
Hazel Ct 7 CB6 .210 F5
Hazel Gdns 1 PE13 .245 D4
Hazel Way PE27 .144 B4
Hazelwood Cl CB4 .83 D6
Head Fen Dro CB6 .224 F3
Headford Cl CB5 .84 D4
Headington Cl CB1 .65 F5
Headington Dr CB1 .65 F5
Headlake Dro CB5 .128 E1
Headland Ave CB9 .23 E7
Headlands
Fenstanton PE28 .121 C5
Huntingdon PE29 .141 C3
Headlands Way PE7 .189 D8
Headley Gdns CB2 .49 B4
Headley's La CB6 .217 A2
Heasman Cl CB8 .110 F5
Heath Ave SG8 .5 C6
Heath Farm Rd IP28 .213 F1
Heath Ho CB4 .84 A5
Heath La PE28 .163 A7
Heath Rd Bottisham CB1 .87 B4
Burwell CB5 .109 D5
Exning CB8 .110 B6
Gamlingay SG19 .41 A4
Helpston PE6 .231 C2
Mildenhall IP28 .239 E5
Newmarket CB8 .111 C3
Swaffham Bulbeck CB5 .108 B2
Swaffham Prior CB5 .109 A3
Warboys PE28 .165 C6
Heath Row PE1 .205 B1
Heathbell Rd CB8 .111 C3
Heathcote Cl 6 PE15 .243 F4
Heather Ave PE1 .198 A8
Heatherdale Cl PE7 .187 C5
Heatherset Way
1 Red Lodge IP28 .213 F1
2 Red Lodge IP28 .214 A1
Heathfield SG8 .5 B6
Heaton Cl Ely CB6 .240 F7
Peterborough PE3 .197 B3
Heaton Dr CB6 .240 F7
Hectare The CB2 .48 F7
Heddon Way PE27 .144 B6
Hedgelands
Peterborough PE4 .204 C5
1 Wisbech PE13 .245 C8
Hedgerley Cl CB3 .83 A2
Heffer Cl CB2 .49 C4
Heights Drove Rd PE26 .170 D6
Helen Cl 3 CB5 .84 E4
Helens Cl PE26 .171 B1
Helions Bumpstead Rd CB9 .23 F5
Helions Park Ave CB9 .24 A7
Helions Park Gdns CB9 .24 A7
Helions Park Gr CB9 .24 A7
Helions Service Rd CB9 .24 A7
Helions Wlk CB9 .24 A7
Helmsdale Gdns PE4 .204 B2
Helmsley Ct 1 PE7 .187 F5
Helpston Rd Castor PE5 .195 D2
Etton PE6 .203 C8
Glinton PE6 .203 D8
Heltwate Specl Sch PE3 197 B7
Hemingford Cres PE2 .187 E6
Hemingford Grey Prim Sch PE28 .143 D2
Hemingford Rd
Cambridge CB1 .65 B8
Hemingford Grey PE27 .143 F2
Hemington Cl 10 CB4 .208 D1
Hemlocks The 5 CB3 .47 B5
Hemmerley Dr PE7 .189 E8
Hempfield Pl CB6 .242 D4
Hempfield Rd CB6 .242 D4
Hempsals 12 PE19 .74 C6
Hempsals Rd or Meadow Dro CB4 .209 C1
Hempstead Rd 2 CB9 .38 C1
Hen Brook PE19 .74 F4
Henderson Cl CB9 .38 C1
Henford Gdns PE15 .243 D5
Henley Rd CB1 .84 B2
Henley Way CB7 .240 F6
Henry Crabb Rd CB6 .242 A6
Henry Morris Rd
Histon CB4 .104 C3
Sawston CB2 .33 A8
Henry Orbell Cl 3 PE15 243 E4
Henry St
Peterborough PE1 .198 A4
Wisbech PE13 .245 C5
Henry Warby Ave 8 PE14 .236 A5
Henshaw PE1 .198 E6
Henson Cl 3 PE13 .245 C8
Henson Rd PE15 .243 C5
Herbert Human Cl 3 CB7 .212 B4
Herbert St CB4 .83 E4
Hercules Cl 3 CB4 .83 E8
Hereford Cl 7 PE28 .208 C8
Hereward 5 PE28 .208 E6
Hereward Ave IP28 .239 C5
Hereward Cl
Haddenham CB6 .209 E4
Histon CB4 .104 C3
2 Peterborough PE1 .198 B2
Hereward Rd
Peterborough PE1 .198 B2
1 Wisbech PE13 .245 D5
Hereward St Ely CB6 .240 B4
March PE15 .243 D5
Hereward Way PE6 .231 F8
Heritage Park Prim Sch PE7 .187 F5
Hermitage Rd PE28 .208 E6
Herne Rd PE26 .220 D4
Heron Cl PE7 .189 F8
Heron Ct 1 PE19 .75 B6
Heron Pk PE1 .198 F6
Heron Rd PE13 .245 D2
Heron Way PE27 .143 F7
Heron Wlk PE15 .243 F5
Heronry Dr PE6 .196 E2
Heron's Cl CB1 .65 D4
Herons Cl 6 Ely CB6 .240 B5
Tallington PE9 .230 F6
Heronshaw PE16 .241 C6
Herrick Cl PE1 .197 E8
Herring's Cl CB5 .85 F5
Herringswell Rd
Herringswell IP28 .214 B2
Kentford CB8 .134 B4
Herschel Rd CB3 .83 B1
Hertford Cl CB6 .240 A3
Hertford La SG8 .8 E5
Hertford St CB4 .246 A4
Hervey Cl 3 CB6 .240 B3
Hethersett Cl CB8 .110 E8
Hetley PE2 .186 A4
Hexham Ct 3 PE1 .198 D3
Heydon La Elmdon CB11 .8 F4
Heydon SG8 .8 B5
Heydon Rd SG8 .7 E2
Heyford Ct 5 IP28 .239 B5
Hicks La Girton CB3 .82 E8
Peterborough PE7 .186 F5
Hicks Way 4 CB9 .24 E5
Hide Cl CB2 .32 F6
High Barns CB7 .240 E6
High Broadgate PE13 .237 F7
High Cl SG8 .8 A5
High Cswy PE7 .189 E7
High Ditch Rd CB5 .85 A4
High Fen Crooked Dro PE28 .215 B5
High Fen Straight Dro PE28 .215 B6
High Gn 2 Abbotsley PE19 57 B6
Great Shelford CB2 .49 A6
High Haden Rd PE28 .175 B1
High Leys PE27 .143 F5
High Mdw Harston CB2 .47 F3
Ramsey PE26 .172 A3
High Piece Cres CB4 .208 C1
High Rd Downham CB6 .217 F6
Gorefield PE13 .237 E3
Newton PE13 .238 A5
Tydd St Giles PE13 .237 F6
Wisbech St Mary PE13 .235 A6
High Sch Cl PE15 .243 D6
High Side PE13 .235 A8
High St Abbotsley PE19 .57 B6
Abington Pigotts SG8 .11 F5
Alconbury PE28 .150 F4
Alconbury Weston PE28 .150 D6
Ashley CB8 .91 F8
Ashwell SG7 .2 D4
Babraham CB2 .33 D8
Balsham CB1 .53 A2
Barley SG8 .6 F2
Barrington CB2 .29 E8
Barton CB3 .63 B4
Bassingbourn SG8 .12 F4
Benwick PE15 .222 A5
Bluntisham/Colne PE28 .208 C5
Bottisham CB5 .86 F5
Bourn CB3 .60 C6
Bourn CB3 .79 B3
Boxworth CB3 .101 B5
Brampton PE28 .140 E2
Brinkley CB8 .70 D2
Buckden PE19 .117 A4
Burwell CB5 .109 B8
Cambridge CB1 .65 F5
Cambridge CB1 .66 A7
Cambridge CB1 .66 C8
Cambridge CB4 .84 A4
Castle Camps CB1 .22 E3
Castor PE5 .195 F2
Catworth PE28 .136 D7
Chatteris PE16 .241 C5
Cheveley CB8 .91 C7
Chippenham CB7 .132 E8
Chrishall SG8 .8 D3
Conington CB3 .121 C1
Coton CB3 .82 B2
Cottenham CB4 .125 E4
Croxton PE19 .76 F4
Croydon SG8 .27 A7
Doddington/Wimblington PE15 .223 A5
Dry Drayton CB3 .102 B1
Earith PE28 .208 E5
Ellington PE28 .139 A4
Ely CB7 .240 D4
Eye PE6 .232 A1
Eyeworth SG19 .10 A8
Fen Ditton CB5 .84 E5
Fen Drayton CB4 .121 F5
Fenstanton PE28 .121 A6
Fowlmere SG8 .15 E8
Foxton CB2 .30 B5
Fulbourn CB1 .66 F5
Girton CB3 .103 E1
Glinton PE6 .203 E8
Grantchester CB3 .64 A4
Graveley PE19 .97 F5
Great & Little Abington CB1 34 C6
Great Chesterford CB10 .18 E2
Great Eversden CB3 .45 E8
Great Paxton PE19 .96 D4
Great Shelford CB2 .48 E3
Great Shelford CB2 .49 A5
Great Wilbraham CB1 .67 F7
Guilden Morden SG8 .10 F4
Haddenham CB6 .209 E4
Hail Weston PE19 .74 B8
Harlton CB3 .46 D5
Harston CB2 .47 F3
Haslingfield CB3 .47 B5
Hauxton CB2 .48 C5
Haverhill CB9 .24 A7
High St continued
Hemingford Abbots PE28 .143 A3
Hemingford Grey PE28 .143 C2
Hildersham CB1 .34 E5
Hilton PE28 .120 B1
Hinxton CB10 .18 B7
Histon CB4 .104 B4
Holywell-cum-Needingworth PE27 .144 F5
Horningsea CB5 .106 A1
Huntingdon PE29 .141 D4
Kimbolton PE28 .113 F4
Knapwell CB3 .100 E3
Landbeach CB4 .105 D6
Linton CB1 .35 C2
Little Paxton PE19 .95 F2
Little Staughton MK44 .93 B1
Little Wilbraham CB1 .86 E1
Littleport CB6 .242 D4
Lode CB5 .107 C2
Longstowe CB3 .59 F2
Madingley CB3 .81 F5
2 Manea PE15 .224 C4
March PE15 .243 D3
Market Deeping PE6 .231 D8
Maxey PE6 .231 C7
Melbourn SG8 .14 C5
Meldreth SG8 .14 B8
Mepal CB6 .216 E3
Mildenhall IP28 .239 C4
Milton CB4 .105 D2
Needingworth PE27 .208 A3
Newmarket CB8 .110 F3
Oakington/Longstanton CB4 .103 C6
Oakington/Longstanton CB4 .123 F3
Offord Cluny PE19 .96 F8
Orwell SG8 .45 E1
Over CB4 .208 D1
Pampisford CB2 .33 B5
Peterborough PE2 .187 A6
Pidley cum Fenton PE28 .155 E8
Rampton CB4 .124 E5
Ramsey PE26 .171 B2
Ramsey PE26 .172 A6
Royston SG8 .5 D6
St Neots PE19 .74 E5
Sawston CB2 .32 F6
Sawtry PE28 .168 B4
Shepreth SG8 .29 E4
Soham CB7 .212 B4
Somersham PE28 .208 C8
Spaldwick PE28 .137 F6
Stamford PE9 .244 B5
Stetchworth CB8 .90 A2
Stilton PE7 .176 A7
Stretham CB6 .210 F5
Sutton CB6 .216 D1
Swaffham Bulbeck CB5 .108 B1
Swaffham Prior CB5 .108 D5
Swavesey CB4 .122 E6
Tadlow SG8 .26 A3
Tilbrook PE28 .113 B6
Toft CB3 .61 D4
Tuddenham IP28 .214 D2
Warboys PE28 .164 F5
Waterbeach CB5 .106 B8
West Wickham CB1 .37 A7
West Wratting CB1 .53 F5
Whittlesford CB2 .32 C5
Wicken CB7 .211 E1
Wilburton CB6 .210 C5
Willingham CB4 .209 A1
Wisbech PE13 .245 C5
Witcham CB6 .217 A3
Wrestlingworth SG19 .25 B4
Wrestlingworth & Cockayne Hatley SG19 .25 B3
Yelling PE19 .98 C1
High St Back 2 CB7 .240 D4
High Street St Martin's PE9 .244 C4
Higham Rd IP28 .214 E1
Highbury St PE1 .198 A5
Highclere Cl CB8 .110 D8
Highclere Rd PE7 .186 D3
Highdene Rd CB1 .66 A6
Highfield Ave
Alconbury Weston PE28 .150 D6
Cambridge CB4 .83 E5
Highfield Cl CB2 .17 D8
Highfield Cotts SG8 .4 B7
Highfield Gate CB1 .66 F6
Highfield Rd Histon CB4 .104 C1
March PE15 .243 D7
Highfield Sch CB6 .240 C5
Highfields Rd CB3 .80 C2
Highgate Gn PE8 .178 D8
Highlands SG8 .5 E6
Highlands The CB8 .110 D8
Highlees Prim Sch PE3 .197 C6
Hightown Dro
Burwell CB5 .129 C4
Reach CB5 .129 B4
Highway The PE19 .94 A6
Highworth Ave CB4 .83 F5
Hilda Clarke Cl 1 PE16 241 C3
Hilda St CB4 .83 D4
Hildersham Rd CB1 .34 D7
Hill Cl
Brington & Molesworth PE28 .147 C5
Little Stukeley PE28 .151 F1
Newmarket CB8 .110 E3
Peterborough PE1 .198 D5
Sawtry PE28 .168 B3
Hill Cres CB9 .39 A1
Hill End Ramsey PE26 .172 B4
St Ives PE28 .143 B5
Hill Farm Rd CB2 .32 B3
Hill La CB9 .24 F3
Hill Rd Over CB4 .208 E1
Wistow PE26 .164 A8
Hill Rise St Ives PE27 .143 E7
St Neots PE19 .75 A5
Hill Row CB6 .209 E6
Hill Row Cswy CB6 .209 A6
Hill St 5 PE13 .245 C5
Hill View
Dry Drayton CB3 .102 D1
Lidgate CB8 .73 F8
Hillary Cl PE9 .244 D6
Hillburn Rd PE13 .245 B4
Hillcrest CB3 .102 C3
Hillcrest Ave PE7 .181 E5
Hillcrest Dr 3 PE13 .235 A2
Hillfield Alconbury PE28 .150 F5
Foxton CB2 .30 C5
Hillfield Rd CB3 .62 D6
Hills Ave CB1 .65 B5
Hills La CB6 .240 B4
Hills Rd CB2 .246 C1
Hills Road Sixth Form Coll CB1 .65 A6
Hillside Orwell SG8 .45 E2
Royston SG8 .5 D5
Sawston CB2 .32 F8
Sutton CB6 .216 D1
Hillside Cl Ellington PE28 138 F4
Ufford PE9 .230 F2
Hillside La SG8 .44 C4
Hillside Mdw CB7 .212 F1
Hillside Rd PE15 .243 B5
Hillward Cl PE2 .186 C6
Hillway CB1 .35 C2
Hilsdens Dr PE29 .142 A1
Hilton Rd PE28 .120 E3
Hilton St CB4 .208 D1
Hilton Turf Maze* PE28 .120 C1
Hinchcliffe PE2 .185 E2
Hinchinbrooke Rd PE28 117 D8
Hinchingbrooke Ctry Pk* PE29 .140 F4
Hinchingbrooke Dr PE16 .241 B4
Hinchingbrooke Ho* PE29 .141 B3
Hinchingbrooke Hospl PE29 .141 B5
Hinchingbrooke Pk* PE29 .141 B4
Hinchingbrooke Sch PE29 .141 A4
Hines Cl CB3 .63 A4
Hines La CB3 .62 C5
Hinkins Cl SG8 .14 D6
Hinton Ave CB1 .65 C5
Hinton Cl PE7 .189 D8
Hinton Rd CB1 .66 D5
Hinton View CB6 .210 A6
Hinton Way
Great Shelford CB2 .49 C6
Wilburton CB6 .210 C6
Hinxton Rd CB2 .17 E8
Hinxworth Rd SG7 .2 B4
Histon Jun Sch CB4 .104 B3
Histon Rd Cambridge CB4 .83 C4
Cottenham CB4 .104 C8
Histon Sch CB4 .104 B4
Hitches St 4 CB6 .242 D4
Hitherford CB4 .208 E1
Hive Rd CB6 .217 A4
Hives The PE19 .74 D4
HM Prison Littlehey PE18 .115 E1
HM Prison Whitemoor PE15 .228 B6
Hoadly Rd CB3 .83 B5
Hobart Ct PE15 .243 C5
Hobart Rd CB1 .65 C7
Hobbledodds Cl CB4 .122 E6
Hobson St CB1 .246 B3
Hockland Rd PE13 .237 F7
Hod Fen Dro
Denton & Caldecote PE7 .177 A7
Yaxley PE7 .181 F2
Hod Hall La CB6 .210 A5
Hodgson Ave PE4 .204 B6
Hodney Rd 2 PE6 .232 A1
Hodson's Dr PE29 .141 E5
Hodwell SG7 .2 D4
Hog Fen Dro PE7 .182 A5
Hogarth Cl PE27 .144 A7
Hogarth Pl 2 PE19 .74 D5
Hogens La PE13 .238 A5
Hogherd's La 9 PE13 .245 C5
Hoghill Dro CB6 .209 F3
Hog's La SG8 .8 D3
Holbein Rd PE27 .144 A7
Holben Cl CB3 .63 B3
Holborn Ave IP28 .239 B6
Holbrook Rd
Cambridge CB1 .65 B4
Haverhill CB9 .23 E6
Holburn View PE28 .168 B2
Holcroft PE2 .186 B3
Holdfield PE3 .197 B6
Holdich St PE3 .197 E2
Holdsworth Valley CP Sch CB8 .110 F3
Holgate La PE4 .204 B7

Holkham Mead CB5 . . . . .130 C2
Holkham Rd PE2 . . . . . .185 D3
Holland Ave PE4 . . . . . .204 D1
Holland Pk CB8 . . . . .91 C7
Holland Rd PE9 . . . . . . .244 C6
Hollands Rd CB9 . . . . . . .24 A6
Hollesley Ave CB9 . . . . . .23 C8
Holliday's Rd PE28 . . . . .208 D5
Hollies Cl SG8 . . . . .5 E6
Hollies The PE15 . . . . . .243 E7
Hollmans Cl CB1 . . . . . . .66 F4
Hollow Hill CB9 . . . . .38 B4
Hollow La PE26 . . . . . . .172 E6
Hollow Rd Chrishall SG8 . . .8 C1
Elmdon CB11 . . . . .9 C4
Ramsey Forty Foot PE26 . . .221 C2
Hollow The PE29 . . . . . .142 B6
Holly Cl Newborough PE6 207 C1
Red Lodge IP28 . . . . . . .213 F1
Holly Dr **4** PE15 . . . . . .223 A6
Holly Way **7** PE6 . . . . . .231 E8
Holly Wlk Ely CB7 . . . . . .240 F5
3 Mildenhall IP28 . . . . . .213 F8
Peterborough PE7 . . . . . . .186 D3
Hollybush Way CB1 . . . . . .35 D3
Hollycroft Cl PE14 . . . . . .236 D5
Hollycroft Rd PE14 . . . . .236 D5
Hollytrees CB3 . . . . .102 C3
Holme CE Jun Sch PE7 . .177 A4
Holme Cl Castor PE5 . . . .195 D2
Oakington/Longstanton
CB4 . . . . .103 C5
Holme Dro PE28 . . . . . .208 E7
Holme Fen Dro PE28 . . . .208 D7
Holme La **1** CB6 . . . . . .218 A6
Holme Rd Ramsey PE26 . .220 C3
Yaxley PE7 . . . . .181 E4
Holme Way CB2 . . . . .32 F8
Holmehill PE29 . . . . . . .118 F8
Holmes Dr PE13 . . . . . . .245 E6
Holmes La CB7 . . . . .212 B5
Holmes Rd PE6 . . . . . . .203 F7
Holmes The CB6 . . . . . . .242 E4
Holmes Way PE4 . . . . . .204 E2
Holmewood Cres PE7 . . . .176 F4
Holmewood Cres PE7 . . . .176 F4
Holmsey Gn IP28 . . . . . .213 F8
Holmsey Green Gdns **2**
IP28 . . . . .213 F8
Holt Cl **8** PE8 . . . . .230 B1
Holt Fen CB6 . . . . .211 B7
Holyrood Cl CB4 . . . . .83 C6
Holywell Cl **1** PE3 . . . . . .197 A1
Holywell Ferry Rd CB4 . . .121 F6
Holywell Front PE27 . . . .144 F2
Holywell Sch PE27 . . . . .208 A2
Holywell Way PE3 . . . . . .196 F2
Home Cl Grafham PE28 . . .116 A6
Histon CB4 . . . . .104 A4
Home End CB1 . . . . .67 A4
Home Farm Cl
Abbotsley PE19 . . . . .57 B6
Rampton CB4 . . . . .124 F4
Home Farm Rd PE28 . . . .143 B5
Home Pasture PE4 . . . . .204 B5
Homefield Cl CB4 . . . . . .104 C3
Homefield Rd CB9 . . . . . . .23 F5
Homerton Coll CB2 . . . . . .65 A5
Homerton St CB2 . . . . . . .65 A6
Homestall Cres CB9 . . . . . .38 B4
Homestead **12** PE28 . . . .215 C1
Homestead Dr **6** IP28 . .213 F8
Homing The CB5 . . . . .84 E3
Honey Dro PE15 . . . . . . .223 E4
Honey Hill
9 Cambridge CB3 . . . . . .83 C3
Fen Drayton CB4 . . . . . . .122 A4
Fenstanton PE28 . . . . . . .121 B6
Gamlingay SG19 . . . . . . .41 D4
West Wratting CB1 . . . . . .53 E5
Honeydon Ave PE19 . . . . . .74 B5
Honeyhill PE4 . . . . .205 A1
Honeyhill Rd PE13 . . . . . .237 C2
Honeysome Rd PE16 . . . .241 A5
Honeysuckle Cl
Haverhill CB9 . . . . .38 E1
Red Lodge IP28 . . . . . . .134 A8
2 Soham CB7 . . . . .212 B4
Honeysuckle Ct PE2 . . . . .186 D7
Honeyway SG8 . . . . .5 E6
Hoo Cl PE19 . . . . .117 B4
Hoof Cl CB6 . . . . .242 D3
Hook Dro PE15 . . . . .228 B1
Hook La PE15 . . . . .223 C7
Hook Rd PE15 . . . . .223 C7
Hook's Dro PE13 . . . . . . .234 C4
Hooper St CB1 . . . . .84 A1
Hop Row CB6 . . . . .210 A6
Hopbine Ct PE26 . . . . . . .171 F5
Hope St CB1 . . . . .65 B8
Hopkins Cl CB4 . . . . .84 A6
Hopkins Hospl* PE9 . . . .244 B4
Hopton Rise CB9 . . . . .38 B1
Horn La Kirtling CB8 . . . . .72 B5
Linton CB1 . . . . .35 B2
Hornbeam Rd IP28 . . . . .239 D5
Horningsea Rd
Fen Ditton CB5 . . . . .84 F6
Horningsea CB5 . . . . .85 A8
Horse & Gate St CB4 . . . .121 F5
Horse Common Cl PE29 141 E5
Horse Common La PE29 141 E5
Horse Dro PE26 . . . . .221 A1
Horse Fair **2** PE13 . . . . .245 C5
Horse Ware CB4 . . . . . . .208 D2

Horsegate
Market Deeping PE6 . . . . .231 E8
Whittlesey PE7 . . . . .189 D7
Horsegate Gdns PE16 . . . .241 C5
Horsegate La PE7 . . . . . .189 C7
Horsehead Dro PE14 . . . .229 F4
Horseheath Gn CB1 . . . . . .37 C1
Horseheath Rd
Linton CB1 . . . . .35 D2
Withersfield CB9 . . . . .38 A4
Horsemoor Rd PE15 . . . .223 D8
Horseracing Forensic
Laboratory CB7 . . . . . . .131 E6
Horseshoe Cl
Balsham CB1 . . . . .53 C2
Haverhill CB9 . . . . .9 B4
Horseshoe La
2 Haverhill CB9 . . . . .23 E7
4 Stamford PE9 . . . . . . .244 B5
Horseshoe Terr PE13 . . . .245 B7
Horseshoes La CB1 . . . . . .54 D5
Horseshoes Way PE28 . . . .140 D2
Horsey Hill (Civil War Fort)*
PE7 . . . . .188 A4
Horsham Cl **3** CB9 . . . . . .38 C1
Horsley Hale CB6 . . . . . .242 D6
Hospital Rd PE15 . . . . . .222 E6
Hostmoor Ave PE15 . . . .243 A7
Hotel La PE28 . . . . .151 F3
Houghton Ave PE2 . . . . .187 F5
Houghton Gdns CB6 . . . .240 B4
Houghton Hill Rd PE28 . .143 B5
Houghton Mill National
Trust* PE28 . . . . .143 A4
Houghton Prim Sch
PE28 . . . . .143 A5
Houghton Rd PE27 . . . . .143 E5
Houghtons La CB7 . . . . . .213 B5
Housman Ave SG8 . . . . . . .5 C8
Howard Cl CB5 . . . . .84 D4
Howard De Walden Way
CB8 . . . . .111 A4
Howard Rd Cambridge CB5 84 E4
Eaton Socon PE19 . . . . . . .74 C1
Meldreth SG8 . . . . .14 A8
Howard's La CB1 . . . . .37 A2
Howe Rd CB9 . . . . .38 F1
Howes Pl CB3 . . . . .83 A5
Howitt's Gdns PE19 . . . . . .75 A2
Howitt's La **5** PE19 . . . . . .74 F3
Howitts La PE19 . . . . .74 F4
Howland PE2 . . . . .186 A3
Howlett Way CB5 . . . . .86 E6
Howletts Hill PE13 . . . . . .245 C4
Hoylake Dr PE7 . . . . .187 C5
Huddleston Way CB2 . . . . .33 A7
Hudson Cl CB9 . . . . .24 C6
Hudson L Ctr PE13 . . . . . .245 A5
Hulatt Rd CB1 . . . . .65 C4
Humber Rd PE29 . . . . . . .141 F7
Humberdale Way PE28 . . .164 F5
Humberley Cl **1** PE19 . . . . .74 F3
Humberstone Rd CB4 . . . .246 C4
Humphreys Rd CB9 . . . . . .83 E6
Humphries Way CB4 . . . .105 D3
Hunchback La PE15 . . . . .238 E2
Hundred Rd PE15 . . . . . .243 C8
Hundreds Rd PE6 . . . . . . .232 C6
Hungate Rd PE14 . . . . . .236 E6
Hunsbury Cl PE7 . . . . . . .189 F6
Hunters Chase PE15 . . . .243 E2
Hunters Way
Kimbolton PE28 . . . . .113 F5
Royston SG8 . . . . .5 E6
3 Sawtry PE28 . . . . . . .168 B3
Hunting Ave PE2 . . . . . . .186 F7
Hunting Gr CB3 . . . . .101 B5
Huntingdon Boat Club
PE29 . . . . .141 F4
Huntingdon Cty Jun & Inf Sch
PE29 . . . . .141 E6
Huntingdon Rd
Boxworth CB3 . . . . .101 E7
Brampton PE28 . . . . .141 A2
Cambridge CB3 . . . . .83 A5
Chatteris PE16 . . . . .241 B4
Fen Drayton CB4 . . . . . . .121 D2
Houghton & Wyton PE28 . .142 F5
Lolworth CB3 . . . . .102 B5
Ramsey PE26 . . . . .171 C2
St Neots PE19 . . . . .75 A8
Sawston SG8 . . . . .33 A8
Huntingdon Recn Ctr
PE29 . . . . .141 D6
Huntingdon St PE19 . . . . . .74 F6
Huntingdon Sta PE29 . . . .141 C4
Huntingdonshire Regional
Coll
Huntingdon PE29 . . . . . . .141 E6
St Neots PE19 . . . . .74 F6
Huntings Dr **5** PE28 . . . .168 B4
Huntley Cl PE5 . . . . .84 E4
Huntly Gr PE1 . . . . .198 B4
Huntly Rd PE2 . . . . .186 F2
Hunt's Gate PE12 . . . . . .237 F8
Hunts Cl **4** PE15 . . . . . .222 F5
Hunts End PE19 . . . . . . .117 B4
Hunts La CB10 . . . . .18 B7
Hunts Rd CB2 . . . . .17 D8
Huntsmans Gate PE1 . . . .196 F3
Huntsmill CB1 . . . . .66 E4
Hurdle Dro IP28 . . . . . . .213 D8
Hurdleditch Rd SG8 . . . . . .28 D8
Hurn Rd PE6 . . . . .203 E3

Hurrell Rd CB4 . . . . .83 C6
Hurrell's Row CB2 . . . . . . .47 C2
Hurricane Cl PE29 . . . . . .141 B8
Hurrys Cl CB2 . . . . .32 E7
Hurst Ave **1** PE15 . . . . . .243 E4
Hurst La **1** CB6 . . . . .240 A6
Hurst Park Ave CB4 . . . . . .83 E5
Hurts Croft **1** CB7 . . . . . .212 E1
Hut Field La CB1 . . . . .99 A3
Hyholmes PE3 . . . . .196 F7
Hyll Cl CB10 . . . . .18 D3
Hyperion Way CB8 . . . . . .110 D8
Hythe Cl CB1 . . . . .130 A3
Hythe La CB5 . . . . .130 A3
Hythe The CB6 . . . . .242 D5
Hythegate PE4 . . . . .204 D4

I

Ibberson's Dro PE15 . . . .221 F4
Ibbott Cl PE2 . . . . .187 E5
Ibbott Cres **7** PE28 . . . .215 C1
Iceni Way CB8 . . . . .110 B8
Icewell Hill CB8 . . . . .111 A4
Ickleton Cl Duxford CB2 . .17 E7
Elmdon CB11 . . . . .9 A4
Great Chesterford CB10 . . .18 C2
Hinxton CB10 . . . . .18 B6
Icknield Cl Cheveley CB8 . .91 C5
Ickleton CB10 . . . . .18 A3
Icknield CP Sch CB2 . . . . .33 A8
Icknield Walk Fst Sch SG8 . .5 F7
Icknield Wlk CB2 . . . . .30 C5
Ida Darwin Hospl CB1 . . .66 D5
Ihlee Cl PE4 . . . . .204 E1
Ilex Cl PE7 . . . . .186 C3
Ilex Rd PE27 . . . . .144 B6
Illing's Lane La PE28 . . . .164 A1
Illingworth Way CB2 . . . . .30 C5
Impala Dr CB1 . . . . .66 A7
Imperial War Mus* CB2 . .31 F1
Impett's Cl **1** CB7 . . . . . . .67 A4
Impington La CB4 . . . . . .104 C3
Impington Village Coll
CB4 . . . . .104 D3
India La PE28 . . . . .151 F2
Infield Rd PE28 . . . . .167 C7
Ingham Hall Gdns **2**
PE13 . . . . .234 D7
Ingham Rd CB9 . . . . .24 A8
Ingle Rd **3** PE14 . . . . . .236 B5
Ingle's La **14** PE15 . . . . .223 A5
Ingoldsby Cl **3** PE15 . . . .243 D2
Ingram St PE15 . . . . .141 E4
Inham's Rd PE7 . . . . .189 E6
Inhams Cl **1** PE14 . . . . . .234 D5
Inhams Way PE28 . . . . . .116 A7
Inkerman Rise PE19 . . . . . .74 C5
Inley Dro PE12 . . . . .237 A8
Institute of Astronomy
CB3 . . . . .83 A3
Institute of Criminology
CB3 . . . . .83 C1
Institute of Public Health
CB2 . . . . .65 B2
International Extension Coll
CB1 . . . . .65 A8
Inverness Cl CB4 . . . . .84 A5
Iram Dro CB4 . . . . .209 B1
Ireton Cl PE19 . . . . .74 F3
Ireton Way PE15 . . . . . . .243 D2
Ireton's Way
Chatteris PE16 . . . . .241 F2
Mepal PE16 . . . . .216 C6
Irnham Rd PE9 . . . . .244 C4
Ironmonger St **2** PE2 . .244 C5
Irving Burgess Cl PE7 . . .189 C8
Isaacson Rd CB5 . . . . . . .109 C8
Isham Rd **1** PE3 . . . . . . .197 D4
Isherwood Cl **3** SG8 . . . . . .5 B8
Isinglass Cl CB8 . . . . . . .111 E2
Isle Bridge Rd PE14 . . . . .236 F2
Isle Coll PE16 . . . . .241 C5
Isle of Ely Way
Chatteris PE16 . . . . .241 C7
March PE15 . . . . .243 A4
Isleham CE Sch CB7 . . . .213 A5
Isleham Rd CB7 . . . . .212 F2
Isons Cl SG8 . . . . .15 E8
Itter Cres PE4 . . . . .197 E8
Ivan Clark's Cnr CB1 . . . . .34 C7
Ivatt St CB4 . . . . .125 E5
Ivatt Way PE3 . . . . .197 C7
Ivel Cl PE19 . . . . .74 C4
Ivelbury Cl PE19 . . . . . . .117 A3
Iver Cl CB1 . . . . .65 F7
Ives Dro PE7 . . . . .189 A2
Ivesdyke Cl **4** PE13 . . . .238 B2
Ivett's Cl CB3 . . . . .45 E7
Ivy Field CB3 . . . . .63 B4
Ivy Gr PE4 . . . . .204 D2
Ivy Way PE28 . . . . .138 A6
Ixworth Cl **8** PE6 . . . . . .232 A1
Ixworth Rd CB9 . . . . .23 E6
Izaak Walton Way CB4 . . . .84 C5
Izzard Rise PE19 . . . . .96 C3

J

Jack Haws La **4** PE9 . . . .230 D4
Jack Hunt Sch PE3 . . . .197 B3
Jack Hunt Swimming Pool
PE3 . . . . .197 B3
Jack Jarvis Cl **5** CB8 . . .111 A3

Jack Warren Gn CB5 . . . . .84 F3
Jack's Corner Dro PE26 172 E3
Jackson Cl CB2 . . . . .48 C5
Jackson's La CB10 . . . . . . .18 D3
Jackson's Sq SG10 . . . . . . .18 D3
Jackson's Way SG8 . . . . . .15 E8
James Carter Rd IP28 . . . .239 A6
James Ct PE19 . . . . .74 F2
James Essex Dr **1** CB6 .240 E7
James Gage Cl PE16 . . . .241 B3
James St CB5 . . . . .246 C3
Janus Cl CB9 . . . . .24 D6
Jarman Way SG8 . . . . .5 B7
Jarman's La IP28 . . . . . . .213 D7
Jarvis Way CB8 . . . . .110 E5
Jasmin Cl PE13 . . . . .245 F7
Jasmine Ct PE2 . . . . .185 E2
Jasmine Way PE7 . . . . . . .181 F6
Jay Cl CB9 . . . . .24 C7
Jaywick Rd CB9 . . . . .24 A8
Jeavons La **6** CB3 . . . . . .79 C3
Jedburgh Cl **3** CB4 . . . . .83 E7
Jefferson Cl **22** PE6 . . . .230 B1
Jeffery Ave **4** PE13 . . . . .245 E7
Jeffrey Cl **2** SG8 . . . . . . .5 C8
Jellicoe Pl **3** PE19 . . . . . .74 A2
Jenkins Cl **4** PE19 . . . . . .74 B2
Jenyns Cl CB5 . . . . .86 E7
Jepps La SG8 . . . . .5 A5
Jermyn Cl CB4 . . . . .83 D6
Jerusalem Dro CB6 . . . . .217 A5
Jesus Coll CB5 . . . . .246 B3
Jesus La CB5 . . . . .246 B3
Jesus Terr CB1 . . . . .246 C3
Jetty The **2** PE13 . . . . . .235 C7
Jew House Dro PE14 . . . .235 E3
Jim Mollison Ct **2** IP28 239 B5
Job's La **2** PE15 . . . . . . .243 C1
John Amner Cl CB6 . . . . .240 D6
John Breay Cl SG8 . . . . . . .29 D4
John Clare Sch PE6 . . . . .231 B4
John Clarke Ct CB4 . . . . . .84 A6
John F Kennedy Ct **2**
PE13 . . . . .245 D4
John Falkner Inf Sch
CB2 . . . . .32 E7
John Impey Way CB5 . . . . .14 D6
John Mansfield Sec Sch
PE1 . . . . .198 B8
John Paxton Jun Sch
CB2 . . . . .32 F8
John St Cambridge CB1 . .246 C2
Royston SG8 . . . . .5 D6
John Thompson Rd **3**
PE13 . . . . .245 D4
John's Cl **5** SG8 . . . . .15 E8
Johnson's Dro PE13 . . . . .234 B7
Joiner's Cl CB1 . . . . .35 B2
Joiner's Rd CB1 . . . . .35 B2
Jolley Way CB4 . . . . .83 F6
Jones Cl **1** PE15 . . . . . .243 B3
Jones Ct PE26 . . . . .172 B7
Jones La PE7 . . . . .190 C7
Jones's Dro PE7 . . . . .221 F8
Jopling Way CB2 . . . . .48 C4
Jordan Mews **2** PE1 . . . .198 B3
Jordans Yd CB1 . . . . .246 A3
Jorose St **4** PE3 . . . . . . .197 A3
Joscelynes CB2 . . . . .49 C4
Josiah Ct CB5 . . . . .106 C8
Joyce's Cl CB2 . . . . .32 F6
Jubilee Ave PE28 . . . . . . .164 D6
Jubilee Cl Isleham CB7 . . .213 A5
Little Paxton PE19 . . . . . . .95 F2
Waterbeach CB5 . . . . . . .106 A8
Jubilee Cl CB8 . . . . .90 A1
Jubilee End SG8 . . . . .11 B2
Jubilee St PE2 . . . . .186 F8
Jubilee Terr CB7 . . . . . . .240 D3
Jubilee Way SG8 . . . . .11 B2
Judson Ct **3** PE29 . . . . .141 F8
Julian Cl CB3 . . . . .24 D7
Julius Martin La CB7 . . . .212 A4
Junction Rd IP28 . . . . . . .239 B5
Juniper Cl IP28 . . . . .239 E5
Juniper Cres PE3 . . . . . . .197 A2
Juniper Dr CB7 . . . . .240 F5
Jupiter Cl **2** CB9 . . . . . . .24 C6
Justinian Cl CB9 . . . . .24 D6
Jutland Rise PE19 . . . . . . .74 C5

K

Kathleen Elliot Way CB1 .65 F7
Kay Hitch Way CB4 . . . . .104 B2
Keates Rd CB1 . . . . .66 A5
Keats Cl **1** SG8 . . . . .5 C8
Keats Ct PE19 . . . . .74 C5
Keats Way PE1 . . . . .197 D7
Keble Cl PE9 . . . . .244 A7
Kedleston Rd PE7 . . . . . . .187 F6
Keeton Rd PE1 . . . . .197 E7
Kefford Cl SG8 . . . . .12 F5
Kelful Cl PE7 . . . . .190 D7
Kelsey Cres CB1 . . . . .66 A7
Kelsey Kerridge Sports H
CB1 . . . . .246 C1
Kelsey Way PE15 . . . . . . .243 D2
Kelvin Cl CB1 . . . . .65 D5
Kemmann La CB3 . . . . . . .79 B3
Ken Stimpson Comp Sch
PE4 . . . . .204 B4
Kendal Cl PE4 . . . . .204 F2
Kendal Way CB4 . . . . .84 A6
Kendrick Cl PE2 . . . . .187 D6
Kenilworth Ave PE7 . . . . .188 C4
Kenilworth Cl **3** PE19 . . . .74 C5

Kenlan Rd PE13 . . . . .245 D6
Kennedy Rd CB7 . . . . .213 A5
Kennels Rd PE6 . . . . .196 D4
Kennet Gdns PE4 . . . . . .204 E1
Kennetside CB8 . . . . .73 C1
Kennett Prim Sch CB8 . .133 F5
Kennett Rd or Moulton Rd
CB8 . . . . .112 F7
Kennett Sta CB8 . . . . . . .133 F3
Kennulphs Cl **3** PE6 . . . .232 C8
Kent Cl Ely CB6 . . . . .240 B5
St Ives PE27 . . . . .143 E7
Kent Rd Huntingdon PE29 141 E8
Peterborough PE3 . . . . . . .197 E2
Kent Way CB4 . . . . .83 F7
Kentings CB3 . . . . .62 B5
Kentmere Pl **1** PE4 . . . . .204 F2
Kents La CB7 . . . . .212 B4
Kentwell Pl CB5 . . . . .130 C2
Kenwood Gdns CB1 . . . . . .35 E2
Kerridge Cl CB1 . . . . .84 A1
Kesters Cl CB3 . . . . .81 B2
Kesteven Cl **6** PE6 . . . . .231 E8
Kesteven Rd PE9 . . . . . . .244 B7
Kestrel Cl Cottenham CB4 125 E5
Huntingdon PE29 . . . . . . .142 A7
Kestrel Dr **2** PE14 . . . . .245 D2
Kestrel Pl **4** PE19 . . . . . .75 B7
Kestrel Rd CB9 . . . . .24 C7
Kestrel Way **7** SG8 . . . . . .5 B8
Keswick Cl **1** PE4 . . . . . .204 F3
Kettering Rd PE9 . . . . . . .244 B2
Kettlefields CB8 . . . . .89 F1
Kettles Cl CB4 . . . . .103 C5
Keynes Rd CB5 . . . . .84 D4
Keyston Rd PE28 . . . . . . .135 D2
Kidmans Cl Hilton PE28 . .120 B1
Newton CB2 . . . . .31 B7
Kigezi Int Sch of Medicine
CB1 . . . . .246 B2
Kildare Dr PE3 . . . . .197 C4
Kilham PE2 . . . . .185 C2
Kilkenny Ave CB6 . . . . . . .240 E7
Kilmaine Cl CB4 . . . . .83 F8
Kiln Cl
2 Little Downham CB6 . .218 B7
St Ives PE27 . . . . .143 E6
Kiln House Yd SG8 . . . . . . .5 C6
Kiln La CB7 . . . . .240 F5
Kilverstone PE4 . . . . .204 B6
Kim Rd PE28 . . . . .114 A7
Kimberley Rd CB4 . . . . . .246 C4
Kimbolton Ct PE1 . . . . . .197 F3
Kimbolton Rd
Hail Weston PE19 . . . . . . .74 A8
Pertenhall MK44 . . . . . . .113 D1
Kimbolton Sch PE28 . . . .113 F4
Kinderley Cty Prim Sch
PE13 . . . . .237 F6
Kinderley Rd PE13 . . . . . .245 C8
King Cob CB6 . . . . .210 F5
King Edgar Cl CB6 . . . . . .240 D7
King Edward Rd PE16 . . .241 C5
King Edward VII Rd CB8 110 E5
King George Ave CB8 . . . .110 B8
King Hedges Prim Sch
CB4 . . . . .83 F7
King James Way SG8 . . . . .5 D6
King St Cambridge CB1 . .246 B3
Doddington/Wimblington
PE15 . . . . .223 B7
Mildenhall IP28 . . . . .239 C4
14 Over PE28 . . . . .208 D1
1 Peterborough PE1 . . . .198 A2
Rampton CB4 . . . . .124 E4
Somersham PE28 . . . . . . .215 B1
West Deeping PE6 . . . . . .231 A8
Wisbech PE13 . . . . .245 C5
Kingdon Ave CB7 . . . . . . .219 B5
Kingfisher Cl Bourn CB3 . . .60 C6
Chatteris PE16 . . . . .241 C6
Haverhill CB9 . . . . .24 C8
March PE15 . . . . .243 E5
Sawston SG8 . . . . .32 E6
Yaxley PE7 . . . . .181 D5
Kingfisher Dr
Burwell CB5 . . . . .130 B4
6 Wisbech PE14 . . . . . .245 D2
Kingfisher Rd PE7 . . . . . .189 F8
Kingfisher Way
Cottenham CB4 . . . . .125 D5
The Stukeleys PE29 . . . . .141 A6
Kingfishers PE2 . . . . .185 D6
King's Ave CB7 . . . . .240 E7
King's Delph Dro PE7 . . .187 E2
King's Dyke PE7 . . . . . . .188 E6
King's Gate CB3 . . . . .78 E1
King's Gdns
Huntingdon PE29 . . . . . . .141 D5
Peterborough PE1 . . . . . .198 A5
King's Hedges Rd CB4 . . .83 D7
King's La Cambridge CB1 .246 A2
Elmdon CB11 . . . . .9 A3
St Neots PE19 . . . . .75 A5
King's Par CB2 . . . . .246 A2
King's Rd CB3 . . . . .64 B7
King's Wk **7** PE13 . . . . . .245 C5
Kings Cl Huntingdon PE29 142 A7
Mildenhall IP28 . . . . .239 C5
Kings Coll CB2 . . . . .246 A2
Kings Coll Sch CB3 . . . . . .83 C1
Kings Delph PE7 . . . . . . .188 C5
Kings Dr CB8 . . . . .111 B1
Kings Dyke Cl PE2 . . . . . .187 E6
Kings Gr CB3 . . . . .63 B4
Kings Hedges PE27 . . . . .144 A6
Kings Mill La
Great Shelford CB2 . . . . . .48 F4

Kings Mill La continued
[2] Stamford PE9 ......244 B4
Kings Par CB7 ......212 B3
Kings Rd Eaton Socon PE19 74 B3
Hardwick CB3 ......81 A2
Peterborough PE2 ......187 B6
St Ives PE27 ......144 A4
St Neots PE19 ......74 F6
Stamford PE9 ......244 B6
Wisbech PE13 ......245 C4
Kings Ripton Rd PE29 ......152 D1
Kings Sch Ely CB6 ......240 C5
Peterborough PE1 ......198 A4
Kingsbridge Ct PE4 ......204 A5
Kingsbrook PE27 ......144 A5
Kingsland Way PE9 ......2 D4
Kingsley Ave PE13 ......245 B4
Kingsley Cl [1] PE9 ......230 D3
Kingsley Rd PE1 ......198 C4
Kingsley St PE15 ......243 D5
Kingsmead Ct CB6 ......242 E4
Kingston Cl PE29 ......141 E8
Kingston Dr PE2 ......187 E6
Kingston Pas [2] CB8 ......111 A3
Kingston Rd CB3 ......61 D1
Kingston St CB1 ......65 A8
Kingston Vale SG8 ......5 E5
Kingston Way PE28 ......163 F6
Kingsway
Duxford Airfield CB2 ......31 F1
Leverington PE13 ......245 F7
Mildenhall IP28 ......239 C4
Newmarket CB8 ......110 F4
Royston SG8 ......5 D8
Kingswood Rd PE15 ......243 C3
Kinnaird Way CB1 ......65 C4
Kinnears Wlk PE2 ......185 F2
Kinross Rd CB4 ......84 A5
Kintbury PE2 ......17 D8
Kipling Ct PE1 ......197 E8
Kipling Pl [1] PE19 ......74 D5
Kipling Rd [1] SG8 ......5 E8
Kirby Cl CB4 ......83 F5
Kirby Cross Ave CB6 ......242 B5
Kirby Rd CB5 ......127 C1
Kirby Terr CB5 ......127 B1
Kirby Wlk [2] PE3 ......197 C5
Kirby's Cl [12] CB4 ......208 D1
Kirk Ogden Cl PE15 ......243 D3
Kirkgate PE13 ......237 F7
Kirkgate St PE13 ......245 E7
Kirkham's La PE14 ......236 C4
Kirkmeadow PE3 ......197 A8
Kirk's La PE14 ......235 B3
Kirkstall PE2 ......186 B3
Kirkton Gate PE3 ......197 A1
Kirkwood Cl PE3 ......197 E2
Kirkwood Rd CB4 ......83 F7
Kirtling Rd Kirtling CB8 ......72 D1
Wooddtton CB8 ......71 F8
Wooddtton CB8 ......90 A1
Kisby Ave PE29 ......142 A1
Kite Cl PE29 ......142 A7
Kitson Gdns CB6 ......210 F5
Knapp Rise CB3 ......47 A5
Knapp The [2] CB3 ......47 A5
Knaresborough Ct [10]
PE19 ......74 F1
Knarr Fen Rd PE6 ......202 D8
Knaves Acre Dro CB7 ......212 E5
Kneesworth Ho Hospl
SG8 ......13 C5
Kneesworth Rd SG8 ......13 C8
Kneesworth St SG8 ......5 C7
Knight's Cl [11] PE15 ......223 A5
Knight's End Rd
March PE15 ......222 C8
[1] March PE15 ......243 C1
Knights Cl
Eaton Socon PE19 ......74 B4
[13] Leverington PE13 ......238 B2
Knights Way CB4 ......105 D3
Knipe Cl PE29 ......141 B7
Knowle Ct CB6 ......242 B5
Knowles Ave PE28 ......164 E5
Knowles Cl PE28 ......140 E2
Knutsford Rd SG8 ......12 E4
Kooreman Ave PE13 ......245 D7
Kyle Cres PE28 ......140 D2
Kym Rd PE19 ......74 C4

L

Laburnum Ave
Mildenhall IP28 ......239 E5
Yaxley PE7 ......181 F6
Laburnum Cl
Cambridge CB4 ......83 F4
Red Lodge IP28 ......213 F1
[5] Wisbech PE13 ......245 E4
Laburnum Gr
March PE15 ......243 C6
Peterborough PE1 ......198 B8
Laburnum La CB5 ......130 A3
Laburnum Way PE27 ......144 A5
Lacey's La CB8 ......110 B7
Lacey's Way CB2 ......32 D1
Lacks Cl CB4 ......125 D3
Laddus Bank Elm PE14 ......236 C1
Upwell PE14 ......236 D1
Laddus Dro PE14 ......229 B8
Lady Adrian Sch CB4 ......83 C1
Lady Charlotte Rd PE7 ......186 D3
Lady Lodge Dr PE2 ......186 A5
Lady Margaret Rd [1]
CB3 ......83 C3
Lady Smith Ave PE7 ......189 F8

Lady Way PE19 ......74 B4
Ladybower Way PE4 ......204 E3
Lady's Dro PE14 ......236 D6
Ladywalk CB4 ......123 F3
Lake Ave PE14 ......229 F3
Lake Ct PE13 ......245 D4
Lake Dro PE7 ......190 E6
Lake Way PE29 ......141 F6
Lakefield Ave PE19 ......96 A2
Lakes Dro CB6 ......209 F3
Lakeside
Peterborough PE7 ......186 C2
Peterborough PE4 ......204 D4
Lakeside Cl
Little Paxton PE19 ......96 A2
Perry PE28 ......115 D3
Lakeside L Ctr PE2 ......186 A5
Lakeway [8] PE28 ......215 C1
Lambert Mews PE9 ......244 C4
Lambeth Wlk PE9 ......244 A6
Lamble Cl IP28 ......213 F8
Lambourn Cl [1] CB2 ......64 D3
Lambourne Rd CB3 ......81 A3
Lamb's La
Cottenham CB4 ......125 D3
Glatton PE28 ......175 D2
Lamb's Pl PE15 ......243 D4
Lambs Hill Dro PE15 ......228 B1
Lammas Field [4] CB3 ..64 C7
Lammas Gdns PE29 ......141 D5
Lammas Rd PE1 ......198 A7
Lammas Way
St Ives PE27 ......143 F4
St Neots PE19 ......74 E6
Lamport Dr PE29 ......141 F8
Lancaster Cl
Old Hurst PE28 ......154 D6
Warboys PE28 ......164 F4
Lancaster Ct PE7 ......181 F6
Lancaster Dr PE27 ......144 A6
Lancaster Rd
Mildenhall IP28 ......213 E8
Ramsey PE26 ......171 E3
[10] Stamford PE9 ......244 B6
Lancaster Way Ely CB6 ......217 F1
Godmanchester PE29 ......141 E4
Huntingdon PE29 ......141 B8
Yaxley PE7 ......181 F6
Lancaster Way Bsns Pk
CB6 ......217 F1
Lancelot Way PE28 ......121 C5
Lancing Cl PE4 ......204 C3
Landbeach Rd CB5 ......105 D3
Landcliffe Cl PE27 ......144 B5
Lander Cl [5] CB4 ......105 C3
Landwade Rd
Exning CB8 ......131 B4
Fordham CB8 ......131 D5
Lane The Easton PE28 ......138 B4
Hauxton CB2 ......48 B4
Old Hurst PE28 ......154 E6
Stow Longa PE28 ......137 B2
West Deeping PE6 ......231 B7
Lanes The
Great Wilbraham CB1 ......67 F8
Over CB4 ......208 D1
St Ives PE28 ......143 A5
Langdale Cl [5] CB1 ......66 A7
Langdyke PE1 ......198 F6
Langford Rd PE2 ......187 A3
Langham Rd CB1 ......65 C6
Langham Way Ely CB6 ......240 E2
Haverhill CB9 ......38 B1
Langley PE3 ......197 B8
Langley Cl PE27 ......144 A4
Langley Way PE28 ......143 B1
Langton Rd PE1 ......198 D7
Langwood Cl [7] PE19 ......74 C6
Langwood Fen Dro
PE16 ......216 D8
Langwood Hill Dro
PE16 ......216 B7
Lankester Rd SG8 ......5 C5
Lansbury Cl [4] PE19 ......74 E4
Lansdowne Cl CB6 ......240 B3
Lansdowne Rd
Cambridge CB3 ......82 F3
Yaxley PE7 ......181 F6
Lansdowne Way PE2 ......186 D7
Lantree Cres CB2 ......64 D1
Lapwing Ct IP28 ......239 D4
Lapwing Dr PE7 ......190 A8
Larch Cl PE7 ......181 F6
Larch Gr PE1 ......198 C6
Larham Way PE16 ......241 B5
Lark Cl IP28 ......213 F4
Lark Cres PE29 ......142 A6
Lark End PE19 ......117 B3
Lark Hill CB8 ......112 E5
Lark Rd IP28 ......239 D4
Lark Rise CB3 ......80 F3
Lark Way PE28 ......150 E4
Larkfield Rd CB7 ......240 E6
Larkhall Rd CB7 ......212 D1
Larkin Cl Cambridge CB4 ......84 A6
Royston SG8 ......13 D1
Larkins Rd SG8 ......26 F6
Larks Cl CB9 ......24 C7
Larksfield PE13 ......245 C4
Larkspur Cl
[4] Red Lodge IP28 ......213 F1
[3] Red Lodge IP28 ......214 A1
Latham Ave PE2 ......186 C6
Latham Cl CB2 ......64 D6
Latham Rd Cambridge CB2 64 D6
Huntingdon PE29 ......141 C8
Latimer Cl CB5 ......84 E3
Latin Cl PE19 ......118 A2

Lattersey Cl PE7 ......189 F7
Laundress La CB3 ......246 A2
Laundry La CB1 ......65 D5
Laureate CP Sch CB8 ......110 E6
Laureate Gdns CB8 ......110 E6
Laureate Paddocks CB8 110 E6
Laureate Sch Rd CB8 ......110 E6
Laurel Cl Haverhill CB9 ......38 D2
Mepal CB6 ......216 E3
[9] Red Lodge IP28 ......214 A1
Sawtry PE28 ......168 A3
Yaxley PE7 ......181 D4
Laurel Dr [2] PE6 ......232 F3
Laurels Cl [3] PE28 ......213 F1
Laurels The PE15 ......243 E7
Lavender Cl [3] PE28 ......213 F1
Lavender Cres PE1 ......198 B8
Lavender Field CB9 ......23 D8
Lavender Rd CB4 ......84 A7
Lavenham Ct PE2 ......186 C7
Lavington Grange PE1 ......198 E6
Law Cl CB6 ......242 D3
Lawn Ave PE1 ......198 A7
Lawn La
Little Downham CB6 ......218 A7
Sutton CB6 ......216 E1
Lawn The CB2 ......32 C5
Lawns Cres CB6 ......218 A4
Lawns The Cambridge CB3 ......83 A4
[2] Everton SG19 ......40 A3
Melbourn SG8 ......14 C5
Wisbech PE13 ......245 B6
Lawrance Lea CB2 ......47 F2
Lawrence Ave PE7 ......187 C2
Lawrence Cl CB3 ......82 D8
Lawrence Rd
Eaton Socon PE19 ......74 C5
Ramsey PE26 ......172 C7
Wittering PE8 ......230 B1
Lawrence Way CB4 ......83 F7
Law's Cl PE6 ......206 F1
Laws Cres PE28 ......140 C4
Lawson Ave PE2 ......187 D6
Laxton Ave CB3 ......81 A3
Laxton Cl PE19 ......74 C4
Laxton Grange [8] PE28 208 C5
Laxton Way CB4 ......84 C6
Layer Rd CB9 ......23 E7
Layton Pk SG8 ......5 D5
Layton Cres PE28 ......140 D2
Lea Brooks Cl PE28 ......164 F4
Lea Gdns PE3 ......197 F1
Lea Rd PE28 ......143 C1
Leaden Hill SG8 ......28 D8
Leaden's La PE19 ......117 C3
Leader's Way CB8 ......110 E4
Leading Dro PE7 ......181 E4
Leafere Way [1] PE13 ......238 B2
Leather La PE19 ......23 E7
Lebanon Dr PE13 ......245 E7
Ledbury Rd PE3 ......197 C3
Ledger Cl PE14 ......144 A6
Ledham PE2 ......185 D4
Ledo Rd CB2 ......31 F2
Lee Cl CB4 ......125 D3
Lee Rd PE7 ......181 E4
Leechcroft PE28 ......121 C6
Lees La PE19 ......95 E5
Lees Way CB3 ......103 E1
Leete Pl SG8 ......5 C7
Leete Rd CB1 ......65 F5
Leete's La CB3 ......46 A8
Leeway Ave CB2 ......49 B5
Legg Rd [21] PE8 ......230 B1
Leicester Cl CB6 ......240 A3
Leighton PE2 ......186 C4
Leighton CP Sch PE2 ......186 C4
Leinsters Cl PE3 ......197 D3
Leiston Rd CB9 ......23 E7
Lemur Dr PE1 ......66 B7
Lensfield Rd CB2 ......246 B1
Lenton Cl PE28 ......140 D2
Lents Way CB4 ......84 C5
Leonard Cl [2] CB5 ......84 E4
Leopold Wlk CB4 ......125 E3
Lerowe Rd PE13 ......245 E7
Les Baux Pl [5] PE13 ......245 E3
Leslie Green Rd PE28 ......143 B5
Lessingham PE2 ......185 D4
Lester Dr CB6 ......210 A6
Lester Piggott Way [3]
CB8 ......110 F6
Lethbridge Rd PE4 ......204 E2
Lettice Martin Croft CB2 32 D5
Levellers La PE19 ......74 F3
Levens Wlk PE3 ......197 A3
Leverington Comm
PE13 ......235 B8
Leverington Cty Prim Sch
PE13 ......238 B2
Leverington Rd PE13 ......245 A6
Levers Wr PE29 ......141 C5
Levitt's Dro PE6 ......200 C4
Lewes Gdns CB4 ......204 C3
Lewis Cl
Great & Little Abington CB1 34 C5
March PE15 ......243 B3
Lewis Cres CB8 ......34 C5
Lexington Cl [3] CB4 ......83 C5
Ley Rd CB8 ......90 A1
Leyburn Cl [1] CB1 ......66 A7
Leys Ave CB4 ......83 F5
Leys Rd Cambridge CB4 ......83 F5
St Neots PE19 ......74 E6
Leys Rectory PE19 ......117 F2
Leys Sch The CB2 ......246 B1
Leys The Alconbury PE28 ......150 F4

Leys The continued
Little Gransden SG19 ......58 E3
Peterborough PE3 ......197 A1
Sawtry PE28 ......168 C3
Leys Wlk CB2 ......48 C4
Leyton Ave IP28 ......239 B6
Liberator Rd PE26 ......171 E3
Lichfield Ave PE4 ......204 B3
Lichfield Rd CB1 ......65 B6
Licking's Dro PE13 ......245 A2
Lidgate Cl PE2 ......186 C7
Lidgate Rd CB8 ......92 E7
Lilac Cl Haslingfield CB3 ......47 B5
Wisbech PE13 ......245 F7
Lilac Ct CB1 ......65 C5
Lilac End CB3 ......47 B4
Lilac Rd PE1 ......198 C7
Lilac Way PE27 ......144 B6
Lilyholt Rd PE15 ......222 A5
Lime Ave PE13 ......245 C7
Lime Cl IP28 ......239 E5
Lime Gr March PE15 ......243 C6
Royston SG8 ......5 E8
St Neots PE19 ......74 F6
Lime Rd PE26 ......172 A8
Lime Tree Ave PE1 ......197 F4
Limekiln Cl SG8 ......5 E5
Limekiln Rd CB1 ......65 E3
Limes Ave [1] PE14 ......236 A5
Limes Cl Bassingbourn SG8 12 E5
Littleport CB6 ......242 C4
Limes Ct PE27 ......143 F1
Limes Park Rd PE27 ......143 F1
Limes Rd CB3 ......81 A3
Limes The
Bassingbourn SG8 ......12 C5
Castor PE5 ......195 F1
Harston CB2 ......47 F2
Sawston CB2 ......32 F8
[5] Wittering PE8 ......230 B1
Limestone Cl [7] CB7 ......213 A5
Limetree Cl
[3] Cambridge CB1 ......65 D5
Yaxley PE7 ......181 F7
Linclare Pl [7] PE19 ......74 E4
Lincoln Ave PE27 ......143 F7
Lincoln Cl PE19 ......117 A5
Lincoln Rd
Deeping Gate PE6 ......231 E7
[4] Mildenhall IP28 ......213 E8
Peterborough PE4 ......197 C8
Ramsey PE26 ......171 E3
Stamford PE9 ......244 D2
Wyton Airfield PE28 ......143 A8
Linden Cl Cambridge CB4 ......83 C4
[6] Haddenham CB6 ......210 A5
Linden Dr PE16 ......241 C4
Linden End [3] CB6 ......210 A5
Linden Gr PE29 ......141 F8
Linden Way CB6 ......210 A5
Lindens Cl PE13 ......234 A2
Lindisfarne Cl [9] PE19 ......74 F1
Lindisfarne Rd PE6 ......232 A1
Lindridge Wlk PE3 ......197 A2
Lindsay Cl SG8 ......13 C1
Lindsells Wlk PE16 ......241 C5
Lindsey Cl PE4 ......204 D1
Lindsey Rd Stamford PE9 244 C6
[5] Uffington PE9 ......230 C6
Ling Garth PE1 ......198 B8
Lingfield Rd [7] SG8 ......5 E5
Lingholme Cl [2] CB4 ......83 C5
Lingmoor [2] PE29 ......141 A6
Lingrey Ct CB2 ......64 D2
Lingwood Pk [5] PE3 ......197 D3
Link Dr PE28 ......140 C3
Link La CB6 ......216 E1
Link Rd Peterborough PE1 197 F3
Sawston CB2 ......32 F8
Links Cl IP28 ......213 F4
Links The CB8 ......89 D8
Links Way PE27 ......143 F4
Linkside PE3 ......204 B1
Linley Rd St Neots PE19 ......74 E3
Whittlesey PE7 ......189 E6
Linlithgow Cl CB3 ......99 A3
Linnet PE2 ......185 D6
Linton CE Inf Sch CB1 ......35 C2
Linton Cl CB1 ......110 F6
Linton Heights Jun Sch
CB1 ......35 D2
Linton Liby CB1 ......35 C2
Linton Rd Balsham CB1 ......52 F2
Great Abington CB1 ......34 D6
Hadstock CB1 ......20 B8
Horseheath CB1 ......36 F3
Linton Village Coll CB1 ......35 B2
Linton Zoo & Gdns* CB1 35 B1
Linwood La PE15 ......223 A8
Lion Cl PE26 ......220 D3
Lion Wlk PE26 ......172 A5
Lion Yd PE26 ......172 B6
Lionel Walden Sch
PE15 ......223 A5
Lions Cross PE29 ......119 A8
Lisburn Rd CB8 ......111 B3
Lisle Cl CB7 ......240 E5
Lisle La CB7 ......240 E4
Lister Rd PE1 ......197 F7
Lister's Rd PE14 ......236 F1
Litchfield Cl PE7 ......181 F5
Litlington Rd SG8 ......11 E1
Little Back La The CB5 ......129 C1
Little Casterton Rd PE9 244 A6
Little Chishill Rd SG8 ......1 C6
Little Cl PE6 ......232 A1
Little Dowgate PE13 ......245 A7
Little End Rd PE19 ......74 B1

Little Farthing Cl PE27 ......144 B4
Little Fen Dro
Burwell CB5 ......129 E6
Swaffham Prior CB5 ......129 A1
Little Fendyke La PE14 ......236 E6
Little Gn 91 C5
Little Gransden La SG19 ......58 D4
Little Hasse Dro CB7 ......212 C6
Little Heath SG19 ......41 C4
Little How PE27 ......143 E6
Little Johns Cl PE3 ......196 F3
Little La Ely CB6 ......240 D4
[1] Great Gransden SG19 ......58 E4
Melbourn SG8 ......14 C2
Little London Dro CB7 ......212 F5
Little London La CB7 ......212 F5
Little Marefen Dro CB6 ......242 A7
Little Mdw PE28 ......102 B2
Little Moor PE28 ......121 C5
Little Northfields [3]
PE9 ......230 D4
Little Paxton CP Sch
PE19 ......95 F1
Little Paxton La PE19 ......95 F2
Little Ramper PE13 ......238 B4
Little Setchel Dro CB4 ......209 F2
Little St CB6 ......218 B6
Little St Mary's La CB2 ......246 A1
Little Thetford CP Sch
CB6 ......211 B7
Little Whyte PE26 ......172 B7
Little Wilbraham Rd CB1 86 D4
Littlechild Dr [5] PE3 ......238 E2
Littlecotes Cl PE28 ......137 F7
Littlefield Cl
Godmanchester PE29 ......118 F8
Wilburton CB6 ......210 C6
Littlemeer PE2 ......185 F4
Littleport Sta CB6 ......242 E6
Littleport Village Coll
CB6 ......242 B4
Littleworth Dro PE12 ......233 F8
Littleworth End PE19 ......118 A1
Livermore Gn PE4 ......204 A6
Locks Cl PE6 ......206 B7
Locks Gn PE6 ......183 A8
Locksgate [1] PE28 ......215 C1
Lockspit Hall Dro CB4 ......125 F8
Lode Cl PE7 ......212 B3
Lode La CB7 ......211 E1
Lode Rd Bottisham CB5 ......86 D7
Lode CB5 ......107 D1
Lode Way Chatteris PE16 ......210 A5
Haddenham CB6 ......210 A5
Loder Ave PE3 ......196 F2
Lodes End Dro PE26 ......220 F2
Lodge Cl PE29 ......141 C4
Lodge Gdns CB6 ......210 A6
Lodge Rd SG8 ......31 A1
Loftsteads [3] PE28 ......215 C1
Logan's Way CB4 ......84 A3
Lomax Dr PE24 ......140 C3
Lombardy Dr PE1 ......198 B8
London La PE19 ......96 E4
London Rd Barley SG8 ......6 F1
Chatteris PE16 ......241 C2
Fenstanton PE28 ......120 E7
Fowlmere SG8 ......15 D5
Godmanchester PE29 ......141 F1
Great Chesterford CB10 ......18 C2
Great Shelford CB2 ......49 B4
Harston CB2 ......48 B3
Hemingford Grey PE27 ......143 F1
Kimbolton PE28 ......114 A4
Peterborough PE7 ......186 F3
Royston SG8 ......5 D4
Sawston CB2 ......32 F5
Wansford PE8 ......194 B2
Yaxley PE7 ......181 C5
London St
Godmanchester PE29 ......141 F1
Whittlesey PE7 ......189 D6
Lone Tree Ave CB4 ......83 C8
Long Cswy
Peterborough PE1 ......198 A2
Witcham CB6 ......217 C2
Long Dolver Dro CB7 ......212 B6
Long Dro Bury PE26 ......172 F5
Cottenham CB4 ......125 F3
Downham CB6 ......224 F3
Elm PE14 ......235 B1
Feltwell PE38 ......226 F6
Haddenham CB6 ......209 C5
Holme PE7 ......177 D5
Over CB4 ......208 D3
Parson Drove PE13 ......234 B5
Ramsey PE26 ......221 D2
Somersham PE28 ......215 D2
Waterbeach CB5 ......106 D8
Whittlesey PE7 ......200 F3
Long Furlong CB4 ......208 D1
Long Holme Dro CB4 ......208 E3
Long La Coveney CB6 ......217 C4
Fowlmere SG8 ......15 D8
Gamlingay SG19 ......41 F6
Hemingford Grey PE28 ......120 E1
Linton CB1 ......35 C1
Over CB4 ......208 E2
Spaldwick PE28 ......137 F5
Willingham CB4 ......124 A8
Long Lots PE14 ......236 F8
Long Meadow Rd CB5 ......107 F2

Long Nightlayer's Dro
PE16 ....241 E8
Long North Fen Dro
CB6 ....216 A4
Long Pasture PE4 ....204 B5
Comberton CB3 ....81 D2
Long Rd Cambridge CB2 ....64 F4
Long Reach Rd CB4 ......84 C6
Longfellow Ave 5 PE19 ..74 D5
Longfield Rd CB6 ....242 B5
Longfields CB6 ....240 A3
Longhead La PE14 ....238 D3
Longhill Rd PE15 ....228 B6
Longholme Rd PE26 ......171 A4
Longmere La CB7 ....212 A5
Longsands Com Coll
PE19 ....75 A6
Longsands Par 3 PE19 ...75 A6
Longsands Rd PE19 ....75 A5
Longstaff Way PE29 ......142 A6
Longstanton CP Sch
CB4 ....123 F2
Longstanton Rd
Oakington/Longstanton
CB4 ....103 A6
Over CB4 ....123 B7
Longthorpe Cl 3 PE3 ....197 A2
Longthorpe CP Sch PE3 .197 A2
Longthorpe Gn PE3 ......197 B1
Longthorpe House Mews 11
PE3 ....196 F2
Longthorpe Parkway
PE3 ....186 A8
Longueville Ct PE2 ....186 B5
Longview CB6 ....216 D1
Longwater PE2 ....186 B6
Lonsdale CB1 ....35 E2
Loop Rd PE28 ....146 A4
Lophams Cl 1 CB9 ....38 F2
Lord's Croft La CB9 ....24 A7
Lord's Gd Dro CB5 ....128 D2
Lord's La PE13 ....235 D6
Lords La PE13 ....235 D7
Lordship Orwell SG8 .....45 E1
Willingham CB4 ....209 A1
Lordship Dr SG8 ....14 C7
Lordship La CB4 ....125 D4
Loris Ct CB1 ....66 A7
Lornas Field PE7 ....186 D2
Losecoat Cl 1 PE9 ....244 D7
Lotfield St SG8 ....45 E1
Lottings Way PE19 ....74 C6
Loughrigg Cl 4 PE29 ....141 B7
Louthe Way PE28 ....168 C3
Love La Ashwell SG7 ....2 A5
Houghton & Wyton PE28 ....143 A5
Wisbech PE13 ....245 C4
Lovell Rd CB4 ....84 A7
Lovers La PE5 ....194 F2
Love's Cl CB4 ....104 C2
Love's Hill PE5 ....195 F1
Low Cl PE7 ....189 E8
Low Cross PE7 ....189 D8
Low Fen Drove Way CB5 .85 B4
Low Gate PE13 ....237 F8
Low Rd Burwell CB5 .....130 B2
Crowland PE6 ....207 F7
Fenstanton PE28 ....121 A7
Hemingford Grey PE27 .....144 A1
Little Stukeley PE28 ....151 D3
The Stukeleys PE28 ....140 C7
Wisbech PE14 ....245 E1
Low Side PE14 ....236 E2
Lowbury Cres CB4 ....103 B6
Lowburyholme Rd CB4 ..208 C1
Lower Downs Slade CB9 .24 A8
Lower Dro CB7 ....211 D3
Lower End CB5 ....108 E5
Lower Gower Rd SG8 ....5 D8
Lower King St SG8 ....5 D6
Lower Park St CB5 ....246 A3
Lower Rd Croydon SG8 ...26 D5
Ely CB7 ....218 D1
Wicken CB7 ....211 E2
Lower St SG8 ....31 B1
Loweswater PE29 ....141 C5
Lowfields CB3 ....46 B8
Lowick Gdns PE3 ....197 C5
Lowry Cl Haverhill CB9 ...38 D1
St Ives PE27 ....144 A7
Lowry Rd PE19 ....74 C6
Lowther Gdns PE4 ....204 D2
Lowther St CB8 ....110 F3
Loxley PE4 ....204 A4
Loxley Gn PE28 ....142 F5
Luard Cl CB2 ....65 A4
Luard Rd CB2 ....65 A5
Lucas Ct PE29 ....141 F7
Lucas La SG7 ....2 E4
Lucerne Cl Cambridge CB1 .66 A6
Red Lodge IP28 ....213 F1
Lucketts Cl CB4 ....104 B5
Luck's La PE19 ....117 A4
Lucombe Dr PE13 ....245 F7
Lucy Cavendish Coll CB3 .83 C3
Luddington Cl PE19 ....96 E4
Luddington Rd
Great Gidding PE28 ....166 C3
Peterborough PE4 ....204 D1
Ludlow La CB1 ....67 A5
Lug Fen Droveway CB5 ..107 A5
Luke St PE19 ....74 E4
Lulworth Dr CB9 ....23 E8
Lumen SG8 ....5 D7

Lumley Cl CB6 ....240 E8
Lundy Cl CB7 ....24 D7
Lutton Gate Rd PE12 ....234 A8
Lutton Gr PE3 ....197 C6
Lye Cl PE19 ....94 A6
Lyles Rd CB4 ....125 D4
Lymage Rd CB28 ....115 D3
Lyme Wlk 3 PE3 ....197 C6
Lynch La SG8 ....15 E8
Lynchwood PE2 ....185 C5
Lyndale Pk PE2 ....185 C6
Lyndewode Rd CB1 ....246 C1
Lyndhurst Cl CB4 ....105 C1
Lynfield La CB4 ....84 A4
Lynn Rd Ely CB6 ....240 D6
Littleport CB6 ....242 F6
Wisbech PE13 ....245 C6
Lynton Cl CB6 ....240 D6
Lynton Dr CB6 ....240 D6
Lynton Rd PE1 ....197 F6
Lynton Way CB2 ....33 A8
Lynx The CB1 ....66 A7
Lyon's Dro PE15 ....223 F4
Lysander Cl 5 PE27 .....143 F7
Lythemere PE2 ....186 C4

M

Macaulay Ave CB2 ....49 B6
Macbeth Cl PE29 ....141 F6
McCalmont Way CB8 ....111 E2
Mace Rd PE2 ....187 D5
Macfarlane Cl CB4 ....104 C2
Mackenzie Rd 5 CB6 ....241 A4
Mackerel H SG8 ....5 B6
Macpherson Robertson Way
IP28 ....239 A5
Maddingley Way CB6 ....210 A7
Madecroft PE28 ....165 A5
Madeley Ct PE28 ....143 C2
Madingley H★ CB3 ....81 E5
Madingley Rd
Cambridge CB3 ....83 B3
Dry Drayton CB3 ....102 B1
Madingley Sch CB3 ....81 F5
Madras Rd CB1 ....65 C7
Maffit Rd PE5 ....195 D3
Magazine Cl PE13 ....245 A4
Magazine La PE13 ....245 A4
Magdalene Cl CB4 ....123 F2
Magdalene Coll CB4 ......246 A4
Magdalene St CB2 ....246 A3
Magee Rd PE4 ....204 D1
Magna Cl CB1 ....34 C6
Magnolia Ave PE3 ....197 A2
Magnolia Cl
Cambridge CB1 ....65 B5
2 Red Lodge IP28 ....213 F1
Magrath Ave CB4 ....246 A4
Maiden La PE9 ....244 C5
Mailes Cl CB3 ....63 B4
Main Dro CB6 ....225 A2
Main Rd Etton PE6 ....203 B8
Little Gransden SG19 ....58 D3
Parson Drove PE13 ....234 E7
Uffington PE9 ....230 D6
Upwell PE14 ....229 E7
Wisbech PE14 ....245 E1
Main St Ailsworth PE5 ...195 D2
Barnack PE9 ....230 D3
Bythorn & Keyston PE28 ...146 D4
Caldecote CB3 ....61 B6
Castor PE5 ....195 D3
Coveney CB6 ....217 B5
Downham CB6 ....217 D8
Ely CB7 ....219 B5
Farcet PE7 ....187 C2
Great Gidding PE28 ....166 D3
Hardwick CB3 ....81 A1
Hatley SG19 ....43 A3
Huntingdon PE29 ....142 A6
Little Downham CB6 ....218 A6
Littleport CB6 ....242 D4
Old Weston PE28 ....147 F7
Shudy Camps CB1 ....21 F6
Southorpe PE9 ....230 E1
Stow cum Quy CB5 ....85 F5
Thetford CB6 ....211 B7
Ufford PE9 ....230 F3
Welney PE14 ....225 A8
Wentworth CB6 ....217 B1
Witchford CB6 ....217 E1
Yarwell PE8 ....183 A8
Yaxley PE7 ....181 E5
Maio Rd CB4 ....83 F5
Maitland Ave CB4 ....84 B6
Malborne Way PE2 ....186 B4
Malcolm St CB1 ....246 B3
Malcolm Way CB8 ....111 B5
Malden Cl CB5 ....84 D3
Maldon Rd PE13 ....245 E5
Malecoff PE29 ....118 F7
Males Cl CB3 ....125 E5
Malin Cl CB9 ....24 D7
Mallard Cl
Chatteris PE16 ....241 C5
Whittlesey PE7 ....189 F8
Mallard Ct PE9 ....244 B4
Mallard La PE19 ....75 A4
Mallard Rd
Peterborough PE3 ....204 A1
Royston SG8 ....5 C6
Mallard Rise 2 CB6 ......210 A6
Mallard Way PE15 ....243 F5
Mallards The
Peakirk PE6 ....206 B1

Mallards The continued
St Ives PE28 ....143 F7
Mallett Cl PE15 ....243 F4
Malletts Rd CB1 ....66 A5
Mallory Rd PE1 ....198 C2
Mallow La PE7 ....175 D8
Mallow Wlk 1 SG8 ....5 E5
Mallows Cl 2 CB3 ....62 D6
Malory Pl CB3 ....99 A3
Malt Dr PE13 ....245 B3
Malta Rd CB1 ....65 B7
Maltby Cl 17 PE6 ....230 B1
Malthouse Cl PE29 ....141 D4
Malthouse La PE26 ....171 F5
Malthouse Way CB2 ....29 F8
Malting End CB8 ....72 D4
Malting La Cambridge CB3 .64 C8
Ellington PE28 ....139 A4
Foxton CB22 ....30 C5
Isleham CB7 ....213 A5
Litlington SG8 ....12 A2
Malting The PE26 ....171 F5
Maltings Cl Moulton CB8 .112 E5
Royston SG8 ....5 C7
Maltings La SG8 ....7 E2
Maltings The
Alconbury PE28 ....150 E5
Eaton Socon PE19 ....74 C5
St Martin's Without PE9 ...244 C2
Sawtry PE28 ....168 B4
3 Thorney PE6 ....233 A3
Maltmas Dro PE14 ....235 F2
Malton La SG8 ....29 B4
Malton Rd SG8 ....45 F1
Maltsters Way CB4 ....84 A4
Malvern Cl CB8 ....111 B2
Malvern Rd
Cambridge CB1 ....65 E6
Peterborough PE4 ....204 E2
Manasty Rd PE2 ....185 D2
Manchester Rd PE28 .....117 D8
Manchester Way 10
PE27 ....144 A8
Mandene Gdns SG19 ......58 E4
Mander Way CB1 ....65 C5
Manderston Rd CB8 ......110 E4
Mandeville Burwell CB5 ..109 B8
Peterborough PE2 ....185 F4
Mandeville Rd PE28 ......140 C3
Mandrill Cl CB1 ....66 A7
Manea Prim Sch PE15 ...224 C4
Manea Rd PE15 ....223 D6
Manea Sta PE15 ....224 B6
Maners Way CB1 ....65 C4
Mangers La CB2 ....32 D1
Manhattan Dr CB4 ....246 C4
Manners Cl 4 PE9 ....230 C6
Manor Ave PE2 ....187 B7
Manor Cl Brampton PE28 140 E2
Buckden PE19 ....117 A3
Graveley PE19 ....98 A5
2 Great Staughton PE19 ..93 F6
Harston CB2 ....47 F3
Little Paxton PE19 ....95 F2
St Ives PE28 ....142 F5
18 Somersham PE28 ....215 C1
Witchford CB6 ....217 E1
11 Wittering PE8 ....230 B1
Yaxley PE7 ....181 D5
Manor Com Coll CB4 ......83 F6
Manor Court Rd CB6 .....217 E1
Manor Cres CB3 ....81 A1
Manor Dr
Fenstanton PE28 ....121 B6
Peterborough PE6 ....205 A3
Sawtry PE28 ....168 C4
Manor Est 18 PE15 ......223 B6
Manor Farm Cl CB4 .....103 C6
Manor Farm Ct PE28 ....115 D2
Manor Farm La PE5 .....195 C2
Manor Farm Rd
"Beck Row, Holywell Row
& Kenny Hill" IP28 ....213 D7
Girton CB3 ....103 E2
St Neots PE19 ....75 A5
Waresley SG19 ....57 E2
Manor Gdns
Buckden PE19 ....117 A4
Peterborough PE2 ....187 C7
Wisbech PE13 ....245 A4
Manor Gr PE19 ....75 A5
Manor House Cl 1 PE19 .74 C2
Manor House St PE1 ....198 A3
Manor La Alconbury PE28 150 F5
Boxworth CB3 ....101 C6
Great Chesterford CB10 ...18 D2
Great Gransden SG19 ......58 D4
Manor Pk CB4 ....104 A4
Manor Rd
Folksworth PE7 ....180 D1
Gamlingay SG19 ....41 D6
Haverhill CB9 ....24 B7
Hemingford Grey PE28 ....143 B1
Little Shelford CB22 ....48 E4
Meldreth SG8 ....29 A1
Mildenhall IP28 ....239 B4
Sutton PE5 ....194 F2
Witchford CB6 ....217 E2
Manor Sch CB6 ....210 C6
Manor St Cambridge CB1 246 B3
Wistow PE28 ....164 A7
Manor View
Barton Mills IP28 ....239 D2
Whittlesey PE7 ....189 D6
Manor Way
Hail Weston PE19 ....95 A1
Market Deeping PE6 ....231 F8

Manor Wlk CB1 ....67 A5
Manse Dr CB4 ....125 C3
Mansel Way CB4 ....83 E6
Mansell Rd PE13 ....245 D3
Mansfield Cl CB4 ....105 C2
Mansfield Ct PE1 ....198 C5
Manton PE3 ....197 A3
Maple Ave Sawston CB2 ..32 F5
Wisbech PE13 ....245 C7
Maple Cl
5 Bluntisham/Colne
PE28 ....208 C6
Bottisham CB5 ....86 F5
4 Bourn CB23 ....79 C3
Cambridge CB4 ....83 F5
Linton CB1 ....35 B3
Sawtry PE28 ....168 A3
Maple Ct Gamlingay SG19 .41 C5
Yaxley PE7 ....181 F6
Maple Dr
Huntingdon PE29 ....141 E8
Little Stukeley PE28 ....151 E3
Maple End PE28 ....150 F4
Maple Gr March PE15 ....243 C5
Peterborough PE1 ....198 C5
Royston SG8 ....5 B8
Maple Way Melbourn SG8 .14 C5
Royston SG8 ....5 B8
Maple Wlk PE7 ....186 C2
Maples The Fulbourn CB1 .66 E5
Peterborough PE1 ....198 F5
March La CB1 ....65 F8
March Rd
Coates/Eastrea PE7 ....191 A8
Elm PE13 ....227 F8
Elm PE13 ....235 A2
Elm PE14 ....235 D2
Welney PE14 ....229 F1
Whittlesey PE7 ....191 D7
Wimblington PE15 ....223 B4
March Riverside PE14 ...229 C8
March Sta PE15 ....243 D6
March Trading Est PE15 243 B7
Marchioness Way 3
PE19 ....74 B4
March's Cl CB1 ....66 E5
Marcus Cl CB9 ....24 D7
Mardale Gdns PE4 ....204 F2
Marefen Dro CB6 ....225 C3
Marfleet Cl CB2 ....48 F7
Margett St CB4 ....125 E4
Margetts PE28 ....143 D1
Marholm Rd Castor PE6 .196 B3
Peterborough PE3 ....204 B3
Ufford PE9 ....231 A2
Marian Way PE16 ....241 C7
Marigold Dr IP28 ....133 F8
Marina Dr PE15 ....243 A5
Mariner's Way CB4 ....84 A3
Marion Cl CB3 ....83 B4
Maris Gn CB2 ....49 A6
Maris La CB2 ....64 C2
Markby Cl CB2 ....17 D8
Market Hill
Cambridge CB2 ....246 A2
Chatteris PE16 ....241 C5
Haverhill CB9 ....24 A8
Royston SG8 ....5 D6
St Ives PE27 ....144 A3
Market La Linton CB1 .....35 C4
3 St Ives PE27 ....144 A3
Market Mews PE13 ....245 C5
Market Pas CB2 ....246 A3
Market Pl 5 Ely CB7 .....240 C6
Mildenhall IP28 ....239 C4
St Neots PE19 ....74 E5
Wisbech PE13 ....245 C5
Market Rd PE27 ....144 B3
Market Sq
Cambridge CB2 ....246 A2
8 Ely CB7 ....240 C6
Market St Cambridge CB2 246 A3
Ely CB7 ....240 C6
Fordham CB7 ....212 E1
3 Newmarket CB8 ....111 A3
12 Soham CB7 ....212 B4
Swavesey CB4 ....122 C6
Whittlesey PE7 ....189 D7
14 Wisbech PE13 ....245 C5
Market Way CB6 ....217 A2
Markfield Rise CB6 ....216 D6
Markham Cl CB4 ....84 A7
Markham Ret Pk PE9 ....244 D7
Markhams Cl 3 CB9 ......38 F1
Mark's Way CB3 ....103 E1
Marlborough Cl
2 St Ives PE27 ....143 F7
Yaxley PE7 ....181 E5
Marlborough Coll The
CB2 ....64 E7
Marley Rd PE13 ....143 F8
Marlowe Ct 2 PE19 ......74 D6
Marlowe Gr PE4 ....197 E8
Marlowe Rd CB3 ....64 C7
Marmora Rd CB1 ....65 B7
Marne Ave PE4 ....204 C1
Marne Rd PE7 ....189 F5
Marquis Cl PE7 ....74 B4
Marriott Ct PE1 ....198 C5
Marriott's Dro PE26 ......221 A4
Marriotts Cl PE26 ....221 A4
Marritt Cl PE16 ....241 B6
Marroway La 4 CB6 ......217 D1
Marsh La PE15 ....143 D1
Marsh Rd Outwell PE14 ..236 F4
Walpole PE14 ....238 F4
Marsh The PE14 ....238 F8
Marshall Rd CB1 ....65 A5
Marshall's Bank PE13 ...234 D8

Marshall's Cl CB1 ....85 A1
Marshall's Way PE7 ......187 C2
Marsham PE2 ....185 F3
Marshfields Sch PE1 .....198 D7
Marshland High Sch
PE14 ....238 E4
Marshland Prim Sch
PE14 ....238 F4
Marston Rd PE19 ....75 A3
Martin Ave PE15 ....243 A7
Martin Cl
Godmanchester PE29 ......119 A8
Mildenhall IP28 ....239 D3
Soham CB7 ....212 A5
Martin Ct PE4 ....204 C4
Martin Rd CB5 ....130 B3
Martindale Way CB2 ......32 E8
Martingale Cl 3 CB4 .....83 C6
Martingale Rd 4 SG8 ....5 E6
Martin's La 2 CB6 ....218 A6
Martins La Linton CB1 ....35 E2
Witcham CB6 ....217 A3
Martins Way PE2 ....185 F5
Martinsbridge PE1 ....198 F7
Marwick Rd PE15 ....243 D7
Mary Armyne Rd PE2 ....187 E5
Mary Walsham Cl PE2 ...187 E5
Maryland Ave
Huntingdon PE29 ....141 F8
Swaffham Bulbeck CB5 ....108 B2
Marylebone Rd 3 PE15 243 C4
Masefield Ave PE19 ....74 C6
Masefield Way 3 SG8 ...13 D1
Maskew Ave PE1 ....197 E6
Mason Gdns IP28 ....213 D6
Mason Rd CB5 ....130 B5
Master Dike PE28 ....237 D8
Masterton Cl PE9 ....244 D7
Masterton Rd PE9 ....244 C7
Matley PE2 ....185 E5
Matt Dawson Cl 4 CB8 .110 F6
Matthew Parker Cl CB4 .105 D7
Matthew Wren Cl 3
CB6 ....218 A6
Matthews La CB8 ....55 F6
Maule Cl PE29 ....141 E6
Maurice Cl PE28 ....113 F5
Mawson Cl CB6 ....240 B3
Mawson Rd CB1 ....246 C1
Maxey Rd Helpston PE6 .231 C5
Peterborough PE6 ....231 D7
Maxey View 10 PE6 ......231 E8
Maxham's Green Rd
PE6 ....203 B6
Maxwell Rd PE2 ....186 D6
May St SG8 ....7 E2
Mayfair Gdns 1 PE15 ...235 C7
Mayfield PE1 ....117 A3
Mayfield Cl 2 CB6 ....240 B5
Mayfield Cres PE29 .....141 F6
Mayfield Prim Sch CB4 .83 C5
Mayfield Rd
Coates/Eastrea PE7 ....190 D7
Girton CB3 ....82 F4
Huntingdon PE29 ....141 F6
Peterborough PE1 ....198 A6
Mayflower Rd 1 PE13 ...245 E3
Mayfly Cl PE16 ....241 B3
Maynards CB2 ....32 C5
Mayner's Dike PE28 ......237 E8
Mayor's Wlk PE3 ....197 E3
Mayors Cl PE15 ....243 D7
Maypole Croft CB1 ....37 C8
Maypole La CB8 ....90 E3
May's Ave CB1 ....53 A2
May's La PE13 ....238 A2
Mays Way CB4 ....84 C5
Maysfield Dr 8 PE13 ....238 B2
Maytrees PE27 ....143 F1
Maze Rd PE28 ....120 C1
Mead Cl CB3 ....204 B1
Mead The PE4 ....204 B1
Mead View CB4 ....103 B5
Meadenvale PE1 ....198 F5
Meadlands Main Dro
CB6 ....215 F1
Meadow Bsns Ctr The
PE27 ....144 B2
Meadow Cl
Chatteris PE16 ....241 C3
Little Paxton PE19 ....95 F2
1 St Ives PE27 ....144 B3
2 Soham CB7 ....212 B3
Stilton PE7 ....175 F8
Witchford CB6 ....217 E2
Meadow Ct CB4 ....242 B5
Meadow Dr PE15 ....243 F5
Meadow Drift CB3 ....100 B5
Meadow Dro PE28 ....208 E6
Meadow Farm Cl CB4 ...103 D6
Meadow Gr PE1 ....205 B1
Meadow How PE27 ......143 F6
Meadow La Earith PE28 .208 C6
Hemingford Abbots PE28 .142 F3
Hemingford Grey PE28 ....143 D3
Houghton & Wyton PE28 ..143 B4
Linton CB1 ....35 D2
Newmarket CB8 ....111 D1
Offord Darcy PE19 ....117 F2
Over CB4 ....208 D1
Ramsey PE26 ....172 B4
St Ives PE27 ....144 C3
Thornhaugh PE8 ....193 F5
Meadow Prim Sch CB1 ...53 B2
Meadow Rd
Great Chesterford CB10 ...18 D3
Great Gransden SG19 ......58 B5
Newborough PE6 ....204 D8

Meadow Rd *continued*
Peakirk PE6 . . . .**206** C1
Ramsey PE26 . . . .**171** B1
Upwood & The Raveleys
PE26 . . . .**171** A1
Willingham CB4 . . . .**209** B1
Meadow Rise CB3 . . . .**60** C6
Meadow View PE19 . . . . . .**77** E4
Meadow Way
Doddington/Wimblington
PE15 . . . .**223** B3
Earith PE28 . . . .**208** E6
Great Paxton PE19 . . . .**96** E4
Harston CB2 . . . .**48** A3
Warboys PE28 . . . .**164** F5
Meadow Way S 7 PE15 **223** B7
Meadow Wlk CB1 . . . .**34** C6
Meadowbrook CB6 . . . . . .**209** E4
Meadowcroft CB6 . . . .**210** F5
Meadowcroft Way SG8 . . .**28** E8
Meadowfield Rd CB2 . . . . .**32** E6
Meadowgate PE9 . . . .**230** F5
Meadowgate La PE14 . . . .**245** E2
Meadowgate Sch PE13 . . .**245** E3
Meadowground PE28 . . . .**116** A7
Meadowlands
Burwell CB5 . . . .**130** B1
March PE15 . . . .**243** A6
Meadowlands Rd CB5 . . . .**84** E3
Meadows Cl 5 PE19 . . . . .**74** F5
Meadows The
Haslingfield CB3 . . . .**47** B5
Worlington IP28 . . . .**213** F4
Meadowsweet PE19 . . . . . .**74** B6
Meadowsweet Cl CB9 . . . .**38** E1
Meals Gate PE4 . . . .**204** F2
Medallion Ct 1 PE19 . . . . .**74** F5
Medcalfe Way SG8 . . . . . .**14** D6
Medeswell PE2 . . . .**186** C4
Medland Gr 6 PE19 . . . . . .**75** A5
Medway Cl PE13 . . . .**245** E4
Medway Rd PE29 . . . .**141** E7
Medworth PE2 . . . .**185** F3
Meeting La Litlington SG8 . .**12** A2
Melbourn SG8 . . . .**14** C6
Meggan Gate PE3 . . . .**197** A1
Megg's Dro PE26 . . . .**221** D2
Megs Cl PE28 . . . .**208** D5
Melbourn Cty Prim Sch
SG8 . . . .**14** C6
Melbourn Rd SG8 . . . .**5** D7
Melbourn St SG8 . . . .**5** D6
Melbourne Village Coll
SG8 . . . .**14** C7
Melbourne Ave PE15 . . . .**243** B7
Melbourne Dr IP28 . . . . . .**239** B5
Melbourne Pl CB1 . . . .**246** C2
Melbourne Rd PE9 . . . . . .**244** D6
Meldon Pl 2 CB6 . . . .**240** D5
Meldreth Manor Sch &
Orchard Ho PE28 . . . .**29** A1
Meldreth Rd
Shepreth SG8 . . . .**29** A1
Whaddon SG8 . . . .**28** C1
Meldreth Sta SG8 . . . .**14** B7
Meldrith Prim Sch SG8 . . .**14** B8
Melford Cl Burwell CB5 . . .**130** C2
Peterborough PE3 . . . .**197** A2
Mellis Cl CB9 . . . .**38** B1
Mellows Cl PE1 . . . .**198** C3
Melrose Dr PE2 . . . .**187** A4
Melrose Gdns CB8 . . . . . .**110** E4
Melton Cl 1 CB8 . . . .**111** B2
Melvin Way CB4 . . . .**104** A4
Mendip Gr PE4 . . . .**204** E2
Mepal Long Highway
CB6 . . . .**216** C4
Mepal Prim Sch CB6 . . . .**216** D3
Mepal Rd CB6 . . . .**216** E2
Mepal Short Highway
CB6 . . . .**216** C5
Mercers Row CB5 . . . .**84** F4
Mercian Ct PE2 . . . .**187** D7
Mere Cl PE26 . . . .**221** A4
Mere Dro Ramsey PE26 . . .**221** D4
Yaxley PE7 . . . .**181** F4
Mere Mill Dro CB6 . . . . . .**210** F4
Mere Side CB7 . . . .**212** A4
Mere Side Dro PE26 . . . . .**221** B4
Mere View PE7 . . . .**182** A5
Mere Way Cambridge CB4 . .**83** E6
Hemingford Grey PE28 . . .**120** B5
Houghton & Wyton PE28 . .**143** A6
Merelade Gr PE4 . . . .**204** B5
Meridian CP Sch CB3 . . . . .**62** C5
Meridian Sch SG8 . . . .**5** E7
Merlin Cl
Huntingdon PE29 . . . .**142** B7
St Neots PE19 . . . .**75** B7
Merlin Dr 4 CB6 . . . .**240** B5
Merritt St PE29 . . . .**141** C5
Merton Rd CB4 . . . .**104** B3
Merton St CB3 . . . .**64** C7
Metcalfe Rd CB4 . . . .**83** D5
Metcalfe Way 5 CB6 . . . .**210** A5
Mewburn PE3 . . . .**204** A1
Mews Cl PE26 . . . .**172** B7
Meynell Gdns CB8 . . . . . .**111** A5
Meynell Wlk PE3 . . . .**197** B3
Michael's Cl CB3 . . . .**103** E1
Mickle Gate PE3 . . . .**197** A1
Mickle Hill PE28 . . . .**135** D7
Mid Fetter PE26 . . . .**221** B3
Middle Broad Dro PE13 **237** D5
Middle Cl 5 CB6 . . . .**210** F4
Middle Drift SG8 . . . .**5** C6
Middle Dro Newton PE13 **237** E3
Ramsey PE26 . . . .**171** A7

Middle Dro *continued*
Soham CB7 . . . .**211** F3
Wimblington PE15 . . . .**223** C5
Middle Pasture PE4 . . . . .**204** B5
Middle Rd Crowland PE6 . .**207** E4
March PE15 . . . .**227** E4
Newborough PE6 . . . .**205** C7
Middle St Elton PE8 . . . . .**178** D8
Farcet PE7 . . . .**187** C2
Great Gransden SG19 . . . . .**58** E4
Litlington SG8 . . . .**12** A2
Thriplow SG8 . . . .**31** B1
Middle Watch CB4 . . . . . .**122** E5
Middle Way CB2 . . . .**50** A1
Middlefield PE7 . . . .**186** D3
Middlefield Cty Prim Sch
PE19 . . . .**74** F2
Middlefield Rd PE28 . . . . .**168** B3
Middleham Cl 2 PE7 . . . . .**187** F5
Middlemiss View PE29 . . .**118** F8
Middlemoor Rd
Ramsey PE26 . . . .**220** D3
Whittlesford PE2 . . . .**32** A5
Middleton PE3 . . . .**197** A4
Middleton Jun Sch PE3 . .**197** A4
Middleton Way CB4 . . . . .**121** E4
Middletons Rd PE7 . . . . . .**181** E5
Midgate PE1 . . . .**198** A2
Midhurst Cl CB4 . . . .**84** A5
Midland Rd PE3 . . . .**197** E3
Mikanda Cl PE14 . . . .**245** C2
Milburn Dro CB8 . . . .**112** E5
Mildenhall Airfield IP28 **239** B4
Mildenhall Rd
Barton Mills IP28 . . . .**239** C2
"Beck Row, Holywell Row
& Kenny Hill" IP28 . . . . . .**239** C8
Ely CB7 . . . .**219** E8
Fordham IP28 . . . .**213** A2
Freckenham IP28 . . . .**213** D3
Icklingham IP28 . . . .**214** E4
Littleport CB7 . . . .**242** F6
Mildenhall Swimming Pool
IP28 . . . .**239** C4
Mildenhall Upper Sch
IP28 . . . .**239** E4
Mildmay Rd PE4 . . . .**197** D8
Mile Dro Glinton PE6 . . . . .**231** F5
Yaxley PE7 . . . .**182** B5
Mile End Rd CB7 . . . .**219** C6
Mile Rd CB2 . . . .**50** C4
Mile Tree La PE13 . . . . . .**235** E7
Miles Hawk Way IP28 . . .**239** A5
Milford St CB1 . . . .**84** A1
Military Rd CB7 . . . .**212** C2
Militia Way CB7 . . . .**240** C4
Milk & Water Dro PE7 . . .**188** A4
Milk & Water Dro Ramsey Rd
PE7 . . . .**188** A2
Milking Hills Dro CB7 . . . .**209** B2
Milking Nook Rd PE6 . . . .**206** E1
Milking Slade Rd PE28 . . .**167** A4
Mill Cl Burwell CB5 . . . . . .**130** B1
Exning CB8 . . . .**110** B8
Hemingford Grey PE28 . . .**143** D2
Huntingdon PE29 . . . .**142** A6
The Stukeleys PE28 . . . . .**151** D3
Wisbech PE13 . . . .**245** C6
Mill Cnr CB7 . . . .**212** A4
Mill Comm PE29 . . . .**141** C3
Mill Cres PE2 . . . .**185** E4
Mill Croft CB7 . . . .**212** B3
Mill Cswy SG8 . . . .**8** C5
Mill Ct CB2 . . . .**49** A5
Mill Dro Crowland PE6 . . . .**207** F7
Lode CB5 . . . .**128** A1
Ramsey PE26 . . . .**221** A2
Soham CB7 . . . .**212** A3
Southery PE38 . . . .**226** E8
Mill End Cl CB1 . . . .**65** F5
Mill End Rd CB1 . . . .**65** E6
Mill Field 3 CB6 . . . .**216** E2
Mill Field Cl PE6 . . . .**231** C4
Mill Gn PE28 . . . .**165** A5
Mill Hill Downham CB6 . . .**175** E1
Glatton PE8 . . . .**175** E1
Haverhill CB9 . . . .**23** F7
Newmarket CB8 . . . .**111** A4
Royston SG8 . . . .**5** E4
Swaffham Prior CB5 . . . . .**108** E5
Weston Colville CB1 . . . . . .**54** C6
Mill Hill End 3 PE28 . . . .**120** B1
Mill Hill Rd 7 PE19 . . . . . .**74** D5
Mill La Arrington SG8 . . . . .**44** C3
Barrington CB2 . . . .**29** E8
Bassingbourn SG8 . . . .**12** D5
Bluntisham/Colne CB6 . . . .**208** D5
Burwell CB5 . . . .**130** B1
Cambridge CB2 . . . .**246** A2
Castor PE5 . . . .**184** F7
Duxford CB2 . . . .**32** E1
Exning CB8 . . . .**110** B8
Fordham CB7 . . . .**212** F1
Gorefield PE13 . . . .**235** B8
Hauxton CB2 . . . .**48** A6
Hemingford Grey PE28 . . .**143** D3
Hinxton CB10 . . . .**18** A7
Histon CB4 . . . .**104** D6
Ickleton CB10 . . . .**18** B4
Impington CB4 . . . .**104** D5
Linton CB1 . . . .**35** C2
Little Paxton PE19 . . . .**95** E1
Newton PE13 . . . .**237** F5
Potton SG19 . . . .**40** D1
Ramsey PE26 . . . .**172** B8
St Neots PE19 . . . .**74** F8

Mill La *continued*
Sawston CB2 . . . .**32** E7
Shingay cum Wendy SG8 . . .**27** B4
Stetchworth CB8 . . . .**89** F1
Swaffham Bulbeck CB5 . . .**108** B3
Tallington PE9 . . . .**230** F7
Toft CB3 . . . .**61** D5
Water Newton PE8 . . . . . .**184** C7
West Walton PE14 . . . . . .**238** F4
Whittlesford CB2 . . . .**32** D5
Mill Pit Furlong CB6 . . . .**242** D3
Mill Rd Alconbury PE28 . . .**150** E4
Ashley CB8 . . . .**91** F8
Buckden PE19 . . . .**117** C3
Cambridge CB1 . . . .**246** C2
Emneth PE14 . . . .**236** D6
Fen Drayton CB4 . . . .**121** D5
Glatton PE28 . . . .**175** E1
Great Gidding PE28 . . . . .**166** E3
Great Wilbraham CB1 . . . . .**67** F7
Haverhill CB9 . . . .**24** A7
Histon CB4 . . . .**104** B1
Huntingdon PE29 . . . .**142** A6
Kirtling CB8 . . . .**72** E5
Little Gransden SG19 . . . . .**58** E4
Little Stukeley PE28 . . . . .**151** D4
Little Wilbraham CB1 . . . . .**86** D1
Lode CB5 . . . .**107** C2
Maxey PE6 . . . .**231** C7
Nassington PE8 . . . .**183** A4
Oakington/Longstanton
CB4 . . . .**103** D6
Royston SG8 . . . .**5** D7
Stilton PE7 . . . .**175** F8
Walpole PE14 . . . .**238** F6
Waterbeach CB5 . . . .**106** A7
West Walton PE14 . . . . . .**238** D4
West Wickham CB1 . . . . . .**36** E8
West Wratting CB1 . . . .**53** F2
Whittlesey PE7 . . . .**189** E6
Wisbech St Mary PE13 . . .**234** C5
Wistow PE28 . . . .**163** F6
Mill Reef Cl CB8 . . . .**110** D7
Mill St Ashwell SG7 . . . .**2** D4
Cambridge CB1 . . . .**246** C1
Gamlingay SG19 . . . .**41** D5
Isleham CB7 . . . .**213** A5
Mildenhall IP28 . . . .**239** B3
St Ives PE28 . . . .**143** A5
Mill View March PE15 . . . .**243** D4
Peterborough PE7 . . . . . .**185** A5
Sawtry PE28 . . . .**168** A4
Mill Way Grantchester CB3 **64** A3
Holywell-cum-Needingworth
PE27 . . . .**144** F3
Stretham CB6 . . . .**210** E6
Swavesey CB4 . . . .**122** C6
Wisbech PE14 . . . .**236** A4
Mill Yd PE29 . . . .**141** E2
Millards La CB5 . . . .**107** D2
Millbank CB8 . . . .**110** F4
Miller Cl
2 Doddington/Wimblington
PE15 . . . .**222** F5
Godmanchester PE29 . . . .**118** F8
Offord Cluny PE19 . . . . . .**118** A2
Miller Way PE28 . . . .**140** C3
Miller's Rd CB3 . . . .**61** D5
Miller's Way PE28 . . . . . .**173** C3
Millers Cl 4 CB1 . . . .**35** D3
Millfield Littleport CB6 . . .**242** C3
Upwell PE14 . . . .**236** E2
Willingham CB4 . . . .**124** A8
Millfield Cl PE16 . . . .**241** B2
Millfield CP Sch CB6 . . . .**242** C3
Millfield La CB6 . . . .**210** C5
Millfield Pl CB6 . . . .**210** D5
Millfield Rd
Market Deeping PE6 . . . . .**231** F8
Maxey PE6 . . . .**231** D8
Millfield Way PE7 . . . .**189** F6
Millfields PE26 . . . .**172** B8
Millfields Way CB9 . . . .**24** B8
Millington Rd CB3 . . . .**64** C7
Mills La Longstanton CB4 . .**124** A1
Witchford CB6 . . . .**217** D1
Millstone La PE9 . . . .**230** D3
Millyard CB6 . . . .**210** A6
Milner Cl March PE15 . . . .**243** D5
Sawston CB2 . . . .**32** E7
Milner Rd Comberton CB3 . .**62** D6
Wisbech PE13 . . . .**245** C4
Milnyard Sq PE2 . . . .**185** C2
Milton Ave PE19 . . . .**74** C6
Milton Cl
Huntingdon PE29 . . . .**141** E6
Ramsey PE26 . . . .**171** F5
Royston SG8 . . . .**13** C1
St Ives PE27 . . . .**143** F6
Milton Ctry Pk ★ CB4 . . . .**105** D1
Milton Dr CB3 . . . .**238** D1
Milton H ★ PE6 . . . .**196** D4
Milton Rd Cambridge CB4 **246** A4
Impington CB4 . . . .**104** F4
Peterborough PE2 . . . . . .**187** A7
Milton Road CP Sch CB4 **83** E4
Milton Sch CB4 . . . .**105** C2
Milton Way PE3 . . . .**196** E3
Mina Cl PE2 . . . .**187** D4
Minden Ct 8 PE19 . . . .**74** C5
Minerva Cl CB9 . . . .**24** D6
Minerva Way CB4 . . . .**83** E8
Mingle La CB2 . . . .**49** B5
Minster Pl 4 CB7 . . . .**240** D4
Minster Rd Haverhill CB9 . .**39** A1
Royston SG8 . . . .**5** C8
Mint La PE19 . . . .**96** E4
Minter Cl CB5 . . . .**86** A5

Missleton Ct CB1 . . . .**65** C5
Misty Mdws CB5 . . . .**84** D4
Mitchells Cotts CB10 . . . . .**20** B1
Moat La
Abbots Ripton PE28 . . . . .**152** C8
Melbourn SG8 . . . .**14** D7
Perry PE28 . . . .**115** D1
Moat Way CB4 . . . .**122** E6
Moats' Way PE28 . . . .**119** E7
Mole Dro PE12 . . . .**233** F8
Molewood Cl CB4 . . . .**83** C6
Molls Dro CB4 . . . .**236** C3
Molteno Inst CB2 . . . .**246** B2
Monarch Ave PE2 . . . .**187** A6
Monarch Rd PE19 . . . .**74** B4
Moncrieff Cl 1 CB4 . . . . . .**83** E7
Monet Cl PE27 . . . .**144** A7
Money Bank PE13 . . . . . .**245** E4
Moneypiece Cl
1 Haverhill CB9 . . . .**38** F1
3 Haverhill CB9 . . . .**38** F2
Monkfield La CB3 . . . .**79** C3
Monkfield Park Prim Sch
CB3 . . . .**79** B4
Monks Cl PE7 . . . .**189** D8
Monks Dr 17 PE6 . . . .**232** A1
Monks Gr PE4 . . . .**204** A5
Monks Mdw PE6 . . . .**232** B8
Monks Way PE28 . . . .**168** B2
Monks Wood Nature
Reserve ★ PE28 . . . .**161** B4
Monkswell CB2 . . . .**64** D3
Monkswood CB6 . . . .**242** C5
Montagu Ct 2 PE19 . . . . . .**74** E4
Montagu Gdns PE28 . . . .**113** E5
Montagu Rd
Huntingdon PE29 . . . .**141** D6
Little Stukeley PE28 . . . . .**151** F2
Peterborough PE4 . . . . . .**197** D8
Montagu St PE19 . . . .**74** E4
Montague Rd PE28 . . . . . .**117** D8
Monte Long Cl PE15 . . . . .**243** E1
Montgomery Rd CB4 . . . . .**83** E6
Montreal Rd CB1 . . . .**65** C7
Montrose Cl CB4 . . . .**83** E7
Monument St PE1 . . . .**198** A3
Moon Hall La CB9 . . . .**24** A6
Moor Pasture Way CB9 . . .**39** B4
Moor Rd
Great Staughton MK44 . . . .**93** B1
Newborough PE6 . . . .**206** E2
Moor The SG8 . . . .**14** C7
Moore Cl CB4 . . . .**84** A6
Moore's La 4 PE6 . . . .**232** A1
Moorfield Rd Duxford CB2 **32** E3
2 Peterborough PE3 . . . .**197** D3
Moorfield Way PE28 . . . . .**151** F2
Moorhen Rd PE7 . . . .**201** A1
Moorhouse Dr PE29 . . . . .**141** E7
Moory Croft Cl PE19 . . . . .**94** A6
Moot Way PE28 . . . .**155** A5
Morborne Cl PE2 . . . .**187** D6
Morborne La PE7 . . . .**180** C2
Morborne Rd PE7 . . . .**180** C2
Morden Rd CB3 . . . .**99** B3
More's Mdw CB2 . . . .**48** F6
Moreton Cl PE7 . . . .**189** F8
Morland Way PE27 . . . . . .**144** A7
Morley Cl 7 IP28 . . . .**213** F8
Morley Meml Prim Sch
CB1 . . . .**65** B5
Morley Way PE2 . . . .**186** C5
Morpeth Cl PE2 . . . .**186** C6
Morpeth Rd PE3 . . . .**197** C3
Morris Cl PE19 . . . .**117** A3
Morris St PE1 . . . .**198** B3
Mortimer La IP28 . . . .**213** C3
Mortimer Rd
Cambridge CB1 . . . .**246** C2
Royston SG8 . . . .**5** C6
Mortimers La CB2 . . . .**30** C5
Mortlock Ave CB4 . . . .**84** B6
Mortlock Cl SG8 . . . .**14** C6
Mortlock Gdns CB1 . . . . . .**34** C5
Mortlock St SG8 . . . .**14** C6
Morton Ave PE15 . . . .**243** E3
Morton Cl CB6 . . . .**240** E8
Morton St SG8 . . . .**5** D7
Morton Way 6 PE15 . . . . .**223** B7
Mosquito Rd PE26 . . . . . .**171** E3
Moss Bank CB4 . . . .**84** C5
Moss Cl PE26 . . . .**171** B1
Moss Dr CB3 . . . .**47** C5
Mostyn Cl 2 CB6 . . . .**216** E1
Moules La CB1 . . . .**20** C6
Moulton Ave CB8 . . . .**134** A2
Moulton CE VC Fst Sch
CB8 . . . .**112** E6
Moulton Gr PE3 . . . .**197** C6
Moulton Rd Ashley CB8 . . .**112** D1
Cheveley CB8 . . . .**91** D8
Cheveley CB8 . . . .**111** D4
Mount Dr PE13 . . . .**245** E4
Mount Pleasant
3 Cambridge CB3 . . . . . .**83** C3
Great Paxton PE19 . . . . . .**96** E4
Peterborough PE2 . . . . . .**187** C7
Spaldwick PE28 . . . .**137** E6
Mount Pleasant Rd
PE13 . . . .**245** C7
Mount Pleasant Wlk 2
CB3 . . . .**83** C3
Mount Rd CB9 . . . .**24** A7
Mount The Barley SG8 . . . . .**6** C1
Toft CB3 . . . .**61** D5
Mountbatten Ave
Stamford PE9 . . . .**244** A6

Mountbatten Ave *continued*
Yaxley PE7 . . . .**181** D5
Mountbatten Ct 6 PE19 . . .**74** C4
Mountbatten Dr PE13 . . . .**245** A7
Mountbatten Way
Peterborough PE3 . . . . . .**197** B6
Whittlesey PE7 . . . .**190** A6
Mounteagle 2 SG8 . . . .**5** D5
Mountford Cl CB2 . . . .**48** C4
Mountford Ct 3 PE19 . . . . .**74** F3
Mountsteven Ave PE4 . . . .**204** C1
Mouth La PE13 . . . .**235** B4
Mowbray Cl PE13 . . . .**235** B7
Mowbray Rd Bretton PE3 **203** F1
Cambridge CB1 . . . .**65** C4
Mowfen Rd CB6 . . . .**242** D5
Mowlam Cl CB4 . . . .**104** C2
Moyne Cl CB4 . . . .**83** D7
Moyne Rd PE28 . . . .**168** C3
Muchwood La PE26 . . . . . .**221** B1
Mudd's Dro PE14 . . . .**229** F6
Mugglestons La PE26 . . . .**172** B6
Mulberry Cl Bottisham CB5 **86** F6
Cambridge CB4 . . . .**83** F5
Mildenhall IP28 . . . .**239** E4
Whittlesey PE7 . . . .**189** F5
Yaxley PE7 . . . .**182** A5
Mulberry Way CB7 . . . . . .**240** F6
Mullein Cl 4 PE19 . . . .**74** C5
Mumby's Dro PE14 . . . . . .**229** C6
Munnings Cl CB9 . . . .**38** D1
Muntjac Cl 5 PE19 . . . .**74** B5
Murfitt Way SG19 . . . .**41** D6
Murfitt's La CB7 . . . .**212** E2
Muriel Cl CB3 . . . .**99** B2
Murrell Cl PE19 . . . .**74** F7
Murrow Bank PE13 . . . . . .**234** D6
Murrow Cty Prim Sch
PE13 . . . .**234** D5
Murrow La PE13 . . . .**234** F5
Murton Cl CB5 . . . .**234** A1
Museum of Archaeology &
Anthropology ★ CB2 . . .**246** B2
Museum of Classical
Archaeology ★ CB3 . . . . .**64** C8
Museum of Technology ★
CB5 . . . .**84** B3
Museum of Zoology ★
CB2 . . . .**246** B2
Musgrave Way
Fen Ditton CB5 . . . .**84** F6
7 St Neots PE19 . . . .**74** F5
Muskham PE3 . . . .**196** F4
Musticott Pl PE13 . . . .**245** F6
Mustill's La CB4 . . . .**123** B8
Muswell Rd PE3 . . . .**197** E4
Myrtle Ave PE1 . . . .**198** C7
Myrtle Ct PE1 . . . .**198** C7
Myrtle Gr PE1 . . . .**198** C7
Myrtle Way PE27 . . . .**144** A5

N

Nansicles Rd PE2 . . . .**186** D6
Napier Pl PE2 . . . .**185** C6
Napier St CB1 . . . .**246** C4
Narrow Dro
Whittlesey PE7 . . . .**188** C5
Yaxley PE7 . . . .**182** C5
Narrow La CB4 . . . .**104** B4
Naseby Cl PE3 . . . .**197** C5
Nash Rd 7 SG8 . . . .**5** D5
Nat Flatman St CB8 . . . . .**111** B3
Natal Rd CB1 . . . .**65** C7
Nathan Cl PE3 . . . .**197** B2
National Extension Coll
CB2 . . . .**64** F7
National Horse Racing Mus ★
CB8 . . . .**111** A3
Navigation Wharf 6
PE19 . . . .**74** E5
Nayland Rd CB9 . . . .**23** C6
Neale Cl CB1 . . . .**65** F7
Neale Wade Com Coll
PE15 . . . .**243** D1
Neaverson Rd PE6 . . . . . .**203** F7
Nedderworth Rd 2
PE27 . . . .**144** B3
Needham Bank PE14 . . . . .**236** C4
Needingworth Rd PE27 . . .**144** B4
Nelson Gdns PE13 . . . . . .**245** D6
Nelson Rd
Eaton Socon PE19 . . . .**74** B3
Huntingdon PE29 . . . .**142** A6
Nelson's La CB6 . . . .**210** A5
Nene Cl Wansford PE8 . . . .**194** A3
2 Wittering PE8 . . . .**230** B1
Nene Par March PE15 . . . .**243** E4
Wisbech PE13 . . . .**245** B7
Nene Parkway PE3 . . . . . .**196** F1
Nene Pk ★ PE2 . . . .**185** C7
Nene Quay PE13 . . . .**245** C5
Nene Rd Eaton Socon PE19 **74** C4
Huntingdon PE29 . . . .**141** E8
Kimbolton PE28 . . . .**114** A7
Whittlesey PE7 . . . .**189** E6
Nene Sch The PE13 . . . . . .**245** D4
Nene St PE1 . . . .**198** B2
Nene Way St Ives PE27 . . .**144** A7
Sutton CB6 . . . .**194** F2
Neneside 1 PE15 . . . .**222** A5
Neptune Cl CB4 . . . .**83** E7
Ness Rd CB5 . . . .**130** C3
Nether Gr CB4 . . . .**123** F2

Netherhall Sch The CB1 .65 E4
Netherhall Way CB1 . . . . . .65 D4
Nettle Bank PE14 . . . . . .235 C4
Neve Gdns IP28 . . . . . . .213 E6
Neville Rd CB1 . . . . .65 C6
New Barn Dro PE28 . . . .173 D4
New Barns Ave CB7 . . . .240 D6
New Barns Rd CB7 . . . . .240 D5
New Bridge La Elm PE14 235 F6
Wisbech PE14 . . . . .245 A1
New Bridge Rd PE14 . . . .236 E1
New Cangle Sch CB9 . . . .38 F1
New Cheveley Rd CB8 . .111 C2
New Cl SG8 . . . . .12 E3
New Close Rd CB6 . . . . .211 A7
New Cross Dro CB6 . . . .216 B3
New Cross Rd PE9 . . . . .244 B5
New Cut PE6 . . . . .233 D5
New Dro Soham CB7 . . . .211 E4
🔳 Wisbech PE13 . . . . . . .245 D2
Wisbech St Mary PE13 . .235 C4
New England CB1 . . . . . .120 B2
New Farm Cl 🔳 SG8 . . . . .15 E8
New Farm Cotts CB1 . . . .20 E7
New Fen Dike PE12 . . . .237 A6
New Fen Road La PE26 .171 C8
New H CB3 . . . . .83 C3
New La PE8 . . . . .183 C8
New Long Dro PE7 . . . . .177 F6
New Meadow Dro PE7 . .187 D1
New Park St CB5 . . . . . .246 A4
New Path 🔳 CB7 . . . . . .212 E1
New Pk PE15 . . . . .243 E5
New Rd Barton CB3 . . . . .63 B4
Burwell CB5 . . . . .130 B3
Chatteris PE16 . . . . . . .241 E5
Cottenham CB4 . . . . . . .125 C4
Exning CB8 . . . . .110 B8
🔳 Eye PE6 . . . . .232 A1
Great & Little Chishill SG8 .15 E8
Guilden Morden SG8 . . . . .11 A5
Haddenham CB6 . . . . . .210 A6
Harston CB2 . . . . .47 F3
Haslingfield CB3 . . . . . . .47 B5
Hemingford Abbots PE28 .143 A1
Hinxton CB10 . . . . .18 B6
Histon CB4 . . . . .104 C3
Impington CB4 . . . . .104 C2
Littleport CB6 . . . . .242 D5
March PE15 . . . . .243 E4
Melbourn SG8 . . . . .14 E4
Mepal CB6 . . . . .216 E3
Offord Cluny PE19 . . . . .118 A2
Outwell PE14 . . . . .236 E1
Over CB4 . . . . .208 D1
Peterborough PE2 . . . . .185 E4
Peterborough PE2 . . . . .186 E7
Ramsey PE26 . . . . .172 B7
St Ives PE27 . . . . .144 B3
Sawston CB2 . . . . .32 E8
Shudy Camps CB1 . . . . . .22 C7
Upwell PE14 . . . . .229 E8
Warboys PE28 . . . . .165 F6
Whittlesey PE7 . . . . . . .189 F6
Wood Walton PE28 . . . . .161 E7
New River Bank CB7 . . .242 F5
New River Gn CB8 . . . . .110 B8
New Road CP Sch PE7 . .189 F6
New Row 🔳 PE6 . . . . . .231 E8
New Sch Rd CB4 . . . . . .104 B3
New Sq SG8 . . . . .246 B3
New St Cambridge CB1 . .84 A2
Chippenham CB7 . . . . . .132 E8
Doddington/Wimblington
PE15 . . . . .222 F5
Godmanchester PE29 . . .141 F1
Mildenhall IP28 . . . . . . .239 C4
St Neots PE19 . . . . .74 E5
Stamford PE9 . . . . .244 C4
New Town Rd CB6 . . . . .209 F6
Newark Ave PE1 . . . . . .198 C6
Newark Cl SG8 . . . . .5 C8
Newark Hill CP Sch
PE1 . . . . .198 D6
Newark Rd PE1 . . . . . . .198 F4
Newbey Cl PE3 . . . . . . .197 B3
Newborn Cl PE2 . . . . . .187 E5
Newborough Prim Sch
PE6 . . . . .207 C1
Newborough Rd PE4 . . .205 C2
Newboults La 🔳 PE9 . . .244 A5
Newcastle Dr PE2 . . . . .186 D6
Newcombe Way PE2 . . .185 D2
Newell Cl SG8 . . . . .44 D1
Newgate Rd PE13 . . . . .237 F6
Newgate St PE15 . . . . . .222 F5
Newgates 🔳 PE9 . . . . . .244 C5
Newghant Dro PE15 . . . .223 F4
Newham Rd PE9 . . . . . .244 A7
Newington CB4 . . . . . . .124 B8
Newlands Ave PE15 . . . .243 D5
Newlands Rd
Chatteris PE16 . . . . . . .241 E6
Parson Drove PE13 . . . .234 D7
Whittlesey PE7 . . . . . . .190 A8
Newman Ave CB6 . . . . . . .5 F6
Newman CI 🔳 PE8 . . . . .230 B1
Newmarket Cl PE1 . . . . .198 B6
Newmarket Com Hospl
CB8 . . . . .111 A5
Newmarket Rd
Ashley CB8 . . . . .91 E8
Barton Mills PE28 . . . . .239 D1
Burwell CB5 . . . . .130 C1
Cambridge CB5 . . . . . . .246 C3

Newmarket Rd continued
Cheveley CB8 . . . . .91 C8
Cowlinge CB8 . . . . .73 D3
Fen Ditton CB1 . . . . .85 D3
Fordham CB7 . . . . .131 D7
Great Chesterford CB10 . .18 C3
Lidgate CB8 . . . . .73 C6
Moulton CB8 . . . . .112 E5
Royston SG8 . . . . .5 F6
Snailwell CB8 . . . . .132 B2
Stow cum Quy CB5 . . . . .85 F4
Stretham CB6 . . . . .211 A3
Newmarket Sports Ctr
CB8 . . . . .110 F4
Newmarket Sta CB8 . . . .111 A2
Newmarket Swimming Pool
CB8 . . . . .110 F3
Newmarket Upper Sch
CB8 . . . . .110 F4
Newnham Cl
Huntingdon PE29 . . . . . .142 A7
Mildenhall IP28 . . . . . . .239 D5
Newnham Coll CB3 . . . . .64 C8
Newnham Croft Prim Sch
CB3 . . . . .64 C7
Newnham Croft St 🔳
CB3 . . . . .64 C7
Newnham Dro CB5 . . . . .129 C5
Newnham La CB5 . . . . . .130 B3
Newnham Rd CB3 . . . . . .64 C7
Newnham St 🔳 CB7 . . . .240 D4
Newnham Way SG7 . . . . . .2 B2
Newnham Wlk CB3 . . . . . .64 C8
Newport Ave CB7 . . . . . .213 A1
Newstead Cl PE5 . . . . . .232 A2
Newstead Rd PE9 . . . . . .230 A8
Newton Cty Prim Sch
PE19 . . . . .77 E3
Newton Rd Cambridge CB2 64 E5
Great Shelford CB2 . . . . .48 D3
Harston CB2 . . . . .47 F1
Newton CB2 . . . . .31 A8
Sawtry PE28 . . . . .168 C4
Newtown
Hail Weston PE19 . . . . . .74 B8
Kimbolton PE28 . . . . . . .113 F5
Newtown La CB3 . . . . . .113 F5
Newtown Rd PE26 . . . . .172 B7
Nicholas Taylor Gdns 🔳
PE3 . . . . .196 F3
Nicholls Ave PE3 . . . . . .197 E3
Nigel Rd CB6 . . . . .240 E8
Nightall Rd CB7 . . . . . . .212 A4
Nightingale Ave
Bassingbourn SG8 . . . . . .13 A5
Cambridge CB1 . . . . .65 C3
Nightingale Cl IP28 . . . .239 D4
Nightingale Ct PE4 . . . . .205 A2
Nightingale Dr PE7 . . . . .181 D6
Nightingale Way 🔳 PE19 75 B7
Nightingale Wlk 🔳
PE15 . . . . .224 B4
Nimbus Way CB8 . . . . . .110 E8
Nine Chimneys La CB1 . . .53 B2
Nipcut Rd PE6 . . . . .232 C2
Nixhill Rd PE15 . . . . . . .223 B6
Noble Gdns PE15 . . . . . .243 E3
Nobles Cl PE7 . . . . .190 F8
Nobles La PE28 . . . . . . .208 C5
Noel Murless Dr CB8 . . .110 F5
Nook The PE6 . . . . .231 C4
Norburn PE3 . . . . .197 B8
Norfolk Ave CB8 . . . . . . .110 E5
Norfolk Rd Ely CB6 . . . .240 A3
Huntingdon PE29 . . . . . .141 E8
St Ives PE27 . . . . .144 A8
Wyton Airfield PE28 . . . .143 B8
Norfolk Sq 🔳 PE9 . . . . .244 B6
Norfolk St Cambridge CB1 .84 A1
Doddington/Wimblington
PE15 . . . . .223 B7
Wisbech PE13 . . . . .245 C4
Norfolk Terr CB1 . . . . . . .84 A1
Norgett's La SG8 . . . . . . .14 D6
Norham Ct PE7 . . . . . . .188 A5
Norico Bay PE15 . . . . . .243 E2
Norman Cl PE7 . . . . . . .189 E8
Norman Dr PE7 . . . . . . .175 F8
Norman Pk CB3 . . . . . . .102 C4
Norman Rd PE1 . . . . . . .198 C4
Norman Way
🔳 Doddington/Wimblington
PE15 . . . . .223 B7
Over CB4 . . . . .208 D1
Norman's La 🔳 SG8 . . . . . .5 D5
Normanton Rd PE1 . . . . .198 D7
Normanton Way CB4 . . .104 B5
Normoor Dro PE16 . . . . .223 B2
Nornea La CB7 . . . . .211 F8
North Bank PE6 . . . . . . .199 D1
North Bank Rd 🔳 PE1 . .198 D3
North Brink PE13 . . . . . .245 A4
North Cambridgeshire Hospl
PE13 . . . . .245 D5
North Cl SG8 . . . . .5 D8
North Cotts CB2 . . . . . . .64 D4
North Dr March PE15 . . .243 E4
Newmarket CB8 . . . . . . .110 F5
Soham CB7 . . . . .212 B5
North End
Bassingbourn cum Kneesworth
SG8 . . . . .12 D6
Exning CB8 . . . . .130 F3
Meldreth SG8 . . . . .29 B2

North End continued
Wisbech PE13 . . . . .245 B6
North End Rd CB10 . . . . .18 A8
North Fen Dro CB6 . . . . .218 B8
North Fen Rd PE6 . . . . .231 F5
North La SG19 . . . . .41 B7
North Pl IP28 . . . . .239 C4
North Rd
Alconbury Weston PE28 . .150 D5
Brampton PE28 . . . . . . .140 D1
Great Abington CB1 . . . . .33 F5
St Ives PE27 . . . . .144 A4
Whittlesford CB2 . . . . . . .32 B6
North Side PE6 . . . . . . .200 F5
North St Burwell CB5 . . .130 B4
Cambridge CB4 . . . . .83 C4
Folksworth & Washingley
PE7 . . . . .181 A1
Freckenham IP28 . . . . . .213 C3
Huntingdon PE29 . . . . . .141 E5
March PE15 . . . . .243 D5
Peterborough PE1 . . . . .198 A4
Stamford PE9 . . . . .244 B5
Stilton PE7 . . . . .176 A8
Wicken CB7 . . . . .211 E1
Wisbech PE13 . . . . .245 C5
North Terr
Mildenhall IP28 . . . . . . .239 C4
Peterborough PE1 . . . . .198 E7
Sawston CB2 . . . . .32 F5
Northam Cl PE6 . . . . . . .232 A2
Northampton Cl 🔳 CB8 .240 A3
Northampton St CB3 . . . .83 C2
Northborough CP Sch
PE6 . . . . .231 F6
Northey Rd PE6 . . . . . . .199 C2
Northfield Fulbourn CB1 . .67 A5
Girton CB3 . . . . .103 C2
Northfield Cl SG19 . . . . .41 C6
Northfield Pk CB7 . . . . . .212 A5
Northfield Rd Ashwell SG7 . .2 C7
Peterborough PE1 . . . . .197 F7
Soham CB7 . . . . .212 A5
Wyboston PE19 . . . . .74 A1
Northfields Ave CB4 . . . .83 E7
Northfields Rd CB5 . . . . .107 D2
Northgate PE7 . . . . .189 D8
Northgate Cl PE7 . . . . . .189 D8
Northminster PE1 . . . . . .198 A3
Northumberland Ave 🔳
PE9 . . . . .244 A6
Northumberland Cl 🔳
CB4 . . . . .83 D6
Northumbria Cl CB6 . . . .210 A7
Northwold CB6 . . . . .240 C5
Norton Cl Cambridge CB5 .84 D3
Papworth Everard CB3 . . .99 A2
Norton Rd Haverhill CB9 . .23 E6
Peterborough PE1 . . . . .197 F6
Norwalde St PE15 . . . . .243 C6
Norwich Rd PE13 . . . . . .245 E5
Norwich St CB2 . . . . .64 E7
Norwood Ave PE15 . . . .243 D5
Norwood CP Sch PE4 . . .204 E2
Norwood Cres PE15 . . . .243 C6
Norwood La PE4 . . . . . .205 B2
Norwood Rd March PE15 243 C6
🔟 Somersham PE28 . . . .215 C1
Notley Dr CB9 . . . . .38 C1
Nottingham Way PE1 . . .198 C6
Nuffield Cl CB4 . . . . .84 B7
Nuffield Rd
Cambridge CB4 . . . . .84 B7
St Ives PE27 . . . . .144 C6
Nunns Way 🔳 CB6 . . . . .216 E1
Nun's Orch CB4 . . . . . . .104 B4
Nuns Way CB4 . . . . .83 F7
Nursery Cl Isleham CB7 .212 F4
Peterborough PE1 . . . . .198 A4
Nursery Dr March PE15 .243 B5
Wisbech PE13 . . . . .245 E8
Nursery Gdns
Little Paxton PE19 . . . . . .96 A2
St Ives PE27 . . . . .144 B5
Whittlesey PE7 . . . . . . .189 F6
Nursery La PE1 . . . . . . .198 D2
Nursery Rd
Huntingdon PE29 . . . . . .141 E4
St Neots PE19 . . . . .74 F4
Nursery Way 🔳 CB3 . . . .62 C5
Nursery Wlk
Brampton PE28 . . . . . . .140 C3
Cambridge CB4 . . . . .83 C5
Nutholt La CB6 . . . . .240 D5
Nutters Cl CB3 . . . . .64 A4
Nuttings Rd CB1 . . . . . . .84 D1

O

O Furlong Dro CB6 . . . .224 F1
Oak Cl PE19 . . . . .75 A5
Oak Dr Brampton PE28 . .140 C4
Little Stukeley PE28 . . . .151 F3
Mildenhall IP28 . . . . . . .213 F8
Outwell PE14 . . . . .236 F3
Oak End PE28 . . . . .150 F4
Oak Farm Cl PE7 . . . . . .176 A7
Oak La Cheveley CB8 . . . .91 C4
Littleport CB6 . . . . .242 A2
Oak Rd Glinton PE6 . . . .231 E5
Stilton PE7 . . . . .176 A7
Oak Tree Ave CB4 . . . . . .83 F5
Oak Tree Cl March PE15 .243 C5
St Ives PE27 . . . . .143 F5
Oak Tree Way CB4 . . . . .104 B3
Oak View PE3 . . . . .196 F2
Oakdale Ave PE2 . . . . . .187 D4

Oakdale CP Sch PE7 . . . .187 C4
Oakington CE Prim Sch
CB4 . . . . .103 C5
Oakington Rd
Cottenham CB4 . . . . . . .125 B1
Dry Drayton CB3 . . . . . .102 D2
Girton CB3 . . . . .103 E3
Oakington & Westwick
CB4 . . . . .103 E3
Oaklands PE28 . . . . .121 B5
Oaklands Ave PE6 . . . . .163 F7
Oaklands Dr PE13 . . . . .245 F7
Oakleaf Rd PE1 . . . . . . .198 C6
Oakleigh Cres PE29 . . . .141 F1
Oakleigh Dr PE2 . . . . . . .186 C6
Oakley Cl PE13 . . . . .245 E4
Oakley Dr 🔳 PE28 . . . . .168 B3
Oakrits SG8 . . . . .14 B8
🔳 Manea PE15 . . . . . . .224 B4
Oaks Dr CB8 . . . . .110 F7
Oaks The Milton CB4 . . .105 C2
Soham CB7 . . . . .212 B3
Oaktree Rd CB4 . . . . .31 A7
Oasthouse Way PE26 . . .172 A5
Oates' La CB6 . . . . .216 E1
Oates Way PE26 . . . . . .172 A5
Oatlands Ave CB3 . . . . .102 B4
Occupation Rd
Cambridge CB1 . . . . .84 A2
Peterborough PE1 . . . . .197 E6
Ockendon Cl PE19 . . . . . .74 B3
Octagon Dr 🔳 CB8 . . . .245 A6
Octavia Cl PE13 . . . . . . .245 F6
Octavia Hill Birthplace Mus★
PE13 . . . . .245 C5
Odecroft PE3 . . . . .197 C7
Offa Lea CB2 . . . . .31 B7
Offord Prim Sch PE19 . .118 A2
Offord Rd PE19 . . . . .97 F6
Ogden Cl SG8 . . . . .14 D6
Oil Mill La PE13 . . . . . . .245 B5
Oilmills Dro PE26 . . . . . .220 F4
Oilmills Rd PE26 . . . . . .220 E6
Old Auction Yd PE16 . . .241 C5
Old Bank CB7 . . . . .219 B4
Old Brewery Cl 🔳 CB7 . .240 E4
Old Church La CB8 . . . . .208 C7
Old Clements La 🔳 CB9 .23 F7
Old Court H PE29 . . . . . .141 E1
Old Farm Cl Histon CB4 .104 B5
🔳 Needingworth PE27 . . .208 A3
Old Fen Dike PE12 . . . . .237 B6
Old Ford La PE19 . . . . . .114 B2
Old Forge Way CB2 . . . . .32 E8
Old Glebe PE28 . . . . . . .150 E5
Old Great North Rd
St Martin's Without PE9 . .244 C3
Sibson cum Stibbington
PE8 . . . . .194 C2
Old Haverhill Rd CB9 . . . .39 E4
Old Houghton Rd PE29 . .142 B6
Old House Rd CB1 . . . . . .53 C2
Old Knarr Fen Dro PE6 . .233 C2
Old Leicester Rd PE8 . . .194 A3
Old Lynn Dro CB6 . . . . .217 C2
Old Lynn Rd PE13 . . . . .245 C7
Old Mill Ave PE28 . . . . .165 A5
Old Mill Cl CB2 . . . . .29 D7
Old Mill La IP28 . . . . . . .239 F2
Old Mkt PE13 . . . . .245 C5
Old North Rd
Bassingbourn cum Kneesworth
SG8 . . . . .13 B4
Longstowe CB3 . . . . .60 A3
Royston SG8 . . . . .5 C7
Sawtry PE28 . . . . .168 D4
Wansford PE8 . . . . .194 A3
Old Oundle Rd PE8 . . . .193 A4
Old Pinewood Way CB3 . .99 B4
Old Pond La PE5 . . . . . .195 E2
Old Pools Dro CB6 . . . . .225 C4
Old Pound Cl PE28 . . . . .143 D2
Old Ramsey Rd
St Ives PE28 . . . . .143 E8
Woodhurst PE28 . . . . . .154 E2
Old Rectory Dr
Dry Drayton CB3 . . . . . .102 B1
🔳 Tallington PE9 . . . . . .230 F7
Thornhaugh PE8 . . . . . .194 A6
Old Rope Wlk CB9 . . . . . .23 E7
Old Sch The PE28 . . . . .160 C2
Old School Cl
Burwell CB5 . . . . .130 C3
Littleport CB6 . . . . .242 D5
🔳 Soham CB7 . . . . .212 B5
Old School Gdns 🔳 PE19 74 C2
Old School La
Brinkley CB8 . . . . .70 E1
Milton CB4 . . . . .105 D2
Wicken CB7 . . . . .211 B1
Old Stable Wlk 🔳 PE26 .172 A4
Old Station Rd CB8 . . . . .111 B4
Old Sunday Sch CB5 . . .106 B7
Old West Est PE15 . . . . .222 A5
Old Weston Rd PE28 . . .158 A5
Oldbrook PE3 . . . . .204 A1
Oldeamere Way PE7 . . .190 A7
Oldfield Ave 🔳 PE14 . . .236 B5
Oldfield Gdns PE7 . . . . .189 D7
Oldfield La PE13 . . . . . . .245 B6
Oldhurst Rd PE28 . . . . . .155 E8
Olive Rd PE1 . . . . .198 C2
Oliver Cl PE26 . . . . .171 F6
Oliver Cromwell Ho★
CB7 . . . . .240 C4
Oliver Rd 🔳 PE27 . . . . .144 B3
Olivers Way PE15 . . . . .243 D4
Olivia Rd PE28 . . . . .140 C3

Ollard Ave PE13 . . . . . . .245 D7
Onyx Ct 🔳 PE13 . . . . . .245 C4
Open Univ The CB2 . . . .246 C1
Opportune Rd PE13 . . . .245 C6
Orange Gr 🔳 PE13 . . . . .245 C4
Orchard Ave CB4 . . . . . . .83 E5
Orchard Cl 🔳 Balsham CB1 .52 F3
Bassingbourn SG8 . . . . . .13 A5
Cottenham CB4 . . . . . . .125 C3
Eaton Socon PE19 . . . . . .74 C4
Elsworth CB3 . . . . .100 B4
Girton CB3 . . . . .103 E1
Hail Weston PE19 . . . . . .95 A1
Haverhill CB9 . . . . .23 F7
Lidgate CB8 . . . . .73 E8
Little Wilbraham CB1 . . . .86 E2
Littleport CB6 . . . . .242 D4
🔳 Manea PE15 . . . . . . .224 B4
March PE15 . . . . .243 E3
🔳 Market Deeping PE6 . .231 E8
Peterborough PE3 . . . . .197 D3
Stilton PE7 . . . . .176 A7
Warboys PE28 . . . . .164 F6
Warmington PE8 . . . . . .178 B3
🔳 Wisbech PE13 . . . . . .236 A5
Orchard Cres 🔳 PE28 . . .208 E6
Orchard Ct 🔳 PE6 . . . . .232 F3
Orchard Dr Girton CB3 . . .82 E7
Waterbeach CB5 . . . . . .127 B1
Wisbech PE13 . . . . .245 E4
Orchard End
🔳 Bluntisham/Colne
PE28 . . . . .208 C5
Rampton CB4 . . . . .124 E4
Orchard Est
Cambridge CB1 . . . . .65 F7
🔳 Little Downham CB6 . .218 B7
Orchard Gate 14 C6
Orchard Gdns PE28 . . . .121 B5
Orchard La
Brampton PE28 . . . . . . .140 E3
Huntingdon PE29 . . . . . .141 E4
🔳 Haslingfield CB3 . . . . .47 B5
Histon CB4 . . . . .104 C5
March PE15 . . . . .243 E3
Melbourn SG8 . . . . .14 C5
Royston SG8 . . . . .5 B7
Sawston CB2 . . . . .32 F7
Stamford PE9 . . . . .244 B5
Orchard Mews PE2 . . . .186 F8
Orchard Pightle CB8 . . . . .20 B6
Orchard Rd Barnack PE9 .230 E4
Eaton Socon PE19 . . . . . .74 C4
Great Shelford CB2 . . . . .49 B6
🔳 Haslingfield CB3 . . . . .47 B5
Histon CB4 . . . . .104 C5
March PE15 . . . . .243 E3
Melbourn SG8 . . . . .14 C5
Royston SG8 . . . . .5 B7
Sawston CB2 . . . . .32 F7
Stamford PE9 . . . . .244 B5
Orchard Rd S PE15 . . . .243 E3
Orchard Row CB7 . . . . .212 C2
Orchard St
Cambridge CB1 . . . . . . .246 B3
Peterborough PE2 . . . . .186 F7
Stow cum Quy CB5 . . . . .85 F5
Whittlesey PE7 . . . . . . .189 D7
Orchard Terr CB2 . . . . . .32 C4
Orchard The Ashley CB8 . .91 F7
Fen Drayton CB4 . . . . . .121 F5
Little Paxton PE19 . . . . . .95 F2
Peterborough PE4 . . . . .204 C3
Orchard View CB5 . . . . .127 B1
Orchard Way
Burwell CB5 . . . . .130 B3
🔳 Doddington/Wimblington
PE15 . . . . .223 B7
Godmanchester PE29 . . .141 F2
🔳 Haddenham PE6 . . . .210 A5
🔳 Manea PE15 . . . . . . .224 B4
Melbourn SG8 . . . . .14 D6
Oakington/Longstanton
CB4 . . . . .103 C5
Offord Cluny PE19 . . . . . .97 A8
Ramsey PE26 . . . . .172 A7
Royston SG8 . . . . .5 C8
Orchard Way Cl CB2 . . . .47 F2
Orchards The
Chatteris PE16 . . . . . . .241 D5
Great Shelford CB2 . . . . .49 B6
Peterborough PE2 . . . . .185 F4
Sutton CB6 . . . . .216 E2
🔳 Wilburton CB6 . . . . . .210 C6
Witcham CB6 . . . . .217 A2
Orchid Cl
🔟🔳 Eaton Socon PE19 . .74 C6
Yaxley PE7 . . . . .181 F7
Orford Rd CB9 . . . . .23 F6
Orkney Cl CB9 . . . . .24 D7
Orme Rd PE3 . . . . .197 D4
Orthwaite PE29 . . . . . . .141 B6
Orton Ave PE2 . . . . .186 E7
Orton Dr CB6 . . . . .217 D1
Orton Longueville Sch
PE2 . . . . .186 A5
Orton Matley Prim Sch
PE2 . . . . .185 E5
Orton Mere PE2 . . . . . . .186 B7
Orton Parkway PE2 . . . .185 D4
Orton Wistow Prim Sch
PE2 . . . . .185 C6
Orwell Cl PE27 . . . . .144 A6
Orwell Dr PE15 . . . . .243 B6
Orwell Furlong CB4 . . . . .84 C7
Orwell Gr PE4 . . . . .204 F1
Orwell Rd CB2 . . . . .29 C8
Osborn Cl 🔳 CB4 . . . . .209 A1
Osborne Pk PE13 . . . . . .245 C8
Osborne Rd PE13 . . . . . .245 B7
Osier Cl 🔳 CB7 . . . . . . .240 E4
Osier Ct 🔳 PE19 . . . . . . .74 C6
Osier Holt 🔳 PE28 . . . . .208 D6
Osiers The PE28 . . . . . . .117 A3
Oslar's Way CB1 . . . . . . .66 E5

Osprey PE2 ....185 F2
Osprey Cl PE29 ......142 A7
Osprey Rd CB9 ......24 C7
Otago Cl PE7 ......189 F8
Otago Rd PE7 ......189 F8
Othello Cl PE29 ......142 A7
Otter Cl CB3 ......102 B4
Otter Way 9 PE19 ......74 B5
Otterbrook PE2 ......185 D5
Oundle Rd Elton PE8 ......183 F1
 Peterborough PE2 ......185 E6
Ouse Fen Rd or Bank
 CB4 ......208 D3
Ouse Rd Eaton Socon PE19 ..74 C4
 Kimbolton PE28 ......114 B7
 St Ives PE27 ......144 A7
Ouse Washes Nature
 Reserve★ CB6 ......224 D2
Ouse Wlk 1 PE29 ......141 A1
Outfield PE3 ......204 A1
Outwell Rd Elm PE14 ......236 C5
 Emneth PE14 ......236 D4
 Outwell PE14 ......236 E3
Over CP Sch CB4 ......208 D1
Over Hall La CB10 ......21 D2
Over Rd Swavesey CB4 ......122 F8
 Willingham CB4 ......208 F1
Overchurch Cl CB9 ......23 F7
Overcote La PE27 ......208 B2
Overcote Rd CB4 ......208 D1
Overend PE8 ......178 D8
Overhills CP Sch PE28 ...173 C5
Overstone Ct PE3 ......197 C6
Overstone Dr 1 PE14 ......235 D1
Overstone Rd 2 PE14 ......235 D1
Overton Way PE2 ......185 F4
Overwater Cl 1 PE29 ......141 A6
Owall Wlk 8 SG8 ......5 E3
Owen Cl 3 PE9 ......230 D3
Owen Dr SG8 ......13 D1
Owl End
 The Stukeleys PE28 ......151 F2
 Yaxley PE7 ......181 D5
Owl Way PE29 ......142 B7
Owls End PE26 ......172 A4
Owlstone Rd CB3 ......64 C7
Oxburgh Cl
 3 Peterborough PE7 ...187 F5
 1 Wisbech PE13 ......245 A7
Oxclose PE3 ......197 A8
Oxford Cl
 Bassingbourn SG8 ......12 F7
 Mildenhall IP28 ......239 A5
Oxford Rd Cambridge CB4 ..83 D4
 Peterborough PE1 ......197 F5
 St Ives PE27 ......144 A4
 Stamford PE9 ......244 A7
Oxford St CB8 ......110 B8
Oxholme Dro CB4 ......209 F1
Oxney Rd PE1 ......198 D5
Oyster Row CB5 ......84 B3

P

Pacific Cl PE15 ......243 C6
Paddock Cl CB4 ......104 C4
Paddock Row CB3 ......100 B4
Paddock St CB7 ......212 B4
Paddock The
 Eaton Socon PE19 ......74 D4
 Ely CB6 ......240 D5
 Harston CB2 ......47 F2
 Huntingdon PE29 ......141 E5
 15 Somersham PE28 ...215 C1
 Stamford PE9 ......244 A5
Paddock Way
 1 Haddenham CB6 ......210 A6
 Sawston CB2 ......32 F7
Paddocks Chase PE19 ..118 A3
Paddocks CP Sch CB8 ..110 E4
Paddocks Dr CB8 ......111 A1
Paddocks The
 Alconbury PE28 ......150 F5
 Burwell CB5 ......130 B1
 Cambridge CB1 ......84 C1
 Folksworth PE7 ......175 D8
 Hilton PE28 ......120 B2
 Little Wilbraham CB8 ...68 F5
 Whittlesey PE7 ......189 E7
 Worlington IP28 ......213 F4
Padgett's Rd PE14 ......229 C3
Padgetts Cl PE28 ......165 A5
Padholme Rd PE1 ......198 C3
Padholme Rd E PE1 ......198 C3
Padlock Rd CB1 ......53 F4
Padnal Bank CB7 ......219 B6
Padnal Dro CB6 ......242 E3
Padney Rd CB6 ......211 D5
Pages Way 3 PE28 ......140 C3
Paget Cl CB2 ......64 E3
Paget Pl CB8 ......111 A6
Paget Rd CB2 ......64 D2
Painter's La PE28 ......216 D1
Pakenham Cl CB4 ......84 C5
Palace Gdns SG8 ......5 C6
Palace La CB7 ......132 D8
Palisade Ct 3 CB6 ......211 B7
Palmer Cl PE7 ......189 F6
Palmers Cl CB1 ......35 D3
Palmers La
 Alconbury PE28 ......150 F4
 Chrishall SG8 ......8 C4
Palmers Rd PE1 ......198 F5
Palmers Way SG8 ......14 D6
Palmers Wlk CB1 ......246 C2
Palmerston Rd PE2 ......186 F7
Pamment's La IP28 ......213 D6

Pampisford Rd CB1 ......34 C5
Pamplin Ct 1 CB1 ......65 F6
Panswell La PE13 ......235 C8
Panther Way 1 CB1 ......66 A7
Pantile La CB5 ......130 A3
Panton St CB2 ......246 B1
Papley Grove Farm Cotts
 PE19 ......77 E7
Papworth Hospl CB3 ......99 C2
Papworth Rd
 Graveley PE19 ......98 A5
 March PE15 ......243 F4
Papyrus Rd PE4 ......203 F3
Papyrus Way PE28 ......168 B4
Parade La CB7 ......240 C4
Paradise Ctr & Pool
 CB7 ......240 D5
Paradise La
 Northborough PE6 ......231 F6
 3 Whittlesey PE7 ......189 D6
Paradise St CB1 ......246 C3
Paragon Rd PE27 ......144 A5
Parcell Wlk PE7 ......118 F8
Parish Bush Dro CB7 ...219 C1
Park Ave Histon CB4 ......104 A4
 Little Paxton PE19 ......95 F1
 Newmarket CB8 ......111 B3
 St Ives PE27 ......144 B4
 Wisbech PE13 ......245 C4
Park Cl Bassingbourn SG8 ..12 E5
 Holme PE7 ......176 F4
 Little Paxton PE19 ......95 E1
 Moulton CB8 ......112 F5
 1 Thorney PE6 ......233 B3
 Yaxley PE7 ......181 D5
Park Cotts CB8 ......111 B3
Park Cres
 Little Paxton PE19 ......95 F2
 Peterborough PE1 ......198 B5
 Thorney PE6 ......233 B3
 Waterbeach CB5 ......106 C8
Park Dr Histon CB4 ......104 C3
 Little Paxton PE19 ......95 F1
Park Est 1 PE6 ......231 F8
Park Farm Cotts CB10 ...18 F6
Park Farm Cres PE7 ......187 F5
Park Farm Dr IP28 ......214 A2
Park Farm La SG8 ......1 A2
Park Farm Rd PE6 ......196 E5
Park Farm Way PE7 ......187 F6
Park Hill CB1 ......37 C2
Park La Brampton PE28 ...117 D8
 Castle Camps CB1 ......22 F3
 Dry Drayton CB3 ......81 C8
 Fen Drayton CB4 ......121 F6
 Godmanchester PE29 ...141 F2
 Histon CB4 ......103 F4
 Kimbolton PE19 ......113 F2
 Langley CB11 ......1 F2
 Leverington PE13 ......238 A3
 Little Downham CB6 ......217 F6
 Longstowe CB3 ......59 F3
 Madingley CB3 ......81 F6
 Newmarket CB8 ......111 B3
 Peterborough PE1 ......198 C4
 Ramsey PE26 ......171 F6
 St Ives PE27 ......144 B4
 St Neots PE19 ......74 F6
 Sawston CB2 ......32 F5
 Sawtry PE28 ......168 B5
 Sutton CB6 ......216 E2
 Tydd St Giles PE13 ......237 D7
 Wisbech PE13 ......245 D5
Park Side PE19 ......95 E1
Park St Cambridge CB5 ...246 A3
 Chatteris PE16 ......241 C4
 Dry Drayton CB3 ......102 C1
 Peterborough PE7 ......186 F7
 2 Wisbech PE13 ......245 D5
Park Street Prim & Jun Sch
 CB5 ......246 A3
Park Terr CB1 ......246 B2
Park View
 Bassingbourn SG8 ......12 E5
 Little Stukeley PE28 ......151 F1
 Needingworth PE27 ......208 A2
Park Way
 Little Paxton PE19 ......95 F1
 Offord Cluny PE19 ......118 A2
 St Neots PE19 ......74 F7
Parker Rd PE8 ......230 B1
Parker St CB1 ......246 B2
Parker's Cl PE16 ......241 B5
Parker's Dro PE28 ......213 D6
Parker's Terr 2 CB1 ......84 A2
Parkers Wlk CB8 ......110 E8
Parkfield La PE15 ......223 B6
Parkgate PE29 ......141 C6
Parkhall Rd PE29 ......141 C6
Parkinson's La 1 PE7 ...189 D6
Parklands SG8 ......5 E6

Parkside Cambridge CB1 .246 C2
 Chippenham CB7 ......132 E8
 Mildenhall IP28 ......214 A8
 Peterborough PE2 ......186 B6
Parkside Com Coll CB1 .246 C2
Parkside Pools CB1 ......246 C2
Parkway St Ives PE27 ...144 B4
 Shudy Camps CB1 ......22 C6
 The Stukeleys PE29 ......141 A5
Parkway Mid Sch CB9 ...23 D8
Parliament St PE1 ......197 F5
Parlour Cl CB4 ......104 B5
Parnwell CP Sch PE1 ...198 E7
Parnwell Way PE1 ......198 F6
Parr Cl 3 CB4 ......104 C3
Parrens Rd 4 PE28 ......208 E6
Parson Drove La PE13 ...238 B2
Parsonage Barns CB5 ...86 F5
Parsonage Cl PE6 ......130 B2
Parsonage Farm La CB8 .90 C7
Parsonage La CB5 ......130 B2
Parsonage St
 Cambridge CB5 ......246 C3
 Wistow PE28 ......163 F6
Parsonage Way CB1 ......35 D2
Parson's Ct CB5 ......246 A2
Parson's Dr PE28 ......139 A4
Parson's La CB6 ......242 C4
Parson's Land Dro PE15 222 D6
Parsons Gn PE27 ......144 C4
Parthia Cl SG8 ......5 E6
Partridge Cl PE7 ......181 D5
Partridge Dr CB3 ......102 B3
Partridge Gr PE4 ......204 A5
Partridge Hill SG7 ......2 C3
Paske Ave CB9 ......23 F7
Passage The 10 CB7 ......240 D4
Paston La PE4 ......197 D8
Paston Parkway PE4 ......204 E4
Paston Ridings PE4 ......204 E1
Paston Ridings Cty Jun & Inf
 Sch PE4 ......204 F1
Pasture Cl PE28 ......165 A5
Pasture La PE6 ......231 F6
Pasture The PE28 ......208 B8
Pastures The CB3 ......81 A1
Pates Cl CB3 ......47 A6
Pathfinder Way
 Ramsey PE26 ......171 F5
 Warboys PE28 ......164 F4
Patterdale Rd 2 PE4 ......205 A2
Paulsgrove PE2 ......185 D5
Pavement The PE27 ......144 A3
Pavilion Ct CB9 ......24 B7
Paxton Cl CB4 ......125 E3
Paxton Hill PE19 ......96 D2
Paxton Rd
 Offord Darcy PE19 ......96 F7
 Peterborough PE2 ......185 D4
Payne Ave PE13 ......245 D7
Payne Rd PE13 ......234 D7
Paynells PE2 ......186 A3
Paynesholm PE4 ......205 A1
Payton Way CB5 ......106 B7
Peacock Dr CB5 ......86 F7
Peacock Way PE3 ......196 F2
Peacocks CB2 ......49 A4
Peake Cl PE2 ......186 F6
Peakes Dr PE7 ......201 F1
Peakirk cum Glinton CE Prim
 Sch PE6 ......203 E8
Peakirk Rd
 Deeping Gate PE6 ......231 F8
 Glinton PE6 ......203 F8
 Northborough PE6 ......206 A4
Peakirk Wildfowl Trust★
 PE6 ......206 B2
Peaks Ct PE29 ......141 A5
Pear Tree Cl
 Fenstanton PE28 ......121 A5
 Haddenham CB6 ......210 A5
Pear Tree Cres PE13 ...238 A2
Pearce Cl CB3 ......64 B8
Pearces Rd PE6 ......199 B5
Pearl L Ctr PE5 ......195 E1
Pearmain Ct CB4 ......84 C5
Pearmains Cl SG8 ......45 E1
Pearson Cl CB4 ......105 D1
Peartree Way 10 PE14 ..236 A5
Peas Hill CB2 ......246 A2
Peas Hill Rd PE15 ......243 A5
Pease Way CB4 ......103 F4
Peate Cl PE29 ......141 F1
Peatlings La PE13 ......245 A7
Peckover Cl 4 PE7 ......187 F5
Peckover Dr PE13 ......245 E4
Peckover Ho★ PE13 ......245 B5
Peckover Prim Sch
 PE13 ......245 B6
Pecks Cl PE28 ......120 C1
Pecks Yd PE16 ......241 C5
Peddars Way PE3 ......197 A2
Pedley La PE13 ......245 A6
Peer Rd PE19 ......74 B4
Pegler Ct 5 PE28 ......209 A1
Peldon Dr PE13 ......245 E2
Pelham Cl
 Cottenham CB4 ......125 D3
 Peterborough PE3 ......196 F2
Pelham Ct CB4 ......83 C6
Pelham Way CB4 ......125 D3
Pelican Prep Sch CB1 ...65 B4
Pemberton Terr CB2 ......246 B1
Pembroke Ave
 Peterborough PE2 ......185 F5
 9 St Neots PE19 ......74 F7
 Waterbeach CB5 ......105 F8

Pembroke Cl
 Huntingdon PE29 ......141 F7
 Mildenhall IP28 ......239 C5
 2 Newmarket CB8 ......111 B2
Pembroke Coll CB2 ......246 A2
Pembroke Gr PE6 ......203 F8
Pembroke La 2 CB1 ......35 E2
Pembroke Rd PE9 ......244 A4
Pembroke St CB2 ......246 A2
Pembroke Way CB1 ......85 B1
Pen Cl CB1 ......66 A6
Pen Hills Nature Reserve★
 SG8 ......4 E3
Penarth Pl CB3 ......64 A8
Pendleton PE3 ......197 B6
Pendragon Com Prim Sch
 CB3 ......99 A3
Pendragon Hill CB3 ......99 A4
Pendula Rd PE13 ......245 E2
Pennine Way PE4 ......204 D2
Pennington PE2 ......185 E3
Pennington Rd PE29 ......142 C1
Pennway 11 PE28 ......215 C1
Penrose Gdns PE13 ......245 E4
Penrwyn Ct 5 PE19 ......74 F1
Pentelowes The PE28 ...135 D2
Pentlands Cl CB4 ......246 C4
Pentlands The PE4 ......204 E2
Pentlow Hawke Cl CB9 ...24 B7
Penwald Ct 7 PE6 ......232 B8
Penyale 3 PE3 ......197 A1
Pepper Cl SG8 ......12 F4
Peppercorn Cl PE1 ......197 E6
Peppercorns La 2 PE19 .74 C2
Pepperslade CB2 ......31 F1
Pepys Ho★ PE28 ......140 F2
Pepys Rd Brampton PE28 .140 F2
 St Neots PE19 ......75 A4
Pepys Road Sch PE19 ...75 A4
Pepys Terr CB4 ......104 C1
Pepys Way 3 CB3 ......82 E8
Percheron Cl CB4 ......104 D3
Percheron Dr PE15 ......243 E2
Percival St PE3 ......197 E2
Peregrine Cl PE29 ......142 A7
Perkins La 7 PE6 ......231 C7
Perne Ave CB1 ......65 C6
Perne Rd CB1 ......65 C6
Pernys Cl PE7 ......186 D3
Perowne St CB1 ......84 A1
Perry Cl CB6 ......210 A6
Perry Ct CB3 ......83 A2
Perry Dr SG8 ......5 E7
Perry Rd Buckden PE19 ..116 F3
 Leverington PE13 ......238 B2
Perse Boys Sch The CB2 .65 A4
Perse Prep Sch CB2 ......64 E4
Perse Sch for Girls The
 CB2 ......246 B1
Perse Way CB4 ......83 D5
Pershore Rd CB3 ......81 A3
Persimmon Wlk CB8 ......110 E8
Peterborough Airport
 (Conington) PE7 ......176 F3
Peterborough Coll of Adult
 Ed PE1 ......198 B3
Peterborough District Hospl
 PE3 ......197 E2
Peterborough Dr
 Bretton PE6 ......196 E2
 Castor PE6 ......196 D3
Peterborough High Sch
 PE3 ......197 D2
Peterborough Rd
 Castor PE5 ......195 E1
 Crowland PE6 ......232 B8
 Eye PE6 ......205 F1
 Newborough PE6 ......205 D8
 Peterborough PE7 ......187 C3
 Wansford PE8 ......194 A3
 Warmington PE8 ......178 A4
 Whittlesey PE7 ......189 B7
Peterborough Regional Coll
 PE1 ......198 A3
Peterborough Sta PE3 ...197 F2
Petergate 1 PE9 ......244 B4
Peterhouse CB2 ......246 A1
Peterhouse Cl 1 PE9 ...244 B7
Peterhouse Cres PE15 .243 E6
Peterhouse Dr CB8 ......111 A2
Petersfield 3 CB1 ......246 C2
Petersfield Rd CB2 ......17 D8
Petersfield Sch SG8 ......28 D8
Petingo Cl CB8 ......110 D7
Pettis Rd PE27 ......143 E6
Pettit Rd PE29 ......142 A1
Pettits Cl CB1 ......66 F4
Pettitt's Cl CB3 ......102 C2
Pettitt's La CB3 ......102 C2
Petts Cl 3 PE13 ......245 E7
Petts La CB10 ......19 E1
Petty Cury CB2 ......246 A2
Petworth St CB1 ......84 A2
Peverel Cl CB5 ......84 D3
Peverel Rd CB5 ......84 D3
Peveril Rd PE1 ......197 F6
Peyton Ave PE15 ......243 B6
Peyton Cl PE15 ......223 A5
Pheasant Gr PE4 ......204 A5
Pheasant Rise CB3 ......102 A3
Pheasant Way PE7 ......181 D5
Philip Gdns PE19 ......74 F2
Philippa Cl CB6 ......240 E7
Philipps Cl CB8 ......110 D4
Phillips Ave CB5 ......5 C8
Phillips Chase 1 PE15 .243 C4
Phillips Ct PE9 ......244 C4
Phillips' Fen Dro CB7 ...219 B6

Phoenix Sq PE19 ......74 E6
Phorpres Cl PE7 ......186 D3
Phorpres Way PE7 ......186 E4
Pickards Way PE13 ......245 A6
Pickle Fen Dro PE16 ......215 E6
Picknage Rd SG8 ......7 A2
Pidley Hill PE28 ......208 A8
Pidley Sheep La PE28 ...155 F7
Pieces La CB5 ......106 B8
Pieces Terr CB5 ......106 B7
Pierce Cres PE8 ......178 C3
Pierce La CB1 ......66 F5
Pig La PE27 ......144 B5
Pigeons Cl SG8 ......31 C2
Pightle Cl Harston CB2 ...47 D2
 Royston SG8 ......5 C7
Pightle The
 2 Bottisham CB5 ......86 E6
 Grafham PE28 ......116 A2
 Haverhill CB9 ......24 A8
Pilgrims Cl CB10 ......18 D2
Pilgrims Way CB6 ......240 A3
Pilton Cl 4 PE4 ......204 F2
Pinder Cl PE7 ......118 F7
Pine Gr CB4 ......122 E3
Pine Tree Cl PE1 ......198 B8
Pine Trees Ave IP28 ......239 E4
Pinewood Ave
 Whittlesey PE7 ......189 E7
 Wittering PE8 ......230 B1
Pinfold La
 Godmanchester PE29 ...141 F1
 Stamford PE9 ......244 D5
Pinfold Rd PE14 ......236 E1
Pingle Bank PE7 ......177 A4
Pingle Dro CB6 ......216 E6
Pingle La PE6 ......231 F6
Pinkeneys SG8 ......8 D5
Pinza Cl CB8 ......110 E8
Piperell Way CB9 ......24 A5
Pipers Cl CB9 ......24 C7
Pipers La PE29 ......141 F1
Pipistrelle Ct 6 PE4 ......204 C3
Pippin Cl
 Offord Darcy PE19 ......117 C1
 Over CB4 ......208 D1
Pippin Dr CB4 ......84 C6
Pippin Pl PE13 ......245 E2
Pippin Wlk CB3 ......81 A3
Pitfield Cl PE28 ......121 C5
Pits La PE15 ......243 D1
Pits The CB7 ......213 A4
Pitsdean Rd PE19 ......57 A4
Pittneys PE4 ......204 F1
Pius Dro PE14 ......236 E2
Place Farm Sch CB9 ......23 F8
Plains La CB6 ......225 C3
Plaistow Way SG8 ......7 E2
Plane Tree Cl SG19 ......41 C6
Plank Dro PE6 ......232 B8
Plantation Gate CB6 ......210 F5
Plantation Rd CB2 ......33 A7
Plantwater Dro PE15 ...227 D5
Plash Dro PE13 ......234 F4
Playles Yd SG8 ......12 E5
Plough Cres PE7 ......189 C8
Plough La PE6 ......207 D1
Plover Cl PE16 ......241 C5
Plover Dr 2 PE15 ......243 F5
Plover Rd PE7 ......189 F8
Ploverly PE4 ......204 C4
Plowright Cl 5 PE15 ...243 B3
Plum Tree Cl 3 CB4 ......83 D7
Plumian Way CB3 ......53 C2
Plumpton Ave IP28 ......239 C5
Polecat La PE28 ......150 E5
Poles Ct PE7 ......189 D7
Police HQ
 Cambridge CB1 ......246 C2
 Peterborough PE3 ......196 F1
Pollards La IP28 ......213 D7
Pond Cl
 Pidley cum Fenton PE28 .165 D1
 The Stukeleys PE29 ......140 F5
Pond Gn CB7 ......211 E1
Pond La 2 CB6 ......218 A6
Pond The CB6 ......210 A7
Pont's Hill CB6 ......242 D5
Pooley Way PE7 ......181 D6
Pools Rd CB6 ......210 D8
Poorsfield Rd 2 CB5 ...106 A7
Pope Rd PE19 ......74 E4
Pope Way PE1 ......197 E8
Pope's La PE13 ......238 A2
Popes Ct 3 CB9 ......24 E5
Popes La Thetford CB6 ...211 B7
 Warboys PE28 ......164 E4
Popham Ct PE19 ......74 A3
Poplar Ave PE1 ......198 C8
Poplar Cl
 Great Gransden SG19 ...58 D4
 Great Shelford CB2 ......49 A5
 Haverhill CB9 ......38 D1
 Huntingdon PE29 ......141 D5
 March PE15 ......243 C5
 Royston SG8 ......5 E7
Poplar Dr SG8 ......5 E7
Poplar Dro PE6 ......242 F8
Poplar Farm Cl SG8 ......12 D4
Poplar Rd CB4 ......104 B3
Poplar Way CB2 ......49 C4
Poplars Cl CB5 ......130 B2
Poplars The PE28 ......208 C6
Popple Dro PE13 ......235 A8
Poppy Fields 7 CB7 ......212 B5

Poppyfields Ave PE15 .224 B4
Porch Cl PE29 .141 F1
Porson Rd CB2 .64 D5
Port La PE5 .195 E1
Portchester Cl PE2 .187 F5
Porters Yd PE16 .241 C6
Portland Ave PE1 .197 F7
Portland Pl
  Cambridge CB1 .246 A3
  Whittlesey PE7 .189 E6
Portland Rd CB8 .110 E3
Portman Cl PE3 .197 C4
Portobello La CB2 .32 E7
Portugal Pl CB2 .246 A3
Portugal St CB2 .246 A3
Portway SG8 .14 E7
Portway Rd CB3 .81 A1
Post Office La **10** PE13 .245 C5
Post Office Terr CB1 .246 B2
Post St PE29 .141 E2
Pott Hall Rd IP28 .213 E6
Potter's La CB7 .240 D3
Potters Way PE1 .198 B1
Potton End PE19 .77 E3
Potton Rd Everton SG19 .40 D2
  Fenstanton PE28 .120 C3
  Gamlingay SG19 .40 F3
  Gamlingay SG19 .41 D3
  Guilden Morden SG8 .10 F6
  Hilton PE28 .99 B8
  St Neots PE19 .74 F2
  Wrestlingworth SG19 .25 B4
Potton Wood (National
  Trust)★ SG19 .25 A8
Poulter Ave PE2 .187 D5
Poulter's Dro PE14 .229 D5
Pound Cl Bottisham CB5 .86 E7
  Burwell CB5 .130 B2
  Hail Weston PE19 .95 B1
  Spaldwick PE28 .137 F6
Pound Gn SG8 .10 F5
Pound Hill CB3 .83 C3
Pound La Isleham CB7 .213 A5
  Kimbolton PE28 .113 F4
  Sutton CB6 .216 E2
Pound Rd Chatteris PE16 .241 B6
  Hemingford Grey PE28 .143 D1
  Ramsey PE26 .172 A4
Pound The PE27 .144 A5
Pound Way CB5 .108 B2
Powell Cl CB3 .61 D5
Powis Pl **2** PE19 .74 F1
Pratt Ave PE4 .204 F2
Pratt St PE12 .212 B4
Prentice Cl CB4 .123 F2
Presses Cl **7** PE28 .208 C5
Preston Cl CB3 .61 D5
Pretoria Rd CB4 .246 C4
Priam's Way CB2 .49 B4
Prickwillow Rd Ely CB7 .240 F5
  Isleham CB7 .212 F7
  Soham CB7 .219 D3
Priest La CB4 .209 A1
Priestgate **4** PE1 .198 A2
Priests Meadow Ct CB6 .240 C5
Primary Cl CB4 .84 B5
Prime Cl SG8 .14 C6
Primrose Cl
  Cambridge CB1 .66 A5
  Peterborough PE1 .198 A4
Primrose Dr PE7 .181 F7
Primrose Farm Rd CB1 .86 E2
Primrose Hill
  Doddington PE15 .222 A5
  Haverhill CB9 .23 F7
  Little Gransden SG19 .58 E3
Primrose La
  Huntingdon PE29 .141 E5
  5 Soham CB7 .212 E6
  Waterbeach CB5 .106 A8
Primrose St CB4 .83 D4
Primrose View **3** SG8 .5 F5
Prince Andrew's Cl **1**
  SG8 .5 D5
Prince Cl PE19 .74 B5
Prince of Wales Cl
  PE13 .245 D8
Prince St PE13 .245 D5
Prince William Cl **6** CB4 .83 C4
Prince William Way CB2 .32 F6
Prince's St
  Huntingdon PE29 .141 E4
  Peterborough PE1 .198 A4
  Ramsey PE26 .172 A4
Princes Cl CB1 .53 C1
Princes Dr PE19 .75 A6
Princes Gate PE1 .198 B4
Princes Gdns PE1 .198 B4
Princes Mews SG8 .5 C6
Princes Rd
  Peterborough PE2 .187 A7
  Stamford PE9 .244 B6
  Wisbech PE13 .245 C4
Princess Dr CB2 .49 F1
Princess of Wales Hospl
  CB6 .240 E7
Princess Way
  Haverhill CB9 .23 E8
  Newmarket CB8 .110 E4
Pringle Cl PE7 .189 C7
Pringle Ct PE28 .151 D4
Pringle Way PE28 .151 D4
Prins Ave PE13 .245 D7
Prins Ct **3** PE13 .245 D7
Prior's Cl CB4 .104 B4

Prior's Ct **8** CB6 .216 E2
Priors Gate PE4 .204 A4
Priors Rd
  Hemingford Grey PE28 ..143 C1
  Whittlesey PE7 .189 C7
Priory Ave Haverhill CB9 .23 F7
  Swavesey CB4 .122 E5
Priory Cl Burwell CB5 .130 B2
  Ickleton CB10 .18 A3
  7 Market Deeping PE6 .231 F8
  Royston SG8 .5 E6
Priory Dro CB5 .129 D7
Priory Gdns
  Peterborough PE7 .184 F3
  Stamford PE9 .244 D5
Priory Gr PE29 .141 E5
Priory Hill PE19 .75 B7
Priory Hill Rd PE19 .75 A7
Priory Jun & Inf Sch CB4 .84 D2
Priory Jun Sch PE19 .75 A6
Priory La
  Huntingdon PE29 .141 E5
  Royston SG8 .5 D5
  St Neots PE19 .74 E5
Priory Mews PE19 .74 E6
Priory Park Inf Sch PE19 74 F6
Priory Rd Cambridge CB5 .84 A3
  Holywell-cum-Needingworth
    PE27 .208 A3
  Horningsea CB5 .106 A1
  Huntingdon PE29 .141 E5
  Needingworth PE27 .144 F5
  Peterborough PE3 .197 E3
  St Ives PE27 .144 A2
  St Neots PE19 .74 E6
  Stamford PE9 .244 D5
Priory St **3** CB4 .83 C4
Priory The PE19 .74 E5
Proby Cl PE7 .181 D5
Prospect Pl PE13 .245 C3
Prospect Rd PE15 .243 B5
Prospect Row
  Cambridge CB1 .246 C2
  9 St Neots PE19 .74 F5
Prospect Way PE16 .241 C6
Prospero Cl PE2 .186 F6
Prospero Way PE29 .141 F7
Provence Pl **2** PE13 .245 E3
Provence Rd PE29 .141 A6
Providence Cl **16** PE28 .215 C1
Providence Pl PE15 .224 B4
Providence Way CB5 .127 A1
Pryor Cl CB4 .105 D2
Pudding Bag La PE9 .230 C4
Pudding La SG8 .7 A1
Puddock Hill PE28 .165 A8
Puddock Rd
  Ramsey PE28 .221 F1
  Warboys PE28 .165 A8
Pudgell The CB5 .7 C2
Pump La **2** Hardwick CB3 .81 A3
  4 Stretham CB6 .210 F5
Purbeck Rd CB2 .65 A5
Purl's Bridge Dro PE15 .224 B4
Putney Hill Rd CB7 .219 B4
Pyecroft PE1 .198 B6
Pyhill PE3 .197 B8
Pymore (Pymoor) La
  CB6 .224 A1
Pyrethrum Way **2** CB4 .209 A1

Q

Quadrangle The PE28 .208 D7
Quadrant The
  4 Royston SG8 .5 C8
  St Ives PE27 .144 B3
Quainton Cl CB5 .84 D3
Quaker Cl PE28 .153 C6
Quaker La PE13 .245 E3
Quaker Way PE16 .241 C5
Quaker's Dro PE7 .191 F5
Quaker's La CB9 .24 A7
Quakers' Rd IP28 .239 F5
Quanea Dro CB7 .240 F1
Quarry La Haslingfield CB3 47 B4
  Maxey PE6 .231 C6
  Swaffham Bulbeck CB5 .108 B1
Quay Hill **1** CB6 .242 E4
Quay The PE27 .144 A3
Quayside CB7 .240 E3
Queen Adelaide Way
  CB7 .240 E3
Queen Edith Cty Prim Sch
  CB1 .65 C4
Queen Edith's Way CB1 .65 D4
Queen Eleanor Cl PE7 .176 A8
Queen Eleanor Sch PE29 244 B6
Queen Elizabeth Dr
  PE13 .245 D3
Queen Emma Wlk **2**
  CB6 .240 E6
Queen Mary Cl PE26 .172 C7
Queen St Cowlinge CB8 .73 C1
  Haverhill CB9 .24 A8
  Newmarket CB8 .111 B3
  2 Peterborough PE1 .198 A2
  Whittlesey PE7 .189 D7
  Wisbech PE13 .245 C6
  Yaxley PE7 .192 C1
Queen Street Cl PE15 .243 D6
Queenholme Way CB4 .209 C2
Queen's Cl Holme PE7 .176 F4
  1 Over CB4 .208 D1
Queen's Dr
  Mildenhall IP28 .239 B4
  Wisbech PE14 .236 A3

Queen's Dr W PE1 .198 A5
Queen's Gdns PE1 .198 A5
Queen's Mdw CB1 .65 F7
Queen's Rd CB3 .64 C8
Queen's Wlk PE9 .244 A5
Queens Cl Balsham CB1 .52 F2
  Harston CB2 .48 A3
  St Ives PE27 .144 A5
Queens Coll CB3 .246 A2
Queens Ct PE19 .74 B3
Queens Dr PE2 .141 F5
Queens Drive Inf Sch
  PE1 .198 A5
Queens Gdns PE19 .74 B4
Queens Rd Littleport PE28 242 B5
  Peterborough PE2 .187 B7
  Royston SG8 .5 D7
  Somersham PE28 .215 C1
  Wisbech PE13 .245 C4
Queens Sch PE13 .245 D3
Queens St March PE15 .243 D6
  Stamford PE9 .244 B6
  Withersfield CB9 .38 C4
Queens View CB8 .110 A8
Queens Way CB4 .103 D6
Queens Wlk PE7 .186 F8
Queensberry Rd CB8 .111 A4
Queensgate Ctr PE1 .198 A2
Queensway
  Cambridge CB2 .64 E6
  Chatteris PE16 .241 D5
  Exning CB8 .110 B8
  Haverhill CB9 .23 E8
  Mildenhall IP28 .239 B4
  Royston SG8 .5 D7
  St Neots PE19 .74 F7
  Sawston CB2 .32 F8
  Soham CB7 .212 B4
Quickset Rd CB11 .9 B5
Quince Rd CB3 .81 A3
Quinion Cl PE7 .189 F6
Quorn Cl PE6 .205 C8
Quy Rd CB5 .86 B8

R

Rachel Cl **1** CB5 .84 E4
Rackham Cl CB4 .83 C4
Radcliffe Cl **1** PE19 .244 B5
Radcliffe Rd **2** PE9 .244 A5
Radegund Rd CB1 .65 B7
Radegunds CB2 .32 C5
Radford Cl **3** PE8 .230 C1
Radwinter Rd CB10 .21 B1
RAF Molesworth PE28 .147 C8
RAF Wyton PE28 .143 A8
Railway La PE16 .241 C5
Railway Rd PE13 .245 C3
Railway St CB1 .65 F7
Railway Mus★ PE2 .197 F1
Raine Ave PE28 .23 D8
Raleigh Cl **1** PE19 .74 A2
Raleigh Way PE3 .197 A5
Ramnoth Rd PE13 .245 D4
Ramnoth Road Prim Sch
  PE13 .245 D4
Rampart The CB6 .210 A6
Ramper Rd CB4 .123 A3
Rampley La PE19 .95 F2
Rampleys The PE28 .143 D2
Ramply Cl PE19 .95 F1
Rampton Drift CB4 .124 B2
Rampton End CB4 .209 A1
Rampton Rd
  Cottenham CB4 .125 B4
  Longstanton CB4 .124 C3
  Oakington/Longstanton
    CB4 .123 F1
  Willingham CB4 .124 B7
Ramsden Sq CB4 .84 A7
Ramsey Abbey Sch
  PE26 .172 C7
Ramsey Cty Jun Sch
  PE26 .172 A7
Ramsey Hollow Dro
  PE26 .173 B7
Ramsey Rd Benwick PE15 221 F4
  Ely CB7 .240 E6
  Kings Ripton PE28 .153 C5
  Old Hurst PE28 .154 D6
  Ramsey PE26 .221 C2
  St Ives PE27 .143 F7
  Upwood & The Raveleys
    PE26 .171 D2
  Warboys PE28 .164 E6
  Whittlesey PE7 .220 F7
Ramsey Rural Mus★
  PE26 .172 C7
Ramsey Sports Ctr
  PE26 .172 C7
Ramsey Way PE2 .187 F6
Ramshill Cotts PE6 .203 A2
Randalls La CB4 .208 D1
Rangefield PE2 .185 E4
Ransome's Cl PE14 .236 E2
Ransonmoor Dro PE15 .222 D7
Raptor Foundation The★
  PE28 .155 E4
Rasen Ct **2** PE1 .198 D3
Ratfords Yd CB1 .68 A8
Rathmore Cl CB1 .65 A6
Rathmore Rd CB1 .65 A6
Raveley Fen Rd PE28 ..162 D8
Raveley Rd PE28 .161 F6
Raven Cl Mildenhall IP28 .239 D4
  St Neots PE19 .75 B7

Ravenhill Dr PE15 .243 C3
Ravens Ct CB6 .240 C5
Ravenscourt **6** PE27 .208 A3
Ravensdale PE7 .175 F7
Ravensthorpe Prim Sch
  PE3 .197 C2
Ravensworth Gdns CB1 .65 A7
Rawlyn Cl CB5 .84 D3
Rawlyn Rd CB5 .84 D3
Rayes La CB8 .111 A4
Rayleigh Cl CB2 .64 E5
Raymond St **14** PE13 .245 C4
Rayner Ave PE7 .187 E5
Rayner's Cl SG8 .30 D1
Ray's Dro PE26 .220 B1
Rayson Way CB5 .84 D3
Reach Dro PE7 .189 B5
Reach Rd Burwell CB5 .109 B8
  Reach CB5 .129 F1
Reaches The PE6 .232 C3
Read's St CB6 .210 F5
Recreation Cl PE28 .140 E1
Recreation Ground Rd
  PE9 .244 B6
Recreation Rd PE9 .23 F7
Recreation Way IP28 .239 C4
Rectors Way **3** PE4 .204 F2
Rectory Cl
  Brampton PE28 .140 E2
  Great Paxton PE19 .96 E4
  Oakington/Longstanton
    CB4 .123 F1
  Sawtry PE28 .168 C3
Rectory Farm Rd CB1 .86 F2
Rectory Fields CB6 .216 E3
Rectory Gdns
  Glinton PE6 .203 E8
  Godmanchester PE29 .141 F2
  Peterborough PE7 .187 B7
Rectory La Ashdon CB10 .21 A1
  Etton PE6 .231 E5
  1 Fowlmere SG8 .15 C5
  Glinton PE6 .203 E8
  Kingston CB3 .61 B3
  Peakirk PE6 .206 B2
  Somersham PE28 .215 B1
  Southoe & Midloe PE19 ..95 D6
Rectory Rd
  Bluntisham/Colne PE28 ..208 D5
  Duxford CB2 .17 A8
  Newton PE13 .238 B5
  Outwell PE14 .236 F2
Rectory Way PE7 .175 F7
Red Barn PE7 .191 E6
Red Cross La CB2 .65 B3
Red Dock La CB8 .73 F1
Red Fen Rd CB6 .210 F7
Red Hill Cl CB2 .48 E8
Red Hill La CB2 .48 E8
Red Lion Cl PE28 .150 F4
Red Lion La CB6 .216 E1
Red Lion Sq **5** PE9 .244 B5
Red Lion St PE9 .244 B5
Red Well The★ CB3 .100 F2
Redbridge PE4 .204 A6
Redcaps La CB6 .217 E6
Redcot Gdns **8** PE9 .244 B6
Redebourne La PE26 .171 F4
Redfern Cl CB4 .83 E6
Redgate Rd Girton CB3 .82 E8
  Tydd St Giles PE13 .238 C8
Redhouse Gdns **3** CB7 .212 B3
Redit La CB7 .211 E1
Redlands Rd CB3 .101 E5
Redman Cl PE7 .240 F7
Redmoor Bank PE14 .235 E8
Redmoor Cl PE27 .144 B2
Redmoor La PE14 .235 F5
Redshank Cl Haverhill CB9 24 C7
  Whittlesey PE7 .201 A1
Redwell PE27 .143 E5
Redwing Cl PE2 .187 E7
Redwing Dr Royston SG8 .5 F8
  5 Wisbech PE14 .245 D2
Redwing Pl **2** PE19 .75 B7
Redwongs Way PE29 .141 D7
Reed Cl Cambridge CB2 .64 E1
  Chatteris PE16 .241 D5
Reedmace Cl PE6 .205 C8
Reeds La CB9 .24 A8
Reepham PE2 .185 D4
Rees Thomas Sch CB4 .83 F6
Reeves Pightle SG8 .7 F3
Reeves Way PE1 .198 D5
Regal Dr CB7 .212 C3
Regal La CB7 .212 C3
Regal Rd PE13 .245 B2
Regatta Ct CB5 .84 B4
Regency Way PE3 .197 E1
Regent Ave PE15 .243 D5
Regent Cl PE19 .74 E4
Regent Pl **1** CB7 .212 B3
Regent St CB2 .246 B1
Regent Terr CB2 .246 B1
Rembrandt Way **3**
  PE27 .144 A7
Renoir Cl **8** PE27 .144 A7
Resbury Ct PE22 .50 A1
Retreat The **8** PE6 .231 C7
Reubens Rd CB4 .105 C2
Reynold's Cl CB9 .38 D1
Reynolds Cl **4** PE27 .144 A7
Reynolds Cl **6** PE19 .74 D6
Reynolds Dr PE19 .95 F1
Reynolds' Dro CB4 .124 D3
Rhee Lake Dro PE28 .208 E8
Rhees The PE28 .208 D6

Rhone Pl **3** PE13 .245 E3
Rhugarve Gdns CB1 .35 D2
Rhymers Gate PE28 .142 F5
Ribble Cl PE27 .144 B6
Ribston Way CB4 .84 C6
Richard Young Cl **2**
  PE13 .245 C4
Richards Cl PE15 .243 B5
Richardson Way PE7 .189 E7
Richmond Ave
  March PE15 .243 C3
  Peterborough PE4 .204 C2
Richmond Cl
  Huntingdon PE29 .141 E8
  7 St Neots PE19 .74 F1
Richmond Ct PE13 .245 A4
Richmond Rd CB4 .83 D4
Richmond Way **6** PE13 .238 B2
Rickard Cl CB1 .65 E6
Rickwood Cl CB6 .216 C5
Rickyard The SG7 .2 D3
Riddiford Cres PE28 .140 C2
Riddy Cl CB2 .48 B5
Riddy La CB3 .60 C5
Rideaway PE28 .119 F8
Ridge Way PE2 .187 B8
Ridgeway
  Papworth Everard CB3 ...99 A4
  Perry PE28 .115 D2
  St Neots PE19 .74 F2
Ridgeway The CB1 .35 E2
Ridley Hall Rd CB3 .64 C8
Rigg Cl **2** PE13 .245 B3
Rightwell E PE3 .197 A5
Rightwell W PE3 .197 A5
Ringers La PE13 .238 B2
Ringstead Rd PE4 .204 F1
Ringwood PE3 .196 F3
Ringwood Cl **4** PE26 .172 A4
Ripon Cl PE4 .204 B3
Rippons Dro PE6 .231 F7
Risby PE3 .197 B8
Riseholme PE2 .185 E3
Rivar Pl CB1 .84 A1
Rivendale PE4 .204 B2
River Cl Little Paxton PE19 .95 F1
  Mepal CB6 .216 E4
River Dr PE15 .243 E4
River Dro PE7 .191 C5
River La Brampton PE28 .140 E1
  Cambridge CB5 .84 A3
  Elton PE8 .178 C8
  Fordham CB7 .212 E1
  Great Paxton PE19 .96 D3
  Haslingfield CB3 .47 C5
  Peterborough PE3 .197 F2
River Mdw PE28 .142 F3
River Rd Eaton Socon PE19 .74 A4
  Kimbolton PE28 .114 B7
  West Walton PE14 .238 D4
River Terr
  3 St Neots PE19 .74 E5
  Wisbech PE13 .245 A8
Riverbank Cl **12** PE6 .231 F8
Riverdene CB5 .84 B3
  11 Market Deeping PE6 .231 F8
Riverside Cl Ely CB7 .219 B5
  Mildenhall IP28 .239 B4
  Whittlesey PE7 .189 D6
Riverside Gdns
  Parson Drove PE13 .234 C7
  Peterborough PE3 .197 D1
Riverside Mead PE2 .187 B8
Riverside Mid Sch IP28 239 A4
Riverside Park★ PE29 .141 E4
Riverside Rd PE29 .141 E4
Riverside Spinney PE8 .194 A3
Riverside Way **1** PE13 .245 B4
Riverside Wlk CB7 .240 E3
Riversmead PE19 .74 E6
Rivey Cl CB1 .35 D3
Rivey Way CB1 .35 D2
Roan Wlk **8** SG8 .5 E6
Robbs Wlk PE27 .144 B3
Robert Arkenstall Prim Sch
  CB6 .210 A6
Robert Ave
  Peterborough PE1 .197 F8
  4 Somersham PE28 .215 C1
Robert Jennings Cl CB4 .84 A6
Robert May Cl CB1 .65 D7
Robert Rayner Cl PE2 .186 D6
Robin Cl Bar Hill CB3 .102 C4
  Haverhill CB9 .24 C7
  Mildenhall IP28 .239 D4
Robin Goodfellow's La
  PE15 .243 D5
Robin Hood Cl PE3 .196 F2
Robin Mews **4** PE14 .245 D2
Robingoodfellow's La
  PE15 .243 C6
Robins Cl **5** Ely CB6 .240 B5
  8 Isleham CB7 .213 A6
  Peterborough PE2 .186 E8
Robins Field PE8 .194 A4
Robins' Cl CB3 .101 F5
Robins Wood PE8 .194 A4
Robinson Coll CB3 .83 B1
Robinson Way CB2 .65 A3
Robshaw Cl **4** PE15 .243 E4
Rocester Way SG8 .5 D8
Rochford Wlk **5** PE13 .245 E4
Rochfort Ave CB8 .110 E5
Rock Rd Cambridge CB1 .65 A6

Roc – San 267

Rock Rd *continued*
Peterborough PE1 197 F6
Royston SG8 5 C8
Stamford PE9 244 B5
Rockall Cl CB9 24 D7
Rockingham Gr PE4 204 C2
Rockingham Rd PE28 168 B3
Rockmill End CB4 209 A1
Rodham Rd PE15 228 F5
Rodings The CB5 84 E4
Rodney Rd PE29 142 A6
Roe Gn PE19 74 B5
Roedeer Cl CB1 66 A7
Roe's Cl CB2 32 F8
Roger's Cl CB3 100 B4
Rogers Rd CB5 108 E6
Rogues La CB3 99 D5
Roland Cl CB4 83 E5
Rollys La SG7 2 D4
Roman Bank
Newton PE13 238 B4
Stamford PE9 244 A4
Roman Cl Burwell CB5 130 A2
Whittlesey PE7 189 F8
Roman Dr PE8 194 D2
Roman Hill CB3 63 C4
Roman Way Haverhill CB9 24 D7
March PE15 243 E6
Perry PE28 115 D2
Stilton PE7 176 A8
Roman Way Fst Sch SG8 5 D8
Romany Gdns PE2 187 D5
Romney Cl PE27 144 A7
Romney Ct 2 PE19 74 C5
Romsey Jun Sch CB1 65 B8
Romsey Rd CB1 65 C8
Romsey Terr CB1 65 B7
Ronaldsway 5 PE15 222 F5
Rook Gr CB4 209 A1
Rookery Cl
Great Chesterford CB10 18 D3
St Ives PE27 144 C4
Waterbeach CB5 106 A8
Rookery Pl PE28 121 C5
Rookery The Balsham CB1 53 A2
Little Paxton PE19 95 F2
Peterborough PE2 185 C7
Yaxley PE7 181 D5
Rookery Way PE28 121 B5
Rooks St CB4 125 E4
Rookswood Rd 4 PE15 243 C4
Rookwood Way CB9 24 A6
Roscrea Terr PE29 141 D4
Rose & Crown Rd CB4 122 C3
Rose Ave PE2 187 C7
Rose Cres CB2 246 A3
Rose Croft PE28 115 E2
Rose Ct 8 PE19 74 C4
Rose Green La 10 IP28 213 F8
Rose Hill CB9 38 D5
Rose La 4 Elm PE14 236 A5
Great Chesterford CB10 18 E2
Melbourn SG8 14 C6
Rose Wlk Royston SG8 5 C7
1 Wisbech PE13 245 A6
Rosebay Gdns 6 CB7 212 B5
Roseberry Rd 4 PE14 236 B5
Rosebery Way CB8 110 E5
Rosedene Dr PE15 243 D3
Rosefinch Cl CB9 24 C7
Roseford Rd CB4 83 D6
Roselea CB4 104 C3
Rosemary Cl 7 IP28 214 A1
Rosemary Gdns PE1 197 F8
Rosemary Greene Cl CB3 78 E2
Rosemary La
Cambridge CB1 65 E7
Sutton CB6 216 C1
Rosemary Rd CB5 106 B7
Rose's Cl PE15 243 D2
Rosie Maternity Hospl
CB2 65 A3
Ross Cl CB9 24 D6
Ross Piers Sports Ctr The
CB7 212 B3
Ross St CB1 65 B8
Roswell View CB7 240 E5
Rosyth Ave PE2 185 D3
Rotherwick Way CB1 65 C3
Rothleigh Rd 2 CB1 65 D5
Rothwell Way PE2 186 C7
Round Church St CB2 246 A3
Round Hills Way PE28 168 A5
Round House Dro PE28 222 A1
Roundhills View PE28 167 E8
Roundhouse Cl PE1 198 D3
Roundhouse Dr PE28 115 D3
Rous Rd CB8 111 B3
Row The CB6 216 E1
Rowan Ave
Peterborough PE1 198 C6
Sawston CB2 32 F6
Rowan Cl Bottisham CB5 86 F6
Huntingdon PE29 141 C5
Wisbech PE13 245 F7
Rowans The
2 Doddington/Wimblington
PE15 223 A6
Milton CB4 105 C1
Rowe Ave PE2 186 D7
Rowell Cl CB9 39 A2
Rowell Wlk 2 PE26 172 A4
Rowells The CB4 125 C3
Rowland Ct PE4 204 B6
Rowlands Cl CB2 30 C5
Rowley Ct 1 CB9 24 E5
Rowley Dr CB8 110 F4
Rowley Gdns 4 CB5 86 E6
Rowley Mile Course
CB8 109 E2
Rowley Rd PE19 75 B7
Rowlinson Way CB4 84 A3
Rows The CB8 110 F3
Roxburgh Rd CB4 83 E7
Royal Anglian Regiment
Mus★ CB2 16 F8
Royal Ct 2 PE19 74 B4
Royal Oak La PE28 143 A2
Royal Pal Cl CB8 110 D7
Royal Pl 2 PE13 245 C4
Royce Rd
Peterborough PE7 185 A4
Peterborough PE1 198 D3
Royle Cl PE2 186 C5
Royse Gr SG8 5 D4
Roysia Mid Sch SG8 5 D8
Royston & District Hospl
SG8 5 D4
Royston Ave
Peterborough PE2 186 C6
Spaldwick PE28 137 F6
Royston La
Comberton CB3 62 C3
Elmdon CB11 9 C6
Royston Mus★ SG8 5 C6
Royston Rd Barley SG8 6 F3
Caxton CB3 59 F7
Duxford CB2 32 D3
Foxton CB2 30 A5
Harston CB2 47 D1
Litlington SG8 12 B1
Royston Sta SG8 5 C7
Royston Swimming Pool
SG8 5 D6
Rubens Way PE27 144 A7
Ruddles La PE28 142 E6
Rudlands Cl 3 CB7 213 A5
Rudyard Gr PE4 204 E3
Rush Gr CB1 66 A6
Rushbrook Cl CB3 59 F3
Rushington Cl PE27 144 B5
Rushmere PE2 185 F6
Rushton Ave PE4 204 A4
Ruskin Cl 2 CB9 38 D1
Russell Ave PE15 243 B6
Russell Cl
Steeple Morden SG8 11 B2
7 Thorney PE6 233 A3
Russell Ct CB2 64 E7
Russell Hill PE8 193 F6
Russell St
Cambridge CB2 246 C1
Peterborough PE1 197 F3
St Neots PE19 74 E6
Wisbech PE13 245 C6
Russet Cl PE27 144 B5
Russet Ct CB4 84 C6
Russet Way SG8 14 D6
Russet Wlk 3 CB3 81 A3
Russets The PE14 236 E2
Russett Ave PE27 208 A2
Rustat Rd CB1 65 A6
Rustons Rd PE14 236 F7
Rustons The CB2 32 D1
Rusts La PE28 150 F4
Rutherford Rd CB2 64 E4
Rutland Cl Cambridge CB4 83 D6
St Ives PE27 143 F7
Rutland Gn 2 PE28 120 B1
Rutland Rd PE9 244 D7
Rutland Terr PE9 244 A4
Rutland Way PE15 224 B4
Rycroft Ave
3 Deeping St James PE6 231 F8
St Neots PE19 74 E6
Rydal Cl PE29 141 B6
Rydal Ct PE4 204 E3
Rye Cl 4 PE19 74 F1
Ryecroft La SG8 15 E8
Ryhall Rd PE9 244 D6

S

Sable Cl CB1 66 A7
Sackville Cl CB4 83 E7
Sackville St CB8 111 B4
Sacred Heart RC Prim Sch
PE3 197 A5
Sacrewell Farm & Ctry Ctr★
PE8 194 C5
Saddlers Cl PE6 203 E8
Saddlers Pl SG8 5 C7
Sadlers Cl Coton CB3 82 B2
Hardwick CB3 81 A1
Sadlers Way PE28 143 D1
Saffron Cl CB6 242 C2
Saffron Piece 3 CB6 216 E1
Saffron Rd Histon CB4 104 B3
Sawston CB2 33 A8
Saffron St SG8 5 F5
Sage's La PE4 197 C8
Saggers Cl SG8 12 D6
Sainfoin Cl CB2 33 A8
St Alban's Dr 20 PE6 232 A1
St Albans CB8 111 A6
St Albans RC Sch CB2 246 B1
St Albans Rd CB4 83 D6
St Andrew's Church★
PE28 169 D1
St Andrew's Cl CB2 49 C4
St Andrew's Hill CB5 106 B7
St Andrew's Pk CB4 104 B5
St Andrew's Pl PE7 189 D6
St Andrew's Rd CB4 84 A3
St Andrew's St
Cambridge CB2 246 B2
Mildenhall IP28 239 C4
St Andrew's Way CB6 240 B6
St Andrews CE Jun Sch
Cambridge CB4 84 C6
Soham CB7 212 B3
St Andrews Cl 1 CB7 213 A5
St Andrews Hill CB5 106 B7
St Andrews La 2 PE28 113 F4
St Andrews Rd 4 PE6 231 F7
St Andrews Way
Histon CB4 104 E4
Sawtry PE28 168 C4
St Annes CE Prim Sch
PE29 118 F8
St Ann's La PE29 141 F1
St Anns Dr IP28 239 B4
St Anselm Pl 1 PE19 74 E5
St Audleys La PE27 144 A5
St Audrey Cl
Peterborough PE2 187 D6
St Ives PE27 144 B5
St Audrey's Cl CB4 104 A4
St Audrey's Way CB6 240 D6
St Augustine's Wlk PE2 186 E8
St Augustines Inf Sch
PE13 245 D8
St Augustines Jun Sch
PE2 186 F8
St Augustines RC Prim Sch
PE9 244 C7
St Augustines Rd PE13 245 C5
St Barnabas Ct 3 PE29 141 F7
St Barnabas Rd CB1 65 A8
St Bede's Cres CB1 65 D6
St Bede's Gdns CB1 65 E6
St Bedes Comp Church Sch
CB1 65 D6
St Bee's Dr 18 PE6 232 A1
St Benedict's Cl PE6 203 F7
St Benet's Gdns 5 PE6 232 A1
St Botolph La PE2 186 C6
St Botolph's Way
Haverhill CB9 23 F8
1 Thorney PE6 233 A2
St Botolphs Prim Sch
PE2 186 B6
St Catharine's Coll CB2 246 A2
St Catharines H CB3 82 C2
St Catharines Sq CB4 83 C7
St Catherine's CB6 240 C5
St Catherines Cl IP28 239 D6
St Catherines Prep Sch
CB2 64 D7
St Christophers Ave 2
CB4 83 C4
St Clement Cl PE14 236 F2
St Clement's PE9 244 A5
St Clements Pas PE29 141 E4
St Colettes Prep Sch CB1 64 F7
St David's Sq PE1 198 D1
St David's Way 4 PE28 168 C4
St Denis's Church★ SG19 43 B2
St Edmunds Coll CB3 83 C3
St Edmunds Dr PE14 236 D5
St Edmunds Fen★ CB7 211 E1
St Edwards Pas 4 CB1 246 A2
St Ethelwolds Cl CB6 240 B4
St Fabians Cl CB8 110 F5
St Faiths Sch CB2 64 E6
St Felix CE VC Mid Sch
CB8 110 F6
St Felix RC Prim Sch
CB9 23 D7
St Felix Rd 1 PE26 221 C2
St George Ave PE2 187 E6
St George's Rd
3 St Ives PE27 144 A4
14 Wittering PE8 230 B1
St George's Sq 5 PE9 244 C5
St George's St PE9 244 C5
St Georges Ave PE9 244 D6
St Georges Cl PE28 140 E1
St Georges Sch
Peterborough PE1 198 A7
Stamford PE9 244 C7
St Georges Way CB4 104 E4
St Germain St PE29 141 D4
St Gilberts Sch PE9 244 B5
St Giles Cl PE7 176 F4
St Giles Gr 1 PE14 236 B5
St Helena Wlk IP28 239 C7
St Helens CP Sch PE28 208 D6
St Hugh's Rd PE19 117 A4
St Ives Rd Eltisley PE19 77 E6
Hemingford Grey PE28 143 D2
Old Hurst PE28 154 D6
Papworth Everard CB3 98 F2
St Ives PE28 143 A5
Somersham PE28 208 B8
St Ives TH PE27 144 A3
St Ivo Recn Ctr PE27 143 F4
St Ivo Sch PE27 143 F5
St James Ave PE1 197 F7
St James Cl 3 CB6 210 F5
St James Rd PE19 95 F3
St John Fisher RC GM Sch
PE1 198 C4
St John's Chase PE15 243 D5
St John's Cl
Mildenhall IP28 239 D6
10 Needingworth PE27 208 A2
7 Needingworth PE27 208 A3
Waterbeach CB5 106 B7
St John's Coll CB2 246 A3
St John's La CB5 106 A2
St John's Pl
Cambridge CB4 83 C3
Wistow PE28 163 F7
St John's Rd
Cambridge CB5 246 A4
Coton CB3 82 B2
Ely CB6 240 A4
March PE15 243 D5
13 Wittering PE8 230 B1
St John's St
"Beck Row, Holywell Row
& Kenny Hill" IP28 214 A8
Cambridge CB2 246 A3
Duxford CB2 32 D1
Mildenhall IP28 213 F8
Peterborough PE1 198 B2
St Johns Ave CB8 111 A1
St Johns CE Prim Sch
PE29 141 E7
St Johns Church Sch CE
Aided PE2 185 E3
St Johns Cl PE28 155 B5
St Johns Coll Sch CB3 83 C2
St Johns La CB3 99 B2
St Johns Mews 2 PE19 96 E4
St Johns Prim Sch PE2 187 C7
St Johns Rd PE2 187 B7
St Johns Sch CB6 240 A4
St Johns St PE29 141 D5
St Judes Cl PE3 197 C4
St Judith's La PE28 160 B6
St Kilda Ave CB4 84 A7
St Laurence Rd CB2 30 C5
St Laurences RC Sch
CB4 83 D7
St Lawrence Way 2
PE9 230 F7
St Leonard's Rd 2 PE13 238 B2
St Leonard's St 4 PE9 244 C5
St Louis RC VA Prim Sch
CB8 111 A4
St Lukes C of E Prim Sch
CB4 83 C4
St Lukes St CB4 246 A4
St Margaret's Rd CB3 82 F6
St Margaret's Sq CB1 65 B5
St Margarets Pl 2 PE2 186 F6
St Margarets Rd 1 PE2 186 F6
St Margarets Way PE29 141 C6
St Mark's Ct 3 PE1 198 A3
St Marks Ct CB3 64 C8
St Marks Rd PE13 237 E3
St Marks St PE1 198 A3
St Martin's Cl
Chatteris PE16 241 D5
Exning CB8 110 C7
Stamford PE9 244 C4
St Martin's Rd
Chatteris PE16 241 D4
Newborough PE6 205 B8
Wisbech PE13 245 F7
St Martin's St PE1 197 F5
St Martins Wlk CB7 240 D5
St Mary's Earith PE28 208 E6
Gamlingay SG19 41 E5
St Mary's Ave PE8 230 B1
St Mary's CE Prim Sch
PE19 75 A5
St Mary's Cl Bainton PE9 230 F5
Bluntisham PE28 208 D5
Farcet PE7 187 C2
Peterborough PE1 198 B4
2 Thorney PE6 233 A2
3 Wisbech St Mary PE13 235 C7
St Mary's Dr March PE15 243 C5
Peterborough PE2 185 F4
St Mary's Gn PE28 164 E6
St Mary's Hill 9 PE9 244 C5
St Mary's Rd
5 Bluntisham/Colne
PE28 208 C5
Ramsey PE26 220 E2
Sawston CB2 33 A7
Stilton PE7 175 F8
West Walton PE14 238 E4
St Mary's St Ely CB7 240 C4
Farcet PE7 187 C2
St Neots PE19 74 E4
Stamford PE9 244 C5
Whittlesey PE7 189 D6
St Mary's Wlk
1 Everton SG19 40 C3
3 Fowlmere SG8 15 E8
St Marys CE Prim Sch
IP28 239 C5
St Marys Jun Sch CB7 240 F6
St Marys Pas 2 CB1 246 A2
St Marys Pk SG8 5 D6
St Marys RC JMI Sch SG8 5 D7
St Marys Sch CB2 64 E7
St Mary's St 1 CB1 246 A2
St Marys St PE29 141 D4
St Matthew's Ct 5 CB1 84 A2
St Matthew's Prim Sch
CB1 246 C2
St Matthew's St CB1 84 A2
St Michael's Ave PE13 245 C7
St Michael's Gate PE1 198 F7
St Michael's Rd 12 PE8 230 B1
St Michaels CB4 103 A8
St Michaels La
Longstanton CB4 124 A1
Oakington/Longstanton
CB4 103 A8
St Neots Rd
Abbotsley PE19 57 A7
Comberton CB3 81 D3
Coton CB3 82 B3
St Neots Rd *continued*
Eaton Socon PE19 74 C4
Eltisley PE19 77 D4
Hardwick CB3 80 E4
Knapwell CB3 79 D5
Madingley CB3 81 F3
St Neots Sta PE19 75 B6
St Olave's Dr 19 PE6 232 A1
St Paul's Cl
Gorefield PE13 237 E2
5 Wisbech PE13 245 C4
St Paul's Rd
Cambridge CB1 246 C1
Peterborough PE1 197 F7
St Paul's St PE9 244 C5
St Pauls CE Sch CB2 246 B1
St Pauls Dr PE16 241 D6
St Pega's Rd PE6 204 A8
St Peter's Cath PE1 198 A2
St Peter's Dr 10 PE15 223 B7
St Peter's Hill 8 PE9 244 B5
St Peter's Rd Coton CB3 82 B2
Huntingdon PE29 141 D7
March PE15 243 D3
4 Wisbech PE13 245 C4
St Peter's St
Cambridge CB3 83 C3
Caxton CB3 59 E8
Duxford CB2 17 D8
Stamford PE9 244 B4
St Peter's Vale PE9 244 B4
St Peter's Way
Ellington PE28 139 A4
3 Thorney PE6 233 A2
St Peters Ave CB8 112 F4
St Peters Cl CB8 112 F5
St Peters Dr PE16 241 D5
St Peters Pl CB7 212 F1
St Peters Rd
Outwell PE14 236 E1
Peterborough PE1 198 A2
St Peters Sch
Huntingdon PE29 141 D6
Wisbech PE13 245 E6
St Philip's Rd CB1 65 B8
St Philips CE Prim Sch
CB1 84 C1
St Philips Rd
Cambridge CB1 65 C8
Newmarket CB8 110 E4
St Stephen's Dr PE16 241 C6
St Stephen's Pl 1 CB4 83 C4
St Thomas PE19 77 E4
St Thomas Cl CB3 62 D6
St Thomas Dr PE15 243 C3
St Thomas Moore RC Prim
Sch PE1 198 D4
St Thomas' Pl CB7 240 C2
St Thomas's Sq CB1 65 D6
St Tibb's Row CB2 246 B2
St Vigor's Rd CB1 66 F4
St Vincent's Cl CB3 82 E8
St Vincent's Cross★
PE6 232 D6
St Wendreda's Dr 3
PE15 243 C1
St Wendred's Way CB8 110 B7
Salcott Dr PE13 245 E5
Salisbury Cl 3 PE27 143 F8
Salisbury Rd PE4 204 B3
Sallowbush Rd PE29 141 D6
Sallows 2 PE28 121 C6
Sallows Rd PE1 198 B6
Salmon La CB1 246 C3
Salon Way PE29 141 B7
Saltergate PE1 198 E7
Salters Way Sawtry PE28 168 B5
Wisbech PE13 245 A2
Saltersgate PE1 198 F7
Saltmarsh PE2 186 C4
Salts Rd PE14 238 F4
Sambar Cl 3 PE19 74 B5
Sames Ct CB4 125 E5
Samuel Ward Upper Sch
CB9 39 B1
Samworths Cl PE5 195 F2
Sancton Wood Sch CB1 246 C1
Sand Acre Cl IP28 239 D5
Sand Bank PE13 235 A7
Sand Dro CB5 127 C8
Sand La CB6 209 E4
Sand Rd SG19 58 F5
Sand St CB7 212 B3
Sandall Rd PE13 245 C3
Sanderling Cl IP28 239 D4
Sanders Cl PE28 151 D3
Sandfields Rd PE19 74 F4
Sandford PE3 197 B5
Sandown Rd PE13 245 A2
Sandpiper Cl
Haverhill CB9 24 B7
Whittlesey PE7 190 A8
Sandpiper Dr PE2 187 E6
Sandpit Rd PE6 233 A3
Sandringham Ave PE13 245 D6
Sandringham Cl 3 PE9 244 B7
Sandringham Dr 2
PE26 221 C2
Sandringham Rd 2
PE4 197 C8
Sandwich Cl
Huntingdon PE29 141 E7
St Ives PE27 143 F8
Sandwich Rd
Brampton PE28 140 D1

Sandwich Rd continued
St Neots PE19 . . . . .75 A5
Sandy Dro IP28 . . . . . .214 D3
Sandy Gate PE12 . . . . . .237 A7
Sandy La Cambridge CB4 . .83 F4
Kimbolton PE28 . . . . .113 C6
Tydd St Giles PE13 . . . . . . .238 B7
Wisbech PE13 . . . . .245 F4
Sandy Rd Everton SG19 . . . .40 E2
Lode CB5 . . . . .107 C6
Sandyland PE13 . . . . .245 B5
Sandys Cres CB6 . . . . . . .242 E3
Sanfoin Cl 5 IP28 . . . . . .214 A1
Sapcote Way PE28 . . . . . .168 B3
Sapley Pk PE29 . . . . .141 F8
Sapley Rd PE29 . . . . .152 F1
Sapperton PE4 . . . . .204 B6
Sargent's Ct PE9 . . . . . . .244 A6
Sascombe Vineyard★
CB8 . . . . .72 F3
Saunders Cl PE29 . . . . . . .141 D6
Saunders Ct CB3 . . . . .79 B3
Savile Way SG8 . . . . .15 E8
Savile's Cl PE19 . . . . .74 D7
Saville Rd PE3 . . . . .197 C5
Savory Rd PE13 . . . . .245 B7
Sawpit La PE28 . . . . .159 A4
Sawston H★ CB2 . . . . .32 F7
Sawston Rd CB2 . . . . .33 D8
Sawston Village Coll PE28 32 E8
Sawtry Com Coll PE28 .168 C4
Sawtry Rd
Conington PE28 . . . . .167 F8
Sawtry PE28 . . . . .168 A6
Sawtry Sports Ctr PE28 .168 B3
Sawtry Way PE28 . . . . . . .153 E2
Sawtry Way Cotts PE28 .143 C6
Saxby Gdns PE1 . . . . .198 C8
Saxon Cl Ely CB6 . . . . . . .240 C5
Exning CB8 . . . . .110 D8
Godmanchester PE29 . . . . .141 F1
Sawtry PE28 . . . . .168 C3
Saxon Dr CB5 . . . . .130 B1
Saxon Pl PE19 . . . . .74 D7
Saxon Rd
5 Barnack PE9 . . . . .230 D3
Cambridge CB5 . . . . .84 A3
Peterborough PE1 . . . . . . .198 C4
Whittlesey PE7 . . . . .189 C7
Saxon St SG8 . . . . .246 B1
Saxon Street Rd CB8 . . . .91 D4
Saxon Way Bar Hill CB3 . .102 B2
Melbourn SG8 . . . . .14 C4
3 Waterbeach CB5 . . . . . .106 A7
Sayer Cl PE28 . . . . .185 F2
Sayer St PE29 . . . . .141 C6
Sayers Ct 3 PE28 . . . . . .208 C5
Scaldgate PE7 . . . . .189 E6
Scales Park★ SG9 . . . . . . .1 C1
Scalesgate Rd PE12 . . . . .237 A8
Scalford Dr PE1 . . . . .198 C8
Scaltback Mid Sch CB8 . .110 E5
Scarfield La 1 PE14 . . . .236 C6
Scargell's Yd PE15 . . . . . .243 D3
Scarlett's La CB1 . . . . .53 D4
Scarsdale Cl CB4 . . . . .84 B6
Scholars Ave PE29 . . . . . .141 C4
Schole Rd CB4 . . . . .209 A1
School Cl Cheveley CB8 . . . .91 C6
Gamlingay SG19 . . . . .41 D8
5 Maxey PE6 . . . . .231 C7
Peterborough PE3 . . . . . . .197 A5
2 Wisbech St Mary PE13 .235 B7
School Dro PE26 . . . . .171 A4
School Farm Rd PE26 . . . .171 E8
School Hill CB4 . . . . .104 B4
School La Alconbury PE28 150 F5
Barley SG8 . . . . .7 A1
Barton CB3 . . . . .63 B4
Bourn CB3 . . . . .79 B3
Boxworth CB3 . . . . .101 B5
Buckden PE19 . . . . .117 B4
Burwell CB5 . . . . .130 B1
Bythorn & Keyston PE28 . .146 C4
Conington CB3 . . . . .121 C1
Coveney CB6 . . . . .217 D5
Downham CB6 . . . . .218 A7
Downham CB6 . . . . .224 D1
Eaton Socon PE19 . . . . . . .74 C2
Elton PE8 . . . . .178 D8
Fenstanton PE28 . . . . .121 B6
Fulbourn CB1 . . . . .66 F4
Glinton PE6 . . . . .203 B8
Haslingfield CB3 . . . . .47 B5
Haverhill CB9 . . . . .23 D8
4 Histon CB4 . . . . .104 C3
Kings Ripton PE28 . . . . . . .153 C6
Little Paxton PE19 . . . . . . .96 A2
Longstanton CB4 . . . . .123 F1
Longstowe CB3 . . . . .60 A3
Manea PE15 . . . . .224 B4
4 Maxey PE6 . . . . .231 C7
Mepal CB6 . . . . .216 E3
Ramsey PE26 . . . . .172 B7
St Neots PE19 . . . . .74 E4
Swavesey CB4 . . . . .122 C6
Thriplow SG8 . . . . .31 B2
Toft CB3 . . . . .61 D4
3 Uffington PE9 . . . . . . .230 C6
Warmington PE8 . . . . .178 B3
Waterbeach CB5 . . . . .127 B8
Wilburton CB6 . . . . .210 C5
1 Wisbech PE13 . . . . . . .245 C5
School Rd
5 Barnack PE9 . . . . .230 D4

School Rd continued
Broughton PE28 . . . . .153 F8
3 Earith PE28 . . . . .208 E6
Great Wratting CB9 . . . . . . .39 E5
Newborough PE6 . . . . .205 D8
Outwell PE14 . . . . .229 D8
Warboys PE28 . . . . .164 F5
West Walton PE14 . . . . . . .238 E4
Woodditton CB8 . . . . .91 A3
School St CB10 . . . . .18 D2
Scolding Dro PE6 . . . . . .233 E5
Scorney 3 PE28 . . . . . . .121 C6
Scotenoon PE2 . . . . .185 E3
Scotgate PE9 . . . . .244 A5
Scotland Cl CB4 . . . . .84 B5
Scotland End CB7 . . . . . .213 C1
Scotland Rd
Cambridge CB4 . . . . .84 A5
Dry Drayton CB3 . . . . .81 A6
Scotney St PE1 . . . . .197 E7
Scotney Way PE28 . . . . . .168 C3
Scotred Cl CB5 . . . . .109 B8
Scotsdowne Rd CB2 . . . . .64 D3
Scott Ave IP28 . . . . .239 C5
Scott Cl
Peterborough PE2 . . . . . . .187 E6
4 Royston SG8 . . . . .13 D1
Scott Polar Research Inst
CB2 . . . . .246 B1
Scott's Cl PE14 . . . . .229 C2
Scotts Cl PE28 . . . . .120 B1
Scotts Cres PE28 . . . . . . .120 B1
Scotts Gdns CB2 . . . . .32 C5
Scotts Rd PE6 . . . . .203 F8
Scotts Yd 7 CB3 . . . . . . .47 B5
Scrolans PE27 . . . . .143 E6
Seadyke Bank PE13 . . . . .235 A7
Seadyke Rd PE13 . . . . . . .234 F6
Seafield Rd 7 PE13 . . . . .238 B2
Sealey's La PE13 . . . . . . .234 D8
Sealodes Rd CB7 . . . . . . .211 E5
Seargeants Cl PE6 . . . . . .207 C1
Searjeant St PE1 . . . . . . .197 E5
Searle St CB4 . . . . .83 D4
Searles Ct PE7 . . . . .189 D8
Searles Mdw CB3 . . . . . . .102 B1
Sears CB7 PE19 . . . . .118 F8
Seathwaite PE29 . . . . . . .141 B6
Seaton Cl PE7 . . . . .181 D6
Sebrights Way PE3 . . . . . .196 F3
Second Ave
Warboys PE28 . . . . .164 E6
Wisbech PE13 . . . . .245 D4
Second Broadpool Dro
PE28 . . . . .165 D8
Second Drift PE9 . . . . . . .244 B2
Second Dro
Downham CB6 . . . . .218 A8
Ely CB7 . . . . .218 F5
Peterborough PE1 . . . . . . .198 D1
St Ives PE27 . . . . .144 C2
Second Marsh Rd PE14 238 C3
Sedge Fen Rd PE38 . . . . .226 E7
Sedge Way CB6 . . . . .217 D2
Sedgwick Mus of Earth
Sciences★ CB2 . . . . .246 B2
Sedgwick St CB1 . . . . .65 B8
Sedley Inf Sch CB1 . . . . . .65 C7
Sedley Taylor Rd CB2 . . . .64 F4
Sefton Ave PE13 . . . . . . .245 E6
Sefton Cl CB2 . . . . .64 D3
Sefton Way CB8 . . . . .110 D5
Selby Ct 2 PE29 . . . . . . .141 F7
Sellers Grange PE2 . . . . .186 B4
Selsingen Way CB2 . . . . . .32 F7
Selwyn Cl
Great Shelford CB2 . . . . . . .49 A5
Mildenhall IP28 . . . . .239 D6
Newmarket CB8 . . . . .111 A1
Selwyn Coll CB3 . . . . .64 B8
Selwyn Gdns CB3 . . . . . . .64 B8
Selwyn Rd Cambridge CB3 .64 B7
Stamford PE9 . . . . .244 A7
Senate House Pas CB2 246 A2
Senes Calls 9 PE27 . . . . .208 A3
Seppings Cl 2 CB6 . . . . .210 C6
Serby Ave SG8 . . . . .5 C8
Serjeants Cl PE26 . . . . . .172 A6
Serpentine The PE7 . . . . .186 D3
Setchel 11 PE28 . . . . .74 C6
Setchel Dro CB4 . . . . . . .125 F7
Setchell Cl PE19 . . . . .97 F5
Setchfield Pl PE2 . . . . . . .186 F7
Sevenacres PE2 . . . . .185 E5
Seventh Ave PE13 . . . . . .245 E4
Seventh Dro CB6 . . . . . . .225 A3
Severn Cl PE4 . . . . .204 E1
Severn Pl CB1 . . . . .84 A2
Seymore Dr CB9 . . . . .23 D7
Seymour Cl 2 CB8 . . . . .111 C3
Seymour Pl PE4 . . . . .205 B2
Seymour St CB1 . . . . .65 C8
Seynory Dro PE7 . . . . . . .177 F7
Shade The CB7 . . . . .212 A5
Shadowbush Cl CB9 . . . . .38 F1
Shady Wlk 2 PE19 . . . . . .74 F5
Shaftenhoe End Rd SG8 . .7 A1
Shaftesbury Ave
March PE15 . . . . .243 E5
St Neots PE19 . . . . .74 F5
Shaftesbury Rd CB2 . . . . .64 F6
Shaftesbury Way SG8 . . . . .5 E5
Shakespeare Cl PE28 . . . .143 F6
Shakespeare Ave PE1 . . . .197 D8
Shakespeare Rd
Eaton Socon PE19 . . . . . . .74 C3
St Ives PE27 . . . . .143 F6

Shamrock Cl PE2 . . . . . . .187 C7
Shannon Cl CB9 . . . . .24 D7
Shardlow Cl 1 CB9 . . . . . .38 C1
Sharma Leas PE4 . . . . . . .204 A3
Sharman's Rd CB7 . . . . . .212 F5
Sharps La PE28 . . . . .150 F3
Shaw Dr PE15 . . . . .243 D3
Shawley Rd PE28 . . . . . . .168 A4
Sheep Mkt 6 PE9 . . . . . .244 B5
Sheep St PE28 . . . . .148 D3
Sheepfold PE27 . . . . .144 C5
Sheepwalk PE4 . . . . .205 A1
Sheldrick's Rd CB7 . . . . .213 B5
Shelford Park Ave CB2 . .49 A5
Shelford Rd
Cambridge CB2 . . . . .48 E8
Fulbourn CB1 . . . . .66 C3
Harston CB2 . . . . .48 C3
Whittlesford CB2 . . . . .32 A6
Shelford Sta CB2 . . . . . . .49 B5
Shelford's Rd CB4 . . . . . .209 A3
Shelley Cl
Huntingdon PE29 . . . . .141 F6
Royston SG8 . . . . .13 D1
Shelley Pl 5 PE19 . . . . . . .74 D6
Shelly Gdn CB3 . . . . .83 C3
Shelly Row 4 CB3 . . . . . . .83 C3
Shelton Rd PE2 . . . . .187 D6
Shepherd Cl SG8 . . . . .5 E5
Shepherd's Cl
Cambridge CB1 . . . . .66 A6
Fen Ditton CB5 . . . . .84 F5
Shepherd's Dro CB7 . . . .226 B2
Shepherds Cl 2 PE4 . . . .204 C4
Sheppard Way CB1 . . . . . .85 B1
Sheppard's Dro PE6 . . . .232 D8
Sheppersons Gr 2
PE15 . . . . .243 E4
Shepreth Rd
Barrington CB2 . . . . .29 D7
Foxton SG8 . . . . .30 A4
Shepreth SG8 . . . . .30 B3
Shepreth Sta SG8 . . . . . . .29 E5
Sheralds Croft La SG8 . . .31 A2
Sherborne Rd PE1 . . . . . .198 D6
Sherbourne Cl CB4 . . . . . .84 B6
Sherbrooke Cl PE15 . . . . .243 D1
Sheridan Rd PE1 . . . . . . .197 F8
Sheriffs Ct CB8 . . . . .70 F3
Sheringham Way PE2 . . . .186 C6
Sherlock Cl CB3 . . . . .83 B4
Sherlock Rd CB3 . . . . .83 B5
Sherwood Ave
4 Peterborough PE2 . . . . .186 F7
Wisbech PE13 . . . . .245 D7
Shetland Rd CB9 . . . . .24 D8
Shi Tennoji Buddhist High
Sch IP28 . . . . .214 B1
Shillow Hill PE26 . . . . . . .172 B1
Shingay La CB2 . . . . .32 F7
Ship Gdns IP28 . . . . .239 B3
Ship La CB7 . . . . .240 D3
Shippea Hill Rd IP28 . . . .213 C8
Shirdley Rd PE19 . . . . . . .74 F4
Shire Gr PE1 . . . . .198 C5
Shires The
1 Bluntisham/Colne
PE28 . . . . .208 C5
March PE15 . . . . .243 E2
Royston SG8 . . . . .5 E6
Shirley Cl CB4 . . . . .105 E2
Shirley CP Sch CB4 . . . . . .84 B5
Shirley Gr CB4 . . . . .84 B5
Shirley Rd CB4 . . . . .104 B3
Shores Cl IP28 . . . . .213 C3
Short Cl PE8 . . . . .178 B3
Short Cswy CB6 . . . . .217 C4
Short Dr PE15 . . . . .224 B5
Short Dro Cottenham CB4 125 F2
Downham CB6 . . . . .217 C8
Downham CB6 . . . . .217 F5
Downham CB6 . . . . .224 F3
Earith PE28 . . . . .208 F6
Holme PE7 . . . . .177 A4
Ramsey PE26 . . . . .221 A2
Somersham PE28 . . . . . . .215 D3
Short La
Bluntisham/Colne PE28 . . .208 C5
Coveney CB6 . . . . .217 C4
Willingham CB4 . . . . .209 A1
Wisbech PE13 . . . . .238 A1
Short Nightlayer's Dro
PE16 . . . . .241 C6
Short Rd Exning CB8 . . . . .131 F2
Snailwell CB8 . . . . .132 A3
Stretham CB6 . . . . .210 E5
Short St Bourn CB3 . . . . . .60 C5
Cambridge CB1 . . . . .246 B3
Shortacres Rd PE2 . . . . . .186 F7
Shortfen PE2 . . . . .186 C4
Shortland 6 PE28 . . . . . .215 C1
Shortsands Yd 3 PE19 . . .75 A5
Shrewsbury Ave PE2 . . . .186 D5
Shrub House Cl PE28 . . . .213 F8
Shrubberies The CB8 . . . .111 D1
Shrubbery Gr SG8 . . . . . . .5 D4
Shrubbery The PE16 . . . .241 D4
Shrublands IP28 . . . . . . .239 C4
Sibberton Lodge★ PE8 .193 E4
Sibson Aerodrome PE8 .183 E6
Sidgwick Ave CB3 . . . . . . .64 C8
Siding Dro PE28 . . . . . . .215 C5
Sidney Farm Rd CB1 . . . . .65 E6
Sidney Gdns CB3 . . . . .47 B6
Sidney St CB2 . . . . .246 A3
Sidney Sussex Coll CB1 246 B3
Siggin's La CB1 . . . . .20 D6
Silhalls Cl CB8 . . . . .91 F7

Silt Rd Littleport CB6 . . . .242 D5
March PE15 . . . . .243 F4
Upwell PE14 . . . . .229 C5
Silver Birch Ave PE27 . . .143 F6
Silver Birch Cl PE27 . . . . .141 E7
Silver Hill PE7 . . . . .186 D3
Silver St Ashwell SG7 . . . . .2 A1
Buckden PE19 . . . . .117 B4
Burwell CB5 . . . . .130 B4
Cambridge CB3 . . . . .246 A1
Ely CB7 . . . . .240 C5
Godmanchester PE29 . . . . .118 E8
Guilden Morden SG8 . . . . . .10 F4
Litlington SG8 . . . . .12 A2
March PE15 . . . . .243 C7
Peterborough PE2 . . . . . . .186 F7
Ramsey PE26 . . . . .172 B7
St Neots PE19 . . . . .74 E4
Willingham CB4 . . . . .209 A1
Wisbech PE13 . . . . .245 C6
Witcham CB6 . . . . .217 A2
Withersfield CB9 . . . . .38 A4
Silverdale Ave CB3 . . . . . .82 B2
Silverdale Cl CB3 . . . . . . .82 A2
Silverley Way CB8 . . . . . . .91 F7
Silver's La PE13 . . . . .234 E7
Silverweed PE7 . . . . .174 C5
Silverwood Cl CB1 . . . . . . .84 B2
Silverwood Rd PE1 . . . . . .197 F5
Silvester Rd PE5 . . . . . . .195 E2
Simeon Cl CB6 . . . . .240 F7
Simmer Piece PE28 . . . . .121 C5
Simpkin Cl PE19 . . . . .74 D2
Singerfire Rd PE5 . . . . . . .195 D2
Sir Harry Smith Com Coll
PE7 . . . . .189 F7
Sir James Black Rd
CB2 . . . . .240 C2
Six Bells 14 PE28 . . . . . . .215 C1
Six Mile Bottom Rd CB1 .69 A1
Sixteen Foot Bank
Christchurch PE14 . . . . . . .229 C4
Wimblington PE15 . . . . . . .223 E5
Sixth Ave PE13 . . . . .245 E4
Skaters Way PE4 . . . . . . .204 C4
Skeggles Cl PE29 . . . . . . .141 B5
Skeifs Row 4 PE15 . . . . .222 A5
Skelton Pl PE27 . . . . .144 B5
Skelton's Dro IP28 . . . . . .213 F8
Skipper's La
West Wickham CB1 . . . . . . .37 E8
West Wratting CB1 . . . . . . .54 E1
Withersfield CB9 . . . . .38 A5
Skiver Cl CB2 . . . . .32 F6
Skylark Pl 9 SG8 . . . . .5 E8
Slade Cl PE26 . . . . .172 A7
Slade The Witcham CB6 . .217 A2
Wrestlingworth & Cockayne
Hatley SG19 . . . . .25 B3
Slade Way PE16 . . . . .241 C5
Slatebarn Dro PE7 . . . . . .221 C8
Sleaford St CB1 . . . . .84 A1
Sleford Cl CB1 . . . . .53 B2
Sleights Dr 4 PE14 . . . . .238 F1
Slid La CB2 . . . . .29 F2
Slipe Cotts PE28 . . . . . . .146 A6
Small Lode PE14 . . . . . . .236 F1
Smallwood PE3 . . . . .197 B5
Smeefield PE28 . . . . .99 B8
Smeeth Rd Emneth PE14 .236 E6
Marshland St James PE14 236 F7
Smith Dr PE19 . . . . .117 B3
Smith St CB3 . . . . .100 A4
Smithey Fen Engine Dro
CB4 . . . . .209 E2
Smithfield 2 PE6 . . . . . . .233 B4
Smith's Dr PE15 . . . . .243 F3
Smith's Dro PE38 . . . . . . .226 F4
Smith's End La SG8 . . . . . .6 E1
Smiths Chase PE15 . . . . . .243 B5
Smiths Yd PE19 . . . . .94 A6
Snailwell Rd
Fordham CB8 . . . . .131 F5
Newmarket CB8 . . . . .111 B6
Snailwell Short Rd CB8 .131 E1
Snoots Rd PE7 . . . . .189 B7
Snowberry Way 3 CB7 .212 B5
Snowden Cl 1 PE6 . . . . .232 C8
Snowdonia Way PE29 . . . .141 A4
Snowley Pk PE7 . . . . .189 B8
Snowy Way PE29 . . . . . . .142 B6
Soham Rd Ely CB7 . . . . . .211 D8
Fordham CB8 . . . . .212 D2
Soham Village Coll CB7 212 B3
Soke Parkway PE3 . . . . . .197 A3
Soke Rd PE6 . . . . .207 B1
Sokemans Way PE28 . . . .117 D8
Somerby Cl 2 PE9 . . . . . .244 B7
Somers Rd PE13 . . . . .245 B4
Somerset Cl CB4 . . . . .83 D7
Somerset Rd Histon CB4 104 A3
Wyton Airfield PE28 . . . . . .143 B8
Somersham Rd
Bluntisham PE28 . . . . .155 E2
Colne PE28 . . . . .208 C8
Holywell-cum-Needingworth
PE27 . . . . .144 C7
Somerville PE4 . . . . .204 A5
Somerville Rd 1 PE9 . . . .244 A6
Somes Cl 1 PE9 . . . . . . .230 C6
Sorrel Cl 4 SG8 . . . . .5 F5
South Brink Elm PE14 . . . .235 B4
Wisbech PE13 . . . . .245 A3
South Cl SG8 . . . . .5 B7
South Dr March PE15 . . . .243 E4
Newmarket CB8 . . . . .110 F4
South End SG8 . . . . .12 E3

South Green Rd CB3 . . . . .64 C7
South La 3 CB3 . . . . .62 C5
South Par PE3 . . . . .197 E3
South Park St PE16 . . . . .241 C4
South Rd Brampton PE28 117 D8
Great Abington CB1 . . . . . . .33 F4
Histon CB4 . . . . .104 B1
South St Comberton CB3 . .62 C4
Great Chesterford CB10 . . . .18 D2
Huntingdon PE29 . . . . .141 F5
Litlington SG8 . . . . .12 A2
Peterborough PE1 . . . . . . .198 B2
Woodhurst PE28 . . . . .155 A4
South Terr CB3 . . . . .32 F5
South View PE2 . . . . .186 F7
South View Rd PE4 . . . . . .197 D8
Southacre Cl CB2 . . . . . . .64 E6
Southacre Dr CB2 . . . . . . .64 E6
Southampton Pl PE16 . . . .241 C3
Southbrook Field CB3 . . . .99 A2
Southbrooke Cl 2 CB2 . . .64 E6
Southdown Rd PE7 . . . . . .181 F5
Southerns The 7 CB6 . . . .216 E1
Southey Wood Forest
Walks★ PE6 . . . . .231 A1
Southey Wood (National
Trust)★ PE9 . . . . .231 A1
Southfield CB10 . . . . .18 A3
Southfields Ave PE2 . . . . .187 D5
Southfields Cl 2 CB8 . . . .110 E4
Southfields Dr PE2 . . . . . .187 D6
Southgate Ave IP28 . . . . .239 B7
Southgate Way PE2 . . . . .185 C2
Southlands Ave PE1 . . . . .198 A6
Southoe Rd PE7 . . . . .187 D2
Southside Ct CB4 . . . . .84 A5
Southwell Ave PE4 . . . . . .204 A4
Southwell Rd PE13 . . . . . .245 C8
Sovereign Cl 3 PE13 . . . .245 A6
Sovereign Pl PE3 . . . . . . .197 E2
Sovereign Way CB4 . . . . . .125 E3
Spalding Way CB1 . . . . . . .65 D4
Spaldings La CB4 . . . . . . .105 D7
Spaldwick Prim Sch
PE28 . . . . .137 F5
Spaldwick Rd PE28 . . . . . .137 C3
Sparkes Cl 2 CB7 . . . . . .213 A5
Sparrow Cl PE29 . . . . . . .141 E5
Sparrow Dr PE28 . . . . . . .150 E4
Sparrow Way PE28 . . . . . .120 B1
Sparrowgate Rd PE14 . . .238 F1
Sparrowhawk Way
PE29 . . . . .142 B7
Sparrows Cl PE28 . . . . . . .117 B8
Speechley Rd PE7 . . . . . . .181 F6
Speechley's Dro PE6 . . . .207 F2
Speed La CB7 . . . . .212 B4
Speedwell Cl CB1 . . . . . . .66 A6
Spencer Ave PE2 . . . . . . .187 D5
Spencer Cl
3 Eaton Socon PE19 . . . . .74 D6
West Walton PE14 . . . . . . .238 E4
Spencer Croft 4 CB7 . . . .240 E6
Spencer Dr Melbourn SG8 .14 D6
St Ives PE27 . . . . .144 A7
Spencer Dro
1 Guyhirn PE13 . . . . .235 A2
Soham CB7 . . . . .212 A4
Spencer Rd CB10 . . . . .18 D3
Spens Ave CB3 . . . . .64 B8
Spenser Cl SG8 . . . . .13 D1
Speyside Cl 1 PE2 . . . . . .185 D4
Spiggots Cl CB4 . . . . .123 E2
Spindle Rd CB9 . . . . .38 D1
Spinney Cl
2 Brampton PE28 . . . . . .140 D3
Warboys PE28 . . . . .164 F5
Warmington PE8 . . . . .178 B2
Spinney Dr CB2 . . . . .49 A4
Spinney Field PE28 . . . . . .138 F5
Spinney Fields PE7 . . . . . .176 F4
Spinney La PE28 . . . . .150 F5
Spinney Prim Sch CB1 . . .65 E6
Spinney The Bar Hill CB3 .102 B3
Cottenham CB4 . . . . .125 E5
Huntingdon PE29 . . . . .142 B6
Spinney Way 5 PE27 . . . .208 A3
Spires End PE28 . . . . .150 D6
Spitfire Cl PE29 . . . . .141 B8
Spittals Way
Huntingdon PE29 . . . . .141 C7
The Stukeleys PE29 . . . . . .152 C1
Splash La Castor PE5 . . . .184 E8
St Ives PE28 . . . . .142 F6
Split Dro CB3 . . . . .129 A4
Spong Dro CB4 . . . . .209 B1
Spooners Cl CB8 . . . . .70 F8
Springall PE3 . . . . .196 F4
Spring Cl Burwell CB5 . . . .130 B1
Histon CB4 . . . . .104 C4
Huntingdon PE29 . . . . .141 E6
Spring Dr PE7 . . . . .187 B2
Spring Hill MK44 . . . . .93 A3
Spring La
Bassingbourn SG8 . . . . . . .12 F3
Bottisham CB5 . . . . .86 F6
Spring Pl PE19 . . . . .95 A1
Springbrook PE19 . . . . . . .74 F4
Springfield
Huntingdon PE29 . . . . .141 E5
Peterborough PE2 . . . . . . .187 A7
Somersham PE28 . . . . . . .215 C1
Springfield Ave PE15 . . . .243 C2
Springfield Cl
Buckden PE19 . . . . .117 A3
2 St Neots PE19 . . . . .75 A5
Springfield Rd
Alconbury Weston PE28 . .150 D5

Springfield Rd continued
Cambridge CB4 . . . . .83 E4
🔲 Parson Drove PE13 . .234 D7
Peterborough PE1 . . . . . .197 F5
Sawston CB2 . . . . .32 F5
Yaxley PE7 . . . . .181 E5
Springfield Terr 🔲 CB4 . .83 E4
Springfields PE7 . . . . . .190 C7
Springfields Sch PE29 . .141 F8
Springhead SG7 . . . . .2 D4
Springhead La CB4 . . . . .240 E5
Springhill Rd CB4 . . . . .121 C6
Spruce Dr PE28 . . . . . . .151 F2
Spurgeon's Cl CB1 . . . . . .85 B1
Spurgeons CB5 . . . . . . .106 B8
Spurling Cl CB8 . . . . .91 C5
Square The
🔲 Barnack PE9 . . . . . . .230 D4
Stow cum Quy CB5 . . . . .86 A6
Squire's Dr PE14 . . . . . .229 F7
Squire's Field The CB1 . . .67 F7
Squires Cl 🔲 PE28 . . . .215 C1
Squires Ct 🔲 PE19 . . . . .74 B4
Squires Gate PE4 . . . . .204 F3
Stackyard The
Ickleton CB10 . . . . .18 A3
Peterborough PE2 . . . . .185 E5
Stafford Rd PE7 . . . . . .189 F6
Staffordshire St CB1 . . . .84 A2
Stagsden PE2 . . . . .185 F4
Stagshaw Dr PE2 . . . . .187 B8
Staithe Rd PE13 . . . . . .245 E6
Stake Piece Rd SG8 . . . . . .5 C6
Stakings The CB2 . . . . . .32 D7
Stallebrass Cl PE2 . . . . .187 E5
Stamford & Rutland Hospl
PE9 . . . . .244 D6
Stamford Ave SG8 . . . . . . .5 D7
Stamford Coll PE9 . . . . .244 D6
Stamford Endowed Sch
PE9 . . . . .244 C5
Stamford High Sch PE9 244 C4
Stamford High Sch Juns
PE9 . . . . .244 B4
Stamford L Ctr PE9 . . . .244 D6
Stamford La PE8 . . . . . .178 E3
Stamford Lodge★ PE6 .196 C5
Stamford Lodge Rd
PE6 . . . . .196 B4
Stamford Mus★ PE9 . . .244 C5
Stamford Rd
Barnack PE9 . . . . .230 C4
Easton on the Hill PE9 . .244 A1
Helpston PE6 . . . . .231 C1
Marholm PE6 . . . . .203 B2
Market Deeping PE6 . . . .231 D8
Tallington PE9 . . . . .231 A8
West Deeping PE6 . . . . .231 B8
Stamford St 🔲 CB8 . . . .111 B2
Stamford Sta PE9 . . . . .244 B4
Stamford Yd SG8 . . . . . . .5 C6
Stamper St 🔲 PE3 . . . .196 F3
Stan Rowing Ct PE2 . . .187 C2
Stanbury Cl CB5 . . . . . . .84 E6
Stanch Hill Rd PE28 . . .168 C3
Stanegate 🔲 PE28 . . . .168 C2
Stanesfield Rd CB5 . . . . .84 D3
Stanford Bus Pk PE9 . . .244 D7
Stanford Wlk 🔲 PE3 . . .197 C7
Stanground Coll PE7 . . .187 C5
Stanground Cty Inf Sch
PE2 . . . . .187 D5
Staniland Way PE4 . . . .204 B5
Stanley Ct CB5 . . . . .84 B3
Stanley Rd Cambridge CB5 84 D3
Great Chesterford CB10 . . .18 E3
Newmarket CB8 . . . . . . .111 C3
Peterborough PE1 . . . . .198 A3
Stanley St PE9 . . . . .244 C5
Stanpoint Way PE27 . . .144 A5
Stansfield Gdns CB1 . . . .66 F5
Stansgate Ave CB2 . . . . .65 D7
Stanton Mere Way CB4 .124 A6
Stanton Sq PE7 . . . . . . .186 D2
Stapledon Rd PE2 . . . . .185 D2
Stapleford Com Prim Sch
CB2 . . . . .49 C4
Staples La CB7 . . . . . . .212 B3
Star Cl PE1 . . . . .198 C3
Star La Ramsey PE26 . . .172 A8
Stamford PE9 . . . . .244 C5
Star Mews PE1 . . . . . . .198 C2
Star Rd PE1 . . . . .198 C2
Starling Cl
Alconbury PE28 . . . . . . .150 E4
🔲 Milton CB4 . . . . .105 D3
Starlock Cl CB6 . . . . . . .210 E4
Stathern Rd PE1 . . . . . .198 D7
Station App March PE15 .243 D6
Newmarket CB8 . . . . . . .111 A2
Somersham PE28 . . . . . .208 C8
Station Ave 🔲 PE13 . . .234 D5
Station Dr Wisbech PE13 245 C4
Wisbech St Mary PE13 . .235 C7
Station Gdns PE26 . . . . .172 A4
Station La PE19 . . . . . . .117 F3
Station Rd
Abbots Ripton PE28 . . . .162 B1
Ailsworth PE5 . . . . .184 C8
Ashwell SG7 . . . . .3 A3
Barnack PE9 . . . . .230 E4
Bluntisham PE28 . . . . . .208 C4
Cambridge CB1 . . . . .64 F7
Catworth PE28 . . . . .136 D5
Chatteris PE16 . . . . .241 C4
Deeping St James PE6 . .206 D4
Dullingham CB8 . . . . .70 D8
Dullingham CB8 . . . . .89 C2

Station Rd continued
Elm PE14 . . . . .235 C2
Ely CB7 . . . . .240 D3
Fordham CB7 . . . . .131 A8
Foxton CB2 . . . . .30 B6
Fulbourn CB1 . . . . .67 A5
Gamlingay SG19 . . . . . . .41 E5
Gedney Hill PE12 . . . . . .233 F8
Great Shelford CB2 . . . . .49 A5
Haddenham CB6 . . . . . . .210 A6
Harston CB2 . . . . .47 F2
Haverhill CB9 . . . . .24 A8
Histon CB4 . . . . .104 C3
Holme PE7 . . . . .177 A4
Isleham CB7 . . . . .213 A4
Kennett CB8 . . . . .133 F5
Linton CB1 . . . . .35 B2
Littleport CB6 . . . . .242 E4
Lode CB5 . . . . .107 C2
Longstanton CB4 . . . . . .123 F4
Manea PE15 . . . . .224 B5
March PE15 . . . . .243 D5
Meldreth SG8 . . . . .14 B6
Oakington & Westwick
CB4 . . . . .103 D7
Over CB4 . . . . .122 F8
Pampisford CB2 . . . . .33 F6
Peterborough PE3 . . . . .197 F2
Ramsey PE26 . . . . .172 A7
St Ives PE27 . . . . .144 B3
St Neots PE19 . . . . .75 B5
Shepreth SG8 . . . . .29 E5
Soham CB7 . . . . .212 B4
Stamford PE9 . . . . .244 B4
Steeple Morden SG8 . . . . .3 B7
Stow cum Quy CB5 . . . .106 C3
Sutton CB6 . . . . .216 F1
Swaffham Bulbeck CB5 . .108 A2
Swaffham Prior CB5 . . . .108 C5
Swavesey CB4 . . . . .122 E7
Thorney PE6 . . . . .233 A4
Tilbrook PE28 . . . . .113 B7
Walsoken PE14 . . . . .236 E8
Warboys PE28 . . . . .164 F7
Waterbeach CB5 . . . . . . .106 B7
Whittlesey PE7 . . . . .189 E5
Wilburton CB6 . . . . .210 C7
Willingham CB4 . . . . . . .124 A7
Wisbech St Mary PE13 . .235 C7
Station Rd E CB2 . . . . . . .32 E3
Station Rd W CB2 . . . . . .32 E3
Station St PE16 . . . . . . .241 B4
Station Yd IP28 . . . . . . .239 B3
Staughton Pl 🔲 PE19 . . .74 C4
Staunch Hill PE28 . . . . .148 C3
Staverton Rd PE4 . . . . .204 A3
Staxton Cl PE4 . . . . . . .203 C1
Stearne's Yd 🔲 CB3 . . . .47 B5
Steeple Morden Sch SG8 11 B2
Steeple View PE15 . . . . .243 C1
Stephen Dr CB4 . . . . .23 F8
Stephens Way 🔲 PE6 . .231 F8
Stephenson Cl SG8 . . . . . .5 B7
Stephenson Rd PE27 . . .144 B6
Stepping Stones PE28 . .143 D1
Stepping Stones Sch
PE4 . . . . .197 D8
Stermyn St 🔲 PE15 . . .245 C5
Sterndale Cl CB3 . . . . . . .82 E8
Sterne Cl CB1 . . . . .65 B6
Sternes Way CB2 . . . . . . .49 C4
Stetchworth Rd
Dullingham CB8 . . . . .70 F8
Stetchworth CB8 . . . . . . .71 C8
Stevens Cl CB4 . . . . . . .125 D4
Stevens Way PE15 . . . . .243 D6
Stevenson Ct
Cambridge CB5 . . . . .84 A3
Eaton Socon PE19 . . . . . .74 D6
Steward Cl CB7 . . . . . . .211 D8
Steward's La CB6 . . . . . .216 E1
Stewart Cl PE28 . . . . . . .140 C2
Steynings The PE4 . . . . .204 C3
Stibbington H★ PE8 . . . .194 D2
Stickle Cl 🔲 PE29 . . . .141 B7
Stiles The PE29 . . . . . . .141 F1
Still The Wisbech PE13 . .235 E8
Wisbech PE13 . . . . .238 B1
Stilton CE Sch PE7 . . . . .175 F7
Stirling Cl
"Beck Row, Holywell Row
& Kenny Hill" IP28 . . .213 D6
Cambridge CB4 . . . . .84 A5
Warboys PE28 . . . . .164 F4
Stirling Dr CB9 . . . . .23 E8
Stirling Gdns CB8 . . . . .110 E4
Stirling Rd PE27 . . . . . .144 A7
Stirling Way
Peterborough PE3 . . . . .204 A1
Witchford CB6 . . . . .217 F1
Stirtloe La PE19 . . . . . . .117 A2
Stitch The PE14 . . . . . . .236 B4
Stitchfield Riding Sch
PE14 . . . . .236 A5
Stocking Fen Rd PE26 . .221 A1
Stocking La
Nuthampstead SG8 . . . . . .1 A2
Spaldwick PE28 . . . . . . .114 E8
Stockley Cl CB9 . . . . .24 C7
Stocks Cl CB5 . . . . .86 E5
Stocks Hill PE5 . . . . . . .195 F1
Stocks La Gamlingay SG19 41 D4
Orwell SG8 . . . . .45 L1
Stockwell St CB1 . . . . . . .65 B8
Stokes Cl CB4 . . . . .123 F1
Stokesay Ct 🔲 PE3 . . . .197 B1
Stonald Ave PE7 . . . . . .189 D8

Stonald Rd PE7 . . . . . . .189 C8
Stone Field CB3 . . . . . . .102 A3
Stone La Meldreth SG8 . . .29 C3
Peterborough PE7 . . . . .197 F5
Stone St CB1 . . . . .84 B1
Stonea Camp★ PE15 . . .223 E8
Stonebridge CB2 . . . . . .186 C5
Stonebridge La CB1 . . . . .67 A4
Stonebridge Lea PE2 . . .186 C5
Stonecross Way PE15 . .243 D3
Stonehill PE29 . . . . .141 C7
Stonehill Rd CB2 . . . . . . .48 C7
Stonehouse Rd
Upwell PE14 . . . . .236 E1
Yaxley PE7 . . . . .181 E5
Stonely Rd PE28 . . . . . .138 B3
Stoney Cl PE29 . . . . .141 F8
Storbeck Rd 🔲 PE13 . . .245 C7
Storers Wlk PE7 . . . . . . .190 C6
Stores Hill CB8 . . . . .92 E8
Storey's Bar Rd PE6 . . . .199 A3
Storey's Way CB3 . . . . . . .83 B3
Storrington Way PE4 . . .204 C3
Stott Gdns CB4 . . . . .84 A6
Stour Cl PE27 . . . . .144 A6
Stour Valley Rd CB9 . . . . .24 B7
Stourbridge Gr CB1 . . . . .84 C1
Stow Gdns PE13 . . . . . .245 E4
Stow La PE13 . . . . .245 E4
Stow Rd Kimbolton PE28 . .113 F5
Spaldwick PE28 . . . . . . .137 F6
Stow cum Quy CB5 . . . . .85 F5
Wisbech PE13 . . . . .245 F5
Stowehill Rd PE4 . . . . . .204 F2
Stowgate Rd PE6 . . . . . .206 B7
Straight Dro Bury PE26 . .172 D3
Coveney PE15 . . . . .217 C7
Farcet PE7 . . . . .187 E1
Sawtry PE28 . . . . .168 A3
Wistow PE28 . . . . .172 A2
Straight Furlong CB6 . . .224 E2
Straight Rd PE15 . . . . . .224 B3
Strangeways Rd CB1 . . . .65 D4
Stratfield Cl CB4 . . . . . . .83 B5
Stratford Pl 🔲 PE19 . . . .74 C3
Strawberry Cl 🔲 PE13 .245 A6
Strawberry Fields CB9 . . .23 D7
Street The
Barton Mills IP28 . . . . . .239 E2
"Beck Row, Holywell Row
& Kenny Hill" IP28 . . . .214 A8
Dalham CB8 . . . . .92 E8
Freckenham IP28 . . . . . .213 C3
Great Bradley CB8 . . . . . .55 F7
Great Wratting CB9 . . . . .39 E6
Kirtling CB8 . . . . .72 D6
Lidgate CB8 . . . . .73 D8
Mildenhall IP28 . . . . . . .213 E8
Moulton CB8 . . . . .112 F5
Snailwell CB8 . . . . .132 A4
Westley Waterless CB8 . . .70 C5
Woodditton CB8 . . . . .91 B2
Worlington IP28 . . . . . . .213 F4
Streetly End CB1 . . . . . . .37 B5
Stretham Old Engine★
CB6 . . . . .210 F4
Stretham Rd Wicken CB7 211 D2
Wilburton CB6 . . . . .210 D5
Stretten Ave CB4 . . . . . . .83 D4
Stretton Ave CB8 . . . . . .111 B2
Stricklands Dr 🔲 PE6 . .232 B8
Strollers Way CB8 . . . . . .90 A2
Stroud Hill PE28 . . . . . .165 E4
Stuart Cl
Godmanchester PE29 . . .142 A1
Peterborough PE2 . . . . .187 C6
Stuart Dr SG8 . . . . .5 D8
Stubbs Cl 🔲 Haverhill CB9 38 D1
St Ives PE27 . . . . .144 A7
Studlands Park Ave
CB8 . . . . .110 D6
Studlands Rise SG8 . . . . . .5 E6
Studlands Rise Fst Sch
SG8 . . . . .5 E6
Stukeley Cl
Cambridge CB3 . . . . .64 A8
Peterborough PE2 . . . . .187 D5
Stukeley Meadows Ind Est
PE29 . . . . .141 C8
Stukeley Meadows Prim Sch
PE29 . . . . .141 C6
Stukeley Rd PE29 . . . . . .141 C6
Stulp Field Rd CB3 . . . . . .64 A4
Stumpacre PE3 . . . . . . .197 A8
Stumpcross 🔲 PE28 . . .168 C2
Stuntney Cswy CB7 . . . .240 E2
Sturmer Cl CB8 . . . . .23 C7
Sturmer Rd Haverhill CB9 .24 B7
Kedington CB9 . . . . .24 F7
Sturrock Way PE3 . . . . .197 C8
Sturton St CB1 . . . . .84 A1
Sudbury Ct PE7 . . . . . . .187 F5
Sudeley Gr CB3 . . . . .81 A3
Suet Hills Dro PE7 . . . . .188 E1
Suez Rd CB1 . . . . .65 C2
Suffolk Cl 🔲 Ely CB6 . . .240 A3
Huntingdon PE29 . . . . . .141 F6
Peterborough PE3 . . . . .197 B2
🔲 St Ives PE27 . . . . . . .144 A8
Suffolk Ho★ CB8 . . . . . . .73 B8
Suffolk Rd 🔲 SG8 . . . . . . .5 D8
Suffolk Way March PE15 .243 E2
Newmarket CB8 . . . . . . .110 E5
Sulehay Rd PE8 . . . . . . .193 C1
Sumerling Way PE28 . . .208 C6
Summerfield CB3 . . . . . . .64 C8
Summerfield Cl PE13 . . .245 A6
Summerfield Rd PE1 . . .197 F4

Summerhayes 🔲 CB7 . .240 F6
Sun Hill SG8 . . . . .5 C5
Sun La 🔲 CB8 . . . . .111 A3
Sun St 🔲 Cambridge CB1 . .84 A2
Isleham CB7 . . . . .213 A5
Sunderland Ave CB2 . . . .33 A8
Sundew Cl PE19 . . . . .74 B6
Sunfield Rd PE26 . . . . . .172 A4
Sunningdale PE2 . . . . . .185 E6
Sunningdale Ave IP28 . .239 B4
Sunnybank 🔲 PE19 . . . . .75 A5
Sunnymead PE4 . . . . . . .204 A6
Sunnyside CB5 . . . . .84 E2
Sunnyville Rd PE7 . . . . .190 F8
Sunset Sq 🔲 CB4 . . . . . .83 D7
Surrey Rd PE29 . . . . . . .141 E8
Sussex Rd Stamford PE9 .244 B6
Wyton Airfield PE28 . . . .143 B8
Sussex St CB1 . . . . .246 B3
Sutcliffe Rd PE8 . . . . . . .193 D8
Sutton Cl CB4 . . . . .105 D3
Sutton Cl 🔲 CB6 . . . . . .216 E2
Sutton Gate PE12 . . . . .237 D8
Sutton Mdws PE13 . . . .245 A8
Sutton Pk CB6 . . . . .216 E2
Sutton Rd Eyeworth SG19 . .10 A8
Haddenham CB6 . . . . . . .210 A8
Mepal CB6 . . . . .216 E3
Newton PE13 . . . . .238 B6
Wentworth CB6 . . . . . . .217 C1
Wisbech PE13 . . . . .245 A7
Witchford CB6 . . . . .217 C1
Sutton Way 🔲 PE15 . . . .223 A5
Sutton's La PE6 . . . . . . .231 E8
Suttons Cl PE14 . . . . . . .236 F2
Svenskaby PE2 . . . . . . .185 C6
Swaffham Bulbeck Prim Sch
CB5 . . . . .108 B1
Swaffham Heath Rd
CB5 . . . . .108 C1
Swaffham Prior CE Com Prim
Sch CB5 . . . . .108 C5
Swaffham Rd
Bottisham CB5 . . . . .107 E1
Burwell CB5 . . . . .109 A7
Reach CB5 . . . . .108 E8
Swain's Dro PE13 . . . . . .238 C8
Swale Ave PE4 . . . . .204 E1
Swallow Cl PE7 . . . . . . .201 A1
Swallow Cl 🔲 PE19 . . . . .75 B6
Swallow La PE13 . . . . . .238 B8
Swallow Way
🔲 March PE15 . . . . . . .243 F5
🔲 March PE15 . . . . . . .243 F5
Swallowfield PE4 . . . . . .204 A4
Swan Cl St Ives PE27 . . . .143 F7
Whittlesey PE7 . . . . .189 F8
Swan Ct PE15 . . . . .243 D6
Swan Dr PE16 . . . . .241 D5
Swan End PE19 . . . . . . .117 B4
Swan Gdns PE28 . . . . . .121 B5
Swan Gr CB8 . . . . .110 B8
Swan La Exning CB8 . . . .110 B8
🔲 Guilden Morden SG8 . .10 F4
Haverhill CB9 . . . . .24 A8
Swan Rd Fenstanton PE28 121 B5
Whittlesey PE7 . . . . .189 F6
Swan St 🔲 SG7 . . . . .2 D4
Swanhill PE8 . . . . .194 A4
Swann's Cl CB8 . . . . .26 A3
Swann's Rd CB5 . . . . .84 A4
Swann's Terr 🔲 CB1 . . . .65 A8
Swanspool PE3 . . . . . . .197 B6
Swanton Cl PE15 . . . . . .243 D7
Swasedale Dro CB7 . . . .219 A5
Swavesey Cty Prim Sch
CB4 . . . . .122 E6
Swavesey Village Coll
CB4 . . . . .122 E5
Sweetbriar La PE4 . . . . .204 A6
Sweeting Ave PE19 . . . . . .95 F1
Sweetings Rd PE29 . . . .118 F8
Swift Cl 🔲 March PE15 . .243 F5
Market Deeping PE6 . . . .231 E8
Royston SG8 . . . . .13 D6
St Neots PE19 . . . . .75 B6
Swifts Cnr CB1 . . . . .66 F5
Swinburne Cl SG8 . . . . . .13 D1
Swinnell Cl SG8 . . . . .13 A5
Sybil Rd PE13 . . . . .245 C6
Sycamore Ave PE1 . . . . .198 C6
Sycamore Cl
🔲 Cambridge CB1 . . . . .65 D5
March PE15 . . . . .243 C3
Sycamore Dr PE29 . . . . .141 E8
Sycamore La CB7 . . . . . .240 F5
Sycamore Rd PE7 . . . . .189 F6
Sycamores The
🔲 Bluntisham/Colne
PE28 . . . . .208 C6
Little Paxton PE19 . . . . . .95 F2
Milton CB4 . . . . .105 C2
Sydney Rd PE2 . . . . .198 D5
Syers La PE7 . . . . .189 D7
Sylton Cl PE29 . . . . .141 F1
Sylvden Dr PE13 . . . . . .245 D6
Sylvester Rd CB1 . . . . . . .83 B1
Symington Cl PE2 . . . . .186 F8
Symonds Cl CB4 . . . . . .104 B4
Symonds La CB1 . . . . . . .35 B3
Sywell Gr 🔲 PE14 . . . . .225 B3

T

Tabrum Cl CB3 . . . . .63 F4
Tadlow Rd SG19 . . . . .25 C3

Tait Cl PE1 . . . . .198 C5
Talbot Ave PE2 . . . . .186 D6
Talbot Cl PE7 . . . . .144 B6
Tall Trees 🔲 SG8 . . . . .5 E6
Tallington Lakes L Pk★
PE9 . . . . .231 A8
Tall's La PE28 . . . . .121 B6
Tamar Cl PE27 . . . . .144 B6
Tamarin Gdns CB1 . . . . . .66 A6
Tan House La CB5 . . . . . .109 B8
Tan Yd PE7 . . . . .74 E5
Tanglewood
Alconbury Weston PE28 .150 E6
Peterborough PE4 . . . . .204 B6
Tanhouse PE2 . . . . .186 C5
Tanners La CB7 . . . . . . .212 B3
Tannersfield Way CB8 . .110 F4
Tannery Cl SG8 . . . . .5 C6
Tannery Drift SG8 . . . . . . .5 C6
Tannery Drift Sch SG8 . . . .5 C6
Tannery Rd CB2 . . . . .32 F6
Tansor Garth PE3 . . . . .197 C5
Tansor Ct PE19 . . . . .74 F8
Tansy Cl 🔲 PE19 . . . . . . .74 B5
Tantallon Ct 🔲 PE3 . . . .197 B1
Tanyard The SG8 . . . . . . .12 E4
Tarrant PE4 . . . . .204 A6
Tasman Rd CB9 . . . . .24 C7
Tatwin Dr 🔲 PE6 . . . . . .232 B8
Taunton Cl 🔲 CB1 . . . . . .65 D7
Taverners Dr 🔲 PE26 . . .171 F5
Taverners Rd PE1 . . . . . .197 F4
Tavistock Cl 🔲 PE6 . . . .233 A3
Tavistock Rd
Cambridge CB4 . . . . .83 C6
Wisbech PE13 . . . . .245 D5
Tawny Cres PE29 . . . . . .142 B7
Tay Cl PE27 . . . . .144 B7
Taylor's Dro PE12 . . . . .237 C8
Taylor's La CB4 . . . . .122 D6
Taylors Field CB8 . . . . . . .70 F8
Taylors Gn PE8 . . . . . . .178 A3
Taylors La PE19 . . . . . . .116 F5
Taymor Pl PE14 . . . . . . .225 A8
Tea Kettle La CB8 . . . . . . .89 F1
Teal Cl Chatteris PE16 . .241 C6
St Ives PE27 . . . . .143 F7
Teal Rd PE7 . . . . .189 F8
Teanby Ct 🔲 PE3 . . . . . .196 F3
Teasdale Cl SG8 . . . . . . .13 D1
Teasel Cl
🔲 Eaton Socon PE19 . . . .74 C6
🔲 Royston SG8 . . . . .5 E5
Teasel Way CB1 . . . . .66 A5
Tebbutts Rd PE19 . . . . . .74 E5
Tedder Way CB4 . . . . .83 C6
Telegraph St CB4 . . . . . .125 E4
Temple Cl Duxford CB2 . . .32 D1
Huntingdon PE29 . . . . . .141 E4
Temple End
Great Wilbraham CB1 . . . .68 A3
Little Thurlow CB9 . . . . . .55 F2
Temple Grange PE4 . . . .204 B6
Temple Rd CB7 . . . . .212 F4
Tempsford Rd SG19 . . . . .40 A4
Ten Acre Dro PE7 . . . . . .220 C8
Ten Bell La 🔲 CB7 . . . . .212 B4
Ten Mile Bank CB6 . . . . .242 F6
Tenby Cl CB1 . . . . .66 A6
Tenby Way 🔲 PE19 . . . . .74 F1
Tenison Ave CB1 . . . . . . .64 F7
Tenison Manor CB4 . . . .125 D4
Tenison Rd CB1 . . . . .65 A8
Tennis Ct Ave PE29 . . . .141 E5
Tennis Ct Rd CB2 . . . . . .246 B1
Tennis Ct Terr CB2 . . . . .246 A1
Tennyson Ave PE27 . . . .143 C6
Tennyson Cl
Huntingdon PE29 . . . . . .141 F6
Royston SG8 . . . . .13 D1
Tennyson Pl PE19 . . . . . .74 D6
Tennyson Rd PE1 . . . . . .197 F7
Tenter La PE9 . . . . .244 C5
Tenterleas PE27 . . . . . . .144 B3
Tern Cl CB9 . . . . .24 C7
Tern Gdns PE16 . . . . . . .241 C6
Tern Way 🔲 PE19 . . . . . .75 B6
Terrace The CB8 . . . . . . .111 A3
Terrington Cl PE14 . . . . .236 D6
Tetworth Hill SG19 . . . . .41 A7
Teversham CE Prim Sch
CB1 . . . . .85 B2
Teversham Drift CB1 . . . .66 A7
Teversham Rd CB1 . . . . . .66 E6
Teversham Way CB2 . . . .50 A1
Teynham Cl 🔲 CB1 . . . . .65 D7
Thackeray Cl SG8 . . . . . .13 D1
Thackers Cl PE8 . . . . . . .194 A4
Thackray Cl PE29 . . . . . .141 E7
Thames Rd PE29 . . . . . .141 F8
Tharp Way CB7 . . . . .213 C1
Thatcher Stanfords Cl
SG8 . . . . .14 C2
Thatchers Cl PE26 . . . . .171 B2
Thatchers Wood CB4 . . .123 F1
Thatchwood Ave 🔲
PE14 . . . . .236 C6
Thetford Rd IP28 . . . . . .239 E4
Thetford Terr CB5 . . . . . .84 E2
Thicket Rd PE28 . . . . . .143 B4
Thickwillow 🔲 PE29 . . .118 F8
Third Ave Warboys PE28 .164 E6
Wisbech PE13 . . . . .245 E5
Third Dro Downham CB6 .225 B1
Peterborough PE1 . . . . .198 E2

Third Marsh Rd PE14 . . .238 C3
Thirlby Gdns CB7 . . . . . .240 E7
Thirleby Cl PE14 . . . . .83 D5
Thirlmere PE29 . . . . .141 B6
Thirlmere Gdns **3** PE4 . .204 E3
Thirlwall Dr CB7 . . . . . . .213 A1
Thistle Dr PE2 . . . . .187 C7
Thistle Gn CB4 . . . . .122 E6
Thistlemoor Rd PE1 . . . . .197 C7
Thoday St CB1 . . . . .65 B8
Thodays CB4 . . . . .209 A1
Thomas Christian Way
CB5 . . . . .86 E7
Thomas Ct **7** PE3 . . . . .196 F3
Thomas Eaton Sch
PE15 . . . . .223 B7
Thomas Rd CB1 . . . . .66 D5
Thomas Way **2** SG8 . . . . .13 D1
Thomas Wlk CB11 . . . . .9 F1
Thompson's La CB2 . . . . .246 A3
Thompsons Gd PE7 . . . . .186 D3
Thompsons Mdw SG8 . . . .11 A4
Thongsley PE29 . . . . .141 F1
Thongsley Cty Jun & Inf Sch
PE29 . . . . .141 F1
Thorby Ave PE15 . . . . . . .243 A7
Thorleye Rd CB5 . . . . .84 C2
Thorn Cl CB7 . . . . .212 A4
Thorndown Inf Sch
PE27 . . . . .143 E6
Thorndown Jun Sch
PE27 . . . . .143 E6
Thorney Dyke PE6 . . . . . .201 C6
Thorney Rd Eye PE6 . . . . .232 E1
Newborough PE6 . . . . . . .206 E2
Wisbech St Mary CB4 . . . .234 C2
Thornham Way PE7 . . . . .190 C6
Thornhaugh H★ PE8 . . . .193 C6
Thornhill Pl CB4 . . . . . . .123 F2
Thornleigh Dr PE2 . . . . . .186 C6
Thornmead PE4 . . . . .204 D4
Thornton Cl Girton CB3 . . .83 A6
Peterborough PE4 . . . . . .204 E3
Thornton Rd Girton CB3 . . .82 F7
March PE15 . . . . .243 D6
Thornton Way CB3 . . . . . .83 A6
Thorolds Way PE5 . . . . . .195 D2
Thoroughfare La PE7 . . . .218 F1
Thoroughfare Way **3**
CB6 . . . . .242 E4
Thorpe Ave PE3 . . . . .197 C4
Thorpe CP Sch PE3 . . . . .197 B3
Thorpe H★ PE3 . . . . .197 C2
Thorpe Lea Rd PE3 . . . . .197 F1
Thorpe Mdws PE3 . . . . . .197 C1
Thorpe Park Rd PE3 . . . . .197 C3
Thorpe Rd PE3 . . . . .197 B1
Thorpe The PE28 . . . . . . .143 B1
Thorpe Way CB5 . . . . .84 F4
Thorpe Wood PE3 . . . . . .196 F1
Thorseby Cl PE3 . . . . .197 B3
Thrapston Rd
Brampton PE28 . . . . .140 B4
Catworth PE28 . . . . .147 C2
Kimbolton PE28 . . . . . . .113 F5
Spaldwick PE28 . . . . .137 F6
Three Cups Wlk CB7 . . . .240 D4
Three Shire Stone★
PE28 . . . . .135 B1
Three Shires Way PE28 . . .135 E4
Thrifts Wlk CB4 . . . . .84 A4
Thriplow CE Prim Sch
SG8 . . . . .31 B2
Thriplow Rd SG8 . . . . .30 F1
Throckmorton PE28 . . . . .164 E5
Throckmorton Rd PE28 . . .117 D8
Throstlenest PE7 . . . . . . .187 C3
Thruffle Way CB3 . . . . . . .102 C3
Thulborn Cl CB1 . . . . .85 B1
Thurland's Dro PE14 . . . .229 C8
Thurlaston Cl PE3 . . . . . .197 B2
Thurley Cl PE19 . . . . .95 E5
Thurlow Rd PE29 . . . . .39 C6
Thurnall Ave SG8 . . . . .5 D5
Thurning Ave PE7 . . . . . . .187 C6
Thurning Rd PE28 . . . . . . .157 F7
Thuro Gr PE2 . . . . .186 A3
Thursfield PE4 . . . . .204 C4
Thurston Gate **2** PE3 . .197 A1
Tiberius Cl Haverhill CB9 . . .24 D7
Sturmer CB9 . . . . .24 C7
Tilbrook Rd PE28 . . . . . . .113 D6
Tillbrooks Hill CB8 . . . . . .73 C1
Tillyard Way CB1 . . . . .65 D4
Tilton Ct PE1 . . . . .198 C2
Tindall Cl PE13 . . . . .245 C8
Tinker's Dro PE13 . . . . . .245 D8
Tinker's La CB3 . . . . .61 C2
Tinkers La PE28 . . . . .168 B4
Tintagel Ct
7 Peterborough PE3 . . .197 B1
2 St Neots PE19 . . . . . .74 F2
Tintern Rise **3** PE6 . . . .232 A1
Tinwell Rd PE9 . . . . .244 A4
Tinwell Road La PE9 . . . . .244 A4
Tipplers' Rd CB4 . . . . .122 C2
Tiptree CB5 . . . . .84 F4
Tirrington PE3 . . . . .197 A3
Tithe Ave IP28 . . . . .213 F8
Tithe Cl PE28 . . . . .120 B2
Tithe Rd PE16 . . . . .241 C2
Tithe Way CB3 . . . . .79 C3
Tiverton Rd PE3 . . . . .197 C3
Tiverton Way CB1 . . . . . . .65 C7
Toates Cl CB6 . . . . .210 C6

Toft La CB1 . . . . .67 F7
Toftland PE2 . . . . .186 D5
Tolethorpe Sq **4** PE9 . .244 B6
Toll Bar La PE28 . . . . .146 B5
Toll Dro PE15 . . . . .224 A3
Toll Rd PE7 . . . . .188 A5
Toll House Rd PE2 . . . . . .186 C7
Tollfield PE28 . . . . .113 F4
Tollgate PE3 . . . . .197 A5
Tom Jennings Cl **2**
CB8 . . . . .110 F5
Toneham La PE6 . . . . .232 F1
Top La PE19 . . . . .57 B5
Top St CB6 . . . . .210 F5
Topcliffe Way CB1 . . . . . . .65 C3
Topham Cres **9** PE6 . . .233 A3
Topham Ct PE19 . . . . .74 F7
Topham Way CB4 . . . . .83 D6
Topmoor Way PE4 . . . . . .204 F1
Torkington Gdns **3**
PE9 . . . . .244 B5
Torpel Way **2** PE6 . . . . .231 C7
Tort Hill PE28 . . . . .168 C5
Toseland Rd PE19 . . . . . . .97 E4
Tothill Rd CB5 . . . . .108 D4
Touthill Cl PE1 . . . . .198 A2
Tower Cl
Bassingbourn SG8 . . . . . . .12 F5
Cottenham CB4 . . . . .125 D3
Huntingdon PE29 . . . . . . .141 D8
11 Over CB4 . . . . .208 D1
Whittlesey PE7 . . . . .189 B8
Tower Ct CB6 . . . . .240 B3
Tower Rd Downham CB6 . .217 F7
Elm PE14 . . . . .236 A3
Ely CB7 . . . . .240 B3
Sawston CB2 . . . . .33 A8
Sutton CB6 . . . . .216 E2
Tower St PE2 . . . . .186 F8
Tower View CB1 . . . . .35 D3
Towgood Way PE19 . . . . . .96 D4
Towler St PE1 . . . . .198 A3
Town Bridge PE13 . . . . . .245 B5
Town Cl CB2 . . . . .32 E7
Town Green Rd SG8 . . . . . .28 D8
Town La CB2 . . . . .33 B5
Town Orch PE19 . . . . .95 E5
Town St Newton CB2 . . . . .31 B7
Outwell PE14 . . . . .236 E1
Towne Rd SG8 . . . . .5 D5
Townley Cl PE14 . . . . .236 E1
Townley Sch The PE14 . . .229 D3
Townsend CB7 . . . . .212 A5
Townsend Cl **3** CB4 . . . .105 D3
Townsend Rd
Needingworth PE27 . . . . .208 A3
Upwell PE14 . . . . .229 E4
Wittering PE8 . . . . .230 A1
Townsend Way
Folksworth PE7 . . . . .175 D8
Folksworth & Washingley
PE7 . . . . .175 E8
Townshend Rd PE13 . . . .245 D6
Toyse Cl CB5 . . . . .130 C4
Toyse La CB5 . . . . .130 B4
Trafalgar Dr
Cambridge CB4 . . . . .246 B4
Eaton Socon PE19 . . . . . . .74 C5
Trafalgar St CB4 . . . . .246 B4
Trafalgar Way CB3 . . . . . .102 B5
Trafford Pk **1** PE13 . . . .245 E6
Trafford Rd PE13 . . . . . . .245 D5
Tram Sta La PE14 . . . . . . .236 B6
Tramar Dr **7** CB6 . . . . . .216 E2
Trap Rd SG8 . . . . .11 A4
Travellers Sch The PE1 . . .198 F5
Treading Bank PE13 . . . . .237 C4
Tredegar Cl CB4 . . . . .83 E6
Treeway PE16 . . . . .241 B5
Trent Cl PE27 . . . . .144 A7
Trent Rd PE8 . . . . .193 D8
Tresham Rd PE2 . . . . .185 D3
Trevone Pl CB5 . . . . .65 D7
Trienna PE2 . . . . .186 B5
Trigg Way SG8 . . . . .14 D6
Trinity Ave IP28 . . . . .239 C5
Trinity Cl Balsham CB1 . . .53 B2
Bottisham CB5 . . . . .86 F6
Ely CB6 . . . . .240 C5
Fordham CB7 . . . . .212 F1
1 Great Paxton PE19 . . . .96 E4
Haslingfield CB3 . . . . .47 B5
Trinity Coll CB2 . . . . .246 A3
Trinity Conduit Head★
CB3 . . . . .82 F4
Trinity Dr CB8 . . . . .111 B2
Trinity H CB2 . . . . .246 A2
Trinity La CB2 . . . . .246 A2
Trinity Link CB9 . . . . .39 A1
Trinity Pl PE29 . . . . .141 E4
Trinity Rd Stamford PE9 . .244 A6
Wisbech PE13 . . . . .245 E6
Trinity St Cambridge CB2 . .246 A2
3 Peterborough PE1 . . .198 A2
Troughton Way **12** PE13 .238 B2
Troutbeck Cl **2** PE4 . . . .204 F3
Truman Ave PE15 . . . . . . .243 A5
Trumpington H★ 64 C3
Trumpington High St
CB2 . . . . .64 D3
Trumpington Rd CB2 . . . . .64 E5
Trumpington St CB2 . . . . .246 A2
Trundle The PE28 . . . . . . .215 C1
Tucker's Yd PE2 . . . . .187 C2
Tuckers Nook **1** PE6 . . .231 C7
Tuddenham Rd IP28 . . . . .239 F7

Tuddenham VC Sch
IP28 . . . . .214 E2
Tudor Cl PE4 . . . . .204 E2
Tudor Ct
Bassingbourn cum Kneesworth
SG8 . . . . .13 B4
Kimbolton PE28 . . . . .113 F5
Tudor Rd PE29 . . . . .141 F2
Tunbridge Cl
3 Bottisham CB5 . . . . . .86 E6
Burwell CB5 . . . . .130 B2
Tunbridge La CB5 . . . . .86 E6
Tunkers La PE26 . . . . .171 F4
Tunwells Cl CB2 . . . . .49 A5
Tunwells La CB2 . . . . .49 A5
Turberville Ct PE28 . . . . . .143 C1
Turf Dro PE7 . . . . .191 C5
Turf Fen La PE15 . . . . . . .222 F5
Turf Fen Rd PE26 . . . . . . .170 F3
Turf Lot Dro PE14 . . . . . .229 E1
Turnbull Rd PE15 . . . . . . .243 B3
Turner Cl CB9 . . . . .38 D1
Turner Rd
Eaton Socon PE19 . . . . . . .74 C5
St Ives PE27 . . . . .144 A7
Turners La PE7 . . . . .189 D6
Turningtree Rd PE7 . . . . . .190 A3
Turnpike Cl **2** PE13 . . . .245 E6
Turnpike Hill CB9 . . . . . . .38 C4
Turnpike La IP28 . . . . .133 E8
Turnpike Rd IP28 . . . . . . .133 E8
Turnpike The CB7 . . . . . . .240 B3
Turnpole Cl **2** PE9 . . . . .244 D7
Turnstone Cl IP28 . . . . . . .239 D4
Turnstone Way PE2 . . . . . .187 D7
Turpin's Ride
4 Royston SG8 . . . . .5 D5
Stilton PE7 . . . . .176 A4
Turvers La PE26 . . . . .172 B7
Turves Rd PE6 . . . . .232 A2
Tuyar Wlk CB8 . . . . .110 E8
Tweed Cl CB8 . . . . .112 F6
Tweedale CB1 . . . . .65 F5
Twelvetree Ave PE14 . . . . .204 A5
Twenty Foot Rd PE15 . . . .227 F8
Twenty Pence Rd
Cottenham CB4 . . . . .125 F6
Wilburton CB6 . . . . .210 B3
Two Pole Dro Farcet PE7 . .187 F1
Soham CB7 . . . . .211 E7
Two Tree Hundred Dro
PE15 . . . . .228 A6
Tydd St Giles Golf & L Ctr
PE13 . . . . .238 A7
Tyrrell Pk PE1 . . . . .198 D2
Tythe Piece PE28 . . . . . . .121 C5

U

Uffen Way CB2 . . . . .32 E8
Uffington Rd
1 Barnack PE9 . . . . . . .230 D4
Stamford PE9 . . . . .244 D5
Uffington Sch PE9 . . . . . .230 C6
Ufford H★ PE9 . . . . .230 F3
Ugg Mere Ct Road
PE26 . . . . .220 D1
Uldale Way PE4 . . . . .204 F2
Ullswater PE29 . . . . .141 C5
Ullswater Ave PE4 . . . . . .204 D2
Underwood Cl PE7 . . . . . .190 D7
Union La CB4 . . . . .83 F5
Union Pl **13** PE13 . . . . . .245 C5
Union Rd CB2 . . . . .246 B1
Union St **4** CB2 . . . . . . .245 C5
Univ Arts Sch CB2 . . . . . .246 A2
Univ Botanic Garden★
CB2 . . . . .64 F7
Univ Concert Hall CB3 . . . .83 C2
Univ of Cambridge
Cambridge CB1 . . . . .84 A2
Madingley CB3 . . . . .81 E6
Univ Sch of Music CB3 . . .83 C1
Unwin's La **13** CB4 . . . . .208 D1
Uphall Rd CB1 . . . . .84 D1
Upherd's La CB6 . . . . .240 C5
Uplands PE4 . . . . .204 C5
Upper Delph Dro CB6 . . . .209 A5
Upper Gwydir St **1** CB1 . .84 A1
Upper King St SG8 . . . . .5 D6
Upton Cl
Peterborough PE2 . . . . . .187 C5
Peterborough PE3 . . . . . .197 A2
Upton Hill PE28 . . . . .160 C1
Upton La CB6 . . . . .242 C4
Upton Pl CB6 . . . . .242 C4
Upware Rd
Swaffham Prior CB7 . . . . .128 D8
Wicken CB7 . . . . .211 C1
Upwell H★ PE14 . . . . . . .236 D1
Upwell Prim Sch PE14 . . .229 D8
Upwell Rd
Christchurch PE14 . . . . . .229 C4
March PE15 . . . . .243 E3
Upwood Airfield
Polebrook PE28 . . . . .174 A2
Ramsey PE26 . . . . .171 D4
Upwood CP Sch PE26 . . . .171 D3
Upwood Rd
Ramsey PE26 . . . . .171 B5
Upwood & The Raveleys
PE26 . . . . .171 A5

V

Valarian Cl **14** PE19 . . . .74 C6

Valence Rd PE2 . . . . .185 F4
Valerian Ct CB1 . . . . .66 A5
Valiant Rd PE27 . . . . .143 F7
Valiant Sq PE26 . . . . .171 F3
Valley Rise SG8 . . . . .5 E6
Valley The CB3 . . . . .62 D6
Valley Way CB4 . . . . .110 A4
Valparaiso Univ CB3 . . . . . .83 C3
Van Diemans Way PE28 . . .116 A7
Van Dyke Pl PE27 . . . . . . .144 A7
Van Gogh Pl PE27 . . . . . .144 A7
Vanners Rd CB9 . . . . .24 A7
Varrier Jones Dr CB3 . . . . .99 A3
Varrier Jones Pl CB3 . . . . .99 A3
Veasey Rd PE2 . . . . .142 A7
Vence Cl PE9 . . . . .244 A5
Ventress Cl CB1 . . . . .65 D5
Verdun Rd PE13 . . . . .245 D5
Vere Rd PE1 . . . . .197 F7
Vergette Rd PE6 . . . . .203 F8
Vergette St PE1 . . . . .198 B4
Vermont Gr PE3 . . . . .197 E1
Vermuyden **8** PE28 . . . .208 E6
Vermuyden Gdns **5**
CB6 . . . . .216 E2
Vermuyden Way CB4 . . . .121 F5
Verulam Way CB4 . . . . . . .83 D6
Vester's Hill Dro PE26 . . .171 B7
Vicarage Ave CB2 . . . . . . .32 F7
Vicarage Cl
Dullingham CB8 . . . . .89 C1
Holme PE7 . . . . .177 A4
Melbourn SG8 . . . . .14 C6
Oakington/Longstanton
CB4 . . . . .103 D6
Swaffham Bulbeck CB5 . . .108 A1
Waterbeach CB5 . . . . . . .106 A7
Vicarage Dr CB3 . . . . .64 A3
Vicarage Farm Rd **5**
PE1 . . . . .198 D3
Vicarage Farm Yd PE19 . . .57 B6
Vicarage La
Swaffham Prior CB5 . . . . .108 D4
Whittlesford CB2 . . . . .32 B5
Woodditton CB8 . . . . .90 D3
Vicarage Rd
Newmarket CB8 . . . . .111 B3
Waresley SG19 . . . . .58 A2
Vicarage Terr CB1 . . . . . . .84 A1
Vicarage Way PE7 . . . . . . .181 D5
Vicarage Wlk PE19 . . . . . . .93 F6
Viceroy Cl PE19 . . . . .74 A3
Victor Cl PE27 . . . . .144 A7
Victoria Ave CB5 . . . . .246 B3
Victoria Cl SG19 . . . . .25 B4
Victoria Cres Royston SG8 . . .5 D7
St Ives PE28 . . . . .143 A5
Victoria Gn **3** CB6 . . . . .217 D1
Victoria Pk CB4 . . . . .83 D4
Victoria Pl
Peterborough PE1 . . . . . .197 F4
Sutton CB6 . . . . .216 D1
16 Wisbech PE13 . . . . .245 C4
Victoria Rd
Cambridge CB4 . . . . .83 D4
Haverhill CB9 . . . . .23 D7
Stamford PE9 . . . . .244 B6
Wisbech PE13 . . . . .245 C4
Victoria Sq **2** PE29 . . . .141 E4
Victoria St
Cambridge CB1 . . . . .246 B2
Chatteris PE16 . . . . .241 C4
Ely CB7 . . . . .240 D3
Littleport CB6 . . . . .242 E4
Peterborough PE2 . . . . . .186 C4
Peterborough PE1 . . . . . .198 A5
Victoria Way CB8 . . . . . . .110 C7
Victory Ave PE7 . . . . .189 F7
Victory Rd PE13 . . . . .245 B3
Victory Way CB4 . . . . .125 C4
Victory Wlk **7** SG8 . . . . . .5 E5
Viersen Platz PE1 . . . . . . .198 A1
Viking Cl CB1 . . . . .53 E5
Viking Way Bar Hill CB3 . . .102 B4
Whittlesey PE7 . . . . .189 E8
Villa Pl CB4 . . . . .104 C2
Villa Rd CB4 . . . . .104 C2
Village Col SG19 . . . . .41 E5
Village The PE2 . . . . .186 B5
Vine Cl Great Shelford CB2 . .49 C4
Hemingford Grey PE27 . . .143 E2
Vine St PE9 . . . . .244 C5
Vinegar Hill PE28 . . . . . . .150 E7
Vinery Ct PE26 . . . . .172 B7
Vinery Rd CB1 . . . . .65 C8
Vinery Way CB1 . . . . .84 C1
Vineyard Rd PE1 . . . . .198 B2
Vineyard The PE28 . . . . . .208 C2
Vineyard Way
Buckden PE19 . . . . .117 B3
Ely CB7 . . . . .240 E5
Vineyard Wlk CB5 . . . . .86 F6
Vineyards The CB7 . . . . . .240 D4
Vintner Cl PE3 . . . . .99 A3
Vintners Cl PE3 . . . . .197 D3
Violet Cl CB1 . . . . .66 A5
Virginia Cl **1** PE3 . . . . . .197 A2
Virginia Rd **3** IP28 . . . . .213 E8
Virginia Way PE27 . . . . . . .143 E6
Viscount Ct PE19 . . . . .74 B3
Viscount Rd PE2 . . . . .187 A6
Vixen Cl PE7 . . . . .181 D6
Vulcan Way PE19 . . . . .74 B1

W

Wadbury's Folly PE27 . .208 B4
Waddelow Rd CB5 . . . . . .106 A8
Wade Park Ave **4** PE6 . .231 E8
Wadloes Rd CB5 . . . . .84 D4
Wagstaff Cl CB4 . . . . .83 F7
Wainman Rd PE2 . . . . . . .186 D5
Wainwright PE4 . . . . .204 A5
Waits The PE27 . . . . .144 A3
Wake Ave IP28 . . . . .239 C5
Wake Rd March PE15 . . . .243 C6
Peterborough PE1 . . . . . .198 B2
Wakefield Cl CB10 . . . . . . .18 D3
Wakelin Ave CB2 . . . . .49 F1
Wakelyn Rd PE7 . . . . .189 C7
Wakerley Dr PE2 . . . . .186 C7
Walcot Rd PE9 . . . . .230 E2
Walden Cl **17** PE15 . . . .223 A5
Walden Gr PE29 . . . . .141 A4
Walden Rd
Great Chesterford CB10 . . .18 E3
Hadstock CB1 . . . . .20 B6
Huntingdon PE29 . . . . . . .141 D4
Walden Way CB2 . . . . .48 F6
Wales Bank Elm PE14 . . . .236 A5
Wisbech PE14 . . . . .236 A5
Walgrave PE2 . . . . .186 A5
Walker Rd PE6 . . . . .203 F7
Walkers Way PE3 . . . . . . .196 F3
Walkling Way CB4 . . . . . . .105 D1
Wallace's Dro PE6 . . . . . .233 D4
Waller's Cl SG8 . . . . .7 A5
Wallman's La CB4 . . . . . . .122 E6
Walnut Cl
Newborough PE6 . . . . . . .205 C8
Royston SG8 . . . . .5 D6
Walnut Gr IP28 . . . . .213 E4
Walnut Tree Ave CB5 . . . . .84 A3
Walnut Tree Cl
Bassingbourn SG8 . . . . . . .12 F5
4 Little Downham CB6 . .218 A6
8 Stretham CB6 . . . . . .210 F5
Walnut Tree Cres PE28 . . .121 B5
Walnut Tree Dr PE29 . . . .141 C6
Walnut Tree Way CB3 . . . . .83 C7
Walnut Way PE7 . . . . .175 F7
Walpole Bank PE14 . . . . . .238 F7
Walpole Rd CB1 . . . . .65 D6
Walsingham Ct **2** PE13 .245 A7
Walsingham Way
Ely CB6 . . . . .240 B5
10 Eye PE6 . . . . .232 A1
Walsoken Rd PE14 . . . . . .236 E7
Walton Cl **5** CB7 . . . . . .212 C1
Walton Comp Sch PE4 . . .204 C1
Walton Hill PE28 . . . . . . .161 D5
Walton J & I Sch PE4 . . . .204 C1
Walton Pk PE4 . . . . .204 C1
Walton Rd
9 Leverington PE13 . . .238 B2
Marholm PE6 . . . . .203 E1
Wisbech PE13 . . . . .245 E1
Wamil H★ IP28 . . . . .213 F5
Wamil Rd IP28 . . . . .213 F5
Wamil Way IP28 . . . . .239 B4
Wandlebury Ctry Pk★
CB2 . . . . .50 B8
Wansford Rd Elton PE8 . . .183 D5
Wansford PE8 . . . . .194 A3
Yarwell PE8 . . . . .193 F2
Wantage Gdns PE19 . . . . . .96 C3
Warbon Ave PE1 . . . . .197 F7
Warboys Airfield Ind Est
PE28 . . . . .164 D2
Warboys Cl CB3 . . . . .61 D5
Warboys CP Sch PE28 . . .164 E5
Warboys Rd PE28 . . . . . . .155 E8
Ward Cl Ramsey PE26 . . . .172 A5
St Ives PE28 . . . . .143 A5
Ward Rd CB1 . . . . .65 D6
Ward Way CB6 . . . . .217 D1
Warden Hill SG19 . . . . .40 C3
Ware La PE28 . . . . .142 F5
Ware Rd PE19 . . . . .74 E6
Wareley Rd PE2 . . . . .197 F1
Waresley Rd
Gamlingay SG19 . . . . .41 D8
Great Gransden SG19 . . . .58 B3
Warkworth St CB1 . . . . . .246 C2
Warkworth Terr CB1 . . . . .246 C2
Warmington Sch PE8 . . . .178 B3
Warner's Dro
Pidley cum Fenton PE28 . .215 B3
Somersham PE28 . . . . . . .215 C2
Warners Gr PE27 . . . . .144 A4
Warren Cl PE28 . . . . .142 F6
Warren Croft PE28 . . . . . .168 B5
Warren La
Bythorn & Keyston PE28 . .146 D4
Titchmarsh PE28 . . . . . . .156 F1
Warren Rd Cambridge CB4 . .84 A6
Herringswell CB8 . . . . . . .134 A7
Red Lodge IP28 . . . . .214 A1
St Ives PE27 . . . . .144 B4
Wothorpe PE9 . . . . .244 B1
Warren The
3 Royston SG8 . . . . .5 D5
Witchford CB6 . . . . .217 C1
Warrington St CB8 . . . . . .111 A2
Warwick Ct **6** PE19 . . . . .74 C3
Warwick Dr CB6 . . . . .240 C6
Warwick Rd
Cambridge CB4 . . . . .83 C5
Peterborough PE4 . . . . . .204 C1
Wasdale Gdns PE4 . . . . . .205 A2
Wash La PE7 . . . . .189 E8

Wash Rd PE14 . . . . .225 B8
Washbank Rd PE19 . . . . . .74 E4
Washingley La PE7 . . . . .175 B7
Washingley Rd
　Folksworth PE7 . . . . . . .175 D8
　The Stukeleys PE29 . . . . .141 C8
Washington Cl CB6 . . . . .242 D5
Washington St IP28 . . . . .213 E8
Washpit La CB3 . . . . .46 D7
Washpit Rd CB3 . . . . .82 C8
Wastwater PE2 . . . . .141 B6
Water End Alwalton PE7 . .185 A5
　Marholm PE6 . . . . .203 D1
　Wrestlingworth SG19 . . . . .25 B3
Water Gdns The PE13 . . .245 A5
Water La Bourn CB3 . . . . .60 D6
　Cambridge CB4 . . . . .84 B5
　Castor PE5 . . . . .195 F1
　Great Bradley CB8 . . . . . .55 F8
　Histon CB4 . . . . .104 C3
　Melbourn SG8 . . . . .14 C5
　Oakington/Longstanton
　　CB4 . . . . .103 C5
　Sturmer CB9 . . . . .24 F5
Water St Cambridge CB4 . .84 B4
　Stamford PE9 . . . . .244 C4
Waterbeach CP Sch
　CB5 . . . . .106 B8
Waterbeach Rd CB4 . . . .105 E7
Waterbeach Sta CB5 . . . .106 C6
Watercourse The CB8 . . .111 A4
Waterfields PE16 . . . . . .241 B3
Waterfurlong PE9 . . . . . .244 C4
Watergall PE3 . . . . .197 B8
Watergall CP Sch PE3 . . .197 A8
Watergate 6 PE9 . . . . . .244 C4
Waterlees Rd 2 PE13 . . .245 E7
Waterloo Cl
　1 Brampton PE28 . . . . .140 D3
　Newmarket CB8 . . . . . . .110 A3
Waterloo Dr 2 PE19 . . . . .74 F3
Waterloo Rd PE1 . . . . . .198 A5
Watermead CB3 . . . . . . .102 C3
Waterside Ely CB7 . . . . .240 E4
　Isleham CB7 . . . . .213 A5
Waterside Gdns CB5 . . . .243 E5
Waterslade Rd PE7 . . . . .181 C4
Waterton Cl 6 PE6 . . . . .231 F8
Waterwick Hill CB11 . . . . .1 F1
Waterworks La PE6 . . . . .203 D6
Waterworks Rd 5 PE28 . .213 E8
Watsons La 1 CB6 . . . . .211 B7
Watt Cl PE4 . . . . .204 E2
Wavell Way CB4 . . . . .83 E6
Waveney Dr PE15 . . . . . .243 B5
Waveney Rd 2 PE9 . . . . .244 C2
Waveney Rd PE27 . . . . . .144 A7
Waveney Terr CB9 . . . . . .24 B7
Waverley Cl PE13 . . . . . .235 A3
Waverley Gdns 3 PE9 . . .244 A6
Way Head Dro CB6 . . . . .217 C6
Way La Waterbeach CB5 . .106 B8
　Wicken PE7 . . . . .211 D2
Wayford Cl PE3 . . . . . . .197 C4
Wayne's La PE3 . . . . .62 C5
Weasenham La 1 PE13 . .245 C2
Weatheralls Cl 4 CB7 . . .212 B4
Weatheralls CP Sch The
　CB7 . . . . .212 B4
Weatherthorn PE2 . . . . . .186 C5
Weavers Field CB3 . . . . . .82 E7
Webb's Rd CB1 . . . . .36 F5
Webbs Mdw SG19 . . . . . .58 D4
Webster's Way CB4 . . . . .208 D1
Websters Cl PE6 . . . . . . .203 F8
Weddell Rd CB9 . . . . .24 C6
Wedgewood Dr CB1 . . . . .65 F6
Wedgwood Dr PE13 . . . . .245 D5
Weir Cl Buckden PE19 . . .117 A3
　Hemingford Grey PE28 . . .143 D1
Weir Rd PE28 . . . . .143 D1
Weirs Dro CB5 . . . . .129 F1
Welbeck Rd PE13 . . . . . .245 E4
Welbeck Way PE2 . . . . . .186 D7
Welbourne PE4 . . . . .204 C4
Welbourne Prim Sch
　PE4 . . . . .204 C4
Welby Cl PE28 . . . . .115 D3
Welches Dam Visitor Ctr★
　CB6 . . . . .217 A8
Well Bottom CB8 . . . . . . .112 B8
Well Creek Rd PE14 . . . .236 F2
Well End PE14 . . . . .236 A3
Welland Bank PE6 . . . . . .207 D7
Welland Cl PE1 . . . . .198 A7
Welland CP Sch PE1 . . . .198 C8
Welland Ct 9 PE19 . . . . . .74 C4
Welland Mews PE9 . . . . .244 C4
Welland Rd
　Peterborough PE1 . . . . . .198 B8
　Wittering PE8 . . . . .230 B1
Welland Way 5 PE28 . . .231 F8
Wellbrook Way CB3 . . . . .82 F7
Wellington Ave 4 PE27 . .143 F7
Wellington Cl
　Old Hurst PE28 . . . . . . .154 E7
　Thistley Green IP28 . . . . .213 D6
　Warboys PE28 . . . . .164 F4
　Waterbeach PE5 . . . . . . .106 B7
Wellington Ct 3 CB1 . . . . .84 A2
Wellington Pl SG8 . . . . . . .13 B5
Wellington Rd Ely CB6 . . .217 F1
　1 Mildenhall IP28 . . . . .213 E8
Wellington St
　4 Cambridge CB1 . . . . . .84 A2
　Littleport CB6 . . . . .242 D4
　4 Newmarket CB8 . . . . .111 A3
　Peterborough PE1 . . . . . .198 B2

Wellington St continued
　St Ives PE27 . . . . .144 A3
Wells Bridge PE26 . . . . . .221 C3
Wells Cl Haslingfield CB3 . .47 A5
　Peterborough PE4 . . . . . .204 B3
Wells Ct IP28 . . . . .239 B5
Wells Way PE7 . . . . .177 A5
Wellside PE29 . . . . .141 E6
Welmore Rd PE6 . . . . . . .203 F8
Welstead Rd CB1 . . . . . . .66 A6
Wenny Est PE16 . . . . . . .241 D3
Wenny Rd PE16 . . . . . . .241 E3
Wensum Cl PE27 . . . . . . .144 B6
Wentworth Dr IP28 . . . . .239 B4
Wentworth Rd CB4 . . . . . .83 C4
Wentworth St 1 PE1 . . . .198 A1
Wenvoe Cl PE13 . . . . .65 F6
Werrington Bridge Rd
　PE6 . . . . .204 E7
Werrington Cty Prim Sch
　PE4 . . . . .204 C3
Werrington Gr PE4 . . . . .204 B2
Werrington Jun Sch
　PE4 . . . . .204 C3
Werrington Mews 5
　PE4 . . . . .204 C3
Werrington Park Ave 2
　PE4 . . . . .204 C3
Werrington Parkway
　PE6 . . . . .203 E5
Werrington Sports Ctr
　PE4 . . . . .204 B4
Wertheim Way PE29 . . . .141 B6
Wesley Dr PE16 . . . . . . .241 D5
Wesley Ho CB3 . . . . . . .246 B3
Wesleyan Rd PE1 . . . . . .198 A7
Wessex Cl PE2 . . . . .187 D7
West Ave PE26 . . . . .171 F4
West Brook PE28 . . . . . . .120 B4
West Brook Cl PE28 . . . . .120 B2
West Cl
　Alconbury Weston PE28 . .150 D6
　March PE15 . . . . .243 B6
　Waresley SG19 . . . . .57 F2
West Delph PE7 . . . . . . .189 D6
West Dr Highfields CB3 . . .80 C2
　March PE15 . . . . .243 F4
　Mildenhall IP28 . . . . . . .239 B4
　Soham CB7 . . . . .212 B4
West Drive Cres 2 CB7 . .212 A4
West Drive Gdns 1
　CB7 . . . . .212 A4
West Dro S PE12 . . . . . . .233 E8
West End Ashwell SG7 . . . .2 C3
　Brampton PE28 . . . . . . .140 C3
　Ely CB6 . . . . .240 C4
　Gorefield PE13 . . . . .237 E3
　Haddenham CB6 . . . . . . .209 F6
　March PE15 . . . . .243 B4
　Whittlesey PE7 . . . . .189 C7
　Whittlesford CB2 . . . . . . .32 B4
　Wilburton CB6 . . . . .210 B5
　Woodditton CB8 . . . . . . .71 D8
　Yaxley PE7 . . . . .181 D4
West End Cl PE16 . . . . . .241 B4
West End La CB9 . . . . . . .38 E8
West End Rd
　Fenstanton PE28 . . . . . .121 A4
　Maxey PE28 . . . . .231 C7
West Fen Dro
　Downham CB6 . . . . .218 A6
　March PE7 . . . . .227 A1
　Whittlesey PE7 . . . . .191 F3
West Fen Rd
　Coveney CB6 . . . . .217 E4
　Ely CB6 . . . . .240 B5
　Willingham CB4 . . . . . . .208 F2
　Witchford CB6 . . . . .218 A3
West Field CB1 . . . . .34 B7
West Field Rd PE15 . . . . .224 A3
West Gn CB2 . . . . .29 D7
West Hill Rd CB2 . . . . . . .30 B4
West Leys PE27 . . . . .143 F4
West Lodge La CB6 . . . . .216 D1
West Moor Ave CB2 . . . . .32 C4
West Newlands PE28 . . . .208 B8
West Par
　Peterborough PE3 . . . . . .197 D3
　Wisbech PE13 . . . . .245 B7
West Park St PE16 . . . . .241 C4
West Perry PE28 . . . . . . .115 D2
West Rd Cambridge CB3 . .83 C1
　Gamlingay SG19 . . . . . . .41 C4
　Histon CB4 . . . . .104 B3
　3 Tallington PE9 . . . . . .230 F7
　Tydd St Giles PE13 . . . . .238 B8
West Row Prim Sch
　IP28 . . . . .213 D7
West Row Rd
　"Beck Row, Holywell Row
　　& Kenny Hill" IP28 . . . .213 F6
　Mildenhall IP28 . . . . . . .239 A5
West St Chatteris PE16 . . .241 B3
　Godmanchester PE29 . . . .141 E1
　Great Gransden SG19 . . . .58 D4
　Helpston PE6 . . . . .231 B4
　Huntingdon PE29 . . . . . .141 E5
　Isleham CB7 . . . . .212 F5
　Over CB4 . . . . .123 A8
　St Ives PE27 . . . . .144 A4
　St Neots PE19 . . . . .74 E5
　Stamford PE9 . . . . .244 B4
　Toft CB3 . . . . .62 B5
　Wisbech PE13 . . . . .245 C4
West Stonebridge PE2 . . .186 C6
West Street Gdns PE9 . . .244 A5
West Town Cty Sch PE3 . .197 E3
West View PE28 . . . . .151 F1

West Way Meldreth SG8 . .28 F1
　Sawston SG8 . . . . .50 A1
West Wickham Rd
　Balsham CB1 . . . . .53 C1
　Horseheath CB1 . . . . .37 A3
West Wlk CB5 . . . . .86 F6
West Wratting Rd CB1 . . .53 B2
Westbourne Cl PE16 . . . .241 B3
Westbourne Dr PE6 . . . . .203 E8
Westbourne Rd PE16 . . . .241 B4
Westbrook Ave 1 PE2 . . .186 F7
Westbrook Cl
　1 Brampton PE28 . . . . .140 C3
　Steeple Morden SG8 . . . . .3 B8
Westbrook Park Cl 2
　PE2 . . . . .186 F7
Westbrook Park Rd PE2 . .186 F7
Westbury Rd PE27 . . . . . .143 F4
Westcombe Sq PE1 . . . . .198 D4
Westcott House Theological
　Coll CB3 . . . . .246 B3
Westcroft 4 CB3 . . . . . . .62 B4
Westering The CB5 . . . . . .84 E2
Westerman Cl PE28 . . . . .168 B5
Western Ave Haverhill CB9 .38 E1
　Peterborough PE1 . . . . . .198 B7
Westfield CB4 . . . . .124 A6
Westfield La CB4 . . . . . . .83 C4
Westfield Prim Sch CB9 . .24 B7
Westfield Rd
　Fowlmere SG8 . . . . .15 D8
　Great Shelford CB2 . . . . . .48 E7
　Newton PE13 . . . . .237 F5
　Peterborough PE3 . . . . . .197 E4
　Ramsey PE26 . . . . .171 F4
　Sawtry PE28 . . . . .168 B4
　Wisbech PE13 . . . . .245 E4
　Yaxley PE7 . . . . .181 D5
Westfield Sch PE27 . . . . .144 A4
Westfields CB3 . . . . .99 A2
Westgate PE1 . . . . .197 F2
Westhawe PE3 . . . . .196 F7
Westhorpe PE3 . . . . .130 B4
Westlands CB5 . . . . .62 B4
Westley Bottom Rd CB8 . .69 B8
Westmead Ave PE13 . . . .245 E2
Westmeadow Cl CB4 . . . .208 F1
Westminster & Cheshunt
　Colls CB3 . . . . .83 C3
Westminster Gdns 18
　PE6 . . . . .232 A1
Westminster Pl PE1 . . . . .198 F5
Westmoor Comm CB6 . . .217 E8
Westmoor Dro
　Chatteris PE16 . . . . .222 D2
　Littleport PE6 . . . . .225 B4
Weston Ave SG8 . . . . .5 C7
Weston Cl PE19 . . . . .95 A1
Weston Colville Rd CB8 . .70 D1
Weston Ct PE19 . . . . .74 C4
Weston Gr CB1 . . . . .66 E5
Weston Miller Dr PE13 . . .245 C7
Weston Rd 17 PE13 . . . . .245 C3
Weston Way CB8 . . . . . . .110 F6
Westry Ave PE15 . . . . . . .243 A7
Westry Cl 3 PE13 . . . . . .238 F1
Westway PE15 . . . . .217 A2
Westwood 5 PE3 . . . . . . .197 C8
Westwood Ave PE15 . . . .243 C5
Westwood Jun Sch
　PE15 . . . . .243 C5
Westwood Park Cl PE3 . . .197 C3
Westwood Park Rd PE3 . .197 D2
Westwood Rd 1 PE27 . . .144 A4
Wetenhall Rd CB1 . . . . . . .65 B8
Wetherby Way 1 PE1 . . .198 D3
Weymouth Way 4 PE1 . . .198 D6
Whaddon Gap SG8 . . . . . .28 A1
Whaddon Rd SG8 . . . . . . .28 E2
Whaddons The PE29 . . . .141 F6
Whalley St PE1 . . . . .198 B3
Wharf Rd PE9 . . . . .244 C4
Wheat Croft CB1 . . . . .35 D3
Wheatfield Cres 2 SG8 . . .5 E6
Wheatfield Dr 1 PE26 . . .171 F5
Wheatfield Jun & Inf Sch
　PE2 . . . . .144 A6
Wheatfields PE27 . . . . . .144 A6
Wheatley Bank PE14 . . . .238 F2
Wheatley Cres 3 PE28 . . .208 C6
Wheats Cl 1 CB6 . . . . . .217 D1
Wheatsheaf Cl 1 CB6 . . .240 A3
Wheatsheaf Dro PE14 . . .229 C3
Wheatsheaf Rd
　Alconbury Weston PE28 . .150 D6
　Eaton Socon PE19 . . . . . .74 C3
　Woodhurst PE28 . . . . . . .155 C4
Wheatsheaf Way CB1 . . . .35 D3
Wheatsheaves 2 PE28 . . .168 C2
Wheel Yd PE1 . . . . .198 A2
Wheeler St CB2 . . . . .246 A2
Wheeler's Cl CB3 . . . . . . .46 A7
Wheelers CB2 . . . . .49 B6
Wheelwright Way CB5 . . . .86 A5
Whichcote Rd PE6 . . . . . .206 E6
Whines La CB4 . . . . .123 B8
Whinfell Cl 3 PE29 . . . . .141 A7
Whipple Science Mus★
　CB2 . . . . .246 A2
Whippletree Rd CB2 . . . . .32 A5
Whistler Rd 5 PE19 . . . . .74 C5
Whistlers The 5 PE27 . . .144 A7
Whiston Cl
　Peterborough PE4 . . . . . .204 F2
　4 Somersham PE28 . . . .208 C8
Whitacre PE1 . . . . .198 E6
Whitby St 3 PE13 . . . . . .245 C5

White Acres PE7 . . . . . . .189 E8
White Croft PE3 . . . . .197 B6
White Cross Rd CB6 . . . .210 E7
White Droveway CB5 . . . .108 A3
White Fen Droveway
　CB5 . . . . .107 B5
White Field Way CB2 . . . .32 D8
White Hall Cl PE2 . . . . . .215 C1
White Hart 5 PE15 . . . . .222 A5
White Hart La
　Godmanchester PE29 . . . .142 A1
　6 Littleport CB6 . . . . . .242 D4
　4 St Ives PE27 . . . . . . .144 A3
　13 Soham CB7 . . . . . . .212 B4
White Horse La 5 CB6 . . .218 A6
White House Rd CB7 . . . .226 C2
White Lion Cl 1 PE15 . . .243 D2
Whitecroft Rd SG8 . . . . . .14 A8
Whitecross PE27 . . . . . . .144 A4
Whitecross Stone★
　PE7 . . . . .190 E7
Whitegate Cl CB4 . . . . . .122 D6
Whitegates CB8 . . . . .111 C3
Whitehall Gdns CB2 . . . . .31 E1
Whitehall Sch PE28 . . . . .215 B1
Whitehall Way PE28 . . . .115 D2
Whitehill Cl CB1 . . . . .84 D2
Whitehill Rd CB5 . . . . . . .84 C2
Whitehouse La CB3 . . . . . .83 A5
Whitehouse Rd PE28 . . . .168 A4
Whitemill Rd PE16 . . . . . .241 D3
Whitemoor Rd PE15 . . . .227 C4
Whitepost Rd
　Borough Fen PE6 . . . . . .207 F1
　Newborough PE6 . . . . . .205 F6
Whiteway Dro CB5 . . . . .107 F8
Whiteways PE2 . . . . .185 D6
Whitfield Cl CB4 . . . . .83 E7
Whitgift Rd CB1 . . . . .85 B1
Whiting Way SG8 . . . . . . .14 C3
Whitman Cl 7 PE9 . . . . . .230 D3
Whitmore St PE1 . . . . . . .189 D7
Whitmore Way CB5 . . . . .106 B6
Whitsed Rd PE6 . . . . . . .207 D1
Whitsed St PE1 . . . . .198 B3
Whittets Cl 2 SG19 . . . . .58 D4
Whittington Cl PE1 . . . . . .198 E7
Whittlesey Rd
　Benwick PE15 . . . . .221 E6
　March PE15 . . . . .243 A5
　Peterborough PE2 . . . . . .187 B4
　Thorney PE6 . . . . .200 F7
Whittlesey Sta PE7 . . . . .189 F5
Whittlesey TH PE7 . . . . . .189 D7
Whittleford Rd
　Little Shelford CB2 . . . . . .48 F2
　Newton CB2 . . . . .31 D7
Whittlesford Sta CB2 . . . .32 E3
Whitton Cl CB4 . . . . .122 E5
Whitwell PE4 . . . . .205 A2
Whitwell Way CB3 . . . . . .82 A2
Whybrows La 1 PE28 . . .208 E6
Whydale Rd 4 SG8 . . . . . .5 E5
Whytefield Rd PE26 . . . . .172 A7
Wicken Fen Nature Reserve
　(National Trust)★ CB7 . .211 D1
Wicken Rd CB7 . . . . .212 B1
Wicken Way PE3 . . . . . . .197 C6
Wiggin Cl IP28 . . . . .239 D2
Wigmore Cl PE29 . . . . . .141 E1
Wigmore Rd PE7 . . . . . . .187 F5
Wigstone's Rd PE15 . . . .243 E5
Wilberforce Rd
　Cambridge CB3 . . . . .83 B2
　Peterborough PE1 . . . . . .197 F2
　Wisbech PE13 . . . . .245 D5
Wilbraham Rd
　Bottisham CB1 . . . . .86 F3
　Fulbourn CB1 . . . . .67 C7
Wilburton Prim Sch
　CB6 . . . . .210 C6
Wilburton Rd
　8 Haddenham CB6 . . . . .210 A6
　Stretham CB6 . . . . .210 E5
Wild Acres CB5 . . . . .130 B1
Wildber Cl PE19 . . . . .74 B1
Wilderspin Cl CB3 . . . . . . .82 F6
Wilding Wlk CB4 . . . . .83 C8
Wildlake PE2 . . . . .186 C5
Wildmere La IP28 . . . . . .214 A8
Wiles Cl Cambridge CB4 . .84 A7
　Waterbeach CB5 . . . . . . .106 A8
Wilford Dr 3 CB7 . . . . . .240 E6
Wilford Furlong CB4 . . . .209 A1
Wilkin St 1 CB1 . . . . .65 A8
Wilkins Rd PE14 . . . . . . .236 C7
Wilkinson Cl
　Eaton Socon PE19 . . . . . .74 B3
　March PE15 . . . . .243 E5
Willesden Ave PE4 . . . . .197 D8
William Dr 8 PE19 . . . . . .74 F1
William Law PE4 . . . . . . .204 B5
William Rd PE13 . . . . . . .245 C5
William Smith Cl 1 . . . . . .65 A7
William Westley CE Prim Sch
　CB2 . . . . .32 D5
William's Way IP28 . . . . .213 D6
Williams Cl
　Brampton PE28 . . . . . . .140 C3
　Ely CB6 . . . . .240 E7
　Newborough PE6 . . . . . .207 C1
Williams Way 2 PE15 . . .224 B4
Williamson Ave 3 PE3 . . .197 E3
Willie Snaith Rd CB8 . . . .110 F6
Willingham Green Rd
　CB8 . . . . .54 D8
Willingham Prim Sch
　CB4 . . . . .209 A1

Willingham Rd CB4 . . . . .208 E1
Willis Rd CB1 . . . . .246 C2
Willmott Rd SG8 . . . . .12 F5
Willock La PE13 . . . . .235 A5
Willonholt PE4 . . . . .197 C7
Willoughby Ct PE1 . . . . . .198 B7
Willoughby Rd PE9 . . . . .244 C7
Willow Ave PE1 . . . . .198 B7
Willow Cl
　"Beck Row, Holywell Row
　　& Kenny Hill" IP28 . . . .214 A8
　Brampton PE28 . . . . . . .140 C2
　Haverhill CB9 . . . . .38 D1
　Little Paxton PE19 . . . . . .95 F1
　St Neots PE19 . . . . .74 F3
　Stilton PE7 . . . . .175 F7
Willow Cres Milton CB4 . .105 D2
　Newmarket CB8 . . . . . . .111 B2
Willow Ct CB6 . . . . .242 E4
Willow Dr 3 PE15 . . . . . .243 B3
Willow Dro PE6 . . . . .207 C9
Willow End PE28 . . . . . . .150 F4
Willow Farm Cl PE28 . . . .150 D7
Willow Gn PE27 . . . . .208 A3
Willow Gr Ely CB7 . . . . . .240 E4
　Lode CB5 . . . . .107 C2
Willow Hall La PE6 . . . . .199 D6
Willow Holt PE7 . . . . . . .186 C3
Willow La CB3 . . . . .79 C3
Willow Rd PE7 . . . . .182 A6
Willow Way Bottisham CB5 .86 F6
　Haruton PE7 . . . . .48 B4
　Ramsey PE26 . . . . .172 B7
　Wisbech PE13 . . . . .245 D3
Willow Wlk
　Cambridge CB1 . . . . . . .246 B3
　Ely CB6 . . . . .240 E4
Willowbrook Dr PE7 . . . . .201 F1
Willows The Glinton PE6 . .203 F8
　Great Chesterford CB10 . . .18 D3
Willowside Way 5 SG8 . . .5 C3
Wilson Cl CB4 . . . . .84 A7
Wilson Way
　Brampton PE28 . . . . . . .117 E8
　Milton CB4 . . . . .105 D2
Wilson's Rd CB4 . . . . . . .103 A8
Wilsons La SG7 . . . . .2 C4
Wilthorne PE15 . . . . .165 A5
Wilton Cl PE3 . . . . .197 C4
Wilton Dr PE3 . . . . .197 C4
Wilton Gdns CB6 . . . . . . .216 E3
Wiltshire Rd CB3 . . . . .99 A2
Wimbish Rd CB3 . . . . .99 A2
Wimblington Rd
　Doddington/Wimblington
　　PE15 . . . . .223 A5
　March PE15 . . . . .243 C1
Wimborne Dr 2 PE1 . . . .198 E7
Wimbridge Cl SG8 . . . . . . .27 F6
Wimpole Avenue (National
　Trust)★ SG8 . . . . .27 F5
Wimpole H★ SG8 . . . . . . .44 F3
Wimpole Park (National
　Trust)★ SG8 . . . . .44 F3
Wimpole Rd Barton CB3 . .63 A2
　Great Eversden CB3 . . . . .45 E7
Wimpole St PE16 . . . . . . .241 B4
Winchester Way PE3 . . . .197 E1
Winchfield SG19 . . . . .58 E5
Winchmore Dr CB2 . . . . . .64 C3
Windermere Cl 3 CB1 . . . .66 A4
Windermere PE29 . . . . . .141 B6
Windermere Way PE4 . . .204 E3
Winders La CB4 . . . . .104 B5
Windgate Way PE8 . . . . .194 A6
Windlesham Cl CB4 . . . . . .83 E6
Windmill Cl
　Ellington PE28 . . . . .138 F4
　2 Ely CB6 . . . . .240 B3
　Sawston CB2 . . . . .32 F8
　Soham CB7 . . . . .212 C4
Windmill Hill CB8 . . . . . . .110 C8
Windmill La Fulbourn CB1 .66 E4
　Histon CB4 . . . . .104 B4
　8 Sutton CB6 . . . . .216 E1
Windmill Sch CB1 . . . . . . .66 D5
Windmill St
　Peterborough PE1 . . . . . .197 F5
　Whittlesey PE7 . . . . .189 D8
Windmill Wlk CB6 . . . . . .216 E1
Windover Rd PE29 . . . . . .141 D7
Windrush Dr PE4 . . . . . . .204 F1
Windsor Ave 3 PE4 . . . . .197 C8
Windsor Cl
　Chatteris PE16 . . . . .241 E5
　St Ives PE27 . . . . .143 F8
　10 St Neots PE19 . . . . . .74 F2
　Stamford PE9 . . . . .244 B7
Windsor Dr March PE15 . .243 B5
　Peterborough PE2 . . . . . .187 D6
　4 Ramsey PE26 . . . . . . .221 C2
　Wisbech PE13 . . . . .245 D2
Windsor Gdns 9 PE28 . . .208 C8
Windsor Pl PE7 . . . . .190 A7
Windsor Rd
　Cambridge CB4 . . . . .83 C5
　Godmanchester PE29 . . . .142 A1
　Newmarket CB8 . . . . . . .110 E4
　Royston SG8 . . . . .5 C5
　5 Sawtry PE28 . . . . . . .168 B3
　Yaxley PE7 . . . . .181 F6
Windsors The 1 PE15 . . .243 A5
Winfold Rd CB5 . . . . .106 A8
Wingate Cl CB2 . . . . .64 D3
Wingate Way CB2 . . . . . . .64 D3

Wingfield PE2 ....185 F3
Winhills Prim Sch PE19 .75 A4
Winship Rd CB4 ......105 C1
Winslow Rd PE3 ......197 C3
Winston Way PE7 ......187 C2
Wintringham Rd [8] PE19 .74 F5
Winwick Pl PE3 ......197 C5
Winwick Rd PE28 ......158 B8
Winyates Prim Sch PE2 186 A3
Wisbech Castle* PE13 .245 C4
Wisbech Gram Sch
  PE13 ....245 B5
Wisbech Rd
  Littleport CB6 ....242 A6
  Manea PE15 ....224 C5
  March PE15 ....243 A7
  Outwell PE14 ....236 F3
  Thorney PE6 ....233 A3
  Walsoken PE13 ....245 E8
  Welney PE14 ....229 E2
  Whittlesey PE7 ....191 C8
  Wisbech St Mary PE13 ..234 A2
Wistaria Rd
  Leverington PE13 ......245 F7
  Wisbech PE13 ....245 E7
Wisteria Rd PE7 ......181 D4
Wistow Ct [3] PE19 ....74 C6
Wistow Fen Dro PE28 .173 B4
Wistow Fen La PE28 ..164 C8
Wistow Way PE2 ......185 D6
Witcham Bridge Dro
  CB6 ....217 A5
Witcham Rd CB6 ......216 E3
Witchford Rd Ely CB6 ..240 A3
  Witchford CB6 ....217 F1
Witchford Village Coll
  CB6 ....217 E2
Witham Cl
  [9] St Ives PE27 ......144 A7
  Stamford PE9 ....244 C6
Witham Way PE4 ......204 F1
Withers Pl [3] CB7 ....212 E1
Withersfield Rd
  Haverhill CB9 ....38 E1
  Withersfield CB9 ....38 F7
Wittering Airfield PE8 .230 A2

Wittering Rd PE9 ......230 D3
Woburn Cl Cambridge CB4 83 E7
  Peterborough PE3 .....197 A1
Woburn Ct PE7 ......176 A7
Woburn Dr PE6 ......233 A2
Woburn Pl CB2 ....31 F1
Wolf La Gorefield PE13 ..237 F1
  Wisbech PE13 ....235 C8
Wolfson Coll CB3 .....64 B8
Wollaston Rd
  Cambridge CB1 ......246 C1
  Peterborough PE3 .....197 C6
Wolsey Way CB1 ......65 F7
Wood End PE28 ......208 C6
Wood Green Animal
  Shelter* PE29 ....119 C5
Wood La
  Abbots Ripton PE28 ...162 E2
  Broughton PE28 ....163 A2
  Papworth Everard CB3 ..99 A4
  Ramsey PE26 ....172 C8
  Stretham CB6 ....210 F5
Wood St Chatteris PE16 .241 C4
  Doddington/Wimblington
  PE15 ....223 A6
  Huntingdon PE29 ......141 E4
  Wisbech PE13 ....245 B6
Woodbine St PE2 ......187 A8
Woodbrook Cl CB3 .....99 B2
Woodbyth Rd PE1 ....198 A6
Woodcock Cl
  Haverhill CB9 ....24 C7
  Histon CB4 ....104 D3
Woodcote Cl PE1 ....198 A7
Woodcote Pk PE13 ...245 A4
Woodcroft Castle*
  PE6 ....203 C5
Woodcroft Rd Etton PE6 .203 B7
  Glinton PE6 ....203 C3
Woodditton Rd
  Kirtling CB8 ....72 B5
  Newmarket CB8 ....111 A1
  Woodditton CB8 ....90 B8
Woodfen Rd CB6 ......242 A2
Woodfield Ave [5] PE26 .172 A4
Woodfield Dr PE28 ...168 A3
Woodfield Rd PE3 ....197 D3
Woodforde Cl SG7 .....2 E4

Woodgate PE6 ....231 C4
Woodgate La PE6 ....231 D7
Woodgate Rd [3] PE13 .238 B2
Woodhall La CB1 .....53 A1
Woodhall Rise PE4 ...204 B6
Woodhead Cl [4] PE9 .244 D7
Woodhead Dr CB4 .....83 F6
Woodhouse Way CB4 ..84 A7
Woodhurst Rd PE2 ...187 D6
Woodland Lea PE6 ...231 B4
Woodland Rd CB2 .....32 F8
Woodland Wlk [2] CB3 ..79 C3
Woodlands [1] Royston SG8 .5 E6
  St Neots PE19 ....75 A7
  Warboys PE28 ....164 F5
Woodlands Ave PE15 .243 D2
Woodlands Cl CB2 .....49 A4
Woodlands Dr SG8 .....14 B8
Woodlands Pk CB3 ...103 D1
Woodlands Rd CB2 .....49 A4
Woodlands The
  Linton CB1 ....35 B4
  Peterborough PE1 ......198 D5
Woodlands Way IP28 ..239 F5
Woodlark Dr CB4 .....125 D4
Woodlark Rd CB3 .....83 B5
Woodmans Way CB4 ..105 C4
Woodroffe Rd PE8 ...193 D8
Woodside Chatteris PE16 241 C4
  Oakington/Longstanton
  CB4 ....123 F1
Woodside Way PE27 ..144 B5
Woodston Cty Prim Sch
  PE2 ....186 F7
Woodwalton Fen Nature
  Reserve* PE26 ....170 B6
Woodward Cl PE7 ....176 A8
Woodysfield [2] PE15 .223 B7
Woolcroft Cl PE13 ...238 A1
Woolfellhill Rd PE6 ..205 F3
Woolgard PE3 ....197 A3
Woollards La CB2 .....49 A4
Woolley Cl PE28 .....140 D3
Woolley Hill PE28 ...138 D6
Woolley Rd PE28 ....149 B3
Woolpack La [2] PE7 .189 D6
Woolpack Way SG8 ...29 B1
Wooton Field SG19 ...41 D4
Woottens Cl CB3 .....62 C5

Wootton Ave PE2 ......186 F6
Wootton Way CB3 .....64 A8
Worboys Ct SG8 ....10 F5
Worcester Ave CB3 ...81 A4
Worcester Cres [2] PE9 .244 B6
Worcester Rd PE13 ..245 C7
Worcester Way SG8 ..14 E6
Wordsworth Ave PE19 ..74 D6
Wordsworth Cl
  Peterborough PE4 .....197 E8
  [1] Royston SG8 ......13 D1
Wordsworth Gr CB3 ..64 C8
Workhouse La PE14 ..229 D8
Worlington Rd
  Barton Mills IP28 ......214 C3
  Worlington IP28 ....239 A3
Worsley PE2 ....186 A4
Worsley Chase PE15 .243 D2
Wortham Pl [2] CB9 ..24 A8
Wortham Rd SG8 ......5 E4
Worthington Cl PE7 ..176 A7
Worts' Cswy CB1 .....65 C2
Wothorpe Ho* PE9 ...244 B1
Wothorpe Rd PE9 ....244 B4
Wragg Dr CB8 ....111 A6
Wratting Rd
  Great Thurlow CB9 .....39 B8
  Haverhill CB9 ....24 A8
Wren Cl IP28 ....239 D4
Wren Pk CB2 ....32 B4
Wrens Cl CB6 ....240 B5
Wrestlingworth Lower Sch
  SG19 ....25 B3
Wrestlingworth Plantation*
  SG19 ....25 A5
Wright Ave PE2 ......187 D5
Wright's Cl CB5 ......84 E6
Wright's Dro PE6 ....232 B7
Wrights Dro PE7 .....220 B8
Wrights Gr CB1 ......66 F4
Wroe The PE14 ......236 C5
Wulfric Sq PE3 ......197 C8
Wulfstan Way CB1 ...65 C4
Wyatt Cl PE26 ....172 B6
Wyboston Ct [1] PE19 ..74 C4
Wycliffe Gr PE4 .....204 A5
Wycliffe Rd CB1 .....65 C8
Wydham Pk PE2 .....185 D6
Wye Pl PE4 ....204 E1

Wykes Dr [3] PE13 ..235 B7
Wykes Rd PE7 ....181 D4
Wyman Way PE2 .....185 F5
Wynborne Cl CB4 .....83 E5
Wyndham Way CB8 ..111 A6
Wynford Way CB4 .....83 F7
Wype Dro PE7 ....191 A5
Wype Rd PE7 ....190 C7
Wytches The CB6 ....211 A7
Wyton Airfield PE28 ..153 F2
Wyton Cty Inf Sch PE28 143 B8

Y

Yardy Cl PE15 ....243 B4
Yarmouth Pl [1] CB9 ..24 A8
Yarrow Rd CB1 ....66 A5
Yarwell Cl PE2 ......186 D7
Yarwells Headlands
  PE7 ....189 D8
Yarwells Wlk PE7 ...189 D8
Yaxley Jun Sch PE7 ..181 E6
Yaxley Rd PE7 ......177 B4
Yeats Cl SG8 ....13 D1
Yeldham Pl CB9 .....24 A8
Yeomans Cl PE28 ...136 D7
Yerril Gdn [3] CB9 ..23 E7
York Cl
  Godmanchester PE29 ..141 F1
  Mildenhall IP28 ....213 D8
York Gdns PE13 .....245 D6
York Rd Chatteris PE16 .241 C4
  Haverhill CB9 ....23 E7
  Peterborough PE1 ......197 F6
  [9] Stamford PE9 .....244 B6
  Sutton CB6 ....216 D1
  Wisbech PE13 ....245 D6
York Sq PE28 ....143 B8
York St CB1 ....84 A1
York Terr CB1 ....84 A1
York Way Royston SG8 ..5 B8
  St Ives PE27 ....144 A8
Yorke Way CB6 ......240 B3
Young St CB1 ....84 A2
Youngman Ave CB4 ..104 C5
Youngman Cl CB4 ...104 C5

NG	NH	NJ	NK
NM	NN	NO	NP
NR	NS	NT	NU
NX	NY	NZ	
SC	SD	SE	TA
SH	SJ	SK	TF · TG
SM · SN	SO	SP	TL · TM
SR · SS · ST	SU	TQ · TR	
SW · SX	SY	SZ	TV

Any feature in this atlas can be given a unique reference to help you find the same feature on other Ordnance Survey maps of the area, or to help someone else locate you if they do not have a Street Atlas.

The grid squares in this atlas match the Ordnance Survey National Grid and are at 500 metre intervals. The small figures at the bottom and sides of every other grid line are the National Grid kilometre values (**00** to **99** km) and are repeated across the country every 100 km (see left).

To give a unique National Grid reference you need to locate where in the country you are. The country is divided into 100 km squares with each square given a unique two-letter reference. Use the administrative map to determine in which 100 km square a particular page of this atlas falls.

The bold letters and numbers between each grid line (**A** to **F**, **1** to **8**) are for use within a specific Street Atlas only, and when used with the page number, are a convenient way of referencing these grid squares.

Example   The railway bridge over DARLEY GREEN RD in grid square B1

Step 1: Identify the two-letter reference, in this example the page is in **SP**

Step 2: Identify the 1 km square in which the railway bridge falls. Use the figures in the southwest corner of this square: Eastings **17**, Northings **74**. This gives a unique reference: **SP 17 74**, accurate to 1 km.

Step 3: To give a more precise reference accurate to 100 m you need to estimate how many tenths along and how many tenths up this 1 km square the feature is (to help with this the 1 km square is divided into four 500 m squares). This makes the bridge about **8** tenths along and about **1** tenth up from the southwest corner.

This gives a unique reference: **SP 178 741**, accurate to 100 m.

Eastings (read from left to right along the bottom) come before Northings (read from bottom to top). If you have trouble remembering say to yourself "Along the hall, THEN up the stairs"!

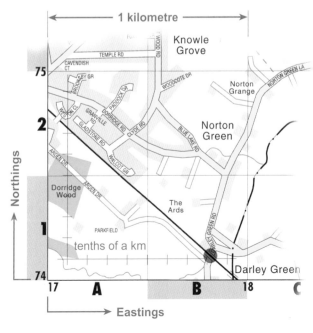

Addresses

Name and Address	Telephone	Page	Grid reference

Name and Address	Telephone	Page	Grid reference

Street Atlases from Philip's

Philip's publish an extensive range of regional and local street atlases which are ideal for motoring, business and leisure use. They are widely used by the emergency services and local authorities throughout Britain.

Key features include:

◆ Superb county-wide mapping at an extra-large scale of 3½ inches to 1 mile, or 2½ inches to 1 mile in pocket editions

◆ Complete urban and rural coverage, detailing every named street in town and country

◆ Each atlas available in three handy formats – hardback, spiral, pocket paperback

'The mapping is very clear... great in scope and value'
★★★★ BEST BUY   AUTO EXPRESS

1 Bedfordshire
2 Berkshire
3 Birmingham and West Midlands
4 Bristol and Bath
5 Buckinghamshire
6 Cambridgeshire
7 Cardiff, Swansea and The Valleys
8 Cheshire
9 Derbyshire
10 Durham
11 Edinburgh and East Central Scotland
12 North Essex
13 South Essex
14 Glasgow and West Central Scotland
15 North Hampshire
16 South Hampshire
17 Hertfordshire
18 East Kent
19 West Kent
20 Lancashire
21 Leicestershire and Rutland
22 London
23 Greater Manchester
24 Merseyside
25 Northamptonshire
26 Nottinghamshire
27 Oxfordshire
28 Staffordshire
29 Surrey
30 East Sussex
31 West Sussex
32 Tyne and Wear
33 Warwickshire
34 South Yorkshire
35 West Yorkshire

How to order

The Philip's range of street atlases is available from good retailers or directly from the publisher by phoning 01933 443863